Spiritual Traditions for the Contemporary Church

EDITED BY

Robin Maas
and Gabriel O'Donnell, O.P.

□

ABINGDON PRESS / NASHVILLE

Spiritual Traditions for the Contemporary Church

Copyright © 1990 by Robin Maas and Gabriel O'Donnell

This book is printed on recycled acid-free paper

Library of Congress Cataloging-in-Publication Data

Spiritual traditions for the contemporary church/
edited by Robin Maas and Gabriel O'Donnell.
    p. cm.
Includes bibliographical references.
        ISBN 0-687-39233-0 (alk. paper)

   1. Spirituality—History. 2. Spiritual life. 3. Christianity—20th century.
I. O'Donnell, Gabriel, 1943–   II. Maas, Robin, 1939–
BV4490.S72   1990
248'.09—dc20   89-48943

Grateful acknowledgement is made for the use of excerpts from the following:

From *The Jerusalem Bible,* published and copyright 1966, 1967 and 1968 by Darton, Longman and Todd Ltd. and Doubleday & Co. Inc., and is used by permission of the publishers.

From *The New American Bible,* copyright © 1970 by the Confraternity of Christian Doctrine, Washington, D.C. Used by permission. All rights reserved.

From *Francis and Clare: The Complete Works,* translated by R. Armstrong and I. Brady, Classics of Western Spirituality, copyright © 1982 Paulist Press. Used by permission of Paulist Press.

From David Watson, *Accountable Discipleship,* pp. 60-61. Copyright © 1984 Discipleship Resources, P.O. Box 840, Nashville, TN 37202. Used by permission.

From Robert Murray, S.J., *Symbols of Church and Kingdom: A Study in Early Syriac Tradition,* copyright © 1975 Cambridge University Press. Used by permission.

From Bruce Vawter, *This Man Jesus,* copyright © 1973 Bruce Vawter. Used by permission of Doubleday, a division of Bantam, Doubleday, Dell Publishing Group, Inc.

From Ntozake Shange, *For Colored Girls Who Have Considered Suicide When the Rainbow Is Enuf.* Copyright © 1975, 1976, 1977 by Ntozake Shange. Reprinted by permission of Russell & Volkening as agents for the author.

From *Luther's Works,* Vol. 43, copyright © 1968 Fortress Press. Used by permission of Augsburg Fortress.

From *The Collected Works of St. Teresa of Avila Volume I,* translated by Kieran Kavanaugh and Otilio Rodriguez, copyright © 1976 Washington Province of Discalced Carmelites ICS Publications, 2131 Lincoln Rd., NE, Washington, D.C. 20002

From *The Collected Works of St. Teresa of Avila, Volume II,* translated by Kieran Kavanaugh and Otilio Rodriguez, copyright © 1980 Washington Province of Discalced Carmelites ICS Publications, 2131 Lincoln Rd., NE, Washington, D.C. 20002

From *The Collected Works of St. Teresa of Avila, Volume III,* translated by Kieran Kavanaugh and Otilio Rodriguez, copyright © 1985 Washington Province of Discalced Carmelites ICS Publications, 2131 Lincoln Rd., NE, Washington, D.C. 20002

MANUFACTURED IN THE UNITED STATES OF AMERICA

94 95 96 97 98 99 00 01 02 03 04 — 10 9 8 7 6 5 4

Elizabeth was filled with the Holy Spirit after conceiving a son; Mary was filled before. "You are blessed," said Elizabeth, "because you have believed."

You too are blessed because you have heard and believed. The soul of every believer conceives and brings forth the Word of God and recognizes his works. Let Mary's soul be in each of you to glorify the Lord. Let her spirit be in each of you to rejoice in the Lord. Christ has only one Mother in the flesh, but we all bring forth Christ by faith.

Saint Ambrose, Bishop

* * *

For our mothers,
the first to teach us to glorify and rejoice in the Lord:
Gertrude Elizabeth O'Donnell
and
Dorothy Lloyd Hill

CONTENTS

ACKNOWLEDGMENTS

Such an ambitious undertaking as this book has proven to be can only be the result of many sources of cooperation and support. The project was made possible in the first place by a generous grant from the Association of Theological Schools and the forbearance of our faculties, The Dominican House of Studies and Wesley Theological Seminary, both in Washington, D.C. We are grateful to our colleagues in the theological guild for the confidence, the expertise, and, of course, the funds that they invested in us and our enterprise. We are especially grateful for the existence of the Washington Theological Consortium, which sponsored our collaboration as teachers and permitted us to share the fruits of our research with assembled consortium colleagues. The wonderfully curious and enthusiastic students who trustingly allowed us to tamper with their prayer lives provided the vision and impetus for our work.

We have been fortunate indeed to have the enthusiastic support of a fine editorial team. Davis Perkins, an astute and scholarly critic involved in the initial stages of the work, encouraged us to expand the project to include the earlier centuries. Ulrike Guthrie, with us for the long haul, has been unfailingly patient and cheerful, as well as precise and painstaking in her attention to detail. Sr. Mary Paul Murphy, O.P., member of a local community of cloistered Dominican nuns, provided invaluable clerical assistance and, perhaps even more important, much moral support through her prayers.

Finally, we need to acknowledge that this was very much a mutual enterprise and that neither one of us could have done this on our own. The collaboration that began in the fall of 1985 with a team-taught course has yielded a very rich harvest indeed and has led us both in directions we never expected to go.

CONTRIBUTORS

Barbara Bedolla, a laywoman with more than sixteen years' experience in directing various forms of the Spiritual Exercises, has served on the Executive Council of the National Federation of Christian Life Communities and has written for *The Way* magazine.

Mark S. Burrows, Assistant Professor of the History of Christianity at Wesley Theological Seminary, Washington, D.C., has recently completed a book on the theology of Jean Gerson.

Eamon R. Carroll, O. Carm., a Carmelite priest and Professor of Theology at Loyola University of Chicago, is an international lecturer whose works have appeared in the *New Catholic Encyclopedia, Theological Studies,* and *Carmelus.*

T. Hartley Hall IV became the president of Union Theological Seminary in Virginia in 1981. A Calvinist by predisposition, he has served pastorates in North Carolina, Texas, and Tennessee. He has had a lifelong involvement with the Presbyterian Church.

Bengt Hoffman, a Lutheran priest and a native of Sweden, was for many years Professor of Ethics and Ecumenics at Lutheran Theological Seminary at Gettysburg, Pennsylvania. His writings in English include his edition of *The Theologica Germanica of Martin Luther.*

Robin Maas, Associate Professor of Christian Education at Wesley Theological Seminary, Washington, D.C., is the author of *Church Bible Study Handbook* and *Crucified Love: The Practice of Christian Perfection.*

William B. McClain, Professor of Homiletics and Worship at Wesley Theological Seminary, Washington, D.C., is an ordained United Methodist minister. His writings include *Travelling Light* and *Black People in the Methodist Church.*

John P. McIntyre, S.J., a Jesuit priest who taught English literature and composition for many years in Jesuit schools in New England, is presently teaching at St. Paul's University, Ottowa, in the area of canon law.

Ronald M. Mrozinski, O.F.M. Conv., a Franciscan priest, is Vice President for Academic Affairs at Mount Marty College in Yankton, South Dakota. He has written and lectured on Franciscan spirituality throughout North America.

Gabriel O'Donnell, O.P., a Dominican Priest and Associate Professor of Spiritual Theology and Liturgy at the Dominican House of Studies, Washington, D.C., is currently writing a book on the tradition of spiritual guidance in the Church.

Douglas F. Ottati, a Ruling Elder in the Presbyterian Church, is Associate Professor of Theology at Union Theological Seminary in Virginia. He is the author of *Meaning and Method in H. Richard Niebuhr's Theology.*

Steven Payne, O.C.D., a Discalced Carmelite priest, is currently editor of *Spiritual Life* magazine and an instructor in philosophy and spirituality at the DeSales School of Theology in Washington, D.C.

Jamie Phelps, O.P., is an African-American Catholic and an Adrian Dominican Sister since 1959. Formerly involved in education, she is presently teaching systematic theology at the Catholic Theological Union in Chicago.

Marjorie Procter-Smith is Assistant Professor of Liturgy and Worship at Perkins School of Theology, Southern Methodist University. She is author of *In Her Own Rite,* soon to be published by Abingdon Press.

Boniface Ramsey, O.P., is a Dominican priest currently assigned to Sacred Heart Parish, Jersey City, New Jersey, and teaching part-time at Seton Hall University. He is the author of *Beginning to Read the Fathers,* an introduction to the Fathers of the Church.

Stephen Rossetti, a priest of the Roman Catholic Diocese of Syracuse, New York, has most recently been Director of Education for the House of Affirmation. His writings include *I Am Alive* and *Fire on the Earth.*

Dominic Tortaro, S.J., a Jesuit priest who teaches high school religion, has been directing the Spiritual Exercises since 1873 and for many years has been closely associated with Christian Life Communities.

Robin Darling Young is Assistant Professor of Patristic Theology at the Catholic University of America, Washington, D.C. Her research concentrates on the areas of patristic Christology, early monasticism, and early Greek and Oriental Christian theology.

John N. Wall, an Episcopal priest and Associate Professor of English at North Carolina State University, is the editor of *George Herbert.* His particular interest is the relationship between Christianity and the literature of the English Renaissance.

The Theory That Undergirds Our Practice

Recently a Protestant seminary professor published an account of his three-month stay at a Trappist monastery. A self-proclaimed "functional atheist," he describes his state of mind as he was about to embark on this new venture:

> I am going to a Trappist monastery high in the Rockies, to be a monk for three months. And what does it offer? I only dimly know, after having tried for months to explain my decision. I am a theologian—I spend my life reading, teaching, thinking, writing, about God. But I must be honest—*I have never experienced God*, not really. I am embarrassed by piety; I am ill at ease with those who thrive on God talk; I have no awareness of what one might mean by the "presence of God."[1]

Is such a thing possible? Can one spend an adult lifetime reading, teaching, thinking, and writing about God and have no vital *experience* of God, no sense of God's presence? Indeed it is, as anyone who has spent much time in a seminary can attest. In this brief, very poignant and distressing description of one professor's spiritual dilemma, we see in microcosm the accurate reflection of a problem of much larger dimensions. It is not an entirely new problem, but it is a persistent one, and it is likely to continue (indefinitely) to plague the Church in general and theological education in particular, barring some radical changes in the way theology is taught and seminarians are prepared to serve as spiritual leaders.

This one professor's quest for spiritual rootedness in a longer tradition is not an isolated instance of religious *angst*. Our seminaries are increasingly populated with people who come not knowing who

11

they are, because they do not know where they come from. It goes without saying, they have very little notion of where they are headed. What they *do* know is that they are hungry and they want to be spiritually fed. And what is true of would-be pastors is true of the laity in general. Our churches, just like our seminaries, are filled with laypersons haunted by a need they have difficulty even naming, let alone satisfying.

For some, this hunger takes expression in a wave of romantic nostalgia for a past in which religious certainty appeared unchallenged by the dominant culture, but this attitude is naïve. Culture is as fallen as human nature itself and has always challenged authentic Christian piety at one level or another. The answer to our lack of rootedness does not lie in the return, through the replication of a particular set of conditions, to some golden age of devotional practice. Rather, our need is to recover an understanding of the value systems of our spiritual ancestors, to discern not only what is compatible with current trends and conditions but also what, in the end, is absolutely essential for the nurture of a human community of significance and meaning.

In the context of Christian life, such a search for rootedness must include both historical considerations and doctrinal issues, for the Church of Christ expresses itself primarily in the active faith of its members and in that community's sacramental celebrations and confessional formulations. Ironically, continuity with our history is essential if we are to prepare the way for the Church's ministry in the twenty-first century, for there can be no relevance without rootedness, and only the deepest taproots can anchor and support life under harsh and arid conditions.

Spiritual Theology as First- and Second-Order Theology

Spiritual theology, like all theology, is simply the act of reflecting on the mystery of God and his relationship with the created universe, especially the *human* experience of God.[2] In our time, religious thinkers speak of first- and second-order theology. First-order theology is the act of reflecting upon the meaning of God—who God is—by the ordinary believer. In this sense, first-order theology implies that every Christian must be a theologian. Every Christian who practices his or her faith by going to church and thinking about or talking to God is, in effect, doing first-order theology.

Second-order theology involves reflecting upon the experience of faith in a more conceptual or scientific way.[3] Prior to the sixteenth century, theology was understood as holy wisdom, and it was assumed that one could not engage in second-order theology unless one was in the first place a practicing Christian. What this means, simply, is that there cannot be a theologian who is not also a believer. The notion that there can be one without the other is a relatively new idea in the Christian Church. That one could be a professional theologian without *necessarily* being engaged in a personal relationship with God is foreign to the long-held view that the theologian is one who is called to a life of wisdom—a life of wholeness and holiness. But that, of course, was the dilemma of the Protestant seminary professor quoted above. He had no personal experience of God.

Spiritual theology suggests—and in fact requires—a particular way of integrating first- and second-order theology, for it is impossible to speak of mystical union with God or contemplative prayer without the correlative admission of the reality of God and the truth of union with him. Spiritual theology is about more than the observable phenomena of Christian piety and its attendant prayer forms. It is about reflecting upon the reality of God as *both* a first- and second-order experience.

Spiritual theology is that part of the science of theology that deals with the relationship between the individual human person and God. It must therefore be concerned for the external aspects of that relationship—our life of communal worship and service to our neighbor—as well as the internal or interior aspects of that relationship—private prayer and communion with God in the depths of the heart. The literature of spiritual theology typically focuses on questions of the "interior life," a phrase that describes the inner search for God and the development of a relationship with Christ that is hidden within our hearts and minds.

Since the seventeenth century, it has been the custom to divide the study of theology into two basic categories, relating (roughly) to theory and practice. In Roman Catholicism, these categories are designated "dogmatic theology" and "moral theology." In Protestantism, with both the nomenclature and methodology differing, one speaks of "systematic theology" and "Christian ethics." Dogmatic theology and systematic theology deal with confessional statements. Their goal is precise and careful definition of all forms of doctrinal formulation. Moral theology and ethics deal with how the Christian person lives out the implications of the doctrinal confession. While these are very convenient categorizations and typically represent two areas of academic specialization, they must nevertheless be understood as closely interrelated.

Historically, the study of Christian spirituality or spiritual theology was begun in the context of this division. What was originally seen as a convenient conceptual division between two closely related parts of the theological project often enough became—especially in the sixteenth and seventeenth centuries—an almost unbridgeable chasm. Consequently, instead of seeing these two parts of Christian theology as closely interrelated, the Church, even today, remains subject to a persistent and potentially harmful tendency to separate religious belief and moral behavior. When such a division occurs, moral theology becomes less a question of how we live out the doctrines that we profess and more "Is this wrong? How wrong is it? Is it just a little bit wrong? Is it very wrong?" Morality degenerates into a rigid legalism, and spirituality becomes a rarified elitism. This pernicious division of morality and doctrine makes it easier to understand how first- and second-order theology came to be understood independently of each other.

Spiritual Theology as Ascetical and Mystical Theology

In the seventeenth century the Roman Catholic tendency to separate dogma and morality resulted in yet a further division of moral theology into ascetical and mystical theology. While strange-sounding to modern ears, the terms "ascetical" and "mystical" theology are important for our consideration of spiritual theology. They are concerned with the biblical ideal of Christian perfection: "You . . . must be perfect, as your heavenly Father is perfect" (Matt. 5:48); "if you would be perfect, go, sell what you possess" (Matt. 19:21).

The division of theology into dogmatic and moral and the further distinction of moral theology into ascetical and mystical had as its purpose not simply reflection about God in the abstract, but reflection—in the context of Christian community—in order to be formed into holy human beings or "perfect" Christians. The imitation of Jesus' perfect obedience, his perfect surrender, his perfect peace, his perfect compassion and perfect justice, was the concrete goal of all theological reflection.

Most Protestants have been relatively suspicious of mysticism in general and nervous about spiritual practices that appear too interior or private. Yet Christians of every age—with the possible exception of our own—have been preoccupied with the question, How can I be more perfectly Christlike? How does one reach the state of perfection commanded by Jesus of his followers? Today, as we approach the end of the twentieth century, the achievement of personal authenticity and psychological integration seems to be the highest priority. We who wish to shape the beginnings of the twenty-first century are concerned about being "actualized," hoping that all our personal potential will be realized through a healthy and well-ordered existence, and we are willing to do whatever is necessary to achieve this end, whether it entails joining a health club, church, or group therapy program.

This drive for personal actualization is a new way of looking at the purpose of human existence. By contrast, the classic literature of the spiritual tradition of the Church in the West is based upon the idea that there is an *objective norm* for the achievement of true integration and wholeness, namely, Jesus Christ crucified. The phrase "Christian perfection" does not mean that personal resources must be marshaled to make a superhuman effort to overcome evil and human weakness through sheer force of will. Rather, Christian perfection has to do with conformity to the externally imposed ideal of the perfect Christ, and it is the purpose of ascetical and mystical theology to describe the ways in which any person becomes a "perfect" Christian (i.e., conformed to the Crucified One).

The common use of the word "person" in the contemporary American vocabulary suggests this pervasive concern for self-actualization. In the classic literature of spirituality there is a tendency to emphasize the *interior* aspects of the process of perfection. Such phrases as "the soul becomes perfect" are used frequently to emphasize that it is the *essence* of the person about which spiritual theology is concerned and not primarily material and social success or physical well-being. Contemporary theology tends to avoid the term "soul," claiming that it suggests an unhealthy dualism in our understanding of the human person; yet modern theologians have not succeeded in finding a satisfactory substitute for the ancient usage. The word "soul" was and still is used to indicate that personal, *essential* self in relationship to God.

Ascetical theology is concerned with the efforts we as free and responsible individuals have to make to prepare for the visitation of God. It comes from the Greek word *askesis*, which means "training," especially in the context of a military or athletic contest. In the early Church those who lived a life of celibacy were called "ascetics." In the seventeenth century a Polish Franciscan by the name of Dobrosielski introduced this term into Western theological usage; a hundred years later, the famous Italian Jesuit Giovanni Scaramelli established the practice of using the term in conjunction with mystical theology.[4]

Just as to become an Olympic star the athlete gradually learns to swim or run to the limit of endurance, so must we eventually be prepared to push until we find our limits in the spiritual life. Ascetical theology deals with the efforts we all must make to get ready for God. It is about learning how to pray, how to be disciplined in my life in relation to food, to my body, to the bodies of others, to material creation, and so forth. What the Christian tradition calls "asceticism" is, in the first place, about the virtues, habits, and attitudes that are required to know God. It is also about vices, harmful attitudes, and destructive habits that make it impossible to become "perfect" or, in modern parlance, *authentically* Christian. Understanding that the exercise of free will is itself a gift of grace, ascetical theology affirms that part of the responsibility for personal holiness, for knowing God, is *ours*.

Mystical theology, by contrast, is about the hidden mysterious things that belong to God—those things that "eye hath not seen, nor ear heard" (I Cor. 2:9 KJV). Once we have done our best under the influence of God's grace to prepare for the visitation of God, then we are led along a path unknown to us—unknown to anyone—save the Spirit, whose steps are sure. Just as ascetical theology is about what *we* do, mystical theology is about what *God* does *in us*. In mystical theology we learn how the life of asceticism opens us up to a life of prayer, to a new awareness of God's presence and power in our personal lives and in the world. Mystical theology explores the stages of development in prayer, the implications of a more intense life of communion with God, and what Christian service may mean as we move along the path of "perfection."

Spiritual theology, therefore, encompasses both the ascetical and the mystical branches of study. Neophytes in the study of spiritual theology need to know that many authors define these two branches as divisions of moral theology in order to emphasize the unity of the theological project and the proper relationship between doctrine and human behavior. Others suggest that spiritual theology is a third division of theology itself: dogmatic, moral, and spiritual theology. These distinctions become an important question in our current situation since there is much confusion about the relationship between doctrinal formulation or creedal statements and the way in which we live out the Christian life. It is too simple to say, "All that matters is that we live together and that we're good, building a better world for our brothers and sisters." That simply is not enough. We have to live together, be good, and build a better world, all the while saying, "I believe in God, the Father almighty, maker of heaven and earth . . . " If there is one thing the tradition is clear about, it is that creedal formulations or Christian orthodoxy and holiness go together and support each other. We do not pray out of a moral and metaphysical vacuum, any more than we live out of one.

It is a fallacy to think that we can be spiritual or have a meaningful relationship with God without being concerned about the specifics of doctrine. Our belief system shapes, in a definitive way, our relationship with God, as the thrust of each of the paired chapters and practica in this work is meant to demonstrate. It is important to note, too, that the now very popular term "spirituality" has only recently come into common usage.[5] In earlier centuries one commonly spoke only of ascetical or mystical theology. Beginning in the seventeenth century, the term "spirituality" emerged. As it gradually came to include both ascetical and mystical theology, it was linked to the rest of the theological project. In the English-speaking world, it was not until the publication of Pierre Pourrat's four-volume *Christian Spirituality* (1927) that the term came to have such all-embracing meaning,[6] and today we speak not only of "spirituality" but also of "spiritualities." The popularity of the term is such that now many Protestants, previously hostile to the idea, have begun to use "spirituality" to refer to their own devotional practices, though some traditions still prefer the more familiar "piety." (For example, see chapter 7 on the Reformed tradition.)

The great Swiss theologian, Hans Urs von Balthasaar, insists that while there are many "spiritualities," there is, at base, only a *single* spirituality, whose "one, concrete norm is Jesus Christ who endows each of these forms with its own particular meaning derived from the unity of God's triune love."[7] An authentic "Christian" spirituality is one that binds us to Christ and leads us through the power of the Holy Spirit to God the Father. It must therefore be both christological and trinitarian. Within that essential framework there are innumerable ways of meeting Christ, and these are often described as "schools" of spirituality or spiritualities (e.g., Wesleyan or Benedictine spirituality). Sometimes historical periods or geographical locales generate descriptions: medieval or French spirituality. A significant exception to this traditional trinitarian and christological pattern has emerged only recently, with the development of feminist theology. As we see in the final chapter of this book, the still very new and self-conscious effort to construct a feminist spirituality seriously questions and in some cases simply rejects traditional norms for assessing the value and authenticity of Christian spiritual practice.

While today we tend to use the terms "spiritual theology" and "spirituality" interchangeably, we must be careful of the nuances involved. Spirituality tends to be a more universal term, including not only study and scientific research but also, and especially, the *lived* experience (first-order theology). Spiritual theology, while not excluding the lived experience, is the term more often used to indicate the academic consideration of the historical and theological issues that inform the subjective experience and often provide the guidance needed at a given period of time.[8]

In the chapters that follow we will be dealing with *both* spirituality and spiritual theology, but our conviction is that, like the whole of the theological project, they cannot be legitimately separated. Our experience must be tested in the light of reasoned reflection on Scripture, history, and the teaching of the Church, and the communal confession of the Church's faith must be lived out by each of us in a personal love relationship with God.

Healing the Breach: An Experimental Course for Seminarians

Anyone who has ever attended seminary or who, as we do, teaches seminarians is acutely aware of a number of painful divisions. The division between doctrine and morality tends to persist in the training of clergy, despite the efforts of many conscientious faculty, and the demands of academic respectability ensure that second-order theology will receive pride of place in the curriculum. Courses in spirituality, if they are available, are almost always taught in a second-order context, emphasizing academic mastery of the subject matter rather than actual (first-order) practice. Seminarians who profess an interest in the subject commonly conceptualize spirituality in a one-sided way by envisioning it exclusively—and rather romantically—in terms of mystical theology. The less glamorous and more difficult dimensions of asceticism hold little appeal, and its essential relationship to fruitful prayer experiences usually remains undiscovered or ignored.

In the fall of 1985 the editors of this volume taught a course in comparative Western spiritualities for the Washington Theological Consortium, which we hoped would begin to bridge these unwholesome gaps. Our first efforts, in retrospect, appear somewhat haphazard, yet they were surprisingly successful. We combined lectures on the historical and theological dimensions of particular spiritual traditions in both Catholicism and Protestantism with an assignment that required the actual practice of a daily spiritual discipline—in this case, *lectio divina* or sacred reading.

This initial effort generated such an enthusiastic response on the part of the seventeen Catholic and Protestant students enrolled in the course that we decided to try teaching the course a second time in an expanded and more intentionally experiential format. Thanks to a generous grant from the Association of Theological Schools, we were able to offer the course again in the spring of 1987 and produce this manuscript. The revised course included a lecture on each tradition, followed by a "practicum" or actual experience of a prayer technique or devotional practice associated with that tradition. Plenty of time for discussion following the lecture and practicum was provided. As with the previous experience, we continued to require a daily session of *lectio divina* for each student as the major course requirement. We recognized that in adding the hour of actual practice in prayer to our course, we were taking some risks; it was not at all a foregone conclusion that our students would feel sufficiently free to tackle some of the exercises we planned or that the actual practice would, as we hoped, spark their interest in learning more about a given tradition. But tackle them they did, and with good humor and generous spirits, even when they had to swallow hard, as some of our Protestants did when we all prayed the rosary together. All of our students expressed appreciation for—and some amazement over—the experience of actually praying together in class, and most significantly from our perspective, the class was unanimous in their judgment that neither the lectures nor the practica alone would have been sufficient for their needs. The lectures provided the necessary credibility and motivation for pursuing the practice in the first place, and the practice challenged them at a deeper and more personal level than they had previously experienced in the seminary setting.

Those of us who teach in seminaries and theological schools that are part of an ecumenical consortium are exceptionally privileged. Both we and our students have ready access to the riches of a variety of vital theological and spiritual traditions, such as are reflected in this work. But most seminarians are not so fortunate, and the same holds true for laypersons who are serious seekers on a spiritual quest. For this reason, we feel that a book of this nature may help to fill what promises to become a spiritually dangerous void in the life of the Church. A few highly motivated individuals may be able to identify, locate, and study the classics of Western spirituality on their own and then integrate what they have learned into their personal devotional practice, but most people need more guidance—and more company. It is less daunting to meditate when you are surrounded by fellow gropers and stumblers who are willing to share their little victories and larger anxieties.

Spiritual Traditions for the Contemporary Church will be, we hope, an equally valuable resource for seminary faculty and students, Protestant and Catholic clergy, and lay people. It is structured so that the fourteen chapters and practica *can* (but need not) be taught in the form of a course, in a variety of settings. The chapters provide important historical and theological information; the practica provide explanations of actual devotional practices and methods of prayer and meditation. Exercises suitable for groups and/or individuals and discussion questions are included.

Finally, one caveat. It is not our purpose, in presenting our readers with a rich range of spiritual traditions, to encourage a smorgasbord or mix-and-match approach to spirituality. As we have attempted to demonstrate, there are clear doctrinal implications connected with these practices. They are each rooted in a unique set of historical and cultural circumstances and therefore reflect a particular way of thinking about God. In late twentieth-century America some spiritual eclecticism may be inevitable, but we do not consider it our calling to exploit that. Rather, recognizing the deep spiritual hunger in our students and the lay people we work with, we hope to send the following message: The time-tested spiritual traditions in Western Christianity are founded on solid rock—they are proven paths to God. Those of us who want to find God do not need to constantly blaze new trails through the wilderness; the paths are already cut and marked, and though perhaps overgrown in some cases, they are nevertheless still negotiable. So think of this book as a map containing a number of routes to a common destination. It would be foolhardy to set out on such a long and arduous journey *without* a guide such as this, and the journey will be easier if traveled in the company of others. But in the end, each one of us has to put one foot down in front of the other . . .

Gabriel O'Donnell, O.P.
Dominican House of Studies
Washington, D.C.

Robin Maas
Wesley Theological Seminary
Washington, D.C.

Notes

1. W. Paul Jones, "My Days with the Trappist Monks," *International Christian Digest* 1, no. 7 (Sept. 1987): 24.
2. Language about God has become a controversial subject in theological discourse and education, and it is now customary in many quarters to eliminate altogether the use of the masculine pronoun when referring to God. However, for a volume that sets out to represent a variety of historical traditions to ignore those traditions' consistent practice of referring to God in masculine terms would be (we think) to distort the traditions themselves, and this strikes us as intellectually dishonest. But while we are not willing to abandon entirely the use of the personal pronoun for God, we have

taken pains to use it sparingly. Compromises often please no one, but in a fallen world, they are sometimes necessary.

3. For a fuller discussion of this relationship see Geoffrey Wainwright, *Doxology* (New York: Oxford University Press, 1980), pp. 16-23.

4. Jordan Aumann, O.P., *Spiritual Theology* (Huntington, Ind.: Our Sunday Visitor, 1979), p. 14.

5. Jean Leclercq, O.S.B., "Spiritualitas," *Studi Medievali* 3 (1962): 279-86.

6. Cheslyn Jones, Geoffrey Wainwright, Edward Yarnold, S.J., eds., *The Study of Spirituality* (New York: Oxford University Press, 1986), pp. xxiv-xxvi.

7. Hans Urs von Balthasaar, "The Gospel as Norm and Test of All Spirituality in the Church," *Concilium* (1969): 16.

8. Eugene Megyer, "Theological Trends: Spiritual Theology Today," *The Way* 21, no. 1 (Jan. 1981): 55-67.

PART I

The Roots
of Contemporary
Western Spirituality

CHAPTER 1

The Spirituality
of the Early Church:
Patristic Sources

BONIFACE RAMSEY, O.P.

Whoever would save his life will lose it, and whoever loses his life for my sake will find it.

—MATTHEW 16:25

To understand any phenomenon fully, we must look to its origins. In the case of the spiritual theology and practice of Western Christendom, the quest for understanding must begin in the earliest centuries of the Church's existence, when the foundations for all future development were laid. No matter how specific and unique the various traditions surveyed in this volume may be, they all take, as a point of departure, some aspect of the common vision of the earliest Christian communities, and it is in precisely this elemental commonality that their authenticity and enduring value lies.

The early Church, as understood in this essay, includes the time when the earliest nonscriptural Christian writings were produced and—while excluding the Scriptures themselves—extends to about the middle of the eighth century. This period of nearly seven hundred years, known as the patristic era or the age of the Fathers of the Church—as the great theologians of the time were called—runs from at least the late first-century so-called *First Letter of Clement* to the systematic works of John Damascene (d. ca. 750). It is, in fact, the longest relatively cohesive era in the history of Christian thought, given that complete cohesiveness does not exist in any arbitrarily designated historical period. The early Church took in too many discrete geographical areas (e.g., Italy, North Africa, Cappadocia, Palestine, and Persia) and too many different languages (Latin, Greek, Syriac, and Arabic, to name a few), with the different ways of thinking that they

25

implied, for it to be legitimately perceived by us, in retrospect, as an unfragmented whole. Yet, despite this, there is a recognizable continuity in these seven centuries and, consequently, in their spirituality.

The Early Church and the World of Spirits

If we were to say that this continuity of conception and spiritual practice consisted in a general awareness of a spiritual world and a consciousness that this invisible world had a profound and unremitting impact upon the visible world of human activity, then we would be saying too little, although it would be abundantly true. Most people in every age of history—Christians and non-Christians alike—have been convinced of the existence of just such a spiritual realm, inhabited by gods and demons and angels or their near equivalents; and the current age is no exception, despite appearances to the contrary. But it is useful nonetheless to emphasize early Christianity's belief in this invisible world and to mention some of its peculiarities.

First, the sources suggest a greater sensitivity to the presence of demons than to that of good spirits. This is especially true in monastic literature, where demons show up in all sorts of guises and shapes and engage in activities ranging from the mildly mischievous to the utterly heinous—all with a view to diverting the monk or nun from the path to salvation. It is also true elsewhere than in monastic literature, however, even if to a slightly lesser degree. We are told in a treatise dating from the early third century, for example, that when a person was to be baptized, he was warned against taking any foreign object into the water with him, lest a demon somehow attach himself to the object and interfere with the baptism.[1] So pervasive was the influence of demons felt to be in some circles that the great third-century theologian Origen had to insist that they were not responsible for *all* the sins that human beings committed.[2]

But the good spirits—the angels—were not without an influence of their own, even if it seems to have been less remarked upon. They were known to make consoling appearances to people in distress, to steer endangered ships through stormy seas, and to provide food for hungry travelers.[3] Sometimes, though, demons would masquerade as their angelic counterparts. The realization that this took place gave rise to the science of distinguishing between the two, otherwise known as the "discernment of spirits." Already referred to in I John 4:1-3 in an inchoate way, the practice of spiritual discernment was developed by later theologians with the sophistication that came with experience. It was agreed that a demonic visitation brought with it confusion and an upsurge of disturbing, unwholesome thoughts, whereas an angelic one brought peace and a yearning for divine things.[4]

But, as has been said, this belief in an invisible albeit extremely populous and active world was not peculiar to early Christianity. If we wish to distinguish the spirituality of the early Church from that of subsequent generations, we must focus upon three other areas: Christology, liturgy, and martyrdom.

Salvation in Christ: The Basis of the Spiritual Life

The early Church was preoccupied, to a degree unparalleled in later eras, with the mystery of Christ. We can see this in the major christological heresies that dominate the seven centuries with which we are concerned: docetism, which denied that Christ had a real body; adoptionism, which asserted that he was the adopted and not the natural son of God; Arianism, which made Christ at best a minor divinity, inferior to the Father; Apollinarianism, which negated Christ's human soul or mind; Nestorianism, which drastically divided the human and the divine natures in Christ; monophysitism, which denied Christ's human nature; and monothelitism, which claimed that Christ had only one will. Even heresies not specifically christological, like Pelagianism and iconoclasm, had in them significant aspects touching upon the person of Christ. The former saw him as a model for human behavior rather than as the source of grace, whereas the latter, which forbade the use of images in worship, implied a terrible misunderstanding of the Incarnation.

However we may look upon such unorthodox ideas, we must at least concede that they were attempts to take Christ very seriously and to understand the meaning that he had for humankind; for none of those who held these heterodox views would have denied that Christ was the Savior. Quite the contrary, they believed passionately that their view of him was more in keeping with his saving role than was the view of the majority of Christians. If they overemphasized either his humanity or his divinity, it was because they were convinced that either a "more human" or a "more divine" Christ would be a better savior. In other words, *it was the issue of human salvation that propelled their speculations,* just as, for that matter, it did the speculations of the orthodox. We can see this overriding consideration clearly in the famous lines of Gregory Nazianzen, written in the late fourth century, in which he attacks the Apollinarian heresy, which erred on the side of the divine. In denying his human soul, the Apollinarians had invented a Christ who could not save our souls:

> Whatever [Christ] has not taken upon himself he has not healed, but whatever is united to his divinity is also saved. If only half of Adam fell, then what Christ takes upon himself and saves may also be half. But if his whole nature fell, it must be united to the whole nature of him who was begotten and so be wholly saved. Let them not, therefore, deny us our complete salvation, clothing the Savior only with bones and nerves and the appearance of humanity.[5]

Cyril of Alexandria, on the other hand, pointed out some fifty years later that Nestorianism, which erred on the side of the human by separating the human from the divine in Christ, had the effect of removing the element of the divine from the Eucharist and making it the flesh and blood of an ordinary man.[6] This would of course nullify the Eucharist's saving power. The orthodox, in a Christology that was canonized at the Council of Chalcedon in 451, affirmed that Christ was both completely human and completely divine.

This intense interest in the person of Christ, born of a preoccupation with salvation and so evident in the struggle between orthodoxy and heresy, is then necessarily apparent in what we refer to as "spirituality." In short, *Christ was the measure, the model, and the goal of the spiritual life.* He was the measure in that he defined the nature of that life by who he himself was. We may see this suggested in some beautiful words of Ambrose of Milan:

> Christ is the beginning of our virtue. He is the beginning of chastity, he who taught virgins not to look for men's embraces but to dedicate the chastity of their mind and body to the Holy Spirit rather than to a husband. Christ is the beginning of poverty, he who became poor even though he was rich. Christ is the beginning of patience, he who did not revile in return when he was reviled and did not strike back when he was struck. Christ is the beginning of humility, he who took the form of a slave although he was equal to God the Father because of his majestic power. From him each virtue has taken its beginning.[7]

Christ was the model in that his own life attracted imitation. Martyrdom, monasticism, virginity, and poverty—to name four of the great spiritual ideals that gripped the early Church—were all thought of as imitations of Christ. A particularly striking example of this notion is found in the immortal expression of Jerome, for whom poverty was the naked following of the naked Christ.[8] Finally, Christ was the goal in that he was the focus of all longing; hence the numerous references to the beauty of Christ that are scattered throughout the literature of the period. John Chrysostom, for one, speaks of the glorious countenance of the human Christ and remarks that in heaven it will be still more attractive.[9] Augustine, for another, describes Christ's beauty as being desirable to virgins, who have turned away from marriage and from the enjoyment of merely human beauty.[10] Even the heretics looked to Christ in these ways, and their literature, like that of the orthodox, could breathe forth the most tender devotion to him.

Beyond all this, however, Christ was the very *possibility* of the spiritual life. And thus we return to the theme of salvation; for if Christ had not saved the human race and established the Church, which was his body and the mediator of his grace, there could of course have been no talk of a spiritual life at all.

Some words deserve to be said here about the Holy Spirit, lest the impression be given that the Christocentricism of the early Church in any way excludes the Spirit. There were varied opinions about this third person of the Trinity. They ranged from second-century Montanism, which seems to have glorified the Spirit at the expense of Christ and exalted the spiritual gifts, especially prophecy, to fourth-century pneumatomachianism, which denied the divinity of the Spirit. Orthodox belief tended to associate the inner workings of holiness with the Spirit, without implying by this that Christ was not crucially involved in this function as well. Cyril of Jerusalem is typical in this regard. He speaks in great detail of the gifts of the Spirit in his mid–fourth-century *Catechesis,* mentioning (in particular) inner enlightenment, virginity, and martyrdom,[11] but he feels obliged to observe that

> the Father *through* the Son *with* the Holy Spirit bestows all gifts. The gifts of the Father are not one thing, those of the Son another and those of the Holy Spirit something else. For there is one salvation, one power, one faith. There is one God, the Father; one Lord, his only-begotten Son; one Holy Spirit, the Paraclete.[12]

We must admit, however, that the Spirit did not occupy the position in early Christian thought, at least in the Greek and Latin-speaking Church, that Christ did. At the risk of oversimplifying, the reason for this seems to be that the operations of the Spirit were hidden and discernible only with difficulty. Who, after all, can measure—or even define—holiness? Consequently, the Spirit was an elusive figure. The workings of Christ, on the other hand, were at least in part those of a historical figure who had lived a life recorded in the Gospels and who had founded a visible organization, the Church. Yet the discrepancy in the attention paid to each of these persons by early Christians should not disturb us. It is no different today, and the respective emphases appear to be natural to Christianity.

The Preeminence of the Liturgy

The second area upon which to focus is the liturgy. Although noteworthy developments occurred here over the course of the Church's first seven hundred years, such that the austere Roman Eucharist that Justin Martyr describes in the mid-second century[13] hardly seems comparable to the elaborate ceremonies in Constantinople and elsewhere in the fifth and later centuries, one thing remained unchanged: The early Christians were a "liturgical" people in the sense that they were *formed by* and *aware of* the liturgy in a way that Christians in subsequent ages were not. To be sure, we must not idealize the situation of the early Church. Christians then could be as slack, for example, in their attendance at and attention to the Eucharist as they were in the Middle Ages or still are in modern times. Nonetheless, the liturgy loomed larger than it has since; and this was true for several reasons.

First, the ancient Church was, by and large, a Church of relatively small congregations; this was especially the case in its earliest period, before the changes effected by Constantine at the beginning of the fourth century. Initially, a town or city normally had only one place where its Christians gathered together, and the consequences of this were significant. Greater mutuality and more direct access to the celebration itself, as well as to the bishops and priests who performed the liturgy, must have contributed to the sense of active participation that fairly leaps out at us from the pages of early texts touching on the liturgy.

We know that preaching was taken very seriously, for it was a time when rhetorical skill was a much-esteemed gift. The greatest preachers, men like Augustine and John Chrysostom, were highly attuned to the moods of their congregations and were thus in something of a dialogue with them. One cannot read ancient sermons without the feeling that most of the preachers knew their audiences intimately. The urgency of the preaching of the time is reflected in a long passage at the end of one of Chrysostom's homilies. Lamenting his congregation's lack of spiritual progress, he says he is so taken up with their sins that he has no leisure to weep over his own, for "you are indeed everything to me."[14] The same degree of passionate—and personal—involvement with his listeners is reflected in the words of Peter Chrysologus, who also preached in the first half of the fifth century: "You are my life, you are my salvation, you are my glory, and therefore I cannot bear that you should be ignorant of the knowledge that God has imparted to me."[15]

We have every reason to believe that each Eucharist celebrated was accompanied by a homily. However, as the period we are considering drew to a close, preaching became less and less central to the liturgy. For example, by the beginning of the sixth century, preachers in the West were often reading homilies prepared by another person, in some cases relying on those composed earlier by Augustine and other Fathers.[16] By the beginning of the eighth century it is clear from the *Ordo primus romanus*—the earliest work describing the sequence of events in the Roman liturgy—that Roman bishops no longer preached at every Eucharist, for there is no mention at all of a homily.

The importance of the liturgy in Christian antiquity was also a consequence of the fact that the participants, who were closer to the sources of its symbolism, were therefore more alert to its full significance. Liturgical gestures and words were not yet largely incomprehensible or subject to misinterpretation, as unfortunately seems to have been the case by the Middle Ages. The medieval penchant for intricate and complex elaboration and the distance that separated the Middle Ages from the sources were partly responsible for this. Early liturgy could be elaborate, too, as has been remarked, but it was still within the grasp, one suspects, of most ordinary men and women.

It should be noted, too, that the liturgy's preeminent place in early Christianity stemmed from its relatively exclusive claim on the believer's attention. When Christians gathered, it was for no other purpose, as a rule, than to celebrate Baptism or the Eucharist, to pray the psalms, or to hear an instruction of some sort. There was none of what a later age would refer to as "public devotions," such as novenas, holy hours, and the like. This is not to say that people did not pray privately: Numerous private prayers (as well as accounts of superstitious practices) have come down to us from antiquity. But public prayer was *liturgical* prayer.

Finally, inasmuch as not everyone in antiquity knew how to read or, if he did, had an adequate supply of books at his disposal, the liturgy was virtually the sole means of instruction in the faith for a large proportion of Christians. It follows that their understanding of their religion was colored to a great extent indeed by liturgical symbolism and the words that they heard whenever the community gathered.

What were these early Christians likely to have seen and heard? By as early, perhaps, as the late second century, they would have been baptized only after a lengthy period of instruction (known as the catechumenate), sometimes lasting as long as two or even three years. As catechumens they would have had the Christian faith explained to them and, as a regular part of their baptismal preparation, would have undergone repeated exorcisms. These latter would have impressed upon them, as mere words could not, the reality of diabolical influence. The baptismal ceremony itself, with its different gestures, its anointings, its use of water and light, its stripping and revesting in white clothing, and its eucharistic conclusion, was calculated to strike the participants with a sense of the grandeur and mystery of that divine grace into whose realm they had thereby entered.

An ordinary Sunday Eucharist would have been a simpler affair—in the West more so than in the East. To the eyes of faith, however, angels crowded around the altar, whatever the style of celebration.[17] The homily at a eucharistic liturgy might be on almost any religious theme, and the thousands of homilies that survive deal with all sorts of things, from trinitarian theology to concern for the poor. It was through the homily in particular, with the readings that preceded it, that people were exposed to the Bible. The allegorical approach that the preachers of the time favored (and that will be discussed in more detail below) would have hinted to their congregations how unfathomable and multifaceted Scripture was, for this method of interpretation laid bare hidden meanings that the average reader or listener would never have identified. Finally, it is thanks to the liturgy that the Christians of these early centuries lived through the seasons of Lent and Easter (or Pentecost) and the great feasts of the Church in particularly vivid fashion.

A concluding word should be added about liturgical gesture and movement. The people's participation in the liturgy, which has already been alluded to, must have been all the more intense in view of the fact that symbolic gesture was not limited to the principal celebrant. Baptism, for example, involved the person's whole body. The Eucharist, too, at least in the earliest centuries, was celebrated by all with the uplifted hands that are now typical of the priest alone; and the reception of communion seems to have been accompanied in some places by elaborate gestures, as both texts and art indicate.[18] But by the Middle Ages in the West, and perhaps even earlier, this mode of participation had disappeared.

Martyrdom

The third and last area in which early Christianity is distinguished from subsequent spirituality is martyrdom (from a Greek word meaning "witness"). Indeed, if people nowadays were asked to name the most specific or unique characteristic of ancient Christianity, the majority would probably reply without hesitation that it was martyrdom. Martyrs, however, were not quite as numerous as we are often led to believe. They numbered in the thousands, and perhaps even in the tens of thousands, but certainly not more than that. There were long periods when no one was martyred, or very few were, and there were places in the Roman Empire where martyrdom was a rare occurrence. Much depended on the attitude of the local authorities, of the populace, and of the Christians themselves. It is interesting that the author of the most recent critical edition of the martyrdom accounts (known as the "Acts of the Martyrs" or "Passions") of the first three centuries, when martyrdoms were most frequent, could vouch for the authenticity of only twenty-eight such accounts,[19] although we know of more than that from other sources. In any event, the martyrs exerted a profound influence on the mind of the ancient Church and hence on its spirituality.

The martyrs, who took their name from the fact that they witnessed to Christ by the shedding of their own blood, were seen by the early Church as the persons closest to the Lord, and this vital likeness provided the single greatest claim to the respect and reverence that other Christians willingly gave them. They achieved this closeness by imitating Christ's suffering and death, as the anonymous author of *The Martyrdom of Polycarp* observes of his hero at the beginning of his second-century account, and through experiencing contact with Christ, often in the form of visions.[20] So intimate were martyrs with the Lord that it could be said that he was suffering *in* them, and this, in turn, had the effect of alleviating their suffering.[21] The author of *The Martyrdom of Polycarp* even hinted that his saint's death had a salvific result and had extinguished the flames of hell.[22] Origen is far bolder and declares outright that just as Christ had saved some by the outpouring of his blood, so the martyrs save others by the outpouring of theirs.[23]

The supernatural powers and gifts of the martyrs were exceptional. The visions and dreams they received were not restricted to Christ but could be of other holy things, and by these visions they very commonly learned that they were to die and in what manner their death would occur.[24] Many Christians believed that the martyrs, while languishing in prisons, had the ability to forgive sins, which was a function otherwise relegated to bishops alone.[25] By reason of their detachment from the concerns of this world, and particularly from their own agonies, the martyrs were like angels; they were no longer "human" beings.[26] When they suffered, angels were in attendance, and the whole cosmos hung in suspense at the outcome of the struggle.[27] Even in death their bodies might bear remarkable witness to the divine favor they enjoyed.[28] After death they were assured of immediate access to the Divine Vision, whereas others had to wait.[29]

Among the various effects that martyrdom had on those who underwent it was the remission of sins. By the end of the second century we learn that martyrdom was considered a form of baptism for those who had never been baptized, while for those who had already received the sacrament but had fallen into sin, it was an opportunity for forgiveness.[30] By the end of the fourth century, Chromatius of Aquileia places martyrdom even higher than baptism: "Baptism in water is certainly good, but better and best of all is the baptism of the martyr. The former is forgiveness, the latter a reward. The former is remission of sins, in the latter a crown of virtues is merited."[31]

No wonder that, given all these qualities associated with martyrs and martyrdom, the concept of martyrdom would continue to have an influence long after "the age of the martyrs"—the Church's first three centuries—had expired. The standard by which all other attempts to imitate Christ and all other forms of holiness were judged, it was also frequently the image in which they were expressed. Thus the monk was a martyr to his daily routine and his struggle with evil spirits.[32] The virgin was a martyr to the temptations against purity she experienced.[33] Asceticism in general was a martyrdom, and self-imposed exile, according to Ambrose, was even better than martyrdom.[34]

A preoccupation with the role of Christ, a somewhat refined consciousness of the liturgy, and a profound susceptibility to the influence of martyrdom, then, set early Christianity apart from its later manifestations. This is by no means to imply that, from the middle of the eighth century on, these three areas were no longer of any significant concern; but they grew more muted, as indeed they had begun to do some two or three centuries previously. Of these three elements affecting the spiritual practice of Christians, the christological was the most important: Christ was, after all, the High Priest of the liturgy and the exemplar and consolation of the martyr.

The early Church's contribution to the spirituality of later generations was not limited to the three areas in question. We may also mention four other topics that bear at least brief discussion because of their great significance for the whole course of church history. They are the spiritual exegesis of the Bible, virginity, monasticism, and the hagiographic ideal.

The Spiritual Exegesis of Scripture

The Fathers of the Church were concerned when they interpreted Scripture to uncover a meaning that lay hidden beneath the more obvious literal teaching. Christians were not the first to engage in this spiritual kind of exegesis; rabbinical exegesis had already sought and discovered a hidden meaning in the Old Testament, and many pagans had long since interpreted their own myths in spiritual fashion simply because they were too embarrassing when taken literally. The history of the spiritual interpretation of Scripture—sometimes referred to as allegorization—is a complex one. Its first major proponent was Origen, who found three levels of meaning in Scripture—literal, "psychic," and spiritual—and set down rules for when a particular passage was to be interpreted in one way rather than another.[35] Although most Fathers did not follow Origen in his extreme view that *all* of Scripture had a spiritual sense while only part of it had a literal sense,[36] it would be safe to say that they all believed that at least some of the Bible was endowed with a deeper, spiritual meaning.

John Cassian, writing in the early fifth century, distinguished among three different "spiritual" levels of meaning in Scripture in addition to the literal one: the tropological, the allegorical, and the anagogical. The tropological level carried the *moral* sense or meaning of the passage, the allegorical pointed to a deeper mystery, and the anagogical raised the mind to heaven.[37] Cassian's understanding of spiritual interpretation was passed on to the medieval Western Church, and its influence was formidable indeed.

The discovery of a spiritual meaning in Scripture laid bare things that would have otherwise gone unnoticed. This was especially true for the Old Testament, where allegorization was very frequently needed to make "Christian" sense out of the text. To be sure, allegorization brought abuses with it. Biblical exegetes who employed this method were bound by few rules (although Origen, Augustine, and others had provided some), and they found meanings that the human authors of Scripture had not only not intended but would also certainly never have endorsed. Despite this, what the allegorizers generally brought to light was not esoteric doctrine but simply the mystery of Christ and the Church. They redeemed the Song of Songs for Christian readership, for example, by seeing in the bridegroom an image of Christ and in the bride an image of the Church or the Christian soul.[38] They saw baptism in the Flood, the Eucharist in the manna in the desert, the Trinity in Abraham's visitors at Mamre, and numerous other Christian truths scattered throughout the Old Testament. And medieval exegetes, continuing in this tradition, saw still more than did the Fathers.

The significance of the spiritual interpretation of the Bible with respect to the exercise of spirituality in the ancient Church was considerable. We may say, first, and quite simply, that it "Christian-ized" the Bible—specifically, the Old Testament—and made it spiritually fruitful reading for believers. The possibility of finding a spiritual meaning, moreover, gave savor to the reading of the Old Testament in particular and made the reader alert to passages that were otherwise not only incomprehensible but unattractive and even barbarous. In this way the Old Testament could become the object of what we now know as *lectio divina* or "spiritual reading." Finally, the patristic "discovery" of Christ and Christian practices such as virginity and monasticism in the Old Testament helped to justify them by giving them a certain legitimacy and pedigree, even if such practices were not really there.[39] In an era in which novelty was scorned, as was the case in antiquity, it was useful to be able to cite precedents in a work as venerable as the Old Testament for behavior that was, in fact, quite unheard of.

Virginity

Virginity is a second contribution of the early Church to the spirituality of later ages. It was a new thing, at least in its Christian manifestation. Virgins were exceedingly rare in both Judaism and pagan religions, and such virginity as existed in paganism (of which the vestal virgins are the most famous example) was, in any event, not a lifelong commitment. By contrast, in Christianity virginity was understood to be lifelong and enjoyed wide favor.

Virginity was a state in many ways similar to that of martyrdom, with the virgin being explicitly compared to the martyr, as noted above. The virgin, like the martyr, had an enviably close relationship to Christ. Although either men or women could be virgins—and it is the case that virgins were first spoken of in the masculine gender in the writings of the Fathers [40]—virginity was early on given feminine characteristics. Whether intentionally or not, this allowed for the image of the virgin as the bride of Christ, with its concomitant notions of fidelity and even eroticism, borrowed from the language of the Song of Songs.[41]

As the bride of Christ, the virgin symbolized the Church, which was itself virgin and bride. But the virgin, like the Church, was also a mother since she brought forth spiritual children, thanks to her prayers and other spiritual good works.[42] And inasmuch as in heaven there would be no marrying or giving in marriage (cf. Matt. 22:30), the virgin anticipated the Resurrection. So Ambrose could write, addressing virgins: "What is promised to us is present to you, and you have the object of our prayers. You are of this world and you are not in this world. The world merited to have you, but it could not hold you."[43]

There was a danger that attached itself to virginity, however, and it was threefold. First, virginity could engender pride, presumably on account, of the redoubtable effort that was required to maintain it, as well as by reason of all the spiritual advantages that were associated with it. The first nonscriptural text that speaks of virginity speaks of pride in the same breath.[44] So considerable a temptation might this be that Augustine devotes much of his treatise *On Holy Virginity* to the problem.[45]

Second, and linked with this pride, was the possibility of an accompanying disdain for marriage and married people. Jerome is perhaps the best example of this, [46] but unfortunately there are several others like him. Perhaps because virginity as Christians practiced it was a new phenomenon in the world, it needed to be exalted at the expense of marriage and thus ultimately find its true place in the scheme of things. But this "true place"—namely, as an equal and a complement to Christian marriage—took many centuries to achieve.

Third, virginity ran the risk of being viewed exclusively in physical terms. The response to this was to point out that virginity was even more a question of spiritual attitude than it was of physical integrity. Augustine observes when he writes in *The City of God* that the virgins who were raped during the sack of Rome in 410 were still interiorly chaste.[47] As central to the significance of virginity as was real physical integrity, the esteem for which lay at the root of this threefold danger, it was nonetheless only a part of what the early Church ordinarily expected of a virgin. Mere physical integrity made the virgin such in name only. Good works, especially prayer, fasting, and spiritual reading, were also required, as well as appropriate comportment.[48] These practices not only completed virginity, so to say, but also helped to safeguard it.

Monasticism

From virginity we can easily pass on to the third contribution of the early Church that must be mentioned: monasticism. Monasticism, after all, implied virginity, and the monk's model, like the virgin's, was martyrdom. Since a further chapter will deal with monastic spirituality in detail, it is only necessary to say a few words about it here. To virginity monasticism added several other practices, the most important among them being poverty, obedience (which was frequently understood as implied in the much-recommended virtue of discretion), and some sort of reclusion. Although all of these things were recommended for virgins, they actually contributed to the definition of the monk. Monks might live either by themselves (as anchorites or solitaries) or in communities (as cenobites). In either instance, reclusion inclined toward the desert, whether that were the sands of Egypt or the forests of Gaul. In fact, the beginnings of monasticism, as we know it in the late third and early fourth centuries in Egypt, correspond with the discovery of the desert as a place of spiritual retreat.[49] From then on, the history of monasticism and of monastic spirituality is inextricably linked with at least the *idea* of the desert, if not the reality of it.

The Hagiographic Ideal

Early Christianity's fourth and final contribution to spirituality to be discussed here is its hagiographic ideal. By this is meant the model of sanctity or holiness proposed by the ancient writers when they portray the lives of the saints. In addition to the characteristics of martyrdom (or would-be martyrdom of some sort) and virginity, the saint was a person of numerous other qualities, all of which can be distilled from the three most important early Christian hagiographies, or lives of the saints: Athanasius's mid–fourth-century *Life of Saint Anthony* (first and most influential of the genre), Sulpicius Severus's *Life of Saint Martin* (late fourth century), and the life of St. Benedict contained in *The Dialogues* of Gregory the Great (late sixth century).

From these works—in many respects typical—we learn, in the first place, that the saint is close to God. This proximity to the Divine comes through prayer (often characterized as constant), through divine visitations, and through possessing the Spirit of Christ.[50] Intimacy with God is manifested by miraculous powers—sometimes exercised in the most improbable ways, as when Martin stops in mid-air a pine tree about to fall on him.[51] The cultivation of such intimacy demands not only the more usual ascetical practices, such as fasting, but also extended periods of seclusion, as all three hagiographies testify abundantly.

Among the saints' most characteristic virtues are humility, charity even toward enemies, steadfastness in the face of demonic attack (apparent throughout *The Life of Saint Anthony* in particular), absolute single-mindedness about divine matters, a precocious maturity and discretion, and a burning zeal for the faith, whether against heretics or pagans.[52] The saint's rigorous, even off-putting austerity is frequently combined with considerable personal charm.[53] Often saints are compared to the great figures of the Old and New Testaments because of either their ability to work miracles or their virtue.[54]

We may wonder whether the saints described in these and other hagiographies were really as they are portrayed, just as we may ask whether the final hours of the martyrs were as sublime and heroic as depicted. Both kinds of accounts dwell on the marvelous and superhuman. If we were to seek instead a more "normal" story, we would be well advised to read Augustine's *Confessions,* whose popularity is the measure of its conformity to the lives of ordinary people. Yet the ancient lives of the saints, like the acts of the martyrs, bear an important message beneath their masses of fantastic details: *The saint, as bearer of the Divine, is transparent to God.* The elements of the marvelous, the improbable feats of asceticism and deeds of love, are meant to stretch the imagination beyond the particular martyr or saint to the transcendent God. In a way, then, the hagiographies and martyrdom accounts are less about the saints and martyrs than they are about God; and if they are read with this in mind, they prove more fruitful and less unsatisfying.

Origen and Augustine

Should we wish to single out individuals who were especially influential in the development of spirituality in this and subsequent eras, we would be obliged to name two: Origen and Augustine, the former Greek and the latter Latin.

The spirituality of Origen (ca. 185–ca. 254), already mentioned because of his fundamental contributions to the spiritual exegesis of Scripture, is marked by the absolute and explicit primacy of the immaterial and invisible over the visible and material, with the consequent tendency to demean the body.[55] There is for him a whole interior and immaterial world corresponding to the exterior one, especially in the realm of the anthropological, where we may speak of both an inner and outer self, each with its own faculties.[56] To Origen we owe the famous idea of the five interior senses that mirror those of the body.[57] His spiritualizing proclivity leads him to emphasize the invisible word over the visible sacraments and to see the sacraments in terms of the Word who is the second person of the Trinity.[58] Because only a few are capable of penetrating to the spiritual level of reality, where the deepest truths lie, Origen's spirituality has an intellectually elitist cast to it.[59]

Despite this intellectual elitism—so often a characteristic of perspectives that emphasize the spiritual over the material—Origen is also capable of emotional commitment. We may see this in his yearning for martyrdom from his adolescence on,[60] in his elaborate and beautiful theology of martyrdom (developed in his treatise *An Exhortation to Martyrdom*) and in his death from torture inflicted during the persecution of Decius. We see it also in the extreme asceticism he practiced, carried to the point of self-inflicted castration.[61] Origen's passion is evident, finally, in his mystical experiences[62]—experiences that undoubtedly made it possible for him to express (for the first time in Christian literature in any extended fashion) the love of God in an erotic way, as he does in his commentary and homilies on the Song of Songs.

Augustine (354–430) is the inheritor of Origen's spiritual interpretation of Scripture, and he seems to have learned other things from him as well, though probably in an indirect manner. He is perhaps best known as the author of *The Confessions,* a spiritual autobiography unprecedented in its own time and unmatched in its genre to this day. In it Augustine establishes, with a sure grasp of both psychology and theology, the pattern of a conversion to Christianity, with its gradual progress, its fits and starts, and its culmination in the discovery not only of God but of the true self as well. God and the soul, he had remarked in an earlier treatise, were the only things worth knowing.[63]

It is Augustine who, more than any of the other Fathers and later theologians, is responsible for the place that *love* occupies in Christian thought as the central and governing virtue and the measure of all activity.[64] He isolates pride as the chief of the vices and, as a result, lays great emphasis on humility.[65] Augustine not only is an absolutist with regard to truth, having written two treatises that condemn lying of any sort whatever,[66] but also discovers in truth its *affective* element, thus removing it from the solely intellectual sphere.[67]

Of all the Fathers, Augustine is the most unambiguous about grace, and the necessity of grace for accomplishing anything good at all is a theme that recurs throughout his writings, especially in those directed against the Pelagians.[68] The Pelagian heresy, which put the accomplishment of good well within human grasp and radically undervalued the role of grace, relied on ascetical practices to achieve what, for Augustine, could ultimately only be brought about by a divine gift: grace. Hence he gives minimal attention to asceticism. In contrast to

Origen, Augustine is no intellectual elitist. Since grace is God's gift, it is unattainable through human effort, even by the most highly endowed minds, and simpler persons are often readier beneficiaries of it.[69] In fact, Augustine betrays a certain suspicion of the intellect. It is too prone to acquire learning for its own sake and so to succumb to pride.[70]

Indeed, Augustine's very evident and single-minded orientation toward God is suspicious of anything that could detract from a human being's attention to him. Only what is directed explicitly toward the Divine is good and worthy of human interest. Thus art, science, and natural beauty must not be viewed as possessing any autonomy whatsoever; rather, they are all to be pressed into the service of the Divine-human relationship or else lose their raison d'être.[71]

Finally, Augustine is the one chiefly responsible for bequeathing to Western Christianity the language with which it customarily expresses mystical experience, that is, that of the soul's interior ascent to God. This language finds its classic form in Augustine's description of his own and his mother Monica's famous experience at Ostia.[72] Augustine himself seems to have been inspired by neoplatonic descriptions of this sort; but if so, he has thoroughly Christianized his sources.

It is telling that Origen and Augustine should have been not only the two greatest theologians of the ancient Church but also the individuals who most influenced its spirituality. In themselves they succeeded in bridging the gap—artificial in any event—between holiness and learning.

To the names of these two geniuses a few others might be added: Evagrius Ponticus (346–399), an ardent disciple of Origen's thought, who for the first time catalogued the eight capital sins and carefully analyzed the human soul; Basil of Caesarea (ca. 330–379), who wrote highly influential monastic rules and established a socially oriented kind of monastic life that stood in contrast to that of the Egyptian desert; John Cassian (ca. 360–ca. 432), who brought Evagrius's thought to the West; the mysterious fifth- or sixth-century Pseudo-Dionysius, the great theologian of unknowing and divinization; Benedict (ca. 480–ca. 550), who wrote the most important Western monastic rule; and Gregory the Great (ca. 540–604), who made Augustine's ideas more accessible. But all these, and others like them, are somehow influenced either by Origen or Augustine. Although for various reasons Augustine's writings made little or no impact on the East, they were peerless in the West. Origen, for his part, was without parallel in the East and, thanks to the Latin translations of his works by Jerome and Rufinus, made a powerful impression in the West as well. Between the two of them, they determined the course of the spirituality of the

Western Church for more than a millennium, and we still feel their presence in our own day.

Notes

1. Cf. Hippolytus, *Apostolic Tradition* 21.
2. Cf. *On First Principles* 3.2.1-2.
3. Cf. *History of the Monks in Egypt* 8.12; Paulinus of Nola, *Letter* 49.3; Palladius, *Lausiac History* 71.3.
4. Cf. Athanasius, *Life of St. Anthony* 35-37.
5. *Letter* 101.
6. Cf. *Letter to Nestorius* 3.7.
7. *On the Faith* 3.7.52.
8. Cf. *Letter* 125.20.
9. Cf. *Homily on Matthew* 27.3.
10. Cf. *On Holy Virginity* 55.
11. Cf. *Catechesis* 16.16ff.
12. Ibid., 16.24.
13. Cf. *First Apology* 65-67.
14. *Sermon on the Acts of the Apostles* 44.3.
15. *Sermon* 147.
16. Cf. *Synod of Vaison*, canon 2.
17. Cf. Origen, *On Prayer* 31.5
18. For a textual description cf. Cyril of Jerusalem, *Mystagogical Catechesis* 5.21-22; for artifacts, cf. the Riha Paten in the Dumbarton Oaks Collection (Washington, D.C.) and the Stuma Paten in the Archaeological Museum, Istanbul.
19. Cf. Herbert Musurillo, ed. and trans., *The Acts of the Christian Martyrs* (Oxford: Oxford University Press, 1972).
20. Cf. *Martyrdom of Polycarp* 1; *Passion of Perpetua and Felicitas* 12.
21. Cf. Eusebius, *Ecclesiastical History* 5.1.22; ibid., 5.1.56.
22. Cf. *Martyrdom of Polycarp* 16.1.
23. Cf. *Exhortation to Martyrdom* 30, 50.
24. Cf. *Martyrdom of Polycarp* 5.2.
25. Cf. Cyprian, *Letter* 15.
26. Cf. *Martyrdom of Polycarp* 2.3.
27. Cf. Origen, *Exhortation to Martyrdom* 18.
28. Cf. *Martyrdom of Pionius* 22.
29. Cf. Tertullian, *On the Soul* 55.
30. Cf. Tertullian, *On Baptism* 16.
31. *Letter* 14.2.
32. Cf. Athanasius, *Life of St. Antony* 47; Pseudo-Macarius, *On Freedom of Mind* 15.
33. Cf. Ambrose, *Commentary on Psalms* 118.47.
34. Cf. Sulpicius Severus, *Letter* 2; Ambrose, *Letter* 63.70.
35. Cf. *On First Principles* 4.2-3.
36. Cf. ibid., 4.3.5.
37. Cf. *Conference* 14.8.
38. Cf. Origen, *Commentary on the Song of Songs*, passim.
39. Cf. Ambrose, *On Virgins* 1.3.12; Athanasius, *Life of St. Antony* 7.
40. Cf. *1 Clement* 38.2
41. Cf. Ambrose, *On Virgins* 1.7.38ff.
42. Cf. Gregory of Nyssa, *On Virginity* 19.
43. *On Virgins* 1.9.52.
44. Cf. *1 Clement* 38.2.
45. Cf. *On Holy Virginity* 31.31ff.
46. Cf. *Against Jovinianus*, passim.
47. Cf. *The City of God* 1.16, 28.
48. Cf. Ambrose, *On Virgins* 3.4.15ff; Pseudo-Clement, *Letter on Virginity* 1.3.
49. Cf. Athanasius, *Life of St. Antony* 3.

50. Cf. Sulpicius Severus, *Life of St. Martin* 26; Athanasius, *Life of St. Antony* 10; Gregory the Great, *Dialogues* 2.8.
51. Cf. Sulpicius Severus, *Life of St. Martin* 13.
52. Cf. ibid., 9; Gregory the Great, *Dialogues* 2.8; ibid., 2.1; Athanasius, *Life of St. Antony* 68-70; Sulpicius Severus, *Life of St. Martin* 14.
53. Cf. Athanasius, *Life of St. Antony* 47; ibid., 67.
54. Cf. Gregory the Great, *Dialogues* 2.5-8; Athanasius, *Life of St. Antony* 1.
55. Cf. *On Prayer* 17.
56. Cf. *Commentary on the Song of Songs*, preface.
57. Cf. *On First Principles* 1.1.9.
58. Cf. *Serial Commentary on Matthew* 85.
59. Cf. *On First Principles* 4.2.8.
60. Cf. Eusebius, *Ecclesiastical History* 6.2.3-6.
61. Cf. ibid., 6.8.1-2.
62. Cf. *Homily on the Song of Songs* 1.7
63. Cf. *Soliloquies* 1.7.
64. Cf. *On Christian Doctrine* 1.35.39ff.
65. Cf. *The City of God* 14.13; *Letter* 118.3.22.
66. Cf. *On Lying, Against Lying*.
67. Cf. *Confessions* 3.6.10.
68. E.g., *On Nature and Grace*.
69. Cf. *Confessions* 8.8.19.
70. Cf. *Letter* 55.21.39.
71. Cf. *On Christian Doctrine* 2.
72. Cf. *Confessions* 9.10.23-24.

Bibliography

Primary Sources

It can be truly said that all, or virtually all, patristic literature has at least some bearing on spirituality since most of it focuses explicitly on some dimension of Christian faith and life in a quite practical way; and spirituality is precisely practical. If one were to be more specific, however, the following works, all available in one or more English translations and listed in roughly chronological order, would be singled out as particularly important:

Origen's commentary and homilies on the Song of Songs
Athanasius's *Life of Saint Anthony*
Basil the Great's *Longer Rules*
Augustine's *Confessions*
Cassian's *Conferences*
Pseudo-Dionysius's *Ecclesiastical Hierarchy*

Secondary Sources

Bouyer, Louis. *The Spirituality of the New Testament and the Fathers.* New York: Desclée Company, 1963.
Bradshaw, Paul F. *Daily Prayer in the Early Church.* New York: Oxford University Press, 1982.
Chitty, Derwas J. *The Desert a City.* Oxford: Basil Blackwell, 1966.
Daniélou, Jean. *The Bible and the Liturgy.* Notre Dame, Ind.: University of Notre Dame Press, 1956.

Frend, W. H. C. *Martyrdom and Persecution in the Early Church: A Study of Conflict from the Maccabees to Donatus.* Garden City, N.Y.: Anchor Books, 1967.

Jungmann, Josef A. *The Early Liturgy to the Time of Gregory the Great.* Notre Dame, Ind.: University of Notre Dame Press, 1959.

Ladner, Gerhart B. *The Idea of Reform: Its Impact on Christian Thought and Action in the Age of the Fathers.* New York: Harper Torchbooks, 1967.

Louth, Andrew. *The Origins of the Christian Mystical Tradition: From Plato to Denis.* Oxford: Clarendon Press, 1981.

Ramsey, Boniface, O.P. *Beginning to Read the Fathers.* New York: Paulist Press, 1985.

Translations of Patristic Texts

The works cited in the notes to the present essay (with a few exceptions), as well as numerous other patristic writings, can be found in English translation in the following series:

Ancient Christian Writers

The Ante-Nicene Fathers

The Fathers of the Church

Library of Christian Classics

Library of the Fathers of the Holy Catholic Church

A Select Library of Nicene and Post-Nicene Fathers of the Christian Church

Reading for Holiness:
Lectio Divina

GABRIEL O'DONNELL, o.p.

For the word of God is quick, and powerful, and sharper than any twoedged sword, piercing even to the dividing asunder of soul and spirit, and of the joints and marrow, and is a discerner of the thoughts and intents of the heart.

—HEBREWS 4:12 KJV

Today everyone recognizes the great handicap illiteracy can be. To a degree unknown in recorded history, many "ordinary folk" now routinely learn to read and write with some distinction. Mass media and the information explosion of the second half of the twentieth century have made it possible to raise the level of literacy even in remote areas of rural life. To know how to read is to be enabled: The literate citizen has the power to pursue goals and defend his or her rights in ways impossible without this significant tool.

There is a clear parallel in speaking of the spiritual life, for here too one must become "literate" by learning how to read the sacred texts in a specialized and faithfully practiced way. Reading in the quest for God—or reading for holiness—has traditionally been called *lectio divina*. The Latin phrase originated in the fourth and fifth centuries and was associated in its beginnings with the spirituality of the monastic life. Literally, it means "divine reading" or "sacred reading." The primary source of what is read in *lectio divina* is Sacred Scripture. Secondarily, *lectio* refers to the reading of other texts recognized as holy by the Christian community, particularly the writings of the Fathers of the Church. Although Scripture and patristic literature continue to be the primary sources used in the practice of *lectio divina,* in later and, especially, in contemporary times, *lectio divina* has been expanded to include the reading of all spiritual books. Some distinctions are necessary here, however, since to read a book about God or the life of prayer is not necessarily to practice *lectio divina.*

Reading the Book of Memory

Reading in the ancient world was not the same as reading in the modern sense of the word. People did not then pick up a book, silently look at it, and simultaneously mentally register what the text signified. To begin with, books had to be produced individually by hand and were therefore scarce and expensive. Further, reading as practiced in antiquity did not refer to the silent work of the eyes and the mind but rather to the oral speaking of words so that they could be physically heard and taken in. One reads, in the ancient sense of that word, with one's mouth and one's ears. In this context, a text is intended to be heard—since words are meant to be proclaimed and heard—and not, primarily, to be seen. In reading in this ancient sense, the reader becomes both proclaimer and hearer of the word and, in the case of *lectio divina,* of the Word of God.

In *lectio,* the book that is opened to be read is the book of our own memory. *Lectio* as a form of vocalization lends itself naturally to repetition of particular words and phrases, and such repetition does in fact become part of the very technique of reading for holiness. Thus the consoling word, the arresting phrase, the sentence that challenges us to the core, is repeated over and over again and, consigned to memory, remains forever available.

Yet the point of repetition in *lectio* is not memorization for its own sake. Repetition is the means whereby we take in the Word of God and allow ourselves to be nourished and permeated by it. An early metaphor used to describe *lectio* is that of eating. A morsel of food is taken, chewed over, broken apart, and swallowed. *Lectio divina* is like that: A phrase from the Bible is first tasted, then savored and chewed—or repeated over and over—and finally swallowed or consumed. There is a mutual interaction or penetration between reader and text in *lectio* that fulfills a divine promise: "If a man loves me, he will keep my word, and my Father will love him, and we will come to him and make our home with him" (John 14:23).

When the early monks and nuns went about the business of *lectio,* they believed that there was in each text a personal message *for them in particular.* They did not assume that the message indicated the meaning of this scriptural text for the whole Church for all time but felt "Right now, here, today, at this moment, God has something to say to *me.*" So they approached *lectio* with great devotion and a sense of expectation and readiness. If they were disappointed, as they often were, they realized that it was because some inward obstacle or resistance prevented them from being able to truly hear the word being "read." Most important, they never used *lectio divina* for some utilitarian or pragmatic purpose, such as preparing a sermon, learning more "about" the Bible, or even for what we might now call spiritual self-improvement. *Lectio* is a disciplined form of devotion and not a method of Bible study. It is done purely and simply to come to know God, to be brought before his Word, to listen.

Finally, *lectio divina,* practiced habitually and privately, begins to set up a certain dynamic between the individual's personal experience of the Word of God and its proclamation in the Church's liturgy. For example, if we happen to use a particular passage from St. Paul's letter to the Philippians for *lectio* and then hear that text publicly proclaimed on the third Sunday of Advent, a light goes on: "I know that text. I have read that text. I have proclaimed that text. That text is *mine.*" A new dynamism is generated when what is proclaimed in the Church begins to create an urgency, an energy, within the heart of the Christian person.

Learning to Do *Lectio*

In actual practice *lectio* is very simple: One finds some private place and begins repeating a text, either taking it from a printed text or remembering it from the liturgy. Let us suppose that the minister has preached on Psalm 23 ("The Lord is my shepherd; I shall not want"), and it strikes a chord. We begin to think about it. Ideally, we would find a quiet corner and begin actually to "mumble" the text. (In chapter 48 of his famous *Rule,* St. Benedict insists that the monks not do their *lectio* in the dormitory, because they could be heard and might disturb those trying to rest.) While mumbling the phrase we would "ruminate" on it—ponder it, rest in it.

When in the midst of repeating "The Lord is my shepherd" other thoughts creep in—planning the day, remembering to pick up the dry cleaning—what should we do? Traditional practice says: *Go back to the Word,* read on a bit further. Use the Word of God as your safeguard, your guide. Don't fight the devil; don't fight yourself. That is God's business. The only tool Jesus had in the desert was the Word of God—what he had learned "by heart"—and prayer. Calmly, insistently, we must "read" on, and eventually we will be led into discourse with the Divine. Done properly, *lectio divina* is a form of reading that leads to prayer.

Lectio has been described as a prayer that begins as a "dialogue" and ends as a "duet." Thus what begins as God addressing us and our responding leads eventually to an experience of union. Through the power of the Word of God proclaimed and heard, we are drawn into the presence of God, into the heart of God, to be in perfect harmony with the divine will.

One critical issue is choosing the text that will be the subject of our *lectio*. Presumably one begins with the Bible or one of the spiritual classics, a text worthy of the attention that the reader gives to it. The Scriptures and time-tested authors are best, especially in the beginning stages. There should be continuity in our *lectio* from day to day. Choose a text, such as the Gospel of Mark, begin at the beginning, and continue to the end, picking up each day where you left off the previous day. Avoid random selection of passages from a book of the Bible or your favorite spiritual author. The point of *lectio* is to allow the reader to be drawn into the text and to discover its meaning. Textual "roulette" can undermine this purpose and tempt us to use *lectio* for some immediate gratification or tangible spiritual consolation. How far along we get in the text is less important than how open we are to the power and message of the text in leading us to authentic communication with God. Some days we may cover a good bit of ground before we are struck by a word or phrase and "linger" over it by repeating it quietly and peacefully. On other occasions we do not get through more than a sentence or two before we are led into prayer.

Reading for Holiness: A Way to God

A later formulation describes the close connection between *lectio* and prayer: *lectio, meditatio, oratio, contemplatio*. Reading, meditation, prayer, contemplation—each one tends toward the others. Strictly speaking, *lectio* means reading; but when what is read is repeated often enough, it leads to reflection and perhaps even to visualizing in the mind's eye a biblical scene. In the case mentioned above, we might picture a shepherd leading his sheep into lush and peaceful pastures. This is meditation in the ancient sense: to think about something and peacefully turn it over in your mind. If we find ourselves doing this with tension and urgency, if *lectio* becomes something that *has* to get done, then we have lost the sense of sacred reading that leads to meditation. It must remain a leisurely activity.

Such "rumination" on the Twenty-third Psalm may well lead to a desire to speak to the shepherd, to speak to God. Our heart and mind move toward the Lord who is the Good Shepherd, and this movement of the heart toward God is the beginning of prayer. Contemplation is the summit of the prayer experience, a profound communion with God that is all-embracing and changes one's life, perhaps dramatically. Such experiences are rare but not impossible for the beginner. Normally they follow on years of fruitful attendance on God. The word *lectio* (or *lectio divina*) implies all these things, not necessarily as consecutive experiences in the life of prayer but as predictable moments and milestones in the search for God.

The search for God always begins with *lectio:* It begins with the Word of God. It is not simply a matter of exercising willpower but more a constant *turning back* to the Word—a form of repentance, so to speak. When distracted or worried, we are forever offered refuge and strength in the Word of God. Yet sinful human nature as often as not resists the invitation to meet God in *lectio* or tries to find a way to "use" the experience in self-serving ways. Typically we are more concerned with what *we* can get out of the experience than we are about the issue of faithful attendance on God. What *lectio* in fact offers us is a mostly "hidden" form of communion with God. Who knows what our reading for holiness means to God? That it rejoices the heart of God we cannot doubt, but our call is to become proclaimers of the Word, to live in the Word.

Ideally one "does" *lectio* for thirty minutes each day, certainly not less than fifteen minutes. There may be times when longer periods of *lectio* are possible, as on a quiet day or a retreat. We must become calm and recollected to begin sacred reading; our critical, academic, analytical faculties must be suspended and replaced with an attitude of expectancy so that *lectio* may become "our time with God," a time that by worldly standards is "wasted" because it yields no direct or visible return. As a result, we can never be sure how long we will linger over a particular word or phrase or sentence. The point is not to get through the text but rather to "read" it in the deepest meaning of that word. Significantly, for the modern reader *lectio* is a form of surrender, of letting go. God leads the way and sets the agenda; we are never sure where the practice of *lectio* will lead. In a very real sense, we give up control to the sacred text, and only then are we free to enter into that quiet part of the self where we meet God—that place where we can truthfully say whatever needs to be said and listen to Truth in return. All successful relationships require time, effort, and attention. The daily practice of *lectio* establishes a pattern that becomes the foundation for a serious relationship with God.

There is, then, no objective measure of success or failure in the practice of *lectio divina*. The reader is always moving into uncharted waters—a personal encounter with the Word. Perhaps this is why the modern individual, so geared to reading for comprehension and tangible results, has great difficulty in changing gears to develop the habit of *lectio*. Yet the efforts we make in this direction will ultimately bear a rich harvest. This mingling of prayer and reading that we call *lectio divina* brings us into contact with God, and through the liberating power of the Word of God we begin the journey into wisdom. Ultimately, our personal liberation and transformation enables us to encourage a similar liberation in our brothers and sisters who hunger for God and the peace of the kingdom.

EXERCISES

For an Individual

First choose the text you want to use for *lectio*. For beginners it is best to use one of the synoptic Gospels to initiate the practice of *lectio divina*. (*The Imitation of Christ* by Thomas à Kempis is a good non-scriptural choice.) Find a quiet place at a time when you are not likely to be interrupted by the telephone or visitors. Spend the first few minutes getting physically quiet and spiritually centered. Repeating the name of Jesus quietly may be of great help, or one might look at a crucifix, an icon, or some religious image. Invoking the aid of the holy Spirit is another appropriate way to begin.

Once you are quiet and interiorly focused, simply begin to slowly *speak* the text aloud in a low voice. When a particular word or phrase strikes you, often for no apparent reason, let yourself repeat it over and over again in the same slow, peaceful rhythm. Let the text go deeply within you, even though there may well be no clear intellectual activity going on in your mind. When you tire of this repetition or you are distracted with unconnected thoughts, concerns, or anxieties, simply return to the text, pick up where you left off, and go on with your reading until something further strikes you.

Each period of *lectio* should be concluded with a prayer of thanksgiving to God for the graces given in this time of prayer. Both the initial preparation of quieting down and this concluding prayer are important for establishing within one a structure that is consistent, regardless of one's emotional or physical state. A personally devised structure carries us over the times we are not able to be as present as we would like to be to this spiritual practice.

Continue this practice for fifteen minutes a day for one week. The second week, increase your time to twenty minutes. Within a month, you should be able to sustain about thirty minutes of *lectio*.

For a Group

People learn best when they are *shown,* rather than *told,* how to do something. To demonstrate such an intensely personal activity as *lectio* is not easy, but we have found it well worth the effort. The following instructions are offered to assist teachers and group leaders in this challenging task.

Arrange the seating and lighting to create an atmosphere of quiet and calm. Ask the group to close their eyes and concentrate on the variety of sounds they can hear: the traffic, nature, the "breathing" of the building, and the like. Then slowly invite the group to intentionally withdraw from each of those sounds to the core of silence within the self. There one can meet and speak to God.

Once the group is focused in this way, someone begins to read and repeat a scriptural text slowly and carefully in a peaceful tone of voice. The first several lines are repeated several times over; then the reader pauses before offering some personal response to the text, as in the pattern of reading leading to meditation and prayer.

The exercise can also be done effectively with two voices, one reading the text repetitively and the other supplying the meditative responses.

Using Psalm 63 (vv. 1-4 from the Jerusalem Bible), such an exercise might go something like this; notice how the meditation or "rumination" slips imperceptibly into prayer:

First Reader:
(text and repetition)

"God, you are my God, I am seeking you,
my soul is thirsting for you,
my flesh is longing for you,
a land parched, weary and waterless;
I long to gaze on you in the Sanctuary,
and to see your power and glory."
God, you are my God . . . *You* are my God,
I am seeking you. You are my God, I
am seeking *you.* My soul is thirsting for *you,* thirsting
for you. You are my God, I am seeking you. My
flesh is longing for you. You are my God, I am
seeking *you.*

Pause

Second Reader:
(meditation)

Jesus, I *am* seeking you, but I am seeking a lot of other things too, and some of them take me far from you. I am torn and confused.

51

First Reader:
(repetition)

God, you are my God, I am seeking you. My soul is thirsting for you, my flesh is longing for you. God, you are my God, I am seeking you.

Pause

Second Reader:
(meditation)

I need your help to figure out what I really want most in my life, and I need your help to want *you* as the absolute center of my existence. Help me, Lord Jesus.

First Reader:
(text and
repetition)

"Your love is better than life itself,
my lips will recite your praise;
all my life I will bless you,
in your name lift up my hands."
God, you are my God, I am seeking *you*. Your love is better than life itself, *better than life itself*. I am seeking you. Your love is better than life itself.

Pause

Second Reader:
(meditation)

Today I have sought many things that I should not seek: my ambition, my need to control, and my desire to be thought well of by others caused me to seek ways to compromise the truth and disregard the needs and feelings of my co-workers. Forgive me, Lord.

First Reader:

God, you are my God, I am seeking you.

This verbalization of *lectio* should only last about ten minutes or less. When completed, the group should be given copies of the psalm and then dispersed to various rooms or parts of the same room to continue *lectio* for another ten to fifteen minutes. At a stated time the group should reassemble and be given ample time to raise questions and discuss the experience together.

DISCUSSION QUESTIONS

1. How much reading, in the ordinary meaning of that term, do you think the average member of your congregation/parish does? Is most of it for work or for pleasure? Is the notion of reading as a leisure activity attractive to people today, or have various forms of the media usurped the role that quiet reading once played in our lives?

2. Our educational institutions have tended to emphasize a wide range of reading for information on any given topic, with strong emphasis on current, up-to-date material, especially periodical literature. Discuss the impact this is likely to have on our efforts to practice the discipline of *lectio divina*, which emphasizes depth or perception in reading a text. Do you think most moderns could adapt to this style?

3. Most of us like to know exactly where we're going, both in career choices and emotional development. What effects does this need to be always in control have on the development of action and prayer?

4. Draw from the group a list of books and other texts that individuals think would be good to use for *lectio*. It might be that when reading something particularly challenging or helpful, they found themselves wanting to go back over that selection but never got around to it. Do such experiences suggest a nascent awareness on the part of most people of the potential a given text may have for deeper riches and insight? Explore this possibility with the group.

5. Tiredness and distraction are always obstacles to growing in prayer. Some of the group may have dozed off in the experience of *lectio* or mentally wandered far away. This is especially true when the atmosphere is soft and peaceful. Is such weakness incompatible with the practice of *lectio*? Draw from the group their own sense of the obstacles they may face and how they intend to confront them.

Resources

Cousins, Kathryn and Ewert, with Payne, Richard J. *How to Read a Spiritual Book.* New York: Paulist Press, 1981.

Hall, Thelma R.C. *Too Deep for Words: Rediscovering Lectio Divina.* New York: Paulist Press, 1988.

Leclercq, Jean. "Lectio Divina." *Worship* 58, no. 3 (May 1984): 239-48.

_____. *The Love of Learning and the Desire for God: A Study of Monastic Culture.* New York: Fordham University Press, 1974. (See especially chapters 1 and 5.)

Mulholland, M. Robert. *Shaped by the Word: The Power of Scripture in Spiritual Formation.* Nashville: The Upper Room, 1985.

Muto, Susan. *Approaching the Sacred: An Introduction to Spiritual Reading.* Denville, N.J.: Dimension Books, 1973.

_____. *Pathways of Spiritual Living.* Garden City, N.Y.: Doubleday, 1984.

_____. *A Practical Guide to Spiritual Reading.* Denville, N.J.: Dimension Books, 1976.

Wells, Ronald V. *Spiritual Disciplines for Everyday Living*. Schenectady, N.Y.: Character Research Press, 1982. (See especially chapter 1.)

Wesley, John. "Advice on Spiritual Reading." From the preface to Wesley's abridgement of Thomas à Kempis's treatise on the *Imitation of Christ*. In *John and Charles Wesley*, edited by Frank Whaling, pp. 88-89. Ramsey, N.J.: Paulist Press, 1981.

CHAPTER 2

Monastic Life
and the Search for God

GABRIEL O'DONNELL, O.P.

*If you would be perfect, go, sell what you possess and give to the poor, and you will have
treasure in heaven.*

—MATTHEW 19:21

In Athanasius's *Life of Saint Anthony*, there is an often-repeated
vignette that accounts for the beginnings of the monastic life.[1] There
Anthony is portrayed as a young man on the brink of life when he
enters the church and hears the text from Matthew's Gospel being
proclaimed: "If you would be perfect, go, sell what you possess . . ."
That Word takes hold of Anthony's heart, and his life is changed. He
must literally sell his possessions, give the proceeds to the poor, and in
his new state of poverty and need, follow Christ. His quest leads him
into the desert, where in solitude he imitates the forty-day wilderness
sojourn of Christ in prayer, self-denial, and the continual pondering of
that Word which compelled Anthony to seek first the kingdom of God,
promising that all else would then be added.

As Athanasius records it, monasticism begins with the conversion
of Anthony and his subsequent search for perfect communion with
God in the wilderness. Before long, others were inspired to search
out Anthony and persuade him to become their spiritual guide. Thus
his solitary search became a corporate venture, or, one should say,
adventure; for the enthusiastic embrace of a life of self-denial and
constant prayer by this original band of spiritual explorers
represents one of the great experiments in human courage and
endurance.

Although monasticism has taken a variety of forms throughout the ages, the movement as a whole has been characterized by a common set of images and ideals—a common wisdom. We begin this essay by identifying the essential components of that vision of the spiritual life we call "monastic." It is a vision that for centuries has fired the imagination of those who are hungry for God.

The Spiritual Principles of Monasticism

The Imitation of Christ

Although the exact historicity of the Athanasian account is debated, the theological truth communicated is not: Just as Christ was driven into the wilderness by the Holy Spirit for a time of testing and tutelage, so the first monks and nuns were compelled by the power of the Word of God to "leave the world" and begin the search for God in the desert regions of Egypt and Palestine. Whether geographically located in the actual desert or withdrawn into the monastic enclosure, these men and women were less concerned to reject the world and flee from it (*fuga mundi*) than they were to imitate Christ (*imitatio Christi*) in his perfect submission to the Father's will. They hungered for communion with God and peace with one another. Theirs, however, was no moderate hunger. Famished with the desire to love God and neighbor *perfectly*, the first generations of monks and nuns pushed themselves to the limits of their physical and psychological endurance in this great experiment in gospel living.

It was this burning vision of the possibility of knowing God in an intimate way that drew so many women and men to turn from the ordinary pattern of society to the harshness and loneliness of the desert, where they would attempt to recreate the fervor and simplicity of the young church at Jerusalem so vividly portrayed in the Acts of the Apostles. What, then, was the intention of the early fathers and mothers of desert monasticism? Did they hope to create a life apart from the rest of the Christian community, in which a heroic search for God might be mounted? In fact, they were attempting to establish Christian life merely "as it should be." A life of simplicity, focused on the Lord and bearing the fruit of humble service to one another, formed the ethos of the first monastic communities. Far from being extraordinary, life in the monastery, in light of the account in Acts, was *ordinary* Christian life, without all the complications, distractions, and compromises imposed by the situation in which fourth-century Christians found themselves.

Solitude and Community

In his account of the origins of monasticism, Athanasius emphasizes Anthony's initial movement into solitude, where he experiences the blessedness and peace of his hermitage, *O beato solitudo,* and his eventual, reluctantly received call into community. While the name "monk" comes from the Greek word *monos* (meaning "alone," "single," or "unmarried"), monastic life takes two basic forms: the solitary or eremitical life and communal or cenobitical life. As with Anthony, the two tendencies are sometimes in tension, but more often they have been combined with varying degrees of emphasis (on either solitude or community) to produce a range of forms, all of which are termed "monastic life."

The arduousness and risk of a life of solitude were quickly realized by early hermits. Although it was often considered a higher calling than the cenobitic life, the life of solitude required such exacting preparation that the conviction soon arose that the cenobium, or monastery, was the proper training ground for eremitical life. Learning to live with others and to love them—was seen as the prerequisite for entrance into the solitary life.[2]

To live alone, deprived of ordinary social interchange, necessitated a highly developed personal discipline; otherwise one might waste precious hours in daydreaming or mental flights of fancy. On the other hand, tasks that were shared by many in the cenobium fell to the individual hermit alone; and thus the burden of providing for food, light, and heat could occupy all one's time and attention, to the neglect of prayer, reading, and silent waiting for the Lord. Whether through laziness or overactivity, the solitary could slip into unreality, living a self-absorbed existence rather than continuing the journey toward God.

While life in the cenobium involved similar risks, there were more structured safeguards, most especially the regime of the monastery and one's relationship with the superior, who daily observed the monk or the nun in activity and in prayer. To develop a life of discipline and a healthy love and respect for others in the close environment of the cenobium was seen as suitable preparation for the hermitage.

Obedience and Spiritual Parentage

Whether one lives alone or in community, the need for accountability in the spiritual life remains constant. Therefore, in all forms of this life called "monastic," the role of the spiritual leader was central. Just as his early disciples looked to Anthony for guidance and wisdom, the monastic institution became synonymous with spiritual maternity and paternity, formalized in the office of the abbess and abbot. Spiritual formation was centered in the relationship of obedience between the novice and the spiritual mother or father who would guide by word and example to a life of integration and radical openness to God. The opening of one's mind and heart to the influence of the spiritual parent was the crucial first demand of the would-be monk or nun. All secrets had to be laid bare, and it was with great confidence in the holiness and doctrine of the spiritual mother or father that the neophyte began the journey into self-knowledge and humility through the path of obedience. It was the spiritual father or mother who supervised the process of transformation by which one was "begotten" in the monastic life—a process that entailed putting off the old or false self and putting on Christ.

Just as Christ struggled in the desert and in the garden to discover and surrender to the will of the Father, so too the monk or nun saw the relationship of obedience as central to the desert call to communion with God. Obedience, as an expression of humility and leading to the fulfillment of love, rendered one receptive to the movements of the Holy Spirit. This receptivity, in turn, led to intimacy with God. In this way the capacity to do the will of another, even when it was against one's own wishes and better judgment, was seen as an expression of the self-transcendent love that is at the core of the gospel message: "My Father, if it be possible, let this cup pass from me; nevertheless not as I will, but as thou wilt" (Matt. 26:39b).

Every monk or nun strove mightily to achieve the taxing ideal of perfect obedience or surrender. This tradition of practical wisdom born from the experience of the daily struggle in the desert was handed on from generation to generation and has been preserved in a number of texts available to us even today.[3]

Monastic Life as a Substitute for Martyrdom

The ideal of martyrdom, which so animated the early Church, was no stranger to monasticism (see chapter 1). Unable to sacrifice their lives in actual physical martyrdom, the early monks and nuns lived daily a life of sincere self-sacrifice. In time, monasticism came to be seen as a substitute for martyrdom. What the martyr accomplished in the moment of death at the hands of others—namely, conformity to the Lord in his death and resurrection—the monk or the nun achieved over a lifetime. Day by day, one's "blood" was spilled in the rigors of fasting, reading or *lectio divina* (see practicum 1), nocturnal prayer, and manual labor. More significantly, one "died" each day in countless attempts to "put on the mind of Christ" in humility, generous service, and a forgetfulness of self that would open the mind and heart to a new knowledge of God. Thus it was in the secret recesses of the heart that martyrdom was accomplished.

Change in attitudes as well as behavior were the order of the day in the cloister, and this commitment to constant conversion formed the core of life for any man or woman who donned the monastic robe. The external observances of the monastic life were an anchor for the monk or nun. On the surface they appear to severely limit the movements of the individual, while in reality they created the conditions for a radical personal freedom; for it was in the stabilizing rhythms of external activities that the real work of dying and rising could take place. In this way, the externals were intended to free the spirit to embrace a life of spiritual martyrdom, which would lead the individual into perfect conformity with Christ in his martyrdom on the cross. Athanasius described Anthony as a martyr as well as a soldier, fighting the enemies of egoism, pride, and arrogance.

Virginity and the Monastic Life

Further, the martyrdom of virginity or chastity was always understood to be an essential part of the monastic vocation. The struggle to curb and deny the natural impulse toward sexual intimacy and the creation of a family is a strong theme in early monastic literature. The early mothers and fathers of the desert professed an ideal of perfect chastity that was considered impossible by their contemporaries. Unembarrassed by human sexuality, they straightforwardly speak of the temptations and dangers involved in such a lofty calling: "It was related of Amma Sarah that for thirteen years she waged warfare against the demon of fornication. She never prayed that the warfare should cease but she said, 'O God, give me strength.'"[4]

To become eunuchs for the sake of the kingdom not only allows monastics to more perfectly imitate the virginal Christ but also reminds them that the same Christ is the principal love of their lives and all other loves must be measured by this primary relationship. For them, chastity is not simply about sexuality, but about *love*. If chastity hollows out a greater space within for God, then all to the good. No matter how violent the temptations, the virginal heart must always cling steadfastly to Christ. That temptations would occur was presumed by the earliest generations of monastic writers. The call into the desert of monastic life was a call to *face squarely* the impulses of greed, sexual desire, ambition, and pride, which are part of the universal human experience. The monk or nun was to be no exception. Indeed, to deny such drives would be another form of unreality or self-deception— one of the great fears of anyone who has embraced a life of silence and asceticism: "Whoever has not experienced temptation cannot enter into the Kingdom of Heaven. . . . Without temptations no one can be saved."[5] The authentic monk or nun was courageous in naming inner desires and drives that could easily become a temptation to turn from the love of God to a life of indulgence and self-love.

Desert monasticism of the fourth and fifth centuries represents the earliest stratum of this deliberate movement away from self-deception. It was centered on the great commandment of love: a love for God embodied in an intense and exclusive commitment and a love for neighbor that continually sought means to diminish interpersonal hostilities and develop authentic mutual forgiveness and acceptance. "You shall love the Lord your God with all your heart, and with all your soul, and with all your mind. This is the great and first commandment. And a second is like it, You shall love your neighbor as yourself. On these two commandments depend all the law and the prophets" (Matt. 22:37-40). Paradoxically, the monastic quest for martyrdom in the practice of poverty, chastity, and obedience, far from repelling people, attracted them. In their daily and sacrificial search for God, the early monks and nuns were forging a way of life that would draw thousands of members for centuries to come and be a point of grudging fascination for even the most disinterested bystander.[6]

Monastic Silence

"A brother who shared a lodging with other brothers asked Abba Bessarion, 'What should I do?' The old man replied, 'Keep silence and do not compare yourself with others.'"[7] The pervasive atmosphere of the life shared by both the hermit and the monk was that of silence. The silence of the monastery was not meant to be the simple absence of external noise but was to promote an inner silence of the spirit in which a life of communion with God could be sustained, regardless of the various occupations in which one must be engaged. Interior silence should produce self-knowledge and self-acceptance, which, when experienced in light of the gospel, must bring inner peace and joy.

Monks and nuns lived within the silent world of the enclosure in order to sharpen their ability to hear the Word of God. The Rule of St. Benedict warns that "speaking and teaching are the master's task; the disciple is to be silent and listen."[8] Since the monk or the nun was called to be a disciple, permission was required of the superior to engage in conversation; and because of human weakness and the need for speaking in order to carry on the ordinary business of daily life, constant vigilance was required to maintain a life of peace and recollection.

The Development of Cenobitic Monasticism

As the early years of experience became decades, and decades became generations, the great leaders of this movement emerged and often set down their experience in the form of monastic "rules." Rules for monasteries were more than catalogues of regulations for the smooth administration of a community. A rule was intended to embody a particular vision of the monastic journey—a concrete way of living in the Spirit. Some rules emphasized solitude, others community; some provided many practical details, others simply stated general principles of the spiritual and monastic life. Whatever its content or viewpoint, the monastic rule was intended to preserve an atmosphere of single-minded purpose and to safeguard a radical God-orientation—qualities that experience had taught required great vigilance and energy. Some of the most durable of these rules, those of Pachomius, Basil, Augustine, and Benedict, generated whole families of monastic communities and were revered for their balance and spiritual insight. (Other forms of literature were written by the early greats of the monastic tradition—treatises on the ascetical life, virginity, the life of virtue, and the importance of sound doctrine in living an intense Christian life. Further, the lives of these important leaders became, in turn, subjects for spiritual biographies that were intended to edify their followers and spur them on to greater zeal and fervor.)

Pachomius (ca. 290–346) is looked upon as the first great organizer of cenobitic monasticism. Opposed to the solitary life, Pachomius saw the monastic family as a form of "the apostolic life" described in the Acts of the Apostles. The fervor and simplicity of the church of Jerusalem, gathered about the apostles, became the dominant theme of his teaching and of the rule he produced. While taking the form of a lengthy compilation of regulations, the Pachomian Rule communicates an overarching concern for the quality of life in the community. "Pachomian community is not just a grouping of individuals around a spiritual father, but a fellowship of brothers, a *koinonia*."[9] Adopting the term *koinonia* to express the meaning of the monastic life, Pachomius laid the foundation for later understandings of community life that would use his teaching as a starting point.

Like Pachomius, St. Basil (ca. 330–379) was opposed to the strictly eremitical way of life and conceived of monastic life as the imitation of the apostolic community at Jerusalem. His contribution to the developing theology of the monastic vocation is found in his insistence on the great law of love—love of God and love of neighbor—as the context for the whole monastic enterprise. The monk retires to the quiet of the monastery to avoid being distracted from this end; but once within the enclosure of the monastery, he must be an industrious worker, continually occupied in mind and heart with prayer. In his Rule, Basil offers not only regulations but also a clear rationale for every aspect of life in the monastery. His preoccupation with justifying monastic usages through the texts of Scripture begins a whole tradition of searching the Scriptures for echoes of the monastic vocation.

St. Augustine of Hippo (354–430) was an innovator in the tradition of the monastic life in several ways. First, his monasteries were not situated in desert regions or remote locations but in the cities. Thus we see in Augustine the beginnings of urban monasteries where withdrawal into the monastery enclosure is, in effect, movement into the desert. Second, Augustine's overriding concern is the unity of the community. To be of one mind and one heart in God is the goal of the monastic life. He even interprets the name "monk" in this light: "They then who thus live together as to make one man, so that they really possess what is written, *one mind and one heart*, [Acts 4:32] many bodies but not many minds; many bodies, but not many hearts; can rightly be called *Monos*, that is, one alone."[10] Third, the formative relationship of monk to abbot is now, in Augustinian monasticism, superseded by the relationship of the monk or the nun to the community. In Augustine's Rule, while obedience is presumed, the community takes center stage. One's spiritual development is primarily linked with the life of the cenobium. This new formulation of monastic life, radically communitarian, was to have a profound influence on later developments of monastic and vowed religious life. Both because it is less specific in detail and because it has a strong community orientation, many religious orders and congregations adopted this rule as the basis of their life together (e.g., Premonstratentions, Dominicans, Augustinians, and communities of Canons Regular).

The Rule of Augustine does not provide a full outline for daily life in the monastery. Rather, in a form almost anecdotal in style, Augustine addresses the major areas of life in community and offers guiding principles that must then be adapted to a variety of situations. The sharing of all things in simplicity and humility is a prerequisite; and his rule acknowledges the tensions and conflicts that can arise in community living, as well as the ordinary temptation to live a private life even in the monastery.[11]

Of all the figures of early monastic history, the fifth century monk John Cassian (360–435) was destined to become one of the most influential. As a young man, he and his good friend Germanus made the long journey to the Egyptian desert to become monks. Instructed in the rudiments of desert cenobitism, they moved on to the Palestinian deserts and eventually found their way back to the West, founding a monastery in southern Gaul. In forming his own community, Cassian drew upon his vast knowledge of the Eastern fathers and eventually wrote the *Institutes* and *Conferences* in order to communicate this tradition to those outside his own monastery.[12]

In every age, even our own, those engaged in the search for God, who are often lost in the desert of their own weakness and confusion, have turned to Cassian for advice and guidance. His writings, in particular the *Conferences,* became the staple diet of religious men and women everywhere. A book for those more advanced in the practice of monasticism, the *Conferences* records the spiritual conferences given by the great teachers of the desert tradition. St. Benedict, for example, legislated the daily reading of the *Conferences* before compline.[13] The *Institutes,* on the other hand, is a book intended for beginners in the monastic life, a kind of formation program. In it Cassian describes the vices that must be rooted out of one's life and lays down guidelines for liturgical prayer, dress, meals, work, and silence.

For John Cassian the goal of life is love. Everything else is secondary to this one good. Prayer, good works, reading, vigils, fasting—all may become, in time, impossible because of sickness or old age. In the end, it is the condition of the heart that dictates the meaning of one's life here on earth and hereafter.

> For all gifts are given for a time as use and need will require, but . . . they will without doubt presently pass away: but love will never be destroyed. For not only does it work usefully in us in this world; but also in that to come, when . . . it will continue in far greater vigour and excellence, and will never be weakened by any defect, but by means of its perpetual incorruption will cling to God more intently and earnestly.[14]

The whole life of conversion—the stream of constant interior and exterior change—is intended to transform the monk or the nun, to strip each one into that perfect "nakedness" of Christ whereby each may participate in the mysterious loving relationship between Christ and the Father. Purity of heart is freedom from illusion, from excessive self-interest, and from the hostility that makes genuine love for Christ and his people impossible. The love of which John Cassian speaks transcends the boundaries of time and geography. It will last into eternity.

Cassian spends time and attention on the obstacles to this inner freedom, which he calls purity of heart: gluttony, fornication, covetousness, anger, dejection, *accidie* or spiritual boredom, vainglory, and pride. His treatment of each obstacle includes descriptions of symptoms, causes, and remedies. Cassian attempts to educate the individual in the way of constant change, that is, the development of better values, attitudes, and habits. He tutors the novice in the tradition of "desert realism"—a ruthless honesty about the self and one's relationship to God and neighbor. The first premise of such realism is that when problems and conflicts arise, the source of difficulty is always to be found within the self. No matter how objective the wrong or injustice done by another, the reason for the loss of inner tranquillity can only be discovered within oneself. This discovery should lead to change, particularly in attitude.

Today's reader will be pleasantly surprised to find in the *Conferences* and other early monastic literature a psychological awareness and insight that is both profound and reassuring. The spiritual struggles of the monk/martyr are not far removed from the everyday world of emotion and inner conflict. The surge of anger, the impulse to control others, the unprovoked outburst of aggression and retaliation are faced squarely, while the potent antidotes of humility, patience, and obedience, perhaps less appealing to moderns, are offered for those who wish to resolve their inner turmoil, move on to the freedom of self-transcendence, and acquire the ability to focus the mind on God and the things of God throughout the day.

The instability of the mind and heart are recurring themes in the *Conferences*. To "settle down" to prayer, reading, or reflection, to silence or solitude, is difficult because the mind moves about so easily. Even when we are most fervently praying, the mundane concerns of life persistently creep into our minds and hearts: "What's for dinner?" or, "What will I do with my day off?" This dilemma requires us to let go of what we *want* to think about in order to be free for God and available to him. This renunciation, as Cassian calls it, of our immediate concerns and desires only expands our true freedom to hear and receive and eventually to reciprocate with God and neighbor. With it, we are on the way to that purity of heart that makes the mind stable.

Prayer, intended to be the continual remembrance of God throughout the day, requires the discipline of the whole monastic regime. It is all of a piece. To become truly free, for Cassian, is to be liberated from the frantic drives, often enough conflicting, that arise from within the self. The classical doctrine of *apatheia* (Greek for "the quieting of the passions") is central to Cassian's anthropology and spirituality.[15]

Another towering figure in the history of monasticism is St. Benedict (ca. 480–ca. 550), who in his teaching on the monastic life upholds the highest ideals of Christian love and asceticism in an uncompromising yet humane spirit. Developed in sixth-century Italy and dependent on earlier sources, his *Rule for Monasteries* has become the most popular and commonly used rule in the West. In this remarkable little document, Benedict describes the monastery as a "school for the Lord's service" and proceeds to outline the contours of life in a monastic community characterized by balance and simplicity. Continuing the tradition of spiritual paternity in the person of the abbot, he teaches the three foundational virtues of the monk: obedience, silence, and humility. While Benedict's monastic legislation was acclaimed for its moderation, it was unbending in its expectation that each monk would be present at all community gatherings; and his emphasis on the exercises of prayer—the Divine Office, Eucharist, and spiritual reading—illustrates Benedict's conviction that the thoughts of the monk must at all times be occupied with God.

Following the tradition of John Cassian, Benedict recognizes that it is the condition of the heart that is the chief concern of monastic life and formation. Mere external conformity to the rule is never enough.

> As we progress in this way of life and in faith, we shall run on that path of God's commandments, our hearts overflowing with the inexpressible delight of love. Never swerving from his instructions, then, but faithfully observing his teaching in the monastery until death, we shall through patience share in the sufferings of Christ that we may deserve to share in his kingdom.[16]

The seventy-two chapters of the Rule combine practical wisdom with highly developed doctrine in such a way that this rule, perhaps more than any other, has stood the test of time.

The rapid expansion of monastic houses in both East and West is legendary. As with every institution fashioned around a high ideal, some monasteries were more faithful to the original inspiration than others, and some were fortunate enough to draw candidates of a caliber to keep the primitive vision of monasticism alive from generation to generation. The history of monastic foundations is complex, yet for our purposes it is important to note that a variety of sizes and styles emerged during this golden age of the fifth to the seventh centuries.[17] Each house, autonomous from others, was subject to the prevailing winds of political unrest, royal displeasure, or the loss of fervor among its membership. The fortunes of autonomous monastic houses can shift in a relatively brief period of time, less than a century. What begins as a large, strong, secure, and fervent community can end up with a few monks or nuns scrambling to keep the institution afloat. For these and for many other reasons, including the variety of religious orders, the history of monasticism in the West is not easy to plot.

In general terms, we can describe the first two centuries of monastic life as a time of expansion and development. Even before the close of that period, we know of houses where laxity was the order of the day, and loss of religious zeal marked the spirit of some communities. Such a state of spiritual tepidity and perhaps administrative neglect signaled the call for reform, a recurring event that was to become part and parcel of the history of these institutions. The renewed commitment of the monks or nuns to more faithful observance of the monastic traditions was almost always followed by new bursts of life: new members, freedom from economic burdens, and a surge of spiritual vitality felt far beyond the walls of the cloister.

St. Gregory the Great (540–604) occupies a unique position in the history of Christian spirituality. Before he became Bishop of Rome and thus concerned with renewal and reform, he was a monk. Summoned from his monastery by the call to the episcopacy, Gregory introduced into mainstream Christian thought much of the language and concerns proper to the monastic life, always adapting his teaching to the condition and vocations of his hearers. In his homilies, preached in the basilicas of Rome, Gregory presented a high doctrine of contemplation and the need to achieve detachment from the self in order to be a faithful servant of God.

It is in his concern for the struggle that takes place in the human heart and his attention to the virtues and vices of the Christian that Gregory is in direct line with the earlier monastic teachers. His creative genius is manifested in his ability to link the ascetical endeavor with his doctrine on purification through temptation, leading to contemplation: the vision of God. For Gregory, it is our desires that manifest the true condition of our inner selves. Our deepest desires betray our real direction in life. Gregory would have us redirect our desires toward the vision of God. In this way, we are helped by the knowledge of the self (humility) and the knowledge of the awful mercy of God (compunction). Then as we are tempted, we turn to affirm our deepest desire to see God and, of necessity, we change. And we keep changing, progressively, until we are ready for a new epiphany of God.

Gregory brings the doctrine of monastic life and perfection into the minds and hearts of ordinary people, his flock at Rome and beyond. Much of his thought is preserved for us, and he became one of the most influential teachers for later medieval theologians, because he combines the traditions of East and West, monastic and lay. To the end of his life Gregory never ceased mourning the loss of his monastic refuge.[18]

Monastic Reforms

The eighth to eleventh centuries saw both the full flowering and the breakdown of many monastic houses. The business of reform and revitalization was in the air. The observance of enclosure (the great guardian of the spirit of the desert), the keeping of the fasts and silence, fidelity to poverty and *lectio*—all of these required constant vigilance. While a community might not fall into moral error, it could well lose its spiritual vitality and the sense of urgency inherited from the early centuries of monastic life. Individual monasteries underwent reform and were revitalized, some becoming centers from which a movement of renewal radiated.

Cluny

One of the great reforms of the tenth century was that of the monastery of Cluny, located in Burgundy, France. Perhaps for the first time, the possibility of monitoring the conditions of communities was effected by making houses dependent on a mother abbey, in this case Cluny. Since the abbot of Cluny was, in effect, abbot of every dependency, he could, by regularly visiting these monasteries, correct abuses and address problems seen in the offing.

As one of the first experiments in the centralization of autonomous monasteries, Cluny has been the subject of much research in recent years. Following the Rule of St. Benedict, Cluny became the model for all the dependent monastic houses to replicate. In a real sense, a "family" of Cluniac houses developed, and this family became a forerunner of the centralized "orders" that developed at a later date. In this case, the mother house had developed a highly ritualized form of Benedictine monastic life, and the resulting preoccupation with ceremony and detail were carried into the daughter houses. The monk or the nun was called to offer continual praise to God through long and intricate liturgical offices and to observe the austerity of a very formal and stylized way of life. These images of the monk as a cultic figure and the monastic life as highly ritualized became the legacy by which Cluny would influence all later monastic developments.[19]

The Cistercians and St. Bernard of Clairvaux

In reaction to the excessive formalism of Benedictine monasticism, and the perceived opulence of Cluny in particular, the first Cistercians turned away from their original monastery at Molesmes in 1027 to establish monastic life at Citeaux according to the purity of the Rule of St. Benedict and, in the religious spirit of the age, to do so in evangelical poverty and simplicity. The early Cistercians, as did the mendicants in the following century, embraced poverty as a means of union with the poor Christ of the gospel. They deliberately rejected all feudal revenues and resolved to base their economy solely on the manual labor of the monks. To make this possible, a new type of member was accepted in the monastery: the lay brother. The "White Monks," as the Cistercians were later called, renounced the ownership of large tracts of land, which would require the employment of serfs to maintain them. They further determined that every element of monastic life would be marked by radical simplicity, even in the church, the one area where monks might legitimately permit some luxury. Thus the altar, the sacred vessels and vestments, and everything connected with the liturgy would be, for the Cistercians, stripped of any lavish display of riches.

In order to maintain this high ideal of austerity, certain safeguards were necessary. First, the Cistercians reaffirmed their separation from the world by adopting a vigorous form of enclosure and also by maintaining autonomy from the temporal lords on whom monastic houses had come to depend for economic support. No prince could hold court at Citeaux, ensuring not only poverty for the monks but the necessity of hard work as well. Second, the community at Citeaux, not unlike Cluny (and also in Burgundy), was to be the model for all the houses of the Order. Through a system of annual visitations, an external authority would review the spiritual condition and financial stability of a house, and in this way the abbot of Citeaux was able to support and correct those houses in need of his direct influence.

The source of spiritual vitality in the Cistercian reform was always to be found in the psalmody of the Divine Office, the sung Eucharist, and *lectio divina*. In spite of the austerity that marked their foundation, the piety of the White Monks was characterized by a warm devotion to the humanity of Christ. Placing themselves under the tender patronage of the Virgin Mary, the Cistercians became the primary agents for the renewal of the monastic life in the High Middle Ages.[20]

It would be difficult to exaggerate the influence of St. Bernard in the development of the new community of Citeaux. He came to the Order in 1113, and through his efforts at expansion there were more than three hundred Cistercian houses by the time of his death in 1153. Even after his death the development continued, and by the end of the century there were more than five hundred houses following the usages of Citeaux. The sphere of Cluny's influence was generally confined to France, but the radical freshness of the spirit of Citeaux, combined with Bernard's brilliance and fame, caused the Cistercian Order to move beyond cultural and geographical borders to every corner of twelfth-century Europe.

The paradox of Bernard, who was at once monk, statesman, poet, and theologian, is unique in the history of monasticism as well as the history of spirituality. Convinced of the superiority of the monastic vocation and its call to austerity and withdrawal from the world, he was himself often employed by the hierarchy of the Church in matters of Church and State. His sermons to his monks are filled with the highest of spiritual ideals. For Bernard, the life of asceticism and prayer leads one on a journey from humility to ecstasy, a "return to God." Such union with God is only possible when the will so corresponds to grace that all sin and evil are cast out and only good works are possible. So much does Bernard emphasize this need to correspond to God's initiative that he believes with St. Augustine that when faced with several options, all of which are good, one should always choose the *best* action. In resolving to always do the better thing in each circumstance of life, we can be sure that we will be challenged and "stretched" by the gospel of Christ. "No one can be perfect unless he yearns to be more perfect, and we show ourselves to be more perfect as we aspire to a still higher perfection."[21]

Not surprisingly, Bernard understands the starting point of the journey of return to God to be humility: the knowledge of our wretchedness and our potential for communion with God in Christ. This concrete experience of both the poverty and dignity of the Christian becomes the foundation of his teaching on the spiritual life, which is the life of love. Perhaps here Bernard is at his most eloquent. He explores the various forms of love and outlines the movement of the Christian from self-interested "carnal" love to a pure love of God. This purified love manifests itself in a life of continual union, foreshadowing the heavenly banquet where the host, Christ the Lord, will be all in all.[22]

Bernard's influence has been felt not only in his doctrine on the spiritual life but also in his emphasis on devotion to Christ's passion, so typical of the centuries immediately following him, as well as the Marian nature of his piety. It was Bernard who popularized devotion to St. Joseph, husband of Mary and foster-father of Jesus, as well as devotion to the angels. These marks of Bernardine spirituality were to be found in particular in the later fifteenth-century development of *Devotio moderna* (see chapter 4). As a sensitive artist, Bernard had a great appreciation for beauty and the grandeur of the physical world. Through the life of meditation on the passion of Christ and the life of charity and humility, one may come to know the Lord and live in intimacy with him for all eternity.[23]

Conclusion

The monk is one who gives his life to the search for God. Thus the monk, the nun, the monastery itself exist simply to say that *God is.* And this God is "good and forgiving, abounding in steadfast love to all who call on [him]" (Ps. 86:5).

The sheer extravagance of this gesture catches the attention of almost anyone who has come into contact with this mysterious way of life—mysterious because it is so absolutely a way of faith. In this context Thomas Merton's image of the monk is particularly apt: "In the night of our technological barbarism, monks must be trees which exist silently in the dark and by their vital presence purify the air."[24] The monastery gives off the oxygen of faith and hope, of absolute dependence upon God, and of love. If monks and nuns engaged in some kind of ministry or social service, their lives would be judged useful. As it is, their lives have no human purpose but to be for God and in continual remembrance of God for all the world. Paradoxically, this is perhaps the most human of reasons for existence, but one foreign to our society and culture. "You have made us for yourself, O Lord, and our hearts are restless until they rest in you."[25]

It is this possibility of being exclusively "for God" and of "wasting" one's life in the search for God's love and the wisdom required for such an encounter that is so incredible to the modern person. In fact, such a vocation has strained the credulity of every age. In the final analysis, the only explanation can be found in the person of Jesus Christ and the possibility of a love relationship with Christ that demands all of our attention and energy. This relationship transforms the hearts and lives of those who become his disciples. The imitation of Christ is not simply a concept or idea. It is the core of that form of martyrdom called the monastic life.

Notes

1. St. Athanasius, *The Life of Antony*, trans. R. Gregg (New York: Paulist Press, 1980).
2. John Cassian, *Conference* 19, chap. 10, in *The Nicene and Post-Nicene Fathers*, vol. 11, trans. E. Gibson (Grand Rapids, Mich.: Eerdmans, 1982), p. 493.
3. B. Ward, trans., *The Sayings of the Desert Fathers* (Kalamazoo, Mich.: Cistercian Publications, 1975); N. Russell, trans., *The Lives of the Desert Fathers* (Kalamazoo, Mich.: Cistercian Publications, 1980).
4. Ward, *Sayings*, p. 229.
5. Ibid., p. 2.
6. Derwas Chitty, *The Desert a City* (Crestwood, N.Y.: St. Vladimir's Seminary Press, 1966), Introduction.
7. Ward, *Sayings*, p. 42.
8. T. Fry, ed., *RB 1980: The Rule of St. Benedict* (Collegeville, Minn.: The Liturgical Press, 1981), p. 191.
9. Ibid., p. 25.
10. St. Augustine, *On the Psalms*, in *Ancient Christian Writers*, trans. Dame Scholastica Helgin and Dame Felicitas Corrigan (Westminster, Md.: Newman Press, 1960), p. 49.
11. Adolar Zumkeller, *Augustine's Ideal of the Religious Life* (New York: Fordham University Press, 1986), p. 211.
12. Cistercian Publications, Kalamazoo, Mich., is planning a modern translation of the *Institutes* and *Conferences*. For the most complete English translation of these texts, see E. Gibson, trans., *The Nicene and Post-Nicene Fathers*, vol. 11, (Grand Rapids, Mich.: Eerdmans, 1983). For a more contemporary translation of several of the *Conferences*, see Colm Luibheid, trans., *John Cassian: Conferences* (New York: Paulist Press, 1985)
13. Fry, *Rule*, p. 243.
14. John Cassian, Conf. I:XI, Nicene and Post-Nicene, p. 300.
15. Owen Chadwick, *John Cassian*, 2nd ed. (Cambridge: Cambridge University Press, 1968); Philip Rousseau, *Ascetics, Authority, and the Church: In the Age of Jerome and Cassian* (Oxford: Oxford University Press, 1978).
16. Fry, *Rule*, pp. 165-67.
17. For a good overview of the development and expansion of monasticism, see D. Knowles, *Christian Monasticism* (New York: McGraw-Hill, 1969).
18. For a fuller treatment of the teaching of Gregory on the spiritual life, see J. Leclercq, "The Teaching of St. Gregory," in *The Spirituality of the Middle Ages*, J. Leclercq, F. Vandenbroucke, L. Bouyer (New York: Seabury Press, 1968), pp. 3-30; for biographical information, see B. Colgrave, trans., *The Earliest Life of Gregory the Great* (New York: Cambridge University Press, 1968).
19. For further historical and bibliographical information, see Noreen Hunt, *Cluny Under Saint Hugh: 1049–1109* (Notre Dame: University of Notre Dame Press, 1968).
20. For further historical information, see Louis Lekai, *The Cistercians, Ideals and Reality* (Kent State, Ohio: Kent State University, 1977). For further discussion of Bernard's spirituality, see J. Leclercq, "The School of Citeaux," in *The Spirituality of the Middle Ages*, J. Leclercq, F. Vandenbroucke, L. Bouyer, pp. 191-200.
21. Bernard of Clairvaux, "On Consideration," PL CLXXXII:440.
22. For further discussion of Bernard's doctrine on the spiritual life, see Etienne Gilson, *The Mystical Theology of Saint Bernard*, trans. A. H. C. Downes (New York: Sheed & Ward, 1958).
23. For more information on St. Bernard, see Basil Pennington, *The Last of the Fathers* (Still River, Mass.: St. Bede's Press, 1983).
24. Thomas Merton, *The Monastic Vocation* (Gethsemane, Ky.: Abbey of Our Lady of Gethsemane, 1957), p. 3.
25. Augustine of Hippo, Confessions, Bk. I, chap. 1.

Bibliography

Chitty, Derwas J. *The Desert a City*. Crestwood, N.Y.: St. Vladimir's Seminary Press, 1966.

Fry, Timothy, ed. *RB 1980: The Rule of St. Benedict in Latin & English with Notes.* Collegeville, Minn.: Liturgical Press, 1981. (See especially the introduction for an excellent historical introduction to monasticism.)

Knowles, David. *Christian Monasticism.* New York: McGraw-Hill, 1969.

Leclercq, Jean. *The Love of Learning and the Desire for God: A Study of Monastic Culture.* New York: Fordham University Press, 1974.

Luibheid, Colm, trans. *John Cassian: Conferences.* New York: Paulist Press, 1985. (This contemporary translation includes nine of Cassian's twenty-four conferences.)

Russell, Norman, trans. *The Lives of the Desert Fathers.* Kalamazoo, Mich.: Cistercian Publications, 1980.

Vögué, Adalbert de. *Community and Abbot in the Rule of Saint Benedict.* Kalamazoo, Mich.: Cistercian Publications, 1975.

Ward, Benedicta, trans. *The Sayings of the Desert Fathers.* Kalamazoo, Mich.: Cistercian Publications, 1975.

Zumkeller, Adolar. *Saint Augustine's Ideal of Religious Life.* New York: Fordham University Press, 1986.

PRACTICUM 2

The Pure Gold of Silence

STEPHEN ROSSETTI

Be silent, all flesh, before the Lord.

—ZECHARIAH 2:13

I opened the day's mail and found a flier from a Yoga center in the United States advertising its annual ten-day retreat. One of its main emphases was on silence. It said: "The silence—which is observed by all retreatants—shields one from external involvements, allowing the mind to go inward. As the mind goes inward, it becomes still, and the peace each of us holds inside comes into flower."[1]

A month ago, I went on a directed retreat for Christians. When I arrived, I was pleased that a certain director, a well-known author and retreat master, would be my guide. However, I was surprised to find out that the entire week would be spent in silence. I would speak with no one except the director, and with him only twenty minutes each day.

Silence is hard. But every spiritual discipline, East or West, modern or traditional, advocates prolonged periods of silence as part of its spiritual training. For example, it was said of one of the Desert Fathers, the fourth- and fifth-century monks who lived in the deserts of Egypt and Palestine, that he kept a rock in his mouth for three years so that he might learn to be silent.[2] For people like ourselves, who are immersed in the daily whirr and hum of the world, this is a radical idea.

What is silence? Why is it so important? And why is it so hard? Silence is a complex and multifaceted spiritual reality. First of all, we can say that it has an ascetical function: It is an exercise in self-discipline. We are not used to silence. Every moment of our waking day is filled with sounds and noises, and when there is a moment of quiet, we feel uncomfortable.

73

A few years ago, there was a program for young people that took them out of the cities for a few days and brought them into the woods. It was meant to give them a rest from the hustle of the city and to help them learn about and enjoy nature. Unfortunately, it was not always as pleasant an experience as planned. Some of the young people could not sleep at night; it was too quiet. Others had difficulty adjusting to such a drastic change.

Our immediate response to silence is to obliterate it. We reach for the knob on the television set or the button on our car radio. Even more to the point, we are unnerved to sit in silence with other people; it makes us uneasy. We usually make idle conversation to fill the vacuum, like a television droning in the background, saying nothing but soothing one's fear of the void.

Have you ever met someone who could not stop talking? He or she will chat endlessly—talking about everything and nothing. For that person, talking is a compulsion; it acts as a defense mechanism. Actually, such people are afraid of silence. They are afraid of what might come up if they stopped and listened.

In the world, we live amidst a roar, a cacophony of noise that overwhelms our senses. In fact, in these modern times we are overstimulated. Certainly it is unhealthy to live in a vacuum. The human senses need stimulation to feed the mind and the soul. But we live in an age of overstimulation. Our senses are bombarded with sounds that deafen the heart and the mind. Paradoxically, because of this excessive stimulation, we have difficulty hearing the hearts of others and the Spirit of God.

This overstimulation results in our being addicted to the stimulation, and we suffer withdrawal when it is taken away. Like any addiction, we feel that we cannot live without this noise. But in our spiritual "drying out" period, we must suffer this withdrawal. Hence silence is, first of all, an ascetical practice.

However, as we look deeper, we find that it is much, much more. During group retreats for young people, I sometimes ask them to engage in the following exercise. They are told to pick a partner and then sit in silence for one minute and stare into each other's eyes. Inevitably, there is giggling and embarrassment.

Why? I tell them that the eyes are the windows of the soul. In the silence, the outer world is still, and we look deeply into the other's heart. It is an intimate form of communication—like standing naked in front of another. It is little wonder that they are embarrassed. They can only take sixty seconds of such nakedness.

We are not used to this depth of exchange. It is no coincidence that there is a proliferation of courses and a great emphasis on communication today. Counselors and therapists spend much of their time helping people to communicate with others and with themselves. It is ironic, though not unpredictable, that in an era in which there is an overabundance of words, there is little communication.

Perhaps true communication does not consist in the skillful use of words or in their abundance. Rather, it is an exchange of hearts. The speaker opens his or her heart to the other and speaks words that transmit the deepest self. If there is love and a true communication, the listener will receive that self with respect and cherish it. This sort of communication is most difficult.

The first step toward achieving this true communication is to sweep away all the useless words, the endless chattering, and to begin to listen. When we do this, an entire parade of things arise. For instance, when I start a new meditation group, people begin to sit and listen. The initial sessions can be very intense. Some break down and sob; others are filled with rage; still others encounter frightening images of the past. There is much inside ourselves of which we are not even aware.

In silence, we look inside. This is the beginning of the spiritual journey. As the great masters of spirituality tell us, the journey begins with self-knowledge. But I am always amazed at how little we know about ourselves. For example, "professional" religious people sometimes present themselves for spiritual direction. In the course of a few sessions, it becomes clear that many do not even have a rudimentary awareness of their own personalities—of who they are as human beings. People who are perpetually in a rage will smile politely and believe they are meek and gentle. Others who are filled with hurt and pain will appear to feel nothing is wrong; they actually believe the false mask that they are wearing.

In silence, we begin to listen, many for the first time, to who we really are as human beings, not who we wish we were. As we listen to our own hearts, then, we can communicate our true selves. Initially, it may be a message of anger or pain; however, it is the beginning of a real self-revelation. And what is prayer if not such a deep communication with God? Without silence there is no true self-awareness or communication. Without silence, there is no prayer.

First of all, we said that silence is an asceticism—a self-discipline. Second, we spoke of silence as a way of listening to the inner self and facilitating communication with others and with God. Both of these are aspects of silence as a *negation*, as merely a lack of words. In its final two aspects, we shall look at silence as a *positive* presence.

In an unpublished manuscript, a modern-day Carthusian monk

wrote a treatise on the spiritual life entitled "The 12 Grades of Silence." In this manuscript the anonymous Carthusian says, "The interior life might be summed up in this one idea: SILENCE." He then lists twelve grades of silence as ascending rungs on the spiritual ladder. They are, from lowest to highest:

> Speak little with creatures and much with God
> Silence at work and in exterior movements
> Silence of the imagination
> Silence of the memory
> Silence to creatures
> Silence of the heart
> The silence of human nature
> Silence of the mind
> Silence to judgments
> Silence of the will
> Silence with oneself
> Silence with God

The first rungs of silence are, indeed, negations, as aforementioned. Silence is refraining from conversing with the exterior world. However, the grades of silence quickly move to an interior reality. Silence becomes an inner stillness of imagination, memory, intellect, emotions, desires, and the will. This interior stillness is much more difficult!

When the cacophony of exterior noise is silenced, we sadly find out that there is a roar of noise *inside*. We are pulled apart by conflicts, painful memories, overwhelming desires, and a barrage of extraneous thoughts. This is why we had shunned exterior silence; we did not want to face this inner turmoil. Now, when the outside world is still, we are forced to face the inner turmoil.

There are spiritual teachers who will encourage their disciples to ignore these pains and conflicts—to act as if they did not exist. However, this would be a denial of who we are and would invariably lead to serious trouble farther down the spiritual path. Rather, the journey must involve courageously facing the inner self and laboring mightily to find healing and peace.

As each conflict, pain, and disproportionate desire arises, it is a "noise"—a lack of silence. This noise disturbs the inner self and disrupts its harmony and peace. For example, to find "silence of the heart," the sixth grade of silence, the Carthusian author speaks of "desires in what they may have of excess, of one's zeal in what it may have of indiscretion, of one's fervor in what there may be of exaggeration." These excessive desires, indiscreet zeals, and exaggerated fervors are all imbalances in the emotional self that need to be corrected for silence to reign in the heart.

Imbalances can be repressions and lack of fulfillment of healthy desires or obsessions and overindulgence of human needs.[3] As an example, all of us need human warmth. We find this warmth in friendship, in marriage, in family relationships, and in a variety of places—home, work, church, and community organizations. However, some have repressed their desires for human warmth, perhaps with such rationalizations as "I'm too busy to start up a friendship," "I can't trust other people"; "I'll only get hurt."

But the need for human warmth does not go away, even if it is repressed. Our emotions will clamor inside us, begging to be heard. We might have dreams of being isolated, left out in the cold. Other dreams will have us running frantically away from an unknown threat; we find ourselves waking up in a cold sweat. Again and again our insides will cry out to be heard, which creates "noise" and a lack of interior silence.

Conversely, interior silence can also be disrupted by *obsessions*. Again, with regard to the need for human warmth, I can be obsessed with the need to be related to a particular person. I may constantly crave that person's attention and feel I must be near him or her. The attention of every waking moment is riveted on the relationship.

Like the repression of the need for human warmth, this too is a neurotic distortion that causes interior "noise." In both cases, progress in the spiritual journey requires one to face this aberration, to discover its cause, and to find healing at the root. Only then will there be internal harmony and silence.

In the spiritual journey, we go deeper and deeper into ourselves. We uncover layer after layer of our beings and wrestle with the "noises," obsessions, repressions, conflicts, and pains that arise, until each layer is left in balance and harmony. With each passing phase, peace grows within the spiritual traveler.

So far, silence has been discussed as an asceticism, as a listening, and as a harmony and balance inside the person. There is one final truth about silence, one that is perhaps the most important, and certainly the most profound. In a chapter of *The White Paradise* entitled "A Carthusian Speaks," another Carthusian monk uses an illuminating phrase. He speaks of the "pure gold of silence."[4] It is as if silence itself is a special treasure to be sought after and guarded, as indeed the Carthusians do.

Thomas Merton, in his work *Contemplative Prayer,* approaches this same truth from a different angle. He says: "He waits on the Word of

God in silence, and when he is 'answered,' it is not so much by a word that bursts into his silence. It is by his silence itself suddenly, inexplicably revealing itself to him as a word of great power, full of the voice of God."[5]

In these few words, Merton has captured one of the great truths of God and the spiritual life. When we pray, we usually sit quietly and hope that God will grace us. We expect the Almighty to break through the silence with the power of the Word. Thus silence would merely be a medium through which God speaks.

However, for Merton, silence is not a medium that carries the message; silence *is* the message. Silence itself is a revelation of God. As Henri Le Saux, a Benedictine monk who lived many years in an Indian ashram and, later, as a hermit in the Himalayas, realized about God, "He himself is Silence and eternal Quiet."[6]

When those youngsters on retreat looked into one another's eyes, they were embarrassed. But if they had been able to sit longer with someone they loved, they would have found a mutual bonding in the silence of another's eyes.

There is a deep communion of hearts in this silence. Words can only obscure this union. Even an intense emotional sharing is not comparable. It is something to be experienced. It is as if the air is filled with a wonderful presence. Those who feel this presence find warmth and peace.

Have you ever seen two older married people sitting together in silence? It is not simply that they have run out of things to say. Rather, after years of conflicts, sharings, conversations, and struggles, they have come to silence. This is not merely an absence of words but rather a communion beyond the mind and heart; it is a communion of souls.

In the Carthusian's manuscript on silence, the final rung on the spiritual ladder is "Silence with God." In the earlier stages, one was to "speak little with creatures and much with" God. Now, there is silence even here. The author says, "This is the silence of eternity. It is the union of the soul with God."

Silence is the language of God. The power and subtlety of divine self-revelation so far transcends human interaction that, unaided, we cannot commune with God. There is simply no common ground for communication. However, in Jesus this communion of divine and human has already taken place. In the God-man we are given the treasure of communication and communion with God. In this we come to know God as the one who radiates the "pure gold of silence."

This pure gold defies description. In fact, it is impeded by the use of words. St. Thomas Aquinas spent a lifetime speaking about God in his renowned theological texts. However, shortly before his death, he experienced this silent God who brought him to silence as well. "I can write no more," he said. "I have seen things which make all my writings like straw."[7]

Truly, this chapter, and indeed this entire book, pales in comparison to the gold of silence. One can only sigh with the author of the book of Ecclesiastes and say, "Of the making of many books there is no end, and in much study there is weariness for the flesh" (Eccles. 12:12 NAB).

Though these words are insignificant, if they have pointed to a divine truth and enkindled in us a desire to experience it, then they have accomplished their task. But every writer as well as every spiritual traveler must learn, as St. Thomas did, when to let go of his or her own thoughts and desires. There comes a time to step into the silence of God.

In this silence we become as monks of the great desert. As it was in an exchange between brother Zachary and abbot Moses, so will it be with us: "When brother Zachary was dying, the abbot Moses asked him, saying, 'What seest thou?' And he answered, 'Naught better, Father, than to hold one's peace.' And he said, 'It is true, my son: hold thy peace.'"[8]

EXERCISES

Is it possible to live a silent life in the world? Surely if silence were only a lack of human words and noises, it would be impossible. One would be forced to run off to a monastery every free moment or become an antisocial hermit in the world. Unfortunately, some try to do this.

But if silence is not only a freedom from excessive words, but also a balance of the interior life and a communion with God, then it is possible to live a silent life in a noisy world—"to be in the world but not of the world." Here are some exercises to promote this interior silence.

For an Individual

Stop Excessive Noise

Select specific television shows that you desire to watch during the week, and turn on the television only during those times. Similarly, set aside times to listen to music, and turn off your radio or stereo for the remainder of the time. With regard to silence of the tongue, before you speak, think about what you are going to say. Ask yourself, "Is it good for me to say this?" As it says in Scripture, "Say only the good things men need to hear, things that will really help them" (Eph. 4:29 NAB).

Find Periods of Silence

In the morning before everyone is up, or perhaps in the evening after everyone is in bed, sit quietly for at least twenty minutes. Relax. Breathe deeply for a moment and rest your muscles. Let the tensions of the world slip away and sit in peace.

As you sit in silence, what comes to the surface from your own interior self? Perhaps a particular person keeps coming to mind, someone who makes you angry. Or a painful memory may keep coming up. Share these with God and ask for healing and an interior silence. If the same images and memories persist, discuss them with a trusted friend, counselor, or spiritual director. These memories can point the way toward needed growth in the spiritual life.

Listen to the Silence

After a considerable period of days or months, even years, of spending quiet times each day, you may find yourself desiring a deeper silence. Stop listening to what breaks through the silence, and listen to the silence itself. Feel the silence itself touch your innermost being and resonate a Word of warmth and peace. Feel the silence sparkle with life and joy. Feel the presence of God.

For a Group

Sit Together in Silence

There is something special about meditating together. Anthony DeMello points it out in his helpful book entitled *Sadhana*.[9] The very presence of other people's prayer and spirit energizes our hearts and lifts them up to God.

Once a week, have your group meet together. Spend an introductory time saying hello and getting reacquainted. Then take about forty-five minutes to either share about important events in each person's life or engage in a discussion centering on a spiritual topic or passages from Scripture.

Now the group is ready to pray together. Turn the lights off in the room to facilitate an atmosphere of silence. Light at least one candle or, as we do, light many candles and put them around the room. Sit together in silence for twenty to sixty minutes, depending on what the group is able to do.

Use meditative music, perhaps selections from Taizé, or readings from Scripture to occasionally break the silence. This will keep people centered and bolster flagging hearts. Some groups may want to refrain from external music or reading and simply have each person use a prayer word or mantra repeated silently over and over. This too will center the heart and help with distractions.

Provide some time, perhaps at the following meeting, to discuss people's experiences during the previous meditation. People may want to share the intense feelings that may have arisen or the striking spiritual experiences that may have occurred. Others may ask for help with distractions or suggest changes in the group's meditation practices. When it is clear that God has graced someone, remember to give thanks.

DISCUSSION QUESTIONS

1. What are the *external* noises and distractions in our lives? Are there some that are excessive and can be eliminated? What positive steps can we take to live a "silent life," that is, a balanced life, in the world?

2. What are the *interior* noises in our modern lives? What are the interior conflicts, obsessions, repressions, hurts, and pains that leave our insides in turmoil and devoid of an interior silence? What are some of the positive ways we can find help and healing for them?

3. How do I communicate nonverbally with others? What do I see when I look into the eyes of other people? When I sit in silence with my closest friend and/or spouse, what is exchanged in the silence? Are there ways to enhance this nonverbal communication and communion with those that I love?

4. How does God communicate with me? Does God ever "speak" to me without using words? What does it mean to say, "Silence is a revelation of God"? How might I enhance this silence with God?

Notes

1. Satchidananda Ashram-Yogaville, "Annual 10-Day Integral Yoga Retreat," Advertising Flier of Satchidananda Ashram-Yogaville, Buckingham, VA 23921, May 1988.
2. Thomas Merton, *The Wisdom of the Desert* (New York: New Directions, 1961), p. 30.
3. Stephen J. Rossetti, *I Am Awake: Discovering Prayer* (New York: Paulist Press, 1987), pp. 51-52.

4. Peter van der Meer de Walcheren, *The White Paradise* (New York: David McKay, 1952), p. 80.
5. Thomas Merton, *Contemplative Prayer* (New York: Image Books, 1971), p. 90.
6. Abhishiktananda [Henri Le Saux, O.S.B.], *Prayer* (Philadelphia: Westminster Press, 1973), p. 29.
7. G. K. Chesterton, *St. Thomas Aquinas* (Garden City, N.Y.: Image Books, 1956), pp. 142-43.
8. Helen Waddell, *The Desert Fathers* (Ann Arbor: University of Michigan Press, 1957), p. 118.
9. Anthony DeMello, *Sadhana: A Way to God* (Garden City, N.Y.: Doubleday, 1984), pp. 54-55.

Resources

Abhishiktananda. *Prayer*. Philadelphia: Westminster Press, 1973.

_____. *Saccidananda: A Christian Approach to Advaitic Experience*. Delhi, India: Wesley Press, 1974.

A Carthusian. "The 12 Grades of Silence." Mimeograph.

The Carthusians: Origins, Spirit, Family Life. Westminister, Md.: Newman Press, 1952.

DeMello, Anthony. *Sadhana: A Way to God*. Garden City, N.Y.: Doubleday, 1984.

_____. *Song of the Bird*. Garden City, N.Y.: Doubleday, 1984.

Eliot, T. S. *Four Quartets*. New York: Harcourt Brace Jovanovich, 1971.

Guigo II. *The Ladder of Monks and Twelve Meditations*. Translated by Edmund Colledge and James Walsh. Garden City, N.Y.: Image Books, 1978.

Lawrence of the Resurrection, Brother. *The Practice of the Presence of God*. Translated by John J. Delaney. Garden City, N.Y.: Image Books, 1977.

Merton, Thomas. *Contemplative Prayer*. Garden City, N.Y.: Image Books, 1971.

_____. *Silence in Heaven: A Book of the Monastic Life*. New York: Studio Publications in association with Thomas Y. Crowell, 1956.

_____. *The Silent Life*. New York: Farrar, Straus & Cudahy, 1957.

_____. *The Wisdom of the Desert*. New York: New Directions, 1961.

Rossetti, Stephen J. *I Am Awake: Discovering Prayer*. New York: Paulist Press, 1987.

Waddell, Helen. *The Desert Fathers*. Ann Arbor: University of Michigan Press, 1957.

Walcheren, Peter van der Meer de. *The White Paradise*. New York: David McKay, 1952.

Ward, Benedicta, and Russell, Norman. *The Lives of the Desert Fathers*. Cistercian Studies, no. 34. Kalamazoo, Mich.: Cistercian Publications, 1981.

CHAPTER 3

Mendicant Spirituality

GABRIEL O'DONNELL, O.P.

The Lord appointed seventy others, and sent them on ahead of him, two by two, into every town and place. . . . And he said to them, "The harvest is plentiful but the laborers are few; pray therefore the Lord of the harvest to send out laborers into his harvest. Go your way; . . . carry no purse, no bag, no sandals . . . remain in the same house, eating and drinking what they provide, for the laborer deserves his wages.

—LUKE 10:1-8

Once or twice in a week of centuries a culture manages to renew itself and express again its finest ideals and values. In much the same way, the Christian Church has known moments of clarity and insight that became sources of renewal and a new surge of energy. The thirteenth century was one such "moment," in which the urgency of the apostolic calling as found in the Acts of the Apostles and the tenth chapter of St. Luke's Gospel burst upon the Church with fresh spirit and enthusiasm. The result of this great new movement of spiritual renewal was the founding of the mendicant or "begging" orders, particularly the Franciscans and Dominicans.

All of the characteristics of medieval piety outlined by historians can be found in abundance among the mendicants: devotion to the humanity of Christ; tender devotion to the Virgin Mary, Mother of Christ and therefore *Mater Misericordiae* (Mother of Mercy); devotion to the saints and angels; and the new cult of the "Blessed Sacrament." The mendicants inherited these movements and tendencies, but theirs was the challenge to give them and the popular piety they inspired definitive shape and then to carry this new fervor from one corner of civilization to the next.

The restlessness of the Christian people at the close of the twelfth century created a deep hunger for a more authentic way of Christian discipleship, a way marked by a vital preaching of the gospel and a vigorous observance of its demands in a manner less removed from the common man or woman. It was a hunger for a Christianity brought down to earth. This, then, was the brief given to the mendicants at the beginning of a new era, and like a spark of electricity, they lighted up the Christian world of the thirteenth century.

The Spirit of the Medieval World

At the dawn of the thirteenth century, Europe was alive with both the expectation and the confusion that accompany any age of great change. Recall that this period saw the breakdown of the feudal system, the development of the city, the emergence of corporations, and the organization of the university. What we name modern civilization and its accompanying institutions were birthed at the end of the twelfth and the beginning of the thirteenth centuries. Such a transition—the death of one entire social system and the beginning of a new one—must involve a degree of turbulence, upheaval, and, in the case of the thirteenth century, violence. Popular idealizations of the Age of Faith and the building of the Gothic cathedrals as an expression of popular piety can be not only misleading but also a positive obstacle to a true perception of social and religious conditions in the High Middle Ages.

There was often great confusion in the mind of the medieval Christian, a great deal of fear and an overriding sense of what we today call depression or gloom. Perhaps chief among the reasons for this darkness of attitude was the size of the world in which the ordinary person lived. It was very small indeed. Ordinary villages or hamlets were surrounded by not only physical boundaries but also tightly controlled religious and psychological boundaries. If it happened, as it often did, that the religious leader was better educated or informed than the local magistrate, then he was likely to become the more powerful and central person, despite the absence of a political title. Outsiders were not to be trusted and were admitted only with great caution. Under such conditions, an individual rarely left the restricted sphere of village life.

In such a small world, crime was a communal evil. Whenever anything happened in the medieval town or village, it was not only a single person who was to blame but the perpetrator's family and neighbors as well—the entire social unit. There was no privacy as we understand it: Privacy is a modern luxury. Both architecturally and socially, there was little room for hiddenness and solitude. The average person was, quite simply, trapped—physically, socially, and psychologically—in a tiny but very public world. It should come as no surprise, then, that a religious movement that offered a way out of this constricted environment would become popular. By joining one of these new movements one, in effect, escaped. As mobile friars, young men were able to launch out and discover a wide and exciting—if dangerous—world, instead of being caught in the petty affairs of one small village for the rest of their days.

Living the Apostolic Life

The early thirteenth century saw a parallel upheaval within the Church. The crisis that took shape in the life of faith had to do with the ideal of Christian perfection. While "Christian perfection" may not be a very compelling phrase to someone living at the end of the twentieth century, to speak in such terms stirred the spirit of medieval men and women. They understood perfection as the final goal of all human existence and tended to identify it with the attainment of eternal salvation through forgiveness of sins.

By "Christian perfection" the Church of the Middle Ages meant an "apostolic life," or what was often called the perfect "imitation" or the "following" of Christ. In the twelfth and thirteenth centuries these were technical terms and not simply descriptive phrases.[1] They applied specifically to groups of individuals who committed themselves to living the gospel to a radical—one might even say extreme—degree. These words conjured up images of men and women committed to exploring the frontiers of what it means to be a follower of Christ, an imitator of Christ, and to live out the demands of the gospel in a literal way. In particular, the term "apostolic life" referred to those living in an intentional Christian community according to the model of the apostles and disciples of the Church in Jerusalem, described in the Acts of the Apostles: "they devoted themselves to the apostles' teaching and fellowship, to the breaking of bread and the prayers. . . . And all who believed were together and had all things in common; and they sold their possessions and goods and distributed them to all, as any had need" (Acts 2:42-46). In other words, the apostolic life was—and is—the *common* life.

Originally, the foundation of the monastic life in the Egyptian and Palestinian deserts was seen as a fulfillment of this vision of apostolic life and "having all things in common." Monks and nuns, leaving the ordinary pattern of society to live a common life, were considered the best example of what it meant to be a perfect Christian. The idealization of their life and spirituality functioned for many centuries as the paradigm of how best to fulfill the call to perfection: "If you would be perfect, go, sell what you possess and give to the poor, and you will have treasure in heaven; and come follow me" (Matt. 19:21).

The rapid growth of the monastic institution and its consequent expansion during the eighth to the eleventh centuries brought with it extensive social, economic, and political influence. By the twelfth century, the large abbeys of Europe had become a force to be dealt with by bishop and prince alike. As with the expansion of any institution, compromises were often made that seriously affected the public image and popularity of monastic life. By the end of the twelfth century, there was widespread disillusionment over the abuse of power, patterns of conspicuous consumption, and the loss of spiritual vitality in many monasteries. The time was ripe for reform.

The Rise of the Mendicant Orders

The hallmark of the thirteenth-century spiritual renewal was the quest for a simple Christian life lived in poverty of spirit and in common with others for the sake of preaching the gospel of Jesus Christ. Newborn evangelical revivals of that period prompted the devout Christian man or woman to search the Scriptures to rediscover the meaning of Christian perfection and the fullness of the apostolic life. A deeper reading of the Acts of the Apostles and the tenth chapter of St. Luke's Gospel suggested a new form of imitation of Christ: the poor itinerant preacher. As a consequence, the ministry of itinerant preaching combined with stark simplicity of life was added to the original concept of common life in an expanded expression of apostolic spirituality.

This great thirst for holiness was not restricted to an educated elite. The little bands of itinerant preachers living a common life of poverty consisted of ordinary layfolk of humble origins. These little groups, most of which died out, were marked by simplicity of life but also by a certain amount of disorganization. By and large, they did not succeed in perpetuating themselves, and because they were often uninstructed, they sometimes fell into doctrinal error. Errors of doctrine led, in turn, to the danger of moral error. The result was a considerable degree of doctrinal and moral confusion among these early bands of preachers. Since they tended to be spontaneous, that is, founded on an informal and charismatic basis, they remained outside the purview of ecclesiastical approbation. Some were co-opted by various heretical sects that sought to convert whole parishes and regions to some new form of Christian teaching.

In an attempt to read the signs of the times and capture the imagination of the Christian people, the Church hierarchy emphasized the canonical life. In the medieval context, a "canon" was an ordained cleric, a priest who resided in a canonry—very like a monastery—attached to the cathedral church. The bishop, then, had a group of canons around him in the form of a secluded community. Canons were meant to live a life of worship of God through the singing of the various hours of the Divine Office in the cathedral and the study of Scripture to assist the bishop in his work of preaching. As a movement, it did not have the widespread appeal hoped for, but it became an important link in shaping what came to be called the mendicant or "begging" orders. These were groups of men and women who organized themselves according to the ideals of common life, evangelical poverty, and preaching but lived in dependence upon the daily offerings of the people. Unlike monks or nuns, who were to remain enclosed or "cloistered," mendicants were given ecclesiastical sanction to go from door to door, begging their daily bread in the name of Christ's Church.

The two major groups in the mendicant movement that have survived into modern times are the Franciscans and Dominicans. Other mendicant orders survived—and some orders actually became mendicants in order to survive—but these two are the most typical of this age of spiritual revitalization.[2] Innovative as they were, these movements captured the imagination of ordinary folk, and in a hundred years' time, from 1220 to 1320, the Christian world became populated with Franciscans and Dominicans.

Becoming a mendicant offered an alternative to the isolation of medieval village life and gave vent to the desire to live the ideal of the perfect following of Christ. The mendicants went everywhere in the world and drew members from all walks of life. To become a Franciscan or a Dominican was to move from place to place. More important, membership in these orders was open not only to ordained clerics or those who wanted to be lay brothers and nuns but also to the laity.

The Franciscan and Dominican movements were not simply an attempt to answer the need of the Church at an institutional or theological level; they were also intended to draw the faithful into a life of increasingly intense spiritual growth in order to become more perfect disciples of the poor Christ. The ideal of the perfect imitation of Christ was and is strong in these movements. Ultimately, it was at their very core. The passion of the early Franciscans or Dominicans was to be perfect in following the crucified Christ, thus their strong Christological orientation focused on the humanity of Christ and, most of all, on his passion and death. It would not be an exaggeration to say that the passion of Christ shaped the spiritual ethos of the thirteenth century.

The addition of lay membership to the mendicant orders mandated different levels of belonging and commitment. The "first order" was made up of ordained priests and lay brothers (i.e., men who saw to domestic details in order to free the priests to go about the work of study, preaching, and teaching). The "second order" was made up of cloistered women who withdrew totally from the ordinary pressures and demands of human society in order to become perfect imitators of Christ. Finally, in the "third order" lay men and women could either live a publicly organized form of the religious life or remain ordinary Christians living at home with their families while sharing in the tradition and spirituality of these orders. A member of a third order did not become a part-time monk or nun, nor did he or she attempt to live like a vowed religious in the world. The "tertiary" was prepared to live the spirituality of these orders according to a secular way of life. To this end, tertiaries were given formal instruction in prayer and doctrine, as well as practical advice. Such membership placed certain limits on the tertiary in relation to social involvements, for profession as a third order member was aimed at shaping one's entire life, exterior as well as interior.

St. Francis and the Order of Friars Minor

In 1205 no one could have foreseen the way in which the name of the small Umbrian town of Assisi would become an international symbol of love and peace, least of all Francis, son of a middle-class dyer who, in one dramatic gesture in the cathedral square, gave his life to Christ and his Church. Thereafter, the names of Francis and Assisi would be synonymous.[3]

From his birth in 1802 until his capture as a soldier prisoner at Perugia in 1202, Francis had been a happy and adventuresome young man, but his year in prison and the subsequent illness he suffered unleashed a restlessness within him, and soon a strong desire to find meaning to his life sprang up in his heart. In 1206 Francis, a poet and mystic, fell deeply in love with the crucified Christ at the ruined church of San Damiano and set himself to serve the Church and that same crucified Lord in humility and gospel simplicity. To the surprise of many, by 1209 this simple layman had gathered about himself a group of poor brothers. Together, they wed themselves to Lady Poverty and went about serving the needs of the poor and preaching the gospel with new fervor and simplicity.

Thus was the Order of Friars Minor, or "Little Brothers," born. In one sense, it simply "happened" around Francis. His spirit attracted many disciples who desired to join the *Poverello* (or "little poor one") of

Assisi, in the service of Christ crucified and his Church. The joy and exuberance gained by freedom from the goods of this world and the unfathomable peace flowing from the heart of Christ that came to these few brothers, or "friars"[4] as they came to be called, worked like a magnet on those who met or heard of Francis. He and his personal experience of Christ were the heart of this movement, and almost before he realized it, the size of his band of poor friars outgrew the simplicity of his original inspiration. Some organization and structure became necessary.

In 1209 Francis composed a rule of life—now lost—that required absolute poverty of his nascent brotherhood, and by 1221 he had already revised it:

> None of the brothers, wherever he may be or wherever he goes, should in any way carry, receive or have received (by another) either money or coins, whether for clothing or books or payment for any work—indeed, for no reason—unless it is for the evident need of the sick brothers; for we must not suppose that money or coins have any greater value than stones. . . . And if by chance—which God forbid—it should happen that some Brother has collected or is hoarding money or coins . . . all the brothers are to consider him as a false brother and an apostate, and a thief and a robber, as the one who held the purse (cf. Jn. 12:6), unless he has truly repented.[5]

The Friars Minor would own nothing, nor could they use monies or material goods as security against the future. Forsaking the goods of this world and the greed and ambition so often attached to them, the friars would know the joy and pleasure to be found in God's creation—Brother Sun and Sister Moon. To own nothing was, paradoxically, to have everything at one's disposal. Their preaching, informal and aimed at the heart, showed the friars' concern to remain faithful to the authentic message of the gospel. Yet the radical lifestyle and personal evangelical fervor of the movement did not in any way engender disregard for institutional authority. St. Francis's reverence for the hierarchy—particularly the Bishop of Rome—was so uncompromisingly strong, simple, and direct, the contemporary Christian is likely to blanch when confronted with it. But for Francis it was essential that the friars remain deeply attached to the ideal of cooperation with the bishops of the Church.

> All the brothers must be Catholic, [and] live and speak in a Catholic manner. But if any of them has strayed from the Catholic faith and life, in word or in deed, and has not amended his ways, he should be

completely expelled from our fraternity. And we should regard all clerics and all religious as our lord in those things which pertain to the salvation of their souls and who have not deviated from our religion, and in the Lord, we should respect their order and their office and government.[6]

During his own lifetime, conflict and division threatened the existence of Francis's fraternity. The rapid expansion of the Friars Minor and the possibility that some among them should be ordained to the priesthood raised the question of theological education and clerical training. These developments, in turn, required financial resources and some amount of stability, both of which appear to contradict the ideal of a small band of itinerant preachers. Although Francis himself was never a priest, he was likely ordained a deacon. Twice he revised his Rule of Life, but never did he mitigate his call to absolute poverty. Eventually, the issue of further development became so critical that by the time St. Bonaventure became minister general of the friars in 1257, the divisions within the order had become pronounced. Although most of the friars followed the directives and dispensations of Rome, many sought to follow the rule *sine glossa* (without additions).

Yet even while there was internal conflict, the friars continued to draw men of the highest caliber to join their ranks. To serve Christ and his Church through the spirit of Francis was for many—intellectuals as well as prophets, poets, and spiritual leaders alike—an irresistible urge that drew them to the Poor Man of Assisi. It is a phenomenon that has never, even to our own time, failed to repeat itself.

While Lady Poverty was Francis's bride, one can only understand the *Poverello* and the family he established through his passionate love for the crucified Christ. It was the poor Christ of the gospel, on his way to the cross, who introduced Francis to this romance with Lady Poverty. And it was Francis's continued meditation on the mystery of the passion and death of Christ and his tireless preaching of this same mystery that culminated in his reception of an unusual mystical grace, the stigmata, whereby the five wounds of Christ's passion were visibly reproduced in his body and physically experienced at regular intervals.

Francis may not have intended to found a full-blown religious order, but, in the event, such was the case. St. Clare (1193–1253), a young woman of Assisi who was drawn into the circle of gospel simplicity, joy, and freedom that Francis generated, became the foundress of the Franciscan second order. The Poor Clares, as they are called, embraced a life of strict enclosure and radical poverty. They sought to rejoice in the goodness of God made manifest in even the smallest of creatures and events of life:

The sisters shall not acquire anything as their own, neither a house nor a place nor anything at all; instead, as pilgrims and strangers in this world who serve the Lord in poverty and humility, let them send confidently for alms. Nor should they be ashamed since the Lord made Himself poor for us in this world. This is that summit of the highest poverty which has established you, my dearest sisters, as heirs and queens of the kingdom of heaven; it has made you poor in the things [of this world] but has exalted you in virtue. Let this be your portion, which leads you to the land of the living (cf. Ps 141:6). Dedicating yourself totally to this, my most beloved sisters, do not wish to have anything else forever under heaven for the name of Our Lord Jesus Christ and His most holy Mother.[7]

Almost as quickly, the Franciscan third order developed, calling men and women of every walk of life to follow Francis, the perfect imitator of Christ and God's holy jester, into the way of gospel simplicity through deep attachment to Christ crucified.

The third orders of St. Francis and St. Dominic were originally part of the broader lay penitential movement—a quasi-religious order that began in the twelfth century. The Brothers and Sisters of Penance were laypersons who sought to lead a life of Christian perfection and penance in the world while continuing the duties of their state in life. Some, such as the beguines and Beghards, vowed themselves to celibacy and wore a religious habit, thus coming under ecclesiastical jurisdiction. The great majority of lay penitents, however, remained in their homes as ordinary laity. They were not affiliated with any particular religious order but sought spiritual guidance from Franciscans, Dominicans, or other religious, depending on their proximity to particular conventual churches.

While not organized under an official Franciscan rule until 1289, groups of tertiaries began developing in almost every Franciscan church, triggered by the rapid expansion of the friars. In this way, the spirit of Francis embraced all walks of life, and another mode of the Franciscan vocation became a possibility for any Christian who felt so inspired.

The thirteenth century witnessed the remarkable flowering of the Franciscan Order and the spiritual energy it unleashed wherever new foundations were made. Without doubt, a spiritual revolution was in progress. Stemming from the hills of Assisi, it was typified by new devotion to the humanity of Christ: the use of the Christmas crèche, the Stations of the Cross, the systematic meditation on the passion of Christ. In many ways, this was the beginning of what we call modern spirituality, that is, a new inwardness, giving rise to a rudimentary form of discursive meditation or mental prayer. All of this must be associated with the mendicant movement in general and in the Franciscan Order in particular. The barefoot friars tramped across

Europe, begging for their daily bread, and although they had no material goods to share, their larder was far from empty, for they were rich in the precious commodities of faith and zeal for the gospel of Jesus Christ.

St. Dominic and the Order of Preachers

The contours of the mendicant movement as shaped by St. Francis and his Friars Minor produce a rich picture indeed but one incomplete without a consideration of the genius and influence of St. Dominic and his Order of Preachers.[8] Both Francis and Dominic were lovers of evangelical poverty, both were preachers, both were lovers of the crucified Christ. Yet the contrasts between them are significant and not simply a matter of emphasis.

Theirs is a fundamental difference of vision, forged by a variety of cultural and geographical factors, as well as by different theological outlooks. Unlike his Italian contemporary, the Castilian Dominic de Guzman (1170–1221) was, from his early years, destined for the service of the Church. Trained in philosophy and theology at Palencia, Dominic embraced the life of the canons regular at the Cathedral of Burgo de Osma. Here the young priest was steeped in the traditions of religious life: the singing of the conventual Mass and the Divine Office, the practice of *lectio divina* and private prayer, study in preparation for preaching. And here, in the seclusion of the canonical cloister, Dominic was exposed to the sources of the ancient monastic ideal that were to prove so important in forging his own brand of mendicant religious life. His particular charism was to bring together the centuries-old practice of virtue and asceticism with a form of mobile religious life aimed at preaching and the salvation of souls. One of his early biographies describes him at this time:

> He became a model of life for everyone and an exemplary religious, and amongst all the other virtues with which he was endowed he had a special gift of weeping for the afflicted and for people in distress and for souls that were perishing, whose salvation he longed for jealously. He often used to spend the night in prayer, asking the Lord to give him the grace to help the salvation of those who were perishing.[9]

The tradition the Middle Ages inherited from the early Fathers of the Church held preaching to be the exclusive prerogative of the local ordinary. "For them [the Fathers] the preacher was the bishop. To teach the doctrine of Christ by homilies and commentaries on the Sacred Scripture constituted his chief function, the essential as a pastor."[10] The evangelical revival of the late twelfth and early thirteenth centuries saw some broadening of this task of preaching, but by and large, preaching was the exclusive domain of the bishop. At Osma, Dominic the contemplative shared that work with his bishop, Diego, who was in turn to share with the young canon his dream of an order dedicated to the preaching of sound doctrine.

It was the year 1203 that was to change Dominic's life forever. Serving as Diego's companion on a mission for the king, Dominic left Spain for the first time and set off for Denmark. In so doing, Dominic the tenderhearted contemplative became Dominic the apostle. The sights and sounds he encountered left him a changed man. Profoundly disturbing to the young cleric and his bishop were the rapidly proliferating heretical sects, many of them concentrated in southern France. There was to be one more trip to Denmark and then, on his return, Dominic would end his journey in the region of Toulouse where, in response to the religious chaos he had seen, he founded his own unique band of preaching friars in 1216.

The reality of heresy was long known in the Church, but the thirteenth century resurgence of religious fervor brought with it the danger of enthusiastic exaggeration and error. The kind of exaggeration Dominic encountered was Catharism, a rigorist, dualistic sect whose origins are buried in the twelfth century or earlier. Catharist dualism posited the human person as a fallen spirit trapped in matter, the flesh, and wandering the earth in search of purity. Eating and drinking, the needs of the body—indeed, marriage itself—were looked upon as evil and to be avoided. Within Catharism was a class of spiritual elites—the "Perfected"—who observed these regulations to the letter. Dressed in austere black robes, the Perfected became the incarnation of all the fervor and seriousness the heretics could muster.

The Albigensians, a name given to adherents of Catharism in southern France (from the city of Albi) had met with enormous success in the towns and villages where they preached and founded their communities. With whole dioceses being won over, the heresy was no small matter to be dismissed as a passing fad. In the hopes of reclaiming the heretics for the true faith, the Church had already deputed preachers to go to the locale of the Albigensians to preach, reason, and argue with them. Cistercian abbots who traveled with all the pomp and retinue due their dignified offices obediently took up the task given them by the pope; but they were not successful, and Diego and Dominic understood why. Such radical groups can only be reached by those who are themselves radical examples of gospel zeal and fervor and well-prepared for long and tedious theological discourses. In this way, the inspiration for an order of preaching brothers was conceived.

In contrast to the *Poverello* of Assisi, Dominic intended from the beginning to found an international order of preachers. On the face of it, this was an impossibility, since preaching was a uniquely episcopal task; but Dominic was able to convince Church authorities that his band of preachers, grounded in the time-tested observance of religious life and committed to constant and rigorous study, could undertake this mission. And so, to become a member of his order was to become a preacher. Influenced by his own formation as a canon, Dominic envisioned a group of ordained priests living the conventual life, begging for their daily bread, and moving everywhere throughout the world to preach the gospel of Jesus Christ. In short, he conceived of a brotherhood that would combine holiness of life with the preaching and teaching of sound Catholic doctrine. His dream quickly became a reality.

Between 1216 and 1221, the year of his death, Dominic moved about Europe, making foundations of preaching friars and devising a system of democratic government that would give stability, solid organization, and order to his religious family. He never wrote his own rule but chose the Rule of St. Augustine, supplementing it with customs or constitutions that would direct both the mission and administration of the friars preachers. In a revolutionary break with tradition, Dominic conceived the highest authority in his Order to be the community itself, gathered together in a solemn decision-making assembly: the chapter. This body elected their superiors for a fixed term and promised obedience to them rather than to a rule. This decision had serious consequences for the founder of the Order, for when, in 1220, the question arose of softening the practice of evangelical poverty, Dominic himself had to bow in obedience to the superior authority of his brothers, assembled in chapter. He then had to convince the friars, in spite of their hesitations, to adopt mendicancy both in principle and in practice, and convince them he did.

This process of self-government shows us much of the spirit of this great apostle. We possess little by way of his writings or verbal transcripts of his words; nor did he write a rule of life. All the evidence speaks of his appealing to the spontaneous generosity of his brothers at every issue or decision. His strategy was always to reason with them in patient conversation and argumentation. Dominic's confidence in the power of reason and his reluctance to arbitrarily impose his decisions and opinions on others imprinted on the Order of Preachers a spirit unique among such communities. Obedience, the single vow pronounced by the friar preacher, was observed in a communal context and always suggested a reasonable and enlightened process.

Finally, founding his Order for the spread of the truth, Dominic placed great emphasis on study and elevated it to the rank of a religious observance. The intellectual life had to be a priority for a group of men dedicated to engaging in all the contemporary struggles of Church and society. Sending his early friars to the university cities to establish convents of the Order, the founder intended that they equip themselves to engage in dialogue with the men and women of the world in order to win them for Christ. It was this scope for intellectual activity that drew the great thinker St. Thomas Aquinas to the Order of Preachers, much to the consternation of his family.

It was a complex idea, this notion of an order of preachers incorporating elements drawn from the monastic tradition alongside elements new and revolutionary: intense conventual life, serious intellectual activity, and the constant demand for preaching and teaching. The adventure of achieving this balance led men to the Order and, like their mendicant cousins the Franciscans, the Dominican Order expanded rapidly, so that by the end of the thirteenth century there were Dominican houses in every part of the Christian world.

What of the other branches of the typical mendicant order? The second order, the nuns of the Order of Preachers, actually came into existence before the friars. As early as 1206 Dominic organized groups of women, largely converts from Albigensianism, into a monastic community and began instructing them in his own version of the contemplative life. From the beginning, these women, although strictly cloistered themselves, were to be associated, through prayer and penance, with the work of holy preaching, in close relationship with the preaching friars. Later, and before St. Dominic died, other houses of nuns were founded in Rome and Madrid, and Dominic took on the responsibility for their material and spiritual formation. As did the friars, the nuns promised obedience to Dominic and his successors. Thus there would be one order, one mission, but a variety of ways in which it would be lived out. St. Dominic imparted both the contemplative ideal and zeal for the salvation of souls to mobile friars and cloistered nuns alike. The friars would fulfill their vocation in the work of preaching and teaching, while the nuns were deputed to ponder, celebrate, and live the Word of God in the hidden life of the monastic enclosure. And like the friars, so the nuns experienced rapid expansion in the thirteenth century and have continued to be an integral part of the Order of Preachers.

The development of the third order, or the Dominican Order of Penance, paralleled that of the Friars Minor. Various lay groups attached themselves to the Dominicans and carried out the works of charity to which their life committed them under the auspices of the Order. Instructed in the spirit and traditions of Dominican life, they became a powerful force for Christian witness in the world about them.

Perhaps the best-known Dominican tertiary is St. Catherine of Siena, the fourteenth-century lay Dominican and mystic who was to play such a prominent role in church politics during her brief life.[11]

St. Dominic, preacher and apostle, poured his love for the crucified Christ into the work of establishing the Order of Preachers. His own person, universally described as joyous and community minded, was less prominent in his project than his vision for providing the Church with a community of holiness and learning dedicated to preaching everywhere the truth of the gospel. The spirit of his own preaching can be summed up in one word: compassion. He addressed God as "my God, my Mercy," and his constant urging to the early friars was to proclaim the tender compassion of God in every city, hamlet, lecture hall, and pulpit. "God had given him a special grace to weep for sinners and for the afflicted and oppressed; he bore their distress in the inmost shrine of his compassion."[12] Where St. Francis is seen by his followers as an icon of the crucified Christ, St. Dominic reflects, in his mission of preaching and teaching, the compassionate Christ. "He thought he would only really be a member of Christ's Body when he could spend himself utterly with all his strength in the winning of souls, just as the Lord Jesus Christ, the Savior of us all, gave himself up entirely for our salvation."[13]

In his call "to contemplate and to give others the fruits of that contemplation," Dominic desired the spirituality of his order to blend contemplation and action in one harmonious movement. The love of truth and the unceasing proclamation of the gospel was the spiritual heritage he imparted to his sons and daughters. The Dominican must be a man or woman of the Word of God, always pondering the sources of revelation in order to discern there what is of God and will lead all to salvation and, contrariwise, to recognize that what is not of God can lead to falseness, confusion, and doubt. One modern writer comments,

> Both [Franciscans and Dominicans] respond to the same notion of *vita apostolica*, based on the same New Testament texts, but for Francis the emphasis is on *vita* (the term he uses for his rule), and apostolate is envisioned at first only as a potential part of the whole way of life . . . whereas for Dominic the emphasis is rather on *apostolica*, and his followers are fired more by the ideal of the apostolic job.[14]

Dominic, the *vir evangelicus* ("evangelical man"), and Francis, the *vir seraphicus* ("seraphic man"), together form the foundation of that moment of insight and clarity which enlightened the thirteenth century and initiated a renewal that still reminds the Church, even a week of centuries later, that at every level the only source of life and hope is to be found in Jesus Christ the Lord.

Conclusion: The Significance of the Mendicant Movement

A cursory glance at the history of the Christian Church from the thirteenth to the twentieth centuries will indicate the prominence of the mendicant orders in developments on every front: missionary activity, theological research, pastoral leadership and experimentation, education, mystical fervor. Further, a truly lay spirituality, another concern of the modern Church, begins in earnest with the mendicant third orders. However, aside from the catalogue of accomplishments and successful figures, the great contribution of the mendicant movement is to be found in its initiating what we have already referred to as modern theology and spirituality. Born into a world of change and desiring above all else to be open to the deepest needs of the people, the mendicants moved to a confrontation with the contemporary situation, and the synergy created in this meeting between the friars and the people of their time became a force for renewal. As always, the Christian tradition must be rediscovered and reinterpreted for the unique circumstances of every age.

Thus the mendicants illustrate the possibility of continuity of faith and Church life that is restated, and in some cases reshaped, for a new cultural situation. Forging new forms does not mean the loss of gospel values nor the compromising of the spiritual principles that form the bedrock of Christian life in every era. From the Dark Ages to the space age, the proclamation of God's saving work in Christ must be the central vocation of every Christian man or woman. The founders of the mendicant orders and their early followers, whether friars, nuns, or laity, had great confidence in the impulses of the Spirit that led them on and, therefore, great confidence in what they could together accomplish in the name of Christ. That is one of the major lessons of the mendicant movement: that the apostolic ideal lives on in the Church in each age and we must be confident of this mission, *our* mission, if renewal is to come to fulfillment in our time.

Notes

1. M. H. Vicaire, *The Apostolic Life* (Chicago: Priory Press, 1966); S. Tugwell, *The Way of the Preacher* (Springfield, Ill.: Templegate, 1979), pp. 111-14.
2. Originally the term applied only to the Franciscans and Dominicans, but it was later applied to the Carmelites, Augustinians, Servites, and, later still, to several other groups, such as the Trinitarians.

3. For a complete history of the Franciscan Order, see C. Esser, *Origins of the Franciscan Order,* trans. A. Daly and I. Lynch (Chicago: Franciscan Herald, 1970); L. Iriarte, *Franciscan History: The Three Orders of St. Francis of Assisi* (Chicago: Franciscan Herald, 1983). The primary source for Franciscan spirituality is found in the writings of St. Francis: R. Armstrong and I. Brady, trans., *Francis and Clare: The Complete Works* (New York: Paulist Press, 1982).
4. The term "friar" came to be used of the members of the mendicant orders, coming from the Latin *frater,* meaning "brother." All the mendicants were brothers and were addressed as such, in contrast to the monks, who were addressed as "father" or "lord."
5. Francis of Assisi, "The Earlier Rule," Armstrong and Brady, *Francis and Clare,* p. 116.
6. Ibid., pp. 124-25.
7. Ibid., pp. 219-20.
8. For the biography of St. Dominic, see M. H. Vicaire, *Saint Dominic and His Times* (New York: McGraw-Hill, 1964); for a history of the Order of Preachers, see W. A. Hinnebusch, *The History of the Dominican Order,* vols. 1-2, (Staten Island: Alba House, 1965); for Dominican documents, see S. Tugwell, ed., *Early Dominicans: Selected Writings* (New York: Paulist Press, 1982); for Dominican spirituality, see G. Bedouelle, *Saint Dominic: The Grace of the Word* (San Francisco: Ignatius Press, 1987).
9. Jean de Mailly, "The Life of St. Dominic," in Tugwell, *Early Dominicans,* p. 59.
10. Vicaire, *St. Dominic and His Times,* p. 189.
11. Catherine Benincasa (1347–1380) was the twenty-third and last child of her parents. Her early life was marked by a spirit of prayer, asceticism, and generous service to the poor. Magnetic in personality, she had, by 1370, gathered about her a "family" of diverse men and women who looked to her for spiritual guidance. In 1376 she journeyed to Avignon to urge Pope Gregory XI to return to Rome. Her role in Church politics was considerable, but her efforts for peace and the return of the papacy to Rome were overshadowed by her teaching on the spiritual life, her personal agony over the state of the Church, and her life of mystical communion with Christ. For a more thorough discussion of Catherine, see chapter 13 in this volume.
12. Jordan of Saxony, *On the Beginnings of the Order of Preachers,* trans. S. Tugwell (Chicago: Parable, 1981), p. 2.
13. Ibid., p. 3.
14. S. Tugwell, *Early Dominicans,* p. 19.

Bibliography

Armstrong, R., and Brady, I., trans. *Francis and Clare: The Complete Works.* New York: Paulist Press, 1982.

Bedouelle, Guy. *Saint Dominic: The Grace of the Word.* San Francisco: Ignatius Press, 1987.

Esser, C. *Origins of the Franciscan Order.* Translated by A. Daly and I. Lynch. Chicago: Franciscan Herald, 1970.

Hinnebusch, William. *The History of the Dominican Order.* 2 vols. Staten Island: Alba House, 1982.

Jordan of Saxony. *On the Beginnings of the Order of Preachers.* Translated by Simon Tugwell. Chicago: Parable, 1981.

Iriarte, L. *Franciscan History: The Three Orders of St. Francis of Assisi.* Chicago: Franciscan Herald, 1983.

Tugwell, Simon, ed. *Early Dominicans: Selected Writings.* New York: Paulist Press, 1982.

Vicaire, M. Henri. *Saint Dominic and His Times.* New York: McGraw-Hill, 1964.

Poverty and Prayer

RONALD M. MROZINSKI, o.f.m. conv.,
and GABRIEL O'DONNELL, o.p.

Where your treasure is, there will your heart be also.

—MATTHEW 6:21

Who would ever want to be poor? The poverty that our Lord assured us would "always" be with us does not ennoble human existence; it is a harsh, dehumanizing reality that can breed crime and despair. Inevitably, it is the poor who are most easily deceived and exploited. No one wants to be thrust involuntarily into this kind of poverty. And yet, there are some who, quite deliberately, choose to be "poor," and they make this choice out of the conviction that, in the end, their "want" will not be oppressive but rather an occasion of grace: sheer gain.

What the Christian tradition calls evangelical poverty is a means to an end, not an end in itself. This form of poverty is freely chosen rather than imposed by the economic circumstances of life. It is a means by which the one who chooses desires to focus on the one who is chosen: Jesus Christ.

The choice of poverty as a lifestyle is a choice to center one's life on the poor Christ of the gospel. It is a commitment to live unencumbered by property, attachments, relationships, or status, and it is an ideal that has informed the spiritual practice of the Church from the very beginning, when the first Christians contributed their resources to the community for the sake of common needs (Acts 2:44-45). The earliest monastic communities were fired by a vision of total freedom for God, and it was this they sought when they promised to live in poverty. Then, in the thirteenth century, the life of gospel poverty brought with it two innovations for organized religious life: mendicancy and itinerancy.

The mendicants were those friars who lived by begging their daily bread from door to door. Unlike monks, who lived in poverty but depended on their own lands and endowments for income, the mendicant embraced a life of daily insecurity, depending entirely on the spontaneous generosity of the people of God. Again, in contrast to the monks, whose vow of stability required them to remain always in the monastery of their profession, the friars embraced the notion of itinerancy. Unencumbered by material possessions, they were always on the move, preaching the gospel everywhere in humility and poverty.

Just as the poor do not have the security of material possessions, neither did the mendicant. The friars sought only the security that came from their gospel fraternity. Their "home" was their community, the brotherhood of poor friars. Their commitment was to evangelize *in via*—"on the way"—anyone who would listen to their message. In its incarnation of the biblical theme of journey or pilgrimage, the mendicant lifestyle reminded the Church that it too was a "pilgrim people," a community *in via* toward the kingdom of God.

Francis of Assisi began his rule of 1225 by stating, "The rule and life of the Friars Minor is this: to observe the holy gospel of our Lord Jesus Christ by living in obedience, without anything of their own, and in chastity."[1] For Francis and his poor brothers, this divestment of material property was symbolic of the constant change required of the heralds of the Great King. The spirit of constant change, of conversion, marks the poverty and prayer of the friar. Poverty— the absence of *things*—prepares a space in our lives and hearts for the Lord, just as prayer bids him welcome. The gospel demands that we follow the poor Christ, and this is a call not only to change the world about us but also to begin the process of change within ourselves.

St. Dominic saw poverty as a means to more effective preaching. Not only did the absence of material possessions focus the life of the preacher by eliminating distractions and temptations, it established his credibility by visibly and voluntarily linking him with the poor Christ of the gospel and the poor people of God, so dear to Christ's heart and so central to his mission. The Dominican Order was founded from the beginning for "preaching and the salvation of souls." For Dominic, poverty was a "corollary of the will to follow Christ in all things" and equipped the preacher with a most important grace: zeal for souls.[2] He wished to become poor by pouring himself out for the salvation of others, for only in this way could he be considered a true member of Christ.

The evangelical poverty of the mendicants was intended to be countercultural. For Francis and Dominic, this contrast with the world was not simply a matter of having or not having, not merely an issue of acquisition or divestment. Rather, it was a contrast of values. Power, wealth, and freedom from deprivation are values that society has always deemed important in measuring self-worth and social success. In the Middle Ages, evangelical poverty challenged these criteria as determinants of any real worth for the follower of Jesus—child of God and companion on the journey to the kingdom. Evangelical poverty challenges these same worldly values today.

When freely chosen poverty becomes an actuating force in a person's life, it is a powerful agent of change. Of inestimable value, such poverty does not so much free us *from* something as it frees us *to* something. Evangelical poverty frees us to live a Christian lifestyle reflective of Christ's own life. It leads to Christ and seeks to remind us that the exigencies of proclaiming conversion of life and acceptance of the kingdom have precedence over all else. The practice of evangelical poverty reminds the disciple that the Master so gave himself to this task of proclamation that he had "nowhere to lay his head." (Matt. 8:20).

Poverty of Spirit

Evangelical poverty should bring one to greater dependence upon God, just as Jesus was dependent upon his heavenly Father. At the same time, it leads a person who vows or freely chooses this way of life to an increased interdependence with others. This interdependence leads, in turn, to the forming of closer bonds of community where this gospel value can be supported and challenged.

The experience of the man or woman of faith is perfectly echoed in the cry of the psalmist, who repeats over and over again, "As for me, I am poor and needy; but the Lord takes thought for me" (Ps. 40:17). This cry for help, for the constant, tender support of God, is the expression of an incompleteness, a gap within ourselves that is the source of our poverty. Although we may seldom catch a glimpse of it or acknowledge its existence, it is this inner emptiness that causes us to depend on the mercy of God and the compassionate love of our brothers and sisters: "He has pity on the weak and needy, and saves the lives of the needy" (Ps. 72:13).

Often enough we become so engrossed in the accumulation of material possessions that we forget the one who created all these wonderful things. In that sense, we have abused creation, which is intended to lead us *to the Creator*. We must learn again to be led by the created universe to the Lord of Creation, to whom each one of us belongs. Evangelical poverty, then, is an integral part of our awareness of belonging to Christ. We begin to be poor when we realize the givenness of all things, especially of our own essential selves.

Poverty of spirit, which begins in the deep recesses of the heart, is intended to express a relationship *with God* in and through Christ. Any following of Christ requires this interior attitude regardless of the form the exterior expression may take: "Blessed are the poor in spirit, for theirs is the kingdom of heaven" (Matt. 5:3). No matter how vehemently we rend our garments and appear as beggars before the world, such witness will be empty if we do not first rend our hearts.

Francis and Dominic understood the priority of poverty of spirit and placed at the heart of their teaching on evangelical poverty the axiomatic proposition of Jesus in the gospel: "For where your treasure is, there will your heart be also" (Matt. 6:21). To treasure being over having, relatedness over domination, and vulnerability over security allows us to know true discipleship, for then we are attempting to live out the very ideals Jesus taught and lived. What we truly love is what we treasure most in life. In a life of gospel poverty, the beatitude "Blessed are the pure in heart, for they shall see God" is realized (Matt. 5:8). Desiring the single Source of all that exists, and that *alone,* is truly single-heartedness, and the goal of evangelical poverty is precisely that: to see God.

Evangelical poverty or poverty of spirit is about one's relationship with the material world as an expression of the prior relationship with God. Thus poverty and prayer are intertwined in the tradition of Christian spirituality. Poverty frees us to experience creation as God's gift, and prayer frees us to experience God himself. Evangelical poverty unites us to God and to creation.

Incarnational Prayer

God the Creator is at the center of creation, and the creature must find a way through creation to the very center: God. This is a journey inward, made only in the heart. The practice of evangelical poverty helps one see that the journey must be made through a change of heart—a change that allows no creature or created thing to stand in the way of seeking the Creator. Paradoxically, in a poverty that has been freely chosen, all of creation is allowed to praise the Creator. The prayer of the poor in Christ exults in the beauty and abundance given in and through creation.

The joy in creation that so characterizes the Franciscans in particular has led to an emphasis on the affective dimension of Christian prayer. A close identification with the humanity of Christ—especially a strong attachment to the poor and crucified Jesus—enabled a loving reverence for all humanity, a humanity for which Jesus gave his life. And not only humanity is reverenced in Franciscan spirituality, but all of creation; for in the life, death, and resurrection of Jesus, nature itself, fallen with Adam, is renewed and redeemed.

This incarnational understanding of the entire created order leads to a deep reverence for everything that comes from the hand of the Creator. Evangelical poverty does not seek domination, power, or control over creation; rather, it seeks harmony, peace, and unity with it. It is no wonder, then, that we find great emphasis upon the praise of God by all of creation in the prayer life of the mendicant, and nowhere more than in "The Canticle of the Creatures" composed by St. Francis. In this prayer St. Francis calls upon "Brother Sun," "Sister Moon," and "Mother Earth" to praise God simply for having been created. He asks that God be praised *in* and *through* all that he has made. Possessing nothing, Francis could claim everyone and everything as brother or sister. Possessing nothing, Francis was free to be in harmony and at peace with all creation.

Dominicans, in both their preaching and teaching about prayer, were equally incarnational. Poverty of spirit was understood as a prerequisite for a deep relationship with Christ, who was like us in all things but sin. The centrality of the doctrine of grace in the friars' preaching emphasized God's initiative in the work of sanctification. They were convinced that it would be impossible to see and use creation wisely unless one's heart had been captured by Christ, who "though he was rich, yet for [our] sake . . . became poor, so that by his poverty [we] might become rich" (II Cor. 8:9). The external rites of the liturgy became, in the Dominican tradition, the gateway to deep interior prayer. The use of a variety of bodily postures in worship and the employment of traditional symbols of light, incense, and song to appeal to the senses and enhance the proclamation of the Word of God became hallmarks of their prayer style. Even the popular (and very concrete) devotional prayer of the rosary, developed by fifteenth-century Dominicans, carried with it the biblical and liturgical orientations cherished by the order from their beginnings. (See appendix 12, p. 391).

In our own day, whole political and economic systems seem to militate against harmony and peace with the created order. Greed and self-sufficiency create chasms between people and often make the environment a victim of exploitation; or we mistake possession for power and hold creation in bondage, unwittingly and without malice. Yet real power lies in freeing the created order to become what the Creator intended it to be. Thus an incarnational spirituality honors the immanent presence of God through the created order; and evangelical poverty, which fosters respect and love for God in all of creation, "embodies" the freeing power of grace. Marveling at creation with a sense of wonderment and awe, the poor in Christ stand overwhelmed at the power and love of God.

Some questions must now be asked: Am I free enough to marvel at the created order and experience there the presence of God? Am I able to be interdependent with others on my journey through life? Do I view my dependence upon God as a weakness or as a source of grace? Does my need to control people and situations impede my ability to form warm relationships with others? With God? Am I held captive by my possessions?

The experience of gospel poverty conditions both our image of self and our image of God—images that we bring to prayer. Prayer in the mendicant tradition is generally *kataphatic* ("image filled"). Images are important, therefore, and cannot be ignored. Asking ourselves often about our images in prayer can yield deep insight into the authenticity of our prayer. Francis of Assisi is said to have observed, "What a person is before God, that they are and nothing more." Before God, each one of us is "poor." Thus the recognition of our real poverty, in which we see ourselves as *God* sees us, is the basis for authenticity in prayer.

Every spiritual tradition, besides seeking transcendence, also helps those who embrace its wisdom to live more authentically. As we have seen, gospel poverty is not an end in itself but a means to an end: an authenticity that reflects the life of Christ and leads to union with God.

Evangelical Poverty and the Laity

We might want to argue that evangelical poverty is fine for people who are members of religious orders but completely impractical for the layperson. Is this so? Dominic and Francis realized that the scope of their movement was broader than a formal vow of poverty and that the spirit of gospel poverty was a pervasive feature in the process of personal Christian and ecclesial renewal, extending beyond the confines of any one religious order.

To share the spirit of this renewal, both Dominicans and Franciscans founded a third order (see chapter 3). Now called "secular orders," these groups of laity follow a rule of life centered on the gospel, yet those who embrace this rule seek to live the ideals of evangelical poverty while remaining in their current jobs, in a manner compatible with their family situations and vocational responsibilities. Realizing that it is impossible to live radical gospel poverty while caring for a home and family, the secular orders nevertheless provide a community for those who are attracted to mendicant spirituality. Third order members together gain insight, find support, and share their faith on a regular basis so that the ideals of the gospel can be lived in a great variety of settings. Yet a formal affiliation with a group seeking to live a rule of life is not required in order to follow the ideals of the gospel. All are called to live some form of freely chosen poverty, just as Jesus did in his life. All are called to realize, as concretely as possible, the reality of Christian evangelical poverty.

The laity, in particular, are called upon to use their material resources and social and political influence to eradicate the kinds of social injustice that perpetuate dehumanizing, unchosen forms of poverty. Since any concerted or sustained action on behalf of the poor will almost certainly be personally costly, it is essential that the Church equip people for this task, and there is no better way to do this than to teach them the meaning of poverty of spirit. Without a clear understanding of our essential neediness toward God—our absolute requirement for God's sustaining grace—our projects (no matter how unselfishly motivated) are just that: *our* projects. And most of them are headed for shipwreck.

Whether we are part of a religious community or not, living gospel values is the baptismal commitment of every Christian; and embracing evangelical poverty is a means to that end of living out our baptismal commitment to Christ. What elements, then, of the spiritual practice of the great mendicant traditions can the ordinary Christian of today appropriate? Attachment to the person of Christ and detachment from things; cherishing all of the created order as a gift from the Creator; a simple lifestyle; an incarnational, image-filled prayer life; and an aptitude for living every aspect of our lives truthfully—"as we are before God."

Evangelical poverty, properly understood, is a world-affirming value. More than a negative renunciation of wealth, power, and influence, it opens up a whole new way of seeing things, of sharing resources, protecting the environment, and seeking to live in harmony with the created order. It is a process of conversion, of letting go. Perhaps better than any other form of discipline, it focuses our values, enriches a life intensely lived for Christ, and makes of our whole life a prayer.

EXERCISES

For an Individual

Identify your most cherished material possession. Place it in front of you. Spend about ten to fifteen minutes silently before this object. Then slowly and deliberately pray the Our Father, meditating on each phrase of that prayer. Spend the next fifteen minutes evaluating the real worth of this possession for you in light of what you have just prayed.

The next time you feel an impulse to buy something you want, picture that object in your mind and repeat the process described above. What lies behind the impulse to acquire more?

For a Group

Option One

In a natural outdoor setting, pray the Canticle of the Creatures (see below) together. Then have each member of the group *be* the particular verse (i.e., Brother Sun, Sister Moon, Mother Earth). Reread each verse, asking the assigned person to reflect on the verse and share the reflection with the group. In summary, have the group write in their journals what was felt during this time and how this helped them become more in tune with the created order of which they are a part.

Upon completion of this exercise, have the group resolve to concretely do something positive for the poor by choice rather than by chance, and set a time for the group to do this together.

Option Two

Invite one or more members of Franciscan and Dominican third orders to share their insights and experience with your group or class. What are the most important aspects of this affiliation for them? What impact has it had on their family life and careers? Can the ideals of mendicant spirituality be applied in any meaningful way to the life of the laity?

CANTICLE OF THE CREATURES

Most High, all-powerful, good Lord,
Yours are the praises, the glory, the honor, and all blessing.
To You alone, Most High, do they belong,

and no man is worthy to mention Your name.
Praised be You, my Lord, with all your creatures,
especially Sir Brother Sun,
Who is the day and through whom You give us light.
And he is beautiful and radiant with great splendor;
and bears a likeness of You, Most High One.
Praised be You, my Lord, through Sister Moon and the stars,
in heaven You formed them clear and precious and beautiful.
Praised be You, my Lord, through Brother Wind,
and through the air, cloudy and serene, and every kind of weather
through which You give sustenance to Your creatures.
Praised be You, my Lord, through Sister Water,
which is very useful and humble and precious and chaste.
Praised be You, my Lord, through Brother Fire,
through whom You light the night
and he is beautiful and playful and robust and strong.
Praised be You, my Lord, through our Sister Mother Earth,
who sustains and governs us,
and who produces varied fruits with colored flowers and herbs.
Praised be You, my Lord, through those who give pardon for Your love
and bear infirmity and tribulation.
Blessed are those who endure in peace
for by You, Most High, they shall be crowned.
Praised be You, my Lord, through our Sister Bodily Death,
from whom no living man can escape.
Woe to those who die in mortal sin.
Blessed are those whom death will find in Your most holy will,
for the second death shall do them no harm.
Praise and bless my Lord and give Him thanks
and serve Him with great humility.[3]

DISCUSSION QUESTIONS

1. In our society poverty is an evil to be shunned and eliminated, yet Christ chose poverty as a way of life, and for centuries the Church has held up the ideal of gospel poverty as something Christians should embrace. Discuss the distinction between "voluntary" and "involuntary" poverty. Does the ideal of evangelical poverty have any relevance for the Church today? Does it challenge you personally?

2. Some of our contemporaries embrace a life of simplicity and restraint in response to the ecological abuses of our time and in search of greater personal wholeness and inner self-actualization. Is this the same as gospel simplicity or poverty? Could such a life,

embraced for the sake of the gospel, have any impact on our contemporary world?

3. What relationship should exist between those who freely embrace gospel poverty and those who are poor because of economic circumstances? Is a freely chosen poverty *true* poverty? Does economic want per se bring us closer to God?

4. Pinpoint the values implicit in current social customs contrary to gospel poverty. Is evangelical poverty necessarily countercultural? How important is the kind of mutual support and accountability a group such as a third order can provide in the practice of gospel ideals?

Notes

1. "The Later Rule," in R. Armstrong and I. Brady, trans., *Francis and Clare: The Complete Works* (New York: Paulist Press, 1982), p. 137.
2. Guy Bedoulle, *Saint Dominic: The Grace of the Word* (San Francisco: Ignatius Press, 1987), p. 140.
3. Armstrong and Brady, *Francis and Clare*, pp. 38-39.

Resources

Bedouelle, Guy. *Saint Dominic: The Grace of the Word.* San Francisco: Ignatius Press, 1987.

Congar, Yves. *Power and Poverty in the Church.* Translated by J. Nicholson. Baltimore: Helicon Press, 1964.

Engelbert, Omer. *Saint Francis of Assisi: A Biography.* Chicago: Franciscan Herald, 1965.

Flood, David, and Matura, Thadee. *The Birth of a Movement.* Chicago: Franciscan Herald, 1975.

Hinnebusch, William A. *The History of the Dominican Order.* 2 vols. Staten Island: Alba House, 1966.

Metz, Johannes. *Poverty of Spirit.* Translated by J. Drury. New York: Newman Press, 1968.

Mrozinski, Ronald M. *Franciscan Prayer Life.* Chicago: Franciscan Herald, 1966.

Vicaire, M. H. *Saint Dominic and His Times.* Translated K. Pond. New York: McGraw-Hill, 1964.

CHAPTER 4

Devotio Moderna:
Reforming Piety in the
Later Middle Ages

MARK S. BURROWS

Carry the cross patiently and with perfect submission, and in the end, it shall carry you. .
—THOMAS À KEMPIS

During the final decades of the fourteenth and the early years of the fifteenth centuries, a pious renewal of the Church occurred in the Netherlands, which later came to be known as the *Devotio moderna,* or "Modern Devotion."[1] Although the original founder of this movement was himself educated at the University of Paris and eventually associated with the Carthusian order, the influence of Geert Groote's thought and life (1340–1384) was at once broader and more general than these horizons. In his writings, as in his establishment and support of emerging communities of lay women and men, Groote dedicated himself to nurturing a peculiar flowering of the Christian life that one modern historian has enthusiastically characterized as the emergence of "the Christian Renaissance."[2] Already within a generation of Groote's death, he was being hailed as "the fountain of the *Devotio moderna,*" a source of spiritual inspiration and ecclesiastical leadership who "illumined the whole country with his life, words, way, and doctrine."[3] He was, to echo the words of another early biographer, "the first father of this our reformation, the source and origin of the Modern Devotion; he was an apostle in this country who kindled fires of religious fervor in the cold hearts of others, and drew them to God."[4]

But what exactly was this renaissance, or rebirth, that Groote in part helped to initiate? And how was his life's work related to broader movements of ecclesiastical renewal during the period that witnessed the political and social turmoil triggered by the papal move to Avignon—characterized during the Renaissance as the "Babylonian captivity"—and the ensuing papal schism in the Western Church? Indeed, we might well ask whether the emergence of the *Devotio moderna* is not itself a measure of the often stark contrasts of the age, a vibrant sign of the resilience and vitality of Christian piety during a period in which the Church as a whole suffered from both the confusion and rancor of the schism and widespread criticism of the clergy's competence and fitness for their pastoral duties.

This was, after all, the age in which satire directed against the Church and expressed in emerging vernacular literatures flourished. (A poignant expression of this is Chaucer's familiar caricature of the greedy and gluttonous friar, set alongside his gentler portrait of the devout if also simple country parson.) This period witnessed a rising tide of criticism aimed at the stratification of medieval society into three estates—laity, clergy, and the monks—with the monastic order representing the apogee of this social hierarchy. Thus we must at the outset observe that the Modern Devotion was by no means radical but rather a phenomenon very much in keeping with the times. This was a movement of devotion, or better, a *style* of Christian commitment that signified both the restlessness and the efficacy of popular efforts aimed at edifying the Church and renewing the Christian life. As a rebirth, this movement joined a broader effort to re-form the Church, a "reformation in head and members," to recall an oft-repeated conciliar pronouncement of this period.[5]

Yet the Modern Devotion emphasized not so much an institutional reform, since its adherents accepted in basic outline the formal structure and lines of obedience of the medieval Church; rather, its focus was upon a renewal of piety among individuals, and eventually communities, in their journey toward God. It is in the articulation of this simple vision of personal reform and the widespread following this message inspired, first in the Low Countries, that the significance of the Modern Devotion can be clearly seen. We will consider, first, the shape of reform that Groote articulated in both his writings and his acts. Second, our attention will range more broadly upon the establishment of the institutional movement known as the Brothers and Sisters of the Common Life, which Groote inspired but which came into being only after his death. Finally, we will examine the devotional classic that emerged from this movement, *The Imitation of Christ,* the literary product of Thomas à Kempis, an Augustinian canon of the monastery of St. Agnietenberg at Zwolle.

Geert Groote, "the Fountain of the Modern Devotion"

Living as he did during a period of intense and popular interest in the mystical life, Geert Groote's contribution to the piety of the age stood against the rising fascination with abstract forms of mysticism, on the one hand, and the speculative excesses to which some university theologians had carried both the methods and the substance of scholastic theology, on the other. In this, of course, he was anything but unique; his voice sounded with cadences that were also to be heard among other reform-minded churchmen of his and later generations.[6] But the texture and constructive vision of the Christian life that he articulated and the energy with which he promoted it mark him as founder of a movement that effected a peculiar flowering of the Christian life. Yet what was new or modern about this devotion was not that it boasted an originality of theological or spiritual content but that it altered the context of earlier monastic ideals for a broader audience: Within the expansive horizon of the *Devotio moderna,* we find the laity occupying a status alongside those bound by formal religious vows. By encouraging an interest in the interior dimension rather than the external marks of the religious life, Groote's vision of how piety might be renewed spawned a movement with wide popular appeal, a legacy that has been called a democratization of the ascetic tradition of medieval monasticism.[7]

Groote's biography cuts across a rich stratum of the intellectual and ecclesiastical life of northern Europe. Educated at the University of Paris, he eventually associated himself, for a sustained retreat, with the Monnikhuizen community of the Carthusian Order, later refusing ordination to the priesthood in favor of the diaconate, and it was as a deacon that he served as an itinerant preacher of reform in the Yssel valley and its environs. His message, which had mystical elements, nevertheless diverged markedly from that of Ruusbroec and the Rhineland mystics; Groote had little respect for either arid speculation or an exclusively interiorized form of mysticism, abstracted from the mundane dimensions of life. His form of mysticism, or "devotionalism," integrated the active and the contemplative, the practical and the theoretical, offering what has been accurately described as "a very realistic conception of the spiritual life."[8]

This is not to say that Groote was anti-intellectual—far from it. But he was suspicious of an academic theology that had no bearing upon the concrete realities of life or offered little encouragement to progress in virtue. Again and again in his writings we hear him use the language of what is "useful" and "fruitful," insisting that a simple but engaged faith (*fides simplex*) is of more value than a complex and nuanced intellectual grasp that is devoid of charity. His concern was not in the first instance with a strictly "intellectual learning" (*studium intellectuale*) but with a "devout and moral learning" (*studium devotum et morale*)[9] that would shape the *life* and not merely the thought of the Christian. This emphasis upon the union of the intellect and affects, of thinking and living the faith, is one of the hallmarks of Groote's writings and indeed of the broader corpus of "devotionalist" literature of this period. Piety and theology were wed in an indissoluble bond, such that the mark of the theologian, as Groote understood it, had more to do with the broad witness of one's life than with academic speculation or even mystical experience. This was a "theology of piety" that would mark a dominant strain in fifteenth-century thought.[10]

Another key facet of Groote's message was his unwavering emphasis upon the use of the Bible in Christian formation. Measured against the leading strains of scholastic theology during the fourteenth century, this was in the first instance a modulation of method rather than of content; that is, scholastic theologians by no means avoided using the Scriptures in their work, even as the starting point of their argumentation, but unlike Groote, they normally relied upon elaborate rhetorical forms of disputation based on a highly developed application of logic. By contrast, Groote applied a simple, devotional use of the Bible, approaching once again that of Augustine, in which the biblical text as *verbum Dei* became a source of meditation or, in the technical language of monasticism, "rumination" for Christian living.[11]

With Augustine, Groote held that the inherent texture of scriptural language was meant to stimulate the twofold love of God and neighbor; any other use or manner of reading was extraneous and indeed a perversion, a sign of the human fall that led to "vain speculation."[12] "Whatever does not make you a better Christian," he wrote with characteristic brevity, "is itself harmful."[13] His was, therefore, a distinctively scriptural piety, far from any mystical flight into God through visions or revelations. While he allowed for such phenomena, as did most theologians of his day, Groote's clear preference was for a meditation upon scriptural texts as the sure vehicle of spiritual experience, rather than an embrace of the elusive (and often illusive) world of private experience alone.[14] As he once noted, "When I read the psalms, hidden manna is flowing into my inner self, so that I experience no fatigue in reading, but sweet rapture instead."[15] Scripture precedes and, indeed, is the instigating factor behind such experience, and not vice versa. This is no small point: The Bible *as experienced,* and not private experience alone, has here become the point of departure, the means by which we "ought to walk in the way of God," to recall the language of the later constitution written for the Deventer Brethren of the Common Life.[16] The rhetoric of Scripture served to "move the heart and will to the love of virtue and the avoidance of vice." In short, the Bible itself stood as the vehicle of growth in the Christian life.[17]

Alongside his devotion to the Bible, Groote's frequent and eclectic use of the early Church Fathers is another index of his love of "useful" learning. Indeed, just as he preferred Scripture to individual experience, so he also insists upon reading the Bible within the Church's historical context, that is, within the interpretive framework of "tradition." In a practical sense, when Groote identifies individual texts that he held to be beneficial for study, the patristic biblical commentaries often dominate his list.[18] By no means a biblicist, Groote never isolates the Scriptures as the sole source of learning. Rather than *scriptura sola,* the rallying cry of later Protestant reformers during the sixteenth century, Groote's approach entailed a blending of the Bible and interpretations of it by those earlier theologians who came to constitute the Church's "tradition." As one historian has rightly noted, Groote's "spirituality springs from the past and is in no way revolutionary."[19] A further measure of this love of the Fathers can be noted in what has been vividly described as Groote's "unquenchable desire for books," a consuming interest that led to his lifelong project of building a library through borrowing and enlisting scribes to copy manuscripts for this purpose.[20] Indeed, this love of books would come to characterize the work of the Brethren of the Common Life, first in their contribution to the work of copying (a task that had previously fallen largely to the monastic houses but that broadened due to an expanding market for books during this period) and later in their use of printing presses to expedite this process.

Groote's vision of the spiritual life, furthermore, was directly linked with the "external" piety to be found in the Church's sacraments and liturgy. Far from setting the inner life of the spirit over against the institutional forms of devotion, or the private in competition with the official, Groote conceived of these as two valid and necessarily interlinked paths of Christian piety. In a later biography of his life, we learn that he attended Mass each day and received the Eucharist rather than withdrawing as a passive witness into the realm of private devotions, as had become common practice among the laity during this period.[21] This is a testimony that suggests as much about the abiding ideals of the later devotionalists as about Groote himself. We know from the later constitution of the Deventer congregation of brothers that the practice of attending Mass together on Sundays and appointed saints' days and other Church festivals was mandatory.[22] In other words, Groote's lead appears to have established a precedent among later proponents of the devotionalist movement, setting the Christian life squarely within the institutional framework of the Christian Church.

Indeed, in this task Groote's insistence on redefining the meaning of the word "religious," which in medieval usage referred to those who had entered monastic life, contributed to the decided shift in the norms and assumptions structuring the social hierarchy of the late fourteenth century. As he argued, against the widely accepted model of early medieval society,

> if devout women separate themselves from the world, and try to serve God in the privacy of their homes, without taking monastic vows, they are just as "religious" as the nuns in their convents. To love God and worship him is religion [*religio*], not the taking of special vows. For the cause and purpose of things give them their names and forms. If it is, therefore, one's aim to live a religious life, one's way of living becomes religious in God's opinion, and according to the judgment of one's own conscience.

He went on to say, "There are many who are not protected by the name *religio*, and yet they may be more religious than those whom the church calls 'religious.'"[23] This is not to suggest that Groote advocated any relaxing of discipline; he consistently upheld an ordered form of Christian life, but his genius lay in emphasizing the voluntary nature of that life, and in accordance with this he emphasized the role of frequent "resolutions" rather than lifelong vows to hold Christians accountable to the religious life. Yet such views were a decided minority report—a dangerous and disruptive novelty—when viewed from the professional ranks of the hierarchically structured late-medieval Church. Within this horizon it is not difficult to imagine why Groote and his successors ran into difficulties with leaders of monastic communities, a confrontation that eventually came to a pointed crisis when the Dominican Matthew Grabow attacked the legitimacy of such lay forms of "religious" life.[24] In anticipating this critique, Groote held to his conviction that all people in their quest to live pious lives had an inner obligation, in contrast to the external marks of Church status, such as religious vows. *Everyone* was to progress in the virtues on the journey toward God and in this manner to embody the religious life.

For this reason he insisted that the hidden "intention" and not the visible approbation of the Church determined the character of the religious life. That is, Groote valued internal devotion rather than the external designation of vows or the mere performance of devout acts (e.g., pilgrimages, acts of penance, etc.) as the true mark of the Christian life. He reasoned that "the mere name *religio* signifies but little, since it is not the name which determines the nature of a thing; names are conventional."[25] With this sentiment we find a suspicion, but by no means an outright rejection, of the Church's hierarchical distinctions between laity and "religious" (i.e., monks). Significantly, this suspicion prompted Groote not to devalue monastic life per se but to accentuate the opportunities available to, if not also the obligations incumbent upon, the laity. Along this line, Groote promoted "resolutions" and "intentions" as an ordering framework for the laity, rather than the "vows" of the monastic life.[26] This theme would become one of the abiding contributions of the devotionalist movement, since it is during the fifteenth century that we witness a peculiar broadening of the possibilities available to the laity, as well as a heightened attentiveness to the pastoral duties incumbent upon those charged with the "cure of souls." It is not too bold to suggest that already here we note anticipations not of later Protestant efforts to bring about a *theological* reform but of a *Church* reform (*reformatio ecclesiae*); yet this ecclesial reform, by empowering the laity to fuller and more direct participation in the religious life, anticipated such later developments.[27]

In similar fashion, Groote argued that the Christian life did not necessitate rigid isolation from society. Indeed, that this could *not* be the case for those exercising pastoral duties is a conviction dominating not only Groote's position but that of the later Brethren of the Common Life as well. These devotionalists lived squarely *in* the world. In defiance of an exclusively individualistic or privatistic form of piety, Groote chose to devote himself not only to a personal quest for perfection in the monastic tradition but also to the pastoral work of preaching and teaching. Groote's vision of the Christian life, while opposing a worldliness that diminished the religious witness, nonetheless turned decisively toward and not away from the world (*saeculum*) and thus stood in contrast to the cloistered life in exemplifying what might be called a secular spirituality.

For this reason we might well speak of Groote's spirituality as blending the "vertical" quest to love God with the "horizontal" practice of service to neighbor. The integrity of his witness is disclosed in his insistence on the essential integration of these two elements as *together* expressive of true religion. As an aspect of this practical spirituality, and alongside his commitment to prayer and meditation, Groote defended the spiritual value of work as an integral part of Christian formation, an approach echoing the early Benedictine motto exhorting the brothers to "pray and work" (*ora et labora*). Indeed, this theme is carried into an early constitution of the Windesheim community, which concluded that among the *spiritual* exercises that we might expect—"prayer, meditation, watching, fasting"—belonged also "manual labor," an outgrowth of Groote's more modest conviction that "labor is necessary for the well-being of humankind."[28] As a further reflection of this practical spirituality, Groote conceived of the Christian life in concrete communal terms, involving the often gritty tasks of living more peaceably with others. Again, this attempt to fuse together the spiritual and the practical, to integrate religion and life, characterizes not only Groote's writings but also the later constitutions and pious treatises emerging from the devotionalist movement.

As part of his concern about pastoral matters, Groote insisted that just as growth in the spiritual life was a matter of progress, so also instruction in this life needed to be methodical and gradual. This grounding of concrete pastoral responsibilities in pedagogical theory reflects Groote's vision of the Christian life as a journey, a process of growth in the virtues by which one increasingly yields to grace. This developmental theory of spiritual and moral growth is a theme that appears with remarkable consistency in his various sermons, letters, and treatises, prompting him to remind one of his correspondents that "nothing is so dangerous as to preach about God and perfection, and not to point out the way that leads to perfection."[29] It was not enough for preachers to establish the destination of human life; their principal task was to articulate the *way* by which each one of us, as a "pilgrim" in this life, might attain to perfection. And, we might add, Groote could conceive no higher calling than that of the pastoral vocation or the "cure of souls" (*cura animarum*), as it was called throughout the Middle Ages. As he repeatedly argued, echoing Pope Gregory the Great, the yoke of the pastoral office was *ars artium,* the highest of all arts.

With this attention to progress, moral and spiritual, Groote grounded his conception of the Christian life on a voluntarist basis, an emphasis that mirrored what has been called "the golden rule" of nominalist ethics, namely, the theme of the conformity of the human with the divine will (*conformitas voluntatis*).[30] Yet Groote qualifies this theme by insisting that all human effort depends first and last upon divine grace, since it is "God alone who converts the sinner."[31] As he elsewhere reasons, "Man proposes, but God disposes," a thesis that in elegant simplicity intentionally captures the grace-centered and theocentric logic of Paul and the later Augustine. This qualification establishes the theological substratum that leads Groote to advocate humility, a commonplace in late-medieval piety that nonetheless bears mention because of its peculiarity to the modern (anthropocentric) mind.

The centrality of humility for proponents of the *Devotio moderna* has its polemic edge, to be sure: In emphasizing this virtue, Groote draws upon a theme that stood at the heart of earlier monastic sources, but here again he has translated a traditional ascetic concern, born in the narrower limits of the professional cloistered life, to pertain to the laity as well. This translation of humility into a broader arena exposes one of the central emphases among the devotionalists more generally, since they valued an "engaged" piety above the merely external marks of a religious profession.

In keeping with the broader devotional current of the day, the idea of the progressive nature of the Christian life that characterizes Groote's spirituality finds its final mooring not in human achievement but in reference to the humanity of Christ. Indeed, this thematic emphasis upon the "imitation of Christ's humanity" (*imitatio humanitatis Christi*) stands as another characteristic focus in the literature and piety of the Modern Devotion more generally. Blended with Groote's concern regarding progress in the spiritual life, this Christological emphasis eventually found expression in terms of a progressive form of meditation, leading from an orderly "rumination" first upon Christ's humanity, next upon his divinity, and only then leading to union with God. This functional application of Christology, together with the practical forms of devotion that arose from it, came to characterize the devotionalist movement and its literature as a whole.[32] Once again, we must note that themes traditionally articulated within the monastic context—and particularly among Franciscans—now found broad expression in a piety applicable to those seeking simply to live devout lives. While we must recall that Groote's impact also led to a renewal of monastic life itself, specifically with regard to the order of Augustinian canons, the full effect of his work extended beyond such communities to forge new expressions of lay piety, both individual and communal. It is to the latter that we now turn our attention.

The Sisters and Brothers of the Common Life

It is interesting to note that the institution that stands as the immediate product of Groote's vision of renewal was a house for women. At the point of a radical conversion in 1374, Groote abandoned the ecclesiastical prebends that had been supporting him and turned his own home over to a group of pious women who wished to live a communal life, though without vows. Five years later he wrote a brief constitution (*consuetudo*) for this group, insisting on obedience to a papal dictate that this was no new order but simply a group of women wishing to live a Christian life together and worship in peace. From this small beginning we mark the establishment of a popular and partially lay movement that swept across the Low Countries during the early decades of the fifteenth century. This movement provided both laity and religious with intentional Christian communities modeled in their administrative structure and common life upon monastic precedent. In these communities we find early strongholds of copying and later printing. This movement also spawned schools for boys, often remembered for their associations with Agricola, Erasmus, and Luther. In a certain sense, however, it was among the modest community of women which Groote first established in his paternal home that we can see the spirit of his work most clearly. Although these "sisters" took no formal vows and did not engage in the active apostolate of preaching, as did the first "brothers," they embodied the vision of spiritual renewal that Groote espoused and stand as the first institutional example of his influence. For this reason, we must turn our attention first to their experience.

In the early years, the statutes of these women's houses (which recorded their first efforts at organization) did not yet anticipate the experience of a fully communal life, as did the communities of "the Common Life" that emerged only after Groote's death. Yet it is quite clear that their emergence nonetheless evoked considerable suspicion, and this at an early juncture, since the style of their life looked remarkably similar to that of the beguines, which had been repeatedly condemned during the later Middle Ages. What was impressive about this first community of pious women was that it attracted members from a broad spectrum of society—something that would also characterize the later movement as a whole. Not only were there no vows involved, but no dowry was required—a stipulation that had often prevented the poor from entering the Benedictine houses. Within this first community at what came to be called Geertshuis, work occupied a central part of the common life, with members contributing to the enterprise according to their various gifts or abilities. Furthermore, these communities eventually came to operate by electing a "mistress" each year on the feast day of St. Gregory (March 12), an office gained by majority vote and confirmed by the city magistrates.[33] Hence these communities had at least a rudimentary form of democratic governance and placed themselves directly under established social bounds of obedience—ecclesiastical and civil—within the diocese and city. With this modest beginning, therefore, we can recognize the expansion of Groote's vision of renewal beyond the strictly personal plane: The devotionalist movement brought into existence a growing realization of the communal dimensions of Christian life, a vision that was to have broad popular appeal for both women and men, religious and laity.

From these early beginnings the Sisters of the Common Life eventually came into existence, with the first house founded at Deventer in 1400, and again the similarity to monastic life is striking. Indeed, one of the outgrowths of this movement was its unintentional effect upon the so-called tertiary orders; it is particularly noteworthy that many of the laywomen early associated with the devotionalist circles eventually came to embrace the Franciscan life in the third order.

The Brothers of the Common Life have their origin in the years immediately following Groote's death in 1384, and it is here that the simple communal and indeed "communistic" implications of Modern Devotion developed. This movement toward a full communal life, conceived not only in a spiritual vein but also in terms of a full sharing of property and resources for the general communal well-being, finally evolved under the leadership of Groote's two followers, Florens Radewÿns and Geert Zerbold van Zutphen. These two men have become known as the practical co-founders of the movement known as the Brothers of the Common Life, though we must recall that the inspiration directly underlying their work derived mainly from Groote's vision of renewal. Unlike those of the sisters, the "brother-houses" had from the beginning a distinctively clerical character. They proliferated during the late fourteenth century and became known for their work in copying and for establishing grammar schools for boys. These primary schools were not, then, centers for theological study as it was done at the universities of the day; their purpose was of more modest scope, focusing above all on training in Latin and the liberal arts and providing a suitably pious context for growth in the Christian life.[34]

The identity of these communities, for both men and women, derived in large measure not only from the monastic structure of life, with its precedent of an ordered day of work and prayer, but also from the spiritual ideals that had been fostered in this tradition. This can be explained partly in terms of Groote's own early exposure to the Carthusian Order and his dedicated preference for reading and copying books that emerged from the matrix of earlier medieval monasticism, Eastern and Western. A further expression of this dependence can be seen in the frequency with which the brothers—and, occasionally, brotherhouses as a whole—joined themselves to houses associated with the Windesheim congregation of Augustinian canons.[35] Yet what is most striking about this affinity to monastic piety is that the early vision of renewal that Groote shared with his disciples blossomed into a communal movement that included the laity, thereby affecting not only the learned from among the clerical and monastic classes but a broader cross-section of Dutch society as well. This meant that although the devotionalist movement did not seek to be original in terms of the sources of its inspiration, it nevertheless offered a radical innovation by bringing this monastic spirituality into communities in which the laity were now admitted as full and equal participants rather than as members of a separate order.[36]

The communal life and worship of these communities, as recorded in the early constitutions, blends public worship with private devotion and study, particularly the study of Scripture. Yet whatever external forms of piety were maintained, the thrust always fell upon the inner life, upon penetrating outward forms of reading or prayer for their spiritual worth. In addition to regular participation in the Mass, the constitutions also mandated an hour each day devoted solely to the study of the Bible. The method of study, advocated already by Florens Radewÿns and echoed in the earliest constitutions, specified meditative reading, or "rumination," that would lead to growth in virtue and love. In this the devotionalists were merely applying in concrete practice a fundamental axiom of Augustine's, who observed that the language of sacred Scripture was intended to promote charity rather than mere knowledge.[37] Again, study in this tradition had less to do with any specific formal characteristic than with the underlying intent of how the text should be used for meditation: The brothers and sisters were to devote themselves to constant meditation upon a specific biblical passage rather than an occasional or "useless" reading.[38] This simple scriptural piety, marked by a "spiritually pragmatic" attitude toward the Bible and grounded above all in the *imitatio Christi,* would come to characterize the *Devotio moderna* as a whole.

Thomas à Kempis and *The Imitation of Christ*

During the third decade of the fifteenth century an Augustinian canon of the St. Agnietenburg monastery at Zwolle named Thomas Haemerken—usually referred to simply as Thomas à Kempis (after his birthplace at Kempen)—wrote *The Imitation of Christ,* a slender devotional book that has become one of the most widely read treatises in the Church's canon of theological literature. As a classic in its own time, the *Imitation* expressed the devotionalist movement's piety in distilled form, delineating many of its salient themes and capturing its mood in exemplary fashion. In addition, it became and has remained one of the most popular devotional volumes within the Western Church, where it continues to articulate its message to Christian readers, both Roman Catholic and Protestant, with a relevance that belies its obscure fifteenth-century origins. Though it emerged from a specifically monastic setting and was initially read within religious communities, the *Imitation* aimed at promoting personal devotion for the re-forming of the individual. To effect this reform, Thomas carried forth Groote's early vision of a practical spirituality, fusing an introspective piety with an emphasis upon service and an attentiveness to the ingredients needed to establish a peaceful communal life.

There is a peculiar irony in the amount of scholarly discussion that this volume has elicited, particularly since its author is emphatic in criticizing academic learning for its own sake. In a passage that has become something of a commonplace in the literature surrounding this book, Thomas warns that "deep inquisitive reasoning does not make a man holy or righteous, but a good life makes him beloved by God" and concludes that "I would rather feel compunction of heart for my sins than merely to know the definition" of the word.[39] In this he is by no means unique for his time; the expression of scorn for "vain curiosity" in intellectual matters reached something of a zenith during this period, expressed positively as an increased interest in the affective dimensions of theology. As an anti-speculative tradition both outside and within the community of academic theologians, this sustained reaction "against vain curiosity" (*contra vanam curiositatem*) opposed any abstract form of theology that attempted "to search and to know the high things of the Godhead" beyond what had been revealed in Scripture. What was beneficial for devotion was what mattered.[40] Hence in stark and deliberate contrast to the familiar caricature of scholastic theologians as being interested only in determining such esoteric questions as the number of angels that could dance upon a pinhead, Thomas à Kempis and others of his generation called scholars to concentrate upon what was useful in order to edify the individual and the Church. "It is better to have little learning with great humility than great learning and great pleasure in it; it is better to have a little learning with grace than much learning of which you are proud," says the author of the *Imitation*, adding elsewhere that "on the day of judgment we will not be asked what we have read, but what we have done; not how well we have discoursed, but how religiously we have lived."[41] And, as Thomas later notes,

> There is a great difference between the wisdom of a devout man, enlightened by grace, and the learning of a subtle and studious scholar; that learning which comes by the influence and the gracious gift of God is much more noble and worthy than that learning which is gained by human labor and study.[42]

This skepticism toward the compatibility of academic theology and piety, of the learned religion of the head and the simple religion of the heart, is but another expression of a tradition rooted in Hebrew Scripture and in the teaching of Jesus, which cried out against those who would worship "only with their lips, while their hearts are far from God" (e.g., Isa. 29:13; Mark 7:6). In the literature of early Christian apologetics, this assault—ironically often quite learned—upon erudition for its own sake attained classic expression in Tertullian's rhetorical disclaimer, "What has Athens to do with Jerusalem?" This outcry has become a tradition deeply ingrained in Christian theology, erupting again and again in the rhetoric of the Church's preaching and in the literature of those critics who, like Groote, attempted to define theology as a "living" science. Theology was to flower not in thought alone but in what an early sympathizer with the Brethren called an "affective erudition," by which theological knowledge was "transferred through constant rumination of the heart and the execution of good deeds."[43]

The ideal of the imitation of Christ, a central thesis of this treatise and of the devotionalist movement in general, reflects a popular resurgence of interest during this period in Christ's humanness, and particularly his suffering—an interest linked to the devotionalist emphasis upon the affective life. "The cross of Christ," Groote had argued, "should therefore ever be raised before us in meditation; his passion, his contumely, derision, injury, and sorrow should ever move our affections."[44] In devotionalist works, this focus promoted a piety attached to the cross. It was at this juncture that the Stations of the Cross emerged as a prominent devotional exercise, attaining wide circulation, particularly within the preaching of Franciscan friars. During the same period mystery plays devoted to the life and death of Christ and the saints also flourished as a popular expression of communal piety and public drama.

Thomas à Kempis's use of the *imitatio Christi* as a central literary motif thus stands as a sign of a much broader tendency and also points to the practical ambition and method of the devotionalists: As persons concerned with the pastoral rather than the strictly academic dimensions of theology in the first instance, they were intent upon establishing not orthodoxy of thought but the proper mode of living. This they accomplished by offering concrete examples—of Christ, in the first instance, but also of Mary and other holy women and men[45]—as guidance for the struggle to live a virtuous life. Indeed, these examples provided the concrete shape of that life, while Christ himself stood as what one tract called "the source of all virtue and the exemplar of all holiness."[46] Imitation as a means of attaining the virtuous life thus stands at the very heart of the devotionalists' appeal for personal reform and growth in holiness.

Yet it is neither the doctrine nor the moral teaching nor again the virtuous life of Jesus that interests Thomas, as a modern reader might expect from the title. Rather, the emphasis found in this treatise—above all in the first three "books" devoted to the interior life—is upon the suffering and death of Christ, especially since this stands as the expression of God's love for humanity. Addressing the reader as if with the words of Jesus, Thomas contends that "I [Jesus] descended from heaven and for your help have taken your miseries, not compelled to do so by necessity but by my charity, so that you should learn with me to have patience and not to refuse to bear the miseries and the wretchedness of this life, as I have done for you." In response to this declaration, Thomas answers in his own voice, "Oh, how many would have lagged behind, if they had not seen Your blessed example going before?"[47] Imitation is thus no barren moralism but the human response to God's expression of love in the Incarnation, another instance of the convergence of Christology and piety.

The Christology of the *Imitation* is a kenotic one, developing the Pauline claim that Christ "emptied" himself, accepting "the form of a slave" and, in obedience, endured death on a cross (Phil. 2:6-7). Thus Thomas à Kempis focuses throughout this treatise upon the integration of Jesus' passion with all human suffering, a theme that has lately emerged once again and in similar fashion in the literature of liberation theologies. For Thomas imitation is not merely a repetition of but a *participation in* the suffering of Jesus, a liberation through suffering. It is a theme that exposes the activist dimension of the devotionalist spirituality. Suffering takes on a constructive role of central importance here; as he concludes, "If you would suffer no adversity, how can you be the friend of Christ?"[48] Indeed, one might well characterize this tradition as an attempt to incarnate theology, to embody the study of God (*theo-logia*), not primarily in the achievement of virtue but in the life of suffering and the struggle with adversity.

This is a spirituality directly integrated in the struggles of human life (and above all in its tragedy), not one that seeks expression in the realm of the "sweet" inner world of mystical experience. Its emphasis falls not upon orthodoxy, which it assumed, nor even the experiences of the spiritual life, which it also encouraged, but upon what liberation theologians call "orthopraxis." Faithful to the devotionalist tradition, this spirituality defines Christianity in terms that integrate doctrine and life, above all in the adversities facing those who have "lost their [original] innocence," as Thomas expresses the impact of the fall.[49]

At the same time, however, Thomas is vehement in his emphasis upon "inner affection" as the spring from which a good life emerges: "Truly, when our inward affection is corrupt, it must needs be that our deeds which follow are also corrupt, for from a clean heart springs the fruit of a good life."[50] On this basis Thomas, himself a canon living under religious vows, echoes Groote's earlier insistence that outward acts of devotion, or the vows upon which the religious (i.e., monastic) life depended, were not sufficient to establish true obedience. In this vein he concludes that "if we place the end and perfection of our religion in outward observances, our devotion will soon be ended." Once again, we see his insistence on integration, that the inner and outer in the person must be harmonious. And yet he insists that one must establish this balance by first attending to the interior life: "The life of a good religious man should shine in all virtue and be inwardly as it appears outwardly," he concludes, adding that "it should be the much more inward, for Almighty God beholds the heart and we should always honor and reverence Him as if we were always in His bodily presence."[51]

This theme of the inner life establishing the foundation for the outer orients the devotionalist literature in general, such that this spirituality conceives of the life of prayer as the source of vitality for the life of action. Here is no collapse of faith into works, but a recognition that a rightly ordered devotion becomes the true source of outward acts of charity. Furthermore, in keeping with the monastic tradition out of which he wrote, Thomas à Kempis underscores the vital role of contemplation, the task of penetrating through meditative prayer beyond the veil of the flesh to the hidden spiritual world beyond. In this à Kempis reflects the appropriation, especially in Christian monastic theology, of the neoplatonic view that the real lies beyond the shadow world of physical matter. "I see that no man is more at rest in this world," he writes,

> than he who always has his mind and his whole intention directed upward to God, and desires nothing from the world: it behooves him,

124

therefore, who would perfectly forsake himself and behold You, to rise above all creatures and himself, also, and through elevation of mind to see and behold that You, Maker of all things, have nothing like to Yourself among all creatures.[52]

Hence alongside his emphasis upon the external obligations of charity, we find lingering traces of the theme of *fuga mundi* ("flight from the world"),[53] an ascetic tradition rooted in medieval monasticism and rendered coherent by these neoplatonic metaphysics.

We must also note that Thomas, like Groote and Radewÿns before him, grounds the moral voluntarism of his spirituality—the requirement to conform one's life to Christ's suffering—in an Augustinian anthropology, with its pessimistic evaluation of the "natural" human condition. This is a critical point, since it reminds us that the devotionalists did not fall prey to any naïve optimism in their view of the spiritual life. This literature is replete with practical wisdom, and its mood is that of the hortatory voice; yet Thomas insists early and late that without God's assistance moral effort would be empty and imitation of no effect. In an apparently deliberate effort to guard against the suspicion of the heresy of the "Free Spirit,"[54] with its "pelagianizing" tendency to ennoble the natural potential of the human spirit, Thomas insists on contrasting nature and grace in sharp terms: "I have great need of Your grace," he writes,

> and of Your grace in great abundance, if I would overcome this wretched nature, which from my youth has always been ready and prone to sin; after nature was defiled and vitiated by the sin of the first man, Adam, the penalty descended to all his posterity so that man's nature, which was good and just at creation, is now captured for sin and corruption.[55]

The fall of Adam has driven a wedge between the Creator and creation, such that the spiritual quest for God cannot simply presume to return of its own initiative to God. On the basis of this Pauline/Augustinian anthropology, therefore, Thomas insists that the spiritual life depends upon humility and receptivity, upon recovering through obedience to God what all have lost through Adam's disobedience. Indeed, the short prayer that Thomas includes in this treatise conveys the very heart of the devotionalist posture: "O Lord Jesus, make possible to me by grace what is impossible by nature."[56] As a practical spirituality, this was a form of devotion deeply impregnated with the mood of humility and repentance.

Finally, we must remember that Thomas concludes this treatise by moving beyond his opening discussion of the interior life, examining in a brief final book the nature and function of "the sacrament of the altar," or the Eucharist. This is no novelty among the devotionalists, as we have earlier suggested. Just as Groote and the Brothers and Sisters of the Common Life before him had blended private devotion with participation in public forms of worship, so Thomas strikes this note at the crescendo of his book. The thematic development here should not be missed: Thomas leads the reader not merely through an exercise in the virtues gained via imitation of Christ to an inner mystical experience, but rather on a journey of increasing attentiveness to and participation in Christ himself—in this case in the reception of the Eucharist. The focus, in other words, is not upon the self but upon Christ. Just as the third book moves beyond the inner life discussed in general terms to introduce a dialogue between Christ and the soul, in which Christ's voice addresses the pilgrim again and again, the final book moves to a deeper level, exploring how it is that we are to receive Christ sacramentally.

In raising this question, Thomas offers a fascinating exploration of the continuities between Christian worship and the obedience of "the ancient holy fathers" of Israel. As Thomas explains it, the Eucharist is an "unveiling" of the devotion of the Hebrew patriarchs and stands as the most fruitful conduit of grace, the source of life by which virtue is restored "and the beauty that was deformed by sin returns again."[57] It is in this sacrament that God "bows down" to us "from [God's] own goodness and not because of [our] merit," and in this simple gesture the entire history of redemption is manifest. And yet he insists that this sacrament is to be joined with Scripture, since the former "refreshes" us while the latter "guides" us as a lantern upon our way: "These two," he concludes,

> can be called the two tables, set here and there in the spiritual treasure of holy Church: the one is the table of the holy altar, having the living bread that is the precious Body of Christ; the other is the table of the laws of God, containing the holy doctrine which instructs man in the right faith and in the true belief and leads him into the *sancta sanctorum* [holy of holies], where the inward secrets of Scripture are hidden and contained.[58]

Scripture and the sacraments, therefore, serve to guide and strengthen us in our quest for God.

It is not difficult to see why *The Imitation of Christ* early became, and has remained, a classic on the Christian life. In its simplicity of expression and practicality of concern, this work addresses concrete problems of everyday living and suggests how spirituality should be a matter not of the exceptional but of the ordinary, not of the isolated experiences of the distant mystic but of the normal routines facing all people. For this reason, perhaps, this book seems to have a timeless appeal, even while the main outline of its message has much to do with the concerns and convictions of its own age.

Conclusion

Within the confines of this chapter, we have only begun to sketch the basic emphases of the *Devotio moderna* movement, perceiving in this effort at renewal a cluster of issues that would continue to exercise theologians and pastors in later generations. This was a movement for the reforming of the person first and foremost, though this focus upon the individual and the attempt to call Christians to a properly ordered inner life flowered quite intentionally in acts of charity and stable forms of communal life. As we have suggested, the *Devotio moderna* was first of all a movement aimed at rekindling devotion, free of any aspirations to enter the often high-flown and complex world of theological disputation. Yet this choice itself stood as a kind of theological reform, since the devotionalist emphasis upon the integration of intellect and heart, of Christian thought and life, had everything to do with the theological discipline. And because of the emphasis on communal life as a vital facet of spiritual discipline, together with the model—radical for its day—of Christians lay and clerical living a common life, the devotionalist movement anticipated developments of reform to be more fully explored in a later day. As we have noted, the stability sought by the devotionalists did not in the early stages of the movement depend upon formal vows, and it resisted all confidence in the external trappings of the religious life: peculiar forms of dress, outward religious observances, and the like.

We must also note the contribution of this movement to the popularizing of themes previously articulated within and for the monastic community. As a movement aimed at effecting spiritual renewal, advocates of the *Devotio moderna* drew upon both the Scriptures and the great sources of ascetic piety, yet their aspirations had a much broader intention and appeal than the renewal of monasticism per se. They sought to establish forms of Christian community that cut across the grain of the medieval stratification of the "religious" life, identifying monks and laity in their common quest to live quite simply as Christians with proper devotion and a lasting peace. Yet as a reform-minded movement, adherents of this "Christian

Renaissance" did not seek to break with the institutional Church. They did not consider themselves separatists or revolutionaries in any significant sense,[59] even though their message evoked a hostile reaction in the mendicant orders. Rather, they understood themselves as Christians bound by a simple evangelical vision: to seek faithful and widely accessible expressions for the Church's traditional forms of piety and to establish communities in which this vision might be embodied. When all has been said about this pious movement, the voices of its literature and the imprint of its humble expressions of institutional renewal remain vibrant, perhaps because these devotionalists rightly recognized that the truth of the Christian gospel was first and last a simple yet ultimately demanding matter. As Thomas à Kempis put it, "We must . . . make diligent search, both within and without, to leave nothing inordinate unreformed in us, as fully as our frailty permits," adding the apt recognition that "Jesus has many lovers of his kingdom of heaven, but he has few bearers of his cross."[60]

Notes

1. On the origin of this name, see John Van Engen, *Devotio Moderna: Basic Writings* (New York: Paulist Press, 1988), pp. 7-8. Van Engen argues that the term first appeared within a generation after Groote's death (ca. 1440), in a short account written about this movement by the prior of the Windesheim Congregation; during the same period, Thomas à Kempis advocated the reading of "the modern fathers," referring to Groote and Radewÿns. See also Dom François Vandenbroucke, *The Spirituality of the Middle Ages* (New York: Seabury Press, 1982), p. 428; J. Chatillon's article on *"Devotio"* in *Dictionnaire de spiritualité* (Paris: Beauchesne, 1957), vol. 3, col. 714. Van Engen's volume, which appeared only after this chapter had been completed, provides a useful array of texts from this tradition, most of which have been previously unavailable to English readers.
2. Albert Hyma, *The Christian Renaissance: A History of the Devotio Moderna* (London: The Century Co., 1925), esp. pp. 3-7.
3. Thomas à Kempis, *Vita Gerardi Magni* 1.2, cited in Hyma, *The Christian Renaissance*, p. 38.
4. Jan Busch, *Chronicon Windeshemense*, in *Geschichtsquellen der Provinz Sachsen und angrenzender Gebiete*, vol. 19, ed. K. Grube (Halle, 1886), p. 46; cited in Hyma, *The Christian Renaissance*, p. 39.
5. This phrase is to be found in "Sacrosancta," the pronouncement issued by the Council of Constance (1415).
6. For a general discussion of this context, and particularly the role of the so-called secular masters in this movement, see Vandenbroucke, *Spirituality*, pp. 439-46.
7. Heiko Oberman has spoken of a "democratization" later in this century in terms of the mystical tradition; see *The Harvest of Medieval Theology: Gabriel Biel and Late Medieval Nominalism* (Cambridge: Harvard University Press, 1963), pp. 341ff. Van Engen suggests, in similar terms, that participants in this movement, because they associated with these communities in a voluntary fashion and hence did not take vows, occupied a curious middle status between the laity and those bound by monastic vows; see Van Engen, *Devotio Moderna*, p. 14.
8. Vandenbroucke, *Spirituality*, p. 429; the use of "realistic" here is intended to contrast Groote's spirituality with what he calls the "false mysticism" of the age, considered to be "more or less tinged with pantheism."
9. Cf. R. R. Post, *The Modern Devotion: Confrontation with Reformation and Humanism* (Leiden: E. J. Brill, 1968), p. 320. Post notes that Groote's spirituality "has as its main

concern the salvation of the soul and to this end constantly applies norms of utility," such that "this spirituality acquires an anthropocentric-utilitarian character" (*The Modern Devotion*, p. 316). It is this emphasis upon the affective dimension of life and the need to link theology with the affects that characterizes this movement as well as the period as a whole. In a similar vein, Heiko Oberman has suggested that "operative behind and within the fourteenth-century rejection of speculation was a new conception of Christian thought and an alternative ideal of Christian life endowed with its own vigor and inventiveness in uncovering new dimensions in human experience, intuition, and affections. It involved a quest for an *Aggiornamento* of intellectual and spiritual life, and in this sense deserves the epithet 'moderna'" ("Fourteenth Century Religious Thought: A Premature Profile," *Speculum* 53 [1978]: 92).

10. On this general question, see Berndt Hamm, "Frömmigkeit als Gegenstand theologiegeschichtlicher Forschung. Methodisch-historische Ueberlegungen am Beispiel von Spätmittelalter und Reformation," *Zeitschrift für Theologie und Kirche* 74 (1977): 464ff. The intentional manner in which the devotionalists directed others to make progress in virtue, often in various forms of "exercises," has been described as a link with the later Ignatian piety of the Counter-Reformation; see Van Engen, *Devotio Moderna*, pp. 29-30, 50, and "On the Life and Passion of Our Lord Jesus Christ, and Other Devotional Exercises," pp. 187ff. Indeed, "exercising" the person through various forms of meditation—particularly on Jesus' passion—stands as one of the movement's characteristic disciplines. The devotionalists emphasized the effects not in some abstract manner but through a formal program of meditation upon Christ and Christ's passion (e.g., Van Engen, *Devotio Moderna*, pp. 89, 116, 188ff.).

11. See Post, *The Modern Devotion*, pp. 235, 323-24; also, J. Leclercq, *The Love of Learning and the Desire for God. A Study of Monastic Culture* (New York: Fordham University Press, 1961), pp. 72-73.

12. Cf. Augustine, *On Christian Doctrine* 1.36.40; also, Post, *The Modern Devotion*, p. 323.

13. Hyma, *The Christian Renaissance*, p. 35.

14. This same preference, based upon a quite similar rationale, is to be found in the later writings of Jean Gerson; see his *Quae veritates sint de necessitate salutis credendae*, in *Oeuvres complètes*, vol. 6 of *L'oeuvre ecclésiologique*, ed. P. Glorieux. (Paris: Desclée et Cie, 1968), pp. 182ff.

15. Hyma, *The Christian Renaissance*, p. 21.

16. See "The Original Constitution of the Brethren of the Common Life at Deventer," reprinted as appendix A in Hyma, *The Christian Renaissance*, and in *The Dawn of Modern Civilization: Studies in Renaissance, Reformation and Other Topics, Presented to Honor Albert Hyma*, ed. K. A. Strand (Ann Arbor, Mich.: Ann Arbor Publishers, 1962), p. 365.

17. See the entire chapter of this constitution, which is devoted to "the study of Sacred Scripture," in Strand, *The Dawn of Modern Civilization*, pp. 365-66.

18. See Post, *The Modern Devotion*, pp. 106-7, 316-17. Post here notes that Groote's disciple, Radewÿns, also shows a marked preference for patristic sources, above all the writings of John Cassian.

19. Post, *The Modern Devotion*, p. 317.

20. Ibid., pp. 98-107.

21. Thomas à Kempis, *Vita Gerardi Magni* 12.4, 13, cited by Hyma, *The Christian Renaissance*, p. 21.

22. See "Constitution of the Brethren," chap. 36, reprinted in Hyma, *The Christian Renaissance*, pp. 471-72. As one facet of the voluntary character of this movement, the early devotionalist communities did not seek to establish themselves as a new religious order, which was forbidden by Church decree during this period, but sought rather to blend their communal life within the confines of local parish life. While these groups represented smaller intentional communities within the established Church, they in no way considered themselves in opposition to the

broader Church. This was a "non-separatist" renewal, as one historian has argued; see Oberman, "Fourteenth Century Religious Thought," p. 92; also see Van Engen, *Devotio Moderna,* p. 14.

23. These references are to be found in his *De simonia,* as cited in Hyma, *The Christian Renaissance,* pp. 25-26.

24. For a good discussion of this attack and the ensuing controversy, see Christoph Burger, *Aedificatio, Fructus, Utilitas: Johannes Gerson als Professor der Theologie und Kanzler der Universität Paris* (Tübingen: J. C. B. Mohr [Paul Siebeck], 1986), pp. 158ff. Gerson's own response to Grabow's argument is to be found in Glorieux's edition of his *Oeuvres complètes,* vol. 10, *L'oeuvre polémique* (Paris: Desclée et Cie 1972), pp. 70-72.

25. Groote makes this observation in a letter, cited in Hyma, *The Christian Renaissance,* pp. 25-26.

26. On the centrality of voluntary "resolutions" rather than lifelong "vows," see "Resolutions and Intentions, But Not Vows," in Van Engen, *Devotio Moderna,* pp. 65ff. As a later rector of the Hildesheim community, Peter Dieppurch (d. 1491) put it, "We are not 'religious,' but we wish to live religiously in the world" (cited in Oberman, *Werden und Wertung der Reformation* [Tübingen: J. C. B. Mohr (Paul Siebeck), 1979], p. 8).

27. On this point Steven Ozment has argued that "the high degree of religious experimentation by both heterodox and orthodox groups in the later Middle Ages attests a failure of the medieval church to meet the original aims of the lay ascetic movements of the high Middle Ages" (*The Age of Reform 1250–1550. An Intellectual and Religious History of Late Medieval and Reformation Europe* [New Haven, Conn.: Yale University Press, 1980], p. 96). This broadening tendency by which the laity found entrance into communal forms of religious life—either as "third orders" associated with monastic communities or as cell communities of the Modern Devotion—is not only allied to earlier efforts aimed at embodying the "apostolic life" (*vita apostolica*) but also stands as an index of the Church's later social reorganization in Protestant circles. On the flowering of this lay piety in the twelfth century, see Vandenbroucke, *Spirituality,* pp. 257-68.

28. This comment from one of the letters is cited in Hyma, *The Christian Renaissance,* p. 23.

29. Hyma, *The Christian Renaissance,* p. 31; cf. also Post, *The Modern Devotion,* p. 121. Once again, we must note that this theme was in keeping with the broader emphasis upon the disciplined character, through "exercise," of the devout life. The voluntary character of this discipline corresponds with the insistence that spiritual growth required an intentional effort, rather than the external prop of religious vows.

30. See Oberman, *The Harvest,* pp. 463-64.

31. Cited in Hyma, *The Christian Renaissance,* p. 30.

32. On this point, Van Engen has rightly suggested that we might speak of "a Christocentric piety" here (*Devotio Moderna,* p. 25). The devotionalists in general went beyond a distant imitation, encouraging an affective rather than strictly intellectual or doctrinal identification with Christ and particularly with his redemptive suffering; they also often utilized the language of "exercise" in the forms of meditation they created (Van Engen, *Devotio Moderna,* pp. 85-91). The index to Van Engen's volume (p. 329) directs the reader to fifty-two different applications of this term.

33. For a discussion of the early statutes of the Sisters of the Common Life, see Post, *The Modern Devotion,* pp. 262ff.

34. Post has put forth this argument in convincing fashion, concluding that "since the Brothers did not attend universities, they were completely outside the academic world and accordingly their theological training was not of the slightest significance" (*The Modern Devotion,* pp. 677ff.). This is not to suggest, however, that students who received their early schooling in these communities were thereby disposed *against* the theological curriculum as taught at the universities.

35. See Post, *The Modern Devotion*, pp. 293-304. Indeed, one index of the deep impact this movement had upon the religiosity of this period, in both personal and institutional terms, is the tremendous growth of the Windesheim Congregation of Canons Regular, a reform order that Van Engen has called "the legally authorized branch of the Modern Devotion" (*Devotio Moderna*, p. 20).

36. Once again, the "modernity" of this movement lay not in the nature of its message, which drew heavily from ascetic traditions of the early and medieval fathers, but in the new lay context for this spirituality. For this reason recent commentators have pointed out that a more apt translation of the title *Devotio moderna* might be "new" rather than "modern" devotion. One historian correctly notes that the force of *moderna* means "'new' with the sense of 'renewed' or 'present-day'" (Van Engen, *Devotio Moderna*, p. 10).

37. See, for example, *On Christian Doctrine* I.35.39, 36.40, 41.

38. Post, *The Modern Devotion*, pp. 323-24. Once again, the manner in which the devotionalists utilized Scripture had to do with their method of "ruminating" upon the text. See Leclercq, *The Love of Learning*, pp. 72-73.

39. See Thomas à Kempis, *The Imitation of Christ*, ed. with introduction by Harold C. Gardiner, S.J. (Garden City, N. Y.: Doubleday, 1955), pp. 31-32 (I.1). All further citations from this text are cited from this version, with the standard sections designated parenthetically to benefit readers using other editions. On the much-disputed question of the authorship of this treatise, see Van Engen, *Devotio Moderna*, pp. 8-9.

40. See, for example, Thomas à Kempis, *Imitation*, pp. 108-9 (III.4). For a thorough discussion of the history of this thematic tradition "against curiosity," which is one thematic consequence of a nominalist epistemology, see Heiko Oberman, "*Contra vanam curiositatem." Ein Kapitel der Theologie zwischen Seelenwinkel und Weltall* (Zürich, Theologischer Verlag, 1974).

41. Thomas à Kempis, *Imitation*, pp. 115 (III.7), 35 (I.3).

42. Ibid., p. 151 (III.31).

43. See Gerson, *De consolatione theologiae*, in *Oeuvres complètes*, ed. P. Glorieux, vol. 9, p. 234.

44. Van Engen, *Devotio Moderna*, p. 89.

45. In a particularly poignant passage from the "Edifying Points of the Older Sisters," we find the affirmation that "it is good to hold [the elder sisters'] lives before our eyes, for their ways were truly like a candle on a candlestick, casting light upon all those in the house. . . . Since we cannot have their presence among us in the body and it is most important to have their edifying lives present in our memory, we have written down some of their most noteworthy points. . . . Moreover, when we describe and take in the lives and morals of good people, they seem in a certain sense to go on living after death, and they awaken many from living death to true life" (Van Engen, *Devotio Moderna*, pp. 121-23).

46. "On the Life and Passion of Our Lord Jesus Christ, and Other Devotional Exercises," in Van Engen, *Devotio Moderna*, p. 187.

47. Thomas à Kempis, *Imitation*, p. 131 (III.18).

48. Ibid., p. 77 (II.1).

49. Ibid., p. 45 (I.13).

50. Ibid., p. 152 (III.31).

51. Ibid., p. 53 (I.19).

52. Ibid., p. 151 (III.31).

53. It should be noted in this regard that this "flight" had to do with the widely acknowledged frailty and instability of human life, particularly when contrasted to the "solidity" and "unchanging" character of the heavenly realm. The ultimate goal of the human pilgrimage, in other words, was toward a place of perfect "rest," to recall an Augustinian image that saturates medieval literature. As Thomas à Kempis put it, here drawing upon this rich tradition and the biblical language of Hebrews, "You have here no place of long abiding, for wherever you have come you are but a

stranger and pilgrim, and never will find perfect rest until you are fully joined to God. Why do you look to have rest here, since this is not your resting place? Your full rest must be in heavenly things, and you must behold all earthly things as transitory and shortly passing away; beware well not to cling to them overmuch, lest you be seized with love of them, and so perish in the end" (*Imitation*, p. 76 [II.1]).

54. See Vandenbroucke, *Spirituality*, p. 429; Hyma, *The Christian Renaissance*, pp. 18ff.; Post, *The Modern Devotion*, pp. 121ff.

55. Thomas à Kempis, *Imitation*, pp. 189-90 (III.55).

56. Ibid., p. 132 (III.19); the anti-Pelagian edge of this argument is clear enough, as earlier noted, and appears to be aimed against any optimistic evaluation of the human potential vis-à-vis salvation. Cf. Post, *The Modern Devotion*, p. 121.

57. Thomas à Kempis, *Imitation*, p. 206 (IV.1).

58. Ibid., pp. 224-25 (IV.11). Against the rising tendency to emphasize the plain, literal sense of the Bible during this period, the devotionalists insist that there is a "secret" meaning to be found hidden beneath the text; Thomas à Kempis goes so far as to suggest that Christ dwells "within" the text, "secretly hidden in the letter" or literal sense of Scripture (*Imitation*, p. 167 [III.43]). Piety rather than academic learning becomes for the devotionalists the key to discerning this inner meaning.

59. This is a crucial point: Although the literature of this movement also emphasized the theme of "conformity with Christ," it in no sense represented an opposition to the Church. See above, note 22.

60. Thomas à Kempis, *Imitation*, pp. 54 (I. 19), 92 (II.11), and 94-95 (II.12), in which he argues that "you will never find, above you or beneath you, a more high, a more excellent, a more sure way to Christ than the way of the Holy Cross." This thematic emphasis upon the cross would later resound in Luther's attack upon what he called a "theology of glory" (*theologia gloriae*); see his "Heidelberg Disputation," chaps. 20-21, where he argues in a quite similar vein to Thomas à Kempis before him that "God is not to be found except in sufferings and in the cross" (*Luther: Early Theological Works*, ed. James Atkinson [Philadelphia: Westminister, 1962], p. 291). On the formal relationship of Luther and the *Devotio moderna*, see also Robert Stupperich, "Luther und das Fraterhaus in Herford," *Geist und Geschichte der Reformation. Festgabe H. Rückert zum 65. Geburtstag* (Berlin: de Gruyter, 1966), pp. 19-38.

Bibliography

à Kempis, Thomas. *The Imitation of Christ*. Edited and with an introduction by Harold C. Gardiner. Garden City, N.Y.: Doubleday, 1955.

Gründler, Otto. "Devotio Moderna." In *Christian Spirituality: High Middle Ages and Reformation*, edited by Jill Raitt. New York: Crossroad, 1987.

Hyma, Albert. *The Christian Renaissance: A History of the Devotio Moderna*. London: The Century Co., 1925.

Janowski, Hans Norbert, ed. *Geert Groote, Thomas von Kempen und die Devotio moderna*. Freiburg i. B.: Herder Verlag 1978.

Post, R. R. *The Modern Devotion: Confrontation with Reformation and Humanism*. Leiden: E. J. Brill, 1968.

Van Engen, John, trans. and ed. *Devotio Moderna: Basic Writings*. New York: Paulist Press, 1988.

Van Zjil, Theodore P. *Gerard Groote, Ascetic and Reformer (1340–1384)*. Washington, D.C.: Catholic University Press, 1963.

Getting Ready to Pray:
The Practice of Spiritual Disciplines

GABRIEL O'DONNELL, O.P.

All the runners at the stadium are trying to win, but only one of them gets the prize. You must run in the same way, meaning to win. All the fighters at the games go into strict training; they do this just to win a wreath that will wither away, but we do it for a wreath that will never wither. That is how I run, intent on winning; that is how I fight, not beating the air. I treat my body hard and make it obey me, for, having been an announcer myself, I should not want to be disqualified.

—I CORINTHIANS 9:24-27 JB

The contemporary man or woman is no stranger to the rigors of physical discipline. Whether one travels in the United States, Canada, or Europe, the early morning jogger hurries through near-deserted streets; at midday joggers are in the parks, and even after sunset they can be seen in quiet suburban neighborhoods. The omnipresent jogger, properly equipped with running shoes and other expensive paraphernalia, has become a symbol of our culture's physical fitness mania. Beyond jogging, those truly dedicated to improving their bodies join exercise spas and health clubs, consume innumerable books on balanced diets, and otherwise bolster the national advertising blitz about exercise and cosmetic perfection. All of these means of self-development require great effort and a considerable amount of time if they are to be successful.

This investment of interest and energy in the discipline of an exercise and health care regimen is a useful entrée into the business of spiritual disciplines. St. Paul likens the Christian life to an athletic contest—to running a race—and speaks of the effort and concentration that it requires. This is as true today as it was in the time of Paul. The life of prayer entails a relationship between God and the individual believer, and as with any authentic relationship, it requires time, attention, and discipline if it is to grow, stabilize, and mature.

It is clear from observing our culture that many people have the capacity for such discipline but (strangely) seem to lack the motivation. Ironically, most moderns are involved in self-help and self-actualization movements of one sort or another, but in the end, these groups do not yield the satisfaction so earnestly sought: They do not produce the sense of inner rootedness and peace for which we all long. A mobile society such as ours generates the search for a strong "at-homeness" within the self. Yet it is only through a relationship with God and its attendant disciplines that such spiritual wholeness and maturity are possible. Thus the issue of spiritual disciplines, traditionally referred to as "asceticism," is a most contemporary one indeed.

Finding Time for God

To develop a healthy life of prayer and sacred reading (*lectio divina*), we must face the question of time, that most precious of commodities in the modern world. We may not be avaricious with our time, but most of us spend it more carefully than we spend our money. The commitment to prayer requires, in the first place, a commitment of time. How often do we pray? The average Christian is likely to respond, "Whenever I feel the need." How often *should* we pray? Daily.

There are always unforeseen things that change our habits and patterns (e.g., we oversleep, we don't feel well, we have guests in the house); but in the spiritual life, as in any other discipline, fidelity to a regimen is of utmost importance. The experience of many centuries tells us that prayer is not simply a matter of what our feelings and immediate needs may be. To pray for three or four days a week or for five workdays is good, but ultimately we have to realize that one does not have "weekends off" from God. Prayer must be an everyday event. Daily prayer—sometimes longer, sometimes shorter—becomes a life-giving encounter with God—as essential as eating and sleeping.

When we do come to pray, how long should we spend? It is generally agreed that a half hour of prayer each day is a good basis for spiritual growth. This is time for personal, private prayer *aside from* any public liturgical or devotional activities. Ideally, it should be in *one* block of time, not two fifteen-minute periods. One normally begins with a shorter time of ten to fifteen minutes and over a period of several months gradually lengthens the time to thirty minutes or more. This is the basic "unit" of personal prayer. Eventually you may feel the need to extend your prayer time even beyond this "unit," either by increasing the time up to a full hour or by adding another "unit" of prayer at another time of the day.

There is still the question of when to pray. Should it be in the morning or at night? The tradition is heavily weighted on the side of the morning. Some authors warn that if we do not pray in the morning, we are likely to omit it altogether. This time-tested axiom comes out of the experience that our time is outside our control once we begin the ordinary business of the day. Normally, we have to steal the early hours of the day for God, because the demands of the job, an unexpected emergency, or a spontaneous social event may change the shape of our day without warning. However, many reason that because they are "night people," it is best to pray at night; there's little point in trying to pray in the morning when half asleep! The important thing, then, is to *unfailingly dedicate some segment of one's day to God, in spite of the lack of immediate gratification or "getting anything out of it."* Failure to grasp this one point probably accounts for more scuttled efforts at daily prayer than any other single factor, including lack of time.

The point—so simple yet so hard to fully understand—is that we do not pray for ourselves only but *for God.* We pray in order to become more involved with God and to fall, so to speak, more deeply "in love" with the Lord. Ultimately, the stability of a life of prayer is more important than personal reward or satisfaction at any given moment. As our relationship with God deepens, our capacity and hunger for prayer grows.

A common temptation for the person beginning a serious prayer life is the lure of the irresistibly logical suggestion that, if acted on, would interrupt the pattern of prayer: While praying we suddenly remember the laundry, which needs to be moved from washer to dryer. Logically, we would expect to be able to pray better if such tasks were out of the way and off our mind. We may even conclude that the "reminder" is divinely inspired! With that chore done, we can settle down to prayer again without distractions. Beware! The temptation to give away one's time for prayer to other jobs is an extremely seductive one. For most of us, one such practical choice leads to another, and yet another, until it is time to go to work or on to the next errand. We must learn to sit through such "distractions" in prayer and get beyond them.

It is in this area of time commitment that a great deal of self-transcendence is required. Most people who are serious about prayer have to get up an hour earlier than they normally do, and initially that seems like a great sacrifice; but the life of prayer requires many such "stretching" exercises. Eventually what began as sacrifice will be experienced as gift.

Finding a Place for God

Where should we pray? Should prayer be at the kitchen table, in the easy chair in the living room, at the desk, or in bed? There is an increasing and appropriate concern in the Church for environment in worship, and we too should choose the place most conducive to the spirit and concentration required for prayer. This may suggest the creation of a "prayer corner" in one's room, where the Bible is prominently displayed on a table and a candle lighted at prayer time. An icon, cross, crucifix, or other sacred image can be useful as a means of both centering attention and symbolically marking out a special space set apart for prayer.

The recurrent temptation is usually to "do" something rather than "waste time" in prayer. The careful choice of a good prayer environment is helpful in avoiding that pitfall, and the consistent use of such space is a great support in developing a strong habit of personal prayer.

Welcoming God with Our Bodies: The Role of Posture in Prayer

When we pray, should we sit, kneel, or stand? The Christian tradition witnesses to a wide variety of bodily postures for prayer, the most familiar of which are sitting, kneeling, and standing. It will be necessary to experiment in order to discover our own response to praying in different physical postures. We might begin prayer kneeling, the traditional gesture of adoration and penitence. Then for the greater part of our prayer time we may prefer to sit, since this posture symbolizes meditation and receptivity to God's word. Finally, we might conclude by standing with our arms lifted toward heaven, adopting the traditional posture for prayer (*orans*), intercession, and the symbol of the Resurrection.

Varieties of posture keep us awake and alert and involve the whole person, body and spirit, in prayer. More important, after some experimentation we will discover that different prayer postures facilitate and sometimes even induce a particular spirit of prayer: silent adoration, intense intercession, or simple meditation. The body and the spirit pray together, one animating and supporting the other. When the mind is exhausted or barren or the heart is too bruised to pray, the body, through kneeling or prostration, may provide the necessary stimulus for prayer. (In prostration one lies face down on the floor with the forehead resting on one's folded arms.) Whatever posture we adopt, it is important to remember that in prayer we should take a posture that is comfortable but not too relaxed, since drowsiness and sleep are always a danger. Fruitful prayer requires that we be alert and attentive.

There are other gestures that the tradition suggests are conducive to a deeper spirit of prayer: signing oneself with the Sign of the Cross at the beginning and end of prayer, bowing before the cross or crucifix as a sign of reverence or adoration, or kneeling with arms spread out in imitation of Christ's death on the cross.

We should not feel surprised if, initially, we feel awkward and embarrassed in our attempts to approach God in a more direct and intimate way. The average Christian may well feel self-conscious in adopting these practices, but establishing an intimate relationship with God requires the same kind of risk taking that any significant relationship entails, and part of what we are called upon to renounce in the life of prayer is our own comfortable sense of ourselves as self-contained, "dignified" adults. Serious prayer requires personal courage as well as commitment, and it is only through a sometimes less than reassuring process of trial and error that we discover how the Spirit is leading us into new ways of prayer and communion with God.

Forms of Self-Denial as Remote Preparation for Prayer

In addition to the specific disciplines of prayer that we have discussed—time, frequency, place, and posture—there are certain attitudes and practices that provide the necessary support system for a vital life of prayer and are best understood as part of the more remote preparation for prayer. As forms of asceticism, they are intended to train us, much as physical exercise does, for the actual event of prayer.

"Asceticism" refers to practices or disciplines that require considerable effort on our part to learn and continue to perform. One who is ascetical is well schooled in the disciplines of the spiritual life. The principal form of Christian asceticism is fasting, which means to refrain from food and drink for a specific period of time for a spiritual motive. The Fathers of the Church express two reasons for fasting: as preparation for prayer (Since Jesus fasted and prayed in the New Testament) and as a way to identify with the poor. The primitive form of fasting is to omit all eating of solid foods for a specific period of time, usually a day or two.

The decision to give up a meal is a choice to step back from a routine dependence upon food and drink in order to gain perspective on the relationship between material food and spiritual nourishment. The pangs of physical hunger lead us to a new hunger for God, and our own tendency to use creation in selfish and pragmatic ways is uncovered. Thus an increase of time spent in prayer goes hand in hand with fasting, which emphasizes the experience of emptiness and dependence upon God. Many serious Christians fast from solid foods one day a week. The routine and pattern are as important here as in the discipline of taking time for prayer.

Abstaining from a particular food for a spiritual motive is another common form of asceticism, for example, from meat on certain days of the week or in the season of Lent or Advent. Again, this discipline gives us some freedom from our likes and dislikes and helps us to see the patterns of gratification that may be dominating us, cluttering our lives with imaginary need. The presumption of both fasting and abstaining is that all of creation is good and is intended for our enjoyment. We let go of one good thing to experience another good; in this case, our intention is to look more intensely at God and to state, in this ritual way of fasting and abstaining, our highest priorities. Fasting and abstention are spiritual disciplines that quickly and effectively clarify those priorities for us. In the first place, we are mortified to discover how thoroughly captured we are by our physical needs, but the empty "space" left by fasting and abstaining is graciously filled with God and a new sensitivity to the needs of his people.

The final discipline that should be addressed here is self-restraint or self-denial, words that do not sound healthy to modern ears. Self-denial does not mean the negation of the essential self as known and loved by God but rather the disciplining of the self, which tends toward egoistic indulgence and illusory daydreaming. The need to be comfortable, physically and emotionally, is a high priority in our world. The discipline of self-restraint puts such needs much lower on the list of priorities. Discomfort because of heat or cold, the quality of the food, or the consistency of the mattress are all areas where the practice of self-restraint can make us more receptive to God. The disciplined acceptance of the "uncomfortable" situation in silence and inner resignation creates a capacity for a spiritual sensitivity that can be lost by constant complaining or using our energies to look for the most comfortable room, bed, or enjoyable situation.

The practice of self-restraint in the pursuit of comfort leads to greater self-restraint in dealing with drives that are more obviously destructive. The continued practice of small acts of self-restraint develops a kind of spiritual hardiness. Over a period of time, we become less preoccupied with our personal needs and desires. Eventually, we discover that our values have changed in a radical way.

Self-denial is much the same. We deny ourselves something we want, something good, in order to have deeper communion with God. The tendency to sidestep the difficulties of life through indulgence or compensation robs us of opportunities to find spiritual significance in the everyday trials that beset us. The typical antidote for a "down" day may be a modest shopping spree at the local mall, but self-denial calls us to resist such immediate relief and turn to God in prayer, begging for both courage and deliverance. As the practice of self-denial clarifies our motives and patterns of evasion and self-indulgence, it becomes ever more obvious that the Lord is our only refuge in any kind of crisis or time of sorrow.

Personal decisions regarding asceticism, especially those involving fasts or abstinence, are usually made in consultation with someone more experienced in the spiritual life, such as a spiritual director. This is a safeguard against imprudent decisions that could be physically or psychologically dangerous and allows a place for accountability. We tend to take such decisions more seriously when they are shared with another person.

A certain amount of guidance is essential in the area of asceticism. When fasting is first begun, it may induce some physical discomfort (e.g., a headache). Since the physical discomfort often makes us feel irritable and on edge, we might logically conclude that it is better *not* to fast, so we can be pleasant to those around us. Experience has shown, however, that the capacity to bear the physical discomfort or inconvenience, as well as to practice patience and cheerfulness, *is what fasting is all about.* Asceticism unmasks our limits and weaknesses, too often hidden behind the numerous pleasures and compensations we provide for ourselves.

Prayer is not an isolated practice in the Christian life. It depends upon support structures or disciplines, and in turn, it shapes the direction those developing structures take over the months and years of habit and commitment. It is interwoven with all the other aspects of our relationship to God. We cannot be reminded too frequently that *spiritual disciplines, asceticism, even prayer itself, are not ends but means to a deeper communion with God.* We must regularly evaluate our life of prayer and asceticism and probe to discover the leadings of the Holy Spirit, who is the true spiritual director of every human heart.

EXERCISES

For an Individual

Set aside one week during which you experiment with kneeling for the first five to ten minutes of your daily prayer; remain seated for the bulk of your prayer time, and stand with your arms raised and slightly apart in the *orans* position for the last five minutes. The following week continue in the same manner, substituting prostration for the standing posture during the last five minutes of your prayer. After the second week, discuss your experiences with someone more advanced in the practice of prayer. Together, evaluate the experience of the postures and decide on a pattern conducive to your life of prayer.

For a Group

To gain some initial experience of the various prayer postures, plan a thirty-minute period for the actual exercise and additional time (fifteen to thirty minutes) for discussion afterward. Begin by orienting the group toward a cross, crucifix, icon, or some sacred image. Participants should be spaced fairly far apart from one another to allow room for movements and a sense of privacy as well as community. Dimmed lighting may help. For five to ten minutes the group should pray standing with hands open and raised in the *orans* position. It is useful to have someone read a brief prayer or meditation, but this should be done slowly and peacefully. Follow this exercise by another five to ten minutes spent praying in a kneeling posture. Again, the *same* meditation is read. For two or three minutes of this time, the group should extend their arms in the form of the cross. For the final segment of the exercise, the group should lie prostrate on the floor. The same meditation is read for the final time.

Group reflection on the experience is important, and ample time should be allowed. The degree of self-consciousness is usually high in this exercise, and frank exchange about the experience is encouraging to all participants. The choice of material for the meditation is important. Reading a brief passage from the New Testament and a brief reflection on it works well for most groups. The following brief passage from Romans or the longer meditation and prayer of John Henry Cardinal Newman are both suitable for this particular exercise:

> Who shall separate us from the love of Christ? Shall tribulation, or distress, or persecution, or famine, or nakedness, or peril, or sword? . . . No, in all these things we are more than conquerors through him who loved us. For I am sure that neither death, nor life, nor angels, nor principalities, nor things present, nor things to come, nor powers, nor height, nor depth, nor anything else will be able to separate us from the love of God in Christ Jesus our Lord. (Rom. 8:35, 37-39)

MEDITATION

God was all-complete, all-blessed in Himself; but it was His will to create a world for His glory. He is Almighty, and might have done all things Himself, but it has been His will to bring about His purposes by the beings He has created. We are all created to His glory—we are created to do His will. I am created to do something or to be something for which no one else is created; I have a place in God's counsels, in God's world, which no one else has. Whether I be rich or poor, despised or esteemed by man, God knows me and calls me by name.

God has created me to do some definite service. He has committed some service to me which He has not committed to another. I have my mission —I may never know it in this life, but I shall be told it in the next. Somehow I am necessary for His purposes, as necessary in my place as an Archangel in his. If, indeed, I fail, He can raise another, as He could make the stones children of Abraham. Yet I have a part in this great work. I am a link in a chain, a bond of connection between persons. He has not created me for nothing. I shall do good, I shall do His work. I shall be an angel of peace, a preacher of truth in my own place, while not intending it, if I do but keep His commandments and serve him in my calling.

Therefore I will trust Him. Whatever, wherever I am, I can never be thrown away. If I am in sickness, my sickness may serve Him. If I am in sorrow, my sorrow may serve Him. My sickness, or perplexity, or sorrow may be necessary causes of some great end, which is quite beyond us. He does nothing in vain. He may prolong my life, take away my friends, He may throw me among strangers, He may make me feel desolate, make my spirits sink, hide the future from me—still He knows what He is about.

PRAYER

O Adonai, O Ruler of Israel, Thou who guidest Joseph like a flock, O Emmanuel, O Sapientia, O Wisdom, I give myself to Thee. I trust Thee wholly. Thou art wiser than I—more loving to me than I myself. Deign to fulfill Thy high purposes in me whatever they may be—work in and through me. I am born to serve Thee, to be Thine, to be Thy instrument. Let me be Thy blind instrument. I ask not to see—I ask not to know—I simply ask to be used.[1]

DISCUSSION QUESTIONS

1. Do most people in your congregation see the connection between developing a life of prayer and other spiritual disciplines? How

essential do they believe this relationship to be? What is your personal response to the position taken in this practicum?

2. Many modern people perceive the notion of asceticism and self-denial as suggesting a negative view of the human person. In view of contemporary attempts to emphasize the beauty of creation and the goodness of humanity, what role do you see for this tradition in today's Church?

3. In thinking over your recent attempts at prayer, can you identify any specific practice that would help to prepare you for the time of prayer? (Use the practices mentioned in the practicum, or come up with your own.)

4. How important is it for you to have someone to turn to in making decisions regarding your spiritual life, particularly in practical matters such as prayer and discipline? Do you see accountability as an element in such direction?

5. Do you notice that prayer gradually influences the apparently nonreligious aspects of your life, that is, how you spend your time, the quality of your conversation, and so on? Why do you think this is so?

Notes

1. John Henry Cardinal Newman, *Lead Kindly Light: A Devotional Sampler*, comp. and ed. Hal M. Helms (Orleans, Mass.: Paraclete Press, 1987).

Resources

Groeschel, Benedict J., O.F.M. Cap. *The Courage to Be Chaste*. Mahwah, N.J.: Paulist Press, 1985.

Foster, Richard J. *Celebration of Discipline*. San Francisco: Harper & Row, 1978.

Francis de Sales. *Introduction to the Devout Life*. 2nd ed., rev. Translated by John K. Ryan. New York: Harper & Row, 1966.

Maas, Robin. *Crucified Love*. Nashville: Abingdon Press, 1989.

Martin, John R. *Ventures in Discipleship*. Scottsdale, Penn.: Herald Press, 1984.

Muto, Susan Annette. *Pathways of Spiritual Living*. Garden City, N.J.: Image Books, 1984.

The Nine Ways of Prayer (of St. Dominic). In *Early Dominicans: Selected Writings*, edited and translated by Simon Tugwell. New York: Paulist Press, 1982.

Ryan, Thomas. *Fasting Rediscovered*. New York: Paulist Press, 1981.

Thurman, Howard. *Disciplines of the Spirit*. Richmond, Ind.: Friends United Press, 1977.

Watson, David Lowes. *Accountable Discipleship*. Nashville: Discipleship Resources, 1984.

Wimmer, Joseph F. *Fasting in the New Testament*. New York: Paulist Press, 1982.

PART II

□

Distinctive
Spiritual Traditions

CHAPTER 5

Lutheran Spirituality

BENGT HOFFMAN

For I am not ashamed of the gospel: it is the power of God for salvation to every one who has faith, to the Jew first and also to the Greek. For in it the righteousness of God is revealed through faith for faith; as it is written, "He who through faith is righteous shall live."

—ROMANS 1:16-17

Luther's theology gave rise to two ways of apprehending the *kerygma* in the Bible and in Christian life. They did not and do not always coincide. In fact, one can speak of a bifurcation, a dividing of the ways. On the one hand, there is the legacy of cognitive theologizing around the theme of justification by faith, the dogmatic bulwark building against the heresies of humanism and scholasticism. That tradition is called "Lutheran orthodoxy." On the other hand, there is the line of personal appropriation of that same theme of justification, evidenced not least by Luther's closeness to some mystics in the Catholic Church. Without necessarily lacking in dogmatic stringency, the proponents of personal spirituality in Lutheranism emphasized the experiential side of Christianity. That tradition is referred to as "Lutheran pietism."

Orthodoxy and Pietism

It may not be the easiest thing in the world to discover the experiential strand in Lutheran thought. The reasons are several. Luther himself, in his theological battles against certain forms of Catholic life and thought, in his fight against the cautious humanism of Erasmus, and in his battle against the prophets of extreme inwardness

145

called "enthusiasts" (or *Schwärmer*), placed a great deal of emphasis on expressions such as "the external word," "righteousness outside us," and "Christ for us." They all point away from the human person to something objective. And when, under these various contingencies, he spoke of "sanctification," he seemed to conceive of it in an exclusively eschatological fashion. Luther brings out the objective and imputative character of faith. "Since righteousness is imputed"—that is to say, *attributed as merit transmitted by another,* namely Christ—"the individual Christian has done nothing about it himself. The Christian is advised to take hold of the promise of forgiveness offered in the word but think nothing of the movements of the soul which, because they fluctuate, are not reliable guides to God."[1]

But in Luther's thought there is

> another category of terms mirroring personal experience and an awareness of non-rational forces active in faith. These terms convey Luther's persuasion that precisely the external in sign and word reaches and is meant for the internal, for "heart" and "feeling." The imputation of God's righteousness is in fact unavailing without the indwelling of Christ which can be experienced "with mystical eyes," in Luther's words.[2]

Take, for example, Luther's comments on Psalm 51:10, "Create in me a clean heart, O God, and renew a right spirit within me." Here he goes to the heart of his theology, to the experiential side of forensic justification. He writes,

> The Holy Spirit is present and works his gift in us. A gift, yes, for the Holy Spirit himself is at work in us. Since I am indeed justified, I know that my sins are forgiven without my merits. But then it is of the essence that I begin to feel [*sentire*] so that I may in some manner understand.[3]

What kind of understanding does Luther mean? He obviously makes a distinction between knowledge as cognition and knowledge as understanding. Later on in his scrutiny of this same passage he explicates: "The truly pure heart . . . does not harbor a false fantasy about God. It boils down to the understanding of the heart which abides in spiritual things."[4]

Or consider the following statements in which Luther's words challenge the cognitive imperialism of Lutheran orthodoxy:

> A theologian is molded by living, no rather by dying and being judged, not by conceptualizing in itself or by study or speculating.[5] Negative

theology . . . true cabala, is very rare . . . too perfect . . . beyond every thought . . . But not even the affirmative theology can be treated by disputation and numerous words. It rather moves in the highest repose and silence of the mind, as in rapture and ecstasy [*in raptu et extasi*]. That makes for a true theologian.[6]

Like Johann Tauler, one of the medieval mystics he frequently quoted approvingly, Luther makes a distinction between cognitive speculation and feeling-borne knowledge by referring to some scholastics (whom he sometimes called "sophists") as *Lesemeister* ("masters of reading") and to Christians who knew about the presence of God in experiential ways as *Lebemeister* ("masters of living").[7]

This same distinction between ways of knowing cognitively and experientially is evident in two sermons preached on Good Friday 1518 (on Isaiah 53 and Psalm 45), in which Luther claimed that our prayer should be that we might come to see Christ "with the eyes of the soul," and not as Pilate and other onlookers saw him, with their external eyes merely, or "the eyes of those who know according to the flesh," to use Luther's words. All treasures, Luther continues, are "hidden" in Christ (Col. 2:3):

> They are called "hidden" because they can only become visible through mystical and spiritual eyes. In him is love and the fountain of all light through which the feeling [*affectus*] is informed. . . . Christ was made our love to influence our feeling and he was made God's wisdom to help our understanding. Thus, as I have said, we should open our spiritual eyes and lay hold of this beautiful form of Christ which holds in it all virtues, depicted and presented to us in clear, vivid, expressive words and signs.[8]

If we define spirituality as the awareness of the presence of the Holy Spirit mediated by the risen Christ, it is clear from these brief quotations that the tradition emanating from Martin Luther contains an essential element of the inward, personal, and subjective, which is often associated with the term "spirituality."

This inward dimension of Martin Luther's legacy can be termed *sapientia experimentalis,* an expression he himself uses and that may be translated "existential wisdom" or "knowledge by experience." Luther speaks of the "kingdom in us," of the *unio mystica,* of the "mystical Christ," of the spiritual, prayer-borne life that is a paradoxical movement between *gemitus* ("anguish") and *raptus* ("transporting bliss").

So you have, on the one hand, the intellectual interpretation of faith with Luther and interpreters such as Flacius, Calovius, and Quenstedt, and, on the other hand, the "experience theology" that employs the same spiritual vocabulary as many medieval mystics and has its anchorage also in Luther and those of his followers who were later termed "pietists"—Arndt, Spener, and Francke.[9]

The two sides of the gospel proclamation, the Christ-for-us of Lutheran orthodoxy and the Christ-in-us of Lutheran pietism, are integrally related in Luther's thought. But *in practice* the two traditions have gone their separate ways, and in the process, the intellectual structures have prevailed over the inward aspect, so much so that practically all well-known accounts of Luther's Reformation theology, both the ones written within a confessionalistic-orthodox framework and those molded by liberal-rationalistic epistemologies, play down Luther's references to spiritual experience and his kinship with the mystics. Much like the intellectualistic exegesis that accords little theological importance to St. Paul's feeling-laden, shattering encounter with the cosmic, supernatural Lord on the Damascus road and that, instead, derives a theology from an intellectual-theological discourse around the Hebrew notion of Law, these elaborations of Luther's theological thought turn the student's attention away from the experience of God's presence to intellectual-theological deliberations, as though they are capable of standing by themselves.[10]

Spirituality and Knowledge in Lutheran Traditions

Interpretations of Luther's—and the Lutheran—approach to the spiritual depend on the definition one applies to the nature of knowledge. If knowledge as the range of what has been perceived, discovered, or inferred is limited to reason's grasp of the testimonies of the senses, we can speak of a rationalistic-empirical epistemology within which two mutually contradictory propositions cannot both be true. Spirituality as the experience of mystic presence will not find much room within such a context. If, on the other hand, knowledge as the range of what has been perceived, discovered, or inferred is expanded to include the experience involved in intuition, intimation, and spiritual inspiration—exceeding the yardsticks of causality within time and space alone—we can speak of a pneumatic ("spiritual") epistemology within which a purely logical treatment cannot cover what the experiencing person "knows." In that kind of knowledge, two mutually contradictory propositions can indeed be true.

In the wake of the Lutheran Reformation, spirituality as experience of divine presence fared less well inside the rationalistic-empirical framework than within the pneumatic one. This can be seen in three respects. We may, with regard to the place of the spiritual or the mystical, speak of three sorts of censorship.

First, Luther's references to experiences of grace and the presence of the "mystical Christ" have often been—and often are—evaluated only from strictly confessional points of view. The result is that Lutheran orthodoxy, as well as Lutheran liberal theology, tends to view Protestant and Roman Catholic theological thought as antithetical at each essential doctrinal juncture. A spirituality with mystical overtones is considered heretical in many Protestant accounts and is assigned to pietism or Catholicism. The matter of Lutheran spirituality has thus contributed to a censoring Lutheran posture with regard to Catholic doctrine. Out of such a criticism comes a statement like the following: "Only dilettantes in the field of spiritual history can call Luther a mystic." The dictum stems from H. Bornkamm, in this regard echoing A. Harnack.[11] In defense of Protestantism, one endeavors to prove an absolute contradistinction between the Catholic-mystical and the Lutheran-evangelical.

Second, the *gnesio*-Lutheran and Melanchthonian reflection on the gospel often regards as theologically inconsequential Luther's frequent allusions to mystic intimations, especially in expositions on Christology and angelology. The effect of this particular form of censorship is that the term *unio mystica* among the Lutheran schoolmen or scholastics became—and becomes—part of a rational system of propositional truth, the doctrine of imputed righteousness.[12] The term consequently lost—and loses—its intuitive-experiential elements in the name of "objective" verity, firmly set against the "subjectivity" of pietism and mysticism.

Third, spirituality in Lutheran garb has been the object of censoring treatment under the impact of theological thought molded by pragmatic and empirical scientific reasoning. To apprehend this climate of scholarly inquiry, we have to go back to Descartes' (1596–1650) ideas about the absolute centrality of intellectual cognition ("I think, therefore I am"), a philosophy inspired by Newton's (1642–1727) notion of a clockwork universe and Kant's (1724–1804) suggestion that metaphysics, attempting to objectivize reality outside the perception-guiding forms—space and time—cannot be accommodated within the only genuine scientific knowledge there is, namely, pure mathematics and pure natural science. These reflections concerning the nature of human knowledge, so indispensable to the cultural movement called the Enlightenment, have molded much of the epistemology governing theological efforts to understand

Luther. The outcome is often a failure to find an organic locus in his thought for spirituality or inward knowledge. As a consequence, the *ordinary,* the *public,* and the *objective* in the life of faith tend to take precedence over or almost occlude their complementary counterpoints, the *extraordinary,* the *private-personal,* and the *subjective.*

In both orthodox and liberal Lutheran discourses we therefore frequently find an emphasis on "theological faith" as opposed to "actual change" in heart and mind. (This particular choice of words is found in Gerhard Ebeling's interpretation of Luther.[13]) Theology in the former sense deals with "the *nous,* mind, intelligence . . . and has through its unconscious intellectualism often proved a significant restrictive influence, stifling the work of the Holy Spirit."[14] This third kind of censorship, unconscious to be sure, runs the risk of eclipsing the aspect of spiritual and mystical knowledge (*sapientia experimentalis*) in Luther's and Lutheran thought. One may lose Martin Luther himself, and his theological concern, by that omission.[15]

There are those in the theological community who recognize the somewhat crippling consequences of the reductionism alluded to here. One such interpreter is Jesuit scholar Jared Wicks, who asserts that at least the younger Luther's primary concern was not intellectual, dogmatic rampart building around God's self-disclosure. Rather, Luther was about the business of translating into meaningful theological language a radical spiritual experience of Christ's justifying and loving presence.[16] Luther's positive use of the writings of mystics supports this claim. He often quoted with approval Bernard of Clairvaux, Hugo and Richard of St. Victor, Jean Gerson, Johann Tauler, and the anonymous "Frankfurter" who wrote *Theologia Germanica,* to name a few of his mystical kin. In fact, such references throughout Luther's career suggest to us that the kinship in question endured throughout his years as a mature Reformer.

Luther and the Mystics

Luther used expressions like "the mystical Christ," "mystical incarnation," "mystical theology," and "mystical eyes" when he wanted to depict life in God. When he looked for a definition of the mystical life in God, he found it in Bernard of Clairvaux and quoted with approval his definition of mystical theology. "Mystical theology," wrote Bernard, is of the "experimental and experiential" kind. In other words, mystical theology to Luther is *experience* of God.[17] It is the inner, spiritual side of Christian faith. It is what prayer leads to. It is the awesome and joyful knowledge, beyond purely rational knowledge, that God is present. It is heart rather than head, but never the one without the other.

The trouble with *our* trouble with Luther's mystical utterances—that is, his knowledge that God is indeed not very far from us—is that we let the theoretical understanding, the urge for all-embracing theological-logical theorems, so overwhelm the religious quest that intuition, inspiration, intimation, and feeling are not given their due. Hence we find in a goodly part of Luther scholarship the cliché that Luther's view of God and salvation stands in diametrical opposition to that of the mystic.[18]

It would carry us too far in the context of this discussion to compare Luther's views of the image of God in man, man's will in relation to God, the "marriage" between Christ and the Christian, or his position on sin, with those of the mystics to whom Luther felt close. Suffice it to say here that the experience of justification by faith, perhaps beginning with the so-called tower experience, became the yardstick with which Luther meditated on the mystics. And from that point of view it is clear that he felt the closest kinship with Johann Tauler and the writer of the fourteenth-century tract *Theologia Germanica*. He had the latter work printed, apparently without any editing of the contents.[19]

Luther's frequent use of the adjective "invisible" points to his trusting knowledge that faith always moves into dimensions not approachable by reason and logic but available to inner experience. Like the mystics, he assumes the reality of a supernatural or supernormal realm. This becomes evident, for instance, in his angelology. In this respect, Luther's thought essentially coincides with that of Bernard of Clairvaux—mystic, healer, administrator, and theologian—who claimed that to dwell with God in the mystic realm is "as by the hands of angels we both feel the being of God and attribute to angelic ministration whatever similitude in which the feeling was conveyed."[20]

It has been alleged that Luther may have been close to the way of the mystics in his younger days but that he abandoned mystical modes in his maturity. This contention is not sustained by the facts.[21] One illustration from his use of the word "invisible" will have to suffice. Luther commented many times in the course of his life on Hebrews 11:1 ("Now faith is the assurance of things hoped for, the conviction of things not seen"). Both in his younger years and in later days when he was battle-scarred and dogmatically much more contentious, he pointed out that when we are involved with God, we are involved with the invisible, with a Christ who knows us from the invisible and with "the dear angels" who draw close for our protection.[22] This attachment to and feeling for the invisible presence of the Holy Spirit is what Luther had in common with some of the mystics. We Wittenbergians are certainly not saying anything new in this regard, he exclaims in the foreword to *Theologia Germanica*.[23]

Yes, mystical knowledge *was* part of Luther's spirituality, but it was not free-floating; it was rooted in the justifying *kerygma* of Scripture.

Anchorage in the Biblical Word

The scriptural *Word* is both outward and inward, an external sign and an inner experience. Luther says in a Christmas sermon (1515) that the *Logos* is the inner Word, God himself—his wisdom, his thought, his power, his life, his righteousness. For us to understand and absorb it, the Word must assume concrete shape. God's inner Word must come in flesh. That enfleshment is the external Word, Christ, and all that he says and does. Christ in his Word is God's external Word to man.[24]

Later in life Luther prefers to speak of "the outer and the inner clarity" of the Word of God. The outer Word comes first. Only the *Word* communicates the Spirit. Luther's forensic or imputative notion of justification demands that kind of start, the outward address. But the forensic action remains a dead Word if the Spirit does not begin to speak inside the Word, through the Word, to man's heart. Then dawns the inner clarity. Luther writes, "The word is a divine and eternal power, for although the voice and the speech soon vanish, the innermost kernel remains, that is the insight, the truth, contained in the voice."[25] Luther continues, "I bring to my mouth the goblet in which there is wine but I don't press the goblet down into my throat. So it is with the word that brings the voice. . . . It falls down into my heart and comes alive."[26] At another point Luther says that when God's Word opens up to a person, it happens only through the Holy Spirit. And this, he continues, has to be experienced, tried, and felt. The Law and the cross are "media" in the "school of the Spirit." The Virgin Mary, he adds, is a good example of one who has seen the inner side or clarity of the Word. She was "illumined and taught through the Holy Spirit" that "God . . . breaks what man makes and makes from what is broken."[27]

Some years ago I was casting around for a picture that would give some idea of Luther's view of the workings of the Word, especially the Word *about and by* Christ. I found the illustration I sought among my memories of a tour through East Africa. I got out of the car in the steppe-like Masai country with the intention of taking a picture of the javelin-equipped tribesmen herding their cattle. As they shied away from my camera, it was brought home to me that these Africans are persuaded that if you have a picture of them, you have *them*. The picture of a person emanates the specific character of the one it represents. Since they practice magic—black and white—they are never sure what the intentions are of the one who possesses a photograph or effigy of them.

Luther could not, of course, have used such an analogy to make a point about the power of the Word of God. But I believe that we may allow ourselves such an application. Just as a photo of a person emanates the specific character of that person and no one else, the Word in Scripture "vibrates" the one who spoke it. The Holy Spirit uses in a special way the words about and by Christ. These words are preeminently the receivers and channels of his communication with us. The Word calls forth the divine Presence to the one who seeks. No wonder Luther encouraged Christians to be diligent in their reading and contemplation of Scripture! The Word spoken by and about Christ is a bridge between the Lord and his friends, Luther thought. It offers us an eternal Now.

It is from Scripture also that Luther derives his understanding of faith as both "historical" and "inner."[28] A distinction between historical and inner faith exists, but for Luther they are interlocked and should never be separated. Historical faith is readily prepared to make the concession that the creedal confession—"Christ has suffered and certainly also for me"—is proper and true. But, said Luther, historical faith, if left to its own ways, does not add this feeling-laden experiential knowledge metaphorically conveyed by the marital union, an image of man-God togetherness that Luther derived from the Song of Songs, Isaiah, Jeremiah, Matthew, John, and the book of Revelation, as well as from some mystics. The true faith is the necessary inner, nonrational *affect* that prompts the faithful to exclaim, "My beloved is mine, and I reach out for him with gladness!" This feeling-laden faith is not grounded in our natural capacity for emotion but in our discovery of sinfulness and experience of grace.

The important point in the present context is that spiritual knowledge, the knowledge imparted by faith, is more than the apprehension of Jesus Christ as a kind of mathematical cipher aiding our self-understanding or promising eschatological fulfillment. Faith is also an "experiential knowledge," according to Luther: By *experience* does the justified know.

As for *historical* faith, well, "even the devil believes it," but the devil certainly balks at the *inner* faith. He does not follow us there. His aim is to keep us captive in the outward repetition alone. He is quite satisfied with merely historical faith.[29] We are back, then, with Luther's comment on Psalm 51: "It is of the essence that I begin to feel so that I may in some manner understand." *Sola fide*, faith alone, cannot be understood as a repudiation of mysticism with Luther, as is often maintained. Luther speaks of "the ecstasy of faith" and is thereby close to the mystical concept of *raptus*. He also uses the term *sensus fidei*, the knowledge of faith that includes "heart," feeling, and sometimes even a state that is beyond the feelings of the psyche and the senses. That side of faith carries us off (*translatio*) from all known conditions to God as "totally exalted." "Faith causes the heart to be carried away to dwell in things that are invisible" and also unutterable.[30]

Significantly, Luther makes a similar distinction between the historical Christ and *Christus mysticus*. Christ is historical in the sense that he appeared in history, walked on earthly roads, and is the center of the scriptural record. Anyone can study the record; it is public. Christ has indeed been here. But this same Jesus Christ is also what Luther calls "the mystical Christ." Jesus Christ is more than an influential memory. He is, after the Resurrection, the cosmic Lord and mystical Presence. He is in fact the spiritual Sun behind the visible, external sun. The psalmist does not merely speak of the visible sun—"In the heavens, he has set a tent for the sun which comes forth like a bridegroom" (Ps. 19:4-6)—wrote Luther in refutation of some notions among theologians, but the visible sun is the outward sign for the mystical Christ, "the SUN of righteousness who provides light and energies and is all" in his followers.[31]

This double view of Christ has another aspect. As we saw, orthodox Lutheran dogmaticians, as well as Lutheran systematicians of Newtonian modernity, spoke and still speak of the Christ-*for*-you, the forensic for-you, as the basis of faith and Christ allegiance, almost to the exclusion of a Christ-*in*-you. This follows logically from the assumption that if one wants to elevate God absolutely—to the 100 percent level—man's value necessarily declines to zero. Consequently, there cannot be, with such a "low" anthropology, much talk about an indwelling Christ or the possibility of being, as Luther puts it, "formed in Christ" or of "Christ [being] formed in us."[32]

On the other hand, pietistic thinkers emphasized and still emphasize the *in*-you of Christ, almost to the exclusion of the *for*-you. But Luther's theology contained *both* the justifying *for*-you and the sanctifying *in*-you (or "divinizing," to use a mystic term to which Luther did not object when he let *Theologia Germanica* go to print.) Christ was more than an *idea* in Luther's world, yes, more than an eschatological *promise*. He was a loving and protecting *Presence*, often working through his angels.

Worship and Presence

I have underlined the significance of objective and external forms of approaching God in Luther and in Lutheran worship. As early as 1523, Luther drew attention to the importance of the Roman Mass as a historical link. In his pamphlet on the Mass he writes, "The liturgy now in common use everywhere, like the preaching office, has a high, Christian origin." But Luther also found "much that was blameworthy in the service of the mass of his day." The sacrament had been buried under all kinds of additions, and the Mass had become, he thought, "a merciless judge." The sacrifice of the Mass "presumes to save man from the anger of God," but it did not as far as Luther was concerned. To him the Mass had become idolatry. So instead of speaking of "the sacrifice of the mass," Luther spoke of "the mass of Christ." The Mass was not a work of merit, earning grace. It was a gift. The Words of Institution were placed in the center of the Mass, the service was translated into the vernacular, Communion in both forms was introduced for everyone, and the transubstantiation section was removed together with the words about the repetition of Christ's sacrifice.[33]

Order is necessary and useful in worship, said Luther, but do not let it obscure the gospel. He wrote in 1539:

> If the Elector will let the Gospel of Jesus Christ be clearly preached, . . . why, have your procession in the name of God, carry a silver or a golden cross, and wear a chasuble or surplice of velvet, silk, or linen. If your lord the Elector is not content with one chasuble or surplice, put on three of them as did Aaron, the high priest . . . and if your Electoral Grace is not content with one procession in which you go around singing and ringing, then go around seven times, as did Joshua with the children of Israel. . . . And if your lord the Elector is so inclined, let him leap and dance in front with harps, drums, cymbals, and bells, as David did before the Ark. . . . Such matters, as long as they are not abused, do not add to or take anything from the Gospel. But they must not be made a matter of necessity for salvation.[34]

In the very way in which Luther spoke of the "ceremoniacs," we recognize that he did not delimit the range of Christ's presence to established places and ceremonies. The inner man "is free from rites and laws. . . . The outer man for the sake of love is bound to order and form."[35] In Luther's view, we need practice, training, and order, but since God is everywhere, we can pray to God everywhere. In *The*

Bondage of the Will Luther speaks of God's presence everywhere by positing that if "a tyrant would throw me into a cesspool and I would not believe that God is close to me until I return to a stately church," then that would really be both a tragedy and a mistake concerning God.[36] Concerning Christ's presence Luther writes (commenting on Eph. 1:23) that it is right to say "not that He is nowhere but that He is everywhere . . . bound to no particular place." Yes, Christ is everywhere, but he deigns to meet us in a special way "in the bread we break in the Holy Communion." That bread is the "body of Christ."[37]

Finally, to Luther's view of worship and Presence belongs his belief in and experience of the ministry of the angels and in the power of the laying on of hands for healing, issues that cannot be dealt with adequately in this chapter but that are important and deserve mention.

The question naturally arises, How does all this affect our lives as moral beings?

The Relation of the Spiritual to the Moral in Luther

We can safely state at the outset: The moral life is an integral part of life in the mystical Christ; the ethical and the spiritual are interlocked, for as theology is more than mere thought, so ethics is more than mere rational decision making.

The ground of ethics is not confined to material reality and rational consciousness about Christ or anything else. These elements play their necessary parts, but the power, the enabling and the incentive for moral commitment stem from the transrational presence of Christ.[38]

For Luther, the moral is rooted in the mysterious, numinous presence of the cosmic Lord, the Sun of Righteousness. The inner union with Christ that is the mystic element in justification by faith is also the wellspring of moral life, but the "extraordinary" anchorage of the moral does not exclude common sharing in the ordinary life of the world. The formation of a Christian life occurs, for Luther, in "conformation to Christ"—the soul being "formed in Christ." From this spiritual communion with Christ comes active service and the doing of justice.

Man's sinfulness is not the total truth, for through Christ we may speak of "the good in us." Let me enlarge a bit on this statement: Commenting on John 15:2, Luther wrote that some people think it is true and smart to contend that "man can do nothing but emit his odor and stench." Luther riposts that one has got to be "a stupid ass" to picture man exclusively this way. One should be able to see the "good in us" and "not only look for and think about that which is bad in us." Moral goodness is not our own doing; Christ is at work. The moral life begins in humility and continues in disciplined action. Luther writes, "Should God bestow His grace and Christ, His Son, on us and then say: 'You need not do anything at all but follow whatever pleases you'?"[39]

In the spiritual union with Christ a paradoxical tension exists between suspension of the moral law and a new confirmation of the moral law. Christ, says Luther, "who is present especially when He cannot be seen," brings about a new moral posture. "When by faith we consciously take hold of Christ himself, we enter into a kind of new law," and Luther adds, "Paul calls grace itself 'Law.'" What has happened here, Luther asserts, is that Christ becomes a living, present Power, a *sacramentum,* and then he acts in a Christian's ethical world as *exemplum.*[40] These words were written between 1517 and 1522; thirteen years later Luther reminds his readers and listeners that a *sacramental* Christ who is the cosmic Lord, the Sun of Righteousness, works with us in our moral strife as our *exemplum,* our model, our source for imitation. God liberates from Law. Paul knew that, but Paul was certainly no antinomian. Moral deeds are part of the life of the Spirit. If one acts against the Spirit, one "cannot possess the Kingdom of God."[41]

Finally, it is a mystical truth that true Christians play a central moral role in the world. Christian deeds, said Luther, are "the extension of the work that Christ merely initiated." For Christ always remains with his followers in invisible but real and powerful ways. Luther reminds his readers that Christ says to them, "Whatever you ask, I will do it." *Prayer* more than *ideas* empowers Christians to act as upholders of life and moral order. This is a paradox: Christians look like "poor beggars," but (listen to this—it boggles the mind!) it is because of Christians and their prayers and actions that "power, honor and goods" exist among people. The unrepenting world does not understand this and "thanks the Christians poorly for it." When "the Christians' words and wonders cease . . . God will end it all; it will all be consumed by fire." Until that happens, those who are spiritually "glued" to the Lord are called to "suffer the stench" from those who do not know the Christ, "in the same manner as the legs carry the paunch and the reeking belly."[42]

Writings in the Tradition of Lutheran Spirituality

Lutheran piety or spirituality has several roots. When we derive it mainly from Luther's influence, it is largely because the main proponents were anxious to claim a precise allegiance to Luther himself. But it should be added that they were also relating themselves more directly to the Lutheran scholastics of the sixteenth, seventeenth, and eighteenth centuries, because they felt the need of defending themselves against accusations of heresy from such quarters. These so-called pietists also absorbed medieval mystical writers through direct study rather than just through references to them in Luther's legacy. The movements of spirituality in Lutheranism mentioned below are best understood as a reaction against the rationalistic objectivism and institutionalism of the ever-growing confessional bodies.

Johann Arndt (1555–1621) and Christian Scriver (1629–1693) were precursors of what was to be called "pietism." Arndt's *True Christianity* became a much-read and beloved book of Christian nurture and meditation all over northern Europe and is still a spiritual resource in Scandinavia.[43] Scriver wrote *The Soul's Treasure*, which has likewise been widely read in the Lutheran churches of Europe.[44] Both works have, for two centuries, been part of the daily worship in countless Lutheran homes.

The same is true in the case of two great spiritual leaders who made pietism a household word: Spener and Francke. The allusion was originally rather critical and negative; mainline Lutherans did not consider it properly Lutheran to be a pietist. However, the socioethical implications of pietistic teachings eventually gave the term a more positive ring. Both social "inner mission" undertakings and "foreign mission" ventures emanated directly from pietist circles, as in the case of Spener's work.

Philipp Jakob Spener (1635–1705) wrote a foreword to a collection of Arndt's sermons, calling it *Pia Desideria*. In 1675 he published it separately. Besides being a devotional source, it was also a reform program for the Lutheran church. A reform movement grew out of Spener's proposals, but it met with heavy resistance from orthodox Lutherans.

August Hermann Francke (1663–1727) made Halle his center, taught at the university there, served as a much-appreciated pastor, and established many institutions for various groups of underprivileged people. Francke claimed Spener as one of his most influential guides. More than Spener's, Francke's pietism was based on the necessity of sudden conversion, a fact he tended to dogmatize. Like much subsequent pietism, the Halle variety tended to be legalistic.

Parallel with this dogmatically more conservative pietism, there arose on German soil a radical pietism that discounted institutional externality. Gottfried Arnold (1666–1730), its best-known representative, wrote (among other works) *An Impartial History of Churches and Heresies, The Mystery of the Divine Sophia,* and the widely read *True Depiction of Inner Christianity.*

In the eighteenth and nineteenth centuries, movements for spiritual renewal created interest in mission work and in public schools all over Lutheran Scandinavia. Thanks to the influence of pietism, catechetical instruction for confirmation was introduced. Danish hymn writer Brorson, Norwegian revivalist Hauge, Swedish law preacher Rosenius, and the illiterate Finnish farmer Ruotsalainen were prominent leaders of waves of inner awakening that swept over Scandinavian countries in the course of two hundred years. Almost everywhere, but especially in Sweden, these renewals met with stiff and sometimes relentless resistance from the established churches, which often used secular authority to silence pietistic preachers and their extra-ecclesial activities. But it is probably true to say that Lutheran church life has benefited from the erstwhile suspect renewals. In Norway, Finland, and Denmark, pietistic renewals were largely integrated with the traditional church structures, whereas in Sweden they often led to the formation of separate sects or churches. Mission work, public schools, and Sunday schools were inspired by spirituality movements.

In recent times, the charismatic renewals in America have also touched Lutheran churches. It is difficult to say whether Martin Luther would have felt at home in a contemporary Lutheran charismatic meeting, with its emphasis on emotional experience. His situation was different from ours: Whereas he battled against clericalism, we contend with secularism. But it seems clear that he would have seen the significance of the charismatic movement as a reaction against the common theological notion that "the church is institutional, not charismatic." Luther's description of faith as "ecstasy" and "rapture" and his emphasis on *feeling* as part of understanding initiated what we rightfully term Lutheran spirituality.

Notes

1. Bengt Hoffman, *Luther and the Mystics* (Minneapolis: Augsburg Press, 1976), p. 13.
2. Ibid., p. 14.
3. Martin Luther, *D. Martin Luthers Werke*, vols. 1-58, kritische Gesamtausgabe, Weimarausgabe (Weimar: Hermann Böhlaus, 1883–1987), vol. 40, 2; 422, 1-5 (on Psalm 51, 1532).
4. Luther, *Werke*, 40, 2; 423, 6-8 (on Psalm 51, 1532).
5. Luther, *Werke*, 5; 163, 28 (on Psalm 5, 1519–1521).
6. Luther, *Werke*, 3; 372, 13-25 (on Psalm 65, 1513–1516).
7. Luther, *Werke*, 6; 291, 30 (1520). See also Hoffman, *Mystics*, pp. 223-24.
8. Luther, *Werke*, 1; 335-45 (1518).
9. Flacius (1520–1575), Calovius (1612–1686), Quenstedt (1617–1688), Arndt (1555–1621), Spener (1635–1705), Francke (1663–1727).
10. Bengt Hoffman, "On the Relationship Between Mystical Faith and Moral Life in Luther's Thought," *Gettysburg Seminary Bulletin* (Winter 1975): 23.

11. Hoffman, *Mystics*, p. 19; Hoffman, "Mystical Faith," p. 23.
12. Hoffman, *Mystics*, pp. 27-28.
13. Gerhard Ebeling, *Luther: An Introduction to His Thought* (Philadelphia: Fortress Press, 1964), p. 260.
14. H. Emil Brunner, *The Misunderstanding of the Church*, trans. Harold Knight (Philadelphia: Westminister Press, 1953), p. 48.
15. Hoffman, *Mystics*, p. 100.
16. Jared Wicks, *Man Yearning for Grace: Luther's Early Spiritual Teaching* (Washington, D.C.: Corpus Books, 1968), pp. ix, 152, 280; Hoffman, *Mystics*, pp. 126-27.
17. Hoffman, *Mystics*, p. 15.
18. Ibid., pp. 132-33.
19. Ibid., pp. 120-22—a discussion of three kinds of mysticism. See also the introduction in Bengt Hoffman, *The Theologia Germanica of Martin Luther*, Classics of Western Spirituality (New York: Paulist Press, 1980).
20. Hoffman, *Mystics*, p. 15. Bernard of Clairvaux (1090–1153) was abbot at the Cistercian monastery Clairvaux and became very influential in world affairs during the reign of Pope Eugene III, a former monk of Clairvaux.
21. Ibid., pp. 112-19.
22. Luther, *Werke*, 3; 498, 27-36 (1513–1515); 32; 117, 1-18 (1530); 44; 700, 19-21 (1535–1545).
23. Hoffman, *Theologia*, p. 54.
24. Luther, *Werke*, 1; 20-25. See also Lef Erikson, *Inhabitatio—Illuminatio—Unio* (Turku, Finland: Abo Academy, 1986), pp. 41-45.
25. Luther, *Werke*, 12; 300, 15-17; Martin Luther, *Luther's Works*, vol. 30 (Philadelphia: Fortress Press, 1958–1986), p. 45. A further illustration of the conventional "Newtonian" approach to the exclusive "for-you" understanding of Word and justification is provided by Gerhard O. Forde in "Forensic Justification and Law in Lutheran Theology" in *Justification by Faith: Lutherans and Catholics in Dialogue*, vol. VII (Minneapolis: Augsburg Press, 1985), pp. 278-303. In this article support is sought from Teutonic scholars in the rationalist tradition, such as Iwand and Ebeling. Forde frowns on any "shuttle service" between the objective and the subjective and on "psychologization." According to Forde, Luther proclaims a "fundamental discontinuity" between God and everything in a "fallen world." "The spirit," he says, "is not a secret inner sphere"; further, Luther has "a literal, historical sense of Scripture" and the "livingness" of the Word of God lies in its "use." This insistence on a noninteriority in Luther is widespread in theological circles, and Forde has in that sense many supporters. The question is whether his modern intellectualizing grasps Martin Luther. My (minority) opinion is that it does not.
26. Luther, *Werke*, 12; 300, 17-20 (1523); *Luther's Works*, 30; 45.
27. Luther, *Werke*, 7; 546, 24-30 (The Magnificat, 1521); *Luther's Works*, 21; 299.
28. Luther, *Werke*, 40, 3; 738, 2-4 (1544).
29. Luther, *Werke*, 40, 3; 738, 6-20 (1544).
30. Luther, *Werke*, 57, 3; 185, 1-8 (Hebr., 1517); Luther, *Luther's Works*, 29; 185. Hoffman, *Mystics*, pp. 149-51, 155-59.
31. Among many passages, see, for instance, Luther, *Werke*, 548, 5-8, 14-17 (1519–1521).
32. Luther, *Werke*, 39, 1; 204, 12-13 (note on a dissertation, 1537) and 22; 336, 24-31 (sermon on Matthew 22, 1537). These later texts have been chosen to show how vacuous is the prevailing view among modern Luther scholars that only "young" Luther entertained ideas of a "mystical" or "spiritualizing" nature. This view coincides more with the mind-set and epistemology of the theological majority than it reflects Martin Luther's style as a theologian. One really picks up what fits one's framework.
33. Vilmos Vajta, *Luther on Worship* (Philadelphia: Muehlenberg, 1958), pp. 3-57.
34. Ibid., pp. 186-87; Martin Luther, *D. Martin Luthers Werke*, vols. 1-18, Gesamtausgabe, Weimarausgabe, Briefwechsel (Weimar: Hermann Böhlaus, 1930–1985), vol. 8; 625, 11-625, 37.

35. Vajta, *Luther,* p. 177.
36. Luther, *Werke,* 18; 623, 14-20 (*De servo arbitrio,* 1525); *Luther's Works,* 33; 47.
37. Luther, *Werke,* 18; 211, 15-16; 18; 212, 30 (*Against the Heavenly Prophets,* 1525). *Luther's Works,* 40; 220-221.
38. The major portion of these remarks about the relationship between the spiritual and the moral in Luther's thought is contained in my essay "Mystical Faith."
39. Luther, *Werke,* 45; 649, 23-27; 45; 650, 14-15 (1538). *Luther's Works,* 24; 207-208; 24; 254.
40. Luther, *Werke,* 10, 1; 11, 1 (1522); 2; 501, 34-37 (1519); 57, third part of the vol.; 114, 15-19 (1517). *Luther's Works,* 29; 124.
41. Luther, *Werke,* 39, 1; 526, 1-14; 39, 1; 527, 1-4 (1537–1540).
42. Luther, *Werke,* 45; 531, 32-35; 45; 532, 2; 45; 536, 5-10 (1538). *Luther's Works,* 24; 78-79, 83. *Werke,* 45; 535, 27-29 (1538). *Luther's Works,* 24; 82; *Werke,* 45; 536, 16-29 (1538). *Luther's Works,* 24; 82-83.
43. Peter Erb, trans., *Johann Arndt: True Christianity* (New York: Paulist Press, 1979); see especially pp. 4-6.
44. Christian Scriver (1629–1693), *Seelenschatz,* vols. 1-5. See M. Schmidt, "Christian Scrivers Seelenschatz als Beispiel vorpietistischer Predigtweise," in *Kirche in der Zeit,* 17, 1962.

Bibliography

Primary Sources

Arndt, Johann. *True Christianity.* Translated by Peter Erb. New York: Paulist Press, 1979.
Luther, Martin. "The Magnificat." In vol. 21 of *Luther's Works,* edited by Jaroslav Pelikan, pp. 297-358. St. Louis: Concordia, 1956.
_____. "Sermons on the Gospel of Saint John." In vol. 24 of *Luther's Works,* edited by Jaroslav Pelikan and D. E. Poellot, pp. 5-45 (John 14:1-6), 405-22 (John 16:26-33). St. Louis: Concordia, 1961.
_____. "A Simple Way to Pray." In vol. 43 of *Luther's Works,* edited by Gustav Wiencke, pp. 193-211. Philadelphia: Fortress Press, 1968.

Secondary Sources

Hoffman, Bengt. *Luther and the Mystics.* Minneapolis: Augsburg Press, 1976.
_____. "On the Relationship Between Mystical Faith and Moral Life in Luther's Thought." *Gettysburg Seminary Bulletin* (Winter 1975): 21-35.
_____, trans. and comm. *The Theologia Germanica of Martin Luther.* New York: Paulist Press, 1980.
Wicks, Jared. *Luther and His Spiritual Legacy.* Wilmington, Del.: Michael Glazier, 1983. (See especially chapter 7, pp. 120-53.)

A Simple Way to Pray:
Luther's Instructions
on the Devotional Use of the Catechism

ROBIN MAAS

You shall have no other gods before me.

—EXODUS 20:3

If the term "catechism" is an evocative one for you, what it most likely suggests is long hours spent memorizing doctrinal formulae when, as a child, you would much rather have been doing something else. In all likelihood, the possibility of the catechism being an important resource for the prayer life of an adult Christian is something that will not have occurred to you. Yet as formidable a theologian as Martin Luther advocated precisely that. The fullest explication we have of Luther's devotional use of the catechism is found in a letter of instruction to his good friend Peter, the master barber. The essay, which is entitled "A Simple Way to Pray," begins on an autobiographical note:

> When I feel I have become cool and joyless in prayer because of other tasks or thoughts (for the flesh and the devil always impede and obstruct prayer), I take my little psalter, hurry to my room . . . and, as time permits, I say quietly to myself and word-for-word the Ten Commandments, the Creed, and, if I have time, some words of Christ or of Paul, or some psalms, just as a child might do.[1]

Luther wisely advises that prayer be the way in which we begin and end each day. "Guard yourself, carefully," he warns,

> against those false, deluding ideas which tell you, "Wait a little while, I will pray in an hour; first I must attend to this or that." Such thoughts get you away from prayer into other affairs which so hold your attention and involve you that nothing comes of prayer for that day.[2]

Morning prayer should begin with a recitation of either the Creed or the Decalogue word for word and from beginning to end. (The one praying should either kneel or stand with hands folded and eyes directed "heavenward.") Then the Lord's Prayer was to be said, one petition at a time, allowing plenty of time for repetition and discursive reflection. The letter of instruction provides sample reflections for each petition, as, for example, he responds here to the fifth: "Forgive us our trespasses as we forgive those who trespass against us."

> O dear Lord, God and Father, enter not into judgment against us because no man living is justified before thee. Do not count it against us as a sin that we are so unthankful for thine ineffable goodness, spiritual and physical, or that we stray into sin many times every day, more often than we can know or recognize. . . . Do not look upon how good or how wicked we have been but only upon the infinite compassion which thou hast bestowed upon us in Christ, thy dear Son. Grant forgiveness also to those who have harmed or wronged us, as we forgive them from our hearts. They inflict the greatest injury upon themselves by arousing thy anger in their actions toward us. We are not helped by their ruin; we would much rather that they be saved with us. Amen.[3]

The point of this exercise, warns Luther, is never "mindless repetition." We are always free to linger on one petition or to let the Spirit move us freely. His concern is that we think deeply about the *meaning* of what we are saying, and the elements of the catechism are there to provide a helpful framework or focus of attention for our prayer and reflection. "It is now clear to me," he tells his friend Peter, "that a person who forgets what he has said has not prayed well. In a good prayer one fully remembers every word and thought from the beginning to the end of the prayer." Just as a barber must concentrate on what he is doing lest he cut his customer, "how much more does prayer call for concentration and singleness of heart if it is to be a good prayer!"[4]

For Luther, the appropriate conclusion to each and every prayer is always a firm *Amen!* This too is filled with meaning and witnesses to our trust in God's mercy:

> Never doubt that God in his mercy will surely hear you and say "yes" to your prayers. Never think that you are kneeling or standing alone, rather think that the whole of Christendom, all devout Christians, are standing there beside you and you are standing among them in a common, united petition which God cannot disdain. Do not leave your prayer without having said or thought, "Very well, God has heard my prayer; this I know as a certainty and a truth." That is what Amen means.[5]

Luther's Four-Stranded Garland:
A Method for Praying the Commandments and Creed

Luther's instructions to Peter the barber included additional suggestions for praying both the Decalogue and the Creed in well-structured ways. The basic method of approach—repetition and reflection—remains the same, but the reflection for each commandment or article of the Creed is to be focused around four types of functions or responses: instruction, thanksgiving, confession, and prayer. Each of these Luther terms a "strand," which when woven with the others creates a wonderful "garland" of praise to God.[6]

Shown below is Luther's example of how to "weave" a four-stranded garland with the first commandment, "I am the Lord your God. . . . You shall have no other gods before me."

The first strand: instruction
Here I earnestly consider that God expects and teaches me to trust him sincerely in all things that it is his most earnest purpose to be my God. I must think of him in this way at the risk of losing eternal salvation. My heart must not build upon anything else or trust in any other thing, be it wealth, prestige, wisdom, might, piety, or anything else.

The second strand: thanksgiving
Second, I give thanks for his infinite compassion by which he has come to me in such a fatherly way and, unasked, unbidden, and unmerited, has offered to be my comfort, guardian, help, and strength in every time of need. We poor mortals have sought so many gods and would have to seek them still if he did not enable us to hear him openly tell us in our own language that he intends to be our God. How could we ever—in all eternity—thank him enough!

The third strand: confession
Third, I confess and acknowledge my great sin and ingratitude for having so shamefully despised such sublime teachings and such a precious gift throughout my whole life, and for having fearfully provoked his wrath by countless acts of idolatry. I repent of these and ask for his grace.

The fourth strand: prayer
Fourth, I pray and say: "O my God and Lord, help me by thy grace to learn and understand thy commandments more fully every day and to live by them in sincere confidence. Preserve my heart so that I shall never again seek after other gods or other consolation on earth or in any

creature, but cling truly and solely to thee, my only God. Amen, dear Lord God and Father. Amen.[7]

Again, Luther sees this structure as an aid to concentration and not a rigid formula. "If in the midst of such thoughts," he cautions, "the Holy Ghost begins to preach in your heart with rich, enlightening thoughts, honor him by letting go of this written scheme; be still and listen to him who can do better than you can."[8] Further on he adds that anyone who wishes to improve on his schema may do so:

> Let him meditate either upon all commandments at one time or on as many as he may desire. For the mind, once it is seriously occupied with a matter, be it good or evil, can ponder more in one moment than the tongue can recite in ten hours or the pen write in ten days. There is something quick, subtle, and mighty about the mind and soul. It is able to review the Ten Commandments in their fourfold aspect very rapidly if it wants to do so and is in earnest.[9]

Precisely the same fourfold procedure applies in the case of the Apostles' Creed, which Luther deals with in terms of three articles: Creation (God the Father), Redemption (God the Son), and Sanctification (God the Spirit). His treatment of the second article exemplifies another concern: that we directly identify ourselves with the scriptural text. Everything that is written, is written for *our* instruction (Rom. 15:4). Every moment of Christ's suffering availed for *our* salvation:

> Again a great light shines forth and teaches us how Christ, God's Son, has redeemed us from death which, after the creation, had become our lot through Adam's fall and in which we would have perished eternally. Now think: just as in the first article you were to consider yourself one of God's creatures and not doubt it, now you must think of yourself as one of the redeemed and never doubt that. Emphasize one word above all others, for instance, Jesus Christ, *our* Lord. Likewise, suffered for *us*, arose for *us*. All this is ours and pertains to us; that *us* includes yourself, as the word of God declares.
>
> Second, you must be sincerely grateful for such grace and rejoice in your salvation.
>
> Third, you must sorrowfully lament and confess your wicked unbelief and mistrust of such a gift. Oh, what thoughts will come to mind—the idolatry you have practiced repeatedly, how much you have made of praying to the saints and of innumerable good works of yours which have opposed such salvation.
>
> Fourth, pray now that God will preserve you from this time forward to the end in true and pure faith in Christ our Lord.[10]

Lex Orandi, Lex Credendi

The ancient Latin tag *lex orandi, lex credendi* means, literally, "law of praying, law of believing." Its significance in Christian history has been to affirm the ways in which what is prayed and what is believed are inextricably linked or mutually interdependent. Roman Catholics have typically cited it to show that Christian doctrine derives its legitimacy from ancient, apostolically instituted worship practices. Another way of saying this would be that prayer precedes or is formative for doctrine. Protestants are more likely to see this relationship in reverse: Doctrine dictates liturgical practice. What is believed precedes or is formative for prayer.

In Luther we have a particularly clear example of the Protestant perspective on the *lex orandi, lex credendi* principle. It is most obvious, of course, in his choice of the catechism—a digest of Christian doctrine—as the basis for daily prayer, but it is reflected, too, in the actual structure of Luther's catechism, which, contrary to tradition, begins with the Decalogue in order to convince us of our helplessness to satisfy the demands of the Law.

For Luther, who saw the Law and the Gospel in antithetical relationship, one must first encounter the moral imperative and be *defeated* by it before being ready to hear the Word of grace in the Gospel. Hence the new Christian learns first what cannot be achieved by human effort. Luther reasoned that the good news that our sins are forgiven will sound entirely different in this context. So the Apostles' Creed, functioning as a concise summary of the Gospel, follows the Decalogue, and the Lord's Prayer and the sacraments serve as the appropriate response to the experience of sin and redemption. The same doctrinal logic is reflected in his placement of the "thanksgiving" strand before that of confession when praying the commandments or the Creed. (Although Luther composed relatively few prayers, those he penned typically presuppose that we have *already* received God's grace and therefore begin with thanksgiving.)[11]

Luther's explicit use of a credal formula derived from the baptismal liturgy as the basis for prayer was by no means totally novel in Christian tradition. In praying the creed he followed St. Augustine, who also admonished Christians to "say the creed daily. When you rise, when you compose yourself to sleep, repeat your creed, render it to the Lord, remind yourself of it, be not irked to say it over."[12]

This constant rendering of the Creed to the Lord was a way, for both Augustine and Luther, of recalling their baptismal confession of faith. It functioned to remind them that their identity as Christians was rooted in a particular world view or set of beliefs about the nature of ultimate reality. While we are accustomed to having creeds used as tests of orthodoxy, in the sense of correct belief, we are for the most part unaccustomed to recognizing that what orthodoxy actually means in the context of Christian confession is correct worship. Heresy is not an arbitrarily drawn boundary excluding us from Christian community in a purely legal sense; heresy is a deviation from true worship and thus threatens to shake the very foundations of our relationship to God. As Geoffrey Wainwright explains it, "The purpose of 'orthodoxy,' in continued teaching and confession is that God may be truly glorified and true witness borne to his gospel of salvation. The recitation of the creed is meant as doxology [praise] and testimony."[13]

In the same vein, we are accustomed to (simplistically) equating being moral or "good" with adherence to a set of rules arbitrarily set forth either by God or the Church. Seldom do we remember that the rules are in fact the content of a covenantal relationship between God and Israel and that the context of this Divine-human relationship was a *prior* act of divine deliverance. The Ten Commandments are not rules for the sake of rules; they instruct us in an appropriate lifestyle for a *delivered* people. And just as deliverance at the Red sea preceded Sinai, so deliverance (baptism and justification) of each individual Christian precedes faithful obedience. Luther's insistence on the need to "pray" the commandments is a vivid reminder that morality or correct behavior can never be properly understood or practiced *apart from* correct doctrine or correct worship. Each assumes the other.

The Catechism and the Religious Professional

Those of us who are called upon to catechize are especially vulnerable to the kind of doctrinal complacency Luther deplored, so we have much to learn from him. Luther knew that it was not the case that once learned, the catechism could be set aside as if it were some rudimentary teaching easily transcended. Once learned, it was to be lived with, lived out, and prayed over. For Luther, the efficacious Word could be relied upon to bring solace, renew fervor, and stop temptation dead in its tracks, and this was just as true for clergy as for the common Christian. For this reason, Luther urged all ministers to take up, as a spiritual discipline, the daily recitation of the catechism and chastised any who dismissed the document as too elementary or popular to be of value to the ordained: "As for myself," he wrote,

> let me say that I, too, am a doctor and preacher—yes, and as learned and experienced as any of those who act so high and mighty. Yet I do as a

child who is being taught the Catechism. Every morning, and whenever else I have time, I read and recite word for word the Lord's prayer, the Ten Commandments, the Creed, the Psalms, etc. I must still read and study the Catechism daily, yet I cannot master it as I wish, but must remain a child and pupil of the Catechism, and I do it gladly.[14]

Perhaps it is fortunate that we cannot "master" the fundamentals of our faith as we might wish, so that in "praying" them we might be mastered *by* them.

EXERCISES

For an Individual

If you are inexperienced in praying within a set structure, we suggest you begin by praying the Lord's Prayer reflectively, petition by petition, as Luther suggests. Initially you may find your reflections rather thin; if so, don't get discouraged. It is perfectly fine to choose only one petition and work with that.

The same considerations apply when you begin praying the commandments and the Creed: If you find the act of reflection difficult, work with only one commandment or article. Reflect back on your earliest encounters with these sacred documents. How have the experiences of adult life deepened your perspective on their meaning? What new invitations and challenges to faith do you find in them now? What *kind* of prayer is evoked when you reflect on moral imperatives? On affirmations of belief? Do your reflections lead you to consider the *ethical* implications of the basic beliefs set forth in the Creed? What difference do your beliefs make in relation to your faithful obedience to the commandments?

For a Group

Time limitations suggest using the three articles of the Apostles' Creed as an appropriate group exercise. Since not everyone may have memorized it, make sure copies of the Creed are available. The exercise should be preceded by an explanation of Luther's four-stranded garland technique for praying the commandments and the Creed and followed by time for participants to discuss the experience. Allow approximately fifteen minutes for the actual exercise.

THE APOSTLES' CREED

I believe in God, the Father Almighty,
  creator of heaven and earth.

I believe in Jesus Christ, his only Son, our Lord.
  He was conceived by the power of the Holy Spirit
    and born of the Virgin Mary.
  He suffered under Pontius Pilate,
    was crucified, died, and was buried.
  He descended to the dead.
  On the third day he rose again.
  He ascended into heaven,
    and is seated at the right hand of the Father.
  He will come again to judge the living
    and the dead.

I believe in the Holy Spirit,
  the holy catholic Church,
  the communion of saints,
  the forgiveness of sins,
  the resurrection of the body,
  and the life everlasting.

                                    Amen

DISCUSSION QUESTIONS

1. How would most people in your congregation react to Luther's expectation that the catechism should be a resource for daily prayer? What do you remember about the process of being catechized? How do your recollections affect your own response?

2. What difference does it make to your understanding of the Ten Commandments to think of them as being the conditions of a Divine-human relationship and not simply a set of rules for moral behavior? If you began thinking in these terms, how might it affect your prayer life?

3. To what extent is the Apostles' Creed used in public worship in your local congregation? How do you normally respond to a public recitation of the Creed? Do you see it primarily as something requiring your intellectual assent, that is, as a test of doctrinal orthodoxy? Do you see it primarily as a statement of devotion or commitment? Why?

4. Are you aware of ways in which your beliefs about God, Jesus

Christ, and human nature affect the way you pray? What connections can you make?

5. Can you identify changes that have come about in your religious beliefs as a result of particular worship experiences or practices? If so, what were they?

6. What long-term effects on your spiritual life would you anticipate occurring if you were to begin praying the commandments and the Creed daily in the manner Luther suggests?

Notes

1. Martin Luther, "A Simple Way to Pray," in *Luther's Works*, ed. Gustav K. Wiencke (Philadelphia: Fortress Press, 1968), p. 193.
2. Ibid.
3. Ibid., p. 197.
4. Ibid., p. 199.
5. Ibid., p. 198.
6. Ibid., p. 200.
7. Ibid., pp. 200-201.
8. Ibid., pp. 201-2.
9. Ibid., p. 207.
10. Ibid., pp. 210-11.
11. Frank C. Senn, "Lutheran Spirituality," in *Protestant Spiritual Traditions*, ed. Frank C. Senn (New York: Paulist Press, 1986), p. 36.
12. Augustine, *Serm.* 58, II, PL 38, 399-400, quoted in Geoffrey Wainwright, *Doxology* (New York: Oxford University Press, 1980), p. 188.
13. Wainwright, *Doxology*, p. 187.
14. Theodore G. Tappert, ed. and trans., *The Book of Concord* (Philadelphia: Fortress Press, 1959), p. 359, quoted in Frank C. Senn, "Lutheran Spirituality," p. 32.

CHAPTER 6

Ignatian Spirituality

BARBARA BEDOLLA AND
DOMINIC TOTARO, S.J.

Whatever you do, do all to the glory of God.
—I CORINTHIANS 10:31

There seems to be no man in the history of spirituality who evokes as many strong reactions as Ignatius of Loyola. Who was this man? What was the source of his spiritual experience? How does Ignatian spirituality fit into the age in which we now live? And who is living this spirituality today?

In this essay we will respond to these questions by (1) looking at Ignatius the man, (2) exploring the primary source of his spirituality—the Spiritual Exercises, (3) showing how this apostolic spirituality differs from others; and (4) examining the way in which Ignatian spirituality is being lived out today both in the Society of Jesus and in the Ignatian-inspired lay groups known as Christian Life Communities.

The Experience of God in the Life of St. Ignatius

In order to understand Ignatian spirituality, it is important to see that his spirituality was a result of his own life experiences. These experiences, both before and after his conversion, reveal the ways in which God was leading St. Ignatius and give a special character to this particular way of being in relation to God.

Inigo, as he was originally named, was born in 1491 to a family of landed Spanish gentry. Although they were not wealthy, his family shared the characteristics of the nobility, and at an early age he was sent to serve in the court of Juan Velasquez, treasurer general to King Ferdinand in Spain.

171

Inigo was a romantic young man with a very active imagination. He dreamed of doing deeds of great daring and sought to implement these dreams by being truly "noble" as this was defined by the world in which he lived. Thus he lived life to the full as a courtier and a soldier, brawling in local pubs and seeking to win beautiful women by performing brave and risky actions, and, indeed, he succeeded in living his dreams to the full.

In the year 1517 there was a border skirmish between France and Spain. Since the French forces were overwhelmingly larger than the Spanish, the battle was doomed from the beginning. Inigo, however, was chagrined when the Spanish would not put forth the effort to fight, so he rallied the forces together and a skirmish ensued. In the middle of the fray, Inigo was hit with a shell, and his right leg was shattered. The French took him off the battlefield and attempted to tend to his leg, but the injury left him with one leg shorter than the other and a noticeable limp. Vanity drove the young courtier to opt for a second, extremely painful operation on his leg.

It was during his time of recovery that Inigo's life took a different direction. As he lay in bed during the long convalescence, he daydreamed of his lady—though no one seems sure who she was—and of the mighty deeds he would someday accomplish in the service of the king of Spain. But soon the daydreams became redundant, and he asked for books to read. He was given copies of the *Life of Christ* by Ludolph of Saxony and the *Golden Legend,* on the lives of the saints. As he read these books, his fantasies began to move in another direction. He began to imagine himself in the service of Christ the King and to be doing marvelous deeds, such as those accomplished by the heroic saints before him. Moreover, he found that something strange happened when he daydreamed about his lady and doing heroic deeds for her; he discovered that after dreaming about chivalric deeds, he would feel nothing in particular. In contrast, when he dreamed about being in the service of Christ the King, he found himself filled with a peace and joy that lasted long after the fantasizing.

By the end of his convalescence, Inigo had begun to review his life and his goals. His question seemed to be "To what is the Lord calling me?" In light of that question he decided to make a pilgrimage to the Holy Land. In order to prepare himself for this venture, he went to Manresa, a small town near the Benedictine monastery of Montserrat. There he lived a life of prayer, fasting, vigils, and new disciplines. He let his hair and fingernails grow long and wore the robes of a beggar. Initially, he felt many graces. In a short time, however, he began to experience scruples concerning his sinfulness. He would go to his confessor and make a general confession that would last days at a time. Despite absolution, he was filled with despair and even contemplated suicide. As he continued to pray through this despair, he was touched by a grace that moved him to realize that he no longer needed to confess his sins. He was freed from his past in the moment, and as a mark of his conversion, he took the new name of Ignatius in honor of the sainted bishop of Antioch.

Through the exercise of his imagination in prayer and meditation, Ignatius soon began to realize that this new spiritual freedom enabled him to move from sin to an experience of God's call. He began to share his experience of these exercises with other young men. He would go from town to town and spend time leading individuals through this spiritual experience. By the time he had left a town, he would have gathered these men together into a community for prayer and apostolic endeavor. (It was from one such group that the Companions of Jesus, now known as the Society of Jesus, came forth.)

In 1523 Ignatius made a pilgrimage to the Holy Land, and although his deepest desire was to stay there, this was not to happen. The Franciscan superior where he had settled did not allow him to stay, and so he returned to Spain and began to study the classics at the universities of Alcala and Salamanca, in the hope of being ordained. During this period, he suffered much both from bouts with poor health and imprisonment on two occasions by the Inquisition. Nonetheless, he met each setback vigorously and continuously sought God's will. In 1528 he began studying theology under the Dominicans at the University of Paris.

During these years of study, Ignatius continued to lead other students in prayer experiences that he called "the Spiritual Exercises." These men spent long hours in prayer and debate, seeking to discern God's will for them. It was this group of ten men who were destined to become the founding members of the Society of Jesus, and on August 15, 1534, they pronounced vows of poverty and chastity.

As Ignatius had done previously, this group decided to make a pilgrimage to the Holy Land. During their nearly two and a half years of waiting for a ship bound for the Holy Land to come to port, all the members in the community were ordained. They spent that time well in preaching, ministering to the poor, administering the sacraments, giving the Exercises, and working with the sick and hospitalized.

When an outbreak of war in the Mediterranean region made it apparent that the hoped-for pilgrimage was not going to take place, the group came together again to make some major decisions about their future. These decisions, taken in 1538, proved to be revolutionary. They communally discerned that they would not be a traditional monastic community, bound by the stability and observances of the cloister; instead, they decided upon the vow of obedience to one of their members and added another vow of obedience to the pope—to go wherever he should choose to send them. They gave up the right to own property and chose not to be honored by accepting ecclesiastical offices unless it was at the insistence of the Holy Father.

Against his own wishes, Ignatius was named the first superior general of the order. During the years that Ignatius was the superior, he facilitated the movement of the Jesuits, as they came to be called, in all their endeavors. He opened homes for the most neglected members of society, and most important of all, he wrote the Constitutions for the new Society of Jesus. Written with astuteness and foresight, these Constitutions incorporate Ignatius's vision and spirituality into an ordered way of life. At the same time, Ignatius was conscious of the practical needs a diversity of persons and personalities would present for the growing community and realized that the Constitutions would have to be relevant beyond time and place. Thus the document asks members of the Society to look at the influence of the Holy Spirit in their lives in order that the greater glory of God might be achieved.

In 1556, sixteen years after being named superior general, Ignatius died of an illness he had been bearing for many years. The small group of ten had in that time become a thousand, for the seeds of Ignatian spirituality had taken hold wherever the members of the Society had been sent.

The Spiritual Exercises: Fruit of Ignatius's Conversion

As Ignatius's life was being transformed by his own experience of making the Spiritual Exercises, he recorded what was happening to him. These notes later became the book we now know as *The Spiritual Exercises of Saint Ignatius.*[1] The basic purpose of the Spiritual Exercises is to assist an individual in seeking and finding God's will and to serve as a channel for the grace that will enable that person to put God's will, once discerned, into actual practice in life. To this end, Ignatius gave the Exercises in the form of a highly structured retreat that included meditation, contemplation, applications of the senses, and the "examen" (examination) of consciousness. He also recommended the practice of discernment of spirits.

Several logistical considerations require clarification: In the first place, since Ignatius wrote the Exercises out of his own experience, the imagery in some of the meditations illustrates the historical and cultural context of his own times. Second, Ignatius envisioned this experience in a one-on-one setting, that is, making the Exercises requires a director and a directee. Third, the original form of the retreat required a period of thirty days, broken down into stages or "weeks." Various modifications of this structure are possible in the form of eight-, six-, or three-day retreats based on themes in the Exercises. For people whose circumstances do not allow the traditional retreat form, an individualized approach to the exercises, known as an "Annotation 19 Retreat," is possible.[2] In this case, the directee meets with a director once a week over a period of time that may last anywhere from six to nine months. The Exercises are pursued at home and involve a daily, hour-long routine that includes prayer, prayer review, and the examen of conscience.

Various types of prayer are used in the Exercises. For example, a particular type of reflective meditation is characteristic of the Exercises. In an Ignatian meditation, one mentally places oneself in the presence of God, utilizes a scriptural text or a specific meditative prayer from the Exercises, and begins with the basics of who, what, where, how, and when: *Who* is this speaking to me? *What* does this mean to me? *Where* does this apply to my life? *How* and *when* do I respond? The whole experience of the meditative prayer is done in an atmosphere of trust—trust that what God wishes to reveal will become clear in the reflective process. In this type of meditation there are many moments of uncertainty, and yet the one praying becomes comfortable as he or she begins to merge with God's desires. This "comfortableness" is almost physically felt—"felt" in the same way that a baker feels that the bread dough he is kneading has come to the right consistency, or that a potter senses when the clay she is fashioning has reached the right degree of smoothness.

A second type of prayer found in the Exercises, contemplation, is also begun in the presence of God and in requesting a certain grace or understanding from the experience of prayer. In contemplation, as Ignatius understands it, the imagination is used as a source of prayerful understanding of the gospel message. The one praying enters into the scene, sees the images, smells the smells, hears the discussion or words spoken, and takes part in what is happening, either actively or passively, according to what is desired.

In some cases, the individual may choose to refer to a personal life experience wherein a similar or analogous situation occurred, in order to enter the scene more fully. Imagine, if you will, that you have lost an article of great value and have searched for it to the point of exasperation. In doing this, you will more easily understand the

175

consternation of the woman in the parable of the lost drachma. And this insight may lead to another: that God also seeks God's own people with the same diligence and, perhaps, the same sense of frustration!

A third element in Ignatian spirituality is the "repetition." Here, the person praying is invited to return to a previous prayer experience in which either a consolation (peace, joy, or touching of the Spirit) or a desolation (an unsettling feeling, chaos, or fear) was the outcome. In reviewing or repraying these moments, the person may experience a more spiritual sense of what is happening within prayer. The "sense" by which this individual perceives the meaning of prayer will no longer be a natural sense but rather a supernatural one wherein the exercitant actually experiences the "tasting" of the Lord.

Fourth, Ignatius also invites the exercitant to be aware of God in everything. The examen or examination of consciousness is a structured exercise designed to help the individual discover when both the divine presence *and* its *absence* have been manifested throughout the day. By using the examen, the individual experiences not only the grace of being gifted but also the awareness of brokenness.

Finally, the successful completion of the Exercises requires skilled direction. During the retreat, the role of the guide or director is analogous to the role of a waiter at an expensive restaurant. A good waiter does not interrupt the flow of conversation between the parties at the table; rather, the person serving changes the courses quietly and unobtrusively. The guide works in similar fashion, never interrupting the conversation between the Lord and the retreatant but facilitating the fruitfulness of their time together.

The Spiritual Exercises open with a basic truth, expressed in "the First Principle and Foundation": We are loved by God, gifted by God, and called to use those gifts for God's greater glory. Thus we need to step back from our lives and look at the way we use these gifts. Meditating on the First Principle and Foundation helps us realize that we are truly loved as a people and as individuals. Simple though it may sound, it is often difficult for us to recognize this as a truth about *ourselves*. It is often the case that this segment of the Exercises takes the longest time to experience, perhaps because so many of us harbor a false or inadequate image of God, shaped by our own unhappy or loveless lives.

Yet when we pray over the First Principle and Foundation, we experience the first of many graces found in the Exercises: a sense, first, of genuine wonder that *we* are so loved by God and, second, of openness to a divine calling to receive the fullness of God. When we begin to experience this love, we come to an awareness of brokenness and sinfulness. Thus we are moved automatically into the First Week of the Exercises.

During the First Week, Ignatius has us examine sin in its broadest dimensions. We look closely at the sins of the world and our own sins. Beyond this, we are invited to reflect even more deeply on sinful tendencies whereby we habitually get "hooked" into sin. (Overwork, for example, may be very productive for our company but lead to family problems or physical stress.) A charism, or gift, that comes as a result of this reflection is the realization that we need not only to be forgiven our sins but also to correct the disorder or sinfulness that exists in ourselves. At the same time, we realize that we cannot do this by ourselves—we need to become totally dependent on God.

In the First Week there is a special prayer called a "colloquy," or better still, a "conversation." Kneeling before the crucifix, we ask the Lord, "What have I done for you? What am I doing for you? What ought I to do for you?" It is this prayer that leads to a radical turning point or conversion in our lives. The thorough reflection on sin during the First Week is not meant to overwhelm us with guilt and remorse but to help us realize that we are sinners *who are loved by God*. It is in being loved and forgiven that we experience a sense of spiritual freedom that moves us to new openness in hearing God's call.

God's call is the subject of a consideration that serves as a transition to the Second Week of the Exercises. This consideration, entitled "the Kingdom," would have us visualize a king who seeks to conquer infidels and calls upon his subjects to join him in this endeavor. The king informs us that there are conditions to this call: If we truly desire to join the king, we must be prepared to dress as the king dresses, eat what the king eats, drink what the king drinks, work with the king by day, and watch with the king by night, in order to be victorious together. (This particular meditation reflects very clearly the influence of Ignatius's own historical, cultural, and, in all probability, psychological background.) As we imagine this scenario, we are challenged to see it in a new light. Ignatius next has us envision a poor carpenter from Nazareth who comes out of obscurity and asks us to make the same offering he has made. At this point we must decide whether to respond to the call to be free from sin *so that* we will be free for service to the Eternal Majesty.[3]

In order to respond faithfully to this call, we must know, love, and serve the King, who calls in an increasingly intimate way. Thus the Second Week begins with a contemplation on the Incarnation. This prayer invites reflection—with the Trinity itself—on the plight of the world throughout time and the world's need for redemption. It leads into a contemplation on the angel Gabriel's annunciation to Mary that she is asked to be the Mother of God. (In these prayers the Christology is what theologians call a "descending" one; it begins with the divine nature and purposes, rather than with the human condition.) The Second Week continues with contemplations on the Nativity, the Presentation, and the childhood of Christ and his hidden years. We also pray over the public life of Jesus, watching him preach, heal, and challenge unjust situations within his society such as, for example, the status of women, the hypocrisy of Pharisaism, lack of repentance, and the like. (The prayers themselves are based totally on Scripture, and the Christology from this point on is an "ascending" one.)

During the Second Week we frequently find that we are called to make a decision based on the prompting in our prayer. For some of us this decision may deal with our state in life: Should we marry or join a religious community? Others may feel Christ's call to experience certain gospel values more fully through, for example, simplifying their lifestyle, being more involved with social justice concerns, or putting committed time into spiritual growth. To help us make this decision, or "election," well, Ignatius interjects throughout the Second Week meditations designed to help us be totally open to God's will. Since there is a tendency to go to God with our own agendas or prejudgments, these meditations are presented to keep us authentic before the Lord.

The first of these meditations, called "the Two Standards," invites us to look first at the camp of Satan, "the chief of all the enemy in the vast plain about Babylon, seated on a throne of fire and smoke, his appearance inspiring horror and terror."[4] With conscription into his army, he promises riches, honor, and pride. Next, we are invited to survey the camp of Christ: "Consider Christ our Lord, standing in a lowly place in a great plain about the region of Jerusalem, His appearance beautiful and attractive." If we align ourselves with his cause, we are promised poverty, exposure to insults and contempt, and, as a consequence of these things, humility.[5] Again, we survey these two standards within ourselves. What have we not yet committed totally to God? In what situations have we chosen the standard of Satan? It is within this meditation that we experience a choice of concrete commitment to the place of Christ in our lives.

Another meditation, known as "the Three Classes of Men," describes three (hypothetical) men, each of whom has a large sum of money and all of whom wish to love their Lord with all their hearts. Each person responds differently to God's call. The first man loves God with his whole heart and says that *tomorrow* he will consider what he might do with the money. But he procrastinates, nothing happens, and he eventually dies. The second man also wants to make the correct choice. In his love for God he *tells* rather than asks God how he intends to use the money. By contrast, the third man, who has experienced the same gift of wealth, goes directly to the Lord and asks, "What would you have me do with it?" Because it is difficult to view our gifts and the way we use them objectively, these meditations are helpful in allowing us to step back and see our words and actions in light of what will give the greatest glory to God.

Finally, there is the meditation on "the Three Degrees of Humility," recently renamed "the Three Degrees of Love." In this prayer we ask ourselves, first, if our love for God will lead us to reject serious sin and keep the laws of the Lord; next, will it lead us to reject small sins; and, in conclusion, will it lead us to reject *anything* that would keep us from following Christ, in his poverty or in the face of the world's contempt and abuse from our fellow sojourners?

Ignatius designed these meditations so that we can root out any disorder in our lives and thus be *free* to choose what God wants for us. This decision, prompted by God's call and discerned through our contemplative appreciation of Christ's life, will be tested in the prayer of the Third Week and confirmed in that of the Fourth.

As the grace to follow Christ closely is received, we enter the Third Week. Here we contemplate Christ riding triumphantly into Jerusalem, leaving us his eucharistic presence, suffering the agony in the garden, and, finally, dying on the cross. In prayer we change from the active involvement of the previous week to a passive, helpless presence; and we experience with Jesus his painful choice to redeem his people. Plunged into the Paschal Mystery, we learn the Ignatian charism of sacrificial compassion. We also learn whether any hardship or suffering would prevent us from carrying out our decision to do God's will.

But death is not a permanent condition, and the Fourth Week finds us rising with Christ and experiencing the joy of Christ's victory. In the contemplative imagining of Christ meeting his Mother, we touch upon the special poignancy of the suffering and love between a mother and her son. We experience the spiritual consolation of the apostles, the disciples at Emmaus, and Mary Magdalene and her companions, all of whom saw their crucified Lord risen from the dead. We realize that Christ will always be with us as he was with them and that he sends us on a mission to recreate the kingdom now.

The Exercises end with the contemplation on Divine Love wherein we begin to look at the gifts of love we have received. With this process comes the realization that these gifts give us only glimpses of the Divine Lover. In a sense, we return at the end to the very starting point of the Spiritual Exercises in the First Principle and Foundation. The experience of the Paschal Mystery in the Third and Fourth Weeks is one in which the element of spiritual freedom keeps revealing itself; now we have both the freedom to suffer and the freedom to go out and make the good news known.

Ignatian Spirituality Is Apostolic

The evolution of the various forms of the apostolic life is a separate study, but for our purposes it suffices to say that through the centuries men and women were inspired by the example of the apostolic community, as it was portrayed in the Acts of the Apostles, to form Christian communities with various purposes and lifestyles. In each age these communities tended to emphasize different aspects of apostolic life. The monastic communities of the early Middle Ages lived by the rule of common life (Acts 2:42), while the mendicant orders emphasized preaching and poverty of lifestyle (Acts 2, 4, 6). These two forms of apostolic life—monastic and mendicant—were the chief spiritual influences in the period prior to Ignatius and the coming of the Society of Jesus.

Monastic spirituality as found in the Benedictine or Cistercian community was based on a very simple, domestic, and ascetical style of life. Separation from "the world" was emphasized, and within the context of the monastic cloister God was served through the carrying out of the tasks that ordinary life imposed on the monk or nun. God was understood as Father of all in the monastery, while the abbot or abbess was the visible leader, the spiritual father or mother, of the community. Monks' and nuns' life of prayer and service was limited to the structured environment of the monastic enclosure where they ministered to other members of the monastic community and to those who came seeking their aid. Even the chanting of the Divine Office was understood as a principle "work" in this form of apostolic or "common" life.

Mendicant orders, in contrast, did not confine their ministry to the limits of the monastic enclosure. Groups such as the Franciscans, Dominicans, and Carmelites lived a regular or quasi-monastic life at home but frequently went into the world to preach the gospel and minister in a variety of circumstances formerly thought to be outside the realm of the apostolic life, notably service to the poor and teaching in the great universities. While continuing the tradition of daily singing the Divine Office in common, mendicant spirituality emphasized sharing the fruits of contemplation with others as well as the quest for individual perfection in the way of prayer and charity. In place of an abbot or abbess, these communities had a prior or prioress who functioned as a "first among equals" in more democratically run communities.

Most significantly, membership in these mendicant orders was open to the laity through the establishment of the third orders. One could partake of the rich spirituality of these communities and even share in their ministries while remaining in one's proper vocation of marriage or in a particular profession. The formation of such groups of tertiaries led the mendicants to provide more instruction in the ways of private as well as liturgical prayer. In this way the meaning of the apostolic life was gradually broadened and the stage set for Ignatius Loyola and his new insights into the meaning of apostolicity.

With Ignatius, the scope for ministry continued to expand, the locus of authority shifted, and independence and flexibility were emphasized. Ignatius proposed a spiritual teaching and practice that would be readily accessible not only to Jesuits but to the laity and ordinary clergy as well. Those involved in living an apostolic spirituality led a variety of lifestyles: They lived as religious, as married persons, as scholars, or as members of the court. Significantly, Ignatian spirituality became an instrument in the founding of many other religious communities, especially for women.

Ignatian spirituality has a distinctive pattern or process that encourages people to become contemplatives in the midst of action. The pattern is reflected in *The Spiritual Exercises*—the experience of God's gift of grace, being loved by God, sinfulness, the call to be an apostle, death, and resurrection. That pattern becomes a "Way of Life," as seen in the Constitutions of the Society of Jesus and in the General Principles of the Christian Life Communities (see p. 185 below), and has three characteristics.

First, Ignatian spirituality promotes the integration of prayer with daily life. It provides different styles of prayer that people then apply to the world in which they live. Conversely, the world in which each person lives becomes the subject of prayer. Thus there is no separation or compartmentalization between prayer and daily life.

Second, this spirituality helps people to discern God's will and choose appropriate ways to live out what has been discerned. The actual process of discernment is done with the assistance of a spiritual director. This helps one avoid self-deception and affirms the divine influence in decision making. The decision is lived out in terms of lifestyle and service—a lifestyle based on gospel values and service for the sake of God's greater glory and the good of others.

Third, this spirituality leads people to become committed disciples or apostles. They determine their Christian commitments in an incarnational sense: As the Word has become enfleshed within them, they seek to renew, from within, the face of the earth. As committed Christians, they bring the good news of Jesus' resurrection into their homes or communities and into the marketplace and professions. As apostles, they radiate joy, charity, and the love of justice.

Ignatian spirituality is apostolic because it calls people to holiness *and* service. Prayer becomes contemplative even in the midst of the busiest of lives, and all is done *ad majorem dei gloriam*—"for the greater glory of God."

Ignatian Spirituality Is Lived in Two Forms

The spirituality of Ignatius established two distinct religious paths: the Society of Jesus and Christian Life Communities. Historically, Ignatius shared his spiritual approach with lay people at Alacala and Salamanca, but it was not until he gathered a group around him at the University of Paris that a permanent community was formed; in fact, it was this group that later became the original members of the Society of Jesus. These men, in turn, went out and formed groups of lay people in this spirituality. These groups were known as the Marian Congregations or Sodalities.

The founding of the Company of Jesus (later to become known as the Society of Jesus) was indeed counter to what people at that time conceived religious life to be. There was much concern throughout the Church and in various countries about this new approach to spirituality and the ways in which these men sought to live their apostolic lives.

Ignatius was very selective about who entered the community; he sought a particular kind of person. (Many whom he refused entered other communities and were excellent religious.) Ignatius sought people who were completely open to the emptying of their own self-love in order to allow God to move through them. In this way, they were free to use their natural and supernatural gifts for the building up of the kingdom of Christ.

The members of the Society of Jesus took vows of poverty, chastity, and obedience. This last vow was one that the total community discussed, prayed through, and decided, through a process of communal discernment, was God's will for them. In addition, these members pronounced a fourth vow of obedience to the pope with regard to missions. (This vow gave rise to serious problems since the papacy of that time was more engaged in political, cultural, and secular affairs than in spiritual matters.) Ignatius understood that the pope, no matter how corrupt, is the Vicar of Christ on earth.

With regard to the vow of poverty, Ignatius suggested to his men that they "love poverty as a Mother."[6] And yet he urged perfect detachment in poverty, especially when their apostolates would lead some Jesuits into a more secular environment (e.g., universities). Thus they were to adapt themselves to a lifestyle compatible with their ministries but always with the ability to move in another direction. In a recent issue of *Studies in the Spirituality of Jesuits*, Father Joseph Tetlow, S.J., describes the poverty of the early Jesuits in this way: "The Companions did not choose to live for the sake of poverty while doing apostolic work. They chose to do apostolic work in poverty."[7] This freedom to respond to God's call, in whatever way of living it was directed, was essential to Ignatius's vision.

There was much controversy over the fact that there was no common prayer in the life of the Companions. While in training, the members were obliged only to celebrate daily Mass and to spend one hour a day in private prayer. Within that hour they might include the Office of our Lady and two examens or any other devotional prayer.

In particular, the place of the examen was extremely important in the life of Ignatius, and he told his men:

> Twice a day, or at least once, make your particular examens. Be careful never to omit them. Above all, so live as to make more account of your own conscience than you do of others; for he who is not good in regard to himself, how can he be good in regard to others?[8]

The Companions therefore undertook exercises of piety. They also were called to pursue studies that included the humanities and philosophy as well as theology. However, all these practices and activities were regulated to the essential purpose of their apostolate. Ignatius placed this kind of emphasis on individual prayer and on the limited time for prayer because he believed that *everything* a Jesuit did with his life was to be done in a contemplative mode. In this way the Jesuit would find, embrace, and carry out God's will.

In line with this apostolic stance, Jesuits dressed in the ordinary clerical attire of the time, without a special habit to identify them. They lived either in community or individually, depending on the ministry in which they were involved. If they lived as individuals, they were still bound to the superior of the nearest community.

The relationship between the Jesuit and his superior was most important. Once a year members of the Society would enter into a process called "Manifestation," wherein each member would reveal to his superior the entire scope of his life, not only in areas of his sinfulness and need for conversion but also in looking at the deepest desires of his heart; for Ignatius felt that in looking at these deepest desires, one would find the desires that God had implanted there. The nature of this relationship enabled the individual to be a zealous member of the Society and to discover the apostolic area in which he would serve. This approach and, indeed, the whole focus of the Order empowered the Jesuits to have a freedom that allowed them to be "Men for Others."

The Society of Jesus continues to be present in the world today. The role of the Exercises and the Constitutions is still as valid in the twentieth century as it was in the fifteenth century. The ministries have expanded as the world itself has expanded. Jesuits are primarily missionaries; they are still educating, preaching, writing, giving spiritual direction and retreats, and ministering to the poor. They are also working in the areas of science, politics, and the arts and have expanded into areas of communications and technology. But the apostolic dimension continues to be based on the dictum, "The more universal, the more divine."

In the early years of the Society of Jesus, when members were traveling throughout the world, they followed a tradition begun by Ignatius himself. They gave the Spiritual Exercises to lay men and women and formed them into small communities. These communities existed throughout Europe and reached such places as Paraguay, India, and China. The purpose of these communities was to grow in the spiritual life, to be in service for others, and to assist the church with its needs. They were known at that time as Sodalities or Marian Congregations.

During the seventeenth and eighteenth centuries, these communities were closely bound to centers of Ignatian spirituality. They became so important within the life of the Church that even when the Jesuits were suppressed, the pope desired these groups to continue. Thus the Sodalities were taken from the jurisdiction of the Jesuits (except in Eastern Europe, where the Jesuits still maintained some educational institutions) and were placed under the jurisdiction of the local bishops.

The suppression of the Society of Jesus also deprived the Sodalities of their source of spirituality: the Spiritual Exercises of Saint Ignatius. The Sodalities gradually changed into groups for women and children with an emphasis on devotion to Mary, especially with the recitation of the Office of Our Lady, and these groups multiplied.

Sodalities began to return to their primary focus in 1910 when a Jesuit and five of his students in Spain composed the Common Rules. In 1925 the Jesuit General set up a Central Secretariate in Rome to foster this movement throughout the world. In 1948 Pius XII issued the Apostolic Constitution *Bis Saeculari*, in which he upheld the Sodality as Catholic Action. The movement was further strengthened when scholars such as Hugo Rahner in Germany recognized the dramatic impact the Spiritual Exercises had had on the early Sodalists and called their twentieth-century counterparts back to this source of their spirituality.

In 1967, in line with the changes accorded by Vatican II, the World Federation of Sodalities became the World Federation of Christian Life Communities, and the Common Rules were replaced with the General Principles. This change, following the directions of Vatican II, emphasized the charisms of community, spirituality, and service and soon began to have its effect upon the total membership.

At present, Christian Life Communities are part of an international community of small groups of committed (mostly Roman Catholic) Christians. Members strive to integrate the features of Ignatian spirituality within a basic community that has as its mission proclaiming the gospel of justice and love. Although it is a lay movement, Jesuits and other religious are also members and frequently assist the groups with spiritual direction and the making of the Spiritual Exercises.

The General Principles of the Christian Life Communities affirm that "the Spiritual Exercises of Saint Ignatius are the specific source and the characteristic instrument of our spirituality."[9] The Principles go on to state that

> the way of life of a Christian Life Community commits its members to seek, with the help of the community, a continuing personal development that is spiritual, apostolic, and human. In practice this involves: frequent and even daily participation in the Eucharist; an intense sacramental life; daily practice of personal prayer, especially prayer based on Sacred Scripture; discernment by means of a daily review of one's life and regular spiritual direction; an annual interior renewal in accordance with the sources of our spirituality; and a love for the Mother of God.
>
> Furthermore, it requires of each member simplicity in all aspects of living in order to follow more closely Christ in his poverty and to preserve interior liberty in the midst of the world. It demands of each an apostolic commitment, especially to the renewal of society, and an effort to strive to develop human qualities and professional skills so as to become ever more competent and convincing in his or her witness.

> Finally, each one assumes the responsibility for participating in the meetings and activities of the community, and each helps and encourages the other to pursue his/her personal vocation, always ready to give and to receive advice and aid as brothers and sisters in Our Lord.[10]

The members meet regularly, often weekly or bi-monthly, to share prayer and their life experiences in order to deepen their understanding of the way their faith and life can be integrated. Together they discern decisions that relate the life and the mission of the community, and together they celebrate their unity through the Eucharist.

The purpose of a Christian Life Community is not solely that its members grow in holiness and share their faith but also that they engage in mission and service, that they recognize that the call to follow Christ is a call to serve. For example, a community may be involved with the needs of the hungry by seeking ways to establish a food bank in its city; another community may feel that the bishops' letters on peace and economics need to be actively implemented in its diocese and will take steps to collaborate with the Church to provide outreach to its members; a third community may be composed of individuals who are so deeply engaged in service, whether in a parish, professionally, or politically, that a common apostolate would be impossible. In this case, the role of the community would be to support and enable its individual members to continue to carry out their individual calls.

Since Mary is seen as a model of mission, her role continues to be valued in Christian Life Communities. Her ability to be open and responsive to the Lord's call is a much needed example to those living out a Christian Life.

Finally, Christian Life Communities are viably connected with the Church. An ecclesial assistant, appointed by the pope, is to be present to the needs of the World Federation of Christian Life Communities. There are fifty-four nations that belong to this federation, spread throughout the First, Second, and Third World countries. Most dioceses and individual communities have persons who link the members to the body of the Church.

In addition to these two distinct paths, Ignatian spirituality is lived by religious communities of men and women whose Constitutions are modeled on those of the Society of Jesus (e.g., the Religious of the Sacred Heart, the Sisters of Loretto, the Oblates of Mary the Virgin, and the Sisters of Notre Dame de Namur). Significantly, Ignatian spirituality is attractive to non-Catholic Christians, many of whom are drawn to the Spiritual Exercises and apostolic lifestyle.

We began this essay with the assertion that Ignatius of Loyola was—and is—controversial. No doubt he will always be so. He was a man who learned his lessons directly from God's own promptings. Providentially, he recorded his Spiritual Exercises in written form and passed them on to all who would respond, and from that experience were born the Society of Jesus and the Marian Congregations or Sodalities. His spirit was radical, for it invited a whole new way of integrating the spiritual life and the world. This apostolic spirituality is one that continues to give life to the Church throughout the world, both within religious orders and within the Christian Life Communities.

Notes

1. See David L. Fleming, S.J., *The Spiritual Exercises of Saint Ignatius: A Literal Translation and a Contemporary Reading* (St. Louis: The Institute of Jesuit Sources, 1980); Louis J. Puhl, S.J., *The Spiritual Exercises of Saint Ignatius* (Chicago: Loyola University Press, 1951).
2. Ignatius did not write *The Spiritual Exercises* with chapter titles; he used notations for the instruction to the director or directee. Thus the term "annotation" is used to identify specific instruction or rules for discernment. After Ignatius's time, each annotation and paragraph was numbered. The 19th Annotation makes provision for a person to make the Exercises at home.
3. Puhl, *The Spiritual Exercises*, p. 12.
4. Ibid., p. 60.
5. Ibid., pp. 61-62.
6. Ignatius of Loyola, *The Constitutions of the Society of Jesus*, trans. and with an introduction and commentary by George E. Fanss, S.J. (St. Louis: The Institute of Jesuit Sources, 1970), part 3, no. 287.
7. Joseph Tetlow, S.J., "The Transformation of Jesuit Poverty," *Studies in the Spirituality of the Jesuits* 18, no. 5 (Nov. 1986): 3.
8. *Constitutions*, no. 342.
9. *General Principles*, Christian Life Communities, no. 4.
10. Ibid., no. 12.

Bibliography

Primary Sources

Fleming, David L., S.J. *The Spiritual Exercises of Saint Ignatius: A Literal Translation and a Contemporary Reading*. St. Louis: The Institute of Jesuit Sources, 1978.
_____. *Modern Spiritual Exercises: A Contemporary Reading of the Spiritual Exercises of St. Ignatius*. Garden City, N.Y.: Doubleday Image Books, 1983.
Puhl, Louis J., S.J., trans. *The Spiritual Exercises of St. Ignatius*. Chicago: Loyola University Press, 1951.
Tylenda, Joseph, S.J., ed. and trans. *Counsels for Jesuits: Selected Letters and Instructions of St. Ignatius Loyola*. Chicago: Loyola University Press, 1978.
Young, William J., S.J., ed. and trans. *Letters of St. Ignatius Loyola*. Chicago: Loyola University Press, 1959.

————. *St. Ignatius' Own Story as Told to Luis Gonzales de Camara.* Chicago: Loyola University Press, 1956.

Secondary Sources

Broderick, James, S.J. *The Origin of the Jesuits.* Chicago: Loyola University Press, 1960.

Drolet, Francis K., S.J. *New Communities for Christians.* Staten Island, N.Y.: Alba House, 1968.

Egan, Harvey D., S.J. *The Spiritual Exercises and the Ignatian Mystical Horizon.* St. Louis: The Institute of Jesuit Sources, 1976.

English, John, S.J. *Spiritual Freedom: From an Experience of the Ignatian Exercises to the Art of Spiritual Direction.* Guelph, Ontario: Loyola House, 1973.

Fleming, David L., S.J. *Notes on the Spiritual Exercises of Saint Ignatius of Loyola: The Best of the Review.* St. Louis: Review for Religious, 1983.

de Guibert, Joseph, S.J. *The Jesuits: Their Spiritual Doctrine and Practice.* St. Louis: The Institute of Jesuit Sources, 1964.

Ignatius of Loyola: Founder of the Jesuits. St. Louis: The Institute of Jesuit Sources, 1978.

Purcell, Mary. *The First Jesuit.* Chicago: Loyola University Press, 1972.

Rahner, Hugo, S.J. *Ignatius the Theologian.* Translated by Michael Barry. New York: Herder & Herder, 1968.

————. *The Spirituality of St. Ignatius Loyola: An Account of Its Historical Development.* Westminster, Md.: Newman Press, 1953.

Sheehan, John F. X., S.J. *On Becoming Whole in Christ: An Interpretation of the Spiritual Exercises.* Chicago: Loyola University Press, 1975.

Stanley, David M., S.J. *A Modern Scriptural Approach to the Spiritual Exercises.* Chicago: Loyola University Press, 1971.

Villaret, Emile, S.J. *Abridged History of the Sodalities of Our Lady.* Translated by William J. Young, S.J. St. Louis: The Queen's Work, 1957.

Periodicals on Ignatian Spirituality

The Harvest, published by National Federation of Christian Life Communities, 3601 Lindell Ave., St. Louis, MO 63108.

Centrum Ignatianum Spiritualitatis (CIS), published by the Centrum Ignatianum Spiritualitatis, Borgo Santo Spirito, 8, 00195 Rome, Italy.

Progressio (supplements), published by the World Christian Life Community, C.P. 6139– (Borgo S. Spirito, 8) 00195 Rome, Italy.

Studies in the Spirituality of Jesuits, published by the American Assistancy Seminar on Jesuit Spirituality, Fusz Memorial, St. Louis University, 3700 West Pine Blvd., St. Louis, MO 63180.

The Way: A Review of Contemporary Christian Spirituality, The Way Publications, Subscriptions Dept., 114 Mount Street, London W1Y 6AN.

Accountability Before God:
The Examen

JOHN P. McINTYRE, s.j.

God, be merciful to me a sinner.

—LUKE 18:13

In their different ways, theologians such as Karl Rahner, Bernard Lonergan, and Hans Urs von Balthasaar have indicated the precise crisis facing the Church today. It concerns her credibility. Given her large claims and larger assurances, how do we make the Church credible in our world? For many people, the history, structure, and doctrine of the Church establish a psychological as well as a cultural impasse. They easily bracket the Church, relegating her to categories of myth and history. What is it, though, that makes us *Emmanuel,* God-with-us? It is the lived life that the Lord set for us (I John 3:22).

Since the Second Vatican Council has enunciated our common vocation in the universal call to holiness, the Church is pressed to put more and more of her resources in service to the *Christifideles*—the Christian faithful. Catechesis and retreats, liturgical and homiletic practices, days of recollection and other devotions characterize the life of the churches as they respond to the needs of the faithful today. Prayer, however, always remains the principal means for realizing our vocation in Christ, who is, after all, the unity capable of integrating everything. The saints—their life and work—agree on this. So St. Ignatius Loyola, for example, contemplating some mystery in the life of Christ, prays "for an intimate knowledge of our Lord, who has become man for me, that I may love him more and follow him more closely." (See his Spiritual Exercises, no. 104[1]) Once again, we learn that there is no Christianity apart from Christ. If the Church, therefore, is to meet the challenge of our age, she must do so by encouraging us all to follow the example of the Lord and his saints. She asks us, in other words, to pray.

The favorite prayer of St. Ignatius was finding God in all things, and he confided this charism to his companions, to those who follow his "way of proceeding."[2] In addition to his own personal history, Ignatius has left us the Spiritual Exercises, his Constitutions, and twelve volumes containing some seven thousand letters. In all of these materials, he counsels union with God and all the means necessary to achieve what he calls "familiarity with God." As the reports of his early companions and staff consistently attest, Ignatius himself had no difficulty in securing this intimacy as the particular fruit of his own prayer. So he recommends to his followers a certain intimacy with God in order to ascertain the divine good pleasure and the greater glory.

If Ignatius himself resided habitually in advanced prayer, it was not always that way. Like all Christians, he too had to "pay his dues" and make his way through the divine labyrinth. In one of his more famous remarks, he admits that "God was dealing with him in the same way a schoolteacher deals with a child while instructing him."[3] As a result of his own experience, then, Ignatius presents various modes of foundational prayer. In the Spiritual Exercises, for example, we find not only the three methods of prayer (nos. 238–258) but also the more self-reflective meditation and contemplation. Still more foundational than all of these methods, as the Spiritual Exercises and the Constitutions make clear, remains the examen—what Ignatius calls the examination of conscience.

The Foundation for Prayer

Although in the course of the *Constitutions* Ignatius refers to the particular examen some half dozen times, he does not explain himself. Rather, he presupposes that his reader has mastered the exercise. Indeed, so necessary is the daily examen in Ignatius's priorities that no spiritual director in the Society of Jesus can dispense with it. Where, then, does Ignatius explain this exercise? Characteristically, he places these materials at the beginning of the First Week in the book of the Exercises,[4] where they follow (logically enough) the meditation called "the First Principle and Foundation":[5]

> Man is created to praise, reverence, and serve God our Lord, and by this means to save his soul.
> The other things on the face of the earth are created for man to help him in attaining the end for which he is created.
> Hence, man is to make use of them in as far as they help him in the attainment of his end, and he must rid himself of them in as far as they prove a hindrance to him.

Therefore, we must make ourselves indifferent to all created things, as far as we are allowed free choice and are not under any prohibition. Consequently, as far as we are concerned, we should not prefer health to sickness, riches to poverty, honor to dishonor, a long life to a short life. The same holds for all other things.

Our one desire and choice should be what is more conducive to the end for which we are created. (no. 23)

This initial meditation has to do with the use of creatures and requires internalizing two principles. The first of these, *tantum-quantum,* appeals to the intellect and requires that we make use of created things *only insofar* as they assist us in attaining our true end, which is to "praise, reverence, and serve God our Lord, and by this means to save [our] soul." The second principle—that of Ignatian indifference—pertains to a posture of the will and insists that "we should not prefer health to sickness, riches to poverty, honor to dishonor, a long life to a short life. . . . Our one desire and choice should be what is more conducive to the end for which we are created." From these reflections, questions naturally arise: How do I use creatures? What creatures do I abuse? Where am I indifferent? Where am I not? To clarify and even to resolve these questions, the daily examen is a particularly suitable exercise.

In the examen Ignatius is providing us with one of the tools necessary to confront the fact of our human sinfulness. Since the whole First Week is concentrated on sin and its consequences, the individual meditations and the particular examen set up a counterpoint that clearly establishes my complicity in the ruinous history associated with rebellion against God. It is not just the angels who have sinned; it is not just the first parents who have sinned; it is not just some anonymous Christian who has sinned—*I too* have sinned, and to that extent I belong to that group which Ignatius symbolizes as the "unworthy knight," who faces public humiliation for his offenses against a previously beneficant monarch (no. 74). Because the sinner refuses to let God be God, he chooses to enter his own cycle of negativity and destruction. In this First Week, then, Ignatius uses many tactics and techniques in order to illustrate the enormous discrepancy between God the Creator and the human sinner. But the sinner is not just any abstract person; it is the exercitant who, influenced by the grace of God, accepts the fact of personal sinfulness. Moving rather quickly from the essential to the existential, the individual retreatant realizes and acknowledges the fruit of the First Week: shame and confusion. On that grace, Ignatius is able to build the cry of wonder before the

191

Crucified: "How is it that they have permitted me to live, and have sustained me in life?" (no. 60). The surge of overwhelming emotion elicited by this reflection is resolved in a "colloquy" or conversation with God in which the exercitant pours out gratitude for God's mercy (no. 61).

Preliminaries to the Examen

As a foundational exercise, the particular examen enables each one of us to recall, to reenact, the complicated synthesis of sin and death, shame and confusion, pardon and mercy, that inform the First Week. The examen enables us to balance the classical human antinomy—*homo simul peccator et justus*—in which each of us is, at the same time, a sinner, yet justified. Nevertheless, the exercise does not revolve around clichés. Moreover, because Ignatius regards it as a matter of honor, he does not tolerate any carelessness, as is evident in his detailed analysis of thoughts, words, and deeds (nos. 32–42). His attention to this kind of interior detail indicates the quality of his seriousness. Accordingly, if we hope to profit from the examen, we must approach it with equal seriousness. Ignatius signals as much by providing preliminary "additions"—three warm-up exercises that characterize all of his formal prayer.

The three basic helps here include a preparatory prayer and two "preludes" or acts of particular attention. The preparatory prayer simply places us in the presence of God—the same Creator who dominates the First Week, the same Lord whom I have offended and who has continually pardoned me. This type of recollection puts me in continuity with the primary modes of prayer in the Exercises and reflects the adult virtues Ignatius called care and seriousness. The act whereby I situate myself in the presence of God already implies a certain openness or availability to God (*disponibilité à Dieu*), a certain willingness to respond to the divine will. Ignatius, however, does not allow us to relax in this ambiance but indicates two preludes: one for the intellect, one for the will. The first prelude makes us conscious of what we are doing; that is, it is an examination of conscience. In other words, this is not the time to rehearse some spiritual shopping list, recite a litany, or to engage in any metaphysical speculation. One mode of seriousness summons another; the presence of God requires the humility of attention, for the examination of conscience contains two elements: the particular and the general examen. One is directed against a specific sin or fault; the other concerns one's whole demeanor before the Almighty. We have reason, then, for concentration.

The second prelude contains the *id quo volo* or particular grace required: What do I honestly expect as the fruit of this exercise? Ignatius would have us insist on this grace at the outset of each prayer in order to ascertain the quality of its fruitfulness. Here, each of us prays that every act and desire, every thought and operation, redound to the greater glory of God—*ad majorem dei gloriam.* In this way, Ignatius is able to reverse the cycle of sin and death and catch us up in the creative dynamics of the divine will. Whether this part takes two seconds or even two minutes, right from the outset we assent to this divine irruption. As a result of this preliminary stance—one that combines concentration with composure—we are now ready for prayer.

The Examen Proper

The examen itself contains five points or topics that we consider successively, allowing about fifteen minutes for the entire exercise. Briefly, the five moments comprise acknowledging, asking, admitting, repenting, and resolving. This pattern of prayer characterizes my availability to the Lord. In effect, it becomes a pledge of my fidelity, my response to the Lord's generosity. A word now about each of these points.

Acknowledging

After the preliminary exercises, we begin by recalling all of the gifts, both natural and supernatural, we have received over the time period under review.[6] Since the examen is prescribed for Jesuits twice a day, it usually is fixed at noontime and the evening. So we review the calendar, noting the benefits and blessings of the morning or of the day. This focus on God's concrete love for us keeps the material very empirical, historical, and personal, allowing prayer to emanate from truth. In reality, this review of the day acts as a corollary to finding God in all things; for if we do not find God ourselves, he has a way of finding us, and we can now reckon his ways. This opening leap, then, announces an Ignatian realism, one that frankly acknowledges that God gives and we receive. So the formal exercise opens with an explicit awareness of our receptivity, our intrinsic dependence on the divine benevolence. Jesuit poet Gerard Manley Hopkins catches the realism and the wonder in this couplet:

> Thee, God, I come from, to thee go
> All day long I like fountain flow[7]

Ignatian gratitude establishes the context for the first word necessary to achieve human maturity: "thank you."

Asking

The second point begins the movement to self-detachment. Ignatius counsels us to pray for the grace "to see myself as I am seen." We pray for enlightenment, a divine infusion that will enable us to put a divine construction on our day. Neither audacity nor timidity seems to trouble us. After having acknowledged that "all is gift," we can continue "asking for more and yet more." Indeed, the stance recalls one of Meister Eckhart's sayings, "The I whereby God sees me is the same I whereby I see God."

This reciprocity of consciousness, so integral to Ignatius's devotion to the Most Blessed Trinity, enables us to assume a divine perspective—to see ourselves as God sees us—and thereby cooperate in the plan of salvation. Ignatius effects the same kind of juxtaposition in his contemplation on the Incarnation (nos. 101–109). To be sure, as subjects of nature we can make no claim on God; what is more, as sinners we resist divine incursions. So it is important here to turn things upside-down and inside-out (one definition of conversion), lest we tend, however subtly, to rely on our personal strengths and ego. Since we do battle "with principalities and powers" (Eph. 6:12), Ignatius allows us no room at all for self-indulgence. Instead, by recognizing all of our strengths for what they are—gifts of God—we must empty ourselves of ourselves and enter into that kenotic movement of self-emptying in order to achieve the incarnational vantage point. To express it differently: At this point in our prayer, we are doing what we can to put on "the mind of Christ" (Phil. 2:5; I Cor. 2:16).

Admitting

The third point considers our human sinfulness. Essentially, sin is whatever alienates us from God, be it person, place, or thing. To that extent, then, sin defines the status of the creature. Accordingly, if sin—thought, word, or deed—is a problem, then the particular examen aims at eliminating it. That is, by recognizing a precise sin, we determine with God's help to correct it, to put things right. So Ignatius urges us, upon rising each morning, to keep our resolve and "to guard carefully against the particular sin" (no. 24). So clearly focused in consciousness is this defect that every time we commit it, we remember and keep a count for this part of the examen. Following the example Ignatius provides us, spiritual directors advise a written record. In this way, we can estimate our progress or retrogression. It is entirely possible, therefore, to spend three weeks or even three months working on a particular failing, for in the ongoing wrestle we invariably learn something important about our weakness and the human condition. We also learn something about the power of idolatry—how idols have a way of turning us into themselves:

> They have mouths but they cannot speak;
> they have eyes but they cannot see;
> they have ears but they cannot hear;
> they have nostrils but they cannot smell.
>
> (Ps. 115:5-6)[8]

In this way the particular examen is a help in converting "the heart of stone" into "a heart of flesh" (Ezek. 36:26).

The consideration of human sinfulness necessarily emphasizes the negative aspect of the examen, reflecting the contrary nature that characterizes the human animal. But this awareness need not obscure the more positive dimensions of the exercise. As the older fathers liked to express it, the examen eradicates vice and implants virtue. Because this positive dimension presupposes and involves the discernment of spirits, authors today refer to the examen of consciousness rather than conscience.[9] That is, after experiencing how the Lord is leading us into his own heart of love, we look for our ways of resistance. However convinced of God's plan and priorities, we still refuse to accept the fact of our radical incompleteness, which we show by making our own plans and setting our own priorities. The poet T. S. Eliot begins his *Four Quartets* with an epigraph from Heraclitus: "Though there is but one Logos, most people prefer to follow their own expertise." The particular examen acts like a corrector; it leads largely by a way of unlearning:

> In order to arrive at what you do not know
>   You must go by a way which is the way of ignorance.
> In order to possess what you do not possess
>   You must go by the way of dispossession.
> In order to arrive at what you are not
>   You must go by the way in which you are not.[10]

So we tend to our infidelities, our moments of stress, our lapses in faith, hope, and charity, in order to discern a pattern to our vulnerability or resistance. Clearly, this advance in life and prayer parallels the original self-emptying of the Lord—a gift in which he confides himself as a sign of his election. And even if spiritual writers describe this phase using the language of brokenness, fracture, and vulnerability, they too rejoice in the growing identity that lets a new self appear. In short, we do well here to imitate the prayer of the publican: "God, be merciful to me a sinner" (Luke 18:13).

Repenting

The fourth point, naturally enough, concerns repentance. Once again, Ignatius points to the enormous discrepancy between the liberality of God and the narrowness of men. Depending upon our state of soul, we fall into contrition, mindful that God blesses and that we abuse. The Lord, who wishes only good things for us, encounters an obstinacy that we cherish as "imp of the perverse." Having assumed the divine vantage point, we recoil at the ease whereby we frustrate the divine initiative. Ignatius has already prepared us to accept this basic dissimilarity between God and us. In the second exercise of the First Week, he asks us to meditate: "I will consider who God is against whom I have sinned, going through his attributes and comparing them with their contraries in me: his wisdom with my ignorance, his power with my weakness, his justice with my iniquity, his goodness with my wickedness" (no. 59). Under the circumstances, the cry for pardon seems right and just.

Moreover, the Lord's forgiveness heals. So we take comfort in his strength, dispossessing ourselves once again of our own resources and ego. In this way, Ignatius prevents the examen from degenerating into an exercise centered on self and committed to narcissism.[11] "Can modern man become a saint without the help of God?" Camus asks. Ignatius replied with a resounding "No!" As the introductory preludes make clear, Ignatius seeks only the divine honor, the greater glory of God. If the exercise is to bear fruit, we must resist any sentimentality that would distract us from the action of God. For Ignatius, our best posture remains that of the humble gesture. In this repose, we have achieved the second word in our maturing consciousness: "I'm sorry."

Resolving

The final point in the examen turns on resolve. Since we have just experienced the truth of the Lord's saying, "Apart from me you can do nothing" (John 15:5), this final movement might well resemble a Catch-22 situation. Surely if we profit from the exercise so far, the examen impels us to a greater intimacy with the Lord, to a greater reliance on his energies. Still, as Ignatius might paraphrase St. Augustine, if Christ has redeemed us without our consent, he will not save us without our consent. And at this point in the prayer, that is precisely what the Lord wants: our consent.

As we assent to grace, our resolve indicates our willingness to enter into the trinitarian rhythms that Eliot calls "the dance." What can we do? We can watch, and we can cooperate. The previous moments in the examen clarify both of these dimensions. That is, we have to know the situations and the circumstances that are liable to disturb us and lessen our determination to become what we already are by grace. In this, we follow the Lord's injunction to stay awake (Mark 13:33-37). Again, we must follow his lead, living by his truth, accepting his love, and entering into his hope, so that by realizing in ourselves the form of God in this world, we may reveal to all peoples the open secret inherent in Christianity, "that God may be all in all" (I Cor. 15:28 JB). St. Ignatius makes this our responsibility. It presents one answer to his questions: "What have I done for Christ? What am I doing for Christ? What ought I to do for Christ?" (no. 53). If love is shown by action (no. 230), we have now reached a level that makes the third, essentially unpronounceable word of love possible and practical—in deed.

Practical Helps

Ignatius mentions that the examen occurs in three moments: upon rising, at noontime, and after supper (nos. 24–26). Although we actually make it twice a day (at noon and at night), Ignatius wants us to call the particular examen to mind "immediately on rising." In this way, we set a tenor for the day by making our resolve explicit.

A written record actually assists some people in making progress; Ignatius indicates as much (nos. 28–30). The list of G's that decorates the page at number 31 in the *Exercises* is thought to stand for *gula* or gluttony. My master of. novices thought the sin was practically impossible to commit, which says something about Ignatius's discretion in selecting an example. This should not dissuade us in any way from keeping an actual count. (See Figure 6-1.)

Ignatius's outline of the examen permits great flexibility, depending upon one's needs, the liturgical season, and one's apostolate or ministry. The more experience we gain with the examen, the more successful do we become in integrating our entire spiritual life. In this sense, the examen becomes a specific sign of our accountability before God. It helps us to avoid false dichotomies.

The dangers come from turning the form into a formula and making it too rigid to be fruitful. Since the spiritual life follows the laws proper to organic life, it resists the merely mechanical. This means that the examen must always center on the Lord; otherwise, it is liable to the temptation of becoming self-centered, either ignoring or missing the action of God. (See Ignatius's notes on the colloquy with the crucified Christ, nos. 53–54.)

G

G

G

G

G

G

G

Figure 6-1

Ignatius, significantly enough, does not refer to penance in his instructions for performing the examen. He does distinguish, however, between interior and exterior penance (no. 82). There are times, moreover, when penance serves effectively (no. 87), but this must be done only with the permission of a director.

The Importance of Praying the Examen

Despite this elaborate explanation of the particular and general examen, no description can substitute for the prayer itself. That is, it is one thing to know a great deal about prayer; it is quite another to pray. Still, the examen so discloses the metaphysical differences between the Creator and the creature that we gradually perceive that the following of Christ becomes a real impossibility. Given his own unique being, his constitution, his archetypal role in the Church and the world, the Lord is, in effect, inimitable.[12] How could it be otherwise? Yet the New Testament gives us the language of following in the command "Follow me." (Matt. 9:9; Mark 2:14; Luke 5:27; John 1:43). And if we cannot take this command seriously, then we are liable to all kinds of discouragement and resentment. What, then, do we need to resolve the paradox?

We need to pray. Unless we actually pray, we never really enter into the paradoxical dichotomies that constitute the stuff of salvation history. Without prayer, we are satisfied to remain as mere bystanders, refusing the direct engagement with God that extends the Incarnation in space and time. Prayer summons the agency of God that we name the Holy Spirit. And the Spirit of God, who is of both the Father and the Son, is able to reconcile discrepancies and to bridge the abyss. (We know that much about the Spirit's personality and operation.) To the extent, then, that we pray the examen, we summon the Spirit of God to assist us in our shift from the notional to the actual, from the abstract to the concrete, from the essential to the existential. In this, we imitate the very action of God. For this reason, among all the spiritual exercises the saints assign primacy of place to the examen.

Finally, the importance that Ignatius assigns to the examen says something about his character and outlook. Three qualities come to mind: his practicality, his optimism, and his breadth. Ignatius thinks rather directly, usually in terms of means to an end. Where the scholastic theologians had taken over this Aristotelian notion and made it something of a cliché, Ignatius transforms that cliché by adding the *magis*—a requirement to go beyond what is merely adequate or good. Not satisfied with just any means, Ignatius sought the "better," always the better. This preoccupation with the *magis* dictates the economy of his style, the energy behind his desires. Second, the examen reveals Ignatius's supreme confidence in God. He knows in his depths that all creatures are blessings from God, that God remains immanent in creation and that everything succeeds eventually for those who love God (Rom. 8:28). "The height of the adventure" then means finding God in all things. Third, Ignatius does not permit any narrowing of consciousness, which he would associate with sin. We must be as capacious as the Lord and as liberal as the Father, and guided by the Holy Spirit, we take the whole world for our provenance. Indeed, this visionary stance, energized by the *magis*, grounds the Jesuit approach and praxis toward mission. In this respect, Ignatius reveals to us the new "man" or being precisely as anagogic man. From these observations, then, we can conclude that Ignatius, like all the saints, presents his own variation on the "paradox of the following"—on how to obey the impossible command. As a companion of Jesus, he confides the same challenge to us, a challenge that blesses even as it burdens. AD MAJOREM DEI GLORIAM!

EXERCISES

For an Individual

Begin to acquaint yourself with this prayer structure in a gradual way. For example, try practicing a review of the day each evening before retiring, but always in the context of prayers of repentance and thanksgiving. Over time, you will begin to notice habitual patterns of carelessness and lack of love. As specific issues begin to emerge, make an effort to be attentive to these problems at other times of day, especially early in the morning before the daily round of activities begins to occupy you. When it becomes obvious that you have a very specific problem to work on, try keeping track of your lapses in written form, as Ignatius recommends. As you become aware of progress in meeting temptations, resist the further temptation to congratulate yourself and, instead, offer a prayer of thanksgiving to God for the grace that has strengthened you in each instance.

For a Group

Since the examen is normally seen as a private conversation between the person and God, it does not immediately lend itself to group practice. On the other hand, there is no reason why a group formed for a particular purpose or ministry could not engage together in a regular examination of conscience as a form of holding itself accountable for the faithful practice of its ministry or commission.[13] Similarly, a group of persons who meet together regularly for prayer or other forms of spiritual support may find it helpful to raise the issue of personal accountability before God in relation to a variety of issues and contexts. The following discussion questions are offered to assist in this effort.

DISCUSSION QUESTIONS

1. Describe your own experiences in working with the examen as a form of prayer. What makes the examen such an effective instrument for personal prayer? What difficulties have you encountered using it? Can you point to any real changes in your life as a consequence of the heightened self-awareness such a practice produces?

2. St. Ignatius was concerned that the practice of the examen should not become an exercise in self-centeredness and narcissism; hence his strong emphasis on Christ—his vision of us, his virtues compared to ours, and our overwhelming need for his grace. What difference does this strong christological focus make in the actual practice of this kind of self-examination?

3. How long should one stay with the same particular examen? If it is concerned with a sin? With a fault? With acquiring a virtue? With a religious practice?

4. How do you think an examination of conscience would differ from an examination of consciousness?

5. What are the advantages and disadvantages of a group examen? How might such a practice enhance the fruitfulness of a given form of group ministry?

Notes

1. This and similar numbers throughout the practicum refer to the paragraphs of the *Spiritual Exercises* of St. Ignatius of Loyola. Cf. chap. 6, notes 1 and 2, for explanation and publication information.
2. See Thomas H. Clancy, S.J., "The Proper Grace of the Jesuit Vocation According to Jerome Nadal," in *An Introduction to Jesuit Life* (St. Louis: The Institute of Jesuit Sources, 1976), pp. 271-82. On this same matter, see E. Edward Kinerk, S.J., "When Jesuits Pray: A Perspective on the Prayer of Apostolic Persons," *Studies in the Spirituality of Jesuits* 17 (Nov. 1985): esp. 6-7.
3. Joseph N. Tylenda, S.J., ed. and trans., *A Pilgrim's Journey: The Autobiography of Ignatius of Loyola* (Wilmington, Del.: Michael Glazier, 1985), pp. 35-36.
4. Père Ravier indicates that the examen belongs to "the earliest core of the Exercises after Loyola, Montserrat and Manresa." See André Ravier, *Ignatius of Loyola and the Founding of the Society of Jesus*, trans. Maura Daly (San Francisco: Ignatius Press, 1987), p. 458.
5. See Gerard W. Hughes, S.J., "The First Week and the Formation of Conscience," *The Way Supplement* 24 (1975): 6-14.
6. It is possible for certain groups of people to make this part of the substance of their examen. See Louis M. Savary, S.J., "The Thanksgiving Examen," *Review for Religious* 39 (1980): 238-46.
7. W. H. Gardner and N. H. MacKenzie, eds., *Poems of Gerard Manley Hopkins*, 4th ed. (New York: Oxford University Press, 1967), p. 194.
8. Translation found in *The Grail* (London: Collins, 1963).
9. See George A. Aschenbrenner, S.J., "Consciousness Examen," *Review for Religious* 31 (1972): 14-21.
10. T. S. Eliot, "East Coker," in *Collected Poems 1909–1963* (New York: Harcourt Brace Jovanovich, 1934), p. 187.
11. See, in this regard, Jean Pasquier, S.J., "Examination of Conscience and *Revision de Vie*," *The Way* 11 (1971): 305-12.
12. On "the paradox of the following," see Hans Urs von Balthasaar, *Church and World*, trans. A. V. Littledale. (New York: Herder & Herder, 1967): 50-111.
13. See, for example, Gerald E. Keefe, "The Companion Examen," *Review for Religious* 37 (1978): 59-68.

Resources

Brou, Alexandre. *Ignatian Methods of Prayer*. Translated by William J. Young. Milwaukee: Bruce Publishing Co., 1949.

_____. *The Ignatian Way to God*. Translated by William J. Young. Milwaukee: Bruce Publishing Co., 1952.

_____. *Finding God in All Things: Essays in Ignatian Spirituality*. Translated by William J. Young. Chicago: Henry Regnery, 1958.

Maruca, Dominic. *Instruments in the Hands of God: A Study in the Spirituality of Saint Ignatius*. Rome: Gregorian University, 1963.

Peters, Louis. *An Ignatian Approach to Divine Union*. Translated by Hillard L. Brozowski. Milwaukee: Bruce Publishing Co., 1956.

Place Me with Your Son: The Spiritual Exercises in Everyday Life. Booklet prepared for the Maryland Province of the Society of Jesus. Baltimore, Md., 1985.

CHAPTER 7

The Shape of Reformed Piety

T . H A R T L E Y   H A L L   I V

Is there injustice on God's part? By no means! For he says to Moses, "I will have mercy on whom I have mercy, and I will have compassion on whom I have compassion." So it depends not upon man's will or exertion, but upon God's mercy.

—ROMANS 9:14b–16

The recently coined termed "Reformed spirituality" is something of an oxymoron, in that the word "spirituality" is notably absent from the works of all the classical Reformed writers, and when it appears in current articles or lectures by Presbyterians, it does so as a term imported from post–Vatican II Roman Catholicism. In any event, the popular understanding of spirituality as "an individual's interior search for meaning and wholeness," as both concept and practice, stands quite outside the mainstream of Reformed experience of the Christian life. For this experience, when faithful to its heritage, is neither individual nor interior—nor is it a "search" for anything at all.

Frankly, I much prefer the older term "piety," which focuses upon a person's behavior as regards the duties and obligations inherent to religion, as the better word to express what Reformed Christians[1] have in mind when they choose to address the issues of a Spirit-filled life. While piety or spirituality must surely include becoming a certain sort of person, for Presbyterians its primary focus is always upon a manner of living that is consonant with and responsible in relation to one's religious commitments.

Our purpose here will be to identify some of the origins and sources, values and beliefs, that give contour and shape to this particular expression of Christian living, that is, to this Reformed piety. In this context, moreover, a proper "spiritual formation" would embrace those activities and experiences that are useful and helpful to prepare and strengthen persons for living this kind of Christian piety. This statement assumes a recognition that just *any* expression of spiritual formation might not serve to accomplish this end, and that while certain activities—religious or otherwise—might well serve to further other legitimate Christian purposes, they may be less than helpful, or even detrimental, for shaping the piety that Presbyterians and other members of the Reformed family of churches are accustomed to value.

Historical Influences

The shape of Reformed piety was profoundly affected by a number of significant developments in late medieval Catholic Christianity. One of these was the rise of devotionalism as an expression of popular religion, and another was Renaissance humanism, both of which arose in their own way and flourished rather apart from official Church sanction. The Reformed response to each of these two developments was markedly different.

Following Martin Luther's lead, the Reformers stoutly rejected virtually everything associated with popular, and increasingly official, devotional Christian piety, while at the same time they embraced—to a degree that far exceeded Luther's inclinations in this regard—the values of Renaissance humanism. Richard Kieckhefer provides an apt description of the first of these phenomena:

> Perhaps the most significant development in late medieval Christianity was the rise of devotionalism. In the last centuries of the Middle Ages, devotions of all kinds flourished in unprecedented profusion: pilgrimages, veneration of relics, Marian devotions, meditations on the passion of Christ, penitential exercises, and more. Development of the Rosary was essentially a late medieval phenomenon. The Stations of the Cross, which attained their modern form by the early sixteenth century, arose out of devotional practices of the late Middle Ages. Eucharistic devotions, often connected with the feast of Corpus Christi, likewise stem from this age. The image of the Sacred Heart, in literary and artistic manifestation, can be traced to the last centuries before the Reformation. . . . This explosion of devotional forms unmistakably changed the tenor of Christian life.[2]

The major themes coursing through this wide variety of devotional practices centered on the passion of Christ, the saints (through their appropriate relics), Mary, and the Eucharist, with a primary focus of attention on the consecrated Host. The thrust of medieval devotional concern was largely penitential—a concern for one's own soul, either for its salvation or for shortening its travail in purgatory.

There were, of course, a number of pivotal theological issues at stake here, on which the Reformers were unwilling to yield ground. But theological considerations aside, there was also the fact that all of these expressions of religion tended to be so inward and "searching." For the highly educated and very practical Reformers, such practices appeared too individualistic in their orientation, lacking any clear or obvious societal or ethical referent. And it was around these latter considerations—the ethical and the social—that Reformed piety was to take its distinctive stamp.

Renaissance humanism began as an attempt to reform the curricula of the medieval university by shifting from scholasticism's dialectic to classicism's rhetoric. Underlying this shift, however, was a profoundly different way of looking at humankind, knowledge, and the world. These early humanists—and we shouldn't confuse them with the later humanists who arose in the post-Enlightenment era—affirmed an absolutely transcendent God, inaccessible to human understanding or direct human experience. There were no ecstatic encounters with Deity for them or, so far as they were concerned, for anyone else. Rather, God could only be apprehended indirectly in his actions, which were the evidences of his divine will demonstrated through his power at work in the world. Human beings were understood not as occasionally sinning but as essentially sinful and therefore totally dependent upon divine grace both for salvation and for the revelation of divine purposefulness for themselves and for creation. Men and women could, however, participate with God in his divine activity by serving his will in the world and doing good for others, and in this way experience an ever-deepening relationship to God and to other persons.

There are other aspects of humanist thought that the Reformers appropriated as well: their concern for language and texts, their recognition of the complicated wholeness of persons, their focus on the humanity and the essential benevolence of God. But these are enough to signal the humanist values that inform the sort of piety that took shape among Reformed Christians.

Reformed piety was also shaped by the changing political environment associated with the fragmentation of Catholic Christendom. From the beginning, the major Reformers had all understood their work as a renewal not only of the Church but of the whole society as well. In this latter emphasis, they differed from their Lutheran counterparts, and the difference can be explained in that their reform had been

> sparked not by the spiritual anguish of a monk struggling with his salvation but rather by the concerns of pastors who knew themselves to be responsible for their communities, in which Church community and political community coincided. Zurich understood itself as a *republica christiana*. The Zurich reformation encompassed both spiritual and secular realms from the very beginning since it applied not only to liturgy and worship in the narrow sense but also to the problem of the individual's service to the community in the exercise of his or her calling.[3]

Calvin's Geneva was widely acclaimed in its own day as a corporate expression of Reformed piety, and even a cursory examination of Calvin's arguments and efforts on behalf of the larger political and social order is enough to convince the reader that his Geneva was intentional and the result of a particular set of Christian values lived out in the larger body politic. Heinrich Bullinger, in his *Decades*, sketches for us his vision of the ethos shaped by this mutual transformation of both Church and society:

> What is, I pray you, more to be delighted in, than the good platform of a well-ordered city, wherein there is (as one did say) the church well grounded; wherein God is rightly worshipped; and wherein the word of God in faith and charity is duly obeyed, so far forth as it pleaseth God to give the gift of grace; wherein also the magistrate doth defend good discipline and upright laws; wherein the citizens are obedient and at unity among themselves, having their assemblies for true religion and matters of justice; wherein they use [*sic*] to have honest meetings in the church, in the court, and places of common exercise; wherein they apply themselves to virtue and the study of learning, seeking an honest living by such sciences as man's life hath need of, by tillage, by merchandise, and other handy occupations; wherein children are honestly trained up, parents recompensed for their pains, the poor maintained of alms, and strangers harboured in their distress?[4]

Theological Parameters

To this cluster of historical influences should also be added the particular configurations of Reformed theology, which to this day serve to set Presbyterian piety in a biblical and theological framework and provide much of the dynamic for its application to individual and corporate Christian life.

In spite of its clean break with Western Catholicism, there is nothing unique or peculiar about the *content* of Reformed theology. Upon examination, any apparent uniqueness is seen to be a matter of priority and emphasis. The fundamental elements of Reformed theology are all there somewhere, in some form, in the major biblical and historical streams of Catholicism. However, the particular convictions that this wing of the Reformation underscores are such that, when you put them all together, they give Reformed theology its own distinctive shape and flavor.

While issues that are of central importance to Presbyterians are indeed a part of the larger Christian heritage, other Christian communions have chosen not to assign to these aspects of the faith the same significance that Reformed Christians do. At the same time, there are many important and essential elements of Christian theology that are not peculiarly Reformed—the Trinity, the Incarnation, the Atonement, the priesthood of all believers—because they are shared more equally with other Christian bodies. The point is that however persons conceptualize the faith—in this instance, where persons have chosen to stand as Reformed Christians—it informs who they are and serves to shape the nature and direction, as well as the content and style, of their mission, ministry, and Christian life.[5]

Reformed theology has always been understood in terms of *covenant*, which may be contrasted with the more familiar "contract." Covenant is a fundamental biblical concept for expressing a relationship in which one party initiates and establishes its conditions and the other accepts these conditions and receives whatever attendant benefits or liabilities accrue from the relationship. Covenant is a hierarchical relationship of the sort established by a last will and testament/covenant, and it is to be contrasted with the mutuality of parties in the more familiar contract. Moreover, the divine covenant—at least in the biblical sense—always involved God with a *people*. Covenant is a communal affair, and individuals share in its obligations and benefits only insofar as they are a part of the community with which the covenant has been made.

For Reformed theology the fundamental issue is, Where does the initiative lie in the Divine-human encounter? And the answer given to this question, according to its covenant theology, is that *God alone* is the initiating party. God acts, God chooses, God calls, God saves and then commissions those whom he has chosen. Those who have been chosen, called, saved, and commissioned then have the privilege and responsibility of responding to this divine initiative in faithfulness and praise.

Under the overarching framework of covenant, the cornerstone of Reformed conviction is the doctrine of the sovereignty of God. God is, Presbyterians say, sovereign in creation (the doctrine of providence) and sovereign in salvation (the doctrines of election and predestination). It is in terms of election/predestination that Presbyterians, historically speaking, are most often singled out and identified by others.

Election simply affirms that God chooses those who are saved and saves whom he pleases for his own good reasons—which reasons may make little or no sense to me or you. Moreover, this is rather to be expected since God is God and you and I are not. For sinful human beings, salvation remains always a mystery hidden in the far reaches of God's eternal wisdom. According to my own personal way of thinking, God is a very poor judge of human character, in that he chooses to save sinners and not the righteous. This divine predisposition is surely not fair, but it *is* grace. And it is an exercise of divine sovereignty, which is always the flip side of the coin of grace. Moral living, ethical practices, and proper beliefs are altogether unrelated to the divine decision as to who happens to be saved. However, moral living, ethical practices, and sound theology are crucial for how a saved person lives faithfully and responsibly in relation to this sovereign God. The christological counterpart of the sovereignty of God is the Lordship of Christ, which Presbyterians choose to emphasize more than other aspects of Christ's person.

Reformed theology also exhibits a profound distrust (acquired through Paul, Augustine, the Renaissance humanists, and empirical observation) of human nature, which by definition is sinful. The phrase most often used to express this sinful condition is "total depravity," which simply means that no part of any human being is untouched by sin. My best deeds always contain a built-in element of self-interest, and my noblest aspirations always turn out a bit skewed. The whole complicated Presbyterian form of church government, with its many checks and balances, is structured to take seriously this understanding of sinful human nature. For Presbyterians, unbridled human freedom and complete individual autonomy can only spell disaster. Under representative government (which is the Reformed preference for both Church and State), no one is free to have his or her own way. And this is seen as a good thing for all of us, since we are every one sinful; and this in spite of our professed good intentions. This understanding of human nature makes our dependence upon a loving God and the community created by his Spirit all the more necessary. Moreover, this dependence upon God underscores the necessity of our having some understanding of his intentions—as opposed to our own desires—for us. This is why the revelation of God and of his divine purposes through the Scriptures occupy such a central place in the Reformed scheme of things.

Reformed theology affirms the "sufficiency" of God's word given in the Scriptures. It is sufficient, that is, adequate enough, for our salvation, in that Scripture lets us know what we should believe and how we ought to live, both in relation to God and to other human beings. The classic claim for the Bible in American Presbyterianism describes Scripture as "the only infallible rule of faith and practice."[6] This important statement may be interpreted in this manner: The Bible is the *one* source that will not fail you (infallible = unfailing) as a standard or yardstick for measuring what to believe about God or how to live as God's faithful disciple. It is important to note that "infallible" as used in these earlier standards does not mean "inerrant," as the latter term is currently understood. While some persons would like to have it read this way today, that's simply not what these writers intended.[7]

When Presbyterians approach the Scriptures, the fundamental interpretive principle is Jesus Christ, the Word of God Incarnate. Christians may not, therefore, arrive at understandings or draw conclusions from the Bible that contradict what we know of Jesus. This principle of interpretation has precedent in Jesus' own practice of discrimination in addressing particular scriptural texts: "You have heard that it was said [in the holy Scriptures of that day] . . . but I say to you . . ." (Matt. 5).

This approach to the Bible forces an acknowledgement that all Scripture is not of equal value. Scripture has value to the degree that it is consonant with the revelation of God in Jesus Christ, and as the Holy Spirit uses it to draw persons to Christ. Revelation consists in what humankind could not and would not otherwise know or learn unless God revealed it to them. What we are able to discover or learn or refine through our own intelligence or efforts does not fall within its parameters. The infallible quality of Scripture is tied to faith and conduct, that is, what to believe about God and how to live faithfully as a disciple. It is not to be identified with geological, astronomical, scientific, or historical data found in the Bible, the accuracy of which may be tested by our own discoveries and empirical observations.[8] This view of Scripture demands discrimination and discernment—and therefore intelligence and preparation—as well as hard work in the process of studying and understanding it. This is why Reformed churches have always insisted that their ministers, as authenticated interpreters of Scripture, should be an educated clergy, well prepared for the task.

It is in part because of their view of Scripture that Presbyterians underscore the necessity of serving God with one's mind, in addition to heart, soul, and strength. But there are other important theological reasons for this as well. Presbyterians have been pioneers in the support of schools and education, but not for its own sake, or even for the sake of individual enhancement. Rather, sound preparation is seen as a necessary adjunct for useful and faithful living under a sovereign God. Faith unexamined, life uncritiqued, and skills undeveloped will be of little worth to the kingdom. Learning, therefore, becomes a vehicle for responsible discipleship.[9]

Reformed theology makes a very important place for the Christian community, which lives in covenant with God. And the Church is seen as essential to God's purposes for creation. The Church is the present locus of the Spirit of Christ, who is its Head and Lord. The basis for its life and the authority for its ministry, therefore, rests in him. Since God calls and establishes his Church, it is totally his creation, and the proper expression of its government is neither autocratic nor democratic but *theocratic*. While the Presbyterian form and order of the Church reflects a profound distrust of human nature, it also expresses an equally profound trust in the Holy Spirit. Human sinfulness makes Reformed Christians wary of individualism of every sort and underscores the necessity of participation in a community governed and sustained by the Spirit of Christ.

Reformed theology affirms that each person is responsible to God for all of life. The thrust of Christian discipleship, therefore, is to bring every aspect of life under the sovereign lordship of Christ. This understanding of calling and vocation blurs the distinctions between the sacred and the secular, since no dimension of human experience lies outside the sphere of God's sovereignty or its potential redemption. Reformed theology prods Presbyterians to take their discipleship very seriously, wherever, however, and in whatever situation they live. Presbyterians are not particularly adept at a number of things, as, for instance, handling internal theological disputes amicably or reaching out beyond their traditional upper-middle-class constituency. They are, however, very good at being responsible, especially for what goes on in the wider world outside the four walls of the sanctuary. Largely because of their theology, Presbyterians are in general better at "being faithful" than at "having faith."

These Reformed emphases interact to produce a cluster of convictions that give Presbyterians their distinctive lifestyle and character. They may be set over against other aspects and dimensions of the Christian faith that Presbyterians have chosen not to emphasize as much, or at all. The Reformed tradition leads its people to emphasize Christ as Lord rather than Christ as Savior; the world as the arena of God's lordship in preference to the world as evil or the world as inherently good; truth as God's, rather than learning as suspect or learning for self-enhancement; Christian experience as nurture and growth in community in preference to Christian experience as individual conversion or spiritual quest; the Christian life as engagement rather than the Christian life as withdrawal; faithfulness more than faith.

An Example: Honor Thy Father and Thy Mother

As an example of how Reformed piety expressed itself, let us examine a portion of the Westminister Larger Catechism, which together with the other documents framed by the Westminster Assembly during the late 1640s has had the most formative influence on American Presbyterianism. As with all catechisms, this one was prepared for the instruction of church members and was intended to have a major role in shaping the character of their Christian life.

Catechism questions and answers 1 to 90 address what Scripture requires persons to believe concerning God; questions 91 to 196 describe their duty to God. Our concern will be for that portion which relates to the fifth commandment: Honor thy father and thy mother.

Prior to its treatment of the commandments themselves, the catechism has stated that God requires of us obedience to his revealed will (question [Q] 91) as contained in the moral law (Q 92), which is summarily comprehended in the Ten Commandments (Q 98). There then follows a hermeneutic "to be observed for the right understanding of the Ten Commandments," consisting of eight rules (Q 99). The second of these rules is especially instructive for our purposes, in that it affirms the moral law to be "spiritual, and so reacheth the understanding, will, affections and all other powers of the soul."[10] In other words, *keeping the moral law* becomes an expression of (to use the current terminology) spirituality. The catechetical material dealing with the fifth commandment is as follows:

Q. 124. Who are meant by father and mother, in the fifth commandment?

A.   By father and mother, in the fifth commandment, are meant not only natural parents, but all superiors in age and gifts; and especially such as by God's ordinance are over us in place of authority, whether in family, church, or commonwealth.

Q. 125. Why are superiors styled father and mother?

A.   Superiors are styled father and mother, both to teach them in all duties towards their inferiors, like natural parents, to express love and tenderness to them, according to their several relations, and to work inferiors to a greater willingness and cheerfulness in performing their duties to their superiors, as to their parents.

Q. 126. What is the general scope of the fifth commandment?

A.   The general scope of the fifth commandment is, the performance of those duties which we mutually owe in our several relations as inferiors, superiors, or equals.

Q. 127. What is the honor which inferiors owe to superiors?

A.   The honor which inferiors owe to their superiors is: all due reverence in heart, word, and behavior; prayer and thanksgiving for them; imitation of their virtues and graces; willing obedience to their lawful commands and counsels, due submission to their corrections; fidelity to, defense and maintenance of their persons and authority, according to several ranks, and the nature of their places; bearing with their infirmities, and covering them in love, that so they may be an honor to them and to their government.

Q. 128. What are the sins of inferiors against their superiors?

A.   The sins of inferiors against their superiors are: all neglect of the duties required toward them; envying at, contempt of, and rebellion against their persons and places, in their lawful counsels, commands, and corrections; cursing, mocking, and all such refractory and scandalous carriage, as proves a shame and dishonor to them and their government.

Q. 129. What is required of superiors toward their inferiors?

A.   It is required of superiors, according to that power they receive from God, and that relation wherein they stand, to love, pray for, and bless their inferiors; to instruct, counsel, and admonish them; countenancing, commending, and rewarding such as do well; and discountenancing, reproving, and chastising such as do ill; protecting, and providing for them all things necessary for soul and body; and, by grave, wise, holy, and exemplary carriage, to procure glory to God, honor to themselves, and so to preserve that authority which God hath put upon them.

Q. 130. What are the sins of superiors?

A. The sins of superiors are, besides the neglect of the duties required of them, an inordinate seeking of themselves, their own glory, ease, profit, or pleasure; commanding things unlawful, or not in the power of inferiors to perform; counselling, encouraging, or favoring them in that which is evil; dissuading, discouraging, or discountenancing them in that which is good; correcting them unduly; careless exposing or leading them to wrong, temptation, and danger; provoking them to wrath; or any way dishonoring themselves, or lessening their authority, by an unjust, indiscreet, rigorous, or remiss behavior.

Q. 131. What are the duties of equals?

A. The duties of equals are: to regard the dignity and worth of each other, in giving honor to go one before another; and to rejoice in each other's gifts and advancement as their own.

Q. 132. What are the sins of equals?

A. The sins of equals are, besides the neglect of the duties required, the undervaluing of the worth, envying the gifts, grieving at the advancement or prosperity one of another; and usurping preeminence one over another.[11]

It is significant, and typical, that this commandment, which could have been construed and applied in very narrow, personal, pietistic, or even privatistic categories, has instead been broadened to include the whole range of human relationships, touching every aspect of human disposition and action "whether in family, church or commonwealth."

While the egalitarian predispositions of our age might well raise questions for us about the Westminster Catechism's expository framework of "superiors" and "inferiors," it ought not cloud the comprehensive range and outward focus of this understanding of how a Christian fulfills the responsibilities of life under the aegis of a sovereign God.

It is also important to note, as elsewhere among Reformed documents, that while the commandment is clearly understood as "law," it is not then translated into rules for specific acts of behavior but instead into broad principles intended to guide and govern human life. And because Reformed piety always resisted this translation into specific rules, it is not as easy as are some others—Jesuit piety, for instance, or even fundamentalist Protestant piety—to describe or define. It does nonetheless have its own particular characteristics, and while the following observations cannot encompass the whole range of its attributes, they do identify a number of its distinctive contours.

The Shape of Reformed Piety

Whatever else Reformed piety may or may not be, it *is* a function of the entire community, making no distinction in this regard between clergy and laypersons (or, more properly, officers and members) in the Church.[12] Its practice is experienced as a proper service to the transcendent and sovereign God, who draws us to himself through obedience to his will. Reformed piety intends to be grounded in revelation and centered in Christ. Theologically, it is informed more by the Incarnation than by the Atonement and functions within the theological parameters of sanctification rather than justification. In other words, it is far more concerned for the elect to "live right" under God than for sinners to "get right" with God, always insisting, however, that the way saved-but-sinful persons come to fellowship with God is precisely by ordering their lives according to the revelation of his will in the Holy Scriptures. The dynamic that drives Reformed piety is not guilt but gratitude, and compared with other Western Christian pieties, it is remarkably free of concern for individual salvation.

While Reformed piety assumes and requires a deeply personal commitment, its primary focus has always been corporate and social, rather than individual. It is inherently skeptical of any individual religious experiences of a "mystical" or ecstatic sort (including the "enthusiasms" of past awakenings and revivals) that cannot be subjected to scrutiny and authentication on the basis of more normative community experience grounded in Scripture. Moreover, its primary goal is not individual self-improvement but the welfare of the neighbor.

The characteristic designation—it was Calvin's—for good deeds or appropriate Christian behavior is "works of righteousness." This biblical term "righteousness" is essentially a relational one. A righteous person is one who preserves the peace and wholeness of the community by fulfilling the obligations inherent to whatever applicable relationship.[13] A righteous king is one who fulfills the obligation of kingship. A righteous master or servant does what the relationship requires. God is righteous because God faithfully fulfills the obligations inherent in the covenant with his people. Persons in whatever walk of life are expected to do the same, both in terms of their relationship to God and in the complex web of relationships that comprise the fabric of society. Reformed piety and its "good deeds" are understood in this sense: as works of righteousness.

Reformed piety is characterized not by our seeking God but by seeking to do God's will, in the process of which the faithful come to know, as something of a serendipity, fellowship with God and find their lives transformed. The practice of Reformed piety, therefore, has the attributes of a pilgrimage rather than a quest. Moreover, its focus is outward, not inward, so that the Christian life is characterized by an engagement with the world rather than a separation or retreat from it. Reformed piety tends to be active rather than contemplative and places a high value on the usefulness, especially in terms of promoting the common good, of whatever activity is involved. Informing all activity, however, is a deep commitment to actualizing God's sovereignty in the ongoing, daily concourse of life in the world.

By and large, Reformed piety functions in an absence of prescribed forms that might otherwise signal its presence. Once again, it tends to operate in relationship to principles rather than rules. As a result, it has the outward appearance of a rather secular or worldly piety, especially to those who are inclined to see the world divided into spheres of the sacred as over against the profane.[14]

The following paragraphs were written to address the issue of Christian vocation. I offer them here because they also provide helpful insight as to why Reformed piety is so easily unrecognized in a culture that has increasingly come to assume that spiritual activity is by definition inward, individual, and essentially otherworldly.

> The work to which God calls us is not distinctively Christian. In fact, there is no distinctively Christian work. The work to which God calls us is the work that is available to every human being. A Christian work may be any work that enhances human life, serves human needs, and glorifies the Creator. Christians for the most part do the same work that non-Christians do. The difference is not in the work but in the faith, in the disposition, and in the sense of accountability that Christians bring to the task. Christians do their work as those who trust in God: that is, as those who know that the final salvation of life is not in their work but in God. Hence Christians can do their work without falling, on the one

hand, into despair or, on the other hand, into a fanaticism that takes work too seriously. The Christian knows that, in the end, as we commit our persons to the care of God, we also have to commit unto God's care the work that we do.

Christians are distinguished by the disposition they bring to their work . . . [and] . . . the Christian conviction that one's work is a vocation: that is, a calling.[15]

Reformed piety experiences the Christian's life as one completely dependent on the work of the Holy Spirit, who bestows faith, creates an inward disposition of helpfulness to the neighbor, and empowers the will to act accountably toward God, all of which serve to further its proper end, which is not simply obedience as such but rather, through obedience, the transformation of life for the whole person.

Since setting aside one's own self-interest in preference to the neighbor's good can never be a matter of personal achievement, all human accomplishment, even that which has the appearance of being noteworthy or good, may be viewed with a healthy skepticism, and all human plans and projections tend to be relegated to the realm of the subjunctive: "if God be willing" or "if the way be clear." In this regard Bullinger's vision of the ideal commonwealth is instructive. His city, he says, would be a place "wherein the word of God . . . is . . . obeyed, so far forth as it pleaseth God to give the gift of grace."[16]

The fact that this essay has emphasized the outward, active, or "wordly" shape of Reformed piety should not be construed to imply that this tradition has not embraced its specifically religious aspects as well, for it has, and does. Reformed religious life has always been consciously rooted in the Scriptures and historically centered upon keeping the Sabbath as a day devoted entirely to public worship, prayer, and "holy conversations." The means by which grace ordinarily infuses the Christian's life are through the biblical Word, the sacraments, and prayer. Any other extraordinary means of grace are simply that: *extraordinary* and not, therefore, normative for Reformed religious practice. Calvin affirmed that prayer "is the chief exercise of faith," and the prominence accorded prayer helps explain the central place of the Psalter in Reformed worship and devotional life, since the Psalms have from the beginning been understood by Reformed Christians as the people's prayer par excellence. In their scriptural or metrical versions, the psalms, together with the stately tunes to which they were early set, are clearly the heart and soul of Reformed piety.

In an earlier age, the practice of self-examination as a means of uncovering one's own self-deceptions and propensities to sin (as preparation and prelude to the Spirit's indwelling and empowerment to action) played an important role in personal devotional life. During this century, however, self-examination—even the traditional services of self-examination in preparation for receiving the sacrament—has increasingly fallen into disuse, if it has not disappeared altogether from Presbyterian piety. Self-examination, along with private prayer and the study of Scripture, are virtually the only individual acts of religion enjoined by the several Reformers; and even when engaged in these ways, it was clearly understood that the individual did so as a member of the larger community, responsible to it and for its religious life.

No better summary of Reformed piety can be found than the one Calvin himself provided when he declared that "the sum of the Christian life is the denial of ourselves." And what Calvin meant by this self-denial is that

> we are not our own: let not our reason nor our will, therefore sway our plans and deeds. We are not our own: let us therefore not set it as our goal to seek what is expedient for us according to the flesh. We are not our own: in so far as we can, let us therefore forget ourselves, and all that is ours.
>
> Conversely, we are God's: let us therefore live for him and die for him. We are God's: let his wisdom and will therefore rule all our actions. We are God's: let all the parts of our life accordingly strive toward him as our only lawful Goal.[17]

The Lord's Song in a Strange Land

Perhaps now the issue briefly alluded to earlier should be raised again. That is, what particular experiences and activities are useful and helpful to shape and strengthen persons to affirm and practice this particular Reformed expression of piety? And the answer, I trust, has already begun to emerge: an active and wholehearted commitment to the community of faith that recognizes, values, articulates, encourages, and itself practices this kind of Christian life, both *in* the world and *for* the glory of God. Which is also to say that Reformed Christians are not necessarily, nor will they be adequately, formed spiritually solely through the performance of any prescribed set of individual exercises of a religious (or whatever) sort, and perhaps less so by their involvement in even socially useful tasks, when this activity is uninformed by the shared faith and disposition that alone imparts to any work its Christian character. Still less likely, I might add, would it seem that a distinctively Reformed piety should take shape and emerge from the various interior quests for self-help therapies that have become so characteristic of (what purports to be) "new age" religion.

What this says, simply, is that Reformed Christians are typically and ordinarily shaped in a Reformed ethos, and that they become this kind of Christian by an ongoing participation in this particular matrix of Christian experience. And while acknowledging that at first glance this may well seem little more than a truism, it is nonetheless profoundly true. At least it is true, and obvious, to persons who find covenant theology compelling. Yet this response, I'm afraid, is no exception to the general rule in that it, like most answers to theological questions, only serves to raise other questions that are knottier and more difficult still. For instance:

What happens to Reformed piety (which developed as response to a society in which Church and commonwealth were mutually inclusive) when Church and State are "separate," or faith and culture are at cross-purposes? Or where the prevailing ethos is no longer Protestant, or even Christian, in its orientation, and where individualism and self-interest groups obscure any sense of common societal or moral values? In other words, how does a Presbyterian manage to live in terms of Reformed commitments and values in the America we increasingly know today?

And the response to this can only be, with some difficulty, and with a great deal of intentionality, and only by the grace of God within the sustaining fellowship of the Church. Given the circumstances, a Reformed piety simply will not come about in any other way. A useful and helpful life lived for neighbor and for God is not an expression of Christian faith calculated to win approval or reward in any age, and certainly not in our day and time—and this in spite of much current rhetoric to the contrary. Moreover, this piety demands a degree of self-denial quite at odds with now-established values of self-affirmation and so is a way of life with which all too many of us are unfamiliar and for which, consequently, we are unprepared.

Still, difficult circumstances are precisely those for which Reformed faith has repeatedly proven itself peculiarly fitted to equip persons to face and surmount. And besides, God has never required his servants to be popular or successful, only faithful, and his promised Spirit is powerful and available to that end.

When Robert Bellah and his associates made their landmark study of the American character, they outlined the long struggle between our "biblical and republican" traditions of communal obligations and our inherent and growing thrust toward (what they called) "ontological individualism." After five years of intense investigation, Bellah's analysis and prescription for American life sounds much like Reformed convictions that several hundred years earlier had taken root in the biblical word:

> Social ecology is damaged not only by war, genocide, and political repression. It is also damaged by the destruction of the subtle ties that bind human beings to one another, leaving them frightened and alone. . . . We have committed what to the republican founders of our nation was the cardinal sin: We have put our own good, as individuals, as groups, as a nation, ahead of the common good. . . . Personal transformation among large numbers is essential, and it must not only be transformation of consciousness but also involve individual action. But individuals need the nurture of groups that carry a moral tradition reinforcing their own aspirations.[18]

Their study concludes with a suggestion of what our life, if ordered by a different set of values, might possibly become:

> Perhaps life is not a race whose only goal is being foremost. Perhaps true felicity does not lie in continually outgoing the next before. Perhaps the truth lies in what most of the world outside the modern West has always believed, namely that there are practices of life, good in themselves, that are inherently fulfilling. Perhaps work that is intrinsically rewarding is better for human beings than work that is only extrinsically rewarded. Perhaps enduring commitment to those we love and civic friendship toward our fellow citizens are preferable to restless competition and anxious self-defense. Perhaps common worship, in which we express our gratitude and wonder in the face of the mystery of being itself, is the most important thing of all. If so, we will have to change our lives and begin to remember what we have been happier to forget.
> We will need to remember that we did not create ourselves, that we owe what we are to the communities that formed us, and to what Paul Tillich called "the structure of grace in history" that made such communities possible.[19]

Not a vision with the clarity and conviction of Bullinger's ideal commonwealth, to be sure, but nonetheless one in which Reformed Christians may recognize in tentative terms the goal toward which their God beckons and their piety impels.

Notes

1. The World Alliance of Reformed Churches currently includes 157 different denominations that identify themselves as standing within the Reformed tradition of Protestant Christianity. These churches are located in seventy-seven countries and comprise roughly a fourth of all Protestants (i.e., non–Roman Catholic and non–Orthodox Christians) in the world. There are more Presbyterians today in Indonesia than in North America.
2. Richard Kieckhefer, "Major Currents in Late Medieval Devotion," in *High Middle Ages and the Reformation*, vol. 2 of *Christian Spirituality*, ed. Jill Raitt (New York: Crossroad, 1987), p. 75.
3. Fritz Busser, "The Spirituality of Zwingli and Bullinger in the Reformation of Europe," in Raitt, *Christian Spirituality*, p. 301.
4. Ibid., p. 313.
5. Honesty compels the acknowledgement that no more so than Roman Catholic theology is Reformed theology a seamless garment, all of one piece. Over the years some of the most bitter arguments of Reformed theologians have been among themselves. The cluster of emphases noted here seems *to me* to be those that give Reformed theology its distinctive character on the American scene today.
6. In 1788 the Presbyterian General Assembly adopted five "subscription" formulae, framed as questions, to which candidates for ministry were required to give their assent as a condition for ordination. These questions, in their original form, continued in use among Presbyterians until the mid–twentieth century, and the phrase quoted here is taken from the first of them.
7. For a detailed substantiation of the proposition that the dogma of inerrancy was the product of seventeenth-century Protestant scholasticism, which was falsely equated with classical Reformed orthodoxy by the nineteenth-century Princeton Seminary theologians, see Jack Roger and Donald McKim, *The Authority and Interpretation of the Bible* (San Francisco: Harper & Row, 1979).
8. Reformed theology has traditionally resisted the notion that the Bible is the Christian's only source of truth, even about God. Scripture, reason, human experience, and the natural order are all sources of God's truth for humankind, and this truth becomes authoritative for Christians when the various truths gained from each of these sources converge, reinforcing and amplifying the others, so as to make "the truth" persuasive and compelling.
9. Calvin's prayer, intended for students to pray each day before going to school, sets the learning experience in the context of their own Christian vocation in which the "proper end" of an education is to know God in Christ, and everything learned should lead to godliness:

O Lord, who art the fountain of all wisdom and learning, since thou of thy special goodness hast granted that my youth is instructed in good arts which may assist me to honest and holy living, grant also, by enlightening my mind, which otherwise labors under blindness, that I may be fit to acquire knowledge; strengthen my memory faithfully to retain what I may have learned: and govern my heart, that I may be willing and even eager to profit, lest the opportunity which thou now givest me be lost through my sluggishness. Be pleased therefore to infuse thy Spirit into me, the Spirit of understanding, of truth, judgment, and prudence, lest my study be without success, and the labor of my teacher be in vain.

In whatever kind of study I engage, enable me to remember to keep its proper end in view, namely, to know thee in Christ Jesus thy Son; and may everything that I learn assist me to observe the right rule of godliness. And seeing thou promisest that thou wilt bestow wisdom on babes, and such as are humble, and the knowledge of thyself on the upright in heart, while thou declarest that thou wilt cast down the wicked and the proud, so that they will fade away in their ways, I entreat that thou wouldst be pleased to turn me to true humility, that thus I may show myself teachable and obedient first of all to thyself, and then to those also who by thy authority are placed over me. Be pleased at the same time to root out all vicious desires from my heart, and inspire it with an earnest desire of seeking thee. Finally, let the only end at which I aim be so to qualify myself in early life, that when I grow up I may serve thee in whatever station thou mayest assign me. Amen. (*Calvin's Tracts,* vol. 2, trans. Henry Beveridge. [Edinburgh: The Calvin Translation Society, 1881], quoted in *The Christian Life,* ed. John H. Leith [San Francisco: Harper & Row, 1984], pp. 80-81.)

10. For those who might be interested, there follows a complete listing of the interpretive principles that, according to the Westminster divines, should be observed regarding the Ten Commandments. They appear as the Larger Catechism's answer to question 99:

For the right understanding of the ten commandments, these rules are to be observed:
1. That the law is perfect, and bindeth everyone to full conformity in the whole man unto the righteousness thereof, and unto entire obedience forever; so as to require the utmost perfection of every duty, and to forbid the least degree of every sin.
2. That it is spiritual, and so reacheth the understanding, will, affections, and all other powers of the soul; as well as words, works, and gestures.
3. That one and the same thing, in divers respects, is required or forbidden in several commandments.
4. That as, where a duty is commanded, the contrary sin is forbidden; and where a sin is forbidden, the contrary duty is commanded: so, where a promise is annexed, the contrary threatening is included; and where a threatening is annexed, the contrary promise is included.
5. That what God forbids, is at no time to be done; what he commands is always our duty; and yet every particular duty is not to be done at all times.
6. That under one sin or duty, all of the same kind are forbidden or commanded; together with all the causes, means, occasions and appearances thereof, and provocations thereunto.
7. That what is forbidden or commanded to ourselves, we are bound, according to our places, to endeavor that it may be avoided or performed by others, according to the duty of their places.
8. That in what is commanded to others, we are bound, according to our places and callings, to be helpful to them; and to take heed of partaking with others in what is forbidden them. (*The Larger Catechism, Our Confessional Heritage* [Atlanta: Materials Distribution Service, 1978], p. 115.)

11. The Presbyterian Church (U.S.A.). *The Constitution of the Presbyterian Church (U.S.A.). Part 1, Book of Confessions* (New York: Office of the General Assembly, 1983), pp. 7.232-.239–7.240-.246. Capitalizations altered in places.

12. A colleague has made the suggestive observation that one way Reformed piety may be understood is as the paradoxical triumph of the Western monastic ideal. Though rejected as such by the Reformers, monasticism's seriousness and intentionality as a way of life was appropriated by the Reformers in a new, democratized and secularized form, and then universalized as the norm for the entire Reformed Christian community.

13. On the biblical concept of "righteousness," see the excellent article on this subject by Elizabeth Achtemeier in *The Interpreter's Dictionary of the Bible,* vol. 4, ed. G. A. Buttrick et al. (Nashville: Abingdon Press, 1962), pp. 80-85.

14. A classic example of Reformed piety alive and well in a secular context may be found in this story included in an address by Robert Maynard Hutchins and delivered on July 5, 1969: "There was a famous dark day in New England in 1780 when the sun scarcely appeared at all. Thousands of people took it for the end of the world. Among them were many in the Connecticut Assembly, in which Col. Abraham

Davenport was sitting. It was proposed that the Assembly adjourn. Col. Davenport said, 'The Day of Judgment is either approaching or it is not. If it is not, there is no cause for adjournment. If it is, I choose to be found doing my duty. I wish, therefore, that candles be brought.'"

15. John H. Leith, *The Reformed Imperative* (Philadelphia: Westminster Press, 1988), pp. 94-95.
16. Busser, "The Spirituality of Zwingli," p. 313.
17. John T. McNeill, ed., *Calvin: The Institutes of the Christian Religion*, III .7 .1, *The Library of Christian Classics*, vol. 20 (Philadelphia: Westminister Press, 1960), p. 690.
18. Robert N. Bellah, *Habits of the Heart* (New York: Harper & Row, 1985), pp. 284-86.
19. Ibid., p. 295.

Bibliography

Baxter, Richard. *The Reformed Pastor*. Richmond, Va.: John Knox Press, 1963.

Brainerd, David. *The Life of David Brainerd*. Grand Rapids, Mich.: Baker Books, Summit, 1978.

Bunyan, John. *The Pilgrim's Progress*. Nashville: Cokesbury Press, 1963.

Calvin, John. *Institutes of the Christian Religion*. Vol. 3 of *Library of Christian Classics*, edited by John T. McNeill. Philadelphia: Westminster Press, 1960.

Hallie, Philip Paul. *Lest Innocent Blood Be Shed*. New York: Harper & Row, 1979.

The Psalms of David in Metre. According to the Version Approved by The Church of Scotland and Appointed to Be Used in Worship. London: Oxford University Press, n.d.

Stated Clerk of the General Assembly of the Presbyterian Church in the United States. *Our Confessional Heritage*. Atlanta: Materials Distribution Service, 1978: "The Westminster Shorter Catechism," pp. 141-50; "A Declaration of Faith," pp. 157-80.

Recovering Faithfulness in Our Callings

DOUGLAS F. OTTATI

We are not our own: in so far as we can, let us therefore forget ourselves and all that is ours. . . . We are God's: let us therefore live for him and die for him. We are God's: let his wisdom and will therefore rule all our actions.

—JOHN CALVIN

This famous passage from John Calvin's *Institutes of the Christian Religion* (above) communicates an essential feature of Reformed piety. In this tradition, piety is an attitude of reverence and love of God, which entails duties and responsibilities. It does not refer to a segregated portion of life labeled "religious" but to life as a whole. Thus in the authentic practice of Reformed piety, worship and work are inextricably connected.

Piety and Worship

Reformed services of worship typically call forth a variety of emotional responses, or "sensibilities," in the worshiper.[1] For example, Scripture readings and sermons may evoke a wide range of pious sensibilities. Likewise, hymns of praise and prayers of adoration evoke sensibilities of mystery, awe, wonder, and reverence at the One who holds all things in existence. Humility at our faults and shortcomings is expressed by corporate prayers of confession, while prayers of thanksgiving voice gratitude to the One "from whom cometh every good and perfect gift"—whose goodness creates us, whose bounty sustains us, whose discipline corrects us, and whose love redeems us.[2]

What sometimes goes unnoticed, however, is that impulses and dispositions like these have to do with both worship and work, prayer and performance. This concern for linking prayer with the ordinary activities of life comes through, for example, in the Reformed practice of sometimes including the Ten Commandments within the services of worship. According to *The Book of Common Worship* of the United Presbyterian Church in the United States of America (1946), the "Order of the Commandments" may stand as an independent service, an introduction to Holy Communion, or within morning or evening worship. It begins with a short litany and a prayer by the pastor asking God to cleanse our hearts. Then all Ten Commandments are read, the people responding to each with "Lord have mercy upon us, and incline our hearts to keep this law." Following a reading of Jesus' summary of the Law from the Gospel of Matthew, the Order concludes with a Prayer of Confession and an Assurance of Pardon.[3]

In its acknowledgment of sin and request for forgiveness, the Order of the Commandments expresses the axiom of Reformed theology that people tend to be curved in upon themselves, that they put their trust in things other than God, that they suffer from misdirected desires, that they engage in acts of disobedience, and that only the grace of God can save them from ruin. In this way it integrates prayer with senses of wonder, gratitude, repentance, and obligation. These affectivities join worship to life because they engender a faithfulness equally at home in worship and work, in sanctuaries, in commercial transactions, in courtrooms, and in family relationships.

All of this stands in marked contrast to the persistent tendency to think of religion as essentially a series of intensely private experiences, as well as to the more common assumption that the sum total of religion amounts to churchgoing and prayer saying. From a Reformed perspective, popular understandings of spirituality as the search for interior wholeness are seriously flawed, and one ought to be very concerned to know what Sunday morning has to do with the rest of the week. The normal concern of worship is not some specially holy compartment of life but a faithfulness that has its place in midstream.[4]

Faithfulness as Service

Faithfulness means devotion to the reign of God, made known through Israel and disclosed with compelling clarity in Jesus Christ. Historically, Reformed Christians have believed that God orders human life in and through God's universal reign in the world, and that Jesus Christ marks off a way of living correspondent to this reign and characterized by love of God and neighbor. In light of the covenant metaphor, we might say that people respond to God's reign—or that they participate in it—by serving God in their relationships with others. In Pauline terms, faithful followers of Jesus Christ ought to do what is helpful and what builds up (I Cor. 10:23). We ought to look not only to our own interests but also to the interests of others (Phil. 4:2). Near the heart or center of the devout life, there should be a posture or stance of attentiveness to the neighbor. The disposition of Reformed piety is to serve God in the midst of things by attending to the welfare of others.

The traditional idea of calling or vocation underscores this disposition to serve and gives it direction. One is called, says Calvin, not only to respond to God but also to a "kind of living assigned . . . by the Lord as a sort of sentry post."[5] A calling is a particular way of service set by some line (or lines) of relationship and responsibility in which one stands. English Puritans made use of this and other ideas in books of "practical divinity" designed to set forth the marks of Christian spirituality by instructing believers in the conduct of their daily lives. Richard Baxter, who became an immensely popular writer, penned advice for husbands and fathers, wives and mothers, children, servants, magistrates, soldiers, teachers, and more. Selected features of his counsel to physicians may serve as an illustration of what we mean by a "calling."

Baxter says from the outset that he has no intention of intermeddling with the subtleties of medical art. His purpose is only to tell physicians "very briefly, what God and conscience will expect from them." According to Baxter, the particular line of service in which a physician stands has "the saving of men's lives and health" as its chief responsibility. Thus where personal gain and professional honor become the physician's first intention, the physician serves not God and the public good but an isolated personal interest. It follows, then, that a primary test of faithfulness is whether a physician helps the poor as well as those who are able to pay. Moreover, where physicians reach the limits of their skills, pride should not prevent them from advising their patients "to use the help of other, abler physicians, if there be any to be had." Finally, due to the "abstruse and conjectural" character of the medical profession, only those possessed of natural strength of intellect and wisdom, significant reading, a great deal of acquaintance with the techniques of able physicians, and considerable experience of their own should venture to practice medicine.[6]

Whether we are called to be a physician, a parent, or a plumber, the general point is that piety as faithfulness amounts to faithful service of God by attending to the welfare of others. Since this is the case, we should take care to see that we are adequately prepared for the particular line of service in question. Care must be taken also that our efforts do not degenerate into a sinful striving after self-aggrandizement. Given, then, the specific skills and responsibilities of a particular calling—in this case, medicine—certain general directives follow, for example, "Be ready to commit yourself to long hours of study and to provide medical care to the poor."

Recovering Faithful Service Today

The metaphor of service has fallen upon hard times. Isolated individualism encourages us to fashion personal identities detached from loyalties to anything larger than self. In the marketplace, an ideology of wholly unrestrained competition too often loses sight of the common good. Similarly, reductive understandings of the professions sometimes sacrifice all other values to technical competence. In this climate, many Americans regard their careers as little more than avenues for self-advancement, popular media often portray interpersonal relationships as vehicles of individual fulfillment, and perennial scandals surrounding leadership in high places lend negative meanings to public service.

Neither have the churches proved especially resistant to the prevailing ethos. Evidences abound: the retreat structured like an encounter group, in which some theme of personal enrichment becomes the exclusive end of spirituality; the sermon that amounts to self-serving psychotherapy; prayers that promise that Christian believing will ensure individual fulfillment; the conspicuous pursuit of wealth by certain televangelists; and so on. In sum, we are in danger of losing any meaningful appreciation of faithfulness in our callings.

From the perspective of the Reformed tradition, our growing inability to construe the lines of relationship and responsibility in which we stand as sources of personal identity as well as particular vectors of service indicates a serious constriction of heart and lapse of vision. Contemporary "me-ism," with its glorification of isolated individual interests and fulfillment, amounts to a tendency toward inordinate self-love. Moreover, this tendency is promoted by a privatization of religion that begins by segregating piety from politics and business and ends by restricting it to an interior, quasi-mystical quest for individual meaning.[7]

The enlargement of our hearts toward God and neighbor is not something that we can accomplish on our own. Indeed, it waits upon an engendering deed and the affecting presence in our experience of a considerably greater Power than the theological essay. From a

Reformed perspective, the power of regeneration or renewal is the power of God in Christ. Assuming the possibility of some heartfelt enlargement, however, we can explore here how some of the particular relationships in which we stand may be envisioned as callings or lines of service.

Let us begin with our families. Parents of young children ordinarily receive a crash course in what it means to care for entirely dependent creatures. Grown children often feel especially obligated to attend to the welfare of those who brought them into the world and raised them. In these and other ways, then, we begin to see that our families are systems of interdependent relations. Participation in a family calls us to live faithfully in the midst of responsibilities and to serve not only ourselves but also the welfare of a wider community.

Three additional points need mentioning. First, it is a matter of moral importance that fathers and mothers try to be good parents, that they develop their abilities to procure the material resources that their families need, that they heighten their abilities to discern when a child or a spouse needs special attention. It is also important that they learn to plan some time for their children to be with other children, for the children to be with their parents alone, and for themselves apart from the children. Why? Because in the economy of God's world, there are others whose well-being depends upon parents' cultivating these skills and habits in themselves. Thus the same theo-logic that encourages us to attend to others also encourages us to attend appropriately to ourselves.

Second, though faithfulness in our calling as parents requires that we be ready to qualify and even deny some of our isolated interests and needs, it may also furnish profound joys. There are, of course, no guarantees here. We all know that genuine attentiveness to the welfare of families cannot avert tragedy. What attentiveness does promise, however, is a sharing in tribulations and trials as well as in triumphs and joys, which may precipitate a reevaluation of what it means to lead a human life.

Third, members of families typically participate in more than one calling or line of responsibility. One may, for example, be both a mother and a physician, both a husband and a son, both a daughter and a student. The competing claims of our varied callings can become quite difficult to negotiate. So yet another matter of moral importance is how one develops a style of living, a set of habits and skills, that helps to faithfully balance multiple responsibilities and claims.

Once we get past the simplistic rhetoric of "looking out for Number One," it will be evident that similar things may be said about participating in various lines of employment. For example, the specific line of service in which auto mechanics stands entails special skills and responsibilities, because other people depend upon mechanics for sound automotive repairs at a fair price. Where personal gain becomes a mechanic's sole intention, there are ample opportunities to take unfair advantage of persons whose vehicles suffer untimely break-downs by making unnecessary repairs and doing shoddy work. At the same time, within our present society an auto mechanic has a responsibility to operate at a profit in order to stay in business and to continue to offer automotive repairs as a public service. Moreover, since mechanics also stand in other relationships of responsibility—say, as parents or as providers for aging relatives—it is also a matter of moral importance that they make enough money to furnish sufficient material resources for the well-being of their dependents.

Faithfulness and Institutions

Many discussions of calling or vocation end right here, and when they do, a critical matter falls by the wayside. Not only persons but also institutions participate in distinctive lines of responsibility. Schools, hospitals, symphony orchestras, corporations, labor unions, neigh-borhood associations, legislatures—all have particular purposes-in-service. Thus the distinctive purpose of a school is to provide opportunities for education by pursuing knowledge and understand-ing. This chief responsibility helps to shape the ethos, divisions of labor, administrative practices, and patterns of behavior appropriate to a school. By contrast, the chief responsibility of a modern corporation is to contribute to the material well-being of the human community by producing goods or services in a way that makes a profit.[8] This is why, although there are common characteristics of good administration, schools shouldn't be run exactly like businesses, and businesses shouldn't be run exactly like schools. The styles of leadership and patterns of interaction appropriate to schools and businesses differ because their immediate purposes and lines of service differ. Similarly, the skills required of a good teacher are not exactly the same as those required of a good executive.

If we fail to faithfully envision the varied institutions in which we participate and their particular lines of service, we concede public life to disorder or, what is more likely, to an order that serves something other than God and God's reign. Piety needs to see, for example, that something as mundane as an insurance company has special and weighty responsibilities to its policyholders, its investors, and its employees. The service it offers its policyholders helps them to participate more freely and effectively in their own economic affairs and also in the affairs of the wider society. So I may insure my life in order to attend to certain aspects of my family's welfare (e.g., the future education of my children), without hoarding income that my family presently needs for other purposes: bicycles, furniture, straightening teeth, or a trip to grandmother's house.

An insurance company's ability to provide these and like services to the public depends upon its ability to earn money, to reinvest some portion of its earnings in operations, to meet its payroll, and to furnish its shareholders (including everything from private investors to pension funds) with a solid return on their investments. Moreover, if the company fails, then the financial affairs of not only policyholders but also employees and shareholders are thrown into disarray. Providing customers with good-quality products and services in a manner that earns money is the primary way in which many corporations faithfully serve others. And just as the faithful services of physicians and mechanics require that they attend to the development of skills and capabilities in themselves, so the faithful services rendered by corporations and other institutions require that they engage in self-improving and maintenance functions.

Restraining Corruption and Furthering Faithfulness

Parents are often faithful in their callings because they naturally invest so much of themselves and their hopes in their children. Positive as this may be, it also means that self-serving impulses may find a ready foothold. Even the most well-meaning parent may sometimes be led to envision his or her children merely as extensions of parental desires and ambitions.

Again, human needs for accomplishment and recognition often spur ambitious professionals to acquire needed skills. Inordinate self-concern in the guise of professional reputation and achievement may therefore infect the hearts and priorities of even the most committed professors and physicians.

Varied tendencies toward corruption are also present in the lives of institutions. A school animated by profound traditions of rigorous inquiry may foster skewed commitments to academic achievement that distort the personal lives of its students and faculty. Corporations may push beyond the disciplined and strenuous pursuit of profit to engender and require an idolatrous love of monetary gain and success, which brings a train of evil consequences. Congregations and even entire denominations may become so focused upon survival that they lose sight of a vital witness to God's reign in the world. Moreover, in the absence of clearly articulated standards of right and wrong, people in government, business, education, and so on may become satisfied with mere legality or even with whatever is strategic or efficient.[9]

Recognizing, then, that our callings present manifold opportunities for both corruption and service and that the power to change hearts rests finally with a reality greater than ourselves, Reformed Protestantism typically has sought to restrain evil and promote good by two related strategies. One strategy is *the way of education and persuasion,* which takes place within a developing tradition. An example is study that acquaints people with the stories, themes, and literatures of the Bible. Another is the practice of instructing young people in catechisms that include theological and moral teachings. Yet another is the Puritan sermon, which often moved from the exposition of a biblical text, through the statement of a doctrine, to an application in life about truth telling, aiding the poor, child rearing, using time wisely, and so on.[10]

Again, Richard Baxter and others regarded the literature of "practical divinity" as an extension of both preaching and pastoral care. Some of the didactic functions of this literature have been taken up in more recent times by denominational study papers about sexuality and the family, Christian faith and economics, war and military service, and the like. Beginning with the nineteenth century, "special pastoral care" in the form of intentional conversations between minister and parishioner was also introduced.[11] The liturgical use of prayers of adoration and confession, thanksgiving and intercession, the Order of the Commandments, and so on, is another powerful practice. Neither should one neglect the considerable importance of Christian fellowship as well as the effects of engaging in projects of Christian service to the wider community and the world. Practices such as these may be understood in part as efforts to educate and incline persons toward faithful service in God's world.

A second strategy is *the way of institutional construction and reformation.* Over time, and particularly in America, Reformed Christians have learned to structure social relations in accordance with three related and dynamic principles.[12]

The *covenantal principle* institutionalizes clear statements of commonly accepted and mutual responsibilities. One example is the insistence upon constitutional frameworks that spell out and apportion the prerogatives and responsibilities of government in both political and ecclesiastical communities. Another example is the contract that specifies the mutual obligations of parties to a business transaction. But the marriage service furnishes the most moving and effective illustration. Here the bride and groom make a public pledge "in all love and honor, in all duty and service, in all faith and tenderness," to live with and to cherish one another "according to the ordinance of God, in the holy bond of marriage." Then the minister leads each in the following vow:

> I, N., take thee, N.; to be my wedded wife (or husband); And I do promise and covenant; Before God and these witnesses; To be thy loving and faithful husband (or wife); In plenty and in want; in joy and in sorrow; In sickness and in health; As long as we both shall live.[13]

With these words, it becomes clear that the basic point of marriage is neither increased individual freedom nor isolated individual fulfillment, but something more profound. Moreover, covenantal agreements such as these serve to guide appropriately faithful conduct as well as to illumine acts of disobedience and betrayal.

The *principle of participation and the limitation of power* is closely associated with covenantal thinking. It assumes that genuine participation in decision making enhances the development in persons of skills and talents needed for faithful service. It also assumes that perennial human tendencies toward self-aggrandizement and injustice are enhanced by concentrations of power in the hands of a few. For these reasons, Reformed Christianity traditionally has favored representative political structures that include appropriate checks and balances upon the exercise of power. An example is the representative structure of American democracy and its division of power between legislative, executive, and judicial branches of government. Another example is the Presybterian form of government, which divides power among congregational sessions, presbyteries, synods, and the General Assembly, as representative courts of the church.[14] Historically, the principle of participation and the limitation of power has been applied in various forms, not only to states and churches but also to educational institutions and business corporations. It seems wise to disperse power within colleges, universities, and seminaries among boards of trustees, administrations, faculty, and students. Somewhat similarly, responsible corporate polity entails structures of shared power and decision making as well as the participation of labor in setting guidelines for policy.[15]

Finally, the *principle of plurality* affirms the relative independence of basic institutions and their distinctive lines of service. Church and

State, for example, are appropriately separate. Negatively, this keeps the State from having exclusive control over popular bases for the legitimacy of its authority and its practices in the religious and moral visions of its citizens. It also ensures that religious associations will not depart from the way of education and persuasion by wielding civic power. Positively, the separation of Church and State allows the basic functions of piety and civil government to receive the undivided attention and expertise of distinct institutions. Similarly, the merging of corporate business with either Church or State would confuse distinctive lines of service and encourage inordinate concentrations of power. Independent charters, endowments, governing boards, and boards of trustees help to ensure the relative independence and integrity of private, public, and church-affiliated institutions of higher education.

Reformed piety refers human life as a whole to God's reign. Called forth and expressed in worship and work, it is molded to the form of faithfulness displayed in Israel and in Jesus Christ. It therefore issues in a manner of living that attaches religious importance not only to inward passion but also to the faithful service of individuals and institutions. While to some people this way of being Christian may appear mundane or even unspiritual, it has profound roots in the apprehension that we—and all that is ours—belong to the One who rules all things. Where this apprehension holds sway, people will be disposed toward the faithful ordering of all of life under God.

EXERCISES

For an Individual

Especially in its Puritan strand, the Reformed tradition developed the practice of keeping diaries or journals as a way of self-examination. This practice helped persons monitor their devotional lives and bring to mind how they were providentially guided and upheld. But it also helped them recollect what they had done, ask whether and how they had faithfully discharged their callings, and, where needed, amend their ways. You may wish to keep such a diary of your own for a period of time to see whether this practice is helpful to you as an aid for examining your own efforts to be faithful in your callings. Alternatively, you may prefer to pause for fifteen minutes or so at the end of the week in order to recollect ways in which you have handled varied lines of responsibility over the past seven days and to anticipate occasions for faithful service in the week ahead.

For a Group

Option One

Sensibilities and dispositions essential for faithfulness are both formed and expressed in worship and in prayer. Review together the order of worship used by your congregation. How do its various elements both shape and express pious sensibilities that refer to worship and work? How do your family and personal prayers (e.g., mealtime blessings) express this dual concern?

Option Two

In the same vein, consider the Order of the Commandments in *The Book of Common Worship* of the United Presbyterian Church in the United States of America (1946), pages 115-18. How do the Ten Commandments in Exodus 20 and Deuteronomy 5 evoke piety as faithfulness? How do they connect devotion to God with responsibilities in the world? How do some of the commandments relate to basic relationships and institutions in human social life? What long-term effects—on each member of the group and on the congregation as a whole—would you anticipate, were the Order of the Commandments to be used in public worship on a regular basis?[16]

Option Three

One feature of modern life, with its characteristic separation of the home from the marketplace and its specialization of lines of employment, is that people often have little acquaintance with the specific challenges and demands of one another's callings. You may wish to take a friend or family member along with you to work for a day or portion of a day and discuss his or her impressions. Persons who work outside the home may benefit from spending a day discharging the many and varied domestic responsibilities that must be attended to there and later discussing the experience with other members of the group.

DISCUSSION QUESTIONS

1. Talk about some of the relationships of interdependence in which you stand: family, peer group, neighborhood, school, nation, television viewing, reading the newspaper, gainful employment.

How may these be envisioned as callings or lines of service? What habits and skills need to be cultivated if one is to render faithful service in these callings? How may these callings become occasions for corruption? Younger people may wish to discuss not only present relationships but also those in which they may participate in the future.

2. There is no simple formula for balancing the competing claims of the varied lines of service in which we participate, such as caring for children and keeping up with brothers, sisters, parents, and friends, or running an efficient, profitable business and spending time with one's family. How do you and/or members of your group handle the competing claims of multiple callings in daily life? How does an appropriate balancing of these claims express faithfulness to God?

3. Discuss some institution(s) other than the congregation in which you and/or other members of the group participate. What are the primary lines of responsibility of these institutions? How may they become occasions for corruption? What institutional checks and balances safeguard against corruption?

Notes

1. James M. Gustafson discusses senses of dependence, gratitude, repentance, obligation, possibility, and direction in *Can Ethics Be Christian?* (Chicago: University of Chicago Press, 1975), pp. 91-114.
2. *The Book of Common Worship* (Philadelphia: The Board of Christian Education of the United Presbyterian Church in the United States of America, 1946), pp. 11-15.
3. Ibid., pp. 115-18.
4. Robert Lowry Calhoun, *God and the Day's Work* (New York: Association Press, 1943), pp. 7-16. Richard R. Niebuhr includes an illuminating discussion of faithfulness in *Experiential Religion* (New York: Harper & Row, 1972), pp. 25, 36-50.
5. John Calvin, *Institutes of the Christian Religion*, ed. John T. McNeill (Philadelphia: Westminster Press, 1960), book 3, chap. 10, sec. 6.
6. Richard Baxter, *The Practical Works of Richard Baxter,* vol. 1 (London: Henry G. Bohn, 1854), pp. 771-72.
7. An enormous literature deals with individualism and quests for self-fulfillment in modern society. Philip Reiff's *The Triumph of the Therapeutic: Uses of Faith After Freud* (New York: Harper & Row, 1966), pp. 1-107, 232-61, continues to be an important discussion. *Habits of the Heart: Individualism and Commitment in American Life*, by Robert N. Bellah et al. (Berkeley: University of California Press, 1985), is a wide-ranging recent treatment. A helpful discussion of modern religion and identity is Thomas Luckmann's *The Invisible Religion: The Problem of Religion in Modern Society* (New York: Macmillan, 1967). A more recent interpretation of the immediate historical background and current shape of the quest for self-fulfillment in American religion is found in Wade Clark Roof and William McKinney, *American Mainline Religion: Its Changing Shape and Future* (New Brunswick, N.J.: Rutgers University Press, 1987), pp. 11-71.
8. Max L. Stackhouse, *Public Theology and Political Economy: Christian Stewardship in Modern Society* (Grand Rapids, Mich.: Eerdmans, 1987), pp. 133-34.
9. Ibid., p. 134.

10. See William Haller's discussion in "The Rhetoric of the Spirit," chap. 4 of his study *The Rise of Puritanism or, The Way to the New Jerusalem as Set Forth in Pulpit and Press from Thomas Carwright to John Lilburne and John Milton* (New York: Harper & Brothers, 1957), pp. 128-72. See also sermons and occasional essays by Jonathan Edwards in *The Works of Jonathan Edwards,* vol. 2 (Carlisle, Penn.: Banner of Truth Trust, 1974), pp. 130-277.
11. "An Orientation by James Duke and Howard Stone," in Friedrich Schleiermacher, *Christian Caring: Selections from Practical Theology,* ed. James O. Duke and Howard Stone (Philadelphia: Fortress Press, 1988), pp. 13-41.
12. H. Richard Niebuhr mentions constitutionalism, the independence of the Church, and the limitation of power in *The Kingdom of God in America* (New York: Harper & Row, 1959), pp. 59-87.
13. *The Book of Common Worship,* pp. 184-86.
14. *The Book of Order,* part 2 of *The Constitution of the Presbyterian Church (U.S.A.)* (New York: The Office of the General Assembly, 1985). This is one reason why Reformed piety ought to be sympathetic with calls for more genuinely representative and balanced political structures in other churches. See, for example, Dennis P. McCann, *New Experiment in Democracy: The Challenge for American Catholicism* (Kansas City: Sheed & Ward, 1987).
15. Stackhouse, *Public Theology,* p. 135.
16. On the Commandments, see *The Westminster Shorter Catechism,* questions 39–81. Short contemporary discussions may be found in Walter Harrelson, "Decalogue," in *The Westminster Dictionary of Christian Ethics,* ed. James F. Childress and John Macquarrie (Philadelphia: Westminster Press, 1986), pp. 146-47; and Arthur J. Dyck, *On Human Care: An Introduction to Ethics* (Nashville: Abingdon Press, 1977), pp. 92-105.

CHAPTER 8

The Tradition of Prayer in Teresa and John of the Cross

STEVEN PAYNE, O.C.D.

In my Father's house there are many dwelling places.
—JOHN 14:2 NAB

The importance of Teresa of Jesus (1515–1582) and John of the Cross (1542–1591) for modern spirituality and spiritual theology in the Christian West would be hard to overstate. From its first publication, for example, Teresa's autobiographical *Book of Her Life* has enjoyed enormous popularity among devout Catholic and Protestant readers alike. The older scholastic manuals of spirituality (such as Tanquerey's *The Spiritual Life*) are replete with references to the works of John and Teresa, investing them with an authority approaching that of Thomas Aquinas. Within this century, Roman Catholics have officially recognized both Carmelite saints as "Doctors of the Church" for their teachings on prayer; Teresa, in fact, was the first woman ever to be so honored. In our own day Teresa and John retain a broad ecumenical appeal. People of all faith traditions are signing up in unprecedented numbers for seminars and retreats on Carmelite spirituality, while current works on prayer and mysticism almost invariably invoke their names—to the point where certain authors lament the "almost tyrannical" influence of these "great Spanish spiritual writers of the sixteenth century."[1]

Yet to some extent this preeminence has proved a mixed blessing. After four centuries, contemporary readers can have difficulty recognizing the original voices of Teresa and John through the accumulated layers of unintentional misrepresentation or ideological distortion by later commentators.[2] Today the Teresian tradition of spirituality is continuing to undergo far-reaching renewal involving a "return to the sources," with new critical editions of the primary texts and more careful historical studies. Such research still has much to discover about the ways Teresa and John responded to the possibilities and limitations of their own milieu, and what they can teach us in responding to our own.

The Early Carmelite Tradition

Without denying their originality, most experts today would emphasize that the spirituality of Teresa and John cannot be understood apart from their own particular background. Both were Carmelites, members of a Roman Catholic religious family officially known as the Brothers (and, later, Sisters) of Our Lady of Mount Carmel. Both lived during the Spanish "Golden Age," in the wake of the Protestant Reformation and the Council of Trent, under the shadow of the Inquisition. The two saints were clearly shaped by the traditions they inherited, which they in turn creatively adapted as their own legacy to later generations.

The Carmelite Order seems to have originated with a small group of Latin hermits (possibly former crusaders or pilgrims) who gathered on the slopes of Mount Carmel near the so-called fountain of Elijah toward the beginning of the thirteenth century.[3] Sometime between 1206 and 1214 they decided to seek official ecclesiastical recognition and so approached the Latin Patriarch of Jerusalem, Albert of Avogadro, for a "formula of living," a "few points . . . written down" to provide them with a standard "in keeping with [their] avowed purpose."[4] That they requested a *formula vitae* rather than adopting one of the classical Rules (e.g., of Augustine or Benedict) is itself instructive and suggests that they were critical of the way these canonical Rules were being lived at the time, seeking instead a simpler, less structured lifestyle in response to the call of the gospel.

In any case, the Latin Patriarch responded with a brief text known to later generations (somewhat misleadingly and in a modified form) as the Rule of St. Albert. Laced with scriptural references and imbued with the spirituality of the desert that has attracted so much interest today, it sets before each of the hermits as a central precept that he "stay in his own cell or nearby, pondering the Lord's law day and night and keeping watch at his prayers unless attending to some other duty" (cf. Ps. 1:2; Josh. 1:8; I Pet. 4:7). This Rule emphasizes the classic eremitical virtues of obedience, silence, solitude, fasting and abstinence, poverty or common ownership, manual work, and direct combat with the powers of evil; at the same time, any ascetical extremes are tempered by an emphasis on prayer and Eucharist in common (even daily), egalitarianism, and common sense (*discretio*), which is the "guide of the virtues." The stated purpose behind all such observances is simply to foster "a life of allegiance to Jesus Christ" (*in obsequio Jesu Christi*) so that one may serve him faithfully, "pure in heart and steadfast in conscience" (*de corde puro et bona conscientia;* cf. II Cor. 10:5; I Tim. 1:5).

This Rule, particularly as adapted and approved by Pope Innocent IV in 1247, became the fundamental text for all later generations of Carmelites and the touchstone to which all subsequent renewal movements within the Order would spontaneously turn for inspiration. In particular, as we shall see, its main themes reappear dramatically in the spirituality of Teresa and John.

It should also be noted that although the Rule of St. Albert makes no direct mention of Elijah or the Mother of Jesus, Carmelite spirituality assumed a prophetic and Marian character almost from the beginning. The first was suggested by the geographical setting itself. Situated near the "fountain of Elijah," knowing that there had been hermits living on the slopes of Mount Carmel since antiquity, and lacking any other heroic figure comparable to Francis, Benedict, or Dominic to claim as founder, the Carmelites soon came to assume that their group had in fact originated with Elijah, and that they had descended in an unbroken historical succession from the "sons of the prophets" (cf. II Kings 2:3-17; 4:1, 38-44; 5:22; 9:1-11). While modern historiography lends no support to such a belief, it nonetheless conveys an important symbolic truth: that the Carmelites have always looked to the fiery figure of Elijah, with his "zeal for the living God," encountering Yahweh in the "tiny whispering sound" at Horeb (I Kings 19:9-18 NAB), as the Old Testament mirror and model of their vocation.

Similarly, the first Carmelites soon discovered that the apparently simple act of constructing a small oratory "among the cells," as Albert required, and dedicating it to "the Blessed Virgin Mary of Mount Carmel" had far-reaching implications. To the feudal mind, the titular saint of any place was its special lord and patron, under whose protection spiritual battles were fought; the Carmelites likewise knew that without this chapel they would never have received Albert's official recognition. "Interpreting these facts in feudal terms, the hermits came to understand that they had been founded for the cult of the Virgin."[5] At certain times in the Order's later history, this Marian orientation would tend to degenerate into pious myths and exaggerated devotions; nonetheless, its truest focus has always been on the contemplative Mary in the New Testament, the "handmaiden of the

Lord" (Luke 1:38), the first and most perfect disciple who "[pondered] all things in her heart" (cf. Luke 2:19, 51), who "heard the word of God and kept it" (Luke 11:28), who joined the disciples in fervent prayer for the outpouring of the Spirit (Acts 1:14). Once again, the hermits found in Mary a New Testament "mother and sister," model and companion, in the following of Christ. Teresa and John were to retrieve these traditional prophetic and Marian themes for their own time, just as is occurring today on a more ecumenical level in the wake of the Second Vatican Council.

In any case, this young hermit community soon faced two serious threats to its existence. On the one hand, the gradual recovery of the crusader kingdom by the Moslems forced the brothers to abandon Mount Carmel and begin new foundations in Europe. On the other hand, to the Europeans the habit and eremitical lifestyle of these strangers from the East seemed suspiciously unfamiliar and perhaps a violation of efforts within the Church to limit the explosion of new (and often bizarre) religious movements. The Carmelites narrowly escaped suppression at the Second Council of Lyons in 1274 and from that point on took the prudent course of gradually assimilating themselves to the mendicant movement. By the fourteenth century their lifestyle and canonical status had become similar to that of the more popular mendicant groups, such as the Franciscans and Dominicans. Like others, their *formula vitae* was eventually "mitigated" in order to cope with the sad consequences of the Black Death, the Western Schism, and the Hundred Years War. Students of history are all too familiar with the abuses of this period, as popes and anti-popes competed for the allegiance of different orders through the promise of ever greater privileges, while individual religious were casually dispensed from community obligations and allowed to acquire vast personal fortunes and power. Too often, religious communities felt required to lower their standards in order to attract and keep what few potential candidates remained. (Fra Filippo Lippi [1406–1469], the colorful Renaissance artist who made his religious vows at the Carmel of Florence at the age of fifteen and became renowned as much for his love affairs as his paintings, is only the most notorious case among the Carmelites.)

From time to time attempts at reform were made. In 1452, for example, as part of his own renewal efforts, the Carmelite General John Soreth began accepting groups of pious women (*beatas,* beguines, etc.) into the Order as the first Carmelite Sisters. For the most part, however, reform movements tended to break away from the main body of the Order and eventually suffered the same decline they were meant to counteract. Yet even in its darkest moments, the Carmelite ideal remained alive. In 1370 the Carmelite Philip Ribot published *The Book of the Institution of the First Monks*, a mythical account of the Order's Elijan origins that had enormous impact on later generations of Carmelites because it purported to be their earliest Rule, written in A.D. 412. While its allegorical interpretation of the Elijah cycle could scarcely pass muster before the standards of contemporary historians and biblical scholars, the work nonetheless captures much of the Order's spiritual tradition and clearly presents the twofold aim of its way of life, as seen in the following commentary on I Kings 17:3-4:

> One part we acquire, with the help of divine grace, through our efforts and virtuous works. This is to offer God a holy heart, free from all stain of actual sin. We do this when we are perfect and in Carith, that is, hidden in that charity of which the Wise Man says: "Charity covereth all sins" (Pr. 10:12). God desired Elias to advance thus far, when He said to him: "Hide in the torrent of Carith." The other part of the goal of this life is granted to us as a free gift of God: namely to taste somewhat in the heart and to experience in the soul, not only after death but even in this mortal life, the intensity of the divine presence and the sweetness of the glory of heaven. This is to drink of the torrent of the love of God. God promised it to Elias in the words: "And there thou shalt drink of the torrent."[6]

Teresa and John would later develop the same theme at great length: that the contemplative experience of God, though completely gratuitous and unmerited, can be humbly sought and expected if one is properly prepared.

Thus the Spanish Carmelites were heirs to a great mystical tradition, which preserved certain classic eremitical values (silence, solitude, meditation, and healthy asceticism) and an unshakeable conviction that the experience of God is a realistic goal in this life.

Teresa of Avila

Teresa de Ahumada y Cepeda was born in the Castilian city of Avila on March 28, 1515, the fifth child among nine brothers and two sisters. Her parents were deeply religious, though of *judeoconverso* stock. It had been the political genius of Ferdinand and Isabella to join the independent kingdoms of the Iberian peninsula by uniting them against their perceived common enemies: first the Moors, who were gradually driven out of Spain, then the Jews, expelled in 1492. Many Jews in Spain became Christians (*judeoconversos*), at least nominally, in order to remain and avoid confiscation of their property. Thus for

Spaniards a shared faith became as much a political as a religious issue, since Catholicism was one of the few forces that united the nation. There developed a tremendous preoccupation with noble lineage, honor, and purity of blood, untainted by Islamic or Jewish ancestry. Officially, the "new Christians" or *conversos* were barred from many public offices and religious orders, though in fact they were present throughout Spanish society. By contrast, Teresa instinctively rejected all such distinctions and insisted on strict equality among her followers, perhaps aware that her own ancestry was "tainted."[7]

Catholics of the Iberian peninsula likewise developed an almost hysterical fear of Protestantism. They were deeply alarmed by the social and political turmoil in the rest of Europe but often had only the haziest notions of the theological and religious issues involved. Teresa herself, for example, decries "the harm being done in France and . . . the havoc the Lutherans had caused" (*Way* I, 2)[8], though in fact the groups in question were Huguenots.

As a result, the Spanish church became deeply suspicious of mental prayer and "spiritual" associations, detecting latent Protestant or illuminist tendencies in anything that seemed to support an inward experience of grace or the private interpretation of Scripture. In fact, there were significant heterodox spiritual movements in Spain (e.g., among the Alumbrados) that needed correction, but the Catholic reaction went to exaggerated lengths. As Teresa herself sadly notes, most books of spirituality along with vernacular translations of the Bible were placed on the Index of forbidden books (cf. *Life* XXVI, 5). Catholics in general, and women in particular, were discouraged from attempting anything beyond the customary vocal prayers and ascetical practices. Even as strong an advocate of interior prayer as Francisco de Osuna (1492–1540), the Spanish Franciscan whose guide to "recollection" in *The Third Spiritual Alphabet* played such a crucial role in Teresa's own mystical development, could advise in another work that if "you see your wife going about visiting many churches, practicing many devotions, and pretending to be a saint, lock the door; and if that isn't sufficient, break her leg if she is young, for she can go to heaven lame from her own house without going around in search of these suspect forms of holiness."[9] Here again Teresa earnestly supported the right of all Christians, especially women, to a deeper spiritual life. Thus for all her remarks on the weaknesses and limitations of her sex, she was also most eloquent in defense of women (cf. *Way* III, 7) and in her insistence that fidelity to mental prayer is ultimately the cure, not the cause, of spiritual aberrations (cf. *Life* VIII, 5-8; XIX, 4, 10-15).

Despite her intelligence and love of reading, Teresa as a woman of the sixteenth century lacked the opportunity for higher studies. Consequently, her writings and doctrine tend to be more experiential than systematic. For the most part, she simply tells her own story, singing "the mercies of the Lord," a feature many readers now find attractive in an age when narrative theology has come into its own. As she recounts in *The Book of Her Life* (which she herself sometimes called *The Book of God's Mercies*), Teresa had been raised in a devout Christian family of comfortable means and early developed a taste for spiritual things. However, at the age of twelve, after the death of her mother, this lively, outgoing adolescent began to fall under the spell of more worldly companions and was placed by her father in a nearby Augustinian convent school to protect her honor (cf. *Life* II, 3-7). Here, through the "good and holy conversation" of a saintly nun, she first began to consider a religious vocation (*Life* III, 1-2). Shortly after leaving the school because of an illness, she was introduced to the practice of spiritual reading by a pious uncle and was inspired to a decision by *The Letters of Saint Jerome*.

Teresa frankly admits that leaving home for the convent was one of the most difficult struggles of her life. While not immediately inclined toward such a vocation, she saw it as the "best and safest state," given her lively nature, and chose the Carmelite convent of the Incarnation in Avila because she had "a good friend" there (*Life* III, 2–IV, 1).

Though very large, "la Encarnacion" was in other respects fairly typical for its time. With over 170 members (many placed there as the only respectable alternative for unmarriageable daughters), the community was in serious financial straits. As a result, the nuns were often forced to accept bequests with strings attached, obliging them to elaborate devotions stipulated by the donors and leaving little time for mental prayer. In addition, the caste system of the Spanish society at large was reflected within the monastery walls; poorer sisters slept in dormitories and barely found enough to eat, while those of noble background had servants and suites of rooms and could insist on the title "Doña." Later on, Teresa's own vision of community would be partly shaped by the effort to avoid such difficulties.

Yet life at the Incarnation was by no means decadent. The community practiced regular fasting, abstinence, and silence, while celebrating the Divine Office with great solemnity. Teresa was surprised at how quickly she adapted to this new lifestyle and began making progress in prayer, particularly after starting to practice the "recollection" described in Osuna's *Third Spiritual Alphabet* (*Life* IV, 7). Yet after this initial fervor she suffered a complete breakdown in health, and during her long convalescence settled into the ordinary routine of a mediocre nun, torn between her love for the busy chatter of the convent parlor and her attraction to a deeper life of prayer. Finally, at the age of thirty-nine, after years of vacillating, she underwent a second conversion experience prompted by Augustine's *Confessions* and meditation on the sufferings of Christ (*Life* IX, 1-9). Henceforth she began to live "another, new life . . . the one God lived in me" (*Life* XXIII, 1). Teresa once more started praying in earnest, quickly advanced, and was soon having extraordinary religious experiences, much to her own consternation and that of sceptical confessors. Shortly thereafter she took up the idea of founding a new Carmelite community better suited to the practice of mental prayer, in keeping with the original spirit of Albert's Rule (which in fact she knew only in the Innocentian version): a small, praying "college of Christ," an egalitarian community of friends living in silence, solitude, and poverty, free from the encumbrance of endowments and honors. Enclosure and other ascetical practices were seen as a means to this end. Teresa's dream was to blossom in a series of foundations of friars and nuns that would eventually become a new religious family, the Order of Discalced Carmelites.[10] (It should be especially encouraging for older Christians today to realize that Teresa did not really begin any of the projects for which she is now best remembered until the last two decades of her life, before her death in 1582.)

Teresian Spirituality

All of Teresa's major works (including *The Book of Her Life, The Way of Perfection, The Interior Castle,* and *The Book of Foundations*) were composed in spare moments at the command of superiors and spiritual directors who wanted some explanation of her mission and spirit. In identifying some of the chief features of her spiritual legacy, one should certainly begin with Teresa's distinctive personality, which shines through everything she said and did, particularly her constant and spontaneous testimony to the activity of God in her life, which gives her writings their enduring appeal—her compelling conviction that God is as real as anything we can see, hear, or touch. Down through the centuries many have been won over to faith by the sheer persuasiveness of *The Book of Her Life.* Yet however lofty the subject, Teresa's style is always human, warm, down to earth, practical, and laced with a disarming sense of humor. She has a spontaneous aversion to all "sad-faced" sanctity.

A second major characteristic of Teresian spirituality is its strong ecclesial dimension. For Teresa, prayer is no private, self-enclosed affair between herself and her Lord. Rather, she sees it as her own contribution to the welfare of the people of God. If at first she regarded her foundations primarily as support groups for herself and friends, news of the missions and of the religious struggles throughout Europe gradually broadened her horizons. Later she would write of her desire "to be engaged in winning souls," to "please the Lord with my poor prayers and always [endeavor] that the Sisters would do the same and dedicate themselves to the good of souls and the increase of His Church" (*Foundations* I, 6-7).

> O my Sisters in Christ, help me to beg these things of the Lord. . . . This is your vocation. . . . These must be the things you desire, the things you weep about; these must be the objects of your petitions. . . . The world is all in flames . . . and are we to waste time asking for things that if God were to give them we'd have one less soul in heaven? (*Way* I, 5)

Again, in her famous dying words, "At last I die a daughter of the Church," Teresa rightly identifies one of her most remarkable accomplishments, during a period when *spirituales* like herself often ran afoul of the ecclesiastical authorities or drifted into the heterodox fringes. With John of the Cross, Teresa saw clearly that no religious group or movement, no matter how seemingly holy in its origins or purpose, can ultimately remain healthy or produce good fruit if it loses touch with the larger reality of the body of Christ.

Third, in an era that was not always favorable to the idea, Teresa encouraged human friendship as a support in the spiritual journey. Certainly she was aware of the classic dangers of "particular friendships" and unhealthy attachments, particularly in religious communities. Yet she herself was an enormously sociable person and recognized how much influence others had exerted upon her, for better or worse. Unlike many other writers of her time, Teresa sees positive value even in less than perfect relationships, so long as both parties are sincerely seeking to serve God. Today, as Christians increasingly become a "cognitive minority" in the larger society, Teresa reminds us of our growing need for mutual support. "A good means to having God is to speak with His friends," she writes; "love such persons as much as you like" (*Way* VII, 4).

Fourth, Teresian spirituality is marked by an intense devotion to Jesus, to the humanity of Christ. Much of her prayer centers around Christ as our friend and companion. On the basis of her own painful experience of years of frustration in praying, Teresa repeatedly warns against trying to bypass the created humanity of Jesus in our efforts to reach the divinity, as some of the spiritual authors she had read seemed to advocate.[11]

I believe I've explained that it is fitting for souls, however spiritual, to take care not to flee from corporal things to the extent of thinking that even the most sacred humanity causes harm. Some quote that the Lord said to His disciples that it was fitting that He go. I can't bear this. I would wager that He didn't say it to His most Blessed Mother, because she was firm in the faith; she knew He was God and man, and even though she loved Him more than they did, she did so with such perfection that His presence was a help rather than a hindrance. (*Interior Castle* VI, 7, xiv)

She insists that the "method of keeping Christ present with us is beneficial in all stages and is a very safe means of advancing in the first degree of prayer, of reaching in a short time the second degree, and of walking secure against the dangers the devil can set up in the last degrees" (*Life* XII, 3). Teresa in fact defines mental prayer in terms of a friendly conversation with Christ, "an intimate sharing between friends . . . taking time frequently to be alone with Him who we know loves us" (*Life* VIII, 5). This focus on the human Jesus is especially evident in the prayer instructions found in *The Way of Perfection:*

As is already known, the examination of conscience, the act of contrition, and the sign of the cross must come first. Then, . . . since you are alone, strive to find a companion. Well what better companion than the Master Himself . . . ? Represent the Lord Himself as close to you and behold how lovingly and humbly He is teaching you. . . . If you grow accustomed to having Him at your side, . . . you will find Him everywhere. . . .

. . . I'm not asking you now that you think about Him or that you draw out a lot of concepts or make long subtle reflections with your intellect. I'm not asking you to do anything more than look at Him. . . .

. . . If you are joyful, look at Him as risen. . . . If you are experiencing trials or are sad, behold Him on the way to the garden. . . .

. . . I desire to suffer, Lord, all the trials that come to me and esteem them as a great good enabling me to imitate You in something. Let us walk together, Lord. Wherever you go, I will go; whatever you suffer, I will suffer. (*Way* XXVI, 1-6)

Out of such passages later commentators would develop the so-called Teresian method of prayer, though in fact Teresa herself advocated no formal method. Nevertheless, her constant practice of loving attention to Christ as our friend and companion strikes a responsive chord with many today.

But perhaps her greatest contribution to later spirituality is Teresa's careful effort to describe and classify the different stages in the spiritual journey, from beginning to end, more thoroughly than had ever been done before. Throughout her life Teresa kept refining her explanations of the experience of God in all its variety. Her account develops from the "Four Waters" imagery of the *Life* (where she compares the degrees of prayer to four increasingly effective ways of irrigating a garden), to the *Interior Castle's* master symbol (inspired by John 14:2) of the human person as a crystalline palace of seven progressively more interior "dwelling places," through which we advance toward the center where the Lord resides, illuminating the entire structure.

Though her schemas cannot be treated in detail here, Teresa's discussions of the transition to contemplative prayer and the goal of the mystical journey deserve special mention. Regarding the first, she teaches that fidelity to meditation gradually leads to a simpler, more quiet and loving form of prayer that is sometimes called "active recollection." Later authors have confused matters by speaking (somewhat misleadingly) of "acquired contemplation," long a controversial phrase among theologians of spirituality. Teresa herself is not always consistent in her terminology; her way of differentiating this stage from the truly contemplative "prayer of quiet," for example, appears to change from book to book as her thinking develops.[12] Nonetheless, it seems clear enough that, for Teresa, there is a state of peaceful, silent attentiveness (not unrelated to the results of contemporary "centering" prayer, for example), which is the usual outcome of faithful praying over a period of time:

All one need do is go into solitude and look at Him within oneself. . . .

. . . This prayer is called "recollection" because the soul collects its faculties together and enters within itself to be with its God. And its divine Master comes more quickly to teach it and give it the prayer of quiet than He would through any other method it might use.

. . . If we make the effort, practice this recollection for some days, and get used to it, the gain will be clearly seen; we will understand, when beginning to pray, that the bees [i.e., the faculties and senses] are approaching and entering the beehive to make honey. . . . And when the will calls them back again, they come more quickly, until after many of these entries the Lord wills that they rest entirely in perfect contemplation.

. . . This recollection is not something supernatural, but . . . something we can desire and achieve ourselves with the help of God. . . .

. . . We must, then, disengage ourselves from everything so as to approach God interiorly and even in the midst of occupations withdraw ourselves.

. . . I conclude by saying that whoever wishes to acquire it—since, as I say, it lies within our power—should not tire of getting used to what has been explained. It involves a gradual increase of self-control and an end to vain wandering. . . .

. . . I know, if you try, that within a year, or perhaps half a year, you will acquire it, by the favor of God. . . . If then the Lord should desire to raise you to higher things He will discover in you the readiness. (*Way* XXVIII, 2-6; XXIX, 4-8)

Even though we can obtain it through our own graced efforts, this state is the doorway to contemplative prayer in the stricter sense and flows almost imperceptibly into it, as the recollection becomes passive and begins to feel as if it were happening to us, with little effort on our part. It is encouraging to realize that, according to Teresa, authentically contemplative supernatural prayer begins at this point, in a relatively common and familiar form of praying that, nonetheless, if nurtured can carry us to the farthest reaches of mystical union.

Teresa is equally helpful in clarifying the goal of the spiritual journey. Though she herself received in abundance the visions, voices, and other extraordinary experiences often associated with mysticism in the popular mind, she clearly states that these are only secondary helps (and sometimes hindrances) along the way. What characterizes the final phase of spiritual development in this life are not ecstasies and raptures but a constant awareness of the Trinity dwelling within, coupled with total availability to the neighbor without.

> Now then, when His Majesty is pleased to grant the soul this divine marriage that was mentioned, He first brings it into His own dwelling place. He desires that the favor be different from what it was at other times when He gave the soul raptures. . . . In this seventh dwelling place . . . our good God now desires to remove the scales from the soul's eyes. . . . When the soul is brought into that dwelling place, the Most Blessed Trinity, all three Persons, . . . is revealed to it through a certain representation of the truth. . . . Here all three Persons communicate themselves to it, speak to it, and explain these words of the Lord in the Gospel: that He and the Father and the Holy Spirit will come to dwell with the soul that loves Him and keeps His commandments. . . .
>
> You may think that as a result the soul will be outside itself and so absorbed that it will be unable to be occupied with anything else. On the contrary, the soul is much more occupied than before with everything pertaining to the service of God. (*Interior Castle* VII, 1, v-viii)

Even at this stage, then, "Martha and Mary must join together"; we should "desire and be occupied in prayer not for the sake of our enjoyment but so as to have this strength to serve" (*Interior Castle* VII, 4, xii). Here Teresa returns to a perennial Carmelite theme: that the value of one's spirituality before God is measured not by the loftiness of one's mystical experiences but by the quality of one's love for neighbor. Thus Teresa inaugurated a spiritual movement freshly reappropriating the ancient Carmelite tradition of deep contemplative union with God overflowing into apostolic service.

John of the Cross

Teresa was quickly joined by others who recognized the value of her charism. Her great collaborator in the Carmelite "reform" was St. John of the Cross.[13] He too seems to have come from *judeoconverso* stock (though perhaps without realizing it) but in other respects was almost the opposite of the Madre in background and temperament. Born at Fontiveros in 1542, almost thirty years after Teresa, Juan de Yepes was raised in destitute circumstances. One of his brothers died in infancy, probably of malnutrition, and for a while John's widowed mother was forced to place him in a kind of orphanage because of the family's poverty. On the other hand, John had access to some of the finest education of his era, first during his adolescent years as an orderly in a plague hospital at Medina del Campo, where the administrator allowed him to attend the new Jesuit school in his spare time, and later at the University of Salamanca as a young Carmelite student.

Unlike the exuberant and outgoing Teresa, John remained throughout his life much more the introvert, scholar, and poet. Yet they became friends. At the time of his first meeting with St. Teresa in 1567, the recently ordained Juan de Santo Matia (as he was then called) was considering a transfer to the Carthusians, for a life of greater prayer and seclusion. Teresa, recognizing him as "small in stature but great in the eyes of God," persuaded John that he could find what he sought within his own Order by joining her project (cf. *Foundations* III, 17),[14] and John subsequently helped inaugurate the first monastery of friars of the Teresian Reform at Duruelo on November 28, 1568 (cf. *Foundations* XIII–XIV). At this time he took the name John of the Cross and promised observance of the same "Primitive Rule" of St. Albert on which Teresa had based her earlier foundations.

Ironically, though, Teresa's promises to John were never entirely fulfilled, since the demands of the growing movement kept him regularly occupied with administrative duties and ecclesiastical controversies for the rest of his life. He was also heavily involved in the ministry of spiritual direction. His only extended periods of silence and solitude were the terrible nine months spent in the Carmelite monastery prison of Toledo in 1577–1578, when he became caught in the middle of a jurisdictional dispute between the Calced and Discalced parties, and the painful exile of his last days after he had apparently spoken out against the vindictive policies of the Discalced leadership. Like Teresa, therefore, John wrote in his spare time, in the midst of many other pressing concerns, though at a later point in his intellectual development when his thoughts about the spiritual life were more or less fully formed. He died on December 13, 1591, at the age of forty-nine.

Sanjuanist Spirituality

John is widely acknowledged as one of Spain's greatest poets. Perhaps the first and most striking feature of his works, therefore, is that he presents his poetry as the primary expression of the experience of God. All of his major treatises (i.e., *The Ascent of Mount Carmel, The Dark Night of the Soul, The Spiritual Canticle,* and *The Living Flame of Love*) are organized as commentaries on the poems, and despite their length and detail John insists that they capture only a small part of what the symbols mean, and that other interpretations are possible.

> It would be foolish to think that expressions of love arising from mystical understanding, like these stanzas, are fully explainable. The Spirit of the Lord, who abides in us and aids our weakness, as St. Paul says [Rom. 8:26], pleads for us with unspeakable groanings in order to manifest what we can neither fully understand nor comprehend.
>
> Who can describe the understanding He gives to loving souls in whom He dwells? And who can express the experience He imparts to them? . . . Certainly, no one can! . . .
>
> As a result these persons let something of their experiences overflow in figures and similes, and from the abundance of their spirit pour out secrets and mysteries rather than rational explanations. . . .
>
> As a result, though we give some explanation of these stanzas, there is no reason to be bound to this explanation. (*Canticle,* prologue, i-ii)

Perhaps more than any other Christian mystic, John was able to give lyrical expression to the ineffable. Contemporary readers value him as much for the mysterious power of his poetry as for the careful analyses of his prose works.[15]

As a poet and Spaniard of the Golden Age, John seems to have had a special fondness for hyperbole and the dramatic turn of phrase. His all or nothing (*todo y nada*) directives can sound excessive, as Teresa herself humorously notes in saying of her fellow Carmelite, "God deliver me from people so spiritual that they want to turn everything into perfect contemplation, no matter what."[16] Yet it is worth remembering that John wrote at the request of others, and that many of his chapters emerged from maxims written in a pithy style for the friars and nuns (e.g., "To arrive at being all, desire to be nothing," or "To come to the knowledge you have not, you must go by a way in which you know not"), meant thereby to be more memorable. In fact, John composed his texts not to impose additional burdens on his readers but to help them deal positively with the inevitable hazards and hardships of the spiritual journey.

John is sometimes described as "the Doctor of Faith" and a teacher of "theologal" holiness (a European neologism), because he grounds his approach to spirituality in the theological virtues of faith, hope, and charity, rather than in the apparitions, ecstasies, and occult states of consciousness popularly associated with mysticism. For John, faith in its most comprehensive sense includes not just intellectual assent to revealed propositions but also the whole existential attitude of radical openness to God's love. Indeed, contemplative prayer itself is a certain activation and unfolding of the inner reality of faith, which together with hope and love serves as our support, protection, and guide for the entire journey to God (see *Ascent* 1, 2, iii; II, 6, i-vii; *Night* II, 21, iii-xii; *Canticle* 1, xi).[17]

Throughout his works, but particularly in *The Ascent of Mount Carmel* and *The Dark Night of the Soul,* John draws out the radical implications for Christian spirituality of a familiar theological principle: that no creature, no human feeling or experience, no idea or dogma, no vision or spiritual ecstasy, no matter how profound, can ever represent or communicate the full reality of God as God is (cf. *Ascent* II, 4, iv). Therefore, we can never afford to become fixated on such things to the point where we confuse them with the divinity to which they should lead us. And so, for example, John warns against the tendency of his contemporaries to become overly fascinated with particular devotions or private revelations. Such things may be helpful in their place, John concedes, but problems arise when we give them more weight than the normal channels of God's self-communication in Scripture, the Church, and the sacraments. According to the Mystical Doctor:

> God could respond as follows: If I have already told you all things in My Word, My Son, and if I have no other word, what answer or revelation can I now make that would surpass this? Fasten your eyes on Him alone, because in Him I have spoken and revealed all. . . . For He is my entire locution and response, vision and revelation, which I have already spoken, answered, manifested, and revealed to you, by giving Him to you as a brother, companion, master, ransom, and reward. . . . But now anyone . . . desiring that I speak and reveal something to him would

somehow be requesting Christ again, and more faith, yet he would be failing in faith, because Christ has already been given. . . . You shall not find anything to ask or desire through revelations and visions; behold Him well, for in Him you will uncover all these revelations already made, and many more. (*Ascent* II, 22, v)

Today, as we anxiously approach the end of the millennium, and many Christians become caught up in a frenzy of apocalyptic "messages" and expectations, John's words once again have a special relevance.

In a similar vein, without in any way denying the Church's call to teach authoritatively through its pastors under the guidance of the Holy Spirit, John is well aware of the fundamental limitations of all talk of God, and that dogmatic claims conceal as much as they reveal in their "covered and inexplicit articles" (cf. *Ascent* II, 3, iii-iv; 9, i; *Canticle* 12, iv-vi). Thus he would no doubt be wary of any expectation that current crises in the Church can be easily resolved either by "progressive" theological changes or by "conservative" magisterial pronouncements and interventions henceforth eliminating all ambiguity and confusion. The unfathomable God always partly eludes our attempts to delimit the mystery, and we must learn to live by the secure insecurity of "dark faith" (cf. *Ascent* II, 3-4).

Like Teresa again, John has heavily influenced later spiritual theologians in his treatment of the successive stages of the mystical life, though his analysis is somewhat more theological and less psychological than hers. He builds his own distinctive teaching around the classic account of the "three ways." Thus for John we typically start our spiritual journey in the "purgative way" of "beginners," with a very busy style of praying, often accompanied by consolations; these encourage us in practicing the basic virtues to help build good habits and redirect the uncontrolled desires of our "fallen nature" (see *Ascent* I). Gradually, however, our prayer becomes simpler and quieter, while the previous emotional satisfaction ceases, because the work of the first phase is completed and we are being asked to move forward without seeking immediate reward (cf. *Ascent* II, 12, vi–15, v; *Night* I, 8-9). If we can remain quietly attentive, without being dissuaded by the dryness, we soon discover a new, gentle, and much more inward awareness of the Divine (cf. *Ascent* II, 13, vii), which begins to grow and intensify (the "illuminative way" of "proficients"); this contemplative experience may become so strong that it disrupts our normal psychophysical stability, resulting in the raptures, ecstasies, voices, visions, and other extraordinary phenomena that the devout sometimes undergo (cf.

Night II, 1, ii; 2, iii). In fact, there is ordinarily so much conscious and unconscious resistance to God embedded in our sin-distorted nature that "divinization" may require a very painful reorientation and healing process. Yet eventually, if we make it this far, we will be brought to a stable union or "spiritual marriage" (the "unitive way" of the "perfect") in which our whole human nature is harmoniously integrated (cf. *Canticle* 22), and we are able to enjoy a more or less continual awareness of the Trinity within while remaining attentive to creation around us, in a state that John compares to that of Adam and Eve in paradise (cf. *Night* II, 24, ii). This sublime participation in the inner life of the Trinity is what John identifies as the goal of the journey, to be experienced clearly and openly in the life to come.

> In this transformation which the soul possesses in this life, the same spiration passes from God to the soul and from the soul to God with notable frequency and blissful love, although not in the open and manifest degree proper to the next life. . . .
>
> One should not think it impossible that the soul be capable of so sublime an activity as this breathing in God. . . . For granted that God favors her by union with the Most Blessed Trinity, in which she becomes deiform and God through participation, how could it be incredible that she also understand, know, and love—or better that this be done in her—in the Trinity, together with it, as does the Trinity itself! . . .
>
> No knowledge or power can describe how this happens, unless by explaining how the Son of God attained and merited such a high state for us, the power to be sons of God, as St. John says [John 1:12]. (*Canticle* 39, iii)

But John is best known for his treatment of the "dark night," a master symbol that he uses in a variety of ways and that has subsequently entered common parlance, often with little awareness of its origins; writers today casually apply the term to almost any difficulty or disillusionment. In the treatise of the same name, John uses "dark night" to refer primarily to the critical moments of transition in the "three ways": the "passive night of sense" when we move beyond the busy, conceptual prayer of beginners to a more contemplative stance, and the "passive night of spirit" when we undergo a radical purification before arriving at a habitual experience of union. Both "passive nights" are painful, according to John, the latter particularly so. Yet for our purposes it is not necessary to treat them separately, especially since John admits that "not everyone undergoes this in the same way" or according to the same precise sequence (*Night* I, 14, v). The painful process of purification and progressive surrender to God can occur gradually over a lifetime or may be punctuated by certain intense moments of crisis, depending upon our individual personality and particular needs. (To tell the truth, Carmelite scholars have difficulty even reconciling John's stages with what Teresa tells of her own spiritual journey, though the two had frequently shared their thoughts and experiences with each other.)

Here it is sufficient to speak of "dark night" in terms of the human "limit-experiences" of affliction, obscurity, confusion, frustration, and "impasse." Sooner or later we reach a point in our prayer, in our lives, when everything appears to fall apart, "everything seems to be functioning in reverse" (*Night* I, 8, iii). We feel lost, disoriented, abandoned by God and friends, painfully aware of past prosperity yet lacking the strength even to ask for relief.

> Because it seems that God has rejected it, the soul suffers such pain and grief that when God tried Job in this way it proved one of the worst of Job's trials. . . . Clearly beholding its impurity . . . , the soul understands distinctly that it is worthy neither of God nor of any creature. And what most grieves it is that it thinks it will never be worthy, and that there are no more blessings for it. . . .
>
> When this purgative contemplation oppresses a man, he feels very vividly indeed the shadow of death, the sighs of death, and the sorrows of hell, all of which reflect the feeling of God's absence. . . .
>
> . . . A person also feels forsaken and despised by creatures, particularly by his friends. (*Night* II, 5, v; 6, ii-iii)

Or the crisis may be that our comfortable religion now simply seems to dissolve around us; God no longer seems real, faith no longer seems true and meaningful. Since other factors can cause similar experiences, John offers various signs for determining whether this "darkness" is simply the result of ill health, lukewarmness, or newly committed sin (*Ascent* II, 13-15; *Night* I, 9); if so, it will dissipate quickly once health is restored or one returns to serious Christian living. By contrast, while the true "passive night" may indeed be triggered by external traumas that do not seem overtly religious (e.g., loss of job, disability, imprisonment, death of loved ones), its essential characteristic is the pervasive inner anguish and disorientation felt in relation to oneself, the world, and God.

John explains that there is little one can do to directly shorten this ordeal except to cooperate as best one can with the process. What is going on, according to John, is that we are actually being drawn closer into the absolute purity and holiness of the Divine, but like the cave dweller emerging into the sunshine, God's light may at first blind us with its painful brilliance, throwing our defects into sharp relief. The "dark ray" of God's self-communication (which is what John believes the underlying cause of the turmoil to be, though it may not be felt as such), now so terrible, is the same communication that the blessed peacefully enjoy in heaven (cf. *Night* II, 9; 12); the only difference lies in our capacity to receive. John compares the work of God on the soul at this time to the enkindling of a log (*Night* II, 10, i-x). At first, all one notices is the hissing dampness and smoke, as impurities within are driven to the surface of the wood and eliminated; all this is simply a necessary prelude in order for the log to become wholly inflamed. So too (as in psychotherapy), though it may seem that persons in the "dark night" are becoming worse when all their subconscious resistance and secret sinfulness is brought to light, the outcome is a very positive one, exposing only what was already there and allowing it to be dealt with and healed.

> Now with the light and heat of the divine fire, [the soul] sees and feels those weaknesses and miseries which previously resided within it, hidden and unfelt, just as the dampness of the log of wood was unknown until the fire being applied to it made it sweat and smoke and sputter. . . . Once they are driven out, he is illumined and, being transformed, beholds the light within himself, since his spiritual eye was cleansed and fortified by divine light. (*Flame* I, 22)

Among other things, what we discover is that there is literally nothing "out there" corresponding exactly to our religious notions; we must be stripped of all our comfortable illusions and false securities in order to make room for something (or Someone) far greater and more mysterious. According to John, if we can learn to let go, to walk forward in simple trust, the turmoil will eventually give way to a profound and unshakeable union with God that no further suffering can fundamentally disturb.

Thus John offers a consoling message for contemporary readers experiencing darkness, confusion, and crises of faith, because he provides categories of meaning for these tribulations that allow us to deal with them constructively (and to treat others compassionately, since we can never fully know what struggles they are suffering). Certainly it is dangerous to assume that we can pigeonhole ourselves or others on the basis of the spiritual stages described by John or Teresa; it may never be possible to determine infallibly whether one is undergoing the "passive nights" or not. Yet we all have desert experiences, whether it be the idealistic youth confronted for the first time with the overpowering reality of evil, the feminist alienated from the traditional beliefs and practices of patriarchal religion, or the older

Christian troubled by changes in the Church.[18] Today many authors are beginning to show how John's basic teaching can be expanded to apply to the purifying crises that both individuals and societies inevitably undergo. In the anguish and confusion of our own times, John provides a spirituality that helps us to keep our bearings and "travel light." He reminds us that we already possess all that we need in Christ and therefore can confidently move ahead in the darkness guided by faith, hope, and love, without seeking premature security in any ideology, theological system, Church structure, religious experience, or one-sided reading of the gospel. As we learn to let go of all our idols and prejudices, we gradually begin to discover and experience the Trinity already dwelling within our hearts. In this way we can enjoy even now a foretaste of the kingdom, where we become "deified" and drawn ever more deeply into the mystery of God's self-communicating love (cf. *Canticle* 1, v-xii; 39, iii-vi).

The Teresian Spiritual Legacy

Thus both John and Teresa were able to transform the Elijan and Marian desert spirituality they inherited from the early Carmelites, showing how the eremitical values of silence, solitude, detachment, meditation on Scripture, and devotion to the humanity of Christ can be internalized even in the midst of an active life, by those who do not actually live as hermits. For the most part, in fact, their basic teachings presuppose no particular state in life or method of prayer, which is why they have been used as helpful guides by a variety of believers with otherwise widely divergent backgrounds.

And the Teresian movement has continued. Though the first followers of John and Teresa failed to reach the same literary heights, their writings did show a characteristic approach to spirituality identified with the "Carmelite school." Thus to the classic steps of mental prayer outlined by Luis de Granada (preparation, reading, meditation, thanksgiving, offering, and petition), the Carmelites added contemplation as another step after meditation and strongly emphasized the importance of passivity, simplicity, and love in prayer at a time when these were often suspect. As noted above, they taught the possibility of an "acquired contemplation," perhaps better described as a kind of recollection or centered attentiveness that we can obtain by our own efforts with the help of grace. Later authors of the Carmelite school likewise began to elaborate the doctrine of John and Teresa into a scholastic system and defended them against charges of illuminism and quietism.

But among the Carmelites it is those who spoke directly from their own experience whose works have endured. The seventeenth century lay brother Nicolas Herman (known to the world by his religious name, Brother Lawrence of the Resurrection) found the divine in the kitchen of his Paris monastery through the constant "practice of the presence of God"; his maxims and letters were later brought together in a collection of the same name that would be treasured by later generations of Catholics and Protestants alike. Fenelon, Francis de Sales, William Law, and John Wesley were among the later admirers who brought the teaching of Teresa, Brother Lawrence, and John of the Cross to the attention of a wider audience. Closer to our own times, the Carmelites Edith Stein, Titus Brandsma, and Elizabeth of the Trinity (with her Pauline spirituality centered on the indwelling Trinity) have attracted considerable interest.

But by far the best-known modern proponent of Carmelite spirituality is Thérèse of Lisieux, whom Pope Pius XI praised as "the greatest saint of modern times."[19] Only twenty-six years old at the time of her death from tuberculosis in 1897, Thérèse seemed to have lived an outwardly uneventful life, spent mostly within the protective shelter of her French Victorian family and the walls of Carmel. Her autobiography originated in the request of her sisters to record her childhood memories and was therefore composed in an intimate, often sentimental style not always appealing to contemporary tastes. Yet beneath the florid language, an astonishing spiritual depth and maturity shine through. It was Thérèse's genius to rediscover for modern men and women a central biblical theme: that in the end we approach God with empty hands, not relying on our own works or discouraged by our own weakness but with boundless hope and confidence in the Father's compassion.

> I understand so well that it is only love which makes us acceptable to God that this love is the only good I ambition. Jesus deigned to show me the road that leads to this Divine Furnace, and this road is the surrender of the little child who sleeps without fear in its Father's arms. . . .
> . . . Yes, I have found my place in the Church and it is You, O my God, who have given me this place; in the heart of the Church, my Mother, I shall be Love. Thus I shall be everything and thus my dream will be realized. . . .
> . . . I feel that if You found a soul weaker and littler than mine, which is impossible, You would be pleased to grant it still greater favors, provided it abandoned itself with total confidence to Your Infinite Mercy.[20]

With this message of hope, together with the countless favors attributed to her intercession, Thérèse has found a permanent place in the hearts of modern Christians as a spiritual mentor of enduring value.

Teresian spirituality continues as a vital force in the contemporary world, not only through the renewed interest in the original writings of the Spanish saints but also through the personal testimony of those they have influenced. Admittedly, it is not an exhaustive tradition; in recent years Teresian spirituality has sometimes been criticized as overly psychological and individualistic, not sufficiently attentive to the liturgical dimensions of prayer. To some extent this is simply the result of the cultural and religious milieu out of which it arose, and may apply less to John and Teresa than to some of their followers. Certainly Teresian spirituality can be complemented by the insights of more communally and liturgically oriented traditions. Yet contemporary readers still find the writings of Teresa and John rich in pastoral applications and broad in ecumenical appeal. There is every reason to believe that the influence of the Carmelite tradition on the spiritual life of the Church will only continue to grow in the future.

Notes

1. Simon Tugwell, *Ways of Imperfection: An Exploration of Christian Spirituality* (Springfield, Ill.: Templegate, 1985), p. viii.
2. The early biographies of Teresa and John as well as the first histories of the Discalced Carmelites were heavily influenced by the interests of a rigorist faction within the Order and the desire of the Spanish to aggrandize their future patrons. For recent demythologizing research, see Ildefonso Moriones, *The Teresian Charism: A Study of the Origins* (Rome: Teresianum, 1968), and Teofanes Egido, "The Historical Setting of St. Teresa's Life," in *Spiritual Direction*, vol. 1 of *Carmelite Studies* (Washington, D.C.: ICS Publications, 1980), pp. 122-82.
3. The actual details of its origin are still in dispute. For some of the most recent and reliable studies of the beginnings of the Order, see Gabriel Barry, *The Inspiration of Carmel* (Durham, England: Teresian Press, 1984); Elias Friedman, *The Latin Hermits of Mount Carmel: A Study in Carmelite Origins* (Rome: Teresianum, 1979); Joachim Smet, *The Carmelites: A History of the Brothers of Our Lady of Mount Carmel, Ca. 1200 A.D. Until the Council of Trent* (Darien, Ill.: Carmelite Spiritual Center, 1975).
4. "*Iuxta propositum vestrum*": This Rule is available in several English versions. Here we will quote from the widely used translation by Bede [Michael] Edwards, found together with the Latin original in *The Rule of Saint Albert* (Aylesford and Kensington: The Carmelite Press, 1973). The most comprehensive modern study of the Rule can be found in Carlo Cicconetti, *La Regola del Carmelo: Origine-Natura-Significato* (Rome: Institutum Carmelitanum, 1973), which was abridged and translated into English by Gabriel Pausback and Paul Hoban as *The Rule of Carmel* (Darien, Ill.: Carmelite Spiritual Center, 1984). See also *Carmelite Rule* (Almelo, The Netherlands: Commission for Religious Dimension, 1979).
5. Friedman, *Latin Hermits of Mount Carmel*, p. 180.
6. "The Book of St. John, 44," trans. Norman G. Werling, *The Sword* 4 (Jan. 1940): 23-24.
7. For generally reliable biographical information in English on St. Teresa and her

social context, see especially Stephen Clissold, *St. Teresa of Avila* (New York: Seabury Press, 1982); Tomas Alvarez and Fernando Domingo, *Saint Teresa of Avila: A Spiritual Adventure,* trans. Christopher O'Mahony (Washington, D.C.: ICS Publications, 1982); Teofanes Egido, "The Historical Setting of St. Teresa's Life"; several of the articles in *Centenary of St. Teresa,* vol. 3 of *Carmelite Studies* (Washington, D.C.: ICS Publications, 1984); and, of course, *The Collected Works of St. Teresa of Avila,* vols. 1-3, trans. Kieran Kavanaugh and Otilio Rodriguez (Washington, D.C.: ICS Publications, 1976–1985). All references to Teresa's works are from the ICS edition.

8. Here and throughout the text of this chapter selections from the works of St. Teresa are cited using the following abbreviations: *Life* is *The Book of Her Life; Way* is *The Way of Perfection; Foundations* is *Book of Foundations; Interior Castle* is *The Interior Castle.* The numbers following the abbreviated titles refer to the internal divisions proper to each work; their meaning is obvious once one consults a standard edition of the works.

9. Francisco de Osuna, *Norte de Estados* (Seville, 1531), as quoted by Daniel de Pablo Maroto in *Dinamica de la Oracion* (Madrid: Editorial de Espiritualidad, 1973), p. 109, and translated by Kieran Kavanaugh in the introduction to *The Way of Perfection,* vol. 2 of *The Collected Works of St. Teresa of Avila* (Washington, D.C.: ICS Publications, 1980), p. 23. See also Francisco de Osuna, *Third Spiritual Alphabet,* trans. and introduced by Mary E. Giles, Classics of Western Spirituality Series (New York: Paulist Press, 1981).

10. The term "discalced" literally means "without shoes"; like other reform groups, Teresa's nuns and friars adopted the ascetical custom of going barefoot or wearing sandals as a sign of identification with the poor Christ, at a time when shoes were often considered a luxury.

11. Commentators differ on the exact nature of Teresa's difficulties in prayer related to the humanity of Christ (as described in *Life* XXII and *Interior Castle* VI, 7). For modern discussions in English, see E.W. Trueman Dicken, *The Crucible of Love: A Study of the Mysticism of St. Teresa of Jesus and St. John of the Cross* (New York: Sheed & Ward, 1963), pp. 279-88; Tomas de la Cruz, "The Carmelite School: St. Teresa and St. John of the Cross," in *Jesus in Christian Devotion and Contemplation,* trans. Paul J. Oligny (St. Meinrad, Ind.: Abbey Press, 1974), pp. 86-101, 111-13.

12. Compare *Life* XIV-XV; *Way* XXX-XXXI; *Interior Castle* IV, 2. For discussions of Teresa's understanding of the "prayer of quiet," see Dicken, *Crucible of Love,* pp. 193-214; Margaret Dorgan, "The Teaching of St. Teresa of Avila on the Prayer of Quiet," *Word and Spirit* 4 (1983): 63-76.

13. For biographical material in English on John of the Cross, see Bruno de Jesus-Marie, *Saint John of the Cross* (New York: Sheed & Ward, 1932); Crisógono de Jesús Sacramentado [*The Life of St. John of the Cross*], trans. Kathleen Pond (London: Longmans, Green & Co., 1958); Richard P. Hardy, *Search for Nothing: The Life of John of the Cross* (New York: Crossroad, 1982). All quotations from John are taken from *The Collected Works of St. John of the Cross,* 2nd ed., trans. Kieran Kavanaugh and Otilio Rodriguez (Washington, D.C.: ICS Publications, 1979).

14. Here and throughout the text of this chapter selections from the works of St. John of the Cross are cited using the following abbreviations: *Ascent* is *The Ascent of Mount Carmel; Night* is *The Dark Night of the Soul; Canticle* is *The Spiritual Canticle; Flame* is *The Living Flame of Love.* The numbers following the abbreviated titles refer to the internal divisions proper to each work; their meaning is obvious once one consults a standard edition of the works.

15. While many theological commentaries note the primacy of John's poetry, few actually discuss it in any depth. For an important new work that approaches Sanjuanist doctrine through poetry, see George H. Tavard, *Poetry and Contemplation in St. John of the Cross* (Athens, Ohio: Ohio State University Press, 1988).

16. From "A Satirical Critique," para. 7, in *The Collected Works of St. Teresa of Avila,* vol. 3, p. 361.

17. See, among others, Karol Wojtyla [Pope John Paul II], *Faith According to Saint John of the Cross* (San Francisco: Ignatius Press, 1981).
18. For attempts to apply Sanjuanist insights to these and similar contemporary experiences, see, for example, Steven Payne, "To Ask God the Right Questions," *Spiritual Life* 25 (Winter 1979): 204-14; Constance FitzGerald, "Impasse and Dark Night," in *Living with Apocalypse: Spiritual Resources for Social Compassion*, ed. Tilden Edwards (San Francisco: Harper & Row, 1984), pp. 93-116; William M. Thompson, *Fire and Light: On Consulting the Saints, Mystics and Martyrs in Theology* (Mahwah, N.J.: Paulist Press, 1987), chaps. 6-7; Segundo Galilea, *The Future of Our Past: The Spanish Mystics Speak to Contemporary Spirituality* (Notre Dame, Ind.: Ave Maria Press, 1985).
19. For reliable recent biographies of St. Thérèse in English, see Patricia O'Connor, *Thérèse of Lisieux: A Biography* (Huntington, Ind.: Our Sunday Visitor, 1983); and Guy Gaucher, *The Story of a Life: St. Thérèse of Lisieux* (San Francisco: Harper & Row, 1987). See also the introductory materials in the ICS editions of her works, especially *Story of a Soul: The Autobiography of St. Thérèse of Lisieux*, 2nd ed., trans. John Clarke, (Washington, D.C.: ICS Publications, 1976).
20. Clarke, *Story of a Soul*, pp. 188-200.

Bibliography

Brandsma, Titus. *Carmelite Mysticism: Historical Sketches*. 50th anniversary edition. Darien, Ill.: Carmelite Press, 1986.

Egan, Keith J. "The Spirituality of the Carmelites." In *High Middle Ages and Reformation*. Vol. 2 of *Christian Spirituality*, edited by Jill Raitt, pp. 50-62. New York: Crossroad, 1987.

John of the Cross. *John of the Cross: Selected Writings*. Edited and with introduction by Kieran Kavanaugh, O.C.D. Classics of Western Spirituality Series. Mahwah, N.J.: Paulist Press, 1987.

Kavanaugh, Kieran, O.C.D. "St. Teresa and the Spirituality of Sixteenth Century Spain." In *The Roots of the Modern Christian Tradition*. Vol. 2 of *The Spirituality of Western Christendom*, edited by E. Rozanne Elder, introduction by Jean Leclercq, pp. 91-104. Kalamazoo, Mich.: Cistercian Publications, 1984.

O'Connor, Patricia. *In Search of Thérèse*. Vol. 3 of *The Way of the Christian Mystics*. Wilmington, Del.: Michael Glazier, 1987.

Paul-Marie de la Croix. "Carmelite Spirituality." In *Some Schools of Catholic Spirituality*, edited by Jean Gautier, pp. 110-85. New York: Desclée, 1959.

Rohrbach, Peter Thomas. *Journey to Carith: The Story of the Carmelite Order*. Garden City, N.Y.: Doubleday, 1966.

Valabek, Redemptus Maria. *Prayer Life in Carmel: Historical Sketches*. Rome: Carmel in the World, 1982.

Practicing the Presence of God: Recollection in the Carmelite Tradition

ROBIN MAAS

Prayer doesn't consist of thinking a great deal, but of loving a great deal.
—ST. TERESA OF AVILA

Perhaps no biblical writer has both inspired and confounded so many Christians as the Apostle Paul. Much of what he wrote we have to wrestle with, and this has certainly been the case with his injunction to "pray without ceasing" (I Thess. 5:17 JB). Each of the spiritual traditions has had to come to terms with it in some way. Since fallen human existence requires that we must earn our bread by the sweat of our brow, none of us is free to spend every waking minute in prayerful solitude "alone" with God. Yet the biblical injunction stands, and the spiritually hungry of this world have been both persistent and ingenious in finding ways to obey it.

The Carmelite tradition, with its strong emphasis on mental prayer, is the source of a particularly helpful and engaging solution to this dilemma. The specific practice to which we refer is termed "recollection." Recollection, as the re-collecting or re-situating of the self *toward God,* is an affective rather than a discursive form of prayer. In other words, instead of requiring a focusing of the intellect, as the practice of *lectio* or meditation tends to do (at least initially), the will and the emotions are most active. In affective forms of prayer, the mind is quieted. We are no longer busy reading or reciting vocal prayers, concerned to tell God something; rather, we are simply and lovingly *present* to God, and when we are present to the Lord, we are not "thinking about" him; we are looking at him.

The motive power of affective prayer is, quite simply, love. Eventually we reach the point in a close relationship where we do not always have to find something to do or say; we can simply be quietly together. The same holds true for our relationship with God. There comes a time when we seek communion not because we have a problem that needs solving or an intercession to plead. We come out of a deep desire for "holy companionship," as Teresa describes it.

Unfortunately, recollection, as an expression of this hunger to love, does not come naturally to most people. It entails a disciplining of self-centered human nature, an effort both of intellect and (especially) of will, in its initial stages. St. Teresa took pains to instruct her nuns in the practice of recollection, and her writings treat the subject in a thorough way. But it was another Discalced Carmelite, Brother Lawrence of the Resurrection, who was to witness to this particular kind of prayer in a way that has made it irresistibly attractive and accessible to Christians of every persuasion.

Practicing the Presence of God

Nicolas Herman was born to a pious family in Lorraine, France, in the early part of the seventeenth century (ca. 1611). In his youth he became a soldier but was forced to change occupations as a result of a wound. A simple and uneducated man, he served for a while as a footman; but being naturally devout, he eventually turned to religious life and followed an uncle into the Carmelites. He spent the rest of his long life serving his community in the most menial capacities, primarily as cook. And out of this utterly ordinary set of circumstances came a life of profound holiness and a spiritual classic that has captivated Protestants as much as Catholics for over three hundred years.

The Practice of the Presence of God by Brother Lawrence of the Resurrection is a collection of four transcribed "conversations" and letters to religious and lay people. So brief that it can—but never should—be read at a single sitting, it contains the humble friar's deceptively simple teachings about a recollected form of prayer he termed "practicing the presence of God." To the many who eventually came to seek his guidance, he always had the same thing to say:

First: Renounce the Love of Anything That Is Not God

"I know," says Brother Lawrence, "that to achieve this [the presence of God] the heart must be emptied of all other things, for God wishes to possess it alone; and as He cannot possess it alone without emptying it of everything that is not Himself, so neither can He act there and do what He wishes there unless it is empty of all else."[1]

This sacrificial gift of self does not consist simply of a single grand or dramatic gesture; rather, it is a matter of keeping a vigilant "watch over our impulses which affect our spiritual life as well as our mundane activities." Far from having to rely solely on our own resources in a heroic act of the will, we will find that God will graciously assist us in this purification if we "truly desire to be united to Him."[2]

Second: Practice God's Presence Faithfully by Keeping the Soul's Gaze Humbly and Trustfully Fixed on God

Unable to pray effectively according to a set method or pattern, Brother Lawrence found that he could pray most successfully (and consistently) by placing himself, through an act of the imagination and by an impulse of love, in the presence of God. Put simply, he saw himself constantly before the gaze of the Almighty, and he understood that gaze to be a supremely patient and loving one. This meant that nothing he said or did could be separated or hidden from God; conversely, everything he did became a part of that Divine-human relationship.

As the practice of placing himself in God's presence gradually became habitual, he found that the distinction between time set aside for prayer and time designated for work became blurred. Whereas the average person craves silence and solitude for uninterrupted prayer, Brother Lawrence claimed "he was more united to God in his ordinary activities than when he devoted himself to religious activities which left him with a profound spiritual dryness."[3] It is a "great delusion," he says, "to think that time set aside for prayer should be different from other times, [for we are] equally obliged to be united to God by work in the time assigned to work as by prayer during prayer time."[4]

Third: We Should Begin, Continue, and End Every Act We Perform by an "Inward Lifting of the Heart to God"

If it is love that drives us to seek communion with God, then it must be for love of God that we perform every action our human existence imposes on us. For Brother Lawrence, "Our sanctification depends not upon changing works but in doing for God what we ordinarily do for ourselves," trusting that he will provide us with the means and the strength to carry out our assigned tasks.[5] Our day should be punctuated with little moments of mental and emotional withdrawal, when we remind ourselves that we are in God's presence and that what we do, we do for God:

During our work and other activities, during our spiritual reading and writing, even more so during our formal devotions and spoken prayers we should stop as often as we can, for a moment, to adore God from the bottom of our hearts, to savor Him, by steath as it were, as He passes by. Since you know God is with you in all your actions, that He is in the deepest recesses of your soul, why not, from time to time, leave off your external activities . . . to adore Him inwardly. . . . These interior retreats to God gradually free us by destroying that self love which can exist only among our fellow human beings.[6]

Brother Lawrence recommends the use of what the tradition calls "ejaculations," that is, abbreviated prayers that can be said in a moment's time as a method of reminding ourselves of God's presence during the day's activities: "See, my God, I am wholly yours" or "Lord, make me pleasing to your heart." These are small gestures of love, but potent ones.

Fourth: Persevere

The effort of thinking of God frequently throughout the day—let alone constantly—will first strike us as laborious and artificial. If it is to become a habit, then it is something for which we must be trained. Distractions are a major problem for the beginner, but we should not be overly discouraged. The desire to be present to God must not itself become a new source of anxiety. Brother Lawrence explains that when he sometimes went for a considerable period of time without thinking of God, "he did not let it bother him, but after having acknowledged his wretchedness to God, he returned to Him with even more confidence for having suffered such misery in forgetting Him so."[7]

Confession, therefore, is the best remedy for distraction, along with a healthy suspicion of long-winded prayer:

I do not advise much talking in prayer, long discourses often being the cause for wandering. Present yourself in prayer to God like a dumb and paralytic beggar at a rich man's door; concentrate on keeping your mind on the presence of the Lord; if it sometimes wanders and withdraws itself from Him, do not let it upset you; confusion serves rather to distract the mind than to recollect it; the will must bring it back calmly; if you persevere in this way, God will have pity on you.[8]

Sincere, if bumbling, efforts on our part are eventually met with gracious invitations on God's part: If we struggle to approach him, he comes running to us, and what began as a deliberate act of the will on our part ends as an effortless delight.

262

The Effects of Recollection

A constant theme in the history of the Church's spiritual traditions is the linking of prayer with virtue. On the one hand, we are taught that the prayer of the virtuous person is particularly efficacious (James 5:16), and on the other, that the practice of prayer purifies and strengthens the one praying. In the case of recollection, it is particularly easy to see how the practice of this prayer form over a period of time would begin to have ethical consequences. To be precise, most of us are accustomed to having some privacy—time when we believe we are alone and unobserved. Take a moment to consider your behavior at such times. Are there things you would do alone that you would definitely not do in the presence of others? What would it mean, practically speaking, to live as if you were *perpetually* companioned by infinite Love? Doesn't it seem reasonable to expect that the more recollected we are, the more likely the quality of our actions will be affected?

The point is not that we suddenly become spiritual heroes; the changes that occur are much more likely to be small and subtle ones: fewer outbursts of temper, more frequent impulses to offer help to someone in need, a willingness to show warmth when you would prefer to give a cold shoulder. The resources for giving more love don't come from within us; they come as a consequence of our dwelling in the presence of Love, and the more we dwell in this presence, the freer we are from our own emotional responses. This liberation from self costs us something, of course. It costs us our privacy. From now on, everything we do, say, or think will be held up to the pure light of truth. And we will be painfully aware that this is the case.

But with the loss of privacy comes the great gain of "holy companionship." Suddenly, we are no longer alone. Every joy we experience, every pleasurable surprise, is shared. Likewise, every doubt, fear, or sorrow is also shared. In recollection, we know that *God* knows. Loose and very public talk about having a "personal" relationship with Jesus has had the adverse effect of making many people who yearn for an intimate knowledge of God wary of just such a relationship, and this is tragic. We were made to love God—*to fall in love* with God. And this, of course, is what happened to all the great mystics, including Brother Lawrence.

What happens when we fall in love? We go a little bit crazy. We find our world is infused with beauty. Without any effort on our part, we find ourselves thinking about our loved one all the time. When we wake up in the morning, when we go to sleep at night, at work, at play, that person is there; he or she is a constant presence in our life and a source of endless wonder and delight. We cannot simply stop working and spend all our time with our beloved; we cannot abandon the seemingly infinite number of tedious chores that daily life requires. But suddenly these things seem less burdensome, because they are emotionally shared.

Oddly enough, the same thing happens in our relationship to God, if we let it. If we reposition ourselves *toward God,* even though we cannot look directly into the Sun of Love, we can feel the light flooding into our life.

A Word to the Wise

As with any promising approach to prayer, there are always a few pitfalls that need to be identified and avoided. The following suggest themselves in relation to the practice of recollection:

"Humility" as an Obstacle to Recollection

Many people who are comfortable offering formal or set prayers are profoundly uncomfortable at the thought of intimate discourse with the Lord. It strikes them as presumptuous, if not silly: Who am I to bother God with my petty problems? But it is not possible to practice the presence of God without an increase in personal vulnerability and a willingness to risk some "silliness." As St. Paul was willing to be a fool for Christ, so was Brother Lawrence, who wrote that the consolations he received unbidden from the practice of God's presence were sometimes so great that he was forced to behave in a ridiculous manner, "singing and dancing violently like a madman."[9]

The "silliness" we risk, however, is of a much less dramatic sort. The humble friar's instructions to "act very simply with God, and speak to Him frankly, while asking His help in things as they occur," are a blow to our own sense of maturity, independence, and self-esteem.[10] It is as if the call to recollection were a call to a naïve and unsophisticated "littleness." And indeed, it is. Teresa of Avila had a shrewd sense of how the practice of recollection threatens our carefully constructed self-image:

> Avoid being bashful with God, as some people are, in the belief that they are being humble. It would not be humility on your part if the King were to do you a favour and you refused to accept it; but you would be showing humility by taking it, and being pleased with it, yet realizing how

264

far you are from deserving it. A fine humility it would be if I had the Emperor of Heaven and earth in my house, coming to it to do me a favour and to delight in my company, and I were so humble that I would not answer His questions, nor remain with Him, nor accept what he gave me, but left him alone. . . .

Have nothing to do with that kind of humility . . . but speak with Him as with a Father, a Brother, a Lord and a Spouse. . . . He will teach you what you must do to please Him.[11]

This kind of simple but intimate discourse with God, far from being a presumption on our part, is the essential prerequisite, says Teresa, to a state of recollection—to the prayer of "quiet," where a wordless, longing gaze replaces petition.

The Problem of Spiritual Gluttony

Many people are initially attracted to various prayer practices because they hold out a promise of some sort of spiritual satisfaction, or "consolation," as the tradition calls it. Who *wouldn't* want to feel a sense of closeness to God? Who doesn't want to feel inspired, consoled, strengthened, enthused? The practice of recollection, which holds out the promise of a *constant* sense of God's presence, is particularly attractive in that respect. But the desire for inspiration as the motive for prayer quickly melts away in the furnace of ordinary daily living.

The deepest motive for all prayer, including recollection, must not be the "loaves and fishes" Jesus distributes, but Jesus himself. The commitment to be present to Christ means sharing not just consolations but sufferings, pain, and aridity as well. Although he himself was blessed with abundant consolations, Brother Lawrence warns against depending on results:

> There is no mode of life in the world more pleasing and more full of delight than continual conversation with God; only those who practice it and experience it can understand it. I do not, however, advise you to pursue it for this purpose. We should be seeking consolation from this practice, but let us do it motivated by love and because God wishes it.

Our deepest need, he explains, is not for consolation but for a clear and truthful vision of our own fallen condition:

> If only we knew how we need God's grace and assistance, we would never lose sight of Him not even for an instant. Believe me, from this very moment, make a holy and firm resolution never to be wilfully

separated from Him, and to live the rest of your days in His sacred presence deprived, for His love if He deems it proper, of any heavenly or earthly consolation.[12]

In the light of God's presence we will be loved, it is true, and *because* we are loved, we will begin to see the truth about God, ourselves, and the world. Some of what we see will not console us; it will frighten us.

The Temptation to Abandon Other Prayer Forms

The emotional satisfactions of affective prayer can be very strong—so strong that we are tempted to leave behind previous practices of vocal prayer and discursive meditation. Generally speaking, this impulse should be resisted. The point is not to remain tied to forms that no longer seem fruitful; rather, it is a problem of continuing to engage the intellect in relationship to God through regular spiritual reading and meditation on Scripture. This type of prayer serves to *instruct* as well as to inspire and will thereby shape the content of our relationship to God. Our personal experience of God does not stand alone, unchallengeable by external norms. The experience of God's presence should, in fact, drive us to scrutinize the teachings of Scripture and tradition on a regular basis.

EXERCISES

For an Individual

For most beginners, practicing the presence of God will initially require the support of some artificial structure. For example, you might decide that during the course of the day, each time you stand, go up and down stairs, or begin a new task, you will take a moment to recollect yourself and address God. If you find it helpful, choose a brief, set form of address, for example, the Jesus Prayer ("Lord Jesus Christ, Son of God, have mercy on me"), or simply speak frankly to God out of the depths of your heart. As you become aware of missed opportunities, don't berate yourself but simply use these moments to confess your need of God's grace and confidently ask for it.

If you use public transportation, instead of reading or simply staring at your fellow passengers, try making use of this time to recollect yourself. Repeat the name of Jesus during the course of your journey with the intention of interiorly meeting Christ and surrendering to whatever he may wish to communicate to you. The point here is not simply that you are developing a new awareness of God's presence but that you have been willing to let go of some other, perfectly legitimate activity to do so.

Learn Brother Lawrence's prayer (shown below), and use it before beginning a new task:

> O My God, since Thou art with me,
> and I must now, in obedience to thy commands,
> apply my mind to these outward things,
> I beseech Thee to grant me the grace
>   to continue in Thy presence;
> and to this end do Thou prosper me with Thy assistance,
>   receive all my work,
>   and possess all my affections.[13]

For a Group

It is possible to practice the presence of God in a group setting if a thorough explanation of the meaning of recollection is provided prior to the group's normal process (e.g., a lecture for a class, or a meeting, a workshop, etc.). Someone must then take responsibility for activating a signal—a small bell, a digital watch alarm, or some visual clue—about once every ten minutes or so over the course of forty-five to sixty minutes while the group goes about its ordinary business. Be sure to allow time to discuss the experience thoroughly, following the exercise.

DISCUSSION QUESTIONS

1. How do you anticipate your life might change if you were to become *conscious* of God's presence on a much more regular basis? Are these prospects attractive or intimidating?

2. Respond to Brother Lawrence's assertion that "our sanctification does not depend on certain works, but upon doing for God that which we ordinarily do for ourselves." Does this idea suggest new possibilities for understanding your own life's work?

3. Are you personally challenged by St. Teresa's admonition not to be "bashful" before God, and her assumption that this timidity masks a desire to avoid being vulnerable before God?

4. Does it make sense to you to speak of "falling in love" with God? Why or why not?

Notes

1. Brother Lawrence of the Resurrection, *The Practice of the Presence of God*, trans. John J. Delaney (Garden City, N.Y.: Doubleday Image Books, 1977).
2. Ibid., p. 37.
3. Ibid., p. 47.

4. Ibid., p. 49.
5. Ibid., p. 49.
6. Ibid., p. 102.
7. Ibid., p. 45.
8. Ibid., p. 77.
9. Ibid., p. 47.
10. Ibid., pp. 40-41.
11. St. Teresa of Avila, *The Way of Perfection*, trans. and ed. E. Allison Peers (Garden City, N.Y.: Doubleday Image Books, 1964), p. 184.
12. Brother Lawrence, *Practice of the Presence*, pp. 60-61.
13. Tony Castle, ed., *New Book of Christian Prayers* (New York: Crossroads, 1986), p. 98.

Resources

Lawrence of the Resurrection, Brother. *The Practice of the Presence of God.* Translated by John J. Delaney, with a foreword by Henri J. M. Nouwen. Garden City, N.Y.: Doubleday Image Books, 1977. (This work is available in a variety of formats from various publishers.)

Teresa of Avila, Saint. *Interior Castle.* Translated and edited by E. Allison Peers. Garden City, N.Y.: Doubleday Image Books, 1961.

———. *The Way of Perfection.* Translated and edited by E. Allison Peers. Garden City, N.Y.: Doubleday Image Books, 1964.

CHAPTER 9

Anglican Spirituality: A Historical Introduction

JOHN N. WALL

We most heartily thank thee . . . that we are very members incorporate in the mystical body of thy Son, the blessed company of all faithful people.
—BOOK OF COMMON PRAYER

Anglican spirituality, like Anglicanism in general, is richly diverse in expression because of the complex histories and various cultural settings of the many different churches in the worldwide Anglican Communion. Individual Anglicans may find religious significance in the plain and austere or in the elaborate and richly decorated; they may experience the holy in solitary retreat or in the midst of a large charismatic congregation. Some will enhance their encounter with the Divine through prayerful response to the Bible, traditional devotional practices, and meditative techniques; others will explore the insights of psychology or non-Western religions. Nor is this an exhaustive catalogue. No simple definition can encompass the varieties of spiritual life that some Anglicans find meaningful.

Yet Anglicanism's distinctive and unifying concerns are still visible in the very pragmatic way all churches of the Anglican Communion go about the basic practice of their corporate lives. In his opening remarks to the Lambeth Conference of Anglican primates and diocesan bishops in the summer of 1988, the Most Reverend Robert Runcie, archbishop of Canterbury, described Anglican unity as a unity of practice: "Anglican unity has most characteristically been expressed in worship, which includes four essential elements: scripture proclaimed, creed confessed, sacraments celebrated, and order maintained through an authorized episcopal ministry."[1] The defining marks of Anglicanism, therefore, do not reside in adherence to a common system of theology or in an experience of divine favor common to each member; they are found, instead, in the observation of and participation in public rites with a certain content that are conducted in a certain way.

An Anglican spirituality will therefore be recognizable as Anglican when it is practiced in relationship to a discipline of public worship that possesses these four essential characteristics. Indeed, the distinctive character of Anglican spirituality lies in the fact that it locates public and corporate prayer and praise as *prior to* and informing of private or individual prayer and praise, rather than the other way around. Anglicans, *as Anglicans*, share a common life of corporate worship in relationship to which a variety of theological perspectives, styles of living, and traditions of spiritual discipline can coexist, so long as the individual practice is seen as being for the enrichment of the corporate life. To speak, therefore, of Anglican spirituality—when one wishes to distinguish it from other spiritual traditions—is to speak of a corporate spirituality that is developed and sustained through the maintenance of a discipline of public rites performed and occasions observed.

Since we usually think of spirituality as the practice of an inner spiritual discipline or the cultivation of a personal relationship to the Divine, this concept of a public spirituality may seem unusual or difficult to grasp. Yet Archbishop Runcie's description of the unity of Anglican identity as consisting of a life of common prayer based on four essential elements reflects a long-standing consensus among Anglicans. The year 1988 marked the one hundredth anniversary of the adoption by the Anglican Communion of what has come to be known as the *Chicago-Lambeth Quadrilateral,* a document first approved by the House of Bishops of The Episcopal Church meeting in convention in Chicago in 1886 and then approved, in slightly modified form, by the Lambeth Conference of all Anglican bishops in 1888.[2] According to this statement, the "substantial deposit of Christian Faith and Order" consists of the Holy Scriptures, the ancient creeds, the sacraments of baptism and Eucharist, and the historic episcopate.

The original intent of this statement was ecumenical. It was to serve as the basis for Anglican efforts to reunite separated Christian traditions. But the *Chicago-Lambeth Quadrilateral* has taken on a life within Anglicanism that was unanticipated by its proposers. It has, in fact, shaped Anglicans' understanding of themselves and thus influenced the development of Anglican worship and spiritual practice—a situation reflected in Archbishop Runcie's remarks. As a result of the *Chicago-Lambeth Quadrilateral,* we are now (a century later) clearer about what unites Anglicans and gives to Anglicanism its distinctive character. In fact, recent liturgical reforms in The Episcopal Church and in other member churches of the Anglican Communion have resulted in rites that express more clearly than ever the public character of Anglican spirituality and the appropriateness of its expression through Bible reading and sacramental participation. Indeed, the very fact that such a statement of the essentials of Christian identity emerged from within Anglicanism and not from within another Christian tradition suggests that the *Chicago-Lambeth Quadrilateral* points to characteristics of the Anglican tradition that were really there all along, waiting for such a definitive articulation.

The English Reformation: Joining Prayer to Good Works

An examination of the emergence of the Church of England from medieval Christendom will reveal that from the early years of the English Reformation, the goal of the English Reformers was to establish a Church whose spiritual life was grounded in public reading and exposition of the Bible, together with public celebration of the sacraments of baptism and Eucharist, conducted by episcopally ordained clergy, in which the historic creeds were recited and affirmed. Basic to this reform effort was *The Book of Common Prayer*, a work that brought together in one volume all the public rites of the Church and provided instructions for their use.

The original efforts of the English Reformers were controversial in their own day, for they asked the English people to change their understanding of what it meant to pursue a Christian life. The Reformers abolished the monastic system, which had for centuries provided a significant model for Christian living; they also rejected acts of private devotion widely practiced by layfolk, such as the repetition of the rosary, invocation of aid from the saints in times of difficulty, and the use of extraliturgical texts and prayers. They insisted that the Christian life was to be oriented toward community salvation, pursued through attendance at worship conducted in the vernacular and performance of public acts of active charity toward one's neighbor.

The Reformers' efforts at such a reordering of emphasis in the English understanding of the Christian life met with resistance, for many viewed the result as an impoverishment rather than an appropriate return to essentials. The Anglican recovery of monasticism and the rich tradition of private devotion that began in the mid–nineteenth century has to some extent redressed whatever imbalance the Reformers' actions might have created. Yet this recovery has taken place within a continuing effort on the part of Anglicans to live out fully the English Reformers' original vision of the community gathered at the altar for prayer and praise, to be enabled to love and serve their neighbors. In this context, the process of Prayer Book revision leading to the American Prayer Book of 1979 is but the latest step in this effort.

The first major change in worship brought about by the English Reformation was the shift from use of Latin to English, in the replacement of the old Latin Missal by a vernacular prayer book. In attempting to reform England through the institution of vernacular worship, Archbishop Thomas Cranmer fashioned in *The Book of Common Prayer* a liturgical work for all the people of God. In the Prayer Book both clergy and layfolk found everything necessary for worship to occur. Further, the Prayer Book did away with the variety and diversity of liturgical texts in use in England, making possible the participation of all Englishfolk in worship with a common text.

This life of public worship was to assure the faithful that they possessed God's "favor and goodness" as "very members incorporate in [Christ's] mystical body," and that they were thus able to "do all such good works as [God] hast prepared for [them] to walk in."[3] Sermons in the official *Book of Homilies,* a companion volume to the English Bible and the Prayer Book, proclaim that our "justification"—and not our salvation—depends on having "a true and lively faith" that reveals itself in good works of charity. After justification, this life of good works leads to salvation, to "that blessed and eternal life."[4] Rejecting late medieval devotional practices, these official texts of the English Reformation make clear that participation in public worship is the source of grace to enable the offering of prayer and the doing of good works.

This cultivation of a liturgical spirituality stripped of all devotions, which joins prayer and worship on the one hand with the performance of "good works" on the other, represents something essential to Anglicanism that has been present from the beginning. In the preface to the House of Bishops' version of the *Chicago-Lambeth Quadrilateral,* the bishops' statement of purpose for this declaration points to the characteristic emphasis on the life of charity as part of the spiritual discipline of Anglicanism. Writing to define the intent of the *Quadrilateral,* the bishops declared as their goals, in addition to overcoming schism, "to heal the wounds of the Body of Christ, and to promote the charity which is the chief of Christian graces and the visible manifestation of Christ to the world" (*BCP,* p. 84). Their concern with the Body of Christ and with charity was also echoed in Archbishop Runcie's opening remarks to the 1988 Lambeth Conference. Recalling the words of his predecessor Archbishop Michael Ramsey, Runcie affirmed that for Anglicans "the journey towards God in adoration and towards the world in service are not two journeys but one."[5]

A People of the Book

A central issue in coming to grips with Anglican spirituality is that of discerning what Cranmer and his followers meant by creating as the centerpiece of their Reformation a book of "common" prayer for *use,* through which all England would be brought to a common table to hear the Bible read, the creeds recited, intercessory prayer offered, and the sacraments of baptism and Eucharist celebrated in a language "understanded of the people." Although Cranmer and his followers shared with continental Reformers a concern to recover the biblical text in the language of the people, what they intended, clearly, was not private reading of the Bible as an act sufficient unto itself. Early in the seventeenth century, John Donne, dean of St. Paul's Cathedral in London, defined the Church of England's understanding of the role of the Bible in these terms:

> [Salvation] is by the Word; but not by the Word read at home, though that is a pious exercise; nor by the Word submitted to private interpretation; but by the Word preached . . . in a settled Church . . . according to his Ordinance, and under the great Seal, of his blessing [in the Eucharist].[6]

For this reason, to understand Anglican spirituality we need to understand the book that facilitates "the ongoing, corporate, liturgical life of the Church,"[7] namely, *The Book of Common Prayer.* While the very early years of the English Reformation (from the rejection of papal authority in the mid–1530s to the authorization of an English translation of the Bible in 1539) saw essentially administrative changes of little consequence for daily Church life, the distinctiveness of Anglicanism begins to emerge in early attempts to transform public worship. Starting with a rite for public prayer, the Great Litany of 1542, Archbishop Thomas Cranmer began gradually to prepare a complete English text for the public worship of the Church. His efforts bore fruit in the reign of King Edward VI with the appearance of the first *Book of Common Prayer* in 1549. While today many different versions of *The Book of Common Prayer* are in use in the different churches of the Anglican Communion, all are related historically and

273

structurally to this first Prayer Book. Revised and reissued in 1552, *The Book of Common Prayer* was again adopted for official use during the reign of Elizabeth I in 1559. After small revisions in 1604 and 1662, it continues as the official Prayer Book of the Church of England and the model for Prayer Books in use in the other churches of the Anglican Communion.

Anglicans are thus a "people of the book," but for Anglicans it is the Prayer Book that enables everyone, lay or ordained, to participate in corporate worship. *The Book of Common Prayer* has been with us for so long and has served as a source for models and texts for worship in so many Christian traditions that it is often difficult for us to realize how revolutionary and distinctive it was in its own day. For this reason, we will find it worthwhile to reconstruct expectations of worship and the spiritual life in England in the early years of the sixteenth century and then contrast to them the changes brought about by the introduction of *The Book of Common Prayer*. To do so will help us get to the essence of the Anglican vision of the spiritual life.

We need not accept as totally factual the Reformers' critique of the medieval Church to acknowledge that the celebration of worship in Latin had its consequences for medieval worship and spirituality. The majority of people, who were required by law to attend church regularly, were illiterate; thus the great theological and spiritual writings of the medieval Church were the work of a brilliant few whose audience never included the vast majority of the English. Recent studies suggest that for most parishioners in the Middle Ages, religion was at best an uncertain mixture of Christian practice, folk magic, and survivals from the old pagan belief systems.[8] We can never know for sure how much even the versions of Christian beliefs taught by educated clergy were mixed in the minds of their adherents with remnants of a still-powerful pagan culture; thus the popular concept of the Middle Ages as an age of universal faith, a high point in the history of Christian belief, is simply an illusion.

Literate clergy celebrating the Mass in Latin were separated from their often illiterate parishioners by more than barriers of learning. The rite had become less a public gathering of God's people than a spiritual discipline of the clergy, performed for the laity yet done without their active participation. While clergy and monastic choirs recited the ancient texts, the laity watched, said the rosary, or thought of other things. Noncommunicating Masses became the norm and, as a result, medieval Church law required all Christians to receive the Eucharist at least once a year during the Easter season.

Far removed from romanticized myths about communal worship in late medieval religion, the early sixteenth-century Church's celebration of the Mass combined two essentially private actions: the apparently private action of the priest who celebrated, and the more obviously private devotions the laity performed while the Mass was being celebrated. In the first *Book of Homilies* of 1547—a collection of official sermons issued to educate layfolk about essentials of Reformed belief—Archbishop Cranmer attacked private devotional practices such as "beads, Lady Psalters and rosaries, XV O's and Saint Agatha's Letters" as inappropriate substitutes for public prayer.[9] At least from the Reformers' perspective, these practices of medieval spiritual life were regarded by their practitioners as having magical efficacy.

The Bible in Anglican Worship

In the medieval Church, regular reading of the Bible was the work of monastic communities; layfolk knew of the Bible through seeing its narratives depicted in dramatic performance or artistic depiction. While to us the pageantry of medieval ceremonies, religious festivals, and pilgrimages to holy shrines may appear delightful enrichments of the Christian life, to the Reformers these practices seemed to get in the way of more fundamental things, of which the great majority of people remained ignorant. Early texts by the Reformers emphasize the necessity of instructing layfolk in such basic things as the creeds, the Ten Commandments, and the Lord's Prayer. From their perspective, late medieval devotional life was individuating rather than community building; it detracted from participation of all the faithful in the public worship of the Church.

One major effort of the English Reformation must therefore be seen as a process of "Christianization," of education in the basics of the faith, of bringing the faith to the people. Cranmer began this task with the Bible. Taking over the translation prepared earlier by William Tyndale and Miles Coverdale, the archbishop ordered that by All Saints' Day in 1539 every parish priest in England should have a copy of "one Book of the whole Bible of the largest volume in English, and the same set up in some convenient place within the said church that ye have cure of, whereas your parishioners may most commodiously resort to the same and read it."[10] A second edition of this Bible, known as the Great Bible because of its physical size, appeared in 1540 with a preface by the archbishop, in which the intent of the Reformers to make the Bible available to all Englishfolk was dramatically affirmed:

> Here may all manner of persons: men, women; young, old; learned, unlearned; rich, poor; priests, laymen; lords, ladies; officers, tenants, and mean men; virgins, wives, widows; lawyers, merchants, artificers, husbandmen, and all manner of persons, of what estate or condition soever they be; may in THIS BOOK learn all things, what they ought to believe, what they ought to do, and what they should not do, as well concerning Almighty God, as also concerning themselves, and all others.[11]

Cranmer's list of those who are to read the Bible strives for inclusiveness; reaching beyond distinctions of class or economic status, it seeks to bring all Englishfolk within the sphere of the biblically literate. Placing the Bible in the midst of each church where all could read it also made the spiritual discipline of reading the Bible a public action in the Church of England from the outset.

Indeed, one way to talk about *The Book of Common Prayer,* Cranmer's next great project, is to see it as providing a structure for the regular public reading of the Bible. In his preface to the first *Book of Common Prayer,* Archbishop Cranmer points out that with the Prayer Book and the Bible "curates shall need none other books for their public service," so that "all the whole realm shall have but one use" (*BCP,* 1559, p. 16). Thus one goal of the early Reformers was to simplify the number of books that were required for public worship by consolidating the many texts necessary to perform the rites of the medieval Church. But Cranmer goes on to note that in the medieval rites the simple reading of the Bible had become obscured by ceremonial and textual accretions, so that while reading of the Bible was often begun, it was never finished—"never read through"—leaving much of the biblical text "unread" (*BCP,* 1559, p. 15).

The Prayer Book, however, provides "an order, whereby the same shall be redressed," enabling a "continual course of the reading of the Scripture" (*BCP,* 1559, p. 15). To facilitate this, Cranmer took the seven offices of the monastic day and collapsed them into two, the rites of Morning and Evening Prayer, or matins and evensong. For each he provided a coordinated calendar of biblical readings so that at these two Daily Offices the Psalter was read through once every month; the New Testament, three times annually; and the Old Testament, once annually. All clergy ordained in the Church of England were, and continue to be, required to read these two Daily Offices every day, in public if possible and in private if necessary.

This discipline of biblical reading makes of the Bible a special kind of experience. The Psalter, for example, becomes a text that is prayed as much as read, as habitual use makes its phrases familiar ones. Such familiarity came both to clergy and to layfolk—a key point, for the reading of Scripture in public became a spiritual exercise as well as an exercise in Christian education. Since the Prayer Book gives all the faithful access to the Bible in the same way, in a regular, disciplined fashion, this exercise of public reading became one that joined rather than divided lay and ordained Englishfolk. We cannot, if we submit to the discipline of the Daily Office lectionary, ignore biblical texts unfamiliar or uncomfortable. Instead, we must take the whole text as it comes and make of it what we can.

In addition, the regular discipline of reading the Psalter and the other books of the Old and New Testament takes place within the context of the eucharistic calendar of the Church year. The eucharistic lectionary organizes the year into a series of liturgical seasons, beginning in Advent and continuing through Christmas, Epiphany, Lent, Easter, and the Sundays after Trinity, until the year begins again in Advent. This liturgical year recalls the events of Jesus' earthly career and, since it determines the Collect for the Day read at both the Daily Offices and the Eucharist, provides the context both for the biblical lessons read at the Eucharist and for those read at Morning and Evening Prayer.

Cranmer objected to the way the regular reading of Scripture had been crowded out of the medieval Church by interruptions caused by saints' days and by the use of nonbiblical texts. To avoid this, he mandated only readings from the Bible and cut down on the number of saints' days and holy days, limiting them to days of commemoration for the New Testament saints and the major events of Jesus' life. Since then, the churches of the Anglican Communion have enriched their calendars with additional observances of saints' days, but not so many as to obscure the fact that the Daily Office calendar still calls for the regular reading, chapter by chapter, of the Bible. In the American Prayer Book, the calendar for the Daily Office now in use provides a two-year cycle of readings. The eucharistic lectionary in Cranmer's Prayer Book appointed appropriate lessons from the New Testament Epistles and Gospels for each day's celebration of the Eucharist; in the current American Prayer Book, a three-year cycle provides lessons from the Old Testament as well as from the Epistles and Gospels for reading at eucharistic celebrations.

Cranmer's plan for worship in England was to combine daily reading of the Morning and Evening Offices with celebration of the Eucharist on Sundays and holy days. Thus a Sunday morning's worship would have begun with Morning Prayer, continued with the Great Litany, and concluded with the Eucharist, with a sermon preached during the Eucharist. Cranmer insisted that at least two or three people receive the Holy Communion with the celebrant, however, eliminating the private Masses characteristic of the medieval Church. Confronted with a people accustomed to watching the celebration of the medieval Mass and receiving once a year, he tried to encourage further participation in the Eucharist by making the rite of penance a part of the eucharistic rite; but resistance was great. By the reign of Elizabeth I, people were required by law to receive at least three times per year. As a practical result, therefore, in most parish churches in Elizabethan England, the Sunday morning rites began with Morning Prayer, continued with the Great Litany, and concluded with the Liturgy of the Word from the Eucharist. Only recently has regular and more frequent Communion become common practice. In that sense, we are still trying to realize the full scope of Cranmer's original vision of the Church as one corporate body joined at least weekly at one altar through the use of one common rite.

The Eucharist in Anglican Worship

It is in the Eucharist that Cranmer links (literally) the reading of Scripture with the life of active charity. The full Sunday morning worship service as Cranmer envisioned it continued after Morning Prayer and the Great Litany with the full service of Holy Communion. The people of God gathered at the opening invitation of Morning Prayer to hear the Word of God read to them; they left after receiving Communion with the promise that they had received assurance of their membership in Christ's Body and grace to go out to "do all such good works as [God] hast prepared for [them] to walk in" (*BCP* 1559, p. 265). Thus the full performance of Cranmer's Sunday (and holy day) services took parishioners from a disciplined attentiveness to Scripture through response in prayer and praise to reception of the Eucharist, preparing them for a continuing response through charitable behavior. From the very beginning, therefore, Anglican worship performed as well as espoused a public spirituality that linked a discipline of reading, prayer, and praise with a life of charitable action. Participation in this public spirituality both taught such a life and enabled through its communion of grace the practice of that life.

Much has been written in an effort to understand Cranmer's eucharistic theology; what is more important here is to describe the experience of worship that Cranmer's Prayer Book made possible. The rite began with the Collect for Purity, Cranmer's transformation of the

278

preparatory penitential rite of the medieval Mass. Although this rite, said by the priest in Latin, was understood to be done for the laity, Cranmer viewed it as essentially a private devotion of the priest. He therefore made it into a prayer for the preparation of the whole congregation, turning its Confiteor ("I confess") into a petition that God "cleanse the thoughts of *our* hearts," again making clear that his understanding of the Eucharist emphasized the action of the corporate body rather than the action of individuals. This feature of Cranmer's original liturgical revision has remained part of all Anglican Prayer Books.

The rite continued with the recitation of the Ten Commandments (a feature now optional in the recent American Prayer Book) and the Collect for the Day. The reading of the Epistle and the Gospel for the Day followed, leading to the recitation of the Nicene Creed and the delivery of a sermon. The phenomenon of Morning Prayer and sermon still found in some parishes in The Episcopal Church and provided for in the 1979 Prayer Book is not a feature of the early Prayer Books. After the sermon came the offertory, the intercessory prayers, and preparation for Communion through the confession of sin and pronouncement of absolution by the priest. There followed the eucharistic prayer, or Prayer of Consecration, with its versicles and responses, its Proper Preface (or variable seasonal text), the Sanctus, and the Words of Institution (or repetition of the narrative of the Last Supper). This was followed by reception of bread and wine, the Prayer of Thanksgiving, the Gloria ("Glory be to God on High"), and the final blessing of the people. In the most recent Prayer Book, the Gloria has been returned to its traditional position at the beginning of the rite, modern-language texts have been provided, and other slight rearrangements have been made to clarify the action, but otherwise Cranmer's texts for prayers and organization of the rite have remained remarkably unchanged.

Medieval theologies of the presence of Christ in the Eucharist were rich, diverse, and founded on a long tradition of theological reflection. While the authentic patristic and medieval traditions emphasized the real, sacramental presence of Christ in the consecrated elements (transubstantiation), certain heterodox medieval theologies exaggerated the physical or spatial presence of Christ in the eucharistic elements. Cranmer, reacting against popular acceptance of this "exaggerated realist" position, objected to the cult of adoration—typical of medieval eucharistic piety in general—in which the eucharistic elements were "reserved, carried about, lifted up, or worshipped."[12] He emphasized the central importance of the actual reception of the

279

Eucharist as the means of receiving divine assurance and insisted on a life of active charity as the goal of the eucharistic celebration. Even as his theology of the Christian life emphasized the action of the congregation in response to God's gift of himself, so his theology of the real presence emphasized the action of God in and through the eucharistic elements. In the archbishop's words:

> I say (according to God's word and the doctrine of the old writers) that Christ is present in his sacraments, as they teach also that he is present in his word, when he worketh mightily by the same in the hearts of the hearers. By which manner of speech it is not meant that Christ is corporally present in the voice or sound of the speaker (which sound perisheth as soon as the words be spoken), but this speech meaneth that he worketh with his word, using the voice of the speaker, as his instrument to work by; as he useth also his sacraments, whereby he worketh, and therefore is said to be present in them.[13]

God works in history, using his people to further his reconciling work and enabling them to further his work through the liturgy of Word and sacrament. To participate in the Holy Communion is to be made part of Christ and to receive Christ, so as to be assured of God's "fatherly goodness towards us," and thus to be empowered to participate in Christ's ongoing work in the world. Christ is fully and really present in the eucharistic action with the bread and wine through what he does with our use of the bread and wine, using them for his work. Cranmer's theology of presence supported and reinforced his concern for building up the public and visible Body of Christ, the Church community, as the agency for societal reform through charitable action.

The basic structure of Sunday worship, concluded later in the day with reading or singing of Evening Prayer (providing an occasion for instruction in the faith), set the pattern for a public Anglican spirituality, for a religious tradition that takes its sense of identity from participation in the observance of public worship. Like the ancient and medieval Church, the Church of England maintained an episcopally ordained ministry, but Cranmer sought to ensure that clergy did not become a group apart from the whole people of God. His priests were to lead worship in which all participated. Cranmer promoted marriage of the clergy as part of his interest in making the local parish and its constituent families—rather than the monastic community—the model for understanding the Church. He insisted that clergy face the people when celebrating the Eucharist, a tradition we have recently recovered; he also made clear that the charitable behavior of all the people of God was as much a part of the Christian life as was worship itself.

Daily Prayer in the Church and in the Home

In preparing a *Book of Common Prayer* to enable the prayer of the Church community, Archbishop Cranmer thought he was recovering the most ancient models of Church organization. His appeal was to the Church of the first five centuries of the Christian era; this helps explain his retention of the Church's most ancient creeds, the Apostles' Creed in the Daily Offices and the Nicene Creed in the Eucharist. His appeal to Christian antiquity and his affirmation of continuity in faith, organization, and practice with the ancient Church continue in such documents as the *Chicago-Lambeth Quadrilateral* to be characteristic stances and desires of Anglicanism.

This mode of Christian understanding made the gathered community the central focus of the Christian life; it also placed great emphasis on the family as the locus of worship apart from the Church. To facilitate family prayer and to link it to the ongoing prayer of the Church, the Church of England provided Primers that offered set forms of prayer to aid with family devotion. These consisted of simplified versions of the Daily Offices, arranged to make clear that the purpose of family prayer was to involve each individual family's daily devotions in the public prayer of the whole Church.

With time, various elements within the Church of England enriched personal and group prayer life through practices that elaborated on the basic pattern of recitation of the Psalter as part of the office. In cathedrals, chapters of cathedral clergy divided the Psalter among themselves, with each priest assigned a number of the Psalms to recite daily in addition to the reading of the Daily Offices. As a result, when these individual disciplines of Psalm recitation were taken together, the cathedral staff as a group could claim to have recited the entire Psalter every day. In a further elaboration, the group of people who gathered with Nicholas Ferrar at Little Gidding in the 1620s and bound themselves to a rule of life under the protection of John Williams, bishop of Lincoln, resolved to recite the entire Psalter together daily. They would begin in the morning and, weaving their recitation around their other daily activities, continue as late into the evening as necessary until the task was finished for the day. The recitation of the Psalter would resume again on the morning of the next day.[14]

Izaak Walton's account of George Herbert's devotional life will take us directly to the way these emphases of Anglican spirituality worked themselves out in the daily lives of parishes. Walton's account is, of course, an idealized one, but it also represents an account of what was supposed to happen in every English parish if the clergy and layfolk simply followed the instructions spelled out for them in the Prayer Book and in the Canons of the Church of England. Walton describes "Mr. Herbert's own practice" as involving, first of all, the doing of the public offices of *The Book of Common Prayer:*

> [Herbert's practice was] to appear constantly with his Wife, and three Neeces (the daughters of a deceased Sister) and his whole Family, twice every day at the Church-prayers, in the Chapel which does almost joyn to his Parsonage-house. And for the time of his appearing, it was strictly at the Canonical hours of 10 and 4; and then and there, he lifted up pure and charitable hands to God in the midst of the Congregation.[15]

Walton notes that Herbert brought with him into church not only his household but also "most of his Parishioners, and many Gentlemen in the Neighborhood, constantly to be a part of his Congregation twice a day" for his reading of Morning and Evening Prayer (the "Church-prayers"). Because he alerted them by ringing his church bell, even those who could not be physically present organized their devotional life around the rhythm of Herbert's observation of the Daily Offices:

> Some of the meaner sort of his Parish, did so love and reverence Mr. *Herbert,* that they would let their Plow rest when Mr. *Herbert's Saints-Bell* rung to Prayers, that they might also offer their devotions to God with him: and would then return back to their Plow.[16]

By making the public recitation of the Daily Offices the focus of spiritual life for his entire parish, Herbert thus demonstrated, according to Walton, a "most holy life" that

> begot such reverence to God, and to him, that [his parishioners] thought themselves the happier, when they carried Mr. *Herbert's* blessing back with them to their labour. Thus powerful was his reason, and example, to persuade others to a practical piety, and devotion.[17]

No words capture better the nature of Anglican spirituality than Walton's here, for the discipline of daily Bible reading and prayer according to *The Book of Common Prayer,* when linked to regular participation in the Eucharist as Cranmer envisioned, does constitute a truly "practical piety, and devotion."

Herbert rang a bell to summon those of his parishioners who could join him in church and to alert those who could not but who wished to pause in their labors and remember what was going on in church. In English parochial life the bounds of one parish stopped at the point at which its bell could no longer be heard. Thus to a degree now difficult to recover, the daily public prayers and readings of the Church organized English life spatially as well as temporally. This sense of ordering and orienting human action in time and space in relationship to the continuing public work of the Church helps us grasp the heart of Anglican spirituality.

In this light, even to read the offices alone is not to engage in a private, as opposed to a public and corporate, spiritual exercise, but to join one's own voice with the chorus of the rest of the Church, separated in space and time but united in action because the reader, even while alone, knows that the Church is reading the same texts and prayers. Many of the Prayer Book's set prayers reinforce this by using the plural pronouns "we" and "us," so that the people who use them to articulate their address to God are reminded that their prayers are not just for themselves but for the whole body of the faithful gathered in action and orientation, if not literally present in the same building.

Thus what is asked of God becomes effective for the petitioner to the extent that, and precisely when, the person praying becomes aware that his or her prayer is not just *his or hers alone* but is in fact the prayer of the whole Church. In this way, the spiritual life of individual Anglicans is defined in relationship to the ongoing corporate use of the Prayer Book. The promises of God to respond to prayer apply to the corporate body of the Church, and to individuals as they take part in the worship life of that body.

Walton does note that in addition to the Daily Offices George Herbert conducted in public, he also did not "neglect his own private devotions, nor those prayers that he thought himself bound to perform with his family." Yet prayer in Herbert's household, Walton writes, was always according to a "Set-form," including the Collect for the Day. In this way family prayer, done according to the directions provided in the official Primers, became an extension of the public prayer of the Church. About the forms and content of Herbert's purely private prayer, Walton is silent. But what is clear from his account is that Herbert immersed himself in leadership of corporate worship for the Church of England, according to the Prayer Book. What Herbert exemplifies in his personal practice he states eloquently in verse:

> Though private prayer be a brave design,
> Yet public hath more promises, more love:

And love's a weight to hearts, to eyes a sign.
We are all cold suitors; let us move
  Where it is warmest. Leave thy six and seven;
  Pray with the most: for where most pray, is heaven.[18]

Cranmer, too, insists on making private prayer ancillary to public worship:

But if thou wilt needs know where the true church of Christ is, and where the false, and not be deceived, herein take this for a plain and full answer, and wheresoever the word of God is truly preached, without addition of man's doctrines and traditions, and the sacraments duly administered according to Christ's institution, there is the true church, the very spouse of God, Christ being the head thereof.[19]

Archbishop Cranmer thus sought to avoid having the Word of God shut up in a single book, accessible only in the privacy of one's study and the recesses of one's heart. It was, instead, to be a living Word, a "true and lively Word" (*BCP*, 1559, p. 254) proclaimed through reading aloud and acting it out in the world. In the same sense we may approach the public theology of Cranmer's sacraments. Baptism, he believed, should be performed on Sundays as part of the main service of the Church, so that parishioners could be reminded of their own baptismal vows and recognize the rite as one of full incorporation into the Body of Christ. The baptized, he claimed in the Prayer Book, "have all things necessary for their salvation, and be undoubtedly saved" (*BCP*, 1559, p. 283).

Much has happened in the years that separate us from those early days of Anglican history. Most notable for Anglican spirituality has been the revival of Anglican monasticism in the nineteenth century. Yet this and other developments have served primarily to enrich opportunities for Anglicans to develop their individual spiritual lives by giving them access to the great traditions of Western spirituality not distinctively Anglican. Yet the focus of Anglican monasticism has still remained Cranmer's basic emphasis on a common or corporate spirituality centering on the recitation of the Offices.

Liturgical revision in The Episcopal Church and in the other churches of the Anglican Communion has sought to recover for our time the possibility of a truly public spirituality. The new Prayer Book makes clear that the Eucharist is "the principal act of Christian worship on the Lord's Day and other major feasts." The Eucharist and "Daily Morning and Evening Prayer . . . are the regular services appointed for public worship in this Church" (*BCP,* 13). New lectionaries make possible reading the Bible through on a two-year cycle in the Daily Office lectionary and on a three-year cycle in the eucharistic lectionary. New rites invite the increasing interweaving of personal, family, and community lives. For the kind of spirituality given to the Anglican tradition to explore and claim as its own, these are exciting times. Yet for such tradition-minded and history-conscious people as Anglicans tend to be, it is deeply comforting to realize that in enriching our spiritual lives as members of a Christian community, we are but discovering for our own time the same vision of the Christian life that Thomas Cranmer and the early English Reformers glimpsed and set about to realize through the creation of *The Book of Common Prayer* just over four hundred years ago.

Notes

1. Quoted in *The Living Church,* Aug. 7, 1988, pp. 9, 16. According to this statement, the "substantial deposit of Christian Faith and Order" consists of the Holy Scriptures, the ancient creeds, the sacraments of baptism and Eucharist, and the historic episcopate.
2. See *The Book of Common Prayer* (1979), pp. 876-78, for the full statement of the Chicago-Lambeth Quadrilateral. For a helpful review of the history of this statement, see the various articles in *Anglican Theological Review,* supplementary series 10 (Mar. 1988), *Essays on the Centenary of the Chicago-Lambeth Quadrilateral 1886/1888–1986/ 1988.*
3. Cited from the rite of Holy Communion in John Booty, ed., *The Book of Common Prayer, 1559. The Elizabethan Prayer Book* (Charlottesville, Va.: University Press of Virginia for the Folger Shakespeare Library, 1976), pp. 264-65. All further citations from the historic Prayer Book will be from this edition, cited by initials (i.e., "*BCP,*" *Book of Common Prayer*), date, and page number in the text. All quotations from the contemporary Prayer Book will be from *The Book of Common Prayer* of The Episcopal Church (1979) and will be cited in the text by initials and page number but with no date indicated.
4. From *Certain Sermons or Homilies* (1547), ed. Ronald Bond (Toronto: University of Toronto Press, 1987), pp. 81, 113. Modernization mine.
5. Quoted in *The Living Church,* Aug. 7, 1988, p. 9.
6. From John Donne, *Sermons,* vol. 7, ed. George R. Potter and Evelyn M. Simpson (Berkeley: University of California Press, 1960), p. 157.
7. Harvie H. Guthrie, "Anglican Spirituality: An Ethos and Some Issues," in *Anglican Spirituality,* ed. William J. Wolfe (Wilton, Calif.: Morehouse, 1982), p. 4.
8. For discussions, see Keith Thomas, *Religion and the Decline of Magic* (New York: Scribner's, 1971), and Jean DeLumeau, *Catholicism Between Luther and Voltaire* (Philadelphia: Westminster Press, 1977).
9. From *Certain Sermons,* p. 112.
10. From the Royal Injunction of Sept. 5, 1538, cited in F. F. Bruce, *The Bible in English* (New York: Oxford University Press, 1978), p. 68.
11. Cited from Bruce, *The Bible,* p. 71.
12. Article XXVIII, *Articles of Religion.*
13. Quoted from Cranmer's occasional writings in John N. Wall, *Transformations of the Word: Spenser, Herbert, Vaughan* (Athens, Ga.: University of Georgia Press, 1988), p. 46.

14. For a discussion of the spiritual life of Little Gidding, see Stanley Stewart, *George Herbert* (Boston: Twayne, 1986), pp. 57-82.
15. Ibid., p. 302.
16. Ibid.
17. Izaak Walton, "Life of George Herbert," in *Lives* (1670; reprint, London: Oxford University Press, 1927), p. 302.
18. From Herbert's "Perirrhanterium," in *The Country Parson, The Temple,* ed. John N. Wall (New York: Paulist Press, 1981), p. 135.
19. Quoted from Cranmer's occasional writings in John N. Wall, *Transformations of the Word,* p. 46.

Bibliography

Primary Sources

Booty, John, ed. *The Book of Common Prayer, 1559: The Elizabethan Prayer Book.* Charlottesville, Va.: University Press of Virginia for the Folger Shakespeare Library, 1976.
Donne, John. *The Divine Poems.* 2nd ed. Edited by Helen Gardner. Oxford: Clarendon, 1978.
_____. *Devotions upon Emergent Occasions.* Edited by Anthony Raspa. Montreal: McGill-Queen's University Press, 1975.
_____. *Sermons.* Edited by George R. Potter and Evelyn M. Simpson. 10 vols. Berkeley: University of California Press, 1954–1963.
Herbert, George. *The Country Parson, The Temple.* Edited by John N. Wall. New York: Paulist Press, 1981.
More, Paul Elmer, and Cross, Frank L. *Anglicanism: The Thought and Practice of the Church of England, Illustrated from the Religious Literature of the Seventeenth Century.* London: SPCK, 1962.

Secondary Sources

Holmes, Urban T. *A History of Christian Spirituality: An Analytical Introduction.* New York: Seabury Press, 1981.
Jones, Cheslyn; Wainwright, Geoffrey; and Yarnold, Edward, S. J., eds. *The Study of Spirituality.* New York: Oxford University Press, 1986.
McAdoo, H. R. *The Spirit of Anglicanism.* New York: Scribner's, 1965.
Moorman, John R. H. *The Anglican Spiritual Tradition.* 1983; reprint, Springfield, Ill.: Templegate, 1985.
Stranks, C. J. *Anglican Devotion.* London, SPCK, 1961.
Thornton, Martin. *English Spirituality.* London: SPCK, 1963.
_____. *Spiritual Direction.* London: SPCK, 1984.
Wand, J. W. C. *Anglicanism in History and Today.* New York: Nelson, 1962.
Wolf, William J., ed. *Anglican Spirituality.* Wilton, Conn.: Morehouse-Barlow, 1982.

Praying the Office:
Time Stolen for God

GABRIEL O'DONNELL, O.P.

> *Pray without ceasing.*
> —I THESSALONIANS 5:17 KJV

Time is a precious commodity in today's world. The accelerated pace of life in the last quarter of the twentieth century has left us breathless, and the specter of many tasks to be done in such a short span of time is often cause for despair. Each new generation, faced with a multitude of choices about how to use opportunities for leisure, is increasingly concerned about the efficient use of time. Yet even our recreational time is often programmed to the hilt with projects for self-enrichment or improvement. In our quest for "results," we have lost the art of killing time, of simply being, rather than doing.

In the spiritual wasteland that now confronts us, there is no space, no time, for God. Consequently, there is no time for the Church, for our neighbor—even for ourselves. Yet we know that a life of prayer and the development of a deep personal relationship with God requires that we steal some time from our other activities in order to be present to God and listen for the movements of the Holy Spirit.

The Origins of the Office

This "stealing" of time from the ordinary round of activities for God is a practice as old as the Christian Church itself. Inheriting the prayer traditions of Judaism, Christians from apostolic times onward prayed at fixed times of the day. In the Acts of the Apostles we read that Peter and John were "going up to the temple at the hour of prayer, the ninth hour" (Acts 3:1; see also 10:2-3, 30). As observant Jews, the apostles had to steal time from their pressing obligations to engage in a life of prayer, and whenever they did, the ordinary passage of time—where each and every moment is filled with the humdrum duties of life (*chronos*)—was transformed and given significance by those climactic interludes of prayer (*kairos*). What would otherwise have been simply the tedious repetition of responsibilities was given new content and an increased significance by these peak moments of communion with God.

In the first centuries of the Christian era these stolen moments of prayer were private and only gradually became forms of communal worship. Certain texts—psalms, hymns, and prayers—became associated with particular times of the day, and these in turn were sometimes related to specific aspects of the passion of Christ.[1] In the morning, the evening, and at other specified times during the day, Christians were expected to stop their routine tasks to offer praise and adoration to God and to remember the Lord as present in the midst of their existence, saving and calling them to a new and more abundant life. Prayer forms that were attached to set times of the day (e.g., morning, evening, or night) established a rhythm of remembrance of God throughout the twenty-four-hour cycle.

This structured way of praying together at certain times each day came to be known as "the Prayer of the Hours." In this way, the whole day was punctuated with the continual remembrance of God in either private or common prayer. These set times for prayer triggered the deep desire for a life of personal communion with God and new motivation for the work of evangelization. For most Christians, morning and evening were the times to gather with the believing community for prayer. At other fixed times during the day individual Christians stopped their work or even interrupted their sleep at night to pray; yet these private prayers of remembrance were never intended to replace the daily, communal Prayer of the Hours. Tertullian observes, "Of course, these [prayers of devotion] are in addition to our regular prayers [*legitimae orationes*], which are due [*debenter*] without any admonition, at the approach of day and night."[2] At this stage of development, the Prayer of the Hours was a collective and not, as it was later to become, an exclusively clerical responsibility. Clergy might take special roles in leading, but the Hours were the prayer of the whole Church.

Another important feature of the early Prayer of the Hours was its clear christological focus:

> Morning prayer was the daily celebration of the Lord's Resurrection,
> and evening prayer the daily commemoration of his burial and descent

among the dead. The lesser times of prayer, too, private though they were, were saturated with the events of the Passion. Hippolytus of Rome, recalling a first-century Roman practice, told his Christians to stop and pray at mid-morning, "For at this hour Christ was seen nailed to the tree"; at noon, "for when Christ was fastened to the wood of the cross the day was rent in two, and thick darkness came over all"; and at mid-afternoon, for "at the ninth hour Christ poured forth water and blood from his pierced side." In these perspectives, the patristic hours of prayer were a kind of daily votive Office of the Passion.[3]

The psalms of which the various Hours were composed were themselves understood christologically, just as the use of headings or titles for the psalms in the contemporary Liturgy of the Hours reinforces a christological interpretation of them.

The *General Instruction on the Liturgy of the Hours* for the Roman Catholic Church explicates this focus when it describes this practice as "the prayer of the Church with Christ and to Christ."[4] Quoting from Augustine, bishop of Hippo, the *Instruction* presupposes St. Paul's vision of the Church as the mystical Body of Christ:

> When we speak of prayer to the Father, we do not separate the Son from him and when the Son's Body prays it does not separate itself from its Head. It is the one Savior of his Body, the Lord Christ Jesus, who prays for us and in us and who is prayed to by us. He prays for us as our priest, in us as our Head; he is prayed to by us as our God. Recognize therefore our own voice in him and his voice in us.[5]

Eventually, as these times for regular prayer became formalized, the Sunday Eucharist and the daily celebration of the Hours—especially Morning and Evening Prayer—became the paradigm of liturgical prayer for the ordinary Christian. In the more specialized setting of monastic life a fuller observance of the hours of prayer was possible. Here the attempt was made to fulfill in literal fashion the text "Seven times a day I praise you" (Ps. 119:164).[6]

The Office as the Sanctification of Time

Inevitably, the daily observance of the Hours, whether in the local church or in the monastery, became the extension of the great *anamnesis* (remembrance) of the Sunday Eucharist throughout the week (see practicum 13). In this way each day was interwoven with the remembrance of God, and the Prayer of the Hours, or the "Divine" or

"Daily" Office, as it came to be called, was seen as the "sanctification" of time. As the continuing remembrance of the Paschal Mystery at specific intervals of time, the Daily Office was the acknowledgement or proclamation that *all* of time is now of the kingdom of God and that what we celebrate now in the Hours is but the temporal beginning of that life of praise and adoration that will be ours in eternity. Thus the Prayer of the Hours consecrates time, not by changing it and making it other than it is, but by admitting it to be *what it is already*—God's time, God's reign, and in the light of the coming of Christ, the time of salvation.

To make time holy through the Prayer of the Hours is not to rescue it from the alien world of the secular. It is the living out of the mystery of Christ from moment to moment. In a very real sense, the Prayer of the Hours is a *berakah*, a formal blessing (as in Judaism), over this particular stolen moment of time—an offering that is at once thanksgiving and acknowledgement. Praying the Hours, day in and day out, we are drawn into a more God-centered existence and commissioned to go forth into the world to serve our brothers and sisters with a new spirit of faith and hope.

The content of the Daily Office has always been chiefly scriptural—psalms, hymns, canticles, and readings taken directly from the Bible. Other elements have been added over the centuries, such as antiphons, responsories, and nonscriptural hymns and readings, but the mainstay of the Daily Office is Scripture. In his famous rule for monasteries, St. Benedict legislated that each week the entire Psalter should be sung by the monks.[7] Thus the Prayer of the Hours was understood as a celebration of the Word of God. In a variety of forms the Word was sung, proclaimed, and pondered. Most often the celebration included some form of antiphonal prayer: a stylized conversation in which the members of the congregation minister to one another in a call and response formula. Either the cantor calls and the congregation responds, or two sections of the congregation chant or speak alternating verses of the psalm to one another, and all join in the concluding trinitarian doxology "Glory to the Father, and to the Son and to the Holy Spirit." In those moments Christians became dependent in a tangible way on one another for hearing the Word proclaimed and were drawn into a response that was, in its turn, a proclamation of the good news of salvation. This dialogical structure exemplified the exchange between God and his people and became a fitting continuation of the eucharistic liturgy, where a similar structure was employed.

The Daily Office became more than a tradition of prayer; it became a ritual pattern that gave the Christian community a strong identity based upon the daily gathering for the breaking of the bread of the Word of God. As might be imagined, this tradition of community prayer became the springboard for a deeper life of personal prayer. The need to digest the rich fare of the Daily Office caused Christians to linger over the Word proclaimed and to ponder it in secret. While ascendancy was always given to this public liturgical prayer, it was understood to feed a rich life of personal devotion. Indeed, in some locales aspects of this devotional life found its way into the Office itself in the form of popular hymns, prayers, antiphons, and ritual actions that might help to reshape the liturgy.

As the practice of celebrating the Hours grew and became somewhat standardized throughout the West, it came to be known as "the prayer of the Church," and this structure provided a universal norm for common prayer throughout the Church. This notion of the "official prayer of the Church" generated the ideal of a continual activity of praise throughout the world in the churches. The nineteenth-century Anglican poet John Ellerton captured it in a few lines.

The day thou gavest, Lord is ended,
The darkness falls at thy behest;
To thee our morning hymns ascended,
Thy praise shall sanctify our rest.

We thank thee that thy Church, unsleeping
While earth rolls onward into light
Through all the world her watch is keeping,
And rests not now by day or night.

As o'er each continent and island
The dawn leads on another day,
The voice of prayer is never silent
Nor dies the strain of praise away.

The sun that bids us rest is waking
our brethren 'neath the western sky,
And hour by hour fresh lips are making
Thy wondrous doings heard on high.

So be it, Lord; thy throne shall never
Like earth's proud empires, pass away:
Thy kingdom stands, and grows forever,
Till all thy creatures own thy sway.[8]

In the context of the universal Church constantly stealing time for remembering God day and night, liturgical prayer and private devotion are not seen to be in competition. Instead, they mutually support and complement one another, for both are aimed at deepening the life of holiness in the Church of Christ. Yet this natural interplay between liturgical and private prayer began to wane in the late Middle Ages when greater emphasis was placed on the *interior* nature of spiritual life and prayer. Ultimately, in the Roman Catholic tradition, the Prayer of the Hours became the preserve of clerics and members of monastic orders. The daily rhythm of public prayer in the local parish was generally lost, and the Divine Office was celebrated in common by communities of monks and nuns and prayed privately by the clergy. In all cases, the Prayer of the Hours was in Latin.

Reforming the Office

The Protestant Reformers reacted negatively both to the complexity of the medieval offices and to the relegation of this tradition to clerics and members of religious orders. Luther, in his opposition to weekday Masses and his preoccupation with the Word, retained the twofold structure of a morning and evening hour of common prayer—in German—but shifted the emphasis from the psalmody to longer scriptural readings and insisted on preaching at each of the Hours. The 1978 *Lutheran Book of Worship* continues this tradition of two daily offices.

Cranmer, influenced by Luther and the other Reformers, maintained the two Daily Offices of matins and evensong. His purpose, however, was not only to replace the weekday celebration of the Mass but also to preserve the tradition of the Hours as a normal part of Christian life—our *legitimae orationes* ("regular prayers"), in the words of Tertullian. "To its great merit the Anglican communion alone of all Western Christian Churches has preserved to some extent at least the daily services of morning praise and evensong as a living part of parish worship."[9] In his *Book of Common Prayer* Cranmer provided in English the offices that both clergy and faithful were to celebrate together. In eliminating many of the complexities and redundancies of the medieval office, Cranmer, like Luther, highlighted the reading of the Bible. He wanted the Psalter and Scripture lessons to be read in continuous sequence (*lectio continua*) from day to day. In this way, *The Book of Common Prayer* was intended as the instrument for the biblical and liturgical revitalization of English spirituality. This attempt to restore the Prayer of the Hours to the devotional life of the whole

Christian community not only provided a means for the renewal of liturgical prayer in the local parish but also generated, in addition, a vast treasury of vernacular psalms and hymns in both the Lutheran and Anglican traditions that have since become part of the common liturgical repertoire of all the churches.

This practicum is intended to reintroduce the contemporary Christian to the effectiveness of the Prayer of the Hours as a means to steal time for God. Marvelously versatile, the Daily Office is a prayer structure suitable for small groups in the parish, the home, or the workplace.

The contemporary student of theology greatly fears a notion of the human person as dualistic, that is, made up of a body and a soul that are two distinct and somewhat autonomous parts of one person. The integration of public liturgical prayer and private prayer and devotion is an antidote for just such a falsification of sound Christian anthropology. Each form of prayer nourishes the other, with public liturgical celebration serving as a great safeguard and challenge to the tendency to become isolated and idiosyncratic in our spiritual lives. The authority of the Word of God and the authority of the Church at prayer constantly call one to a new level of authenticity with an insistence we are not likely to discover in our own private struggle to maintain and develop a life of prayer and communion with God. The liturgy becomes, in effect, a training ground in the life of Christian prayer and spirituality. Through continual celebration of the mysteries of faith in the Church's sacred ritual, one learns a way of prayer and meditation that is both doctrinally sound and devotionally satisfying.

> The sacred liturgy does not exhaust the entire activity of the church. Before [people] can come to the liturgy they must be called to faith and to conversion. . . . Nevertheless the liturgy is the summit toward which the activity of the church is directed; at the same time it is the fount from which all her power flows. For the aim and object of apostolic work is that all who are made sons of God by faith and baptism should come together to praise God in the midst of his church, to take part in the sacrifice, and to eat the Lord's supper.[10]

EXERCISES

For an Individual

As with any form of prayer, the environment is important. Arrange some corner of a room as a place of prayer. The use of a candle, crucifix, or icon is very effective. You will need a copy of one of the offices listed in the resource list. Each morning for a week, plan to set aside fifteen to twenty minutes for Morning Prayer (lauds). This will take some careful preparation in studying the text and the directions (rubrics). After the first day or two be somewhat adventuresome—if you know it, stand and sing the hymn softly to yourself; sit for the psalms, stand for the canticle of Zechariah (the Benedictus) and the concluding prayer or collect. Be sensitive to how such formal ritual prayer may move you to a few minutes of quiet reflection once it is over. The same practice can be used for Evening Prayer (vespers), depending on your schedule. Ideally, both Morning and Evening Prayer could become part of our remembrance of God, but at least the morning begins the day in the right spirit and direction.

Since an office is essentially a communal form of prayer, using it in private requires a bit of practice and adaptation. It would be a great help initially to find a parish or monastic community where one might experience an office in its full form. After such an introduction to the experience of common liturgical prayer, it might be possible to invite someone you know in your workplace to pray Midday Prayer together during your lunch hour. Inexpensive copies of such daytime prayer are included in the list of resources that follows. A sample noonday office from the 1974 American *Book of Common Prayer* may be found in appendix 9.

For a Group

Divide the group into two sections, facing each other with a few feet of distance between the sides. Ideally a lectern or some sort of stand for the Scriptures should be placed in the center space. Copies of an office, such as Morning, Daytime, or Night Prayer, should be duplicated out of one of the sources listed in the resource section. A thorough study of the structure and directions will have to be made ahead of time. The leader will have to begin the prayer and lead the singing of hymns. The psalms should be read verse by verse (two lines or four lines) by alternating sides. At the end of each psalm the doxology ("Glory to the Father . . .") is added.

In this practicum the use of varied postures is especially useful: Begin the office standing, after the hymn sit for the psalms and reading, and stand for the concluding prayer. The doxology at the end of each psalm could be accompanied with a bow of the head as a gesture of praise and adoration to the Trinity.

It is also possible to organize a field trip to a parochial or monastic community where your group could experience the well-established celebration of the office. Afterward the group would find it easier to imitate the practice and use it as a prayer form at the beginning of a meeting or as a form of closing prayer at regular gatherings. Some Church organizations regularly close their meetings with the celebration of Night Prayer (compline). Inexpensive copies of these offices are included in the list of resources at the end of this chapter.

DISCUSSION QUESTIONS

1. Sunday worship is the mainstay of the prayer life of the Church. In some traditions daily gatherings for Eucharist or other forms of prayer are part of an established pattern. Do members of your congregation/parish show any interest in a weekday celebration of the Prayer of the Hours? This need not replace other forms of liturgical worship but will be complementary to it.

2. Many people consider the development of a life of prayer and devotion a very personal matter. Do you think that those members of your congregation/parish who are serious about a life of prayer and devotion might find in a corporate prayer form such as the Liturgy of the Hours a support for their own efforts and a real sense of connectedness to the larger Church community?

3. Given the highly privatized notion of religion and religious practice in our culture, could the Liturgy of the Hours become instrumental in drawing persons together for an experience of common prayer that is not overly subjective? What obstacles do you see to this idea in your own experience of prayer and Christian community?

4. The Prayer of the Hours is more complex than a simple daily devotional reading of the Bible. Might this be a great aid in helping to sustain one's attention and fervor in the call to daily prayer, or do you think the greater complexity might prove burdensome?

5. The various forms of the Hours involve certain stable parts but also include sections that change with the various liturgical seasons. Can you see this kind of prayer as instrumental in forming a more biblical and liturgical spirituality? Discuss the implications of this approach with the members of your congregation/parish.

Notes

1. Cf. Hippolytus, *Apostolic Tradition* 35.
2. Cf. Tertullian, *On Prayer* 25.5
3. William Storey, "The Liturgy of the Hours: Cathedral versus Monastery," in

Christians at Prayer, ed. John Gallen (Notre Dame, Ind.: University of Notre Dame Press, 1977), p. 65.

4. *General Instruction on the Liturgy of the Hours;* Liturgy Documentary Series 2 (Washington, D.C.: United States Catholic Conference Publications, 1983), p. 5.
5. Ibid., p. 7.
6. *The Grail* (London: Collins, 1963).
7. Cf. St. Benedict, *Rule for Monasteries* 18:23.
8. John Ellerton, "The Day Thou Gavest," *The Hymnal of the Protestant Episcopal Church in the U.S.A.* (New York: The Church Pension Fund, 1940), song 179.
9. Robert Taft, *The Liturgy of the Hours in East and West* (Collegeville, Minn.: Liturgical Press, 1986), p. 323.
10. "Constitution on the Sacred Liturgy," nos. 9 and 10, in *The Documents of Vatican II,* ed. Walter M. Abbot (Baltimore: America Press, 1966), p. 142.

Resources

Prayerbooks

The Book of Common Prayer. New York: Seabury Press, 1979. (Contains the Daily Offices for The Episcopal Church as well as daily devotions for individuals and families based on the offices.)

Christian Prayer: The Liturgy of the Hours. Boston: Daughters of St. Paul, 1976. (Probably the least expensive edition of a full office book or breviary.)

Daytime Prayer: From the Liturgy of the Hours. Washington, D.C.: United States Catholic Conference Publications, 1980. No. 577-1. (Inexpensive paperback of Daytime Prayer throughout the year.)

Lutheran Book of Worship. Philadelphia: Augsburg Press, 1978. (Contains Morning Prayer, Evening Prayer, and Night Prayer, with a full schema of psalms and readings for the whole liturgical year.)

Morning and Evening Prayer: Selections from the Liturgy of the Hours. Edited by D. Joseph Finnerty and George J. Ryan. New York: Regina Press, 1978. (Contains an abbreviated form of Morning and Evening Prayer for those who wish to pray the Daily Office, but tailored to more individual devotional needs.)

Night Prayer: From the Liturgy of the Hours. Washington, D.C.: United States Catholic Conference Publications, 1976. No. 480-5. (Inexpensive paperback of Night Prayer through the year.)

Praise Him! A Prayerbook for Today's Christian. Edited by William G. Storey. Notre Dame, Ind.: Ave Maria Press, 1973. (Inexpensive, abbreviated versions of Morning and Evening Prayer.)

Texts and Historical Studies

Bradshaw, Paul F. *Daily Prayer in the Early Church: A Study of the Origin and Early Development of the Divine Office.* New York: Oxford University Press, 1982.

Gallen, John, S.J., ed. *Christians at Prayer.* Notre Dame, Ind.: University of Notre Dame Press, 1977. (See especially William Storey, "The Liturgy of the Hours: Cathedral versus Monastery," pp. 61-82.)

General Instruction on the Liturgy of the Hours. Washington, D.C.: United States Catholic Conference Publications, 1983. No. 898-3.

Hatchett, Marion J. *Commentary on the American Prayer Book.* New York: Seabury Press, 1981. (See especially pp. 89-153.)

Martimort, A. G. *The Liturgy & Time,* vol. 4 of *The Church at Prayer.* Collegeville, Minn.: Liturgical Press, 1986.

Taft, Robert, S.J. *The Liturgy of the Hours in East and West.* Collegeville, Minn.: Liturgical Press, 1986.

Tugwell, Simon. *Prayer in Practice.* Springfield, Ill.: Templegate, 1974. (See especially pp. 59-73.)

An Order of Service
for Noonday†

Officiant   O God, make speed to save us.
People   O Lord, make haste to help us.

Officiant and People

Glory to the Father, and to the Son, and to the Holy Spirit: as it was in
the beginning, is now, and will be for ever. Amen.
Except in Lent, add Alleluia.

A suitable hymn may be sung.

*One or more of the following Psalms is sung or said. Other suitable selections
include Psalms 19, 67, one or more sections of Psalm 119, or a selection from
Psalms 120–133.*

Psalm 119   *Lucerna pedibus meis*

105   Your word is a lantern to my feet*
           and a light upon my path.

106   I have sworn and am determined*
           to keep your righteous judgments.

107   I am deeply troubled;*
           preserve my life, O LORD, according to your word.

†From *The Book of Common Prayer* (New York: Seabury Press, 1974), pp. 103-7.

108 Accept, O LORD, the willing tribute of my lips,*
and teach me your judgments.

109 My life is always in my hand,*
yet I do not forget your law.

110 The wicked have set a trap for me,*
but I have not strayed from your commandments.

111 Your decrees are my inheritance for ever,*
truly, they are the joy of my heart.

112 I have applied my heart to fulfill your statutes*
for ever and to the end.

Psalm 121   *Levavi oculos*

1   I lift up my eyes to the hills;*
from whence is my help to come?

2   My help comes from the LORD,*
the maker of heaven and earth.

3   He will not let your foot be moved*
and he who watches over you will not fall asleep.

4   Behold, he who keeps watch over Israel*
shall neither slumber nor sleep;

5   The LORD himself watches over you;*
the LORD is your shade at your right hand,

6   So that the sun shall not strike you by day,*
nor the moon by night.

7   The LORD shall preserve you from all evil;*
it is he who shall keep you safe.

8   The LORD shall watch over your going out and your coming in*
from this time forth for evermore.

Psalm 126   *In convertendo*

1   When the LORD restored the fortunes of Zion*
        then were we like those who dream.

2   Then was our mouth filled with laughter,*
        and our tongue with shouts of joy.

3   Then they said among the nations,*
        "The LORD has done great things for them."

4   The LORD has done great things for us*
        and we are glad indeed.

5   Restore our fortunes, O LORD*
        like the watercourses of the Negev.

6   Those who sowed with tears*
        will reap with songs of joy.

7   Those who go out weeping, carrying the seed,*
        will come again with joy, shouldering their sheaves.

At the end of the Psalms is sung or said

Glory to the Father, and to the Son, and to the Holy Spirit:*
    As it was in the beginning, is now, and will be for ever.
        Amen.

One of the following, or some other suitable passage of Scripture, is read

The love of God has been poured into our hearts through the Holy
Spirit that has been given to us. *Romans 5:5*

People   Thanks be to God.

or the following

If anyone is in Christ he is a new creation; the old has passed away,
behold the new has come. All this is from God, who through Christ
reconciled us to himself and gave us the ministry of reconciliation.
2 Corinthians 5:17-18

300

or this

From the rising of the sun to its setting my Name shall be great among the nations, and in every place incense shall be offered to my Name, and a pure offering; for my Name shall be great among the nations, says the Lord of Hosts. *Malachi 1:11*

People　　Thanks be to God.

A meditation, silent or spoken, may follow.

The Officiant then begins the Prayers

Lord, have mercy.

Christ, have mercy.

Lord, have mercy.

Officiant and People

Our Father, who art in heaven,	Our Father in heaven,
hallowed be thy Name,	hallowed be your Name,
thy kingdom come,	your kingdom come,
thy will be done,	your will be done,
on earth as it is in heaven.	on earth as in heaven.
Give us this day our daily bread.	Give us today our daily bread,
And forgive us our trespasses,	Forgive us our sins
as we forgive those	as we forgive those
who trespass against us	who sin against us.
And lead us not into temptation,	Save us from the time of trial,
but deliver us from evil.	and deliver us from evil.

Officiant　Lord, hear our prayer;

People　　And let our cry come to you.

Officiant　Let us pray.

The Officiant then says one of the following Collects. If desired, the Collect of the Day may be used.

Heavenly Father, send your Holy Spirit into our hearts, to direct and rule us according to your will, to comfort us in all our afflictions, to defend us from all error, and to lead us into all truth; through Jesus Christ our Lord. *Amen.*

Blessed Savior, at this hour you hung upon the cross, stretching out your loving arms; Grant that all the peoples of the earth may look to you and be saved; for your tender mercies' sake. *Amen.*

Almighty Savior, who at noonday called your servant Saint Paul to be an apostle to the Gentiles: We pray to you to illumine the world with the radiance of your glory, that all nations may come and worship you; for you live and reign for ever and ever. *Amen.*

Lord Jesus Christ, you said to your apostles, "Peace I give to you; my own peace I leave with you." Regard not our sins, but the faith of your Church, and give to us the peace and unity of that heavenly City, where with the Father and the Holy Spirit you live and reign, now and for ever. *Amen.*

Free intercessions may be offered.

The service concludes as follows

Officiant   Let us bless the Lord.

People   Thanks be to God.

CHAPTER 10

Wesleyan Spirituality

ROBIN MAAS

You shall love the Lord your God with all your heart, and with all your soul, and with all your strength, and with all your mind; and your neighbor as yourself.

—LUKE 10:27

A traditional Wesleyan spirituality has the virtue of being both deliberate and methodical as well as extremely broad and generous in scope and practice. Insofar as it emphasizes "inward religion" and the necessity of a vital, personal appropriation of faith, it is an *evangelical* and *experiential* spirituality. John Wesley's insistence on using the Bible as the primary source for theology and the life of prayer ensures that this expression of the life of the spirit is deeply *scriptural* and therefore "Protestant." Yet a true Wesleyan spirituality is equally "Catholic" and *sacramental* in its assumption that the means of grace, especially frequent Communion, will play a central role in the life of each Christian. Catholic, too, is the broad and generous invitation of grace to all who wish to "flee from the wrath to come": Salvation is a gift freely offered to the whole of creation. Despite its emphasis on inwardness and personal holiness, Wesleyan spirituality is best known today as an *activist* or reforming spirituality. From the very beginning, works of mercy and justice have been considered essential for true discipleship in the Methodist tradition. Finally, a Wesleyan spirituality will honor the *rational* component of religion. A total, self-giving dedication to God requires that we put our intellects as well as our hearts and bodies at the service of the kingdom.

To say all this is to claim a great deal for a single tradition, especially when many contemporary Christians who trace their roots back to

Wesley do not in fact practice such a comprehensive and balanced spirituality. What warrant do we have, then, for making these claims? To respond to this challenge, we must look first at the life of John Wesley.

John Wesley: A Biographical Sketch

Born in 1703, the ninth child of Samuel and Susanna Wesley, John was a precocious, extremely impressionable child and soon marked by his parents for a special role in the Church. Both Samuel and Susanna had been the children of "dissenters," and both had decided early in life, and as a matter of principle, to reunite with the Church of England, with Samuel taking Holy Orders. Very different in talents and temperament, both parents were to have a profound influence on the religious development of young John.

Samuel Wesley was a passionate, impetuous, and temperamental man. A romantic at heart, he was attracted to the mystical and to inwardness in religion as the measure of religious authenticity. From his father Wesley imbibed a love for inward religion and, at the same time, learned to value the sacraments and the importance of religious tolerance. A free-spirited and disorganized individual, Samuel is said to have observed of his son that he "was so committed to arguing his position that he 'would not attend to the most pressing necessities of nature unless he could give a reason for it.'"[1]

By contrast, John's mother was a very rational and highly organized administrator. Bright and ambitious for her children, Susanna Wesley provided the firm center of stability for the family. In addition to the many responsibilities of managing such a large household, she took it upon herself to catechize each child in the Creed, the Decalogue, and other fundamentals of the faith. Each child received Susanna's individual attention and was taught by her to read, using the book of Genesis as a primer. As a catechist, Susanna was stern and efficient; in her description of her philosophy of religious education we can see the beginning of John's extremely sensitive (some would say overscrupulous) conscience:

> In order to form the minds of the children, the first thing to be done is to conquer their will, and bring them to an obedient temper. To inform the understanding is a work of time; and must with children proceed by slow degrees, as they are able to bear it: but . . . subjecting the will is a thing which must be done at once, and the sooner the better; for by neglecting timely correction, they will contract a stubbornness and obstinacy which

are hardly ever conquered. When a child is corrected it must be conquered. . . . I insist upon conquering the will of children betimes, because this is the only strong and rational foundation of a religious education.[2]

A formidable presence, Susanna's attentions to John and his spiritual formation increased markedly after he came close to perishing in the Epworth rectory fire at the age of seven years. A dramatic last-minute rescue of her son convinced Susanna that God must have some special purpose in mind for him. Describing John as a "brand plucked from the burning," she resolved hereafter to be "more particularly careful of the soul of this child, which God had so mercifully provided for."[3] And to be sure, Susanna left her indelible mark on John, who ever after was imprinted with a passion for piety, order, method, and detail.

Once away from home at preparatory school, Wesley described himself (too harshly) as lax in his religious observances and behavior:

The next six or seven years were spent at school [Charterhouse, in London]; where, outward restraints being removed, I was much more negligent than before, even of outward duties, and almost continually guilty of outward sins, which I knew to be such, though they were not scandalous in the eyes of the world. However, I still read the Scriptures, and said my prayers, morning and evening. And what I now hoped to be saved by was 1. Not being so bad as other people. 2. Having still a kindness for religion. And 3. Reading the Bible, going to church, and saying my prayers.[4]

What Wesley is looking back on here is, of course, a tacit, taken for granted religious practice, and one always hopes that what is taken for granted will someday be treasured. But the rich structure of practices and beliefs he inherited stood him in good stead and led, eventually, to a very intentional appropriation of religious identity. Here is Wesley describing himself at the age of twenty-three, when suddenly the full significance of religious commitment bursts upon him:

In the year 1725, being the twenty-third year of my age, I met with Bishop Taylor's *Rules and Exercises of Holy Living and Dying.* In reading several parts of this book, I was exceedingly affected: that part in particular which relates to purity of intention. Instantly I resolved to dedicate all my life to God; all my thoughts, and words, and actions; being thoroughly convinced there was no medium, but that every part of my life (not some only) must either be a sacrifice to God, or myself; that is, in effect, to the devil.[5]

Thus a new vision of *total* dedication to a great cause—holiness—suddenly takes hold. It is a daring and demanding vision, admitting of "no golden mean" of moderation. A year later Wesley the Oxford don discovers yet another devotional classic—*The Imitation of Christ* by Thomas à Kempis. This little book, which has served as the foundation for all modern interiority and spirituality, simultaneously annoyed and intrigued the youthful scholar. In the *Imitation* Wesley discovered the vital significance of what he called "inward" religion: There is more to loving and serving God than outward observances. Describing his encounter with this book, he writes:

> The nature and extent of inward religion, the religion of the heart, now appeared to me in a stronger light than ever it had done before. I saw, that giving all my life to God (supposing it to be possible to do this, and go no farther) would profit me nothing, unless I gave my heart, yea, all my heart to Him. I saw that "simplicity of intention, purity of affection," one design in all we speak or do, and one desire ruling all our tempers, are indeed the "wings of the soul," without which she can never ascend to the mount of God.[6]

The seeds of Wesley's emerging vision of a total, single-minded and single-hearted devotion to God were present in the honest and not always so earnest adolescent; the new vision is certainly not a repudiation of the old. But the new vision is a broader, deeper, and much more compelling one. It asks not much, but *all*, and Wesley the young adult yearned to give his all to some wonderful One. The final confirmation of this new vision comes a year or two later when he read William Law's *A Serious Call to a Devout and Holy Life.* The weight of this text, combined with the *Imitation,* convinced him, Wesley reports,

> of the absolute impossibility of being half a Christian. And I determined, through His Grace (the absolute necessity of which I was deeply sensible of), to be all devoted to God,—to give all my soul, my body, and my substance.
>
> Will any considerate man say, that this is carrying matters too far? or that anything less is due to Him who has given himself for us, than to give ourselves; all we have, and all we are?[7]

Out of this deep desire to give himself totally to God, Wesley, his younger brother Charles, and a few close friends at Oxford formed the Holy Club.

The Holy Club, which John Wesley led from 1729 until 1735, was designed to provide a structure for the living out of this new vision of total self-giving to God, and this small but very earnest group of young men set about the task of trying to imitate Christ with a degree of intentionality that most Christians today would find utterly daunting. Wesley describes his earliest attempts at a reconstructed lifestyle thus:

> I began to alter the whole form of my conversation, and to set in earnest upon a new life. I set apart an hour or two a day for religious retirement. I communicated every week. I watched against all sin, whether in word or deed. I began to aim at, and pray for, inward holiness.[8]

In effect, Wesley and his fellows began to practice what amounted to an extremely frugal, semi-monastic lifestyle that included a type of Daily Office, a (tortuously structured) form of daily self-examination, twice-weekly Communion, serious Bible study, penance and mortification (especially fasting), and works of mercy among the poor of Oxford. The deliberation and rigor with which these pious practices were undertaken evoked much ridicule among the intellectuals of the university community—the group came to be known derisively as the "Methodists"—but it was a harbinger of things to come; Wesley's methodical approach to the life of the spirit was to become for the masses a boon and a blessing.

True to the ancient tradition out of which the young Wesley's vision of holiness was formed, Wesley gave that vision a name, and the name was *"Christian* Perfection." "Be ye . . . perfect, even as your Father in heaven is perfect" (Matt. 5:48 KJV)—be nothing less. Human nature, of course, rebels: Why be perfect? Why struggle for such an impossible goal? What did John Wesley understand to be at stake in this incredible spiritual quest? It was quite simple. What was at stake was our eternal destinies. "The one perfect good shall be your one ultimate end," preached the young Wesley:

> One thing shall ye desire for its own sake—the fruition of Him who is all in all. One happiness shall ye propose to your souls, even union with Him that made them; the having "fellowship with the Father and the Son"; the being "joined to the Lord in one spirit." One design ye are to pursue to the end of time—the enjoyment of God in time and in eternity. Desire other things so far as they tend to this: love the creature, as it leads to the Creator. But in every step you take, be this the glorious point that terminates your view.[9]

What the young John Wesley wanted was God himself, nothing less. Singleness of purpose and unity of intention were the means to the fulfillment of this one consuming vision: union with God. The fact that Wesley had still to learn that perfect faithfulness was not within the grasp of human effort, no matter how dedicated, in no way detracts from the authenticity and power of the vision itself.

Wesley's pursuit of personal holiness continued throughout his years as a fellow at Lincoln College and served him well until he undertook in 1735 to go to Georgia as a missionary. Then, on the voyage to America, he encountered a new spiritual challenge, one that was to affect him as deeply at the age of thirty-five as the *Imitation* had eleven years earlier.

Wesley's initial introduction to Moravian faith and piety left him feeling impressed but quite incredulous. Headed to the colonies on the same ship with Wesley was a group of Moravians whose faith claims seemed to promise more than they could possibly deliver. When a terrifying storm arose at sea, Wesley watched this group carefully to see how they would weather it. As the badly frightened Anglican priest observed, the Moravians sang their way through the storm with a kind of peaceful assurance at which he could only marvel. With all his concern for inward religion and a life free from sin, here was an existential faith that far outstripped his own!

Wesley's first efforts at missionizing were singularly unsuccessful. He suffered considerable disillusionment about the intended subjects of evangelization, the Indians, who seemed to be not the noble savages he had anticipated, and a failed romance led to a hasty and ignominious departure from Georgia in 1737. But this interlude in the colonies was far from a total loss:

> It was here that he began to condense a number of mystical works; it was here that he began the theological work on the Old and New Testaments that would bear fruit later; it was here that he experimented with some of the features of his later organization including societies, bands, lay leaders, extempore prayer and preaching, love feasts, and chapel buildings; it was here that he learned German and beautifully translated a number of German hymns.[10]

The sense of personal failure Wesley sustained in leaving Georgia—as well as simple curiosity—led him to a sustained encounter with Moravian spirituality that included assisting in the founding of the Fetter Lane Society in London, a profound religious experience of "assurance," and a trip to Herrnhut to visit Count Zinzendorf, leader of the Moravians—all within the same year (1738). While he was never able to completely embrace their radical, relatively quietist theological position, this encounter with Moravian piety led to a significant modification of Wesley's own understanding of the place of works in the economy of salvation, to a greatly enhanced appreciation for the place and power of hymns in spiritual development, and to his eventual appropriation of the Moravian "bands" as a structure for mutual accountability in the tasks of discipleship.

Wesley scholars are divided in their assessment of the ultimate significance of the famous "Aldersgate experience." Whether it was indeed a first or second, and deeper, conversion for Wesley, we shall probably never know; but through his contact with the Moravians, he became convinced that, dedicated as he was to the ideal of holiness, he lacked a sense of inward assurance of salvation based on total trust in the merits of Christ. Failing to find that assurance and unable to identify the kind of instantaneous conversion that the Moravians assured him was possible, Wesley went through weeks of prayer and soul searching. Finally, on the eve of May 24, 1738, he went (reluctantly) to a meeting of the Fetter Lane Society at Aldersgate, where Luther's preface to the Epistle to the Romans was being read. Wesley reported that, in response to hearing the great Reformer's words, he suddenly felt his heart "strangely warmed." After what had seemed like a long and difficult search for a genuine and justifying faith, Wesley at last felt an inward assurance that he did indeed trust in Christ—and *only* in Christ—for his salvation.

It is not immediately apparent how this experience of assurance may have changed the character or behavior of John Wesley. Nowhere do we have a detailed account of any particular conversion experience in Wesley's writings. Indeed, the Aldersgate event is very little mentioned. As an evangelical preacher able to evoke intensely strong emotional reactions in others, John Wesley had surprisingly few such peak experiences himself. Pragmatic and experimentalist, he always retained the ability to stand back and observe himself in a relatively detached and objective way, even in the midst of the most fervent sermonizing.[11]

It is all the more amazing, then, to observe the results of Wesley's post-Aldersgate efforts to missionize. Convinced that God had accepted *him* through the merits of Christ, Wesley was finally free to concentrate on facilitating the work of God in the hearts of people who had found little or nothing to sustain them in the established Church of the day. The conversion of thousands upon thousands of hearts and lives as a consequence of Wesley's field preaching is persuasive enough testimony that something remarkable had finally happened to the young scholar who wanted so desperately to dedicate *all* his life to God.

Going on to Perfection

Although Methodism has traditionally resisted efforts at doctrinal definition, Wesleyan spirituality is nevertheless doctrinally rooted and cannot be understood adequately without dealing with John Wesley's "pneumatology," or doctrine of the Spirit.

Wesley confidently preached justification by faith in line with continental Reformation theology, yet he did not stop there. His passion to belong totally to God did not permit him to be satisfied with a purely forensic understanding of salvation. That is, it is not enough that Christ do something *for* us; Christ must also do something *in* us. It is not enough that we be *forgiven* our sins; we must also be *rid* of them. Said Wesley:

> Justification implies only a relative, the new birth a real, change. God in justifying us does something for us; in begetting us again, He does the work in us. . . . The one restores us to the favor, the other to the image of God. The one is the taking away of guilt, the other the taking away the power, of sin: so that, although they are joined together in point of time, yet are they of wholly distinct natures.[12]

Specifically, Wesley taught an *ordo salutis*—a schema of salvation—that begins and ends with grace. It is grace that in the first place draws or invites us to repent by revealing the unpalatable truth about our own sinfulness. Then it is "justifying" grace that pardons us when we are no longer willing or able to rely on our own resources to cure what ails us. The submission to grace that results in pardon produces the long-sought, much-treasured experience of assurance, an inner peace that the world cannot disturb. But the story does not end here; for Wesley, it has barely begun. At the moment of justification, a remarkable and very real change takes place in the believer. Wesley called this moment of transformation the "new birth." What happens after this is (again) the work of grace—"sanctifying" grace. The newly born Christian, supported by the power of the Spirit, sets out on a journey toward perfection. This journey is an extended "novitiate" in discipleship in which the novice is supported and called to account by Scripture, tradition, and fellow pilgrims headed for the same destination. Without this support, embodied in what Wesley scholar David Lowes Watson refers to as the disciplines of "right intent,"[13] the newly born will remain isolated in what was—and still is—almost certain to be a hostile or at least indifferent environment. Not withstanding the "blessed assurance" that came with the experience of justification, the individual believer is required to cooperate fully with the initiatives of grace by adopting a set of spiritual practices and living a particular lifestyle. The journey toward perfection is not an easy one, and a fall from grace is always possible. For the persistent, however, union with the divine will and freedom from sinning is a gift that may be received *this* side of the grave—a gift that, like pardon, can be given and received in a moment's time. Thus Wesley and his followers allowed for "entire sanctification"—a "second blessing." The early Methodists set no limits to God's goodness and generosity. For them, the grace that saves is the gift of a profligate God. Faith—not an end in itself—is the *means* to holiness, the precondition for union with a God who is nothing but Love.

Wesley's idealism may have been innate, but it was given shape and substance, first, by the high expectations of his parents and, second, by his extensive reading of the patristic literature, especially the Eastern fathers—John Chrysostom, Basil, Gregory of Nyssa (through Macarius the Egyptian), and Ephraim Syrus—and the Christian Platonists, Smith and Cudworth of Cambridge.[14]

Important also were the Roman Catholic mystics Wesley read first at Oxford and later in Georgia. Pascal, Scupoli, Fenelon, Quesnel, de Renty, Mmes. Guyon and Bourignon, Tauler, Molinos, Brother Lawrence, John of Avila, Lopez, and the *Theologia Germanica* were all sufficiently impressive to Wesley to rate inclusion in his fifty-volume *Christian Library,* a collection of abridged devotional reading intended for popular consumption. The (perhaps mitigating) influence of Puritanism can be seen in Wesley's choice of Protestant authors to include in the *Christian Library:* Samuel Clark, Robert Bolton, John Preston, Richard Alleine, John Bunyan, Richard Baxter, and Edmund Calamy.[15]

Wesley's eclecticism and marvelously catholic taste in reading gave birth to a spirituality that was popular in the finest sense of the word, a spirituality in which the element of Spirit was a vivid, energizing, and pervasive presence. For Wesley, the goal of the Spirit was nothing less than a total transformation of both the individual and the society. Fallen humanity was called to holiness of heart and holiness of life—to inward perfection and a visible, external expression of love for neighbor that Wesley liked to call "social holiness."

Wesley's choice of the term "Christian Perfection" to describe his vision of the process of sanctification was to cause endless debate and confusion, but he stubbornly resisted any effort to replace it with a more palatable—or innocuous—label. By "perfection" Wesley meant that same single-minded devotion to God that he first found in Taylor and Law—an absolute purity of *intention* that expressed itself in love for the good and an abhorrence of sin. A perfect Christian by this definition was not someone freed from the limitations of the human condition; the perfect man or woman might indeed suffer from ignorance, physical infirmities, and a tendency to be mistaken in word or deed. Rather, perfection, as John Wesley understood it, was reflected in a purity of intention toward God and conferred the freedom to stop committing known or *conscious* sins. This purity of intention is itself not the consequence of human effort; it is the gift of God's overflowing, prevenient grace. Perfection is the work of the Spirit *in* us—a work that requires our full cooperation if the hoped-for transformation is to occur.

Despite his self-conscious eclecticism, it would be a mistake to identify Wesley's understanding of the process of sanctification as a deliberate synthesis of Eastern and Western views:

> To suggest this would be reductionism. What rather happened was that the Wesleys inherited a Christian tradition at the beginning of the eighteenth century that contained a cluster of elements that provided the background wherein they could develop their vision of God. But what developed was *their* vision of God. This vision of God, this spirituality, transcended the influences that helped to produce it and led in turn to a radical renewal of the tradition they had inherited.[16]

Wesley's aim was always to articulate a *practical* spirituality, one which would be accessible to every earnest seeker after truth. Like so many Reformers, he never intended to found a new sect; he saw his mission as entailing the renewal of a cherished tradition, not its eclipse. Despite the defection of his followers from Anglicanism, John Wesley remained a priest of the Church of England all his life.

Accountability in the Spiritual Life

Ordinarily one does not expect to find in a single individual a genius for spirituality and organization both. But the history of the Church makes it abundantly clear that effective organization assists rather than impedes the work of the Spirit, and so it is sometimes the case that these two charisms appear simultaneously. Like Ignatius Loyola, John Wesley was thus doubly gifted in his intense commitment to a spiritual ideal and organizing zeal, and the synergism that resulted made Methodism a kind of spiritual-social leaven in Britain and America. Certainly the evidence suggests that, perhaps more than any other

Protestant religious leader, Wesley understood the *"spiritual* importance of organization."[17]

Here again Wesley's effectiveness lay in his eclecticism. None of the organizational forms he used were entirely original; all had their counterparts either in radical Protestantism or monasticism. But combined together in the context of a vital evangelical movement, they were peculiarly effective. Most significantly, they represent an authentic *structural* response to Wesley's own unique soteriology. Given Wesley's understanding of the process of sanctification, this organizational design makes very good sense.

Wesley's view of salvation as a series of stages, rather than as an all-or-nothing state, suggested a series of groups reflecting various degrees of commitment. Already familiar with the structure used by the religious societies of the Church of England, themselves influenced by the conventicles of German Pietism, Wesley simply took over this form; he then proceeded to subdivide his society members into bands, here borrowing a form, developed by the Moravians, that he had first experimented with in Georgia. The societies were groups of earnest young men who met together for mutual support, edification, and good works. As Wesley was to encounter them, they were an authentic expression of the Anglican emphasis on "inward holiness of intent applied to practical works in the world, on the assumption that the world is also God's sphere of salvation."[18]

As the number of converts from his field preaching grew, Wesley made use of the by then very common religious society structure as a means of offering them guidance and support and proceeded to set up dozens of societies in the areas of London and Bristol. The one requirement for admission was "a desire to flee from the wrath to come, to be saved from [one's] sins."[19] This single requirement made the Methodist Society "at once the easiest and hardest group to join."[20]

The bands, on the other hand, were smaller, more intimate settings where a high level of commitment and mutual trust was expected. Segregated according to sex, age, and marital status, they provided a safe place for soul-searching and confession. Wesley was much attracted to the idea that small groups of converted Christians could serve as strong support for persons who had experienced the new birth. And along with support, he sensed the need for accountability. Peer pressure could be put to God's purposes as well as the Devil's! The bands were to meet weekly, to begin and end with prayer, and to provide opportunity for each member to speak "freely and plainly, the true state of our souls, with the faults we have committed in thought, word, or deed, and the temptations we have felt, since our last meeting."[21] Membership assumed the experience of justification, that is, the experience of assurance and a willingness to be "told of your faults, and that plain and home." "Consider!" warns Wesley's *Rules for Band Societies;* "Do you desire that we should tell you whatsoever we think, whatsoever we fear, whatsoever we hear, concerning you? Do you desire that, in doing this, we should come as close as possible, that we should cut to the quick, and search your heart to the bottom?"[22] To ensure that each heart *was* searched to the bottom, Wesley devised a set of questions for eliciting a truthful account of spiritual progress. The following were to be used at every meeting:

1. What known sins have you committed since our last meeting?
2. What temptations have you met with?
3. How were you delivered?
4. What have you thought, said, or done, of which you doubt whether it be sin or not?
5. Have you nothing you desire to keep secret?[23]

The destruction of the power of sin that occurred in the new birth meant, literally, a *new life* for the believer. Wesley was clear about the specifics of an appropriate lifestyle for those going on to perfection: no spiritous liquor, tobacco, or snuff; scrupulous honesty in business dealings; the renunciation of gossip, faultfinding, and frivolous ornaments that feed vanity. Those rescued from sin were to be generous in almsgiving; gentle but firm in rebuking sin; diligent; frugal; and self-denying. Finally, the testimony of the inward witness did not in any instance do away with the need for making use of the ordinary means of grace. Regular church attendance, frequent Communion, faithful attendance at band meetings, Bible study, private and family prayer, and fasting on Fridays were all non-negotiable obligations. The performance of these disciplines of "right intent" were not a means of earning grace, but they were essential for keeping one open and responsive to the initiatives of grace.[24]

The rapid increase in the size of the Methodist movement continued to pose organizational challenges to Wesley, and it was in responding to a particular financial crisis that the most successful and ultimately durable of Wesley's accountability structures was born. The Methodist class meeting first came into being in 1742 as a convenient and efficient way of collecting contributions to retire a debt incurred by the Bristol Society, numbering by then over a thousand members. The society was broken down into groups of twelve, and a lay leader was assigned to each. His function was to collect a penny a week from all members, and this of course necessitated either paying a call at their homes or meeting together as a group on a weekly basis. Not surprisingly, the latter arrangement was much more efficient. Wesley, seeing at once what *other* useful purpose this arrangement might serve, seized the opportunity. He instructed the lay leaders of each "class," as they were called, to use this occasion not only to receive contributions but also to inquire as to the state of each person's soul and thus "advise, reprove, comfort or exhort, as Occasion may require."[25] The class leaders were to keep in close touch with the stewards of the larger society, who were to receive the funds collected, and the minister, who was to be informed of "any that are sick, of any that walk disorderly, and will not be reproved."[26] Eventually, the class meeting structure became the only point of entry into the larger Methodist societies.

The single entrance requirement—"a desire to flee from the wrath to come"—was to be evidenced in three ways: first, by avoiding all known sin; second, by doing all possible good; and third, by attending all the ordinances of God—the same, basically, as those required of band members, that is, prayer, fasting, frequent Communion, Bible study, works of mercy, and faithful attendance at corporate worship and class meetings. Meetings began with prayer and hymn singing, following which each member reported on his or her spiritual progress during the past week.

Similar in format to the bands but less intense and demanding, the class meeting was an enormous organizational success. Wesley was delighted:

> It can scarce be conceived what advantages have been reaped from this prudential regulation. Many now happily experienced that Christian fellowship of which they had not so much as an idea before. They began to "bear one another's burdens," and naturally to "care for each other." As they had daily a more intimate acquaintance with, so they had a more endeared affection for, each other. And "speaking the truth in love, they grew up into Him in all things, who is the Head, even Christ."[27]

He saw the class meeting as the ideal way of conforming to the biblical injunction to Christians to exhort, comfort, and edify one another, to meet frequently for prayer, instruction, mutual confession, and support. It required a stable, supportive structure such as the class meeting to ensure that the flames of faith that erupted in response to field preaching would not soon be quenched by the deadly ordinariness and relentless worldliness of daily living. So strong was Wesley's emphasis on *applied* spirituality, no one was ever expelled from a meeting for doctrinal heterodoxy, and few for strictly religious reasons. Social sins—cursing, Sabbath breaking, drunkenness, spouse abuse, gossip—were the most serious sins. Interestingly, the chief offense and stumbling block for the largest number was what Wesley called "lightness and carelessness"; by this he meant not taking one's religion *seriously enough.*[28] And Wesley was strict about administering discipline! Yet those who had "made shipwreck of their faith" were to be provided for in special groups composed of penitents.[29]

Even the needs of the *very* spiritually advanced were provided for in the Methodist system. People with whom Wesley felt he could unburden himself became part of a "Select Society." The proceedings of these elite groups were kept strictly confidential. Members agreed to submit to their ministers in all "indifferent things" and to contribute weekly at a sacrificial level to a common fund.[30]

Neither bands nor classes survived into the twentieth century; a tendency toward legalism hastened their demise, and until recently, efforts to revive the forms have met with little or no success. The continuing legacy of this system can still be seen, however, in the strong emphasis put on lay leadership (for men *and* women) in The United Methodist Church and other denominations claiming a Wesleyan heritage. In Wesley we see how high expectations yield high results. Howard Snyder, author of *The Radical Wesley,* writes:

> Now here is a remarkable thing. One hears today that it is hard to find enough leaders for small groups or the other responsibilities in the church. Wesley put one in ten, perhaps one in five, to work in significant ministry and leadership. And who were these people? Not the educated or the wealthy with time on their hands, but laboring men and women, husbands and wives and young folks with little or no training but with spiritual gifts and eagerness to serve. Community became the incubator and training camp for Christ-like ministry.[31]

Prospects for Retrieving a Wesleyan Spirituality

A number of historical factors—social, cultural, and political—can be cited to account for the loss of this remarkable spiritual tradition in twentieth-century American Methodism. *No* European spiritual tradition survived the trans-Atlantic crossing entirely intact. Frontier conditions in America, the scarcity of ordained clergy, and strong anti-British sentiment before, during, and after the Revolutionary War all conspired to dilute the relatively High Church tradition originally associated with Methodist piety. Add to this the notorious anti-intellectual bias of American revivalism and the tendency to *substitute* inwardness for tradition, and the conditions are ripe for the demise of a tradition.

It is important to remember, too, that John Wesley *assumed* a common consensus, if not on doctrinal "niceties" then at least on the theological basics reflected in Scripture and the historic creeds. He never expected the Methodist movement to supplant the established Church of England but only to reform and enliven it. The application of Wesley's generous religious tolerance to issues of theological pluralism *without* this original, very basic consensus has seriously attenuated the spiritual vitality of American Methodism.

Where American Methodism has most succeeded in remaining faithful to the spirit of John Wesley has been in its energetic and pragmatic responses to social evils and political injustices. Now, as the end of the twentieth century approaches, the denomination is making a self-conscious effort to retrieve the forgotten elements of its tradition, and in doing so it is taking the risk of breaking new ground:

> It is not so much that [Wesleyan] spirituality has been tried and found wanting. Certain elements of it have been tried and have borne fruit especially through the medium of the Methodist tradition. Even so, in its wholeness the spirituality of the Wesleys has never been fully tried.[32]

Those among us who are concerned about the retrieval of once-vital spiritual traditions would do well to observe this brave experiment carefully and support it with our prayers.

Notes

1. G. Elsie Harrison, *Son to Susanna*, vol. 1 (Nashville: Cokesbury Press, 1938), p. 44, quoted in James Fowler, "John Wesley's Development in Faith," in *The Future of the Methodist Theological Traditions*, ed. M. Douglass Meeks (Nashville: Abingdon Press, 1985), p. 175.
2. Robert L. Moore, *John Wesley and Authority: A Psychological Perspective.* American Association for Religion Dissertation Series 29 (Chico, Calif.: Scholar's Press, 1979), p. 42, quoted in Fowler, "John Wesley's Development," p. 174.
3. Stanley Ayling, *John Wesley* (Cleveland: William Collins), p. 20, quoted in Fowler, "John Wesley's Development," p. 176.
4. *The Reverend Mr. John Wesley's Journal*, in *The Works of John Wesley*, vol. 1, 3rd ed. (the Wesleyan Conference Office edition, 1872; reprint, Grand Rapids, Mich.: Baker Book House, 1979), p. 98, para. 2, quoted in Fowler, "John Wesley's Development," pp. 178-79.
5. John Wesley, *A Plain Account of Christian Perfection* (London: Epworth Press, 1968), p. 5.
6. Ibid., pp. 5-6.
7. Ibid., p. 6.
8. *Wesley's Journal*, p. 99, quoted in Fowler, "John Wesley's Development," p. 180.

9. Wesley, *Plain Account,* p. 7.
10. Frank Whaling, "Introduction," in *John and Charles Wesley: Selected Writings and Hymns,* The Classics of Western Spirituality Series (New York: Paulist Press, 1981), p. 16.
11. See Ronald Knox, *Enthusiasm* (Westminster, Md.: Christian Classics, 1983), pp. 515-17.
12. Wesley, *Works,* vol. 5, pp. 223-33, *Sermon 14,* "The Great Privilege of Those That Are Born of God," quoted in Whaling, "Introduction," p. 48.
13. David Watson, "Methodist Spirituality," in *Protestant Spiritual Traditions,* ed. Frank C. Senn (New York: Paulist Press, 1986), p. 224.
14. Whaling, "Introduction," pp. 9, 12.
15. Watson, "Methodist Spirituality," p. 222.
16. Whaling, "Introduction," p. 3.
17. Ibid., p. 62.
18. Watson, "Methodist Spirituality," p. 226.
19. Wesley, *Works,* vol. 8, p. 250, quoted in Howard A. Snyder, *The Radical Wesley* (Downers Grove, Ill.: Inter-Varsity Press, 1980), pp. 34-35.
20. Snyder, *The Radical Wesley,* p. 35.
21. David L. Watson, *The Early Methodist Class Meeting: Its Origins and Significance* (Nashville: Discipleship Resources, 1985), p. 200.
22. Ibid.
23. Ibid., p. 201.
24. Ibid., pp. 201-2.
25. "Rules of the United Societies," quoted in Watson, *Class Meeting,* p. 204.
26. Ibid.
27. *Works,* vol. 8, p. 254, quoted in Snyder, *The Radical Wesley,* p. 37.
28. Snyder, *The Radical Wesley,* pp. 57-58.
29. Ibid., p. 62.
30. Ibid.
31. Ibid., p. 63.
32. Whaling, "Introduction," p. 64.

Bibliography

Baker, Frank. *The Heart of True Spirituality, John Wesley's Own Choice.* Vols. 1-3. Grand Rapids, Mich.: Francis Asbury Press of Zondervan Publishing House, 1985.

Chilcote, Paul Wesley. *Wesley Speaks on Christian Vocation.* Nashville: Discipleship Resources, 1986.

Harper, Steve. *Devotional Life in the Wesleyan Tradition.* Nashville: The Upper Room, 1983.

Jeffrey, David Lyle, ed. *A Burning and a Shining Light: English Spirituality in the Age of Wesley.* Grand Rapids, Mich.: Eerdmans, 1987.

Langford, Thomas A. *Practical Divinity: Theology in the Wesleyan Tradition.* Nashville: Abingdon Press, 1983.

_____. *Wesleyan Theology: A Sourcebook.* Durham, N.C.: Labyrinth Press, 1984.

Lindstrom, Harald. *Wesley and Sanctification.* Wilmore, Ky.: Francis Asbury Publishing Co., 1980.

Meeks, M. Douglas, ed. *The Future of the Methodist Theological Tradition.* Nashville: Abingdon Press, 1985. (See chapter 5.)

Outler, Albert, ed. *John Wesley*. New York: Oxford University Press, 1964.

Sangster, W. E. *The Path to Perfection*. London: Epworth Press, 1943.

Snyder, Howard. *The Radical Wesley*. Downers Grove, Ill.: Inter-Varsity Press, 1980.

Watson, David Lowes. *Accountable Discipleship: Handbook for Covenant Discipleship Groups in the Congregation*. Nashville: Discipleship Resources, 1984.

―――. *The Early Methodist Class Meeting*. Nashville: Discipleship Resources, 1985.

―――. "Methodist Spirituality." In *Protestant Spiritual Traditions,* edited by Frank C. Senn, pp. 217-73. New York: Paulist Press, 1986.

Wesley, John. *A Plain Account of Christian Perfection*. London: Epworth Press, 1968.

Whaling, Frank, ed. *John and Charles Wesley: Selected Prayers, Hymns, Journal Notes, Sermons, Letters and Treatises*. New York: Paulist Press, 1981.

Williams, Colin W. *John Wesley's Theology Today*. Nashville: Abingdon Press, 1960.

Accountable Discipleship: Methodism's Quest to Retrieve a Tradition

ROBIN MAAS

Let the word of Christ dwell in you richly, teach and admonish one another in all wisdom, and sing psalms and hymns and spiritual songs with thankfulness in your hearts to God.
—COLOSSIANS 3:16

The recovery of a genuine Wesleyan spirituality, though highly desirable, will not be an easy task. Many cultural factors weigh heavily against it. But the same could be said of Wesley's own time, and he was not one to be daunted by unfavorable conditions! It is *never* easy to be faithful to the demands of discipleship, and that is why Wesley emphasized so heavily the importance of regular, mutual, structured support for individuals struggling to be faithful to Christ in a culturally hostile environment. Such groups were not simply an "aid" to the enhancement of spiritual growth—in fact, they were not about "growth" at all. They were necessary channels of grace and served not to enhance but to *preserve*—to make sure that what was gained in conversion was not destroyed in a workaday world still infested with sin and evil.

Wesley's original vision of moral accountability, particularly in the public sphere, has largely been preserved in the rhetoric of modern-day Methodism. Members of mainstream churches in the Wesleyan tradition are accustomed to calling one another to account through the connectional system over such issues of social justice as racism, sexism, peace, and the eradication of poverty. And this effort has been a persistent one, even in the face of disinterest and resistance at the level of the local congregation. More recently, a concerted effort has been made by The United Methodist Church to recover Wesley's equally strong emphasis on individual moral and spiritual accountability. Specifically, this vision entailed constant recourse to what Wesley called the means of grace: faithfulness in corporate worship, frequent Communion, private and family prayer, daily study of Scripture, and fasting or abstinence.

Covenant Discipleship

The means the denomination has chosen for implementing a truly balanced practice of Wesleyan spirituality have been traditional. Local congregations are being encouraged to develop "Covenant Discipleship" (CD) groups. These groups represent a self-conscious effort to restore the old Methodist class meeting in a modified form, suitable for this day and age. The effort grew out of the work of one individual in particular, a British Methodist named David Lowes Watson. An accomplished Wesleyan scholar and ordained minister, Watson did his doctoral research on the Methodist class meeting and began experimenting with modifications of the form between 1978 and 1987, while associated with Perkins School of Theology in Dallas as associate dean of community life and McCreless Professor of Evangelism. The results of Dr. Watson's efforts to modify the form are detailed in a concise handbook designed for congregational use: *Accountable Discipleship* (cf. list of resources at end of this practicum). Under the direction of Dr. Watson, the Covenant Discipleship model has become a denomination-wide program for spiritual renewal.

Beginning Again: Logistical Considerations

A CD group, like the original class meeting, is open to any seeker of salvation willing to keep himself or herself responsive to the initiatives of grace through the practice of the "disciplines of right intent." Unlike the bands, they are not segregated by sex, age, or marital status. Watson wisely warns us that relatively few church members are ready or willing to have their commitment put to anything that might resemble a test. As a general rule, no more than 15 percent of the active members of a congregation are likely to involve themselves at this level. Ideally, a congregation should begin with a pilot CD group of committed people. Eventually the members of the pilot group would be ready to lead new groups themselves.

Although the original class meetings were lay-led, there is no reason why clergy should not be instrumental in starting such a group. Whoever heads the group needs to be personally committed, compassionate, and relatively directive in leadership style without being autocratic. Once a group is comfortable with the format, Watson suggests the leadership role be shared. The size of the group needs to remain small, seven people or less. The group meets weekly for one hour (only), and that time is spent in calling on each individual member to report on the extent to which he or she has been faithful to the practice of mutually agreed-upon disciplines. The basis for accountability in this area is a group covenant.

The original class meetings operated with a set of specific rules rather than a mutually designed covenant. The "Rules of the United Societies," as they were called, were based on three very broad injunctions. The only condition for membership was a desire for salvation, but it was expected that this desire, if authentic, would manifest itself in

1. doing no Harm, [and] . . . avoiding Evil in every kind. . . .
2. doing Good, . . . by being in every kind, merciful after their Power; as they have Opportunity, doing Good of every possible sort, and as far as it is possible to all Men. . . .
3. attending upon all the Ordinances of God.[1]

Not willing to have anything important fall through the cracks, Wesley spelled out the implications of these three principles with specific obligations. For example, "doing harm" included swearing; Sabbath breaking; drunkenness (including using liquor for anything other than medicinal purposes); quarreling, brawling, or going to law; irregularities in commerce; the use of interest in financial transactions; gossip; vain adornment; frivolous diversions and unedifying entertainment; hoarding and overconsumption of the world's goods; and "softness and self-indulgence."

"Doing good" included—first and most prominently—attending to the physical wants of people: feeding the hungry, clothing the naked, visiting the sick and those in prison. In the second place came attendance on people's spiritual needs through reproof and exhortation. This was to be particularly the case for those of "the household of faith." These should be the beneficiaries of the Methodists' patronage in business and commerce. High on the list too were "diligence" and "frugality," humility and self-denial, and the willingness to suffer slander and persecution for the sake of Christ.

Finally, the "Ordinances of God" were detailed as faithful participation in public worship—both the "Ministry of the Word" and the sacraments—private prayer, searching the Scriptures, and fasting or abstinence.[2] These injunctions were the fire to which early Methodist feet were held.

The first task of any new CD group is the forging of a covenant. The covenant should reflect the *spirit* of Wesley's "Rules" as well as the needs and aspirations of the group members. Normally such a covenant will include Wesley's list of the "Ordinances of God" and other provisions that reflect his concern to do no harm and all the possible good we can. The covenant shown in appendix 10-1 is typical in that respect.

Individual members of the group may add optional, more specific clauses to deal with specific needs they may have:

> I will prayerfully plan my study time.
> I will spend an hour each day with my children.
> I will offer friendship each day to someone of an ethnic background different from my own.

Clauses can always be added, dropped, or made more specific as the issue of what is at stake in accountability becomes clearer to group members. For example, the clause above that speaks about stewardship of resources could be reworked to commit the individual to tithing; some may eventually feel the need for daily, not just weekly, Communion; and some may wish eventually to commit a specific number of hours weekly or daily to helping the poor or disadvantaged.[3]

Once a covenant has been agreed upon, it should be signed and, if possible, ritually recognized in some way. For example, the use of Wesley's covenant service either for the group alone or in the context of congregational worship would be a particularly appropriate way to recognize and solemnize the commitment of CD group members.[4] True to the spirit of John Wesley, CD meetings should begin and end on time with the understanding that a pattern of failure to attend, except for valid emergencies, is a signal that the individual is not yet ready for this level of commitment.

The format of the meeting includes opening and closing with prayer and possibly hymn singing. The bulk of the time is spent in reviewing each person's experience of living out of the covenant during the past week. Usually this proceeds on the basis of taking one clause at a time and having each individual respond before moving to the next clause. Some groups prefer to let each individual respond to the covenant as a whole. Group dynamics in the CD context will be more structured and leader directed than in the typical small group, since the leader is responsible for making sure that each person gets a chance to share. However, this certainly should not preclude other members' adding their own comments of support and encouragement; in fact, mutual admonition and encouragement are likely to increase markedly as the group becomes familiar with the format and with one another.

Issues of Special Concern

As with any new undertaking, there are possible problematic areas that are best identified early on, and initiating a program of covenant discipleship in the local congregation is no exception to this rule. The following issues are ones the group leader should be alert to in advance. Significantly, most of them involve different forms of resistance to accountability in the spiritual life.

Preserving the Original Function of the CD Group

Keeping to the task at hand can be a problem for any small group. It must be remembered that the CD has a special function to perform that will not be dealt with elsewhere if the group itself fails to do so. As the group becomes closer, there is always a temptation to use meeting time for other forms of social exchange—anything from chitchat to intimate personal sharing. It is the leader's task to ensure, without resorting to heavy-handedness, that conversation—at whatever level—remains relevant to the covenant and the issues of accountability in discipleship. This does not foreclose intimate sharing; indeed, eventually this kind of sharing is to be expected and desired. What it does is to set limits to the *scope* of subject matter shared. The leader-directed structure of CD group dynamics, with its emphasis on giving everyone a chance to report back, is a help in this regard since it discourages "monopolies" in an impersonal way. Lack of vigilance here is likely to result in creeping formlessness; unchecked, people's proclivity to simply "share" will erode the original structure and purpose of the group. *The substitution of sociability for accountability is probably the most subtle, and therefore dangerous, threat to the project.*

The Problem of Elitism

The formation of a group within the local congregation committed to the practice of spiritual disciplines may give rise to concerns that spiritual elitism will be fostered. This is not a charge to be dismissed lightly; many congregations and parishes have been badly burned by a kind of smug triumphalism that results when a few are "saved" and the rest are not. A clear case in point has been the havoc wreaked in some places by charismatic groups functioning within the Church. But to level the same charge at a CD group is to misunderstand its basic function. Dr. Watson answers this objection by pointing out that CD groups are in fact analogous to self-help groups such as Alcoholics Anonymous or Weight Watchers,

> where a common weakness is confessed and dealt with through the help of others who have the same problem. Members of covenant groups likewise confess a common weakness: their inability to be obedient disciples of Jesus Christ. Even though they are restored to communion with God in Christ, there remains what the Wesleys described as "inbred sin"—that residual old nature which still resists the gracious initiatives of God. The mark of covenant group members is their recognition of this weakness, and the taking of some elementary steps to deal with it. They have seen the importance of watching over one another in love, and their sense of need is far removed from any feeling of superiority.[5]

We might further add that when any group within a congregation meets for prayer, study, mission, or personal support, *the entire body of Christ benefits.* There is a sense in which the few represent the many, and the grace focused in the lives of those few has a mysterious but inevitable "ripple effect." Those who can, *do,* not simply for themselves but on behalf of those who, for whatever reasons, cannot. Failure to appreciate this means we do not really yet understand what we are saying when we affirm that the Church is "one body."

The Danger of Legalism

A danger facing CD groups that is in fact much more real than spiritual elitism is legalism. Legalism has been blamed for the demise of the class meeting by the turn of the century, and it remains an ever-present danger whenever deeply earnest Christians attempt to get specific and intentional about what it means to be a disciple of Christ. Since these are precisely the distinguishing marks of a Wesleyan spirituality, it is vitally important to guard against the development of a legalistic or censorious attitude in CD groups. Faithfulness is not simply a matter of obeying rules; it is, rather, the maintaining of a *relationship with God* in the company of good friends who are trying also to be "faithful." None of us is going to make it alone—we need all the help we can get!

Fear of being legalistic—the flip side of the coin—can also sabotage the success of a CD group. Having been warned against being judgmental, many of us are paralyzed when it comes to calling someone else to account when it's clear that lack of accountability is a problem.[6]

Routinization

Small groups have life cycles just as individuals do. Charles M. Olsen, author of *Cultivating Religious Growth Groups*, has postulated four predictable stages that groups can expect to experience: discovery, romance, struggle, and investment. At first we can expect a good deal of excitement because of high expectations about what the group will accomplish, but eventually the euphoria wears off, and various forms of rebellion surface. In the case of CD groups, rebellion is likely to focus around the realities—especially the humdrum everyday realities—of accountability.

Another area of struggle may involve the relatively set format of the hour spent together. The covenant may begin to get old and responses to various clauses predictable. It is possible under these circumstances to vary approaches to using the covenant, as has been suggested above, or the problem may lie in clauses that are too general to be challenging. Boredom may be a signal that it's time to renegotiate a more specific set of clauses. But marriages also get old, and a spouse can be very predictable. One of the greatest challenges of the spiritual life is to persist in relating to God faithfully even when we have lost a vital sense of God's presence in our life, to go on loving when there is no apparent response. If covenant groups can be encouraged to persist through dry and difficult spells, says Olsen, "they will move to a deep love and clear covenant. Community will burst upon them as a gift, and not something they have earned or forged for themselves."[7]

The Problem of Resources

A successful CD group will, in effect, create new needs. It will awaken its members to the need for a more intentional prayer life, systematic study of Scripture, opportunities for service, and—if the Wesleyan injunction to commune frequently is taken seriously—it will begin to create a hunger for the Eucharist. Since it is poor pedagogy to create needs without taking into account how these needs will be met, the CD leader must think carefully how to make the necessary resources available. It may be as simple as consulting with the pastor or church librarian to identify good books on prayer and Bible study and then making those easily available, or it may entail ordering new materials for the church library or arranging for book consignments from a local religious bookseller. Since the enormous amount of materials available ranges in quality from excellent to appalling, it is imperative that sound guidance be available to CD group members. Pastors should be aware that the CD experience may create a demand for more classes and workshops relating to the disciplines being practiced.

Similarly, as a desire to serve is nurtured in these groups, it will be important that people find suitable outlets, whether these be rooted in the congregation or the larger community. Again, people may need help in identifying organizations that deal with issues of special concern to them, or they may need encouragement in identifying their own special gifts in the context of voluntary service.

Finally, the most difficult problem in resourcing for many Protestant congregations is likely to be access to the Eucharist. In recent years there has been a trend toward more frequent Communion, and many United Methodist churches, for example, now serve Communion once a month. Since this leaves CD group members in the somewhat uncomfortable position of having to go hunt for mid-week Communion services in other denominations, some of which would not permit intercommunion in any case, Watson suggests a structure that would work well when a single congregation has one or more CD groups meeting at the same time and on the same day of the week. His solution is for the clergy to serve Communion to members of all the groups following their weekly meeting time. It is fervently to be hoped that the opportunities for frequent Communion in churches rooted in the Wesleyan tradition will increase as individuals and groups are awakened to its essential role in the formation of faithful disciples.

EXERCISES

For an Individual

Whether we have access to a spiritual support group or not, we are always accountable to God for being faithful disciples of Jesus Christ. Wesley's "Rules of the United Societies" and the sample CD covenant shown in appendix 10 are useful to individuals in that they can serve as the basis for a regular (weekly or even daily) examination of conscience. Take time this week to look carefully at the way in which you invest your time and your money. How does your investment of these two most precious resources reflect your commitment to Christ? What devotional disciplines do you perform on a regular basis? How does your own program of commitment measure up to the standards Wesley set? What are the major obstacles in your life to the systematic practice of committed discipleship? What new efforts could you undertake on your own? Are there certain disciplines that you know you would need assistance from others in order to practice faithfully? Do you have friends who might be willing to explore the possibility of forming a CD group?

For a Group

After reflecting on the discussion questions below, take time (approximately one hour) to attempt the formulation of a covenant similar to the one shown in appendix 10. (Don't be surprised if you can't complete the task!) Does the sample covenant represent a level of commitment that seems manageable? Does it appear too demanding? What areas are the most difficult in terms of reaching a consensus? Why do you think this is the case? Is your group able to reach the same level of specificity represented by the sample covenant? Can you push beyond this to a greater level of specificity?

Conduct a one-hour meeting in which you follow the leader-directed format described in Watson's *Accountable Discipleship*. Ask each participant to hold himself or herself accountable to the practice of discipleship as he or she currently understands it. Take time following the meeting to reflect on the process you have just experienced. How has it affected each one's motivation to be a faithful disciple of Christ?

John Wesley had very specific things in mind when he wrote "Rules of The United Societies." Review the list of things he included under "Doing no harm and avoiding Evil of every kind." If you were to produce a similar list today, what things would you delete from or add to this list? Do the same thing for his injunction to do "good of every possible sort." Would such a list be generally helpful to Christians today? Why or why not?

DISCUSSION QUESTIONS

1. What are you normally looking for when you join a small group, especially a group sponsored by your local congregation or parish? What is your church looking for from you when it sponsors a particular group? What kind of a reaction does the CD model evoke in you? Why?

2. Where do you currently feel the most need for greater accountability in your life? Is it in any of the areas covered in the sample CD covenant shown in Appendix 10?

3. Wesley's one stipulation for entrance into a class meeting was a sincere desire "to flee from the wrath to come." How might the Church give voice to this same desire for salvation in a modern idiom?

4. Fear of a moralistic legalism is likely to be a principle source of resistance to implementing the CD model in local congregations. How effective is Watson's description of a CD group as analogous to self-help groups such as Alcoholics Anonymous or Weight Watchers in responding to this criticism? Would a CD group be seen as elitist in your church?

Notes

1. "Rules of the United Societies," 1743 ed., quoted in David L. Watson, *The Early Methodist Class Meeting* (Nashville: Discipleship Resources, 1985), pp. 205-6.
2. Ibid.
3. David L. Watson, *Accountable Discipleship* (Nashville: Discipleship Resources, 1984), p. 61.
4. See "Wesley's Covenant Service, Directions for Renewing Our Covenant with God," in *John and Charles Wesley: Selected Prayers, Hymns, Journal Notes, Sermons, Letters and Treatises,* ed. Frank Whaling (New York: Paulist Press, 1981), pp. 134-45.
5. Watson, *Discipleship,* p. 89.
6. See John R. Martin, *Ventures in Discipleship* (Scottdale, Penn.: Herald Press, 1984), p. 137. This very helpful book, written out of an Anabaptist perspective, addresses many issues of common concern to the practice of Wesleyan spirituality, including that of "fraternal admonition." A brief synopsis of his position follows:

   Scripture is full of references to the need for mutual encouragement and admonishment; but to admonish in a way that encourages rather than discourages is truly a spiritual art. Defining admonishment as the giving of "earnest advice," Martin relates it to the baptismal vow, which, in the Anabaptist tradition, is a fully adult, freely given promise implying submission to "the sisters and brothers of the church so that they have the authority to admonish [the believer] if he or she errs." To be baptized is to say, in effect, to the Church, "I *want* you to help me when I stumble, and I call on you to do so" (p. 137).

   The conventional view of admonition starts with the assumption that there is a standard or predetermined model of Christian discipleship one should follow. Anyone who does not measure up to the standard would be in need of admonition. This view assumes clarity and consensus in doctrinal matters and a relatively high view of Church authority. Normally, preaching and "direct admonition" are the means for enforcing the predetermined standard of discipleship. Martin observes that this understanding of admonition works "when members have a high commitment to community and the concept of uniformity. However, it encounters difficulty when members have a strong orientation to individualism, such as is evident in most churches today" (p. 139).

   Given the reality he is describing and the absence of doctrinal consensus in mainstream denominations, a different model of admonition would be called for in most American congregations today. Martin suggests a model that assumes the following:

1) biblical discipleship is a dynamic following of the risen Christ, not following a predefined order; 2) members of congregations are at various levels of spiritual maturity; and 3) members live below the level of their spiritual understanding. (p. 139)

Specifically, he proposes seeing the primary function of admonition as

helping another Christian to clarify his or her spiritual understanding and to become accountable to live that level of knowledge through the grace and power of God. The primary task of the person doing the admonishing is to help the other person live the truth God has shown him or her, not to dictate the details of their life or to enforce a defined order. (p. 139)

This model is a promising one for CD groups since it allows for different levels of commitment within and among groups; at the same time, it assumes that we will know one another well enough to know what our spiritual aspirations and commitments are. While they might not all be identical, they are likely to be more similar than dissimilar. It is helpful, too, in reminding us that what is at stake is a personal relationship with the risen Christ and not simply the ability to obey a set of rules.

7. Charles M. Olsen, *Cultivating Religious Growth Groups* (Philadelphia: Westminster Press, 1984), p. 52.

Resources

Dunnam, Maxie. *The Workbook on Spiritual Disciplines.* Nashville: The Upper Room, 1984.

Foster, Richard J. *Celebration of Discipline.* New York: Harper & Row, 1978.

Harper, Steve. *Devotional Life in the Wesleyan Tradition.* Nashville: The Upper Room, 1983.

Martin, John R. *Ventures in Discipleship: A Handbook for Groups or Individuals.* Scottdale, Penn.: Herald Press, 1984.

Muto, Susan Annette. *Pathways of Spiritual Living.* Garden City, N.Y.: Doubleday Image Books, 1984.

Olsen, Charles M. *Cultivating Religious Growth Groups.* Philadelphia: Westminster Press, 1984.

Watson, David Lowes. *Accountable Discipleship: Handbook for Covenant Discipleship Groups in the Congregation.* Nashville: Discipleship Resources, 1984.

_____. *The Early Methodist Class Meeting.* Nashville: Discipleship Resources, 1985.

Wells, Ronald V. *Spiritual Disciplines for Everyday Living.* Schenectady, N.Y.: Character Research Press, 1982.

A Covenant of Discipleship*

Knowing that Jesus Christ died that I might have eternal life, I herewith pledge myself to be his disciple, holding nothing back, but yielding all to the gracious initiatives of the Holy Spirit. I faithfully pledge my time, my skills, my resources, and my strength, to search out God's will for me, and to obey.

I will pray each day, privately, and with my family or friends.
I will read and study the Scriptures each day.
I will worship each Sunday unless prevented.
I will receive the Sacrament of Holy Communion each week.
I will heed the warnings of the Holy Spirit not to sin against God and my neighbor.
I will obey the promptings of the Holy Spirit to serve God and my neighbor.
I will prayerfully care for my body and the world in which I live.
I will prayerfully seek to help someone in need each day.
I will prayerfully plan the stewardship of my resources.
I will share in Christian fellowship where I will be accountable for my discipleship.

I hereby make my commitment, trusting in the grace of God to work in me that I might have strength to keep this covenant.

Date _____ Signed _____

*From David L. Watson, *Accountable Discipleship* (Nashville: Discipleship Resources, 1984), p. 60.

CHAPTER 11

Black Spirituality

JAMIE PHELPS, O.P.

There is neither Jew nor Greek, . . . slave nor free . . . male nor female; for you are all one in Christ Jesus.

—GALATIANS 3:28

While it is common practice to describe the spiritual life within the context of a particular historical period (early Church or medieval), a commanding figure in religious history (Ignatius Loyola or John Wesley), or a specific theological tradition (Reformed or Roman Catholic), it is also possible to speak of culturally or racially determined spiritualities (French, Spanish, Hispanic, African, Native American). Yet the essence of spirituality—the attempt to encounter the Divine Other—is fundamentally the same for every human being, despite the particularities of gender, race, culture, class, or national heritage.

Black spirituality is a vital and distinctive spirituality forged in the crucible of the lives of various African peoples. Black Africans and those members of the African Diaspora whose ancestors were brutalized by enslavement in the New World all share a common racial heritage, a common relationship to the dominant Western culture, and a common spirit. This common spirit found in people of African descent is an attitude that sees all of life in the context of the encounter with the Divine, and the all-embracing vision of the Divine-human encounter—which is really the essential clue to understanding the nature of black spirituality—is rooted in a distinctive and ancient world view.

The African World View

No matter where or when they live, black people are fundamentally *African* people, whose perspective and way of life have been conditioned by their roots in Mother Africa. Therefore, the study of black spirituality properly begins with a look at the African world view and African traditional religions.

As African and African-American philosophers identify experiences that are uniquely African, they note a distinctive world view in traditional religions' proverbs, oral traditions, social ethics, and moral codes.[1] A foundational aspect of the traditional African world view is the primacy of the group as the basis for identity and survival. This attitude is directly reflected in the communal character of traditional African religions:

> Traditional religions are not primarily for the individual, but for his community of which he is part. Chapters of African religion are written everywhere in the life of the community, and in traditional society there are no irreligious people. To be human is to belong to the whole community, and to do so involves participating in the beliefs, ceremonies, ritual and festivals of that community. A person cannot detach himself from the religion of his group, for to do so is to be severed from his roots, his foundations, his context of security, his kinships and the entire group of those who make him aware of his own existence. To be without religion amounts to a self-excommunication from the entire life of the society, and African peoples do not know how to exist without religion.[2]

Thus Africans and African-Americans tend to both communicate and organize by a process of human and spiritual networks or groups. Work is done more efficiently by groups, and the community is supported by the networks of groups that are, in turn, sustained by community worship. The communal understanding of religion gives rise to a community anthropology whereby the "I" signifies "we."

A second fundamental element of the African world view, which differs significantly from that of the dominant Western culture, is its concept of time and reality. Time, for the traditional African, is the eternal present; that is, the past and present are *now,* and *now* is the most important concern of one's religious activities and beliefs. The concept of the future is absent from traditional African thought. Since the future has not occurred, it does not exist within the context of "actual time." Yet through the influence of Western culture and Christianity, Africans are discovering the future under the rubric of "potential time." This concept of time influences the African understanding of human life, death, and immortality.[3]

333

Edwin Nichols' research into the African world view yielded what he considers to be a distinct axiology (theory of value), epistemology, logic, and way of processing information.[4] His description of the African philosophical perspective identifies interpersonal relationships as the highest value in African society, making community the center of and foundation for all of African life. Further, Africans and African Americans both see all of life as an organic whole, with each thing or being integrally related to every other. Thus the sacred and secular categories typical of traditional Eurocentric Christianity do not exist in the African world view. Because African-rooted logic is a diunital process by which the mind tends to seek the unity of opposites, the African typically does not use categories of "either-or" but rather those of "both-and." God speaks through the roar of the mighty wind or lion as well as through the quietness of a gentle breeze or rabbit. God is found in the midst of community activity as well as in quiet moments of solitude. Life is not complete without the unity of the male and female. The rhythm of life requires activity and rest, laughter and mourning, thought and emotion. In this way, the African way of life tends to unite that which seems to be mutually exclusive.

Africans and African-Americans process thought through the use of symbolic imagery and rhythm. African linguistic expression uses analogy and metaphor extensively to reflect concrete experience and the environment, and information is relayed through descriptive images. For example, in my childhood I heard people describe someone inebriated by alcohol as being "as high as a Georgia pine!" Or a child who was fidgety might be described as having "ants in his pants." In a similar vein, blacks rely on the use of rhythm aids for learning. While teaching black first-graders, I found that singing numerical facts aided their retention of mathematics. In the same way, clapping the rhythm of a word improved their pronunciation.

The philosophical distinctiveness of the African world view gives rise to equally distinct understandings of religion, spiritual expression, and spiritual development. The remainder of this chapter will survey the development and chief characteristics of black spirituality, with its roots in African religions, slave religion, and the black church.

African Religions

Since African religions are tribal and national, theoretically one cannot speak of African religion in the singular. However, a review of the religions of several West African tribes—the Fon of Dahomey, the

Yoruba of Nigeria, and the Akan of Ghana—does reveal similarities in patterns of behavior and belief, and given that most American blacks trace their origins to West Africa, it is appropriate to look briefly at one of these religions in a representative way in order to understand what kind of a God—or gods—Africans typically worship.

The Fon understanding of God is of a Supreme Being who creates all things and participates in a cosmic harmony with human beings and inanimate things. In some tribes the supreme Creator God is assisted by lesser deities who interact in the daily affairs of human life to bring them into conformity with the will of the Supreme God—the all-powerful, ever-present, and all-knowing Creator, Begetter, Originator, Sustainer—the One who orders all things.

This Supreme Creator God is assisted by his two descendants, Mawu, the male god who represents coolness, wisdom, and mystery, and Lisa, the female god who represents the strength and energy of the dialectical rhythm of life. Mawu and Lisa act together as a universal complementary force in nature and are symbolized by the snake. Below Mawu and Lisa, the Fon pantheon contains two levels of deities known collectively as "vodu." These greater and lesser vodu, offspring of Mawu and Lisa, guard land and sea or are involved in everyday human pursuits. In the religious system of Dahomey, "the gods meet man at every point of life."[5]

Besides belief in a Supreme Being, the African religious traditions emphasize belief in the ancestors, the practice of sacrifice, belief in spirits and powers (both good and evil), and, finally, belief in the fullness of the present life. Reverence for ancestors, in particular, is a universally important feature of African religions. These ancestors are the "living dead" who continue to influence the present as long as they are remembered by their kinfolk. Ancestors are not worshiped but are held in respect and reverence similar to that given to the older living members of the family or tribe. The spirit of the ancestors is a vital part of the African concept of community, in which the collective power of all members of the community—the living and the "living dead"—energizes and pervades the daily life of everyone. Those ancestors who exhibited special moral virtue and strength in life are held up as spiritual guides for the living.[6]

Sacrificial ritual was the centerpiece of traditional African worship. Priests and priestesses offered sacrifice on behalf of the people for purposes of "propitiation, substitution, prevention, or purification" and in conjunction with the key events and rites of passage of human life: birth, puberty, marriage, and so on. A second component of African ritual, spirit possession, was a prized experience. The singing and drumming characteristic of African worship was used to invoke the presence of the lesser deities among the assembly, and as possession occurred, the devotees danced. The essential element of African religious expression, spirit possession—with its accompanying music and dance—was maintained in the transfer of African religion to the black church.[7]

The organizing principle of all African religion is the preservation and strengthening of life-force or power. Life is to be lived with great enthusiasm and energy and, simultaneously, protected from evil spirits and human malice. Various kinds of intercessory prayer—chants and invocations—are used to assuage the evil spirits, and medicine men or traditional healers are called upon to cure sickness with incantations as well as with medications.[8]

The power of the gods and spirits, for good or evil, was a central aspect of African life and belief. While African tribes did not share all such beliefs, Albert Raboteau portrays, in general terms, a picture of the interpersonal and relational character of African religions:

> The gods and men related to one another through the mediation of sacrifice, the mechanism of divination, and through the phenomenon of spirit possession. Widely shared by diverse West African societies were several fundamental beliefs concerning the relationship of the divine and the human: belief in a transcendent and benevolent God, creator and ultimate source of providence; belief in a number of immanent gods, to whom people must sacrifice in order to make life propitious; belief in the power of the spirits animating things in nature to affect the welfare of people; belief in priest and others who were expert in practical knowledge of the gods and spirits; belief in spirit possession, in which gods, through their devotees, spoke to men.[9]

Although most Christian missionaries to Africa summarily dismissed these traditional religious beliefs and practices as pagan and idolatrous, one may argue that some points of African belief could have provided a basis for religious dialogue between African religions and Western Christianity. African belief in a supreme, all-powerful, omniscient, and immutable God is suggestive of the Christian understanding of the one true God. "Who is God?" asks the catechism. "God is the Supreme Being who made all things" is the reply. A Christian raised in the Catholic scholastic tradition must also hear in the African definition of the Divine echoes of Aquinas's description of God's attributes in the *Summa Theologica*.

Some aspects of the African ancestor traditions seem to correlate with the Christian doctrine of the "Communion of Saints," in which the living and the dead maintain a spiritual unity before the Lord, and what Catholic Christian worship has traditionally called the "Sacrifice of the Mass" was seen not only as a community celebration of God's presence in our lives but also as an actual reenactment and memorial of the sacrifice of Jesus, who, in our place, died to atone for our sins and to redeem us from the condemnation of original sin. Even the concept of a spirit taking possession of an individual is not totally foreign to Christian concepts of the divine indwelling and the strengthening of one's faith by the celebration of the sacraments. In Confirmation, the Holy Spirit is called upon to strengthen the faith and direct the ministry of the recipient of the sacrament. Sacramental rituals are celebrated to effect the presence and strength of God: Father, Son, and Holy Spirit are asked to protect—"take possession"—of the person in the sacrament of baptism, to forgive the person in the sacrament of reconciliation or penance, and to heal the person in the sacrament of anointing of the sick.

This is not to say that traditional African and Christian beliefs are identical, only that there are inherent in both sets of beliefs some shared meanings that provide a basis for understanding between two religious communities rooted in cultures with distinct world views. Such similarities account for the development of religious syncretism when African religious traditions encountered Christianity in the New World.

Slave Religion

Along with the beliefs and practices of African religions, both medicine men and sorcerers were transported to the New World as slaves. The continued presence of these religious leaders could not, however, ensure that African religions would survive the Atlantic crossing intact, for the very important communal bases of African religious perspectives and practices were more often than not destroyed by slave traders, who separated members of clans and tribes to insure against insurrection and create dependence on the slave master. Some sources argue that these practices, along with the trauma of the "middle passage" from Africa to the American shores, totally eradicated the slaves' cultural and religious traditions by destroying their community. Other scholars suggest that new bonds were forged during the middle passage, allowing a creative integration of the common elements of the tribal rituals and religious perspectives to emerge.[10]

337

Raboteau suggests that both sides of the argument possess some truth, depending on the receptiveness of the receiving cultures. While African belief and ritual endured in the Latin cultures of Cuba, Haiti, Brazil, and the Caribbean Islands, it generally did not survive in the United States, though some residuals of the African pantheons and rituals are evident in the isolated Sea Islands of the Carolinas and in Louisiana. Two factors account for this difference: the cultural systems of the receiving countries and the density of the African population in the New World.[11] For example, in Cuba, Haiti, Brazil, Trinidad, and the Virgin Islands, where the African population is dense, religious cults exhibit recognizable elements of African rituals and ancestor cults.[12]

The new and hostile environment of the slaves inevitably required some transformation of African religious beliefs and practices. The question that dominated the slaves' world was one of survival, seen—as it traditionally had been—in terms of a struggle against evil forces. But these evil forces were (consistently) much more evident now in the day-to-day conditions of slavery than they had ever been in life on the African continent. The medicine man and conjurer now had to focus on conquering the illness and evil that accompanied slavery. The situation was a matter of life and death, and the life-force was to be preserved and strengthened by any means possible. Yet even in slavery, Africans knew that God had not abandoned the community but was in their midst, and the slave was grateful that God had provided means of survival. Thus the rituals of slave religion were a joyous affirmation of God's presence and providence. As the drums beat, slaves opened themselves to receive the Spirit, to become united with that spirit which strengthened their life-force and restored their wounded bodies. Amazingly, in the midst of the violence of slavery, the major theme of slave religion was joy!

> Even carnal pleasure had its prominent place. Such a religion bound men and women to the organic vitalistic powers of creation—to powers that they believed could provide for and sustain those who joyfully acknowledged and served the Creator. Behind the recognition that in existence there is some radically opposing force, some intrinsic mischief that we must somehow overcome or learn to control, was an even greater recognition that life is good and is to be savored and enjoyed while it lasts.[13]

As slave religion encountered Christianity, the slaves integrated those aspects of Christianity that eased "the burden of their captivity and gave little attention to the rest."[14] In Latin America and the Islands, Catholic piety, with its use of sacramentals, veneration of saints, and religious societies, combined with the African propensity for survival and harmony, resulted in the development of an African-Catholic syncretism in which the slaves' popular piety identified the attributes of the lesser gods with the intercession of the saints. This African-Catholic syncretism thrived in the cults of Latin America, where Catholicism and the Latin cultural system were dominant. It was not so well preserved where the dominant cultural system was English Protestantism.[15]

Despite the hostile circumstances of slavery in the New World, the African world view, which affirms the presence of the spirit world in the daily affairs of the community and the individual, was not destroyed. The African slave continued to see all of life as permeated with the Spirit. All of life was sacred. The individual and community were obligated to affirm this divine presence in ritual, prayer, and other forms of worship. Such rituals strengthened the life-force of the community and each of its members. Africans creatively indigenized their new environment through religious syncretism and, in some instances, secret cults. Where African life was harshly restricted and religious expression suppressed, religion became the basis of the struggle for liberation. For example, the vodun cult of Haiti, a syncretistic practice combining the African religion of Dahomey and Catholic Christianity, was the source of spiritual strength for Haitian nationalists who revolted in 1791.[16]

The Black Church

The primary locus for and nurturer of black spirituality has been the traditional black church. The term "black church" designates both those black Christian churches that originated as a consequence of the rejection and second-class citizenship blacks experienced in the mainline Protestant denominations and those independent churches that have roots in the religion of the slave quarters and fields (e.g., Baptist and Pentecostal).[17]

The forms of Christianity the African slaves encountered in captivity had already degenerated by their accommodation to the immoral enslavement of other human beings. These Protestant and Catholic Christians had anesthetized themselves to the immorality of slavery by philosophical and theological rationalizations that "justified" the economic and personal exploitation of their estranged African brothers and sisters. Indeed, few of these Christians would ever

339

concede that Africans were fully human and therefore their equals in the eyes of God. To the contrary, in the eyes of most slave traders and missionaries, Africans were uncivilized barbarians who were being saved and elevated by their mere association with Christian civilization.[18]

In the United States, where English Protestantism was the dominant religious culture, few efforts were made to convert the slaves to Christianity until the eighteenth century, and these efforts increased only when it was guaranteed that baptism would not alter the "property" status of the slave.[19] That these baptisms were often attempts to pacify the enslaved Africans is indicated by one slave catechism from the mid–nineteenth century: The question "What did God make you for?" is followed by the answer "To make a crop." Another question, "What is the meaning of 'Thou shalt not commit adultery'?" is answered "To serve our heavenly Father, and our earthly master, obey our overseer, and not steal anything."[20]

In general, the Christian churches remained indifferent to the spiritual welfare of their African slaves, who were viewed primarily as property. Blacks were thought to be the cursed descendants of Ham. In reality, they were not cursed by God but by the indifference of those Christians who used "their bodies but denied their souls, and . . . turned them away from their churches."[21] Even when the doors of the church were opened, blacks were relegated to the back pews and balconies of the assemblies to prevent social contact. Yet it was in these back pews and balconies that the slaves heard the liberating words of the gospel. While the white preacher attempted to use the gospel to justify the current social and economic relations between the races, the slaves heard the liberating themes of the gospel and integrated them with their traditional African beliefs of a loving, ever-present, and provident God. When their interpretation of the biblical message and its implication for blacks clashed with denominational stances and boundaries, some blacks left their parent churches and formed independent African churches.

Black Christian preachers realized that God's provident love required that human beings be free to develop their humanity to its fullest potential. If God is free, then human beings, created in the divine image and likeness, were meant to be free. Thus Christian responsibility requires those who have been enslaved to recover their God-given freedom so their *force-vitale*, or inner spirit, could be free. Such was the meaning and message of the liberating actions of Henry Highland Garnett, Thomas Fortune, David Walker (who followed in the footsteps of Nat Turner), and Denmark Vessey.[22]

It was not unusual for the early black Christian slaves who assembled in the balconies and back pews of the white Christian churches to reassemble in the backwoods and swamps, where they could express their common experience and common spirituality in more congenial forms of rhythm, song, and prayer. With the emergence of the independent African churches in the eighteenth and nineteenth centuries, the invisible black church of the backwoods became the visible black church in the United States.[23] These churches generally maintained the structures and central doctrines of their originating denominations; nevertheless, they developed a unique black-American religious culture—a blend of both African religion and Euro-American Christianity. This distinctive religious culture, like the African religious cultures that preceded it, sought and still seeks to interpret the meaning of black life in relationship to both God and its environment. The preaching and worship styles of the black church echo and reflect the African world view and understanding of God's love and active presence in the daily affairs of human beings. In varying degrees, the liberating spirit that gave birth to the black church is evident in the content and style of its preaching and song, as well as in the involvement of its members in evangelization and action for social justice.

Although some traditional black Christian churches have maintained a faithfulness to the essential meaning and message of Jesus Christ as apprehended from an African or black perspective, others have become accommodated to a dualistic view that divides the world into the sacred and the secular, thus contradicting their African origin. This culturally alien dualism can give rise to a variety of problems. On the one hand, black churches can be solely havens of emotional security from the world's racial hostility. On the other hand, they can be both comforting and challenging sources of spiritual regeneration, empowering their members to struggle to liberate their families, their community, and the world from moral compromise with personal and social sins such as narcissism, materialism, racism, sexism, imperialism, and militarism. Then again, the black church can be corrupted into an institution that functions solely as a political-economic base for a racially isolated community.[24] The authentic black church must have a holistic approach to its members. It must comfort as well as challenge, and it must address the spiritual as well as the social and political needs of its members.

The Characteristics of Black Spirituality

Black spirituality is characterized by a number of specific emphases and attitudes, none of which are exclusive to it but all of which, taken together, combine to produce a unique vision and practice of the spiritual life.

First, black spirituality, like the African religions in which it is rooted, is community centered. It shapes the community and, in turn, is shaped by the community, which defines itself and its history as being integrally connected with God. It is in the context of the worshiping community that the God-awareness of black spirituality is nurtured. What was true of slave religion of the past is equally true of the black church today: In common worship the community is called by song to be conscious of the Spirit who comes to join the assembly. Just as the drums of the African ritual opened the door for the spirit to enter the assembly, gospel song invites the Holy Spirit to be manifest in the midst of the worshiping community.

Another fundamental element of black spirituality is its strong biblical character. The worship services of the traditional black church are dominated by the dynamic and evocative preaching of the minister, and the starting point of the sermon is always the Word of God. The preacher begins by retelling an entire biblical story or dramatically announcing a few lines from a text taken from the Old or New Testament. After this vivid proclamation of the Scripture, the preacher brings the biblical text to life by indicating how the story has meaning in the lives of the congregation. Often the preaching is a dialogical experience, with the congregation affirming the preacher's truth telling by nods of the head, applause, amens, and the like. When the Spirit of Truth envelops the assembly, some of the worshipers respond in a manner similar to their African ancestors, who experienced spirit possession. The preaching and singing is necessarily emotional, because the worshipers have been touched at the core of their being, moved by the presence of the Spirit deep in their soul.

In African-American culture the emotional is not the opposite of the spiritual, nor is there any separation between the emotional and the intellectual. Both the mind and the heart are needed to grasp the truth. If the preacher does not preach the truth, it will not be long before the congregation calls him to task.[25]

The point of the black church's biblically centered worship is to hear God's word from the past as it is evidenced in the present. This "immediate" interpretive principle or hermeneutic is a reflection of the African concept of time, in which past and present are one and continuous. Thus black spirituality is always concerned to situate itself firmly in the present, in the midst of concrete daily experience. By the same token, the biblical characters are not simply heroes and heroines of long ago; they have joined the ranks of the ancestors, and their lives, like those of the biological ancestors of African-Americans, influence the lives of the living community.

In some worship services, members of the congregation testify to God's action in their lives and those of their extended family during the week. Increasingly, black-Catholic liturgies are incorporating this testimonial aspect through spontaneous prayers of the people during the penitential rite and in the general intercessions during the Liturgy of the Word. In communal worship the assembly gathers up the experiences of its individual members and transforms them into the experience and concerns of the entire community. The suffering caused by unemployment, poverty, hunger, homelessness, rejection, and the human degradation of racism is all brought to the church to be transformed; and all of it *is* transformed by offering the entire community to God for healing, relief, and strengthening.

Most Africans and members of the African Diaspora have an experience of God that is both transcendent and immanent—God who is beyond us but dwells within us. Black believers know experientially ("deep down in my soul") that the Spirit of God dwells within their inner selves, directing their memory, imagination, intellect, feelings, and body. Any person born into the religious tradition of African or African Diaspora cultures is nurtured from birth into a style of life that witnesses to the belief that God is manifest everywhere and in every person, thing, or event. This attitude corresponds to the traditional religions of Dahomey, in which God meets the human being at every point of life; but the involvement of God in human life by way of "the gods" has been replaced, in the black church, by the concept of God being present by means of the Spirit sent by Jesus after his ascension. Thus a person steeped in the black spiritual tradition is trained, so to speak, in a particular kind of mystical tradition. One sees God's hands in every human encounter and event in life and is conditioned by environmental nurturing to abandon oneself, in obedience to God's will, to the movements of the Holy Spirit.

It is not unusual for a black child reared in a religious home to hear family members, especially the mother, talking to Jesus as they mull over family concerns. Nor is it unusual to hear in family and community conversations testimony that a person has been led by God to use his or her talents in a specific way or to do this or that thing, even when the individual involved was initially resistant to such a course of action. The impulse in black spirituality to abandon oneself to the divine will and the indwelling Spirit lends itself to a particularly intimate experience of God.

Yet the kind of abandonment black worship invites is not a somber resignation to or hopeless acceptance of a life over which one has no control. The mystical union to which black spirituality predisposes one is the source of an emotional, energetic, and joyful approach to life and worship. The life experiences of African-Americans attest that God is reliable and benevolent, involved in the daily life of individuals and the community. Blacks in touch with their spiritual traditions are confident about their ultimate well-being, because God is a loving God who, in the last analysis, can be counted upon to give joy, power, and liberation from the debilitating oppressions of sin, racism, or any form of evil. This deep sense of joy finds expression in a correspondingly deep and pervasive sense of peace, even in the midst of great adversity or trial, and it is the same deep joy that overflows in quiet tears, loud shouts, exuberant or emotional songs, dancing, and clapping by choir and congregation gathered in worship.

While the joy of the Spirit's presence manifests itself in vivid and diverse ways in the worshiping community, such expression alone does not authenticate black spirituality. The absolute criterion of authentic black spirituality is its impact on the quality of the believer's life. It assumes that the true nature of our faith is reflected in the way in which we relate to other human beings and the created order, and that our concern for others will naturally generate witness and actions directed toward the realization of freedom for all human beings to live a liberated and joyful life, energized by the power of the Spirit. For example, does the person possessed by the Spirit of God treat his family, neighbor, friends, and enemies with a sense of respect for the presence of God within each and every person? Does this person struggle to establish right relationships with others, regardless of race, gender, or creed? Does this person act right and call others to be right? Does this person struggle for the liberation of oppressed persons, races, nations?

Since the center and organizing principle of all African religion is the preservation and strengthening of the life-force or power of the community, in black spirituality, too, the central focus is the preservation and strengthening of the life-force and power that dwells within each individual and in the community. This life-force is the Spirit of God.

Individuals oppressed by reason of gender, race, class, or nationality have had their authentic freedom, their unique expression of the God-force, suppressed. Thus they are denied their role as cocreators of God's kingdom. Authentic black spirituality leads to prophetic action on behalf of justice, a justice that requires liberation from sin and its effects. This understanding of justice entails a reordering of the false and unjust structures of institutions, nations, and even ecclesial bodies that have become stumbling blocks rather than facilitators of an individual's or community's right relationship between God and one another. A person imbued with the life-force at the center of black spirituality—with the Spirit of God—is willing to struggle for this liberation, knowing that even death is not too high a price to pay for the establishment of those right relationships that characterize the kingdom of God.

In their commitment to the liberation and justice of the poor, the marginalized, and the oppressed, adherents of the prophetic tradition so prominent in authentic black spirituality recognize that they must stand for the truth. The Christian person must walk the path of Jesus Christ, who is the Way, the Truth, and the Life. A man of love who announced the gospel to the poor, the oppressed, and the marginalized of his society (Luke 4:14ff), Jesus not only spoke the good news, he *was* Good News.

The Gospel writers portray a Jesus who, in his love, invited and challenged all he encountered to a way of being and acting that reflected their true dignity and identity as members of the one family of God. Pharisee, Sadducee, Samaritan woman, disciple, Roman governor, tax collector—any and all persons encountered were invited or challenged. No one was (or is) beyond God's call to conversion in Jesus. Thus black spirituality challenges any exclusive interpretation of those invited to the wedding feast of the kingdom. Christ's message of love, justice, and liberation was good news for some and a fear-inducing challenge to others. Those who heard his message as good news became disciples and apostles. Those who heard his message as demanding a change that threatened their security—the rich, the powerful, and the pious—responded by calling for his crucifixion. This Jesus is Love. Out of his love he died and rose from the dead to free humankind from its sin and oppression. His death and resurrection have freed us from fear and empowered us to live for and with God.

Not all black Christians embrace this universal and community-centered understanding of the meaning of Jesus. They, like some other Christians, believe that the life and death of Christ have nothing at all to do with the ecclesial and social structures of human society, even when these structures suppress the spirit of love, truth, and liberation given to each person and community for building up and preparing for God's kingdom.

Black Spirituality and the Churches

It should be apparent that black spirituality transcends and crosses denominational and ecclesial boundaries. Its characteristic cultural expressions are more evident in some congregations and denominations than in others; consequently, it is more or less empirically evident in the lives of individual black Christians.

Many African-American Catholics and other blacks nurtured in predominantly white Christian congregations have become estranged from their cultural religious heritage because they were introduced to an ecclesial form of spirituality by sisters, priests, ministers, or missionaries who were not conscious of the cultural wrappings with which they presented the gift of Christianity to the children of the African Diaspora. The spiritual traditions of the Catholic church, for example, were transmitted to the sons and daughters of Africa without any consciousness of the culture-specific ways—Spanish, Irish, German, English, French, or Italian—in which they were being transmitted. In addition, these ministers of God's good news sometimes maintained a disdain for the natural religious expression of blacks. For them, blacks needed to be elevated and rescued from their immorality by their participation in what was perceived to be a universal spirituality that was, in fact, a particular cultural-ecclesial spirituality and way of life. White missionaries assumed that blacks had no culture worth preserving, and that their religiosity was a natural disposition based primarily on fear and ignorance. Christianity would provide them both with culture and the true faith.[26]

In contrast to the missionary endeavors of the nineteenth century, the writings of St. Paul suggest that the early Church approached Gentile cultures with an implicit sense of the need for cultural adaptation. Unfortunately, this sense of cultural adaptation was absent from the method of evangelization used by many missionaries encountering non-European peoples, whether they were Asians, Africans, Native Americans, or black Americans. Universality was narrowly defined as uniformity, rather than as unity in diversity.[27]

Today, the picture is changing. The twentieth-century shift to a historical consciousness in biblical studies and theological interpretation and the Church's attempt to address the role of God in the modern world call for a shift in evaluating the religious, racial, cultural, economic, and social-political diversity evident within the world and the Church. This shift is obvious in recent Roman Catholic documents relating to liturgy, mission, evangelization, and non-Christian religious, which urge respect for and utilization of cultural expressions, symbols, and practices that are not fundamentally at odds with Christian orthodoxy.[28]

Most significant for our discussion is the emerging theological understanding of the relationship between the natural and the supernatural spheres of reality. Traditionally the Church has taught that "grace builds on nature." Many modern theologians, notably Karl Rahner, would assert that nature itself is "graced." This graced human nature is a reality that is unified and organically interrelated yet manifests itself in diversity of all kinds, and this diversity does not eliminate any person or group from participating in the universal salvific will of God. Everything created by God manifests God's creative Spirit, indeed, *embodies* that Spirit in one form or another. Positions such as Rahner's are in harmony with the African world view, in which the world is not dichotomized into sacred and secular realms.

Taken seriously, these philosophical and theological shifts would lead those engaged in ministry and mission to first seek the manifestation of the Spirit in cultural diversity rather than always thinking in terms of "bringing Jesus" to non-Christian nations and cultures. Further, respect for God-given cultural diversity in the human community requires pastoral ministers to develop religious educational materials that reflect such diversity. Congregational worship or liturgies serving distinct cultural or multicultural constituencies should attempt to integrate the music, symbolic expressions, and theological interpretations of God and Christ so as to nurture the spiritual consciousness of worshipers. At the same time, the Church needs to challenge culturally different populations to deepen their spiritual awareness by prayer and a study of the Scriptures directed toward discerning the authentic meaning and message of Jesus as it affirms and critiques their present way of relating to God and others.

Christian churches engaged in the spiritual nurturance of African-Americans must take seriously the particular culture and context of black life in America. In this regard, they would be wise to take account of the challenges presented in the work of contemporary black theologians, historians, anthropologists, religious leaders, and scholars, who are reexamining the Scriptures and black religious traditions in order to discern how God is being revealed in today's black community and what the black church's mission is in relation to the world and the world Church.[29]

Pope Paul VI, in a historic visit to Kampala, Uganda, urged African Catholics to enrich the Church with their "gift of Blackness," and increasingly, African and black Christians in the United States and throughout the World are ready and willing to share with their black and white brothers and sisters the rich gift of black spirituality given to them by God. They, in turn, will continue to integrate and enrich their African religious heritage and spirituality with the gifts of other Christian traditions and world religions.

Notes

1. John S. Mbiti, *African Religions and Philosophy* (New York: Doubleday Anchor Books, 1970), pp. 1-2.
2. Ibid., p. 3.
3. Ibid., see pp. 19-36.
4. Edwin J. Nichols, Ph.D., a black Catholic philosophical psychologist, is the chief of the Service Systems Technology Transfer Branch at the National Institute of Mental Health. After teaching briefly at the University of Ibadan, Nigeria, he developed a comparative schema that he presented at the World Psychiatric Association and Association of Psychiatrists at the University of Ibadan on Nov. 10, 1976. Nichols consults in the area of cross-cultural management and decision making and has worked with missionaries engaged in cross-cultural interactions to interpret the philosophical aspects of cultural differences between ethnic and racial groups.
5. Leonard E. Barrett, *Soul Force* (New York: Doubleday Anchor Books, 1974), pp. 17-20.
6. Ibid., pp. 22-24; and Albert Raboteau, *Slave Religion* (New York: Oxford University Press, 1978), pp. 12-13.
7. Barrett, *Soul Force*, pp. 24-26; and Raboteau, *Slave Religion*, pp. 10-11, 15.
8. Medicine men are carefully selected and must undergo a minimum of ten years of apprenticeship and training, then pass a test administered by their peers. The Western mind has looked upon these practices as "magic" and nonscientific, yet this does not seem to be the reality. Increasing numbers of scientifically trained doctors have acknowledged the psychosomatic component of much physical illness and are exploring the relationship between diet and disease in what is now termed "holistic medicine." The distinction should be noted that whereas the medicine man seeks to protect the life-force of human beings, the sorcerer or conjurer employs witchcraft to diminish the life-force of persons and thereby hurt or kill them. See Barrett, *Soul Force*, pp. 27-31, 60; and Raboteau, *Slave Religion*, pp. 13-14.
9. Raboteau, *Slave Religion*, pp. 11-12.
10. For a review of this classic discussion, see E. Franklin Frazier's *The Negro Family in the United States*, rev. and abr. ed. (New York: Dryden Press, 1948); and Melville J. Herskovits, *The Myth of the Negro Past* (New York: Harper & Bros., 1941). Frazier suggests that African-American religious practices owe little to African influence, while Herskovits argues for essential continuity evidenced both in African-American culture and religious practices.
11. Raboteau, *Slave Religion*, p. 86.
12. Barrett, *Soul Force*, p. 69.
13. Gayraud Wilmore, *Black Religion and Black Radicalism* (Maryknoll, N.Y.: Orbis Press, 1983), pp. 12-13.
14. Ibid., p. 11.
15. For a detailed look at the parallels made, see Raboteau, *Slave Religion*, pp. 22-23. Raboteau discusses the issue of syncretism on pp. 16-42.
16. Wilmore, *Black Religion*, p. 23. Vodun and its "vodu" rituals have been grossly misunderstood in Western religious traditions as satanic evil. Wilmore gives a more positive view of this tradition; see pp. 20-23.

17. Only recently have blacks in predominantly white churches been included in this designation. As blacks in predominantly white churches begin to identify, embrace, and nurture the spiritual aspect of their African cultural heritage, some are rediscovering the spiritual expressions and experiences characteristic of African peoples. Previously these blacks had adopted the spiritual understandings and expressions of their denominations, as they were expressed in a European or Euro-American mode.

18. C. Eric Lincoln, *Race, Religion and the Continuing American Dilemma* (New York: Hill & Wang, 1984), pp. 28-31.

19. Raboteau, *Slave Religion*, p. 88; Lincoln, *Race, Religion*, pp. 44-49.

20. Wilmore, *Black Religion*, p. 24, quoting Anson West, *A History of Methodism in Alabama* (Nashville: Publishing House, Methodist Episcopal Church South, 1893).

21. Lincoln, *Race, Religion*, p. 39.

22. Ibid., p. 63.

23. Ibid., pp. 33, 64ff. The major independent African churches—the African Methodist Episcopal, the African Methodist Episcopal Zion, the Christian Methodist, the National Baptist Convention, the National Baptist Convention of America, the Progressive Baptist Convention, and the Church of God in Christ—collectively account for 95 percent of the black Christians in our country. Ibid., p. 69.

24. See Joseph Washington, *Black Religion: The Negro and Christianity in the United States* (Boston: Beacon Press, 1964).

25. Clarence Joseph Rivers, *The Spirit in Worship* (Cincinnati: Stimuli, Inc., 1978), p. 5; see also Henry Mitchell, "Black Preaching," in *The Black Christian Experience*, ed. Emmanuel L. McCall (Nashville: Broadman Press, 1972), pp. 43-62; and Giles A. Conwill, "Black Preaching and Catholicism," in McCall, *The Black Christian Experience*, pp. 31-43.

26. Jamie Phelps, "The Mission Ecclesiology of John R. Slattery," dissertation in progress at the Catholic University of America. The dissertation examines Slattery's missiology and his cross-cultural evangelization in the American Catholic Church in the late nineteenth century.

27. See James Dunn, *Unity and Diversity in the New Testament* (Philadelphia: Westminster Press, 1977); also, Marcel Dumais, "La Rencontre de Foi et des Cultures," *Lumière & Vie* 153/154 (July-Sept. 1981): 72-86.

28. See the respective documents in Austin Flannery, ed., *The Documents of Vatican II* (New York: Costello Publishing Co., 1981–1982): "Evangelii Nuntiandi," nos. 40-58; "Ad Gentes," nos. 10-12, 13-18; "Sacrosantum Concillium," nos. 21-40; "Gaudium et Spes," nos. 23-32, 53-62; "Unitatis Redintegratio," nos. 5-12.

29. For example, C. Eric Lincoln, Vincent Harding, James Cone, Gayraud Wilmore, Joseph Washington, DeOtis Roberts, Jackie Grant, Albert Raboteau, Cyprian Davis, Albert Pero, Shawn Copeland, Toinette Eugene, and Thea Bowman, to name only a few.

Bibliography

Barrett, Leonard. *Soul Force: Afro-American Heritage in Afro-American Religion.* Garden City, N.Y.: Doubleday Anchor Books, 1974.

Bowman, Thea. "The Sign of Soul." In *Tell It Like It Is*, pp. 83-95. Oakland: National Black Sisters Conference, 1978.

Bowyer, O. Richard; Hart, Betty; Meade, Charlotte A., eds. *Prayer in the Black Tradition.* Nashville: The Upper Room, 1986.

Chavis, Benjamen E. *Psalms from Prison.* New York: Pilgrim Press, 1983.

Cone, James. *The Spirituals and the Blues.* New York: Seabury Press, 1972.

Davis, Cyprian. "Spirituality." In *Theology: A Portrait in Black,* edited by Thaddeus Posey. St. Louis: St. Cyprian Priory, 1978. (Private distribution from Thaddeus Posey, St. Cyprian Priory, 3731 Westminister Place, St. Louis, MO 63108.)

Dubois, W. E. B. *Prayers for Dark People.* Edited by Herbert Apathekar. Amherst, Mass.: University of Massachusetts Press, 1980.

_____. *The Souls of Black Folk.* New York: Fawcett, 1961.

Hoard, Walter B., ed. *Outstanding Black Sermons.* Vol. 1. Valley Forge, Penn.: Judson Press, 1979.

King, Martin Luther Jr. *Strength to Love.* Philadelphia: Fortress Press, 1981.

_____. *Stride Toward Freedom.* New York: Harper & Row, 1958.

_____. *Where Do We Go from Here: Chaos or Community?* New York: Harper & Row, 1968.

_____. *Why We Can't Wait.* New York: Signet Books, 1964.

Lincoln, C. Eric. *Race, Religion and the Continuing American Dilemma.* New York: Hill & Wang, 1984.

Mbiti, John S. *African Religions and Philosophy.* Garden City, N.Y.: Doubleday Anchor Books, 1970.

_____. *The Prayers of African Religion.* Maryknoll, N.Y.: Orbis Press, 1976.

Mitchell, Ella Pearson, ed. *Those Preaching Women.* Valley Forge, Penn.: Judson Press, 1985.

Oates, Stephen. *Let the Trumpet Sound: The Life of Martin Luther King Jr.* New York: New American Library, 1982.

Owens, Milton E. Jr., ed. *Outstanding Black Sermons.* Vol. 3. Valley Forge, Penn.: Judson Press, 1982.

Pauli, Hertha. *Her Name Was Soujourner Truth.* New York: Avon Books, 1962.

Raboteau, Albert. *Slave Religion.* New York: Oxford University Press, 1978.

Rivers, Clarence J. *Soulful Worship.* Washington, D.C.: National Organization of Black Catholics, 1974.

_____. *The Spirit in Worship.* Cincinnati: Stimuli, Inc., 1978.

Rivers, Clarence J., and Morris, Gertrude, eds. *Freeing the Spirit: The Magazine of Black Liturgy.* Vols. 1-6, 1971–1980.

Smith, J. Alfred, Sr., ed. *Outstanding Black Sermons.* Vol. 1. Valley Forge, Penn.: Judson Press, 1976.

Smith, Luther E. *Howard Thurman: The Mystic as Prophet.* College Park: Maryland University Press of America, 1981.

Thomas, Latta R. *Biblical Faith and the Black American.* Valley Forge, Penn.: Judson Press, 1976.

Thurman, Howard. *The Centering Moment.* Richmond, Ind.: Friends United Press, 1980.

_____. *Disciplines of Spirit.* Richmond, Ind.: Friends United Press, 1977.

_____. *Deep Is the Hunger.* New York: Harper, 1951. Reprint.

_____. *Deep River and the Negro Speaks of Life and Death.* Richmond, Ind.: Friends United Press, 1975. Reprint.

_____. *The Inward Journey.* Richmond, Ind.: Friends United Press, 1980.

_____. *The Growing Edge.* Richmond, Ind.: Friends United Press, 1956.

————. *Temptations of Jesus*. Richmond, Ind.: Friends United Press, 1978. Reprint.

Walker, Wyatt T. *"Somebody's Calling My Name": Black Sacred Music and Social Change*. Valley Forge, Penn.: Judson Press, 1982.

Wilmore, Gayraud S. *Black Religion and Black Radicalism: An Interpretation of the Religious History of Afro-American People*. 2nd ed., rev. and enl. Maryknoll, N.Y.: Orbis Press, 1983.

American Black Worship:
A Mirror of Tragedy and
a Vision of Hope

WILLIAM B. McCLAIN

Let my people go.

—EXODUS 5:1

Any attempt to properly understand the development of Afro-American spirituality and the worship styles it engenders must be done in light of the particular American dilemma—the continuing conflict of racism, morality, culture, and religion. The dilemma derives from the contradiction between the profession of high-sounding Christian concepts as embodied in the American creed and the fact that self-acknowledged Christians consistently act in ways that deny or falsify Christian teachings. It is precisely this dilemma that produced the black religious traditions in their varied forms, of which the black church is only a part.

It is against the backdrop of American racism, a peculiarly heinous and idolatrous chauvinism, that the transplanted African slaves began to develop a spiritual response to their human conditions of suffering: ways of living life in relation to God and neighbor, ways in which the human spirit could transcend the impact of the destructive conditions of racial oppression, ways of allowing the African gods to die and give way to the God of Christianity (while still maintaining some sense of identity and living connection between the present and the past), ways of finding meaning, worth, hope, and purpose in different and decidedly difficult contexts.

If there had not been such blatant racism and pervasive racial xenophobia in American society and its churches, there would probably have been no need for racially distinct churches, black religious traditions, and a black-American style of worship and spirituality. But the fact is that there was, and there is. The problem became acute as increasing numbers of African slaves became Christians. What was typically offered as a solution to the problem in the nineteenth century is revealed in the 1834 minutes of the meeting of the Presbyterian Synod of South Carolina and Georgia:

> The gospel, as things are now, can never be preached to the two classes successfully in conjunction. The galleries or the back seats on the lower floors of the white churches are generally appropriated by Negroes, when it can be done without inconvenience to the whites. When it cannot be done conveniently, the Negroes must catch the gospel as it escapes through the doors and windows.[1]

The Invisible Church

The "gospel as it escapes through the doors and windows" was not enough for black worshipers. They had caught its sound elsewhere and were determined to worship in freedom and dignity. And the sound of the gospel was heard from them elsewhere to a different beat, in a new key, and with a syncopated cadence. Some would even go so far as to say that the gospel "escaped" from the white church and took up residence in the bayous and the canebreaks and swamps where black Christians were gathered in what came to be called the "invisible institution."

Here blacks found a common experience at a single level of human and spiritual recognition. Away from the disapproving eyes of the master and beyond the ears and telltale tongue of the overseer, the shouts that were stifled in their throats like a cork caught in a bottle's neck were released. The agony, so long suppressed, burdened the air with sobs and screams and rhythmic moans. The ecstasy of unstifled praise and celebration in glorious adoration to a God who "builds up Zion's walls" and "sets his people free" and a "God who don't never change and will always be God" were offered without hesitation or shame. His mercy was enjoyed, his justice invoked. And they *had* church! An ex-slave described this "invisible institution":

> Our preachers were usually plantation folks just like the rest of us. Some man who had a little education and had been taught something about the Bible would be our preacher. The colored folks had their code of religion, not nearly so complicated as the white man's religion, but more close observed. . . . When we had our meetings of this kind, we held them in our own way and were not interfered with by white folk.[2]

Thus black religion was born as an expression of soulful worship, a response to suffering and suppression. The black church became that "institution in which is crystallized the whole range of credits and debits of genius and emotion, hope and fear, projection and recoil which characterized the random gathering of peoples of West Africa who were fused in the black experience in America."[3]

These black congregations did not go unmonitored by white folks and were sometimes closed or destroyed when they were considered by them to be a great threat to their interest or well-being. But whites were not able to destroy the Church itself. It was something more than simply the invisible Church made manifest in wood and glass and stone. It was and is the siftings of centuries—a unifying force that made a scattered confusion of slaves a distinctive entity. It was womb and mother to a vast spectrum of people who believed that "troubles don't last always." It was the seminal impetus to and fertilizing hope for freedom and revolution. Whites could not destroy it because it was not flesh of their flesh or substance of their substance. It was a witness against their rejection of the imperative to "do justly, and to love mercy, and to walk humbly with thy God" (Micah 6:8 KJV). And since it could not be destroyed, most eventually left it alone. Amused by its style, confused by its meaning, sometimes a patron to its indigence, but always aloof from its fellowship, the white man kept counsel with his own kind, and the black church was able to become itself without his spiritual taint.[4]

It is this separation that accounts for the unique style of worship that persists in the black church to this day. In a sense, we can say that white racism created the black church and its style of life and perspective. But perhaps in a more profound sense, God has created it for a witness to liberation and reconciliation for all peoples.

The Gathering

At whatever point of the history of black people and their church that one may wish to view, the gathering of the community is central and pivotal to what happens afterward and remains the fulcrum of the souls of black folks.

The civil rights movement of the sixties was the most recent illustration of this. Hundreds of thousands marched to protest segregation and discrimination in the South. They were willing to face firehoses, police dogs, cattle prods, and inhumanly cruel sheriffs, police, and state troopers. Children and adults alike marched in Selma and St. Augustine, in Birmingham and Montgomery, to insist on the unendurability of second-class citizenship and segregation. But always they were in the street because they had *first* gathered in the church, where they had engaged in songs of praise and protest, entreated the God of history to be their Guide, and heard sermons and testimonies that related the gospel to their unjust social situation and challenged them to act.

The gathering of black folks in services of worship reveals the rich culture, the ineffable beauty and creativity of the black soul, and the uniqueness of the black religious tradition, characterized always by passionate preaching and music, both of which elicit an active and spontaneous response from the congregation.

Black Spirituality and White Fundamentalism

Although this very traditional, emotionally charged religious expression takes the biblical message with total seriousness, the use of Scripture in black worship must be distinguished from that of white fundamentalism. There is a basic and critical difference between black Christians, who tend to be religiously conservative yet politically liberal, and white fundamentalists, for whom dogmatic claims of biblical authority typically become the acid test of faithfulness. While many blacks easily can be classified as neo-evangelicals who believe in the inspiration of Scripture, they do not generally make dogmatic statements about inerrancy. One can search in vain through the official statements of faith, even among black Pentecostals, to find references either to "verbal" or "plenary" inspiration of the Bible—common code words used by white fundamentalists. For blacks, authenticity rests always with truthful *practice* of biblical religion, especially in the pursuit of love and justice.

This orientation to scriptural authority leads to a particular manifestation in preaching and the use of the Bible. Black preachers have developed strongly narrative approaches to biblical material. For instance, they take much more liberty than do whites with elaborating or imaginatively embellishing texts for the benefit and enjoyment of their listeners and are much less inclined to make such a fine distinction between the Old and New Testaments, as if the New canceled out the Old. In fact, black preachers tend to preach more often from the Old Testament than from the New, just as they are more likely to preach from the synoptic Gospels than from the Epistles.[5] Such practices are not typical of those who label themselves fundamentalists.

This proclivity for certain portions of Scripture is rooted in the historical experience of slavery; although these black slaves accepted the Christianity offered by the white man and often imitated it, and even though they learned to revere the *book* of white Christianity, they also went beyond that understanding of the faith to fashion it according to their social, recreational, and spiritual needs. In other words, they took from it what was useful and left the rest. They may have been by and large illiterate, but they were not fools.

C. C. Jones, one of the white Presbyterian missionaries in Georgia in the first part of the nineteenth century, reports an interesting incident in Liberty County, Georgia:

> I was preaching to a large congregation on the Epistle to Philemon; and when I insisted on fidelity and obedience as Christian virtues in servants, and upon the authority of Paul, condemned the practice of running away, one half of the audience deliberately rose up and walked off with themselves; and those who remained looked anything but satisfied with the preacher or the doctrine. After dismission, there was no small stir among them; some solemnly declared that there was no such epistle in the Bible; others, that it was not the Gospel; others, that I preached to please the masters; others that they did not care if they never heard me preach again.[6]

The Songs of Zion

Music in the black religious tradition is as close to worship as breathing is to life. It has been the "songs of Zion" in this strange land that have cut a path through the wilderness of despair and have often kept black folk from "starting down the steep and slippery steps of death" in suicide. The Negro spirituals that speak of life and death, suffering and sorrow, love and judgment, grace and hope, justice and mercy, were born out of this tradition. They are songs of a people weary at heart, an unhappy people, yet they are the most beautiful expressions of human experience born this side of the seas. The music is more ancient than the words. These songs are timeless—the work of ages. They tell of exile and trouble, of strife and hiding; they grope toward some unseen power and sigh for rest in the end. "But through all the sorrow of the sorrow songs," as W. E. B. Dubois points out in *The Souls of Black Folks*, "there breathes a hope—a faith in the ultimate justice of things."[7] John Wesley Work's comment on the Negro spiritual is helpful. He says in his book, *Folk Songs of the American Negro*,

> To our fathers who came out of bondage and who are still with us, these songs are prayers, praises and sermons. They sang them at work; in

leisure moments; they crooned them to their babes in the cradles; to their wayward children; they sang them to the sick, wracked with pain on beds of affliction; they sang them over their dead. Blessings, warnings, benedictions and the very heartbeats of life were all expressed to our fathers by their songs.[8]

Another musical genre, the gospel song, was created in the North and became the Northern urban counterpart of the negro spirituals of the South. The gospel song combines the sheer joy of living with a deep religious faith. It arose in the midst of the early exodus from the farms and hamlets of the South, when black folks arrived in Chicago, New York, Detroit, and other northern cities and found themselves in a "strange land." The simple lines of the gospel were written on their minds and hearts and got translated into songs on their lips and praise in their mouths. There is little argument in these times that these gospel songs and the gospel sound arising out of the black religious tradition have supplied the roots for much of contemporary music, from rock symphonies to detergent commercials. Not surprisingly, the American public's listening expectations have been reshaped by this urban creation.

These songs of hope and promise have helped to bring a people through the torture chambers of the last two centuries. The music of the black religious tradition has affirmed that just being alive is good and worth celebrating and singing and shouting about. That music has nourished the black community. It has soothed its hurts, sustained its hopes, and bound its wounds. The music of the black religious traditions has enabled a people to keep on going, to keep on tramping. It is impossible to conceive of black spirituality in any authentic sense without the songs of survival, liberation, hope, and celebration.

The dominant role music plays in black worship has its antecedents in Western Africa, the original home of many black slaves. Black worship in America recreates patterns that have been observed in West African religious practice, reflecting the old African dictum, "The Spirit will not descend without song." In Africa, ritual dances and songs were integral parts of African religious observances. This heritage of emotional religion was one of the strongest contributions African culture made to the Afro-American. The Puritan tradition saw dancing as an evil, worldly excess, but dancing as an integral part of the African's life could not be displaced by the still white notes of the Wesleyan hymnal.

From the earliest times when black slaves sang,

O Freedom, O Freedom over me.
And before I'll be a slave I'll be buried in my grave,
and go home to my Lord and be free.

until the singing of

Go down Moses, way down in Egypt land,
Tell ole Pharaoh to let my people go,

black people were not simply singing songs, they were expressing a definite point of view. That point of view was that the God of justice and the God of Jesus is on the side of the oppressed. This was and is at the heart of—and is the gut of—black spirituality in America.

A Vision of Hope for All

Throughout the development of black spirituality in America there is present the American dilemma. The extraordinary genius of black religion and the black church is that they created new ways of serving God in the face of enduring racial conflict. In a society where significant truths and values are racially determined, issues of identity, a proper relationship with God and other human creatures, and worthiness to be included in the peculiar concern God reserves for those created in God's own image can be clouded and frequently compromised. But the black church perceives itself as an expression of the divine intent that, however nefarious may be the strategies of others, the faith cannot be robbed of its power and the righteousness of God will not be left without a witness. Throughout its winding journey, it has been a voice crying in the wilderness. Its development is a mirror of the American dilemma—a tragedy as well as a vision of hope that the dilemma can be resolved and all flesh can see it together.

EXERCISES

For an Individual or a Group

If you have not yet attended a black worship service, by all means do so. There is simply no way to recapture the essential elements of black worship and spirituality in isolation from the gathering of the black community. Try, if possible, to attend worship services in different denominations, and look for common stylistic elements in music and prayer forms that transcend traditional denominational distinctions. Then reflect on and/or discuss the following questions.

DISCUSSION QUESTIONS

1. Many people are normally accustomed to worshiping in an atmosphere of quiet and emotional restraint. Describe the personal impact of worshiping in a black congregation, where spontaneous emotional responses are expected and encouraged. Does this intensification of congregational involvement enhance or detract from your efforts to commune with God?

2. In what ways does black worship reflect the experience of common suffering? Is there any equivalent expression in white worship? How significant for worship is a *common* experience, either of suffering or deliverance? Are there ways in which this commonality could be heightened in other worship traditions?

3. It has been suggested that most Christians' operating theology is that found in their favorite hymns. Reflect on the extent to which religious music has shaped your understanding of the nature of God and authentic, satisfying worship. What accounts for the religious power of music? Why do we so frequently turn to hymns and spirituals in time of trial? Why do we get so upset when the wording or musical arrangement of a favorite piece of religious music is altered?

4. Compare the black church's understanding of the authority of Scripture with that of your own tradition. To what extent does—or should—the authority of the Bible base itself on its correspondence to human experience, especially in relation to issues of justice and liberation?

Notes

1. W. E. B. DuBois, ed., *The Negro Church* (New York: Arno Press, 1968), p. 27.
2. Robert Anderson, *From Slavery to Affluence: Memories of Robert Anderson Ex-slave* (Hemingfor, Neb.: n.p., 1927), pp. 22-23, quoted in E. Franklin Frazier, *The Negro Church in America* (New York: Schocken Books, 1973); C. Eric Lincoln, *The Black Church Since Frazier* (New York: Schocken Books, 1973), p. 16.
3. C. Eric Lincoln, *Race, Religion, and the Continuing American Dilemma* (New York: Hill & Wang, 1984), p. 65.
4. Ibid.
5. See William B. McClain, "The Genius of the Black Church," *Christianity and Crisis* 30, no. 18 (Nov. 2 and 16, 1970): 250-52. For a longer version of this article, see "What Is Authentic Black Worship?" in *Experience, Struggles and Hopes of the Black Church*, ed. James B. Gadsden (Nashville: Tidings Press, 1975), pp. 69-84. See also James S. Finney, "Doctrinal Differences Between Black and White Pentecostals," *Spirit* 1, no. 1 (July 1977).
6. Charles C. Jones, *Religious Instruction of Negroes in the United States* (Savannah: T. Purse Co., 1842), p. 126.
7. W. E. B. DuBois, *The Souls of Black Folks* (A. C. M. McClurg & Co., 1903; reprint, New York: Fawcett, 1961), p. 380.

8. John Wesley Work, *Folk Songs of the American Negro* (New York: Howell, Soskin & Co., 1940), p. 87.

Resources

Books

Baldwin, James. *The Fire Next Time*. New York: Dial Press, 1963.

———. *Just Above My Head*. New York: Dell, 1980.

"The Black Christian Worship Experience." Special double issue (256 pp.) of *The Journal of the Interdenominational Theological Center* 14, nos. 1 and 2 (Fall 1986/Spring 1987). (See especially pp. 237-52 for an excellent bibliography on the subject.)

Carter, Harold A. *The Prayer Traditions of Black People*. Valley Forge, Penn.: Judson Press, 1976.

Cleveland, J. Jefferson, ed. *Songs of Zion*. Nashville: Abingdon Press, 1980.

DuBois, W. E. B. *Prayers for Dark People*. Edited by Herbert Aptheker. Amherst, Mass.: University of Massachusetts Press, 1980.

Epstein, Dena. *Sinful Tunes and Spirituals*. Chicago: University of Illinois Press, 1977.

Fisher, Mark Miles. *Negro Slave Songs in the United States*. New York: Citadel Press, 1963; New York: Russell & Russell, 1969.

Heilbut, Tony. *The Gospel Sound*. Garden City, N.Y.: Doubleday Anchor Books, 1975.

Hoard, Walter B., ed. *Outstanding Black Sermons*. Vol. 2. Valley Forge, Penn.: Judson Press, 1979.

Johnson, James Weldon. *God's Trombones*. New York: Viking Press, 1927; New York: Penguin Books, 1976.

Johnson, James Weldon, and Johnson, J. Rosamon, eds. *The Books of Negro Spirituals*. New York: Viking Press, 1940; New York: Da Capo Press, 1970.

Kelsey, George D. *Racism and the Christian Understanding of Man*. New York: Scribner's, 1965.

Lincoln, C. Eric. *The Black Experience in Religion*. Garden City, N.Y.: Doubleday Anchor Books, 1974.

McCall, Emmanuel L. *The Black Christian Experience*. Nashville: Broadman Press, 1972.

McClain, William B. *The Soul of Black Worship*. Madison, N.J.: Multi-Ethnic Center, Drew University, 1980.

Mitchell, Ella Pearson, ed. *Those Preachin' Women*. Valley Forge, Penn.: Judson Press, 1985.

Rivers, Clarence Joseph. *This Far by Faith: American Worship and Its African Roots*. Washington, D.C.: National Office for Black Catholics, 1977.

Smith, J. Alfred. *Outstanding Black Sermons*. Valley Forge, Penn.: Judson Press, 1976.

Southern, Eileen. *The Music of Black Americans*. New York: W.W. Norton, 1983.

Thurman, Howard. *Deep River and The Negro Spiritual Speaks of Life and Death*. Richmond, Ind.: Friends United Press, 1975.

Walker, Wyatt Tee. *Somebody's Calling My Name: Black Sacred Music and Social Change*. Valley Forge, Penn.: Judson Press, 1979.

Discography

Black Spirituals and Art Songs. Stereo LP album available from Afro-American Music Opportunities Association, Inc., Box 662, Minneapolis, MN 55440.

Negro Church Music. Atlantic Recording, 1351.

Negro Religious Songs and Services. Library of Congress AAFSL10.

For additional recordings consult the catalogues for *Schwann Long Playing Records* and *Folkways Records*, available from Rounder Distribution, 1 Kanys Street, Cambridge, MA 02410.

PART III

The Feminine Dimension in Christian Spirituality

CHAPTER 12

Marian Spirituality

E A M O N   R .   C A R R O L L ,   O .   C A R M .

Henceforth, all generations will call me blessed, for he who is mighty has done great things for me.

—LUKE 1:48b-49a

Everyone knows that the most coveted role in any Christmas pageant is always the Virgin Mary. Children understand instinctively that it was she who, by her "yes" to God, somehow made Christmas possible. How is it, then, that when these same children are adults, it is in relation to this most ancient and powerful religious symbol—the Mother of our Lord—that they redefine themselves as being one sort of Christian or another? How is it that a figure of such humility and grace could become the focus of so much religious rancor and misunderstanding? Is it reasonable to hope that the object of devotion for millions of Catholic and Orthodox Christians may someday soon no longer be a stumbling block to Christian unity?

The famous eleventh edition (1911) of the *Encyclopedia Brittanica* contained an article on the Virgin Mary that was mainly a litany of the errors of Roman Catholicism; its two authors, Kirsopp Lake of Oxford and J. S. Black of the encyclopedia staff, were prominent contributors. Today we have a ready indication of the improved Christian climate with respect to the Mother of Jesus in the current *Brittanica* entry on Mary by Jaroslav Pelikan, the Lutheran historian of doctrine. It is a balanced and peaceful piece that concludes with this gentle observation:

Even those non-Roman Churches which have most vigorously criticized the "Mariolatry" they claimed to find in the dogmas of the Immaculate Conception and the Assumption have frequently addressed praises to

365

her in their hymnody that they would have hesitated to express in the prose of their dogmatic theology. Thus, in ways she could never have anticipated, all generations have called her blessed.[1]

The starting point for this essay on Marian spirituality is the evidence of primitive Christian veneration of the Virgin Mary in the Bible. There followed gradual development from scriptural testimony through allusions by early authors to the place of the holy Mother of the Savior within Christian worship, in both private prayer and the liturgy, especially at the Eucharist.

Mary in Scripture: Faithful Discipleship

In 1978 a team of twelve scholars produced the book *Mary in the New Testament: A Collaborative Assessment by Protestant, Anglican and Roman Catholic Scholars.*[2] The authors spanned a cross-section of traditions, and their joint study was supported by the ongoing American Lutheran–Roman Catholic consultations. (Substantially the same group produced *Peter in the New Testament.*[3]) The latest published "agreed statement" from these dialogues has been the remarkable document on justification of 1983,[4] which also touches on significant differences in relation to the Virgin Mary. Most recently, the Lutheran–Roman Catholic consultations have taken up the Communion of Saints—a subject to be considered in other interconfessional dialogues such as those between Roman Catholics and Southern Baptists—and under this heading will be considering the place of the Virgin Mary.

The concern of *Mary in the New Testament* was basically biblical, although it did include a chapter on the second century. The kerygmatic thrust of the New Testament portrayal of Jesus the Christ puts the Mother of Jesus in a similar pattern: What the Gospels say about Mary of Nazareth is at the service of a richer Christian life. The consensus reached by the authors of this study was that Mary was the faithful Virgin, completely committed to God's saving work made manifest in her son Jesus. The gospel exemplar of faith, the Mother of Jesus is the perfect disciple. With self-surrendering love, she follows Jesus from his mysterious conception through his birth and childhood, into his young manhood and baffling destiny to proclaim and advance the kingdom of God.

The Mother of Jesus was present still at the apparent failure of all the great hopes on Calvary, and St. Luke places her again in the upper room, praying for the Spirit of Pentecost promised by her risen Son. It is on that note of prayer that the Acts of the Apostles take leave of the Mother of Jesus. Like other members of the family of Jesus—Joseph, Elizabeth, and Zachary (Zacharius)—and like his first followers, Mary is a woman of prayer awaiting the consolation of Israel. The Virgin of Nazareth is committed to her Son's saving work, through compassion and contradiction, through apparent failure and final vindication.

For a long time, in the strained atmosphere of Catholic-Protestant considerations about the Virgin Mary, it was mutually accepted that, after all, there is comparatively little about Mary in the New Testament; thus the controversy turned on the legitimacy of subsequent tradition. With the leaving behind of the "quest for the historical Mary," along with the "quest for the historical Jesus," we have come to a deeper appreciation of Mary's role, as is evident in this quotation from a Fortress Press publication of 1975 by Lutheran author Philip H. Pfatteicher:

> From the biblical record nothing is known of Mary's birth or parents or death. But more is known about her than about most of the apostles. The New Testament shows Mary present at all the important events of her Son's life: the birth cycle, the first miracle at Cana, at the cross, at the tomb, waiting with the apostles for the gift of the Spirit. . . . Through the centuries, Mary has been a principal focus of devotional attention, chosen by God as his servant, the one from whom Jesus took his flesh, the God-bearer, the personification of the old Israel and of the new, obedient to the word of God.[5]

Commenting on the Magnificat, he asserts that

> the Gospel is the song of Mary . . . setting forth the character of God. . . . Mary's song is the Church's song of liberation and of revolution, based on the song put into Hannah's mouth at the birth of Samuel. . . . God's word now spoken is as good as fulfilled. . . . Personal and national concerns merge and Mary's experience is but an example, although the principle one, of God's revolutionary care—moral, social, economic.[6]

Further on in this essay we will take up the ecumenical difficulty of invoking Mary in prayer, but it is appropriate at this point to propose one gospel teaching that is pertinent to Marian spirituality, namely, the meaning of faithful discipleship and the way in which Mary models this for all Christians. We submit that Christians can hold in common and, indeed, often already *do* observe a Marian spirituality without using that phrase or compromising their consciences or respective traditions.

The oldest Gospel material takes up the public ministry of Jesus, culminating in his death and resurrection. St. Mark's Gospel, oldest of the four, has no nativity story, and in this document (with parallel accounts in Matthew and Luke) Mary appears in her Son's public life one time only—the incident of the "true kinsmen," called also "the coming of the mother and the brethren." Without reviewing all the details of the three variants of the story, it is instructive to look at differences in their treatment of Mary.

While Mark does not clearly include Mary among the family members who are upset about the behavior of Jesus, neither does he clearly exclude her. St. Matthew, who has already referred to the virginal conception of Jesus in his nativity account, gives a somewhat warmer portrait of Mary in public life, but it remained for St. Luke to read the "true kinsmen" account as praise of Mary's faith: "My mother and my brothers are those who hear the word of God and act upon it" (see Matt. 12:46-50; Mark 3:31-35; Luke 8:19-21).

St. Luke does the same in another brief narrative from Jesus' public life that is peculiar to him—the incident in chapter 11 of the enthusiastic woman, with its remarkable similarity to the exchange between Mary and Elizabeth. In this incident the anonymous woman calls out, "Blest is the womb that bore you and the breasts that nursed you" and receives from Jesus the reply, "Rather . . . blest are they who hear the word of God and keep it" (11:27-28). In the context, the woman's praise for Jesus, by way of his mother, is contrasted with the failure to understand him that had led some even to wonder if he was in league with the devil. For St. Luke, the Mother of Jesus is the model of perfect understanding, trusting in God's own faithfulness, loving God and neighbor as she loved her Son, the Holy One. In Mary's visit to Elizabeth, the praise of the unnamed woman and the reply of Jesus are both transposed into statements by Elizabeth: "Blessed is the fruit of your womb" and "Blessed are you who have believed."

A number of recent books have shown that Mary's exemplary discipleship is well rooted in the New Testament. Bertrand Buby, S.M., wrote *Mary, the Faithful Disciple* in 1985,[7] and Australian Scripture scholar Francis Maloney, S.D.B., has much on Mary in his book *Woman: First Among the Faithful*.[8] Two Englishwomen consider Mary's role in recent books: Rosemary Haughton, prolific author and mother of a large family, devotes a chapter to our Lady in her book *The Recreation of Eve*,[9] and especially helpful is Rita Crowley Turner's *The Mary Dimension*.[10] Also a mother and a writer for the BBC, Mrs. Turner attempts to link women's concerns with the veneration of the Mother of the Lord.

Along with the two synoptic incidents showing Mary in the public life, the Mother of Jesus is recalled with reverent respect in the Nativity narratives, at Cana and on Calvary in St. John's Gospel, and, finally, in the Cenacle, according to the Acts of the Apostles. In addition, there is at least the possibility that the remembrance of Mary is somehow bound up with the ecclesial figure of the woman clothed with the sun in chapter 12 of the book of Revelation.

So Great a Cloud of Witnesses:
Mary and the Communion of Saints

The Church's teaching with respect to the "Communion of Saints"—the solidarity between us still earth-bound pilgrims and those who have "fallen asleep in the Lord"—is powerfully depicted in the book of Hebrews (chapters 11-12), which presents a great parade of heroes and heroines of faith from the Hebrew Bible, culminating in Jesus himself as our great Pioneer in faith. Reference is made to the great "cloud of witnesses" who watch over us as we run the race in faith (12:1)—a key text in considerations about the Communion of Saints. As recent interconfessional dialogues have shown, the thorny theme of Mary's place in Christian prayer life is bound up with different understandings of the Communion of Saints.

Does the Communion of Saints stop at the gates of death, or is there a vital interchange between the blessed dead and the living on earth? The question of calling on the saints in prayer (technically, "invoking" the saints, with St. Mary at their head) is an important aspect of prayer practice in some Christian churches, though obviously not in all. It is well to note, however, that this is only one facet of Marian spirituality. Acceptance of Mary's role as model of faith is a very important aspect of veneration of the Mother of Jesus and hence of genuine Marian spirituality. High regard for the Mother of the Lord belongs to her biblical theological portrait, and this is an incipient Marian spirituality. Normally, however, the phrase "Marian spirituality" raises the further question of Mary's present place in the Communion of Saints and the expanded veneration that came to be expressed by calling on her in prayer, both public and private.

As J. N. D. Kelly shows in the chapter "Mary and the Saints" in recent editions of his book *Early Christian Doctrines*,[11] the rise of veneration of the saints, especially St. Mary, was a phenomenon of great significance in the patristic period. The martyrs were the first to be honored as heavenly intercessors; by the fourth century other holy people remembered as model Christians were also especially honored "so that by their prayers and intercessions God may receive our supplications."[12] God was clearly regarded as the one who receives all prayers, and the blessed were held to be heavenly helpers, still concerned with their pilgrim brothers and sisters. How soon were supplications for "prayers and intercessions" to God on our behalf addressed to St. Mary? According to present evidence, which Kelly calls "sparse but persuasive," explicit invocation of Mary was already being practiced by the year 400.

During World War I the Egyptian desert yielded a papyrus fragment of an ancient prayer in Greek, which is now in the John Rylands Library in Manchester, England. It is an early form of a prayer that became extremely popular in both East and West. Catholics know it as "We fly to thy patronage, O Holy Mother of God" (Latin: *Sub tuum praesidium*). Opinions about the age of this fragment range from the late 200s up to almost the Council of Ephesus, 431. We do know that the title *Theotokos* (literally, "God-bearer") was already in use in Egypt by 300. The scrap of papyrus seems to have been a private prayer, not yet part of the liturgy, said in troubled circumstances by a Christian with great confidence in the Mother of the Lord.

Virgin Mother: Mary and the Church

Throughout the fourth century, with Christianity no longer proscribed, the form of Christian witness that succeeded martyrdom was consecrated virginity and celibacy. (One recalls the monks of the desert and the house communities of consecrated virgins.) St. Athanasius (d. 373), the hero of Nicea, praises the vocation of virginity, appealing to Mary's example. In the West, St. Ambrose (d. 397) expands Athanasius's thought to the same purpose, again with emphasis on the exemplar role of the Virgin Mary. Sts. Jerome (d. 420) and Augustine (d. 430) form part of the same chorus, and Augustine develops the theme that Mary, Virgin-Mother, is model of the Church as virgin-mother.

What is significant in this Augustinian spirituality is its solid scriptural support. An often-quoted statement from St. Augustine's book on virginity[13] is a commentary on the sayings from the public life, "My mother and my brothers are those who hear the word of God and act upon it" (Luke 8:21 NAB) and "Rather . . . blest are those who hear the word of God and keep it" (Luke 11:27-28 NAB). Here Augustine presents Mary as the model for virgins through her faith and charity. In the sense of the Gospels, Mary is Mother of the Faithful as well as Mother of the Savior, and all Christians are called to imitate Mary's motherhood. Augustine specifically refers also to the spiritual motherhood of wives and mothers of families. Augustine's words (often, alas, quoted without sufficient context to reveal their biblical basis) are as follows:

> [Mary] is evidently the mother of us who are His members because she has cooperated by charity that the faithful, who are members of that Head might be born in the Church. Indeed, she is Mother of the Head Himself in the Body. . . . Both married women of the faith and virgins consecrated to God by holy lives and by charity "from a pure heart and a good conscience and faith unfeigned," [I Tim. 1:5] are spiritually the mothers of Christ because they do the will of His Father.[14]

Mary in the Liturgy

Apart from the reference to Mary and the virginal conception of Jesus in the creeds, the oldest liturgical allusion is her commemoration in the remembrance prayer (*anaphora*) at the Eucharist. In the fourth-century liturgy of St. Basil (still in use in the East) these words occur: "remembering in the first place the Blessed Virgin Mary, Mother of God, and all the saints." Fifty years earlier a similar commemoration of Mary was in the Syrian *anaphora* of the apostles.

The background of this Marian remembrance was the upper room before Pentecost, where Mary the Mother of Jesus is expressly named along with the apostles. It is significant—the *lex orandi-lex credendi* interchange has always been operative—that the liturgy and Christian artists of every age have unhesitatingly rearranged the order of those present in the upper room to put Mary the Mother of Jesus "in the first place." They are, in effect, rereading St. Luke's Acts of the Apostles in a mode consonant with the evangelist's own implicit insights about Mary as model disciple, as ideal recipient of the Holy Spirit, and, now, as part of the heavenly choir around the glorified Redeemer. A great man of prayer, the Spanish Carmelite St. John of the Cross (d. 1591) saw in the Holy Virgin the follower of Christ who responded most perfectly to the inspirations of the Holy Spirit. He wrote in *The Ascent of Mount Carmel*, "Perfect from the first, there was no impression of created things on her soul to turn her aside from God or in any way to influence her; for her every movement always proceeded from the Holy Spirit."[15]

The Marian remembrance at the eucharistic prayer (the *anaphora*) is found in the West in the late fifth century. By then the term *Theotokos* ("Mother of God"), canonized at the Council of Ephesus in 431 for its christological importance, had become common throughout the Church. The anniversary year of the Second Council of Nicea (787), last of the great seven recognized as ecumenical by the Orthodox East, was 1987, and we are reminded again of traditional veneration of the Virgin Mary as *Theotokos*. This is especially true of the worship experience of the East, both at the sacred liturgy and in the rich world of icons as places of prayer, both in churches and in homes. The marvelous balance of Eastern Christianity can serve as a lesson to Western Christians still divided over the place of the Mother of the Lord. Consider, for example, these words from the late G. Florovsky in an essay on the ethos of the Orthodox church, words with which this Roman Catholic writer is in total accord: "Christ is never separated from his Mother, the *Theotokos*, and his 'friends,' the saints. The Redeemer and the redeemed belong together inseparably. In the daring phrase of St. John Chrysostom (d. 407), inspired by Ephesians 1.23, Christ will be complete only when his Body has been completed."[16]

In the context of Christian spirituality, whatever is said about Marian spirituality can only have its proper place in relation to *Christ*. Any form of Marian piety that deviates from the Christian center is at least inadequate and at worst dangerously superstitious. Just as Christian spirituality in general has assumed various forms to meet different needs, so also Marian spirituality in particular has experienced changes at various periods. As we have seen, the Gospels are our primary evidence of the earliest regard for Mary. Her biblical portrait was in terms of God's grace-gifts, especially the theological virtues of faith, hope, and charity; nor can we overlook the evangelical poverty by which the Virgin Mary appears as the model of the poor people of God who look to him for salvation in love, trust, and faith. The Magnificat is the song of Mary the poor woman. It is also the song of the Church, the Body of Christ, and the Church has made it part of liturgical Evening Prayer from early days. It is a biblical prayer members of different Christian churches can still say joyously together, along with the first—and scriptural—part of the Hail Mary prayer.

The Christian community gradually perceived in the Mother of Jesus a model of itself. As early as the mid–second century, Christian authors Justin and Irenaeus began to explore the "New Eve" theme, joyfully contrasting the obedient Virgin Mother of the New Adam to the disobedient first Eve. The concept of the Blessed Virgin as the New Eve, beautiful and richly evocative, continued to attract attention, as this example from the time of St. Ephrem (late fourth century) indicates:

The Church gave us	the living bread
for that unleavened bread	which Egypt gave.
Mary gave us	the bread of refreshment
for the bread of weariness	which Eve gave.[17]

In spite of the exuberant excesses of some early apocryphal writings, with their fantastic stories of the childhoods of Jesus and Mary, a critical sense was not lacking in other early authors. Third-century writers were sensitive to Mary's own need to grow in faith through the trials, even the doubts, of Simeon's "sword," of Cana, of Jesus' public life, and, most of all, of Calvary. Origen (d. 254) did not regard it as contrary to Mary's holiness that she underwent the purification of suffering, associated with the redemptive sacrifice of her Son. In the fourth century, with the Church at peace in the Roman empire, Mary was increasingly proposed as a model of dedicated virginal life in the context of a strong eschatological thrust. By the Council of Ephesus, the Virgin Mary, as *Theotokos,* had an assured place in the eucharistic liturgy.

By the end of the patristic period (ca. the Second Council of Nicea) a double tendency characterized Marian doctrine and devotion. One tendency emphasized Mary's association with the life of Jesus, focusing on the feasts of Annunciation and Christmas. The other tendency might be called the "transcendence" of Mary, her dignity and holiness as Mother of God, her union—body and soul—with the risen Lord in her Assumption, and her role as heavenly helper, even as Queen of Heaven. There was a matching sense of consecration to her service, as in St. Ildefonsus of Toledo (d. 667). In the East, great homilists extolled the Virgin Mother of God, for example, St. Germanus of Constantinople (d. 733) and St. John of Damascus (d. ca. 751), both defenders of the icons.

In the West, St. Anselm of Canterbury (d. 1109) would compose not only his masterworks of philosophy and theology but also magnificent prayers to our Lady.[18] St. Bernard (d. 1153), singer of the love of God, would prove also to be a troubadour for the Mother of the Savior, albeit with a cautionary word against forms of Marian piety he found not supported by the tradition. Thus he scolded the canons of the church of Lyons for keeping a feast of the conception of the holy Virgin, a position that would later be accepted as binding doctrine by Catholics.

Throughout these same centuries liturgies of both East and West, as well as other popular prayers, were reflecting the changing convictions about Mary's place in the life of the spirit. As the fourteenth and fifteenth centuries wound to a close, and in the aftermath of the catastrophe of the Black Death, much Marian piety became divorced from solid Christian spirituality. Mary's power as intercessor, as heavenly Mother, and as Mediatrix of grace was overemphasized. Popular devotions succumbed to sentimentality, sometimes running riot. Leaders such as Gerson (d. 1429) rightly criticized excesses, and the great Reformers Luther (d. 1546) and Calvin (d. 1564) excoriated such abuses, with the church of Rome officially catching up a bit tardily at the Council of Trent (1545–1563). Yet Luther, Calvin, and the other early Reformers continued to preach in praise of the Virgin Mary; collections of these sermons have been published in recent years, and Luther's early commentary on the Magnificat is particularly well known.[19]

Mary and the Problem of Christian Unity: The Search for a Controlling Principle

The rift with respect to the veneration of the Mother of Jesus that took place in the West at the Reformation has not yet been healed. Dr. Donald Dawe, a Presbyterian theologian from Union Seminary (Richmond, Va.) and president of the American Ecumenical Society of the Blessed Virgin Mary, published some years ago a lecture entitled "From Dysfunction to Disbelief,"[20] in which he traced the gradual decline of doctrines involving the Virgin Mary as veneration of her dwindled in Reformed piety. The title of his essay reflects the old axiom *lex orandi, lex credendi*. For if there is a close connection between the pattern of prayer and the pattern of belief, similarly, the elimination of Mary from Reformed prayer led also to reducing her doctrinal role.

Even the overtures between the Western Reformed churches and Eastern Orthodoxy have not overcome the sharp differences about the veneration of Mary and the saints, particularly in relation to the practice of calling on the Mother of the Lord in prayer. The author recalls an unusually clear example of the differences between Protestants on one side and Catholics and Orthodox on the other in the case of a lecture delivered by Dr. Arthur Crabtree to the Ecumenical Society of the Blessed Virgin Mary in Washington, D.C. (1978). The address, a warm appreciation of the biblical Mary, was subsequently featured in an article in *Newsweek* magazine (Jan. 1, 1979), which surveyed changing opinions about the Virgin Mary and her increasingly prominent place in ecumenical interchanges. The article reported that Dr. Crabtree, a Baptist, had begun to include Mary in his prayers "as a unique member of the church and a model for all Christians." A letter of reply by Dr. Crabtree was later published in *Newsweek* (Jan. 22, 1979), which included the following disavowal: "I do not include [Mary] in my prayers, although I do regard her as a 'unique member of the church and a model for all Christians,' as I stated in an address to the Ecumenical Society of the Virgin Mary in Washington, D.C."

There is an important lesson in the letter of Dr. Crabtree: It reminds us that our ordinary religious words have different meanings in different Christian contexts. As a Catholic, this author would regard the phrase "including Mary in my prayers" as covering not only the invocation of Mary but also the reverent remembrance of her as a member of the Church and as a model for all Christians, whereas for Dr. Crabtree and, we would suppose, for most Protestants, including Mary in one's prayers means calling on her in prayer, an approach alien to Protestant piety.

Is there a controlling principle for an authentic Marian spirituality that might overcome our confessional differences four and a half centuries after the Reformation? Some of these difficulties are as much ecclesiological as they are concerned with doctrine and devotion about the Virgin Mary. Perhaps Western Christian churches may yet learn from the joyful liturgy and exuberant prayer life of Eastern churches the lasting place in Christian life of the saints, especially St. Mary. Can a sense of the bond between Mary and the Church be a shared conviction between Rome and Constantinople? Between Tübingen, Edinburgh, and Canterbury?

One controlling principle for an authentic Marian spirituality is a fuller understanding of the Communion of Saints. We acknowledge, of course, that different values attach to the words. For some, it is the mutual assistance of pilgrim Christians; for others, such as Roman Catholics, the Anglican Communion, and Churches in the East, it includes both commemoration and communication between those still on earth and the dead, especially the blessed—the great assembly of the saints united to the risen Christ—led by Mary, Mother of Jesus, first of the redeemed, the *panagia* ("All-Holy One") as Eastern Christians love to call her.

The basic raison d'être of true Marian spirituality is paschal spirituality. For Mary personally, and for all who are influenced by her—in whatever positive manner—the Paschal Mystery is the criterion for authentic spirituality. The suffering, death, and resurrection of Jesus are at the heart of all Christian spirituality. In her life on earth Mary was, like all of us, a pilgrim, discovering ever-new dimensions of the mystery of her Son. And she by no means always understood his words and actions, whether he spoke or performed them at the age of twelve in the temple, or at Cana, in the public life, or in the scandal of Calvary. Yet she was open to God's merciful will even when the divinely appointed hour was at its darkest.

Like her Son, Mary lived a life of loving service to humanity in need of redemption. The Magnificat indicates the communitarian dimension of her God-given dedication. Like the seed of grain that must first enter the cold soil in order to germinate and rise to grow for the harvest, Mary too entered into the passion of her Son, then into the glory of his resurrection, receiving the pentecostal Spirit. Gabriel had greeted her as God's favored one; God's grace was the key to her sharing in the Paschal Mystery. Mary shares still in the paschal victory of her Son, who lives forever to make intercession for us, by her own subordinate heavenly intercession, itself the fruit of her Son's redemptive exaltation.

Since 1950 an international congress on Marian doctrine and devotion has been held every four years in different countries. Since 1965 an ecumenical round table has been part of these congresses, and at the last two meetings (Saragossa, 1979, and Malta, 1983) an interdenominational committee issued an agreed statement about Mary and the Communion of Saints. Another such ecumenical interchange occurred at the international congress at Kevelaer, West Germany, in September 1987.

The overall theme at Saragossa was "Devotion to Mary in the Sixteenth Century," introducing inevitable differences stemming from the Reformation. Two of the six common convictions arrived at in Saragossa are quoted below:

2. We recognize the importance of IMITATION as an element which is common to the traditions of our different Churches concerning Mary. As we find, in particular in the Magnificat, Mary is seen as the humble and most holy servant of the will of God. This invitation involves, in a special way, the Gospel understanding of poverty before God. The spiritual attitude of Mary was her total response to the Word of God, and thus she became the temple of the Holy Spirit who accomplished in her the incarnation of the Son of God (Luke 1:35-38). . . .

4. The problem of the INVOCATION and INTERCESSION of Mary was examined afresh in this congress. We have considered it against the background of the communion of saints. As a Christian can and should pray for others, we believe that the saints who have already entered into the fullness which is in Christ, amongst whom Mary holds the first place, can and do pray for us sinners who are still suffering and struggling on earth. The one and unique mediation of Christ is in no way affected by this. The meaning of the direct invocation of the saints who are alive in God, an invocation which is not practiced in all the churches, remains to be elucidated.[21]

The Malta ecumenical round table also produced a six-point "ecumenical declaration" centered on Mary and the Communion of

Saints by Lutheran, Orthodox, Reformed, Anglican, and Catholic signatories. After stating that "the very fact that Christ prays for us in heaven at the right hand of the Father shows us that death does not break the communion of those who in their lifetime were united by the ties of brotherhood in Christ, and that a communion therefore exists between those who belong to Christ, whether they live on earth, or having left the body, dwell with the Lord (2 Cor. 5:8; Mk. 12:27)," the Malta statement suggested that this is the context in which the intercession of the saints on our behalf should be understood.[22] Item 5 considered Mary's place:

5. Mary Mother of God has a place within the Communion of Saints. It is precisely the relationship to Christ which gives her a singular role in the Communion of Saints, a role that is of christological origin. Further, the prayer of Mary for us should be seen in the context of that worship of the entire heavenly Church described in the Apocalypse, to which the Church on earth wishes to unite itself in its own corporate prayer. Mary prays within the Church, as once she prayed in expectation of Pentecost (Acts 1:14). There is no reason preventing us, even with our confessional differences, from uniting our prayer to God in the Spirit with the prayer of the heavenly liturgy, and especially with the prayer of the Mother of God.

The final section of the Malta statement reads:

6. The inclusion of Mary in the worship of the Lamb that has been sacrificed (the christological aspect) as well as her part in the heavenly liturgy (the eschatological aspect) must not give rise to any interpretation which would attribute to Mary the honor due to God alone. Moreover, no member of the Church can add anything whatsoever to the work of Christ, which remains the only source of salvation; it is not possible to "by-pass" him or to find an "easier" way to come to the Father than through the Son of God. At the same time it is clear that Mary has her place in the Communion of Saints.[23]

In the crypt of the chapel at the Calvinist monastic community of Taizé in France, there is an icon of the Virgin Mary. The prior-founder of the community, Brother Roger Schutz, invites visitors to pause there and join in this prayer, with which we conclude this essay:

Holy and merciful Father, you have revealed to the Blessed Virgin Mary that by the coming of your Son the mighty will be put down and the lowly lifted up. We pray to you for the humble who with Mary cry out to you.

Oh Christ, you who were born of the Virgin Mary, obedient to your Word, grant us also a spirit prompt to obey. With her, the first of all "the cloud of witnesses" (Heb. 12:2) we wish to learn to say to you, "let it be done unto me according to your will."

Oh God, you willed to make of the Virgin Mary the figure of the Church. She has received Christ and has given him to the world. Send on us your Holy Spirit so that we may be soon united visibly in a single body and that we may radiate Christ to men and women who cannot believe. Gather us all in a visible unity so that with the Virgin Mary and with all the saints, witnesses of Christ, we may rejoice in you, our Lord, now and forever and ever. Amen.

Notes

1. *Encyclopedia Brittanica*, 14th ed., S.V. "Mary (the Virgin Mary)."
2. Raymond E. Brown, Karl P. Donfried, Joseph A. Fitzmeyer, and John Reumann, eds., *Mary in the New Testament* (Philadelphia: Fortress Press, 1978).
3. R. E. Brown, K. P. Donfried, and J. Reumann, eds., *Peter in the New Testament* (Philadelphia: Fortress Press, 1973).
4. "Justification by Faith" (Sept. 30, 1983), in *Origins* 13 (Oct. 6, 1983): 227-304.
5. *Proclamation: Aids for Interpreting the Lessons of the Church Year. The Lesser Festivals* (Philadelphia: Fortress Press, 1975), vol. 1, Visitation, Feb. 2 and Mar. 25, and vol. 2, Aug. 15.
6. *Proclamation*, vol. 2, Aug. 15.
7. Bertrand A. Buby, S.M., *Mary, the Faithful Disciple* (Mahwah, N.J.: Paulist Press, 1985).
8. Francis J. Maloney, S.D.B., *Woman: First Among the Faithful* (Notre Dame, Ind.: Ave Maria Press, 1986).
9. Rosemary Haughton, *The Recreation of Eve* (Springfield, Ill.: Templegate, 1985), chap. 8.
10. Rita Crowley Turner, *The Mary Dimension* (London: Sheed & Ward, 1985).
11. J. N. D. Kelly, *Early Christian Doctrines*, 5th ed. (New York: Harper & Row, 1978). See chap. 18, "Mary and the Saints," pp. 490-99.
12. Ibid., p. 490.
13. St. Augustine, *De sancta virginitate* [On Holy Virginity], trans. John McQuade, S.M., in *St. Augustine: Treatises on Marriage and Other Subjects*, vol. 27, ed. C. Wilcox (New York: Fathers of the Church, 1955), quoted at greater length in the joint pastoral of the bishops of the United States, *Behold Your Mother: Woman of Faith* (Washington, D.C.: United States Catholic Conference, 1973).
14. Augustine, *De sancta virginitate*, in *Treatises*, p. 149.
15. Book 3, chap. 2, para. 10. A slightly different translation is found in K. Kavanaugh, O.C.D., and Otilio Rodriguez, O.C.D., eds., *The Collected Works of Saint John of the Cross* (Washington, D.C.: Institute of Carmelite Studies Publications, 1979), p. 217.
16. World Council of Churches, *Orthodoxy: Faith and Order Dialogue*, Faith and Order Paper no. 30 (Geneva: World Council of Churches, 1960), reprinted from *The Ecumenical Review* 12 (Jan. 1960): 48.
17. Robert Murray, S.J., *Symbols of Church and Kingdom: A Study in Early Syriac Tradition* (London: Cambridge University Press, 1975), p. 145.
18. Benedicta Ward, ed., trans., and author of "Introduction," *The Prayers and Meditations of Saint Anselm* (New York: Viking Press, Penguin Paperback, 1984).
19. See *The Magnificat: Luther's Commentary*, trans. A. T. W. Steinhauser, ed. Jaroslav Pelikan, in *Luther's Works*, vol. 21 (St. Louis: Concordia, 1956).

20. Donald Dawe, *From Dysfunction to Disbelief: The Virgin Mary in Reformed Theology*, paper delivered at the meeting of the Ecumenical Society of the Blessed Virgin Mary in Washington, D.C., Apr. 30, 1977, published by the Society, 423 Fourth St. NE, Washington, D.C. 20002, and also in A. Stacpoole, ed., *Mary's Place in Christian Dialogue* (Wilton, Conn.: Morehouse-Barlow, 1983), pp. 142-57.
21. Candido Pozo, S.J., "Does declaraciones ecumenicas marianas De Zaragoza (1979) a Malta (1983)," *Scripta de Maria* 7 (1984): 539-41.
22. "The Ecumenical Agreed Statement" appeared in the English *L'Osservatore Romano*, Sept. 26, 1983.
23. Ibid.

Bibliography

Official Documents

Behold Your Mother: Woman of Faith, Joint Pastoral of U.S. Bishops, Nov. 21, 1973.
Marialis cultis (Paul VI), Feb. 2, 1974.
Lumen gentium, Dogmatic Constitution on the Church, Vat. II, Nov. 21, 1964, chapters 7 and 8.

Books

Allchin, A. M. *The Joy of All Creation: An Anglican Meditation on the Place of Mary.* Cambridge, Mass.: Cowley, 1985.
Brown, Raymond, S.S. *Mary in the New Testament.* Philadelphia: Fortress Press, 1978.
Buby, Bertrand, S.M. *Mary, the Perfect Disciple.* New York: Paulist Press, 1985.
Jelly, F. J., O.P. *Madonna: Mary in the Catholic Tradition.* Huntington, Ind.: Our Sunday Visitor, 1986.
Stacpoole, A., O.S.B., ed. *Mary's Place in Christian Dialogue.* Wilton, Conn.: Morehouse-Barlow, 1983.

Articles or Chapters in Books

Brown, Raymond E., S.S. "Mary in the New Testament and Catholic Life." *America* (May 15, 1982): 374-79.
Louf, Andre. *The Cistercian Way.* Kalamazoo, Mich.: Cistercian Studies Publications, 1983. (See chapter 10, "With Mary, the Mother of Jesus," pp. 135-44.)
deLubac, Henri. *The Splendor of the Church.* San Francisco: Ignatius Press, 1986. (See "The Church and Our lady," pp. 238-89.)
Montague, George T., S.M. "Mary and Learning the Ways of the Spirit." In *Riding the Wind: Learning the Ways of the Spirit,* pp. 91-98. Ann Arbor, Mich.: Word of Life, 1974.
O'Donnell, C. O., O.Carm. "The Holiness of Mary." *Scripture in Church* (Oct.–Dec. 1982): 532-43.
———. "Mary, the True Disciple." In *Sowing the Word: Biblical-Liturgical Essays,* edited by P. Rogers, pp. 230-37. Dublin: Dominican Publications, 1986.

Prayer, Prayers, and Popular Devotion in Roman Catholicism

GABRIEL O'DONNELL, O.P.,
AND ROBIN MAAS

The Spirit too comes to help us in our weakness. For when we cannot choose words in order to pray properly, the Spirit himself expresses our plea in a way that could never be put into words, and God who knows everything in our hearts knows perfectly well what he means, and that the pleas of the saints expressed by the Spirit are according to the mind of God.

—ROMANS 8:26-27 JB

The subject of prayer is an attractive and mysterious one. What earnest Christian would not like to know more about prayer and how to pray "properly"? How many times have we heard people bemoan their inability to express themselves adequately in prayer? How many others are convinced that their lack of faith and virtue renders their prayers ineffective? The frustration so many sincere Christians experience in relation to praying is often due to a fundamental misunderstanding of the meaning of prayer.

One of the most ancient—and satisfactory—explanations of this most important but elusive subject defines prayer simply as the "lifting" of the heart and mind to God: "Let my prayer be counted as incense before thee," wrote the psalmist, "and the lifting up of my hands as an evening sacrifice" (Ps. 141:2). It is an entirely interior gesture, a mute plea to a Power beyond our own meager resources. This desire or hunger for communion with God creates the necessary conditions under which prayer—which is actually the work of the Holy Spirit within us—can occur. By this understanding, it would be a mistake to consider prayer a reflection of our own insight and eloquence, which are sure to be lacking. It is not a "work" we perform on our own behalf. Ironically, it is God the Spirit who performs the work of prayer, who knows our need, the condition of our heart, and how properly to express it. What we commonly call prayer is actually an *invitation* we issue to the Spirit to come and "express our plea in a way that can never be put into words."

This means that the issue of prayer for us is really one of placing ourselves—our hearts and our minds—at the disposal of the Spirit, and it is at this point that specific prayers become extremely significant. Such prayers, whether they are said silently in solitude or communally in a liturgical setting, are a reliable means for placing ourselves at the Spirit's disposal. The Church has long recognized that although true prayer is a purely interior act, externalized words, along with particular postures and gestures, are essential in assisting people to lift their hearts and minds to God. It is, of course, possible to recite a prayer without actually *praying* it, but prayers are meant to be prayed, not said. Those who insist that they want to pray but resist "saying prayers" are reacting out of the experience of having recited prayers without actually praying them. Yet the power of words is such that even the mere saying of prayers can lead to an experience of prayer.

Liturgy: The Bedrock of Devotion

In the liturgy the community gathers together to say and do things that are either the result or the beginning of a new way of relating to God. The Church's liturgy is our primary and original model of what it means to have such a relationship. Its purpose is to provide a structure within which prayer—the *modus vivendi* of the Divine-human encounter—can occur.

But while it is true that the liturgy provides the paradigm for all prayer, it does not exhaust the Church's prayer activity. In fact, good liturgy can be counted upon to generate *other* expressions of prayer and devotion and thus undergird them. Personal prayer, far from being a substitute for the communal liturgy, is, most often, its "superfluity," a kind of inevitable overflowing of love and devotion. The Word proclaimed in community has a *lingering* effect whereby individual Christians seek to explore and reflect on the implications of what has been experienced in prayer for the deepest recesses of personal life. Typically, this overflow of prayer and devotion has tended to focus on concrete things or persons that, in turn, symbolize the ineffable, and just as liturgy gives rise to particular devotional practices, so the most popular of these practices find their way back into the liturgy.

Devotion to the Altar

In the tradition of Christian iconography, as well as in liturgical practice, the altar—always fixed, imposing, and central—is seen as the focus for the presence of Christ. As such, the altar itself very early became an object of devotion. During the sixth through the eleventh centuries, the development by the Church of elaborate liturgical rites based on the altar (e.g., the blessing and consecration of an altar) was as much or more a response to preexisting popular devotion as a conscious effort on the part of the clergy to valorize the altar as a focal point. Significantly, devotion to the altar as evidence of the presence of Christ predates by many centuries any notion of eucharistic reservation.

The pattern of reciprocity seen here in liturgical life and devotions has been replicated many times since: First, a liturgical factor or practice inspires a particular form of popular devotion; next, further liturgical developments respond to popular devotion by incorporating or intensifying devotional acts in formal worship, which in turn leads to increased devotion.

Devotion to the Martyrs

A very early and particularly intense form of Christian piety revolved around the efficacious intercession of the martyrs—those faithful ones whose witness to Christ had led to the sacrifice of life itself. Heroic and sacrificial gestures always capture our imagination, and the martyrdoms of the first four centuries of Christianity in particular had precisely this effect. The places where martyrs were buried quickly became shrines, and their bodily remains were often exhumed and placed in or under altars to further sanctify them.

In both cases—devotion to the altar and devotion to the martyrs—devotion was localized, that is, centered around a particular thing in a particular place: the altar and the tomb. The practice of entombing relics in or under the altar made a tomb of the altar, just as the cult of the martyrs made an altar of their tombs. Popular devotion discerned with great clarity that the martyr is both a Eucharist and an altar, because in the martyr we have the perfect completion of what the individual has undergone sacramentally. To be precise: What happens in baptism? We die with Christ and are raised with Christ (Rom. 6:3-4). What happens in the Eucharist? We are fed with the body and blood of Christ. Just so, in martyrdom the body of Christ is broken again, and the blood of Christ is poured out again on the altar of the world.

Martyrdom—a baptism by blood—ensured those who witnessed even unto death a secure and very high place in heaven. Therefore, martyrs and others who lived lives of sacrificial witness (e.g., monks and nuns) came to be seen as the special friends of God. Their status as special friends was, not surprisingly, seen to give them equally special *access* to God. Thus they quickly came to be seen as powerful intercessors. Just as we are likely to ask people whose faith impresses us to pray for us in times of need, so the early Christians sought an intimate communion with the "friends of God" and relied unhesitatingly on their assistance.

This sense of what amounts to a familial connection with the blessed dead was developed in the Middle Ages to a high degree and formulated in terms of the Communion of Saints—a foundational doctrine that arises out of popular devotion and that is reflected in the early ecumenical creeds. The cult of the saints, which continues to be popular in modern Catholicism and which so baffles Protestants, is grounded precisely in beliefs that most Protestants would nevertheless be likely to share, namely, the conviction that life continues beyond the grave, that those who are baptized into Christ—at whatever time in history—are all of them members of a single Body and therefore gravely concerned with and affected by each other's fortunes, and that the prayer of faithful people is efficacious.

Just as the Church responded to popular devotion to the altar with liturgical elaborations, so the Church, rather than trying to stamp out all apparently questionable or idiosyncratic popular devotions, proceeded instead to "co-opt" much of martyrial piety by establishing feast days for martyrs in the liturgical calendar. In this way, celebrations that were initially extremely localized were universalized and, perhaps more important, *standardized*. This strategy allowed the Church to take an active role, first, in deciding which devotions were authentic and, second, in actually propagating those devotions that it felt would enhance participation in the liturgy. And it needs to be underscored that official sanction of particular devotional practices is always (at least in intent) *in the service of liturgical practice*. Significantly, the Church has consistently recognized that its role in shaping faith and practice involves more than the teaching of doctrine and liturgical celebration. The Church claims, too, the right to shape personal devotion and in this way does much to deter the development of an idiosyncratic "privatization" in the devotional life.

Over the centuries the Roman Catholic church has consistently nurtured devotional practices that focus either on the person and work of Jesus Christ or on the intercession of the saints, especially that of the Blessed Virgin Mary.

Christological Devotions

Christological devotions—the most central of all—are typically focused on either Christ's incarnation or passion, with the latter predominating. Passion-inspired devotions are associated with Fridays, the season of Lent, and, of course, the Mass itself. Significantly, they can be performed corporately as well as individually. A particularly popular one, especially during Lent, is the Way of the Cross, a series of meditations on Jesus' final hours, beginning with his condemnation in the Sanhedrin and ending with his entombment. Originally popularized by the Franciscans, this exercise is usually performed as a kind of pilgrimage by groups of people who stop to pray at specially designated "stations" in Roman Catholic churches, but it may be done privately anywhere. The stations have inspired numerous devout and poetic responses to the experience of an empathetic participation in the crucifixion.[1]

Devotion to the Blessed Sacrament, that is, the reserved Eucharist, is a peculiarly Catholic devotion and a logical response to the Roman Catholic understanding of "Real Presence." The consecrated Host, as the "real" or actual presence of Christ, became itself an object of worship, and its continual presence in the tabernacle behind or adjacent to the altar was responsible for a particularly localized expression of devotion. Even those people who know nothing about Real Presence or the reserved Eucharist comment on the profound silence and the sense of reverence and devotion they commonly observe—and perhaps experience themselves—upon entering a Roman Catholic church. The practices of genuflecting and kneeling upon entering the church are directly attributable to this form of devotion. While it is common practice for Roman Catholics to simply "visit" the church at odd hours during the day in order to spend time in prayer and reflection before the Blessed Sacrament, the Catholic church finds it in its own best interests to promote this particular form of devotion and does so by offering special occasions for devotion, when the Host is exposed in a special container called a monstrance. The Forty Hours Devotion and "holy hours" provide regular opportunities for communal adoration employing particular liturgies, hymns, and meditations. The intent is to answer yes to Christ's plea, "Could you not watch with me one hour?" (Matt. 26:40). The hour of adoration ends with Benediction, a particularly colorful and elaborate rite that has it roots in the evening services in honor of the Virgin Mary.

A third christological devotion revolves around the image of Christ's "Sacred Heart." This too strikes Protestants as being something peculiarly Catholic, but its roots are in the biblical and patristic emphasis on the saving efficacy of Christ's precious blood. Pictured as pierced by a crown of thorns and bleeding, the Sacred Heart is meant to evoke the passion as the supreme sacrifice of love. Following a set of revelations about the nature of the Sacred Heart to a seventeenth-century French nun, St. Margaret Mary Alacoque, the Sacred Heart as a symbol of the human Jesus' compassionate love was vividly contrasted with humankind's sinful indifference toward the Blessed Sacrament, and thus the two forms of devotion were increasingly linked until they tended actually to be fused by the mid–nineteenth century:

> Emerging from this identification of the Sacred Heart and the Blessed Sacrament was the idea of Jesus' presence as a voluntary "prisoner" in the eucharistic wafer. His continuing presence, understood as an extension of his life on earth, was perceived as a manifestation of his continued willingness to suffer out of love for humankind.[2]

In this way devotion to the Blessed Sacrament was seen to be a form of reparation for the coldness and ingratitude of those who ignored or despised the Real Presence. The Society of Jesus in particular has been responsible for promoting devotion to the Sacred Heart.

Marian Devotions

Second only to christological devotions are devotions centering around Mary as the Mother of Jesus, the Mother of God Incarnate. The most popular of these is the rosary, a series of prayers (the Our Father and the Hail Mary) repeated rhythmically with the aid of a string of beads used as counters. The practice of repeating 150 Hail Marys as an analogue to praying the 150 psalms in the Daily Office is an ancient one, but the form as we know it now dates back to the late fifteenth century when it was popularized by the Dominican Alan de La Roche, who attributed this particular form of devotion to St. Dominic.

Long misunderstood by Protestants as a form of "vain repetition," the rosary has become the focus of renewed interest and appreciation for both Catholics and Protestants as a consequence of exposure to Eastern prayer techniques involving the use of a mantra. The rhythmic repetition of brief vocal prayers can be a powerful centering activity that, when mastered, leaves one mentally free to meditate, and this is precisely the point of the rosary. Every decade, or set of ten beads, provides a "space" for meditating on a particular mystery in the lives of Christ and Mary. As with most of the christological devotions, the rosary can be prayed by the individual or by groups and is often recited following Mass.

Devotion to the Immaculate Conception of Mary is another

relatively long-established practice that illustrates the powerful influence popular devotion can have, not only on liturgical practices but also on the development of doctrine itself. The Middle Ages saw the rise of a feast honoring the Immaculate Conception of Mary despite the opposition of many theologians, and it was not until the nineteenth century that the matter was finally settled by papal decree. The vision of the Miraculous Medal to St. Catherine Labouré that occurred just before the papal promulgation, and the appearances of the Virgin to St. Bernadette at Lourdes following right after it, had the effect of heightening enthusiasm for devotion to Mary.

Contrary to popular misconceptions, the Immaculate Conception does not refer to the Virgin Birth but to *Mary's* having been conceived without the stain of original sin. The absence of a clear biblical warrant for this belief has made it particularly controversial in ecumenical contexts; suffice it to say here that, as with so many developments in Mariology, its origin lies in christological concerns to protect the full divinity of Christ and maintain the priority of the divine initiative in bringing salvation to the world. Mary as the Immaculate Conception evokes patristic images of Mary as the New Eve who, because she has not experienced the bondage of original sin, can tread Evil underfoot and give birth to a human being who is indeed made in the flawless image and likeness of God.

The Cult of the Saints

The Roman Catholic proclivity for praying to the saints is rooted, as we have already indicated, in the doctrine of the Communion of Saints. The Pauline image of the Church as the Body of Christ suggests a radically organic or mutually interdependent ecclesiology that is essentially foreign to the individualistic values of Western—especially American—culture. Yet this concept, in which the good of the individual is both subordinated to and inescapably dependent on the good of the whole, underlies the entire Christian enterprise. Nowhere is this concept more vividly expressed and tested than in the life of prayer, most particularly intercessory prayer.

From the earliest centuries Christians called on one another to each pray for the other. When we add to this biblical imperative the social context of antiquity, in which patronage was essential to any successful endeavor in public life, it is not surprising to see a deep and persistent pursuit of supernatural patronage in Christian practice. Particular saints became patrons not only of individuals who were given their names but also of groups, guilds, and people who shared similar circumstances (e.g., Thérèse of Lisieux is the patronness of all foreign missions; Augustine of Hippo, patron of theologians; Luke, patron of physicians and artists; Clare of Assisi, patronness of television!). In addition to assigning feast days for individual saints in the liturgical calendar, special acts of veneration were directed toward saints, for example, novenas. A novena consists of nine days of prayer in which the aid of a patron saint is invoked for the sake of a particular intention. The choice of nine days comes from the nine days between the Ascension of the risen Christ and the arrival of the Holy Spirit on Pentecost. This time is therefore meant to be a period of supplication, intercession, and anticipation of the coming of the Holy Spirit.

Devotion to the Virgin Mary or a particular patron saint is never meant to serve as a substitute for having a direct and personal relationship with Jesus, nor is his love for us in any way enlarged by having many prayers said on our behalf. But one of the great mysteries of grace—and of faith—is that we are commanded to *ask* for this gift in order to receive it. Further, the reception of grace inevitably means the end of our spiritual isolation in the act of being grafted into the "true vine" (John 15). At this point our need becomes the need of all Christians, living or dead; our diminishment injures them just as our enlargement benefits them, and every prayer prayed in heaven or on earth resounds to the glory of God. Having thrown in our lot with the People of God, we have no separate destiny.

The Relationship of Vocal and Mental Prayer

In the literature of devotion, one often meets with a distinction between vocal and mental prayer. Vocal prayer is, by definition, verbal. It consists of words designed to lead us to the lifting of heart and mind to God. Mental prayer may or may not be verbal, and it is certainly not confined to purely intellectual activity. Mental prayer is an inward, interiorized activity; it is precisely the lifting of self to God and may be characterized as much or more by affectivity as by intellect.

The point of vocal prayer is to lead us eventually to mental prayer, and most of us find some vocal prayer to be an absolutely essential aid to mental prayer. The danger lies in reaching the point where we feel we have "got beyond it," so that vocal prayer can finally be abandoned. But the higher reaches of the spiritual life are mined, so to speak, with dangerous periods of dryness and darkness when God seems utterly absent, and prayer is no longer a consolation but a terrible burden. At such times, to be able to return to something as simple as the rosary can be a great salvation. At such times, we must be willing to have others "voice" our prayers for us with words that, if they do not spring from our own affections, *tell the truth* nonetheless. And this, of course, is the point of participating in traditional devotions. In so doing we are joining our prayer to that of millions of other Christians who have prayed before us and who will someday pray after us and letting *them* give voice to our own wordless longings and thereby imprint a family resemblance on our relationship with God.

EXERCISES

For an Individual

Make the twelfth chapter of Paul's first letter to the Corinthians the subject of prayer and meditation over a period of time. Reflect back on the role intercession has played in your prayer life. What assumptions about the nature of God, prayer, and the Church have been reflected in your devotions? How does Paul's image of the Church as a single Body challenge those assumptions? When was the last time you asked someone to pray for you or for someone else? Precisely what were you expecting when you made that request? Have you ever been conscious of being the beneficiary of someone else's prayers?

Begin gradually to broaden your concept of the Communion of Saints and the power of intercession by using the following prayers:

THE MEMORARE

Remember, O most gracious Virgin Mary, that never was it known that anyone who fled to your protection, implored your help or sought your intercession was ever left unaided. Inspired with this confidence, I fly unto you, O Virgin of virgins, my Mother; to you I come, before you I stand, sinful and sorrowful; O Mother of the Word Incarnate, despise not my petitions, but in your mercy hear and answer me. Amen.

PRAYER TO SAINT FRANCIS OF ASSISI

O Blessed St. Francis, lover of Lady Poverty, teach us to love her, too. In these our days when so many of our brothers and sisters suffer so much from the lack of the basic necessities of life, help us who are better off to learn how to share what we have even to the point of depriving ourselves. Raise up in the world leaders who will know how to reshape the economy so that no one will want at the abundant table of the Lord, each content with the wonderful portion the Lord has allotted, just as you found great joy in the common heritage of the human family. O holy Poor Man of Assisi, pray for us now and at the hour of our death. Amen.

PRAYER TO SAINT THOMAS À BECKET

St. Thomas, by your life you showed us that wealth, power, and prestige are nothing compared to following Christ. Pray for us, who are encompassed by the temptations of the commercial world, that we may turn away from it, and turn toward the example of our Savior, Jesus, as you have done. Pray that we may also stand firm in our faith and in our love for Christ and for our fellows as you did when the evil soldiers sank their swords into your flesh at the altar of Christ. Amen.

PRAYER TO MY PATRON SAINT

O Heavenly Patron, in whose name I glory, pray ever to God for me that he may strengthen me in my faith, establish me in virtue, and guard me in conflict, so that I might overcome all evil and attain to everlasting glory with you. Amen.

For a Group

Plan a group Bible study on I Corinthians 12, making use of the discussion questions listed below. Conclude the session by praying the rosary and/or the angelus together as a group. Directions for praying the rosary are found in appendix 12. The angelus, meant to be prayed responsively, is shown below.

THE ANGELUS

Leader: *The angel of the Lord declared unto Mary*

Response: And she conceived by the Holy Spirit.
Hail Mary, full of grace, the Lord is with thee.
Blessed art thou among women and blessed is the fruit of thy womb, Jesus.
Holy Mary, Mother of God, pray for us sinners now and at the hour of our death. Amen.

Leader: *Behold the handmaid of the Lord*

Response: Be it done unto me according to Thy Word.
Hail Mary. . . .

Leader: *And the Word was made flesh*

Response: And dwelt among us.
Hail Mary. . .

Leader: *Pray for us, O Holy Mother of God*

Response: That we may be made worthy of the promises of Christ.

Leader: *Let us pray*

Response: Pour forth, we beseech Thee, O Lord, Thy grace into our hearts: that we to whom the Incarnation of Christ, Thy Son, was made known by the message of an angel, may by his passion and cross be brought to the glory of his resurrection through the same Christ Our Lord. Amen.

DISCUSSION QUESTIONS

1. Is the distinction between prayer and prayers a helpful one for you in interpreting your own experience? Why or why not?

2. Has your participation in liturgical or communal worship had any impact on your personal devotional life? What specific connections can you make?

3. In your own experience, has private prayer enhanced or detracted from your participation in communal worship? Why is this the case?

4. How important is the doctrine of the Communion of Saints in your own faith community? What expressions does it take? Does an understanding of this doctrine help to make sense of Roman Catholic devotional practices? What other implications might it have for the Church? For your own relationship to God?

5. If you do not think of yourself as having a patron saint, whom might you choose to be your patron saint and why?

Notes

1. See, for example, "Prayers on the Way of the Cross," in Michael Quoist, *Prayers*, trans. Agnes M. Forsyth and Anne Marie de Commaille (Kansas City, Kans.: Sheed & Ward, 1963), pp. 151-79.
2. Ann Taves, *The Household of Faith* (Notre Dame, Ind.: University of Notre Dame Press, 1986), p. 34.

Resources

Bishops' Committee on the Liturgy, National Conference of Catholic Bishops. *A Book of Mary: Prayers in Honor of the Blessed Virgin Mary.* Washington, D.C.: United States Catholic Conference, 1987.

———. *Catholic Household Blessings and Prayers.* Washington, D.C.: United States Catholic Conference, 1988.

Dollen, Charles. *My Rosary: Its Power and Mystery.* New York: Alba House, 1988.

Lowery, Daniel L., C.S.S.R. *Day by Day Through Lent.* Liguori, Mo.: Liguori Publications, 1983.

Pennington, M. Basil, O.C.S.O. *Pocket Book of Prayers.* Garden City, N.Y.: Doubleday Image Books, 1986.

Storey, William G., ed. *Praise Him! A Prayerbook for Today's Christian.* Notre Dame, Ind.: Ave Maria Press, 1973.

The Way of the Cross. Compiled and composed from Biblical texts. Baltimore, Md.: Barton-Cotton, 1965.

Ward, J. Neville. *Five for Sorrow, Ten for Joy: A Consideration of the Rosary.* Rev. ed. Cambridge, Mass.: Cowley, 1985. (Reflections on a Catholic devotion by an English Methodist.)

APPENDIX 12

Praying the Rosary

Doubtless the best-known and most popular form of Marian devotion, the rosary provides a simple but highly satisfying vocal and mental prayer form. The vocal aspect of the rosary consists of the rhythmic repetition of the Hail Mary, interspersed with the Our Father (the Pater Noster or Lord's Prayer). The mental aspect involves meditating on the principal mysteries of our salvation, drawn from the Scriptures and focusing on the principal events in the life of Christ. It is a prayer form that can be performed antiphonally with groups (often just before or after weekday Mass) or individually, aloud or silently, with or without beads.

An entire rosary consists of fifteen sets of ten beads (decades), divided by single, often larger, beads, on which the Our Father is said. Most people use a "chaplet," consisting of five decades. Attached to the chaplet is a crucifix, where one begins with the Sign of the Cross and then the Apostles' Creed. Following this is a single bead (for an Our Father), three beads (for three Hail Marys), and the Our Father bead that begins the first decade. The recitation of this first set of prayers and each decade concludes with the Doxology (Gloria Patri), and the entire exercise concludes with an anthem to Mary, usually Hail Holy Queen (Salve Regina), followed by the Sign of the Cross. Praying the rosary, for most people, consists of the recitation of five decades with the accompanying meditations on the particular set of "mysteries" assigned to that particular day of the week.

The first set of five "joyful" mysteries is prayed on Mondays and Thursdays, the five "sorrowful" mysteries are prayed on Tuesday and Friday, and the five "glorious mysteries" are prayed on Wednesday, Saturday, and Sunday. The intention is to meditate on some aspect of these mysteries with each decade prayed. Learning to pray the rosary takes a little practice, and one is likely to find this mental exercise somewhat difficult until the vocal prayers have been fully mastered and can be prayed effortlessly. But the constant repetition of the vocal prayers finally begins to function as a powerful centering device—much like a mantra—and this frees the mind to reflect on the mysteries. Many devotional guides are available to assist in the process of meditation and can be found in any Catholic book or religious goods store. Most Protestants are surprised to discover that the rosary is not simply a matter of "vain repetition" but a substantial and, when the meditations are practiced, very biblical form of prayer, since each of the mysteries (with the exception of the last two) are taken straight from Scripture. Below is a diagram of the chaplet (Figure 12-1), followed by a list of the mysteries and the actual prayers repeated.

The Three Types of Mysteries

1. *The Joyful Mysteries* (Mondays and Thursdays)
   The Annunciation
   The Visitation
   The Nativity
   The Presentation of the Infant Jesus at the Temple
   The Finding of the Child Jesus in the Temple
2. *The Sorrowful Mysteries* (Tuesdays and Fridays)
   The Agony in the Garden
   The Scourging of Jesus
   The Crowning with Thorns
   The Carrying of the Cross
   The Crucifixion
3. *The Glorious Mysteries* (Wednesdays, Saturdays, and Sundays)
   The Resurrection
   The Ascension of Jesus into Heaven
   The Descent of the Holy Spirit at Pentecost
   The Assumption of Mary into Heaven
   The Crowning of Mary, Queen of Heaven

Prayers of the Rosary

THE SIGN OF THE CROSS

In the name of the Father, and of the Son, and of the Holy Spirit. Amen.

ROSARY DIAGRAM

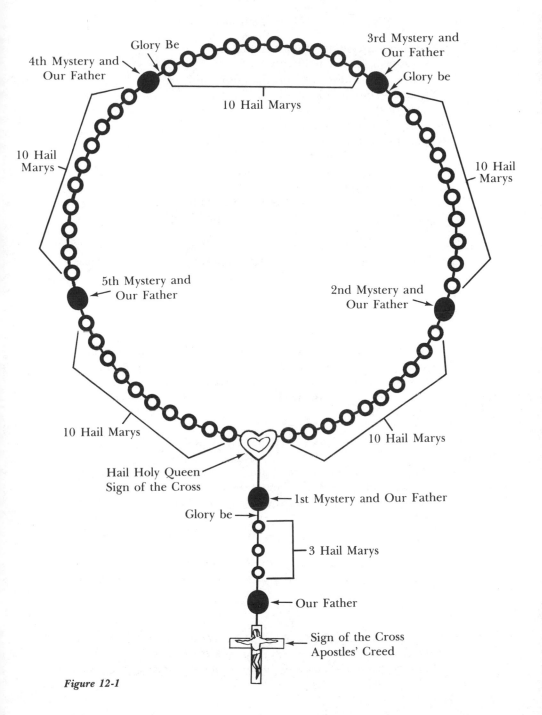

4th Mystery and
Our Father

Glory Be

3rd Mystery and
Our Father

Glory be

10 Hail Marys

10 Hail
Marys

10 Hail
Marys

5th Mystery and
Our Father

2nd Mystery and
Our Father

10 Hail Marys

10 Hail Marys

Hail Holy Queen
Sign of the Cross

1st Mystery and Our Father

Glory be

3 Hail Marys

Our Father

Sign of the Cross
Apostles' Creed

Figure 12-1

THE APOSTLES' CREED

I believe in God, the Father Almighty,
Creator of heaven and earth.
and in Jesus Christ, his only Son, our Lord,
who was conceived by the Holy Spirit,
born of the Virgin Mary,
suffered under Pontius Pilate,
was crucified, died, and was buried.
He descended into hell,
the third day he rose from the dead.
He ascended into heaven
and sits on the right hand of God the Father Almighty.
From thence he shall come to judge the living and the dead.
I believe in the Holy Spirit,
the holy Catholic Church,
the communion of saints, the forgiveness of sins,
the resurrection of the body,
and life everlasting. Amen.

THE OUR FATHER

Our Father, who art in heaven, hallowed be thy name. Thy kingdom come. Thy will be done on earth as it is in heaven. Give us this day our daily bread. And forgive us our trespasses as we forgive those who trespass against us. And lead us not into temptation but deliver us from evil. Amen.

THE HAIL MARY

Hail Mary, full of grace, the Lord is with thee. Blessed art thou among women, and blessed is the fruit of thy womb, Jesus. Holy Mary, Mother of God, pray for us sinners now and at the hour of our death. Amen.

THE DOXOLOGY

Glory be to the Father, and to the Son, and to the Holy Spirit, as it was in the beginning, is now, and ever shall be, world without end. Amen.

HAIL, HOLY QUEEN

Hail, Holy Queen, Mother of Mercy, our life, our sweetness and our hope.
To thee do we cry, poor banished children of Eve.
To thee do we send up our sighs, mourning and weeping in this valley of
tears.

Turn, then, O most gracious Advocate, thine eyes of mercy toward us.
And after this our exile, show unto us the blessed fruit of thy womb,
     Jesus.
O clement, O loving, O sweet Virgin Mary!

Versicle: Pray for us, O holy Mother of God
Response: That we may be made worthy of the promises of Christ.

O God, whose only begotten Son, by his life, death, and resurrection, has
purchased for us the rewards of eternal life, grant, we beseech thee, that
meditating upon these Mysteries of the most holy rosary of the Blessed
Virgin Mary, we may imitate what they contain and obtain what they
promise. Through the same Christ our Lord. Amen.

CHAPTER 13

Holy Women:
Their Spiritual Influence
in the Middle Ages

ROBIN DARLING YOUNG

*I rejoice in my sufferings . . . and in my flesh I complete what is lacking in Christ's
afflictions for the sake of his body . . . the church.*
—COLOSSIANS 1:24

The spirituality of the women of medieval Western Christianity (ca.
500–1500) is not a uniform entity in content, form, or method. Some of
its features are shared with the early Church, and some with the
Church of the Reformation or modern periods; indeed, much of the
religious life of medieval women resembles that of medieval men,
especially among those authors whose daily lives were passed and
spiritual odysseys made in monastic institutions. The variety of women
spiritual authors, or of religious women whose acts were recorded by
others, defeats any strict categorization by content or gender.
However, much of the literature this chapter will survey does bear a
kind of family resemblance that may spring from two circumstances:
the continuity of the spiritual lives of medieval women with that of
early Christian women (insofar as we can know the latter) and the
evident fact that medieval women, although they did not occupy public
and official teaching positions within the Church of the day,
nevertheless experienced a private or hidden kind of authority that
they later found ways to communicate publicly.

The writings of these women, many of whom enjoyed a wide
reputation during their own time and were sought after as spiritual
guides, are currently enjoying a much broader and more general
audience, due to the recent interest in women's history and religious
life during the ancient and medieval periods. This new interest has led
to their "rediscovery" and—in a very important and salutary

development—their republication for an audience interested in coming to hear the voices of those not normally represented in the official Church teachings or "clerical" spirituality of the period.

To the reader expecting to find divergence from and opposition to an established position in the writings of medieval women, it may come as a surprise to learn of the loyalty of many of them to Church authority and teaching. This is not to deny that many women of the medieval period freely chose heresy or schism as best representing authentic Christian teaching; yet it is likely that as many women or more, including those whose writings have become spiritual classics, both desired to be, and truly were, loyal to the institution among whose organizations—convents, beguinages, hermitages—they found a home. If they were dissatisfied with the Church of their day (as were, for instance, Elizabeth of Schonau and Catherine of Siena), it was often because they, like many of the zealous, wished the Church to be truer to its ideal form and to its Lord, for whom they expressed the most fervent devotion.

The Early Christian Roots of Medieval Women's Spirituality

The spirituality of the women under consideration here had its roots in the institutions and spiritual writers of the early Church. From the very beginning, the Church produced numerous women martyrs, solitary ascetics, nuns, and some teachers who transcended their social and natural limitations to become friends or advisors to their male counterparts. In fact, one of the most notable changes from the ancient pagan religious world to that of the Christian world of late antiquity was the new and significant degree of prominence gained by women who joined one or another part of the "third race," that of the Christian Church.[1]

Pagan religion had indeed held a definite place for women and for their divine counterparts, the goddesses, but the various pagan devotions of Greco-Roman antiquity attended primarily to women's roles as wives or mothers and emphasized their relationship to a divinely sanctioned order on earth through the medium of the family. Judaism, on the other hand, insisted on monotheism and rejected the numerous gods, female and male, who guarded the lives of their adherents. Although there is some evidence that women functioned as synagogue leaders, the Judaism of late antiquity had no room for women whose religious devotion might have called them to renounce family and sexual practice and live as virgins. (A possible exception to this would be the Therapeutae, a philosophical-ascetical sect near first-century Alexandria.)[2]

This renunciation of family ties in favor of attachment to Jesus and identification with him was, of course, a strong component in Christianity from the period of Paul's activities and remained strong until it became institutionalized in various forms of ascetic life in the late third and early fourth centuries. In fact, it may have been the extension of this choice to both sexes that attracted so many women to Christianity in the first decades of its existence. The influential presence of women in early Christianity was noted, often with ridicule, by pagan authors and is unmistakable in various Christian authors' descriptions of women's functions in the Church. Although women were not ordained priests, and the female diaconate was a somewhat restricted ministry, we hear many reports of Christian women as religious devotees of great sincerity: martyrs, visionaries, pilgrims, virgins, and counselors to monks, or wealthy financial backers of churches in various cities. One of the most popular hagiographies of the early Church, *The Acts of Thecla*, portrayed a woman who, as the putative follower of Paul in his missionary travels, defied her wealthy family, renounced her impending marriage, and lived an ascetic life as a missionary until an early death as a martyr.[3]

The lives of women ascetics, preserved by various early Christian authors, testify to the wide influence of these women among both their families and the wider Church. Lacking hierarchical status, they gained a reputation for their spiritual discipline and, sometimes, for their mystical devotion. Like male ascetics, many Christian women consciously identified themselves with Jesus and pursued, through the practice of celibacy, the "angelic life." However, no early Christian woman has left an account, written by herself, of her spiritual visions or her counsel to others following the same path. An exception may be Gregory of Nyssa's *On the Soul and the Resurrection*, which he presents as a dialogue with his sister Macrina on her deathbed. The latter, one of the best-known Greek female ascetics, administered a double monastery established in the family villa and counseled her brothers in the spiritual life.[4] Also, the hagiographical *Life of Febronia*, a Syrian Christian martyr and abbess, may have been written by a woman in her convent.[5] More usual, however, is the sort of witness given by Tertullian about the spiritual life of an anonymous woman in his church in Carthage during the first decade of the third century:

> We have now among us a sister whose lot it has been to be favored with . . . gifts of revelation, which she experiences in the Spirit by

ecstatic vision admidst the sacred rites of the Lord's day in the church: she converses with angels, and sometimes even with the Lord; she both sees and hears mysterious communications; some men's hearts she understands, and to them who are in need she distributes remedies. Whether it be in the reading of Scriptures, or in the chanting of psalms, or in the preaching of sermons, or in the offering up of prayers, in all these religious services matter and opportunity are afforded to her of seeing visions. It may possibly have happened to us, while this sister of ours was rapt in the Spirit, that we had discoursed in some ineffable way about the soul. After the people are dismissed at the conclusion of the sacred services, she is in the regular habit of reporting to us whatever things she may have seen in vision (for all her communications are examined with the most scrupulous care, in order that their truth may be proved). "Among other things," she says, "there has been shown to me a soul in bodily shape, and a spirit has been in the habit of appearing to me; not, however, a void and empty illusion, but such as would offer itself to be even grasped by the hand, soft and transparent and of an ethereal color, and in form resembling that of a human being in every respect." This was her vision, and for her witness there was God; and the apostle most assuredly foretold that there were to be "spiritual gifts" in the church.[6]

Tertullian also edited, it is thought, *The Passion of Sts. Perpetua and Felicity*,[7] another text that shows the women of the Carthaginian Church as recipients of visions that the Church in turn received for instruction or consolation. In each case, however, these visions have been transmitted through an amanuensis.

Despite the obvious disparities of place and circumstance between the Mediterranean world of late antiquity and the European setting of the medieval period, there are clear continuities between these hints of early Christian women's spirituality and the piety of women in the Middle Ages. Take, for example, the emphasis in monasticism on virginity and martyrdom or Christlike suffering of various kinds, as well as the willingness to offer teaching or interpretation to the wider Christian Church. These perduring preoccupations connect the women of our period, many of whom wrote or dictated their religious views and experiences, with their early Christian ancestresses.

Although the scope of this chapter precludes a thorough survey of what, by now, is an extensive collection of translated documents covering a long span of time, increasing interest in the contributions of Christian women to the Church's spiritual tradition makes even an abbreviated treatment of the subject a worthwhile exercise. We propose to discuss in some detail and in chronological order the lives and works of six major women authors who are representative of the approaches of medieval women to God but who exemplify the different situations that shaped these responses. Despite these different contexts, several common themes can be described as marking out a particularly medieval, and feminine, spiritual life. Significantly, these derive from the influence of cenobitic monasticism in the transition from the period of the early Church to that of the medieval Church.

Common Features of Medieval Women's Spirituality

The Eastern Christian communities for women, so famous during the fourth and fifth centuries, survived the fifth-century divisions of the Church and the seventh-century Islamic invasions and continued either in lands under Muslim domination (Egypt, Palestine, Syria, and Armenia) or in the territories held by the now-shrunken Byzantine Empire. Their vital spiritual traditions continued, though little of a written record survives, and these groups expanded into the Slavic countries once those nations had converted to Christianity. To some degree, women's communities, and with them a women's spirituality traceable to Christian origins, survive to the present day. Their largely contemplative orientation distinguishes them from numerous women's religious orders in the West.

Inasmuch as medieval women's communities derive from the common stock of the Benedictine monastic movement, they have an organic connection with those Eastern cenobitic communities that were, in part, Benedict's model for the rule he wrote for the community at Monte Cassino. However, women's religious life in the medieval West had naturally to adapt itself to a different set of social conditions. Increasingly, their world resembled the barbarian kingdoms established in place of the Roman Empire, remnants of which had survived in Italy and southern Gaul through the sixth century. As a result, the Church had to adapt itself to differing customs regarding the family and the roles of women therein. Nevertheless, the Church also carried on the work of evangelizing and civilizing the tribes that had settled in northern Europe. It is well known that monastic foundations were fundamental to the extension of the Church in pagan, barbarian territory, just as they had been in fourth-century Asia Minor or would be in the medieval Balkan countries. Along with men's monastic foundations, monasteries for women were established, some of them organized by the Benedictine Rule (which did not become universally required of Western monasteries until approximately 800, and then only for the Frankish domains under the Carolingian revival).

It is not surprising that women generally fared better in early medieval Europe as residents of a cenobitic monastery than as practitioners of a more individualized form of monasticism, if for reasons of safety alone. In early medieval Spain, as in England and Germany, there were double monasteries in which communities for men and women lived in close proximity to one another and under a common rule. This meant that the outward form of the spiritual life for men and women would have been almost identical, emphasizing the devotion to the Divine Office (often called the Opus Dei) and a life balanced between prayer and work. The abbess was the central figure in the monastery, to whom obedience was owed and from whom a motherly and protective guidance was expected. In communities where the Benedictine Rule was in force (a rule that, according to Benedict's hagiography, his sister Scholastica asked be written for women as well), the seven-times-daily community psalmody would have shaped the nuns' self-understanding. Likewise, ascetic practices, always meant in the Benedictine tradition to be a reasonable and orderly discipline for "beginners on the path of salvation," would have included farming, domestic tasks such as care of the sick, cleaning, and maintaining a frequent form of convent service: the hostel for visitors or pilgrims. The tradition of holy women going on pilgrimage, begun in the early Church (and recorded by Egeria in her *Travels,* describing a journey to the Holy Land), was often viewed skeptically by male monastics concerned for the safety and intact chastity of consecrated women; yet it continued, either to Jerusalem or, when that was closed to Western pilgrims, to Rome or other shrines.[8]

Extremely important for the spiritual lives of the women discussed in this chapter was the monastic school that was typically a part of Benedictine and other cenobitic monastic houses. This school existed to educate the children and young women living in the convent, because the performance of the Opus Dei, like the Mass, required literacy; more so did the spiritual counseling and scriptural interpretation that went on in the women's monasteries. Thus along with the copying of manuscripts and teaching, women became scholars of theology and learned their Latin, sometimes to a high degree of erudition. Hilda of Whitby (614–680) is a case in point; a nun from the age of thirty-three, she became abbess of Whitby at forty-three and educated future monks and clerics of the English Church. She was also, according to Bede, a counselor to the royalty and nobility of England.

Lioba

Similar to Hilda of Whitby is another educated English nun, Lioba (700–780), of whom a biography and one letter survive. She was reputed to possess an encyclopedic education, at least in ecclesiastical matters, and was a mistress of Scripture, patristic literature, and early canons of the Church councils. A friend and counselor to Boniface, she left the abbey of Wimborne, England, at his request, in order to aid him in the conversion of the Saxons. The fact of their friendship provides a glimpse of the continuity between early Christian and medieval women's spirituality—that, as brides of Christ, they were free to be friends with male monastics in a way that would have been unusual for wives, as inferior members of a household, in relation to their husbands. In addition, Lioba's conception and birth resemble that of the early Christian virgin, Macrina; her mother realized in a dream while pregnant that she would bear an especially sacred child, and Lioba was consecrated to God at birth. Thus she was raised in a devout Christian family, in which it was expected from her childhood that she would become a nun.

In 748, having left England to join Boniface, Lioba became abbess of Tauberbischofsheim and corresponded with the monks of the important abbey of Fulda. Like other nuns of both early and medieval Christianity, Lioba understood herself as a *sponsa Christi*, "bride of Christ," but this did not deter Boniface from requesting that after his death her bones "should be placed next to his in the tomb, so that they who had served God during their lifetime with equal sincerity and zeal should await together the day of resurrection." Lioba's *Life* portrays her as an abbess who, because of her reputation and virtue, attracted the jealous attentions of the devil, who attacked her through her disciples. The *Life* reports that

> she was a woman of great virtue and was so strongly attached to the way of life she had vowed that she never gave thought to her native country or her relatives. She expended all her energies on the work she had undertaken in order to appear blameless before God and to become a pattern of perfection to those who obeyed her in word and action. She was ever on her guard not to teach others what she did not carry out herself. In her conduct there was no arrogance or pride. . . . In appearance she was angelic, in word pleasant, clear in mind, great in prudence, Catholic in faith, most patient in hope, universal in her charity. But though she was always cheerful, she never broke out into laughter through excessive charity. . . . [Abstemious as to food and drink, she was also zealous in acquiring knowledge.] She read with attention all the books of the Old and New Testaments and learned by heart all the commandments of God. To these she added . . . the writings of the church Fathers, the decrees of the Councils and the whole of ecclesiastical law. She observed great moderation in all her acts and arrangements and always kept the practical end in view.[9]

Despite the attractiveness of this portrait of an abbess, the reader is forced to accept the word of the biographer of Lioba and women like her until the beginning of the second millennium, when religious women from the Benedictine tradition or from the religious orders that were formed later in the High and late Middle Ages record in their own words the shape and details of their spiritual lives.

Hroswit of Gandersheim

Hroswit of Gandersheim (932–1000), a nun of the German Benedictine tradition, wrote religious poetry, prose, epics, and dramas. Working from the extensive library in her convent, her aim was to employ her wide knowledge of Scripture and patristic sources and the Latin classical tradition. The latter, with its habitual denigration of the capabilities of women (especially by Terence), she both imitated and opposed by showing how Christian women, particularly virgins, retained their chastity despite impending martyrdom, or how they conquered the passions of the flesh by means of the spirit. In the play *Abraham* (based on an early Syriac hagiography) Hroswit puts forward her own teaching of the redemptive power of divine love to reconcile the human longing for God with the passions that often cause women and men to stray from that longing; Maria, whom her uncle Abraham raises as a chaste and virtuous girl, is seduced by a monk and becomes a prostitute. Abraham, disguising himself as a potential client, is at last able to see her. She receives the teaching that we may readily conclude was Hroswit's own, put in Abraham's mouth: "Whoever despairs, thinking that God forbears to come to the aid of sinners, sins irremediably. Because just as the spark from a flintstone cannot set the sea on fire, so the bitter taste of our sins cannot likewise aspire to change the sweetness of divine goodwill."[10]

In addition to the typically Benedictine characteristics under discussion, one must note during the High Middle Ages the increasing devotion, particularly among women, to the Eucharist. Attachment to Christ present in the eucharistic bread and wine becomes more and more a central feature in the developing medieval piety, and from this eucharistic orientation there came a broad range of writings that extoll the tenderness and nurturance of God made manifest in the eucharistic manna that comes down from heaven. In fact, it was a woman, Juliana of Liège (1192–1258), who first proposed the thirteenth-century feast of Corpus Christi to specifically honor the eucharistic presence of Christ. Eucharistic visions and miracles multiplied in the High and late Middle Ages, and the increasing association of women with eucharistic activity, especially among

Cistercians and Dominicans, became a commonplace. Just as medieval women were the dispensers and regulators of food in the home, so too in the Church, women became the devotees of the heavenly food of the Eucharist and shaped much of both piety and practice for later centuries. (The practicum following this chapter discusses eucharistic devotion as it emerged from these medieval traditions.)

Visionary Women:
Hildegard of Bingen and Elisabeth of Schönau

By the twelfth century, women who received visions as part of their spiritual lives began to communicate them in writing to their followers as authoritative teaching. Two good examples of this development are Hildegard of Bingen (1098–1179) and Elisabeth of Schönau (1129–1165). Despite the Benedictine life these two nuns have in common with earlier medieval figures, their writings testify to a noticeable change in the religious life of women, even allowing for the difference between works by a woman and those about a woman. In these two figures we see certain features shared in common among women religious writers through Teresa of Avila in the sixteenth century.

1. A period of perceived or real humiliation in which the woman identifies with the suffering of Christ. Eventually, the experience of humiliation is replaced by one of exaltation at the end of progress in the religious life, or else the visionary is rewarded for her humiliation by private revelations.
2. An illness, sometimes arising out of strict self-discipline or as a result of a specific petition for illness, or from natural causes.
3. A sense of authority, based on the experience of suffering in the religious life *and* on status as abbess or teacher in the convent. This apprehension is often combined with either real erudition or a kind of wide-ranging examination of the truths of faith, or with religious experience apart from formal instruction. It is quite common for the authors to assert a harmony or identity between their own teaching and that of the Church.
4. A conviction of intimacy with God based on their particular, and female, appropriation of the sufferings of his Son, Christ.
5. Some message or counsel for a wider audience, whether confessor, community, or (as in the case of Catherine of Siena) the entire Church. Often these are messages of comfort or of urgent need for reform and are thought to be the purpose of the sufferings and revelations experienced by the women.

One of the earliest of these visionary women is also one of the most interesting and learned. Hildegard of Bingen, abbess of Tupertsberg, was granted visions from early childhood. Raised by her aunt, the hermitess Jutta, who resided in a cell on the Diessenberg, she was in 1116 received into the Benedictine community that gathered around Jutta. In 1136 she became abbess and from 1141 to 1151 dictated the *Scivias,* her most famous composition. She was known to Bernard of Clairvaux and to Pope Eugenius III, who in 1147 warily approved of her visions. In the interests of her convent she traveled around the Rhineland, eventually forming a daughter house. The twenty-six visions in the three books of the *Scivias,* many apocalyptic in content, gave her the status of a prophet, even if her predictions were to go unconfirmed. A naturalist and an astute theologian, she wrote treatises to explain the Athanasian Creed, the Gospels, and the Rule of St. Benedict. In addition, she wrote liturgical songs expressing her devotion to Christ, the Trinity, and the Virgin Mary.

The preface to the *Scivias* gives an account of Hildegard's recognition of her own authority to teach on a matter so daunting as the Trinity and other essential doctrines. Although she had since the age of fifteen "felt in [herself] in a wonderful way the power of the mysteries of sacred and wonderful visions,"[11] she divulged them to no one: "Till God wished His favors to be manifested, I repressed them in quiet silence." Apparently a deepening of this religious experience began in Hildegard's early middle age; at forty-two she experienced a mental light, as a result of which she suddenly "knew and understood the explanation of the Psalter, the Gospels, and other Catholic books of the Old and the New Testaments," although grammatical matters remained difficult for her. Finally, at forty-three, Hildegard was expressly commanded by a voice from heaven to communicate her visions just as she heard and saw "in celestial matters from above"; this was because of her simplicity and lack of learning. Hildegard was anxious to have her readers know that her visions were not delusions:

> I saw these visions not in dreams, nor sleeping, nor in frenzy, nor with the eyes of my body, neither did I hear them with my exterior ears, nor in hidden places did I perceive them, but watching them, and looking carefully in an innocent mind, with the eyes and ears of the interior man, in open places, did I perceive them according to the will of God.[12]

Predictably, Hildegard had to suffer from the visions; she represents her heavenly voice identifying her as "one whom I desired, and whom I sought out according to what pleased me in her wonderful gifts, beyond those of the ancients who saw many secrets in Me, but I humbled her to the dust lest she should be elated."

Hildegard's communication of the visions that she thought she was commanded to write down depended on two friends. The first was the monk Volmar, who acted as her amanuensis. His qualifications were his devotion to God and his religious obedience; as the voice said, he was "someone in My love who would run in the way of salvation." Volmar made possible the *Scivias;* "holding fast to him, she labored together with him in all these matters, in the high and earnest endeavor that My hidden miracles should be revealed." Volmar, too, is required to show humility in the endeavor: He "did not exalt himself above her, but yielded to her with many sighs in the height of that humility which he obtained, and in the intention of a good will."

It required an illness to provide the final impetus for Hildegarde to write: She recalls, "[I] refused for a long time the duty of writing, not in obstinacy but in humility, until I fell on a bed of sickness, cast down by the scourge of God, until at length I was compelled to write by many infirmities."[13] Another nun seems to have persuaded her to write the revelations she received, and after some further suffering she took ten years to record her visions. These are remarkable for their combination of rather traditional doctrine with visionary and prophetic illustrations drawn from Scripture, and for their naturalistic metaphors (e.g., the interrelationships of the persons of the Trinity). Here Hildegard reveals herself the beneficiary not only of the voice from Heaven but also of the inspiration of similarly original patristic works as well, and like other medieval writers, she was also able to devote some of her poetic gifts to songs in honor of the Virgin. One of the simplest of these songs describes the effects of the Divine in the world:

> Love overflows into all things,
> From out of the depths to above the highest stars.[14]

This kind of dictation, and the visions behind them, seem to have given Hildegard an authority wider than that due her as a Benedictine abbess; hence she is one of the first to become a regional or international and nonclerical female teacher in the Church.

Elisabeth of Schönau was, like Hildegard, a member of a convent—in this case a double monastery, and it was here she received her visions from 1152–1160, having in 1157 become the magistra of nuns. Her brother Eckbert was her scribe and wrote down the vision she received as a sequel to extreme illness. Elisabeth seems to have been preoccupied with the priestly role (a role the abbess Gertrude the Great of Helfta would also appropriate for herself, at least symbolically), for she received visions, apparently representing the Eucharist, of the Virgin at an altar in priestly vestments, and she regarded herself as a successor to the Hebrew prophetesses Deborah, Jael, and Judith.

Elisabeth was also more conscious, or more expressive, than Hildegard about the difference between the teaching she received in her visions and that which was put forward by clerics:

> Because in these times the Lord deigns to show His mercy most gloriously in the weak sex, such men [who mutter against God] are offended and led into sin. But why do they not remember that something similar happened in the days of the fathers? While the men were given over to sluggishness, holy women were filled with the spirit of God, that they might prophesy, govern God's people forcefully, and indeed triumph gloriously over the foes of Israel.[15]

Unlike Hildegard, Elisabeth not only heard a celestial voice but was also accompanied regularly by an angelic guide to pleasant spots where she saw her visions. These visions were always intended for the instruction of those in her care. For instance, in one vision Elisabeth was transported immediately after the reading of the Gospel on John the Baptist, and through her the double monastery to which she belonged was rebuked: "Persuade them of this, that through those things that the Lord has worked in you, they may be warned and they may zealously attempt to correct themselves in all things."[16] The sisters responded by "doing bodily penance" and thus seemed to have trusted Elisabeth's revelations.[17] Severe physical illnesses precede or accompany her experiences, but Elisabeth regards them as necessary because of the pedagogic function of her visions. On one occasion the heavenly voice explained that "these visions and many others you saw in these wicked times, [are] for no other reason but because of the unbelief of many, and to confirm the faith. . . . It is proper and necessary to reveal such visions, which come opportunely to confirm the faith of Christendom."[18]

An interesting doctrinal development occurred through the visions of Elisabeth; this was the revelation to her in a vision that the Virgin Mary was assumed into the heaven in a bodily as well as in a spiritual way. Elisabeth was accustomed to receiving visits from the Virgin, and on one occasion she asked for "certain information about whether you were assumed into the heavens. . . . I was asking about this because, as they say, this is not set forth clearly in the books of the fathers." Elisabeth had to wait a year for her answer then finally learned of the bodily assumption of Mary from Mary herself. But she was instructed to keep the information secret; she had already concluded that making the vision public would lead to accusation of inventing new doctrines. Mary told her that she had received the revelation "so that my praises may be magnified among those who love me specially." Such caution in Elisabeth is, it would seem, a reflection not only of her instructions in the context of her ecstatic visions but also of her prudence as the magistra of her convent; she knew the difference between divine rebuke, delivered through a chosen servant like herself for the good of the community, and the unrest that could be caused by the introduction of a new doctrine. Again, such an attitude may have been shaped by her Benedictine context.[19]

However, the remainder of the Middle Ages would see a proliferation of new doctrines, some of which attracted numerous women followers, such as the adepts of the Cathari or the nuns who were devotees of Meister Eckhart. Such groups are, however, outside the limited scope of this essay, even though their eventual condemnation doubtless contributed to the doctrinal caution of a Julian of Norwich or a Catherine of Siena. These last two authors show the connection of women's spirituality in the late medieval period to that of earlier eras,. and an examination of their major works makes a fitting conclusion to this chapter.

Catherine of Siena

As a mystic and reformer, a practitioner first of the life of solitude and then of a public life of devotion to the well-being of the Church, Catherine represents a general movement in late-medieval Western piety from the model of monastic withdrawal to that of the religious order. In the latter, the impulse for conversion of souls and reform of the Church led to a modification of the Benedictine model of religious life and an adoption of various organizations allowing for an active apostolate. The primary examples of this are, of course, the Dominican and Franciscan orders, but various other groups, including groups of pious lay people, followed the same pattern. Catherine of Siena was a member of one of these groups, the Dominican tertiaries.

According to the testimony of her biographers, Raymond of Capua and Tommaso de Siena (Caffarini), Catherine's religious life developed in a series of clear stages, beginning from early youth. Born in

1347, the youngest of a large Sienese family, she vowed at the age of seven to remain a virgin; at fifteen, resisting marriage, she cut off her hair; at eighteen she entered the Dominican tertiaries—a "third" order for laity who, though active in the world, desire to follow the example of St. Dominic. In this final action Catherine accomplished two things: She became a part of a lay movement reflecting the religious revival of the cities of Italy in the fourteenth century, and she entered into a life of more profound devotion. A room in her family's house became her cell (from 1363–1368), and until she was twenty-one she practiced solitude and silence punctuated only by attendance at Mass at the nearby Church of St. Dominic. Here began and flourished her devotion to the Eucharist, already a marked feature of later medieval piety, which continued to the end of her life.

During her period of solitude, Catherine experienced conversation with Christ and received the insight that guided her activity once she had left the cell. This conversation culminated in her "mystic espousal" to Christ, an identification with the Lord and his passion that would give distinctive shape to her interior life and to her anxious devotion to the Church, of whose peril she was acutely aware.

After Catherine's period of solitude, she began her work in public, laboring as a nurse and attendant to the poor of Siena while retreating for silent contemplation and fasting for long periods. Catherine, who seems always to have had an attractive personality, drew to herself a group of loyal and enthusiastic disciples with whom she conversed in her room on matters of theology, exegesis, and religious experience. She had thus far been guided by two confessors, and, in a deepening of her religious life, she continued to experience intimate conversation with God. This period culminated in 1370 with her "mystical death" of four hours' duration, in which she received visions of hell, purgatory, and heaven and was instructed by God to enter the world more fully.

The last ten years of her life Catherine spent in activities that might best be termed "apostolic." She undertook a public mission to a Church deeply divided by the Avignon papacy and the Great Schism. It was a Church marred, she realized, with disobedience and sin in all its ranks. From this period date Catherine's almost four hundred letters both to ecclesiastical and public dignitaries and to private citizens or religious; during this time her periods of contemplation and ascetic practices coexisted simultaneously with her extensive travels to promote, for example, the reunification of the papacy, a new crusade to the Holy Land, or the spiritual revival of the countryside around Siena. In 1375 Catherine received the stigmata, confirmation of her identification with the passion of Christ, but she asked that these marks of suffering not be made visible during her lifetime. In the summer of 1378 she dictated the *Dialogue,* her only spiritual work barring a collection of prayers. Catherine died in 1380; she spent the last two years of her life in Rome at work for the end of the schism and living with a group of mendicant men and women. In 1380 she asked Christ to allow her to suffer for the sins of the world and that her body be sacrificed for the unity of the Church. Her prayers were answered, and from January 1380 until the spring she became progressively weaker in body, although her correspondence continued unabated. She consumed only the eucharistic Host as she continued to pray and work from her sickbed.

The *Dialogue* begins with a prologue that characterizes Catherine's spiritual orientation: "A soul rises up," she stated of herself,

> restless with tremendous desire for God's honor and the salvation of souls. She has for some time exercised herself in virtue and has become accustomed to dwelling in the cell of self-knowledge in order to know better God's goodness toward her, since upon knowledge follows love. And loving she seeks to pursue truth and clothe herself in it.[20]

For Catherine, the love of God, possible only through the mediation of Christ, issues in the soul's increased desire for him, and her longing that other souls follow the same path. Furthermore, love follows knowledge and requires truth in order to guard against deception and temptation.

The *Dialogue* may be seen both as a record of Catherine's journey along the path of knowledge and love and as a kind of instruction for others—those souls in need of salvation who may, because of God's providence, follow the same course. The goal of the journey is perfection of the human being, but this may happen only in union with God, which Catherine describes at the end of the book as a kind of self-understanding. Looking into the sea of the Godhead, the soul finds a mirror:

> This water is a mirror in which you, eternal Trinity, grant me knowledge; for when I look into this mirror, holding it in the hand of love, it shows me myself, as your creation, in you and you in me through the union you have brought about of the Godhead with our humanity. This light shows you to me, and in this light I know you, highest and infinite Good.[21]

Between the prologue and the conclusion, however, Catherine describes (in ten sections) a way that leads through various difficulties until it arrives at the stage of obedience. Each section is marked by a petition to God, a response from God, and a thanksgiving to him; as such, each one gives a kind of summary of the life of prayer for the Christian who is being formed in the particular virtues that Catherine considered necessary in the way of perfection.

The content of Catherine's initial petitions, not surprisingly, reflect the general direction of her life and religious devotion. She asked for divine providence in general, and specifically for a particular soul (whose identity still remains unclear).

Following the prologue, Catherine records the answers she received from God on the way of perfection; on a further dialogue with God; on the spiritual journey as the bridge to salvation; on the tears that accompany the progress of the soul; on the truth that must be received on the way to salvation; on the mystic body of holy Church; on divine providence; and on obedience. A conclusion contains God's summary of their conversation and a hymn to the Trinity, which Catherine ends with the memorable sentence: "Clothe, clothe me with yourself, eternal Truth, so that I may run the course of this mortal life in true obedience and in the light of most holy faith. With that light I sense my soul once again becoming drunk! Thanks be to God! Amen."[22]

Although the *Dialogue's* complexity of structure, language, and metaphor almost defies summary, it should be noted that a constant theme within it is the Christ who is Catherine's, and the world's, bridge to God. However, Christ is not only the incarnate Word of God for Catherine; perhaps the primary experience of Christ that she had, and that marks the *Dialogue,* is that of Christ as *food.* Following Catherine's own devotion to the Eucharist, her love for the Church—and perception of God's anger over its disobedience—follows on her appreciation of Christ's self-sacrifice on its behalf. Linked with this is her emphasis upon the passion of Christ, who suffers at the hands of the Church, as well as for it. Again, Catherine identified with Christ crucified and understood her own suffering to be joined with that of Christ in atonement for human sin. Finally, the metaphor of Christ as Bridge from earth to heaven is founded on the doctrine, which Catherine strongly emphasizes, of Christ's human and divine natures; the union between these natures makes possible the reformation of human creatures through obedience, ending finally in perfection.

Julian of Norwich

One of the last female spiritual authors of the medieval period, Julian of Norwich is also one of the most arresting. She combined ancient traditions of asceticism—"anchoritism" or a life of solitary withdrawal, mortification, and spiritual guidance—with features more common to her late-medieval English setting, such as a deep mysticism and identification with Christ and his human suffering. As with Catherine, the passion became her own religious expression as well as the object of her devotion. Like Catherine, she pursued the critical theological questions that arose from her own meditation, but she remained a hermitess and was less concerned to arouse the Church to reform than to offer comfort to those tempted to despair of God's love and mercy.

The details of Julian's life are scanty. Born in about 1342, she spent a considerable portion of her life in an anchorhold, probably in a cell beside the Church of St. Julian in Norwich. She died after 1416. Julian may have been educated in a religious community, where she would have become familiar with the Latin authors of the Western contemplative tradition, but her spiritual writings were composed in Middle English, in which she was an accomplished stylist.

The one document left by Julian, *The Showings* or *Revelations of Divine Love*, exists in two forms, whose composition is separated by twenty years. The first, the "Short Text," was composed soon after she received the revelations in May 1373. The "Long Text," dating from 1393, resulted from Julian's continued meditation upon her religious experience and represents her mature spiritual teaching based on the sixteen revelations she received during an ecstatic state. The latter text is the basis for the following discussion of Julian's spiritual teaching.

The revelations to Julian, which she regarded as corporeal visions, became a vehicle for communicating a teaching that she came to understand over time, namely, the doctrine of divine love, which is the substratum of all human existence but which is forgotten by those who think that evil has a real, concrete existence. In her efforts to share this teaching, Julian was willing to engage in both personal and speculative language—for instance, the doctrine of the "godly will" in the predestined, which preserves from mortal sin and real evil and the understanding of God as "our Mother." However, Julian anchored her teaching (which she thought was "shown by our saviour Jesus Christ for our endless comfort and solace") in tradition and Scripture, as one of the book's final passages makes clear:

> I pray almighty God that this book may not come except into the hands of those who wish to be his faithful lovers, and those who will submit themselves to the faith of Holy Church and obey the wholesome understanding and teaching of men who are of virtuous life, settled age and profound learning; for this revelation is exalted divinity and wisdom, and therefore it cannot remain with him who is a slave to sin and

to the devil. And beware that you do not accept one thing which is according to your pleasure and liking, and reject another, for that is the disposition of heretics. But accept it all together, and understand it truly; it all agrees with Holy Scripture, and is founded upon it, and Jesus, our true love and light and truth, will show this to all pure souls who meekly and perseveringly ask this wisdom from him.[23]

Julian appears, in the text of *The Showings,* as a humble woman and, at the same time, an experienced counselor who understood the particular hunger of the souls to whom she listened. She cautions that "there are many who never had revelations or visions, but only the common teaching of Holy Church, who love God better than I,"[24] but she understands that she has a particular role to fulfill as one who has received a special kind of knowledge. "God wants us always to be strong in our love, and peaceful and restful as he is towards us, and he wants us to be, for ourselves and our fellow Christians, what he is for us."[25]

As did Catherine of Siena, Julian focused upon the passion of Christ as the medium of God's love for us, and her visions, given in response to a set of petitions, revealed to her the most intimate details of Christ's physical suffering; these visions grew in intensity as she herself experienced an acute physical illness for which she had asked, apparently to promote the bond between herself and Christ.

Julian tells her readers at the beginning of the Long Text that she had made three requests to God. Two were conditional, depending upon God's acceptance of them, and one was unconditional; Julian apparently felt within her rights to ask it. The first petition was for a recollection of the passion; the second was for a severe bodily sickness. The third petition was for three wounds ("by the grace of God and the teaching of Holy Church"): "true contrition, loving compassion, longing with my will for God."[26]

God granted Julian's first two requests by granting sixteen visions, as follows: the crowning with thorns, including the teaching of the Trinity, the Incarnation, and the union of God and man's soul; the "discoloration of his face"; the rule of God over creation; the "scourging of his tender body"; the conquest of the devil by Christ; the "thanks with which our Lord God rewards all his blessed servants in heaven"; the "frequent experiences of well-being and woe"; the last sufferings and death of Christ; the delight of the Trinity in Christ's passion; the heart of Jesus "split in two for love"; a showing of Christ's mother; that "our Lord is all sovereign life"; that God wishes men to appreciate his work of creation and redemption, and the adherence to "the faith and truth of Holy Church"; that "our Lord God is the foundation of our beseeching"; that "we shall be taken from all our pain and . . . woe"; and, finally, the indwelling of the Trinity in the human soul "in Jesus Christ," which saves and preserves it, and protects it against the enemy, the devil.[27]

It can be seen that the order of the visions or "showings" reflect the alternation of joy and woe, which Julian thought were the two poles of human life. The visions of the passion, with their painfully realistic description by Julian, are linked with Julian's own insight into God's redemptive activity on our behalf. The knowledge of the Trinity as creative Godhead, dwelling in our souls "in Christ Jesus our Creator," undergirds Julian's emphasis on the worthiness of the created world and its eventual healing. Her eschatology is a confident one of eventual restoration, reflected in the well-known text, "Sin is necessary, but all will be well, and all will be well, and every kind of thing will be well," which sentence Julian received from Jesus himself.[28]

Thus for Julian, human suffering is linked to the suffering of Jesus. Far from making light of the passion, she concentrates upon its effects in Jesus and in her own, voluntary imitation of it. These are real enough; in the eighth revelation, for instance, Julian gives a painful and painstaking description of her vision of the passion, in which she actually saw death seize the body of Christ.[29] Likewise, in the course of her revelations she experienced morbidity and was apparently so near death that she received the last rites. In the midst of this double passion, Jesus' and her own, Julian learned that the "Passion is the overcoming of the fiend," on account of which "we may laugh."[30] The suffering of Christ was changed to joy, just as human suffering will give way to that state.

· Julian seems to have learned through her visions and suffering that Christians who long for God must shift their attention away from self, a fixation that could easily lead to despair and entrapment by the devil, to God. This she took as an insight applicable to all human life—to concentrate upon the joy of the Trinity and understand human suffering as a prologue to this joy. In this context, Julian taught that sin, real enough for those who did not seek Christ, was relative for those being saved:

> And God showed that sin will be no shame, but honor to man, for just as there is indeed a corresponding pain for pains, the more grievous are the sins, so will they be rewarded with various joys in heaven to reward the victories over them, to the degree in which the sin may have been painful and sorrowful to the soul on earth. For the soul which will come to heaven is so precious to God, and its place there so honorable, that God's goodness never suffers the soul to sin finally which will come there.[31]

This view of sin, conditioned by the heavenly destiny of the soul who recognizes its woe and seeks God, is reminiscent of Christian Neoplatonism, exemplified by Origen and the Cappadocian theologians; sin and the devil himself are a reality, but a negative one. Both are "deprivations of the good," having no existence of their own. In the life of the Christian, they are replaced by a slow but progressive education in the friendship with God:

> All our endless friendship, our place, our life and our being are in God. For that same endless goodness which protects us when we sin so that we do not perish, that same endless goodness constantly draws us into a peace, opposing our wrath and our perverse falling. . . . For we cannot be blessedly saved until we are truly in peace and in love, for that is our salvation.[32]

This conditional, or eschatological, view of sin and the goodness of God seems to have provided Julian with the inclination to use the language of motherhood when discussing the Trinity (although this terminology had already been used by William of St. Thierry and among the Benedictine nuns of Helfta). On the other hand, Julian's application of this term to Christ, whose role she specifically states that she has taken upon herself, may be a reflection of her own status as spiritual "mother." Of the "mother" in the Trinity, she says,

> I saw and understood that the high might of the Trinity is our Father, and the deep wisdom of the Trinity is our Mother, and the great love of the Trinity is our Lord. . . . And furthermore I saw that the second person, who is our Mother, substantially the same beloved person, has now become our mother sensually. . . . The second person of the Trinity is our Mother in nature in our substantial creation, in whom we are founded and rooted, and he is our Mother of mercy in taking our sensuality. And so our Mother is working on us in various ways, in whom our parts are kept undivided; for in our Mother Christ we profit and increase and in mercy he reforms and restores us, and by the power of his Passion, his death and his Resurrection he unites us to our substance [i.e., to our divine nature].[33]

Julian's final revelation she regarded as a confirmation of the preceding fifteen; in it she was tempted by a frightening encounter with a palpable devil, after which she received a vision of her own soul, in which Jesus dwelt. This was the final replacement of woe by joy and the occasion for a complete understanding of the conquest of illness and fear by God's grace, in which those two failings are replaced by the longing for him that he stirs up in the soul.

Julian and Catherine, both professedly loyal to the teaching of the

Church, exemplify the different ways in which that doctrine could be understood and applied in the difficult situation of the late-medieval Church. Both lived lives of ascesis and prayer, traditional for holy women since the early Church, and both understood themselves to be teachers by virtue of their training, their suffering, and their conversation with God. The difference in emphasis between the *Dialogue* and *The Showings* derives from the differing temperaments of the authors and from their distinct roles—Catherine's as reformer, at work in the world for the revival of the church, and Julian's as anchoress and guide of souls. Each one, however, places Christ at the center of her life and teaching, and each understands herself, not without cause, as an *alter Christus*.

Notes

1. See E. A. Clark, *Ascetic Piety and Women's Faith* (Lewiston, N.Y.: Edwin Mellen Press, 1986), for studies of the roles of women in the early Church; also *Women in the Early Church* (Wilmington, Del.: Michael Glazier, 1983).
2. See Bernadette Brooten, *Women's Leadership in the Ancient Synagogue* (Chico, Calif.: Scholars Press, 1985).
3. See Stephen L. Davies, *Revolt of the Widows: The Social World of the Apocryphal Acts* (Carbondale, Ill.: Southern Illinois University Press, 1980), for a discussion of the aspirations and social situations implied in the apocryphal literature concerning women.
4. See Gregory of Nyssa, *Life of Macrina*, trans. W. Lowther Clarke (London: SPCK, 1916).
5. For a translation and brief study of the work, see S. Brock and S. Harvey, eds., *Holy Women of the Syrian Orient* (Berkeley: University of California Press, 1987).
6. Tertullian, *On the Soul* 9, in Ante-Nicene Library, vol. 15, trans. P. Holmes (Edinburgh, 1899), pp. 410-541.
7. See J. A. Robinson, *The Passion of St. Perpetua* (Texts and Studies, 1, 2) (Cambridge: Cambridge University Press, 1891).
8. The most famous of nun-pilgrims in antiquity is Egeria, a Spanish nun who traveled to the Holy Land and the Christian Orient in the late fourth century. See J. Wilkinson, trans., *Egeria's Travels* (Jerusalem: Ariel; Warminster, England: Aris & Phillips, 1971 and 1978). See also Gregory of Nyssa, *Letter* 2, for an attempt to dissuade Christian women from traveling to the holy places of Palestine.
9. *Life of Lioba*, para. 10.
10. Hroswit, *Abraham* 6.
11. Hildegard, *Scivias*, Preface.
12. Ibid.
13. Ibid.
14. Hildegard, *Antiphons* 16, from Barbara L. Grant, "Hildegard of Bingen: Liturgical Songs," in *Medieval Women's Visionary Literature*, ed. Elizabeth Avilda Petroff (New York: Oxford University Press, 1986), pp. 157-58.
15. Elisabeth of Schönau, *Visions* 11.1.
16. Ibid., 11.6.
17. Ibid., 11.7.
18. Ibid., 11.8.
19. The account is in *Visions* 11.20.
20. Catherine of Siena, *Dialogue*, Prologue (1).

21. Ibid., Conclusion (167).
22. Ibid.
23. Julian of Norwich, *Showings,* Long Text, chap. 86, trans. and ed. Edmund Colledge and James Walsh (New York: Paulist Press, 1978).
24. Ibid., chap. 9.
25. Ibid., Short Text, chap. 25.
26. Ibid., Long Text, chap. 2.
27. Ibid., chap. 1.
28. For example, chap. 27 (thirteenth showing).
29. Ibid., chap. 16.
30. Ibid., chap. 13 (fifth showing).
31. Ibid., chap. 38.
32. Ibid., chap. 61.
33. Ibid., chap. 58.

Bibliography

Primary Sources

Catherine of Siena. *The Dialogue.* Translated and with an introduction by Suzanne Noffke. New York: Paulist Press, 1980.
Gertrude of Helfta. *The Life and Revelations.* Westminster, Md.: Newman Press, 1949.
_____. *The Exercises of Saint Gertrude.* By a Benedictine nun of Regina Laudis. Westminster, Md.: Newman Press, 1956.
Hadewijch. *The Complete Works.* Translated and with an introduction by Columba Hart. New York: Paulist Press, 1980.
Hroswitha of Gandersheim. *The Plays.* Translated by Larissa Bonfante. New York: New York University Press, 1979.
Julian of Norwich. *Showings.* Edited and translated by Edmund Colledge and James Walsh. New York: Paulist Press, 1978.
Kempe, Marjory. *The Book.* Edited by Sanford B. Meech and Hope Emily Allen. London: Early English Text Society, 1940.

Secondary Sources

Atkinson, Clarissa W. *Mystic and Pilgrim: The Book and the World of Margery Kempe.* Ithaca, N.Y.: Cornell University Press, 1983.
Baker, Derek, ed. *Medieval Women, Dedicated and Presented to Professor Rosalind M. T. Hill.* Oxford: Basil Blackwell, 1978.
Bolton, Brenda. "Mulieres sanctae." In *Sanctity and Secularity: The Church and the World.* Edited by Derek Baker. Oxford: Basil Blackwell, 1973.
Bolton, Brenda. *Women in Medieval Society.* Philadelphia: University of Pennsylvania Press, 1976.
Bouyer, Louis; Leclercq, Jean; and Vandenbroucke, Francois. *The Spirituality* of the Middle Ages. London: Burns & Oates, 1968.
Bradley, Ritamary. "Julian of Norwich: Writer and Mystic." In *An Introduction to the Medieval Mystics of Europe,* edited by Paul Szarmach. Albany, N.Y.: SUNY Press, 1984.

Bynum, Caroline W. *Jesus as Mother: Studies in the Spirituality of the High Middle Ages.* Berkeley: University of California Press, 1982.

Clarke, E. A. *Ascetic Piety and Women's Faith: Essays on Late Ancient Christianity.* Lewiston, N.Y.: Edwin Mellen Press, 1986.

Eckenstein, Lina. *Women Under Monasticism: Chapters on Saint-Lore and Convent Life between* A.D. *500 and* A.D. *1500.* Cambridge: Cambridge University Press, 1896. Rev. ed., New York: Cambridge University Press, 1963.

Goodich, Michael. "Contours of Female Piety in Later Medieval Hagiography." *Church History* 50 (1981): 429-37.

Grant, Barbara L. "An Interview with the Sybil of the Rhine: Hildegard von Bingen (1098–1179)." *Heresies* 3, no. 2 (1980).

Heine, Susanne. *Women in Early Christianity: A Reappraisal.* Translated by John Bowden. Minneapolis: Augsburg Press, 1988.

Leclercq, Jean. "The Spirituality of Medieval Feminine Monasticism." In *The Continuing Quest for God,* edited by William Skudlarek. Collegeville, Minn.: Liturgical Press, 1982.

McDonnell, Ernest M. *The Beguines and Beghards in Medieval Culture.* New Brunswick, N.J.: Rutgers University Press, 1954.

Morewedge, Rosemarie Thee, ed. *The Role of Woman in the Middle Ages.* Albany, N.Y.: SUNY Press, 1975.

Petroff, Elizabeth Avilda, ed. *Medieval Women's Visionary Literature.* New York: Oxford University Press, 1976.

Radcliff-Umstead, Douglass, ed. *The Roles and Images of Women in the Middle Ages and Renaissance.* Pittsburgh: Center for Medieval and Renaissance Studies, 1978.

Reuther, Rosemary, and McLaughlin, Eleanor, eds. *Women of Spirit: Female Leadership in the Jewish and Christian Traditions.* New York: Simon & Schuster, 1979.

Warren, Ann K. *Anchorites and Their Patrons in Medieval England.* Berkeley: University of California Press, 1986.

The Eucharist and the Continual Remembrance of God

GABRIEL O'DONNELL, O.P.,
AND ROBIN MAAS

Do this in remembrance of me.

—LUKE 22:19

All of us want to be remembered. There are special times of the year—birthdays, anniversaries, and family holidays—when it is crucial for us to be remembered. To be forgotten at such times is to be excluded in a particularly painful way. When our presence is not considered essential to a gathering or event, in a certain sense we disappear. It is as if we had never been.

Regularly celebrated family rituals, photo albums, home movies, and scrapbooks make it possible for us to remember the dead. Our ancestors, so long as they are remembered, can continue to influence us by conferring a name, a history, an *identity* on us, and each time we identify ourselves by means of a particular name, history, or ethnic affiliation, we are, whether we realize it or not, invoking our ancestors' presence among us. We are, in effect, bringing them back to life.

The ancient Hebrews attached great significance to this essential and very human kind of "resurrection." Since they did not believe in a life after death, their only hope for immortality was to be remembered by their progeny or, if they had the great misfortune to be childless, by the larger community through some form of lasting memorial, the most important of which was a righteous reputation: a "good name." No worse fate could befall a person than to have his name blotted out—his line destroyed, his life on earth forgotten. This was the ultimate form of personal annihilation.

While individual Israelites earnestly desired to be remembered by their offspring, the nation itself sought unceasingly to be remembered

419

by God. Israel existed only because God mercifully remembered her: first, while she languished in Egypt, then at the Red Sea with Pharaoh's army bearing down on her, and finally in the wilderness when, after forty years of aimless wandering, God led her rejoicing into the Promised Land. This collective memory of deliverance alternately sustained and haunted God's chosen people. It formed—and still forms—the focus and framework of all her prayers, her ritual remembering. Because God remembers their name, the Jews persist. In remembering God, the Jews are reminding themselves of who they are.

Christian Remembering: The Prayer of Pure Praise

The issue of forgetting and remembering God is one that has long occupied Christian men and women. The easy way in which even the most devout person can pass through minutes, hours, and days without thinking about God is a commonplace observation among saints and spiritual writers. For them, being forgetful of God, author of all life and the center of our existence, is seen to cause a serious deprivation, for we are always richer, stronger, more faithful to our true identity when we are living in the conscious awareness of God. God, who is always present to us, offers us a most intimate and reliable friendship. But as is the case with all close relationships, this one also requires *mutual* remembrance, attention, and love. From this point of view it behooves us to remember God, to depend and call upon divine grace and assistance for our personal needs and those of our fellow pilgrims. Just as our lives are a mixture of sorrow and joy, victory and defeat, our remembrance of God necessarily includes prayers of confession and petition, thanksgiving and intercession.

There is yet another, "doxological" motive for the continual remembrance of God—what we might call the prayer of "pure praise." We have been speaking of God's power and goodness in relationship to our own lives and needs, but there is the prior and, in the end, more important need to praise and worship God not for any utilitarian reason but simply because God *is*. The reality that the One we worship is God, through whom all else exists, rightfully requires an unquestioning response of thanksgiving and praise on our part. This act of pure praise is the foundation for the continual remembrance of God that both ancients and moderns have striven to realize.

The daily remembrance of God from moment to moment, however, is not simply the triggering of our personal memories. In the Christian context, our remembrance of God is an extension of the great *anamnesis,* or remembrance of the Sunday Eucharist, into every day of the week, into each moment of every day. *Anamnesis,* the Greek word for "remembrance," designates the action of the community gathered in faith to recall the passion, death, and resurrection of Christ—God's great Passover—and in so doing, to make present the mystery of our deliverance through the words and gestures of the eucharistic celebration. In the Eucharist the Christian community, priest and people, gathers to remember and give thanks for what God has done for us in Christ and for what Christ has done for us in the mystery of his cross and resurrection. The community meets Christ, participates in his sacrifice of himself to the Father, and receives the gift of his body and blood under the visible forms of bread and wine. The eucharistic remembrance is the fulfillment of the Lord's own command, "Do this in memory of me."

It is this anamnetic activity or "remembering" that the great German theologian Karl Rahner has called the primary action of the Church.[1] In remembering, the Church acknowledges the *mirabilia dei*—the wonders God has worked in creation, in salvation history, and (wonder of wonders!) in the Incarnation. In remembering Jesus Christ, the Word made flesh, we Christians are given a name, a history, an identity. In this sense, the Church *becomes* the Church precisely at the moment of remembrance, acknowledgement, and thanksgiving. St. Augustine long ago expressed the precise identification of the eucharistic with the ecclesial body of Christ: "Receiving the body of Christ, the faithful say 'Amen' to indicate that they believe this is indeed what we are."[2]

It is because of this connection that we can never speak of remembrance in worship as a simple jogging of the memory. *Anamnesis,* or the liturgical memorial, always indicates that action of the Christian Church that gathers all of time—past, present, and future—and offers it to God in virtue of the once-for-all event of the Paschal Mystery, which transcends the categories of time and space. In the eucharistic memorial we who live in the present recall the past and look to the future: "Christ has died, Christ is risen, Christ will come again." In this way the Eucharist becomes the declaration that all time is holy, not by changing it and making it other than it is, but rather by admitting it to be what it is already: *God's* time, God's reign, and, in the light of the Paschal Mystery, *the time of salvation.* As the weekly remembrance of the Christ event, the Sunday Eucharist is the acknowledgement or proclamation that all of time is now of the kingdom of God.

The Eucharist does not, therefore, rescue history or time itself from the alien world of the secular but declares that time is *already* God's. It is the living out of the mystery of Christ from moment to moment. Thus the Eucharist is a *berakah,* a formal blessing, as in Judaism, over this particular moment of time—an offering that is at once thanksgiving and acknowledgement. Significantly, the impulse to remember God and his work in Christ could not be contained within the limits of the weekly Eucharist. Very early in the life of the Church this activity overflowed into the Prayer of the Hours. Each day at fixed times Christians still pause to offer praise and adoration to God and to remember the Lord as present in the midst of human existence, saving us and calling us to a new and abundant life.

Food for the Journey

The very structure of the eucharistic rite embodies this theological vision of perpetual praise. In all traditions the narrative of the event of the Lord's Supper is the central focus of the eucharistic rite, but that is never its conclusion. There must be a sending forth, a dismissal, an imperative to become the Body of Christ for the world in which we live and where we must preach the good news and make disciples of all nations.

As Christians, our is a heritage rich in the theology of the Eucharist and the Church as the Body of Christ. Each new age has added insights and clarifications and has expressed its eucharistic theology in new ways. For the Fathers of the Church the Eucharist had, as its primary meaning, the unity of the Church. "Just as the bread broken was first scattered on the hills, then was gathered and became one, so let your Church be gathered from the ends of the earth into your kingdom."[3]

Outside of the celebration itself, the eucharistic species, the consecrated bread and wine, were reserved by the ministers for the purpose of *viaticum* ("traveling money" or "supplies"), to be given to the dying so that the reception of the body and blood of Christ might strengthen them on their last journey from this life into the next. (For practical reasons, it was ordinarily only the eucharistic bread that was reserved.) During the Middle Ages a real transformation took place as Christians became more conscious of the presence of Christ, not only in the celebration of the Eucharist but also in the eucharistic elements of bread and wine.

Because of long debates about the nature of this presence as real, physical, or symbolic, the explanation called "transubstantiation" was developed and became widespread in the Western Church prior to the Reformation. This theological explanation teaches that while they remain the same in outward appearances, the bread and wine used at the Eucharist are changed in substance. Through the words of the priest spoken over these elements, they become the actual body and blood of Christ, while retaining the outward marks of ordinary bread and wine. The eucharistic controversies of the tenth and eleventh centuries and the working out of a detailed explanation of how Christ was truly present, "body, blood, soul, and divinity," under the appearances of bread and wine facilitated a shift in emphasis from understanding the Eucharist as an action of the whole people of God to the celebration as a means to "receive" the eucharistic bread, or the Blessed Sacrament as the species came to be called. This focus on the presence of Christ in the Blessed Sacrament encouraged the practice, already begun, of keeping the species reserved in a public place in the church, even on the main altar.[4] In addition to the ancient reason for reservation, *viaticum* for the dying, there was now a new motive, to reverence the presence of Christ in the eucharistic bread and wine.

The presence of Christ in the reserved sacrament was signaled by the sanctuary lamp, a light kept burning perpetually near the place of reservation. The cult of eucharistic devotion outside of Mass developed quickly and took a variety of forms such as prayer "in the presence of the Blessed Sacrament" and vocal prayers addressed to Christ present in the reserved sacrament. So emphasized was the physical, material presence of Christ in the eucharistic bread or "Host" that *seeing* the Eucharist became as important as receiving it. This need to "see" resulted in the practice of elevating the Host after the institution narrative and in "exposition" of the Blessed Sacrament in a monstrance, a holder for the host that visually displayed the eucharistic bread. Eucharistic processions in which the Blessed Sacrament was carried about the church or through the city streets, with periodic blessings with the monstrance (Benediction) along the way, developed as an expression of devotion to the reserved sacrament.[5] These developments in eucharistic devotion gave rise, in turn, to new hymn texts, prayers of devotion, and eventually to the establishment of a liturgical feast, Corpus Christi, to celebrate Christ's presence in the Eucharist.[6]

Such developments in eucharistic devotion became the extension of the great Sunday celebration of "remembering God" into the days of the week and the hours of the day. In the High Middle Ages it became increasingly common to celebrate Mass on each day of the week and not only on Sundays. By the end of the medieval period, this was standard practice even in parish churches, where the devout were able to attend the celebration of the Eucharist at the beginning of each day. Just as *viaticum* fortified one for the journey into death, so too daily Eucharist was the means of living each day in closer communion with Christ, present in a most unique way in the Host, as well as in the community of believers.

The history of spirituality since the High Middle Ages has been characterized by greater emphasis on interiority, the deep inner union with God possible through prayer and a life of intentional discipline. The fourteenth-century mystical movements of Germany and England as well as the later *Devotio moderna* (see chapter 4) saw the climactic moment of our encounter with Christ to be the time of sacramental Communion. At this sublime moment of oneness with the Savior, words of tender love, surrender, petition, or simply quiet listening take on a new significance and intensity.

As a consequence, preparation for this reception of the sacrament was careful and prolonged; an exaggerated sense of personal unworthiness led to infrequent reception of the Eucharist. Understandably, eucharistic devotions became yet more important both as a substitute and a preparation for the next reception of Holy Communion. The practice of "visiting" the reserved Blessed Sacrament at various times throughout the day brought strength and comfort to the believer. The themes of adoration and fidelity to the eucharistic presence of Christ became very strong in the postmedieval period. Even the practice of making the Sign of the Cross when passing a church was a sign of recognition and reverence for Christ present in the sacrament reserved in the tabernacle. (Gentlemen were always expected to tip their hats.) The making of spiritual communions throughout the day became a commonplace: "My Jesus, since I cannot now receive you sacramentally, come spiritually into my heart and remain there forever."

By and large, the leaders of the Protestant Reformation repudiated the cult of adoration that surrounded the Eucharist and deemphasized the climactic significance of the Mass as it came to be understood during the Middle Ages. A variety of theological explanations for the presence of Christ in the eucharistic species of bread and wine emerged from the churches of the Reformation. Consequently, after the sixteenth century, eucharistic adoration and devotion became associated almost exclusively with Roman Catholicism.

Adoration of the Blessed Sacrament became especially popular with Catholics in the eighteenth and nineteenth centuries. Periods of exposition during which the Host was placed in the monstrance and enthroned above the altar with lighted candles and flowers were accompanied by hymns, prayers, and sermons, and concluded with Benediction, the blessing of the congregation with the monstrance. These periods might be short, a "holy hour," or longer, as in the Forty Hours Devotion. In the latter case each parish in a diocese would, in turn, have exposition of the Blessed Sacrament for forty consecutive hours, day and night. Members of the congregation volunteered to "take the adoration" through this period, since exposition requires that there be always someone present in prayer and adoration. Perhaps the most extreme expression of this devotion is that of "perpetual adoration," whereby exposition continues day and night all year long, interrupted only for daily Mass and during the Triduum of Holy Thursday, Good Friday, and Holy Saturday. This is most commonly practiced by some religious communities who can provide "adorers" for a twenty-four-hour period. Such eucharistic devotions, flowing out of the celebration of the liturgy, are still widely practiced and are, at present, enjoying a revival in many parts of the world.

The Eucharist and the Poor

The liturgical reforms initiated by Vatican Council II have done much to shift our emphasis again to the Eucharist as the action of God's people. Gathered about the altar, the Christian community celebrates the Paschal Mystery wherein the body and blood of Christ become our food and we become one in partaking of that "bread from heaven." Authentic eucharistic devotion must always be in harmony with the liturgical life of the Church; that is, it must *flow from* and *lead back to* the community celebration of the Sunday Eucharist.

Twentieth-century reforms and modifications have been at pains to make all eucharistic devotions more explicitly biblical and liturgical while still maintaining the popular aspects of eucharistic piety. For example, during periods of exposition the current discipline provides for the reading of Scripture and the use of hymns and prayers of a christological and eucharistic nature. Just as the eucharistic rite sends us forth to proclaim the good news, so too eucharistic devotion has been typical of men and women in the nineteenth and twentieth centuries concerned with social issues and the plight of the poor. Founders and foundresses of religious orders who work directly with the poor often spend an hour in eucharistic adoration each day as the source of their strength and outreach. Mother Teresa of Calcutta's Missionaries of Charity—women who minister to Christ in the bodies of the dying—continue this practice in each of their houses. The focus of prayer on Christ as *really present* in the Eucharist appeals to our physical nature. This concrete, divine presence draws us into prayer in the very midst of the suffering and chaos around us, revealing in suffering humanity another form of Real Presence.

It is not so much the case that the Church invents and then promotes particular devotions; rather, it *discovers* devotional practices among its members and recognizes certain of these as being in harmony with the faith rather than detrimental to it. In this sense, devotions are "approved" by Church authority, but because each age produces new devotions or reshapes old ones, these practices and rituals belong to the ordinary people in a unique way. It is they who have insisted on remembering God throughout the week and throughout the day, and it is they whom Christ will remember when he comes again in glory.

EXERCISES

For an Individual

Find a church where the Blessed Sacrament is reserved, and spend time in quiet prayer, say ten or fifteen minutes. Do this for several days running and note any difference you experience in contrast to your usual pattern of prayer. To express sentiments of adoration, try beginning your time of prayer on your knees, the posture of penance and adoration. If the church is locked, as is so often the case, go to the rectory door for access to the church. Also, in many modern or renovated churches the Eucharist is reserved in a separate chapel or room. Look around for the tabernacle (a metal cupboard or box in which the Blessed Sacrament is kept) and for the sanctuary lamp.

Eventually you may wish to spend a longer period of prayer to make a holy hour. The idea of the holy hour was inspired by the words of Christ spoken to the sleeping disciples in the Garden of Gethsemane: "Could you not watch with me one hour?" (Matt. 26:40). During this one hour of watching by the side of the eucharistic Christ, prayer is offered in reparation for the neglect of Christians and for one's own sin and infidelity. Normally the hour is spent in a combination of silent prayer, Scripture reading, and a variety of vocal prayers. There are many formats available, and the holy hour may be done privately or with a group. Use the format provided in appendix 13, and adapt it to your own inclinations and needs.

Finally, try to find a parish, monastery, or convent in your area where daily adoration of the Blessed Sacrament is carried out. Although one visit will not be enough to enter into the spirit of this type of eucharistic prayer, you will find in repeated visits a definite atmosphere of peace and prayerfulness.

For a Group

Search out a parish in your vicinity where a Forty Hours Devotion is being held, and join the congregation for the closing celebration. These ceremonies usually include a sermon on a eucharistic theme and Benediction of the Blessed Sacrament. Meet together following this experience to discuss the questions below.

DISCUSSION QUESTIONS

1. Sunday worship is the mainstay of the prayer life of the Church. In some traditions daily gatherings for Eucharist or other forms of prayer are part of an established pattern. What is the practice of your congregation/parish? Is your church strongly eucharistic? Are you comfortable with its present policy regarding the Eucharist?

2. Have you ever felt drawn to a more explicitly eucharistic spirituality, first, in terms of a stronger emphasis on the liturgical celebration of the sacrament and, second, in terms of a devotional life more centered on the reserved sacrament? Can you account for why you feel this way?

3. Do you see eucharistic devotion as a possible means to overcome our tendency to forget or ignore God? What other means toward the continual remembrance of God do you and others in your congregation/parish practice?

Notes

1. K. Rahner, S.J., *The Church and the Sacraments* (New York: Herder & Herder, 1963), pp. 85-86.
2. St. Augustine, *Sermon* 272 PL 38 (1247–1248).
3. "The Didache," as found in L. Deiss, *Springtime of the Liturgy* (Collegeville, Minn.: Liturgical Press, 1979), p. 75.
4. A. King, *Eucharistic Reservation in the Western Church* (New York: Sheed & Ward, 1965), pp. 75-81.
5. N. Mitchell, *Cult and Controversy: The Worship of the Eucharist Outside Mass* (New York: Pueblo, 1982), pp. 163-72.
6. Ibid., pp. 172-84.

Resources

Bishops' Committee on the Liturgy. *Eucharistic Worship and Devotion Outside Mass: Study Text 11.* Washington: United States Catholic Conference Publications, 1987.

Cabié, R. *The Church at Prayer. Vol. 3 of The Eucharist.* Collegeville, Minn.: Liturgical Press, 1985.

Emminghaus, J. *The Eucharist: Essence, Form, Celebration.* Collegeville, Minn.: Liturgical Press, 1978.

Hellwig, Monika K. *The Eucharist and the Hunger of the World.* New York: Paulist Press, 1976.

Léon-Dufour, X. *Sharing the Eucharistic Bread: The Witness of the New Testament.* New York: Paulist Press, 1987.

Mitchell, Nathan. *Cult and Controversy: The Worship of the Eucharist Outside Mass.* New York: Pueblo, 1982.

Eucharistic Holy Hour

Ordinarily the holy hour begins by kneeling in silent adoration before the Blessed Sacrament. Take a few moments to make the transition from the busy pace of daily life to the silent presence of Christ in the Eucharist.

Opening Prayer

O sacred banquet, in which Christ becomes our food, the memory of his passion is celebrated, the soul is filled with grace, and a pledge of future glory is given to us.

Versicle (leader): You gave them bread from heaven.
Response: Containing every blessing.

O God, in this wonderful sacrament you have left us a memorial of your passion. Help us, we beg you, so to reverence the sacred mysteries of your body and blood that we may constantly feel in our lives the effects of your redemption. You who live and reign forever. Amen.

Prayer to Christ in the Blessed Sacrament
Jesus, my Lord, I believe that you are truly present in the Blessed Sacrament of the Eucharist. I desire to love you above all things and to receive you into my heart. Since I cannot now receive you sacramentally into my heart, come at least spiritually to me and unite me to your way of love and self-sacrifice. Never permit me to stray from you through sin and self-centeredness.

As I read your holy Word, send your Spirit into my mind and heart that I may hear what you wish to speak to me and understand the mission you have for me. I ask this of you who are the Lord, forever and ever. Amen.

O sacrament most holy, O sacrament divine! All praise and all thanksgiving be every moment thine!

Scripture Reading

. Spend ten to fifteen minutes reading John 6, the "bread of life" discourse, or some other eucharistic text from the New Testament.

Meditation

Spend fifteen minutes in silent prayer and adoration. Begin by reflecting on the scriptural passage read and slowly begin to address Christ present in the reserved Eucharist.

The Rosary

Pray the five sorrowful mysteries of the rosary, meditating on the passion of Christ. (These consist of the agony in the garden, the scourging at the pillar, the crowning with thorns, the carrying of the cross, and the crucifixion.)

Silent Adoration

Spend the remainder of the hour in silent prayer before the Blessed Sacrament.

Concluding Prayer

Lord, make me an instrument of your peace!
   Where there is hatred, let me sow love.
   Where there is injury, pardon.
   Where there is doubt, faith.
   Where there is despair, hope.
   Where there is darkness, light
   Where there is sadness, joy.

O Divine Master, grant that I may not so much seek
   to be consoled as to console,
   to be understood as to understand,
   to be loved as to love, for
   it is in giving that we receive,
   it is in pardoning that we are pardoned,
   it is in dying that we are born to eternal life.

(ST. FRANCIS OF ASSISI)

We adore you, O Christ, and we bless you;
because by your holy cross, you have redeemed the world.

Feminism and Spirituality

M A R J O R I E   P R O C T E R - S M I T H

> *i found god in myself*
> *and i loved her/i loved her fiercely.*
>
> —NTOZAKE SHANGE

Spirituality is, in no small part, an imaginative and nonrational enterprise. Feminist spirituality in particular, the subject of this chapter, is involved in freeing and expanding our imaginations about what is real and what is possible. Therefore, this chapter begins with an image: a spider spinning her web. See, with your mind's eye, the way in which she creates out of her own body a world that feeds and protects her, a world unique and adapted perfectly to its environment. Let her spin and weave in your imagination . . .

The Roots of Feminist Spirituality

The feminist spirituality movement is a global phenomenon that is finally inseparable from its political, intellectual, and theological sister-movements. Its origins lie in the struggles of women for political, intellectual, and religious recognition and autonomy and in the feminist critique of existing political, intellectual, and religious structures, rather than in any particular religious tradition. Therefore, it is necessary to understand the basis of the feminist critique in order to understand the history and character of the feminist spirituality movement.

The feminist critique arises out of a process of coming to feminist awareness; this most often begins in the present, includes reexamination of the past, and works for the future. Beginning in the present may take two forms. Many women come to feminist consciousness out of experiences of violation, abuse, or rejection by patriarchal structures, institutions, or individuals they formerly trusted. Others come by way of a more structured process known as "consciousness raising," whereby women begin to recognize that what they had been told were personal and individual problems were in fact structural and social. Consciousness raising names the sources of women's oppression as patriarchy, androcentrism, and misogyny. Patriarchal social and political systems, androcentric language and philosophical systems, and institutionalized violence against women are recognized as part of all women's present daily reality. The grief and anger that this recognition produces in women often leads to a reexamination of the past, in search of the origins of women's oppression or in search of a time or place when women were not oppressed. At the same time, the answer to anger and grief is a determination to bring about change, if not for ourselves then certainly for our daughters.

Because the questions raised in this process are fundamental religious questions, feminism has always had a spiritual element in it, although it has not always been named as such. The recognition of the depths of women's oppression raises questions such as, Why do women suffer? Where is God? Does God care about women's sufferings? Searching the past is motivated by a search for answers to the questions, How did the oppression of women come to be accepted? Was there ever a time when women were free? Shaping the future is an attempt to answer the question, What would the world look like if women were free?

However, when women have asked these religious questions of traditional forms of Christianity or Judaism, they have been forced to recognize that their religion, far from being a source of comfort or power to women, has in fact contributed to women's suffering and oppression. Indeed, according to the prevailing interpretation of Christianity and Judaism, women's oppression seems to be part of the divine plan from the beginning of creation, and therefore women can have no hope of bringing about change, either in the present or in the future.

Feminist Response to Patriarchal Religious Traditions

The response of some women to this recognition has been, not unreasonably, to reject traditional patriarchal religions altogether. But since the religious questions remain, an alternative religious answer must be given. Therefore, many forms of nontraditional "feminist religions" or "feminist spirituality groups" have arisen. The growth and popularity of such groups must be seen in part as a judgment on the traditional religions' lack of adequate response to women's most fundamental religious questions. At the same time, many women have refused to leave the religious traditions in which they have grown up and are continuing to challenge Christianity and Judaism to respond to them and their issues.

This division between those who remain within traditional religions and those who have moved out of them is the most fundamental division among those who practice feminist spirituality. At base is the question of women's relationship to tradition. As long as tradition is understood to be patriarchal and androcentric, within which women are at best marginal and at worst inherently heretical or evil, feminist spirituality is at odds with tradition. Anne Carr makes a useful distinction between "women's spirituality" and "feminist spirituality." Women's spirituality, she notes, is distinct from men's spirituality because women occupy a different social and psychological place in our world. Therefore, their relationship with God, self, and others is accordingly different. Moreover, women's spirituality, like women's nature, has often been defined by men in ways that serve the purposes of men. Thus women's spirituality might be said to be more passive, more emotional, or more nurturing than men's, reflecting patriarchal assumptions about women's nature. Feminist spirituality, by contrast, "is the spirituality of those who have experienced feminist consciousness raising."[1] Feminist spirituality, then, is spirituality defined by women for our own purposes, which must include our own emancipation.

Therefore, the feminist spirituality movement stands at some distance from all androcentric religious traditions. However, even this does not necessarily mean that feminist spirituality can take place only outside established religions. Since the study of women's history within religious traditions has revealed that women are not only victims but also agents of change and creators of their own lives, feminist spirituality has found ways to challenge androcentric traditions by insisting that women's spiritual lives and experiences be considered part of the tradition. This radical reconstruction of tradition allows women to remain within their own religion while also refusing to submit to patriarchal models of spirituality. This same impulse toward self-definition has led many women to construct their own normative religious practices out of imaginatively reconstructed woman-centered traditions. They are convinced that existing religions are fundamentally patriarchal and choose not to spend their energy attempting to change them. "I believe that Christianity and Judaism can only become liberating for women if they are transformed at their cores," says Carol Christ. "This is not a task to which I wish to devote my life and work."[2]

Diversity in Feminist Spirituality

Because of this critical distance, one of feminist spirituality's chief characteristics is its diversity. Unlike mendicant, Ignatian, or Wesleyan spirituality, feminist spirituality has no single definitive leader, founder, or prophet. Unlike most other spiritual traditions, feminist spirituality has no commonly recognized "holy books," since the Jewish and Christian Scriptures are critiqued as androcentric and patriarchal writings. Indeed, some practitioners of feminist spirituality have no interest in organized religion of any kind and instead understand their spirituality as primarily psychological.[3]

But more important, diversity is not just circumstantial; it is purposefully valued. This valuing of diversity is in part a consequence of feminist awareness that orthodoxy has commonly been used to suppress women's religious autonomy. It is also a result of feminist spirituality's connection with the larger feminist intellectual and religious movements.

Together with the intellectual feminist movement, which is concerned with the development of feminist studies, methods, and disciplines, feminist spirituality recognizes gender as a basic category of analysis. However, both experience and critical reflection have emphasized that gender is also experienced within the context of racial, class, and age distinctions as well. As women have rejected men's right to speak for us and have begun to name our own reality and experiences, the immense diversity of women's lives has been made visible. When white women have claimed to speak for all women, women of color have reminded us of the dangers of imposing our definitions of "women's experience" on them. Jacqueline Grant observes, "The critique that feminist theologians make of the classical theologians, namely that they have taken one culture—that of White males—and universalized it, can be turned against them. Feminist theologians have taken one experience, that of White middle-class women, and made that the norm."[4]

Likewise, when educated or elite women have claimed to speak for all women, women of other classes have recalled this basic feminist principle. Therefore, feminist spirituality, like feminist studies and the feminist political movement, is compelled by its own logic to recognize and value the diversity of women's experience.

Given such a commitment, it may seem that it is difficult to generalize about such a diverse movement. Yet by naming some common emphases, one is better able to identify divergences, differing interpretations, and varying practices.

Major Themes in Feminist Spirituality: Women's Experience

The commitment to diversity is itself based on an even more fundamental common commitment of the feminist spirituality movement to the naming and celebrating of women's experience. As Jewish writer Esther M. Broner notes, "We were women before we were Jews, Christians, Moslems. It seems only natural, historical, and just, therefore, to make religion respond to our origins."[5]

However, this assertion is not as simple as it seems. Women's experiences are not only diverse due to education, race, class, age, and so on, but are also subject to varying interpretations. In the writings and practices of some forms of feminist spirituality, centering on women's experience means sacralizing women's bodies and natural cycles, such as birth, menstruation, and menopause.[6] There are also spiritual practices and rituals that have developed in order to respond to crises experienced by women, such as rape, divorce, or battering.[7] Still others focus on empowering women's struggles for affirmation, for ordination, for recognition, and for remembrance.[8]

Synergism

A second important characteristic of feminist spirituality is its synergistic nature. It is possible to group practitioners of feminist spirituality into two broad categories: those who have left organized religion to form feminist, often goddess-centered, religions, and those who remain in traditional Christianity or Judaism in order to infuse these patriarchal religions with feminist content. Although relations among practitioners of these different groups (which may be further subdivided among themselves) have at times been strained, in practice there is a good deal of sharing of practices. For example, a collection of Christian feminist liturgical resources included a feminist version of the traditional Jewish *mikvah* ritual bath and a "croning ritual" that draws on practices of goddess worship known as Wicca.[9]

Wiccan practices such as chanting, spell casting, and, most fundamentally, prayer to a goddess, are not uncommon among Christian and Jewish feminists, who find in such practices some answers to their fundamental questions about religion. Carol Christ argues that worship of a male God can never empower women; only worship of a goddess is capable of legitimating women's power, affirming women's bodies, and valuing women's will and women's bonds with other women.[10] Some feminists see the use of female-specific language about the Deity or the use of woman-centered rituals as a temporary stage in a process of transformation of religious institutions. However, the logic of feminist awareness of the diversity of women's experiences would seem to argue against such an assumption. In any case, for the present there is a dynamic "sharing of energy" among feminists, whether inside or outside the traditional religious structures.

Particularity

Another common theme within feminist spirituality and theology is particularity. Feminist rituals and spiritual practices are often not only diverse but also particular to the individual or to the gathering as well as to the cultural and religious identification. Especially, there is new interest in women's religious traditions in non-European cultures. While Wicca is essentially based on a recovery of old pre-Christian European religions, women of non-European backgrounds have recovered some of their own religious traditions, which are usually inclusive of, if not centered on, goddess worship. Native American feminists have recovered a gynocratic society in which female deities were worshiped before the coming of Christianity.[11] Some black feminists are interested in African goddesses and in practices of Voudou.[12] Such movements enable women of color to celebrate and sacralize not only themselves as women but also their racial and cultural identities.

Feminist Literature

An important factor in this sharing of resources and practices is the value placed on feminist literature within feminist religious communities. In a groundbreaking study of contemporary women's spirituality, Carol Christ argued that "the new stories that women tell each other . . . in fiction, poetry, and other literary forms are key sources for discovering the shape of women's spiritual quest."[13]

Similarly, Naomi Goldenberg views women's fiction and poetry as possible "new sacred texts."[14] Whether such works can rightly be named "feminist canon" yet is debatable, but they certainly constitute a significant body of what in traditional spiritual traditions would be called "devotional literature."

Christ studied the literary work of Kate Chopin, Margaret Atwood, Doris Lessing, Adrienne Rich, and Ntozake Shange. Since Christ's study was published, the works of Alice Walker, Anne Cameron, Audre Lourde, Esther Broner, and Marion Zimmer Bradley (to name but a few) have become religious texts for countless women both within and outside Christianity and Judaism. In some of these works, women encounter for the first time imaginative reconstructions of the past through women's eyes. For example, in *The Mists of Avalon*, Marion Zimmer Bradley recounts the tale of Camelot from the perspective of the pre-Christian inhabitants of Britain, who worship a goddess and are led by priestesses.

Anne Cameron, in *Daughters of a Copper Woman*, tells the mythic stories remembered by the secret women's society of the Canadian Nootkas. Women who read this book in seminary commonly compare it with Christian and Jewish Scriptures and wonder what stories ancient Jewish or Christian women might have passed on if they hadn't been suppressed or distorted. They also find in the stories sources for rethinking their own spirituality. Such literature expands women's imaginations about the ancient past, giving them a new perspective from which to view their own history and tradition and relativizing the power of patriarchal biblical texts that have been used against women. Moreover, by placing women and women's religious questions into the stream of history, women can find authority to search for answers not only in the past but also in the present and in the future.

The spiritual power of women's lives is celebrated in the works of writers such as Alice Walker and Ntozake Shange. Both Walker and Shange do not shrink from speaking of the daily struggles of women, especially black women, for survival and dignity against great odds. The women in their writings are victims of rape and abuse and violence, but they are much more than victims; they are also agents of their own spiritual transformations. At the conclusion of *For Colored Girls,* the Lady in Red, after recognizing that she has been "missin somethin," begins singing a song of joy:

> i found god in myself
> and i loved her/i loved her fiercely.[15]

Similarly, in *The Color Purple,* the heroine Celie comes into her own power at last when she curses the husband who raped and abused her. The power she discovers comes not only from within her but also from beyond her: "Look like when I open my mouth the air rush in and shape words."[16] Out of this powerful experience Celie learns to love herself and to "love folks." This connection between women's struggle and women's spiritual power is summed up in Alice Walker's definition of "womanist": "Loves music. Loves dance. Loves the moon. *Loves* the Spirit. Loves love and food and roundness. Loves struggle. *Loves* the Folk. Loves herself. *Regardless.*"[17] As Walker's definition suggests, it is not only women's literature that is an important source for women's spirituality but also women's whole emotional, political, and intellectual creative life.

Feminist Spirituality and Political Activism

This holistic character of feminist spirituality means that, for many, spirituality has a much broader significance than more traditional forms of spirituality. For some, feminist spirituality means experiencing "the earth as holy, and our true home."[18] This experience of interconnection with all of life fosters concern for an activism on behalf of ecological issues.[19] For others, the experience of or identification with women's struggles for survival leads to concern about poverty, political repression, battering, or rape, which are seen not only as social or political issues but also as spiritual issues.[20] Thus feminist spirituality, because it takes as its starting point women's experience, cannot be content with the spiritual development of women of privilege but must be concerned about the spiritual well-being of all women and of the planet. Therefore feminist spirituality is committed to change, not only of the individual woman but also of the community, of the religious body, and, indeed, of the whole world.

Feminist Spirituality and Patriarchal Religious Traditions

Clearly, the Christian and Jewish scriptural canons do not hold an absolutely authoritative position even for those feminists who have chosen to remain within Christianity or Judaism. Where the canonical Scriptures are regarded as useful, it is a limited and critical usefulness. Texts must be creatively reinterpreted from women's perspective, and those texts that defame women or have been used against women are not granted authority. Noncanonical texts are often regarded as a useful corrective to canonical texts, especially where those texts challenge the scriptural portrayal of women.[21]

Traditional worship forms are also regarded from a critical distance, as women recognize that the language and symbol systems exclude or degrade women and women's experiences. At the heart of the debates within Christianity and Judaism on the use of "inclusive language" in worship is a spiritual question. Women fail to experience God or themselves as part of the community when the language used denies their existence or distorts their experience. The language of patriarchy and domination does not express the fullness of women's experiences of encounter with the Divine, nor does it answer our basic questions of identity. Are women made in the image of God, or not? Are women part of the religious community, or are we peripheral? Even when other statements by religious leaders seem to answer yes to these questions, androcentric religious language and restriction of women's access to religious leadership shout no more loudly. Even when women do experience the presence of God within traditional worship, their experience is rarely confirmed as part of the religious tradition.

This experience has led women to generate a large and growing body of feminist liturgical materials, ranging from litanies remembering our foremothers, to prayers and songs using female images and language for God, to alternative forms of blessing, Communion prayers, and other rituals of Christian or Jewish tradition.[22]

A particularly difficult problem for Christian feminists is the centrality of Jesus Christ as a male savior. Although attempts have been made to redefine Jesus Christ in ways which deemphasize his maleness—as a "feminist," as model of the "new humanity," as liberator or Suffering Servant—such efforts leave two major difficulties unanswered.

The first of these is the use to which the maleness of Jesus has been put by the Church. The historical fact that Jesus was male continues to be used to deny women access to positions of religious and spiritual authority. Implicit, if not explicit, in this position is the message that maleness is more like God than femaleness, since God chose to be incarnate as male rather than female. This view appears to grant spiritual superiority to male embodiment and to devalue female embodiment. Theological claims that Jesus is God or reveals God reinforce this negative view of female bodies. Feminist spirituality, by contrast, affirms and values female embodiment, refuses to define it as a disability, and in some visions of goddess religion, claims that the ability of women's bodies to give birth and nurture young makes female embodiment superior to male embodiment.

The second problem for Christian feminists is the role of Jesus as male savior. The feminist emphasis on women's autonomy and freedom rejects dependence on men as saviors. A male savior appears to deny women's religious authority, autonomy, and moral agency. The further emphasis of some forms of Christian piety on "submitting to Jesus," "yielding to his will," and so on, deepens the dilemma for women who are struggling to name our own experience and claim our own authority. Models of submission to male will and authority are not emancipatory for women. Traditional language naming Jesus as "Lord," "Master," and "King" are not regarded as useful.

These problems have yet to give way to a single satisfactory conclusion. However, models being explored include Jesus as "Lover," "Friend," or "Brother," emphasizing an egalitarian rather than a hierarchical relationship.[23] The biblical connection between the female image of Wisdom (or "Sophia") and Jesus as the Wisdom of God also offers a fresh model of Jesus Christ that includes a female image.[24]

Within both Christianity and Judaism, traditional definitions of holiness, a central concern of spirituality, have excluded or marginalized women. Feminist spirituality focuses more on wholeness than on traditional ideas of holiness. Male-defined norms of holiness that include rejection of bodiliness and sexuality, hatred and fear of women, and an emphasis on control and separation are excluded from feminist spirituality. Holiness is reinterpreted to mean affirmation of the self as body, of femaleness and female sexuality, and of woman-to-woman bonds, as part of the *tikkun olam*, the "repair of the world."[25]

Consequences of Feminist Spirituality

Women who come to feminist spirituality by way of either personal trauma or intentional consciousness raising have already undergone significant behavioral and confessional changes. The very act of questioning one's religious tradition as a woman automatically moves one into a new relationship with other people and with one's religion. In a sense, then, feminist spirituality serves as a means of support for maintaining a critical distance and as a resource for establishing new relationships with others, with the self, and with religious institutions. Feminist spirituality calls forth women's power, which means taking responsibility for one's self and for the just exercise of one's own authority. Because women are commonly unaware of having any power or authority as women, and because women are frequently rebuked (either indirectly or directly) when attempting to exercise power or authority, the act of accepting responsibility for one's self calls for major changes in behavior. It requires that we begin to speak out about our own experiences rather than allow others to speak for us. It means encouraging other women to do the same and learning to listen to and support one another. It means refusing to ignore injustice against other women, the silencing of other women, or the punishing of other women for speaking out. It also means developing nonauthoritarian ways of exercising authority by empowering others and sharing power.

Feminist spirituality demands accountability to all women. The feminist value of sisterhood requires us to recognize both the ways in which we are alike as women and the ways in which we are different. Only by recognizing our own complicity as women in structures of oppression against women can we begin to construct relationships of mutual and honest support. Racism and elitism can divide women, and they will continue to do so unless we are able to claim a sense of accountability to one another over patriarchal systems of oppression from which some women benefit.

Feminist spirituality challenges us to work for change, not only in ourselves but also in the religious institutions and the communities and the world in which we live. Accountability to women and responsibility for ourselves means that the emancipation of women is work that cannot be left to others to do. Feminist spirituality "loves struggle." Feminist spiritual disciplines, then, would include a wide range of practices, from the relatively modest ones of speaking of women as "we" or refusing to laugh at sexist or misogynist humor, to more demanding political activism on behalf of battered women or scholarship focusing on women.

Feminist spirituality is not only challenging. It is also nurturing and empowering. Through the use of literature, poetry, art, and dance, our imaginations are engaged and stretched and our spirits led. Through valued relationships with women, whether those close at hand, those met only once or rarely, or those known only through books or other creative forms, our spirits grow into new stature and strength. "The spider creates a world from her own body."[26] Her web is made strand by strand, not in a straight line but woven to fit the space available and to answer her needs for nourishment and survival. It is slow work, done a bit at a time, often against great odds. The image of the spider's web reveals the complexity, the interconnectedness, and the world-creating potential of feminist spirituality. Poet Muriel Ruckeyser asks, "What would happen if one woman told the truth about her life? The world would split open."[27] Feminist spirituality asks also, What would happen if many women, thousands of women, millions of women, told the truth about their lives? Perhaps together we could weave new traditions, weave new religious communities, weave a new world.

Notes

1. Anne Carr, "On Feminist Spirituality," in *Women's Spirituality: Resources for Christian Development*, ed. Joann Wolski Conn (New York: Paulist Press, 1986), pp. 49-58.
2. Carol P. Christ, "Roundtable Discussion: What Are the Sources of My Theology?" *Journal of Feminist Studies in Religion* 1, no. 1 (1988): 120.
3. See, for example, the work of Barbara G. Walker, *The Skeptical Feminist: Discovering the Virgin, Mother, and Crone* (San Francisco: Harper & Row, 1987); Jean Shinoda Bolen, *Goddesses in Everywoman: A New Psychology of Women* (San Francisco: Harper & Row, 1984).
4. Jacqueline Grant, "A Black Response to Feminist Theology," in *Women's Spirit Bonding*, ed. Janet Kalven and Mary Buckley (New York: Pilgrim Press, 1984), p. 122.
5. Esther M. Broner, "Honor and Ceremony in Women's Rituals," in *The Politics of Women's Spirituality*, ed. Charlene Spretnak (Garden City, N.Y.: Doubleday, 1982), p. 234.
6. See, for example, Penelope Washbourn, *Becoming Woman: The Quest for Wholeness in Female Experience* (San Francisco: Harper & Row, 1977).
7. See Carolyn R. Shaffer, "Spiritual Techniques for Re-Powering Survivors of Sexual Assault," in Broner, *The Politics of Women's Spirituality*, pp. 462-69; Rosemary Radford Ruether, "Healing Our Wounds: Overcoming the Violence of Patriarchy," in *Women-Church: Theology and Practice* (San Francisco: Harper & Row, 1985), pp. 149-81.
8. These emphases are found throughout feminist liturgies, such as those in Ruether, *Women-Church*, and in Miriam Therese Winter, *WomanPrayer, WomanSong* (Oak Park, Ill.: Meyer-Stone Books, 1987).
9. Ruether, *Women-Church*, pp. 220-21, 206-9.
10. Carol Christ, "Why Women Need the Goddess: Phenomenological, Psychological, and Political Reflections," in *Womanspirit Rising*, ed. Carol Christ and Judith Plaskow (San Francisco: Harper & Row, 1979), pp. 273-87.
11. Paula Gunn Allen, *The Sacred Hoop: Recovering the Feminine in American Indian Tradition* (Boston: Beacon Press, 1986).
12. Luisah Teish, *Jambalaya: The Natural Woman's Book of Personal Charms and Practical Rituals* (San Francisco: Harper & Row, 1985).
13. Carol Christ, *Diving Deep and Surfacing: Women Writers on Spiritual Quest* (Boston: Beacon Press, 1980), p. 12.
14. Naomi Goldenberg, *Changing of the Gods: Feminism and the End of Traditional Religions* (Boston: Beacon Press, 1979), p. 120.
15. Ntozake Shange, *For Colored Girls Who Have Considered Suicide When the Rainbow Is Enuf* (New York: Macmillan, 1975), p. 63.
16. Alice Walker, *The Color Purple* (San Diego: Harcourt Brace Jovanovich, 1982), p. 176.
17. Alice Walker, *In Search of Our Mother's Gardens: Womanist Prose* (San Diego: Harcourt Brace Jovanovich, 1983), p. xii.
18. Christ, "Roundtable Discussion," p. 120.
19. See, for example, Elizabeth Dodson Gray, *Green Paradise Lost* (Wellesly, Mass.: Roundtable Press, 1981).
20. See Dorothy Sölle, *The Strength of the Weak: Toward a Christian Feminist Identity* (Philadelphia: Westminster Press, 1984).
21. Drorah Setel, "Roundtable Discussion: Feminist Reflections on Separation and Unity in Jewish Theology," *Journal of Feminist Studies in Religion* 2, no. 1 (1986): 116.
22. Rosemary Radford Ruether, *Womanguides: Readings Toward a Feminist Theology* (Boston: Beacon Press, 1985).
23. See Sallie McFague, *Models of God* (Philadelphia: Fortress Press, 1987), and Carter Heyward, *Our Passion for Justice* (New York: Pilgrim Press, 1984).
24. For a study of the biblical basis for the idea of Jesus as wisdom, see Elisabeth Schüssler Fiorenza, *In Memory of Her* (New York: Crossroad, 1983), pp. 132-99. See also Susan

Cady, Marian Ronan, Hal Taussig, *Sophia: The Future of Feminist Spirituality* (New York: Harper & Row, 1986).
25. See, for example, the liturgies collected in Ruether, *Women-Church*.
26. Adrienne Rich, "Integrity," in *A Wild Patience Has Taken Me This Far* (New York: W.W. Norton, 1981), p. 9.
27. Muriel Ruckeyser, "Käthe Kollwitz," in *By A Woman Writt*, ed. Joan Goulianos (Baltimore: Penguin Books, 1973), p. 377.

Bibliography

Prayers, Liturgies, and Rituals

Iglehart, Hallie Austen. *Womanspirit: A Guide to Women's Wisdom*. San Francisco: Harper & Row, 1983.

Ruether, Rosemary Radford. *Womanguides: Readings Toward a Feminist Theology*. Boston: Beacon Press, 1985.

————. *Women-Church: Theology and Practice*. New York: Harper & Row, 1985.

Starhawk. *The Spiral Dance: A Rebirth of the Religion of the Great Goddess*. San Francisco: Harper & Row, 1979.

Starhawk. *Dreaming the Dark: Magic, Sex, and Politics*. Boston: Beacon Press, 1982.

Swidler, Arlene, ed. *Sistercelebrations*. Philadelphia: Fortress Press, 1974.

Teish, Luisah. *Jambalaya: The Natural Woman's Book of Personal Charms and Practical Rituals*. San Francisco: Harper & Row, 1985.

Winter, Miriam Therese. *WomanPrayer, WomanSong*. Oak Park, Ill.: Meyer-Stone Books, 1987.

Literary Resources

Bradley, Marion Zimmer. *The Mists of Avalon*. New York: Alfred A. Knopf, 1983.

Broner, Esther M. *A Weave of Women*. Bloomington, Ind.: Indiana University Press, 1978.

Cameron, Anne. *Daughters of a Copper Woman*. Vancouver, B.C.: Press Gang Publishers, 1981.

Chernin, Kim. *The Flame Bearers*. New York: Random House, 1986.

Shange, Ntozake. *For Colored Girls Who Have Considered Suicide When the Rainbow Is Enuf*. New York: Macmillan, 1975.

Walker, Alice. *The Color Purple*. San Diego: Harcourt Brace Jovanovich, 1982.

Secondary Resources

Allen, Paula Gunn. *The Sacred Hoop: Recovering the Feminine in American Indian Traditions*. Boston: Beacon Press, 1986.

Cady, Susan; Ronan, Marian; and Taussig, Hal. *Sophia: The Future of Feminist Spirituality*. San Francisco: Harper & Row, 1986.

Christ, Carol. *Diving Deep and Surfacing: Women Writers on Spiritual Quest*. Boston: Beacon Press, 1980.

Christ, Carol. *Laughter of Aphrodite: Reflections on a Journey to the Goddess*. San Francisco: Harper & Row, 1987.

Christ, Carol, and Plaskow, Judith, eds. *Womanspirit Rising: A Feminist Reader in Religion*. San Francisco: Harper & Row, 1979.

Conn, Joann Wolski, ed. *Women's Spirituality: Resources for Christian Development*. New York: Paulist Press, 1986.

Giles, Mary E., ed. *The Feminist Mystic and Other Essays on Women and Spirituality*. New York: Crossroad, 1982.

Kalven, Janet, and Buckley, Mary I., eds. *Women's Spirit Bonding*. New York: Pilgrim Press, 1984.

Morton, Nelle. *The Journey Is Home*. Boston: Beacon Press, 1985.

Sölle, Dorothee. *The Strength of the Weak: Toward a Christian Feminist Identity*. Philadelphia: Westminster Press, 1984.

Spretnak, Charlene, ed. *The Politics of Women's Spirituality*. Garden City, N.Y.: Doubleday Anchor Books, 1982.

Walker, Alice. *In Search of Our Mothers' Gardens: Womanist Prose*. San Diego: Harcourt Brace Jovanovich, 1983.

Wisdom Calls to Her Children

R O B I N   M A A S

Wisdom calls aloud in the streets,
  she raises her voice in the public squares;
she calls out at the street corners,
  she delivers her message at the city gates,
"You ignorant people, how much longer will you cling to your ignorance?"

—PROVERBS 1:20-22 JB

Shortly after the death of his father David, King Solomon had a dream in which God asked him what his heart's desire might be. With extraordinary prudence and tact, the new king replied by first acknowledging the great kindness Yahweh had shown to his father before him; only then did he submit his request:

> Now, Yahweh my God, you have made your servant king in succession to David my father. But I am a very young man, unskilled in leadership. Your servant finds himself in the midst of this people of yours that you have chosen, a people so many its number cannot be counted or reckoned. Give your servant a heart to understand how to discern between good and evil, for who could govern this people of yours that is so great? (I Kings 3:7-9 JB)

God is touched by the humility and unselfish altruism of Solomon's request and gladly grants it: "Since you have asked for this," says Yahweh,

> and not asked for long life for yourself or riches or the lives of your enemies, but have asked for a discerning judgement for yourself, here and now I do what you ask. I give you a heart wise and shrewd as none

before you has had and none will have after you. What you have not asked I shall give you too: such riches and glory as no other king ever had. (I Kings 3:10-14 JB)

Surely the young king was already wise beyond his years, to frame his request as he did! In any case, the wisdom of Solomon became legendary, and foreign potentates like the queen of Sheba, who came to investigate the phenomenon, ended by paying the Hebrew monarch extravagant homage (II Chron. 9:1-12).

We can see from the prominent place he maintained in the Hebrew Scriptures that Solomon's reputed wisdom continued to occupy a place of honor in Israel's memory and imagination, and despite much historical evidence to the contrary, he remains the most visible and popular scriptural symbol of even-handed justice, discretion, and prudent judgment. This symbolic connection is even more evident in the intertestamental literature (found in the Roman Catholic canon but not the Protestant), which includes the book of Wisdom, attributed to King Solomon but written during the last century before Christ.

Far less evident and for the most part forgotten is the character of the wisdom Solomon prayed for, and again this is partly due to the greater prominence of wisdom as a theme in the intertestamental or "deuterocanonical" literature. The figure of Wisdom (in the Hebrew, *hokmah*, and in the Greek, *sophia*), either as an attribute of God or as the crown of creation (scholars differ in assessing Wisdom's identity and significance), was central to a particular genre of biblical theology and literature. Wisdom's general eclipse in Christian tradition represents a serious loss on several accounts, not least of which is the loss of a scripturally sanctioned, prominent, and powerful feminine image of the Divine. The current call of feminist theologians to recover "lost" or hidden dimensions of the tradition in which feminine images of God figure significantly warrants serious attention, and although considerable scholarly research is required in this effort, there is much the individual Christian and the local parish or congregation can do to assist in the process of recovery. The following discussion and exercises are intended to demonstrate how some of this recovery might occur in a grass roots setting.

Wisdom Calls to Her Children:
The Feminine Principle in Creation

The wisdom tradition, as it is called, is most prominently displayed in the Protestant canon in the books of Proverbs, Job, and Ecclesiastes, as well as in many of the psalms. The Roman canon includes, in addition, the books of Wisdom and Ecclesiasticus (or Ben Sirach). Unlike most of

Hebrew Scripture, which deals with the particular historical circumstances of the saving relationship between Yahweh and Israel, the wisdom tradition deals primarily with the universal search for truth, especially as it is lived out in the concrete circumstances of daily life. The delineation of standards of conduct, homely advice about virtues and vices and the fruits of honest living, and exhortations to examine the wonders of the created order permeate this literature. The focus of attention in wisdom is always on *what is;* its method might best be termed "empirical" and its ethos a kind of humane and savvy pragmatism. What is most striking about this tradition for our purposes is what has consistently remained most invisible about it: the personification (or *hypostasization*) of wisdom as female in the figure of Lady Wisdom—Sophia, as she is called. In other words, the divine attribute of wisdom became such a commanding reality in the tradition that it acquired a "personality" of its own. Perhaps because her appearance in Protestant versions of Scripture is limited to sections of the book of Proverbs, Lady Wisdom has languished in the shadows of collective Christian memory and seldom, if ever, makes an appearance in preaching and teaching; yet the fact that she features more prominently in the Roman canon does not mean she fares better in that tradition either.

The origins of this distinctive feminine character in the biblical tradition of wisdom are quite mysterious, but scholars are clear that wisdom literature enjoyed wide popularity in the Mediterranean Basin during the Hellenistic Period (beginning with the conquests of Alexander the Great, ca. 336–325 B.C., and continuing in its effects into the first century A.D.). Informed speculation targets Greece and Egypt in particular as major sources of cross-fertilization. Some scholars have suggested the Egyptian goddesses Isis and Maat or the Hellenistic Demeter and Persephone as prototypes for Wisdom/Sophia. Like these goddesses, Sophia plays a special—and aggressive—role in relation to creation.

The feminine element in religion is typically related to creation, usually in the form of an all-embracing, fecund Earth Mother image. Similarly, Sophia is definitively linked to the creative principle but in a strikingly different way. She is not fecundity or creativity per se. She is the divine order imposed on the primal chaos of the material universe. Source of light and not darkness, she is the rational principle, the blueprint of creation, the plan by which a principled and predictable created order emerges. In Proverbs 8 Sophia is the "unfolding purpose" of Yahweh, present with God before the Spirit begins to hover over the primeval waters (vv. 22-23). Significantly, the ordering principle Sophia represents does not preclude mystery, wonder, or humor; Scripture speaks of her playful presence pervading the entire process of creation (vv. 24-31). That the universe is marked with the distinctive stamp of her divine immanence is evidence that Yahweh could not have done this without her!

It is precisely because Sophia pervades the entire natural order that the biblical tradition must speak of her as "calling" to humankind. Akin to what the Church calls "general revelation," the traces of Sophia's handiwork are everywhere. Her domain is a public one, accessible to any and all who have eyes to see or ears to hear. Her call comes always as a gracious invitation to enter her "house of seven pillars" and there partake of her bread and wine, source of life and protection against the vicious consequences of undisciplined self-indulgence (Prov. 9:1-6).

Significantly—for Israel and for us—public access to the cosmic order underlying creation has clear and obvious ethical consequences. The person taught by Sophia, whether king or peasant, Jew or Gentile, has discovered God's will in the very nature of reality: "Then," Scripture promises—and only then—"you will understand what virtue is, justice, and fair dealing, all paths that lead to happiness" (Prov. 2:9 JB). The profound ethical consequences of the pursuit of Wisdom/Sophia are further clarified by later passages (Ecclesiasticus/Sirach 24:23-25; Baruch 3:37-4:2), which connect her explicitly to Torah, the authoritative "teaching" that explicates Yahweh's covenantal relationship with Israel. For the pious Jew there could be no access to ultimate reality outside the specific cultic and ethical parameters that govern Yahweh's relationship to his people.

Precisely the same understanding of the ethical consequences of the natural order of creation is assumed by Paul in his letter to the Romans. Inveighing against Gentile sinners, who had no access to the revealed Torah, Paul claims that

> what can be known about God is perfectly plain to them since God himself has made it plain. Ever since God created the world his everlasting power and deity—however invisible—have been there for the mind to see in the things he has made. That is why such people are without excuse: they knew God and yet refused to honour him as God or to thank him; instead, they made nonsense out of logic and their empty minds were darkened. The more they called themselves philosophers, the more stupid they grew, until they exchanged the glory of the immortal God for a worthless imitation, for the image of mortal man, of birds, of quadrupeds and reptiles. That is why God left them to their filthy enjoyments and the practices with which they dishonour their own bodies, since they have given up divine truth for a lie and have worshipped and served creatures instead of the creator . . . ! (Rom. 1:19-25 JB)

For those who are diligent in their search for Sophia and faithful to what she reveals, she promises the good life. Security, honor, wealth, and long life are the inevitable consequences of the disciplined quest for Wisdom (Prov. 4:5, 8; 8:18, 35). She is indeed a bringer of salvation, especially in the sense of *shalom*—peace, wholeness, and fulfillment in a life lived according to the divine intention.

Wisdom and the Incarnate Logos:
The Feminine Principle in Redemption

For Christians, the special functions and teaching of Sophia are preserved, but transformed, in the development of a wisdom Christology. To say this is to give an admittedly positive reading to what actually developed. It is equally possible to argue, as many feminists would, that the attribution of Wisdom/Sophia's special role to Jesus, the crucified Messiah, did not serve to "preserve" this feminine dimension of the Divine or to assign it salvific power but in fact destroyed or eclipsed it in a masculine savior. The fundamental ambivalence between the exalted role of Sophia and the jealous demands of strict Jewish monotheism evidenced in the Hebrew Scriptures was almost certain to be reflected in the development of the Christology of the early Church, and the current discussion among feminists about the consequences of this theological development for women in the Church reflects this built-in ambiguity.

Given the method of symbolic reappropriation employed by the New Testament writers, it seems inevitable that such a powerful and attractive symbol as Sophia would be claimed for Christ. Paul does this quite self-consciously when he describes the risen Christ as the "power and wisdom"—sophia—of God (I Cor. 1:24). God's wisdom, a hitherto unrevealed mystery, was nevertheless present as Sophia—as the divine intention or plan, "predestined" from the very beginning of creation for the salvation of all (I Cor. 2:7). The *imago dei*—the "new creation"—that is the stamp of Sophia is for the apostle that very Christ we must each "put on," and this truth must now be broadcast publicly, proclaimed from the rooftops, on street corners—in all those visible places where Sophia has always issued her "call" (Rom. 16:25-27).

In the prologue to the Gospel of John (John 1:1-18) another explicit connection is made. The identification of the Greek *logos* ("word," "reason," "rule") with a preexistent Christ active in creation is reminiscent of Proverbs 8, where Sophia, the "firstborn" of creation, becomes Yahweh's "master craftsman," taking an active—and decisive—role in every creative act. Again, the fact that *logos* is translated "word" (which directly suggests the Hebrew *dabar*, the verbal command by which Yahweh creates in Genesis 1) generally works to obscure the strong influence of the wisdom tradition in this very familiar and most theologically significant text. This obscuration is unfortunate, for the prologue to the Gospel of John is the text par excellence for understanding the meaning of the central Christian doctrine of the Incarnation. To miss the connection with personified Wisdom in New Testament Christology is to overlook the significance of the participation of the feminine not only in creation but also in redemption.

At the same time, the Christian must recognize that the passion of Jesus of Nazareth forever alters what the community of faith designates as "truth." The call of Sophia in the Hebrew Scriptures to live according to the intentions of the Creator through the practice of virtue is radically re-visioned when the Creator is understood to have assumed human nature, to have suffered and died on our behalf. Wisdom of this sort comes only through revelation. As the Apostle Paul said, the good news must be preached, but not "in terms of philosophy, in which the crucifixion of Christ cannot be expressed":

> The language of the cross may be illogical to those who are not on the way to salvation, but those of us who are on the way see it as God's power to save. As scripture says, I shall destroy the wisdom of the wise and bring to nothing all the learning of the learned. Where are the philosophers now? Where are the scribes? Where are any of our thinkers today? Do you see now how God has shown up the foolishness of human wisdom? If it was God's wisdom that human wisdom should not know God, it was because God wanted to save those who have faith through the foolishness of the message we preach. And so, while the Jews demand miracles and the Greeks look for wisdom, here are we preaching a crucified Christ; to the Jews an obstacle that they cannot get over, to the pagans madness, but to those who have been called, whether they are Jews or Greeks, a Christ who is the power and the wisdom of God. For God's foolishness is wiser than human wisdom, and God's weakness is stronger than human strength. (I Cor. 1:17-25 JB)

St. Paul understood that the wisdom of the gospel overturns human priorities, even well-intentioned human effort, with the ironic and playful unpredictability of divine grace. The "public" nature of the divine intention in creation does not disappear, to be sure; Sophia continues to call from the street corners, the marketplace, the city gates, for there is much to be learned from a careful scrutiny of "what is." But in Jesus the elusive, hidden aspect of Wisdom (Job 28) reasserts itself. Against all reason, the intellectual and religious pursuits of the well born, the well educated, and the socially influential are ultimately sterile. It is to the humble, the ordinary, the unlettered worker or the social outcast—persons without skills or stake in the status quo—that the call is first issued and the pearl of great price first offered, for only such as these would be sufficiently "foolish" to accept it. Oddly enough, it is in just such an irrational arrangement that God is glorified and Truth honored. In the Incarnation, the invitation extended by Wisdom to share her bread and wine becomes an invitation to approach the Lord's Table, and her injunction to study and self-disciplined living becomes a call to discipleship and self-surrender. In the Incarnation, the quest for Truth is no longer a process but a relationship.

EXERCISES

For an Individual or a Group

In the wisdom tradition the primary acts of devotion are the pursuit of Truth through study of and reflection on God's Word, an experimental exploration of the natural order as a means of determining the divine intention for creation, and the practice of virtuous living. The following Bible study exercises utilizing material from the wisdom tradition in both the Hebrew Scriptures and the New Testament should be carried out with a sense of zestful enthusiasm and prayerful intent, for nothing is more wonderful than new knowledge about God.

Option One

Study each of the following passages, line by line: Genesis 1–2:4a; Proverbs 8:22-31; John 1:1-18. For each passage answer the following questions:

1. Does the passage say anything about the order or process of creation?
2. Who or what is the means, method, or agent of creation?
3. What does the method or agent of creation imply about the purpose of creation?
4. What does the common vision of creation in these passages seem to suggest about the meaning and means of both sin and salvation?

Option Two

Make a list of the attributes and creative functions of the agent of creation in each of the three passages and then compare and contrast them. How does the assignment of the same or parallel functions to each agent of creation affect your understanding of it/her/him? Does

450

any one of them suffer diminishment or, contrariwise, enjoy enhancement in the process of comparison? If so, how does this occur?

Option Three

The prologue of the Gospel of John is thought by many New Testament scholars to be a Christian redaction (edition or adaptation) of an early hymn to the Greek *Logos* or Sophia. Read New Testament scholar Bruce Vawter's minimalist reconstruction of this original hymn[1] below and compare it to John 1:1-18. Then examine the cross-references associated with each line of the original hymn to see how thoroughly the wisdom tradition has influenced certain strands of New Testament Christology. (Protestants will need to have access to a Bible that contains the Apocrypha in order to do this exercise.) What conclusions do you draw about the relationship of old and new elements in the development of theological ideas? What does this exercise suggest about the power of tradition in relation to the impact of an immediate experience of God?

THE JOHANNINE HYMN

v. 1 In the beginning was the word
and the word was with God,
and the word was god.

v. 2 He was with God in the beginning.

v. 3 All things were made through him,
and apart from him nothing was made.

v. 4 What came to be in him was life,
and this life was the light of men.

v. 5 And the light shines on in darkness,
a darkness that did not overcome it.

v. 9 He was the real light
giving light to every man[,]
coming into the world.

v. 10 He was in the world,
and through him the world was made,
yet the world did not know him.

v. 11 He came to his own,
but his own did not accept him.

CROSS-REFERENCES TO MATERIAL IN THE WISDOM TRADITION

In the beginning was the word
Proverbs 8:22; Sirach 1:4, 24:9
the word was with God
Proverbs 8:27, 30; Sirach 1:1; Wisdom 8:3, 9:4, 6

he was with God in the beginning
    Proverbs 3:19, 8:27
all things were made through him
    Proverbs 3:19, 8:30; Wisdom 7:22, 8:6, 9:1f., 9
what came to be in him was life
    Proverbs 3:18, 8:35; Wisdom 6:18f., 8:12, 17; Baruch 4:1
this life was the light of men
    Sirach 24:30; Wisdom 6:12; 7:10, 26; Baruch 4:2
the light shines on in the darkness
    Wisdom 8:24-30
he was in the world
    Wisdom 8:1; Sirach 24:3, 6
the world did not know him
    Proverbs 1:24f.; Baruch 3:31
he came to his own but his own did not accept him
    Sirach 24:7f.; Baruch 3:11f.

For a Group

Plan a time—before or after a discussion or study such as that outlined above—when the group can participate in the liturgical "meditation" in appendix 14-1. The experience will be most successful if used with a group of men and women both, seated or standing opposite one another to facilitate antiphonal responses. Select a man for the role of King Solomon and a woman for Lady Wisdom. Allow approximately one hour for both the actual meditation and an opportunity following the experience to discuss its impact.

Begin the liturgy with the first two or three verses of the song "Wisdom Has Built Herself a House" (text of song appears in appendix 14-2), and conclude with the final two verses of the song. The music will be particularly effective if male and female voices are alternated (e.g., male voices sing antiphon 1, female voices sing antiphon 2, and everyone sings the verses).

DISCUSSION QUESTIONS

What is the psychological effect of using a liturgy in which prayers are directed to a divine power that is female in character? What new insights or experiences does this generate? What kind of inner obstacles, if any, did you encounter?

2. How do you react to the equation of the feminine principle in the personification of Wisdom with the rational, the orderly, the predictable in nature? What is the effect of giving intellectual achievement a feminine character?

3. Does the equation of Sophia/Wisdom with Jesus in New Testament Christology have the primary effect of eclipsing Sophia or of enriching and elaborating our understanding of who Jesus is?

4. Does the eventual theological development that equates Jesus with God suggest that Sophia/Lady Wisdom may also be granted a similar divine autonomy? Why or why not?

5. In what ways do experiences of oppression shape our understanding of God and our practice of prayer? For women: Does the experience of having been oppressed by a man—or men—make prayer to a masculine God impossible? Why or why not? Some men have experienced oppressive relationships with women. Should we expect them to respond the same way to the prospect of directing prayer to a feminine image of the Divine?

Notes

1. Bruce Vawter, *This Man Jesus: An Essay Toward a New Testament Christology* (Garden City, N.Y.: Doubleday Image Books, 1973), pp. 177-78.

Resources

Cady, Susan; Ronan, Marian; and Taussig, Hal. *Sophia: The Future of Feminist Spirituality*. San Francisco: Harper & Row, 1986.

Engelsman, Joan Chamberlain. *The Feminine Dimension of the Divine*. Philadelphia: Westminster Press, 1979.

Fiorenza, Elizabeth Schüssler. *In Memory of Her: A Feminist Reconstruction of Christian Origins*. New York: Crossroad, 1983.

Mollenkott, Virginia Ramey. *The Divine Feminine: The Biblical Imagery of God as Female*. New York: Crossroad, 1987.

Ruether, Rosemary Radford. *Sexism and God-Talk: Toward a Feminist Theology*. Boston: Beacon Press, 1983. (See chapter 5, "Christology: Can a Male Savior Save Women?")

von Rad, Gerhard. *Wisdom in Israel*. Nashville: Abingdon Press, 1972.

Suggs, M. Jack. *Wisdom, Christology, and Law in Matthew's Gospel*. Cambridge: Harvard University Press, 1970.

Wilkins, Robert, ed. *Aspects of Wisdom in Judaism and Early Christianity*. Notre Dame, Ind.: Notre Dame University Press, 1975.

Vawter, Bruce. *This Man Jesus: An Essay Toward a New Testament Christology*. Garden City, N.Y.: Doubleday Image Books, 1973. (See chapter 5, "The Power and the Wisdom.")

King Solomon and Lady Wisdom: A Liturgical Meditation

Hymn: *"Wisdom Has Built Herself a House" (vv. 1-2)*

Silence: *Solomon prepares to ask for Wisdom.*

Solomon: Like all the others, I too am a mortal man, descendant of the first being fashioned from the earth . . . A wail my first sound, as for all the rest. I was nurtured in swaddling clothes, with every care. No king has known any other beginning of existence; for all there is one way only into life, as out of it. And so I prayed, and understanding was given to me; I entreated, and the spirit of Wisdom came to me (Wis. 7:1, 3-7 JB).

Wisdom: Who is ignorant? Let him step this way. . . . Come and eat my bread, drink the wine I have prepared! Leave your folly and you will live, walk in the ways of perception (Prov. 9:4-6 JB).

Solomon: All that is hidden, all that is plain, I have come to know, instructed by Wisdom who designed them all. For within her is a spirit intelligent, holy, unique, subtle, active, incisive, lucid, invulnerable, . . . sharp, irresistible, . . . loving to man, . . . dependable, . . . almighty, all-surveying, penetrating all intelligent, pure and most subtle spirits. . . . She is a breath of the power of God, pure emanation of the glory of the Almighty. . . . Although alone, she can do all; herself unchanging, she makes all things new. In each generation she passes into holy souls, she makes them friends of God and prophets. (Wis. 7:21-23, 25, 27 JB).

Wisdom: Yahweh created me when his purpose first unfolded, before the oldest of his works. From everlasting I was firmly set, from the beginning, before earth came into being. The deep was not, when I was born, there were no springs to gush with water. Before the mountains were settled, before the hills, I came to birth; before he made the earth, the countryside, or the first grains of the world's dust. When he fixed the heavens firm, I was there, when he drew a ring on the surface of the deep, when he thickened the clouds above, when he fixed fast the springs of the deep, when he assigned the sea its boundaries—and the waters will not invade the shore—when he laid the foundations of the earth, I was by his side, a master craftsman, delighting him day after day, ever at play in his presence, at play everywhere in the world, delighting to be with the sons of men (Prov. 8:22-31 JB).

Solomon: She it was I loved and searched for from my youth; I resolved to have her as my bride, I fell in love with her beauty. . . . Yes, she is an initiate in the mysteries of God's knowledge, making choice of the works he is to do. . . . She knows the past, she forecasts the future. . . . I therefore determined to take her to share my life, knowing she would be my counsellor in prosperity, and my comfort in cares and sorrow (Wis. 8:2, 4, 8a, 9 JB).

Wisdom: I, Wisdom, am mistress of discretion, the inventor of lucidity of thought. Good advice and sound judgement belong to me, perception to me, strength to me. . . . I hate pride and arrogance, wicked behaviour and a lying mouth. I love those who love me; those who seek me eagerly shall find me (Prov. 8:12-14, 17 JB).

Women: She loves those who love her; those who seek her eagerly will find her.

Solomon: Inwardly revolving these thoughts, and considering in my heart that immortality is found in being kin to Wisdom . . . I went in all directions seeking by what means I might make her mine. . . . I turned to the Lord and entreated him, with all my heart I said: (Prov. 8:17, 18, 20b JB) "God of our ancestors, Lord of mercy, who by your word have made all things and in your wisdom have fitted man to rule the creatures that have come from you, to govern the world in holiness and justice and in honesty of soul to wield authority, grant me Wisdom, consort of your throne, and do not reject me from the number of your children."

Wisdom: I love those who love me; those who seek me eagerly shall find me.

Solomon: I am your servant, son of your serving maid, a feeble man, with little time to live, with small understanding of justice and the laws.

Indeed, were anyone perfect among the sons of men, if he lacked the wisdom that comes from you, he would still count for nothing. (Wis. 9:5-6)

Wisdom: I love those who love me; those who seek me eagerly shall find me.

Solomon: With you is Wisdom, she who knows your works, she who was present when you made the world. She understands what is pleasing in your eyes and what agrees with your commandments. Despatch her from the holy heavens, send her forth from your throne of glory to help me and to toil with me and teach me what is pleasing to you, since she knows and understands everything. She will guide me prudently in my undertakings and protect me by her glory. Then all I do will be acceptable, I shall govern your people justly and shall be worthy of my father's throne. (Wis. 9:9-13)

Wisdom: I love those who love me; those who seek me eagerly shall find me.

Solomon: What man indeed can know the intentions of God: Who can divine the will of the Lord? The reasonings of mortals are unsure and our intentions unstable; for a perishable body presses down the soul, and this tent of clay weighs down the teeming mind. (Wis. 9:14-15)

Wisdom: I love those who love me; those who seek me eagerly shall find me.

Solomon: It is hard enough for us to work out what is on earth, laborious to know what lies within our reach; who, then, can discover what is in the heavens? As for your intention, who could have learnt it, had you not granted Wisdom and sent your holy spirit from above? Thus have the paths of those on earth been straightened and men been taught what pleases you, and saved, by Wisdom (Wisd. 9:16-18 JB).

Men: She loves those who love her; those who seek her eagerly shall find her.

Wisdom: And now, my sons, listen to me; listen to instruction and learn to be wise, do not ignore it. Happy those who keep my ways! Happy the man who listens to me, who day after day watches at my gates to guard the portals. For the man who finds me finds life, he will win favor from Yahweh; but he who does injury to me does hurt to his own soul, all who hate me are in love with death (Prov. 8:32-36 JB).

Silence: All pray for Wisdom.

Wisdom: [The answer to your prayer will surprise you. God has promised to] destroy the wisdom of the wise and bring to nothing all the learning of the learned. Where are the philosophers now? Where are the scribes? Where are any of our thinkers today? Do you see now how God has shown up the foolishness of human wisdom? If it was God's wisdom that human wisdom should not know God, it was because God wanted to save those who have faith through the foolishness of the message that we preach. And so, while the Jews demand miracles and the Greeks look for wisdom, here are we preaching a crucified Christ; to the Jews an obstacle that they cannot get over, to the pagans madness, but to those who have been called, whether they are Jews or Greeks, a Christ who is the power and the wisdom of God. For God's foolishness is wiser than human wisdom, and God's weakness is stronger than human strength (I Cor. 1:19-25 JB).

An affirmation of faith, to be recited by all:

[Christ] is the image of the unseen God
and the first-born of all creation,
for in him were created
all things in heaven and on earth:
everything visible and everything invisible,
thrones, dominations, sovereignties, powers—
all things were created through him and for him.
Before anything was created, he existed,
and he holds all things in unity.
Now the Church is his body,
he is its head.

As he is the Beginning,
he was first to be born from the dead,
so that he should be first in every way;
because God wanted all perfection
to be found in him
and all things to be reconciled through him and for him,
everything in heaven and everything on earth,
when he made peace
by his death on the cross.
(Col. 1:13-20 JB)

Hymn: *"Wisdom Has Built Herself a House" (vv. 6-8)*

"Wisdom Has Built Herself a House"*

Antiphon I

Wisdom has built herself a house;
she has prepared her table,
has brought forth her wine;
and she calls to her children.

Antiphon II

Come and eat of my bread,
and drink of my wine;
Come to the feast
I prepared for you.

Verses

1. They have come from the eastern and western lands,
   Gathered around your table
   At the feast of the kingdom.
2. Bread of heav'n is the food that is offered here,
   Bread soon to be your Body,
   Which is Cause for eternal life.
3. Living bread that the Father has giv'n to us,
   Food for our Paschal feasting,
   Sign of the Promise renewed once more.
4. Cup of wine poured to cheer ev'ry troubled heart,
   Free us from ev'ry sadness,
   Blood of Christ, our redeeming Wine.

*From "Wisdom Has Built Herself a House," Lucien Deiss, copyright © 1970, World
Library Publications, Inc. All rights reserved. Used by permission.

5. By your love we are drawn into unity,
   Singing our joyous praises,
   While rememb'ring your tender care.
6. To your table the poor and the humble come,
   Bearing their pain and sorrow,
   And in mercy you dry their tears.
7. In my presence you ready your feast, O Lord;
   Blest with your saving graces,
   They are happy whom you invite.
8. Lead us all to your glorious kingdom, Lord:
   Open the gates of heaven,
   Bringing all to eternal peace.